Readings in Child Development

CAUSES OF BEHAVIOR

Readings in Child Development
CAUSES OF BEHAVIOR

Edited by

JUDY F. ROSENBLITH, *A. Howard Meneely Professor of Psychology,*
Wheaton College,
and Member, Institute of Life Sciences,
Brown University

WESLEY ALLINSMITH, *Professor of Psychology,*
University of Cincinnati

JOANNA P. WILLIAMS, *Visiting Professor of Psychology and Education,*
Teachers College, Columbia University

ALLYN AND BACON, INC., BOSTON

To Sandra, Ronald, Justin, Bryan, Wendy, and Craig

A NOTE ON THE COVER DESIGN

Visual acuity of infants was tested with one row of such stripes: $\frac{1}{8}$, $\frac{1}{16}$, $\frac{1}{32}$, and $\frac{1}{64}$ inch wide. Each pattern was displayed with a gray square of equal brightness, placed 10 inches from the infant's eyes. It had been established that infants preferred patterns to solid colors; so, in this test, the finest stripe pattern consistently preferred to gray showed how narrow a stripe the infant could perceive. Infants under a month old responded to the $\frac{1}{8}$-inch stripes and infants six months old to the $\frac{1}{64}$-inch stripes.

From Robert L. Fantz, The origin of form perception, Scientific American, 1961, 204 (5), 66–72 and 204; copyright © 1961 by Scientific American, Inc., all rights reserved; reprinted with abridgement by permission in the first edition of Causes of Behavior.

Library of Congress Catalog Card Number: 72–92092

Printed in the United States of America.

Contents

CROSS-REFERENCE CHART

Section	See Also	Consult the Index
I. GENERAL INTRODUCTION (Articles 1–4)	III. 10 VII. 39 VII. 42 VII. 43 XI. 59	Behaviorism Cognitive psychology Competence Culture Man Naturalism Psychology Society
II. BIOLOGICAL BASES FOR BEHAVIOR (Articles 5–9)	IV. 18 IV. 23 VI. 35 VII. 40 VIII. 46	Animals (Baboons, Birds, Dogs, Monkeys) Constitutional factors Environment Genetics Heredity Heritability Imprinting
III. LEARNING AS A DETERMINANT OF BEHAVIOR (Articles 10–12)	II. 9 IV. 13 IV. 14 IV. 19 IV. 22 VI. 35 VI. 36 VI. 37 VII. 40	Aggression Anxiety Discipline Drives Personality Punishment Reinforcement Reward
IV. INTERPERSONAL EXPERIENCES AS DETERMINANTS OF BEHAVIOR (Articles 13–25)	II. 8 III. 11 VI. 32 VI. 34 VI. 37 VII. 41 VII. 42 VIII. 46 VIII. 54 XII. 65	Aggression Authority Dependence Identification Imitation Models Mother Parents Peers Permissiveness Siblings Socialization
V. SETTINGS AND SPECIFIC STIMULI AS DETERMINANTS OF BEHAVIOR (Articles 26–30)	III. 12 IV. 20 IV. 24 VII. 42 X. 57 XII. 66	Achievement motivation Classroom Conformity Social influence Social power Street groups Teachers
VI. GROUP MEMBERSHIPS AS DETERMINANTS OF BEHAVIOR (Articles 31–37)	I. 4 IV. 19 IV. 21 V. 29 VIII. 44 VIII. 45 VIII. 47 IX. 52 X. 55	Communication Culture Peer groups Race Social class Socioeconomic status (SES)

Section	See Also	Consult in the Index
VII. AGE OR DEVELOPMENTAL STAGE AS A DETERMINANT OF BEHAVIOR (Articles 38–43)	II. 6 IV. 16 V. 28 VIII. 45 IX. 48 IX. 50 IX. 51	Adolescence Biological bases Competence Crises Critical periods Infants Motivation Newborn infants (Neonates) Psychosexual stages Regression Stability
VIII. SEX AS A DETERMINANT OF BEHAVIOR (Articles 44–47)	II. 6 IV. 17 IV. 19 IV. 20 IV. 24 VI. 35 VII. 42 IX. 49 IX. 53 X. 58	Sex Sex differences Sex role Socialization Women
IX. COGNITIVE DETERMINANTS AND RESULTANTS (Articles 48–54)	VI. 35 VI. 37 VII. 40 XI. 59	Geniuses Intelligence Intelligence quotient (IQ) Testing
X. MOTIVATIONAL DETERMINANTS AND RESULTANTS (Articles 55–58)	VI. 33 VI. 37 VII. 39 VII. 41 XII. 65	Achievement Anxiety Apathy Compulsivity Daydreams Defenses Delay Fantasies Generosity
XI. SPECIFIC EDUCATIONAL IMPLICATIONS (Articles 59–63)	III. 12 IV. 21 V. 26 V. 29 VI. 37 IX. 49 IX. 54 X. 55	Discrimination Fear Motivation Passivity Reading Schools Teaching machines Testing
XII. TEACHERS AND TEACHING (Articles 64–66)	III. 12 IV. 21 V. 26 V. 29 VII. 43 X. 55	Classroom Education Schools Teacher Teaching

PREFACE

This volume, intended for courses that focus on child development, is one of three books compiled concurrently. The other two are *The Causes of Behavior: Readings in Child Development and Educational Psychology,* third edition, and *Readings in Educational Psychology: The Causes of Behavior.*

A number of universities and colleges offer courses that combine educational psychology with child and adolescent psychology or human development. The editors compiled the larger volume, *The Causes of Behavior,* third edition, as a result of their experience in teaching such combined courses. The two smaller volumes are intended for courses that focus on only one of the topics.

While basic articles are repeated in all three volumes or in two volumes, each volume also contains articles not available in either of the others. Thus, the books supplement each other.

Each of the three books is organized as follows. The "Orientation to the Book" explains the organization and gives information to help a reader interpret statistics used in some of the articles. Section I, an introductory section, presents a group of selections that conveys the range of outlooks in the field. Sections II through X each deal with one of the explanations of behavior that have been emphasized by important theorists or schools of thought about developmental psychology or human behavior. Articles applicable to educational issues—matters that no student of child development can afford to ignore—are often presented within the framework of one of these broad avenues to the understanding of behavior. Some of these themes are more basic or inclusive than others. A theme that may be derivative of others is assigned a section of its own when the factor it emphasizes is an important determinant of behavior, either in theory or practice. Complexly interwoven behaviors are discussed primarily in Sections IX and X. The emphasis of all three books is on various approaches to understanding the behavior of children rather than educational psychology in any narrow sense. The final sections of the book (XI and XII), as well as a number of articles in the earlier sections, deal with research and problems that have specific educational implications.

Our experience indicates that most reading assignments provoke a considerable variety of reactions. The article that some students consider the most valuable of all is one that other students rate as having limited merit. As a result of the diversity of opinion, we recognize that not all students (or all teachers) will necessarily be pleased by every article included. We have attempted to offer a collection that changes pace frequently, ranging widely in topics covered, in techniques of investigation used, in levels of difficulty, and in the views espoused by the authors. In order to show the variety of existing methods and to convey some of the information that exists in areas not yet subjected to precise research, we have included work of investigators who, in opening up new areas of study, have used approaches that lack scientific rigor.

In general, we believe that articles in a collection of readings should be reproduced in their entirety. Nevertheless, we have had to abridge some selections. In certain cases we did this almost entirely to save space, but without sacrificing the crucial points. In other cases we considered portions of a selection too difficult for a typical student to follow. In all instances the author's agreement has been obtained. We have also taken care to indicate all deletions so that the interested student or teacher can check the original source. Congruent with our interest in completeness of content, we have usually included the original references and footnotes (our own footnotes are indicated by "Editor"). The inclusion of references is especially important for those students who are preparing a paper or planning and conducting a study.

When introducing articles we have tried to specify the authors' affiliations to show readers where active research in educational and child psychology is being conducted. We expect that students contemplating graduate study, particularly, will want to know the location of people with whom they might like to work. Readers are also enabled to write an author for details of a study or reports of further investigations.

We wish to express our gratitude to the authors and publishers who have allowed us to use their material in this book. They are credited in footnotes at the beginning of each selection.

We are indebted to Wheaton College and the University of Cincinnati for leaves of absence and support in preparation of the manuscript. We are also grateful to the University of Pennsylvania for aid in preparing the manuscript and obtaining the necessary permissions. Rebecca Anderson Huntington of the Institute of Life Sciences, Brown University, gave sage advice, editorial assistance, and help in assembling the manuscript.

The hundreds of students who have given us the benefit of their reactions often made useful suggestions that went beyond standard questionnaire responses. We acknowledge their generosity, as well as that of many colleagues who have commented on the second edition's merits and lacks. For willing and able assistance we thank Ruth Church of Wheaton College; Christine Bebel, Irving Sears, Cheryl Sopko, and Carol Weiss of the University of Pennsylvania; and Wendy Allinsmith.

Judy F. Rosenblith
Wesley Allinsmith
Joanna P. Williams

PSYCHOLOGY AND THE TEACHER

. . . you make a great, a very great mistake, if you think that psychology, being the science of the mind's laws, is something from which you can deduce definite programs and schemes and methods of instruction for immediate schoolroom use. Psychology is a science, and teaching* is an art; and sciences never generate arts directly out of themselves. An intermediary inventive mind must make the application, by using its originality.

The science of logic never made a man reason rightly, and the science of ethics (if there is such a thing) . . . never made a man behave rightly. The most such sciences can do is to help us catch ourselves up and check ourselves more articulately after we have made mistakes. . . .

And so everywhere the teaching must *agree* with the psychology, but need not necessarily be the only kind of teaching that would so agree; for many diverse methods of teaching may equally well agree with psychological laws. . . .

But, if the use of psychological principles thus be negative rather than positive, it does not follow that it may not be a great use, all the same. It certainly narrows the path for experiments and trials. We know in advance, if we are psychologists, that certain methods will be wrong so our psychology saves us from mistakes. It makes us, moreover, more clear as to what we are about.

From William James, *Talks to Teachers on Psychology* (New York: Holt, Rinehart, and Winston Inc., 1920, first published in 1899), pp. 7–11. Reprinted by permission.

* In our observation, where the word "teacher" is used in this passage, one could substitute "parent," and for "teaching," "child-rearing." We are grateful to Professor Gordon Hendrickson of the University of Cincinnati for calling this passage to our attention.—EDITOR

ORIENTATION TO THE BOOK

In describing the purposes of a pioneering investigation in which a number of factors relevant to the prediction of children's actions were taken simultaneously into account, John W. M. Whiting of Harvard University wrote:

> Various positions have been taken as to the major determinants of a child's behavior. Gesell and Piaget, taking a developmental point of view, say the most important thing to know in order to predict a child's behavior is how old he is; Freud and his followers would insist that the most important determinant of a child's behavior is his life history, especially his relationship with his father and mother; the learning theorists would insist that a knowledge of previous rewards and punishments for the particular behavior in question is what is needed. The Gestalt school, as exemplified by Lewin, Baldwin, and Barker and Wright, would take an ahistorical approach and insist that a knowledge of the situation, that is, the setting and instigation, is the thing to have; and, of course, the anthropologists would insist that if you don't know what society the child is a member of, you can't predict a thing.[1]

Whiting goes on to cite one more factor as possibly having some weight, namely, whether the child is a male or a female. He concludes, "We suspect there is a grain of truth in each of these positions."

We believe that Whiting has put his finger on a key characteristic of the social and behavioral sciences today. Because the determinants of behavior are multiple, *each* theoretical view is more or less "true." Full understanding and precise prediction must wait until we have the formula that can assign a suitable weight to each of the factors. Nevertheless, prior to such a Utopian state of affairs, we can increase our understanding of behavior by studying each of its possible determinants. We have accordingly organized this book into parts, most of which deal with a class of determinant.

We realize that our selection of classes of determinants is not the only selection possible. Also, the classes to which we assign a label, and thus a section, are not mutually exclusive or nonoverlapping. We recognize, furthermore, that some factors to which we have assigned a role as primary determinants are themselves a resultant of other determinants. An example is *intelligence* (an aspect of cognition, Section IX), which may be conceived of as a consequence both of biological factors and of learning experiences. However, intelligence plays an important role in educational psychology and in psychology generally; it is frequently viewed as a determinant and used as an independent variable in research studies. Hence, we have chosen to present it in that context.

In addition to discussing the purpose of every section at its outset, we have written editors' comments to precede each of the articles. If an article's open-

---

[1] These statements are from a paper entitled "The Observation of Children's Behavior—A Cross-Cultural Approach," given by Dr. Whiting at the December 1958 Meeting of the American Association for the Advancement of Science.

ing statement or summary does not say all that we think might be of help to students, we give our description or interpretation of the material to be covered. We also call attention to overlap with other articles or sections. Additional readings are listed in the cross-reference chart at the beginning of the book. They will be of interest to students who lack an adequate background for the topic under discussion or who may wish to pursue the topic in greater depth.

HOW TO READ STATISTICS

A number of the articles in this book present numerical findings from psychological research. The reader who has never delved into the research literature of psychology or education may need some help in reading these data papers. The data in such articles are accompanied by statistical statements. In this section we present some information about statistical statements that should help you read and understand the articles even if you do not know statistics.[2]

The statistical tests most frequently used in these articles deal with the question of what probability exists that random error, or chance,[3] could have led to findings or relationships of the magnitude obtained. Such probability statements are pivotal concepts in statistics. The lower the probability of obtaining a result through random error, the more confidence one can have in the finding. For example, an experimental outcome with a probability (p) of $< .05$ (less than five in a hundred) would have occurred by chance less than one time in twenty. If the experiment were run a hundred times, results as extreme as those found would, on the average, occur less than five times out of the hundred if there were no systematic relation between the variables. To put it another way, even if there were no relation between the variables, findings with a p of .05 would still occur, on the average, five times out of a hundred just because of chance.

In psychological and educational research, when a finding is described as "statistically significant" the author usually means "the probability that the result is due to chance is .05 or 'better.'" A "better" probability is a lower one; that is, one which indicates less likelihood of the results having occurred by chance. Better p's would be .02, .01, or .001, which means that such a result would be obtained by chance only two times in a hundred, one time in a hundred, or one time in one thousand.

In psychological writings, the remark that a result is "significant" does not mean that it is "meaningful" or "important," but that it is *statistically* significant. Of course, $p = .06$ and $p = .07$ are not much different in probability from $p = .05$. One can place almost as much confidence in them. Yet, by convention, the term

---

[2] It may help to call attention to the most basic abbreviations used. S is an abbreviation for research subject, Ss for subjects (plural); N is for the number of subjects (N=23 or N23 means there were 23 subjects or Ss); p stands for probability level; $<$ means less than and $>$ more than; $\overline{X}$ stands for the mean or average; ANOVA (or sometimes ANVAR) stands for analysis of variance, a technique discussed below.

We assume that readers are familiar with purely descriptive statistics or that their instructors will acquaint them with measures of central tendency (mean, median, mode), with measures of dispersion (range, standard deviation), and with the basic idea of correlation. The chapters on statistics in many introductory texts constitute valuable sources for review. For a highly readable, non-mathematical account that may aid in better understanding of statistical reasoning, the student is referred to the chapter on statistical thinking in Donald O. Hebb, *A Textbook of Psychology,* 2d ed. (Saunders, 1966), pp. 165–186.

[3] "Random error," or chance, is a factor in research results just as it is in other matters; if you shuffle and deal four bridge or poker hands, you may find some rare, unlikely hands (e.g., a full house) "just by chance." Or, to take one more example, if you flip an unbiased coin ten times, you can get nine heads "just by chance." In the same way, the psychological experimenter may be "lucky" or "unlucky." Statistics provide a means of assessing this luck factor.

"significant" is usually applied only to results that have a *p* value of .05 or less. Some authors give no actual probability figures when the *p* is greater than .05, merely labeling the results N.S. for "not significant." Others report probabilities such as .10 or .12 to indicate trends that might have reached a more acceptable "*p* level" if there had been more cases in the sample or if the results obtained had been a little more striking.

Two qualifications about "*p* values" should be understood by all students of psychology. (1) The fact that a result is significant does not rule out the possibility that it is due to chance, or random error. Out of one hundred findings based on the same experiment, five (on the average) might be significant at the .05 level or better even if only chance were operating. (2) The fact that a finding is "significant" does not, as we have said before, mean that it is important. If there were a difference between the average heights of redheads and blondes, and enough women of each coloring were measured, the difference might be statistically significant, that is, greater than is likely to be accounted for by random errors, even though the actual difference in average heights was only .1 inch. Needless to say, it would be futile under such circumstances to use the information that "redheads are taller than blondes" to predict the relative heights of a particular unknown redhead and blonde who are to be matched with a tall and a short man as blind dates.

The findings that are discussed in terms of their significance or probability level are of three major classes:

1. *Significance of Differences.* The differences may be of various types: (a) between two different performances by the same people (e.g., between history achievement and arithmetic achievement); (b) between two groups of people measured on the same performance or characteristic (e.g., heights of blondes and redheads, arithmetic performance of 6- and 8-year-olds); or (c) between the results of two experimental treatments (e.g., arithmetic performance of those taught by method A and those taught by method B).

2. *Relationship (and Degree of Relationship) Between Two Variables.* The second class of findings discussed in terms of significance levels or *p* values is concerned with the existence of a relationship between two variables. Such findings are frequently assessed by methods such as Chi-square (χ^2). The studies that assess the degree of relation between two variables use correlational techniques of which the Pearson product moment correlation (*r*) is used most frequently. Another way to assess degree of relationship is by use of Rho or rank order correlation. Findings assessing relations, like those examining differences, may be significant without indicating a close or important relationship. To illustrate, two indices or variables such as chronological age and score on a given test may correlate .20 with one another ($r = .20$). This may be a significant association ($p < .05$) if the sample on which the correlation was obtained was sufficiently large. However, the capacity to predict the test score from knowing the chronological age (or vice versa) is low indeed. The amount of variability in one factor that is controlled by the other is found by squaring the correlation coefficient (r^2). In the example just given where $r = .20$, $r^2 = .04$, or 4% of the variance. Thus, only 4% of the variability in test scores may be said to be determined by or covary with chronological age.

3. *Interaction among Variables.* In recent years increasing numbers of studies have looked at more than one variable in relation to the behavior being studied. (This trend reflects the growing maturity of our field and the greater ease of doing necessary computations in the computer age.) Therefore, more of the studies we reprint have these more complex statistical analyses. They can still be under-

stood by the student who lacks real statistical training if the basic principles of probability levels are kept in mind.

In such multivariate studies, one is, however, also concerned with "interactions." These are usually assessed by statistical procedures called analysis of variance, which take into account the fact that it often takes two conditions acting together to affect an organism's behavior. Neither condition alone may suffice. If, in a research study, sex of subject has an effect on the results, but only among middle class *S*s, then one says that social class and gender *interact*. For example, middle class girls may act differently from middle class boys and differently from lower class girls and boys. In this case one would say that social class affects behavior, but only among girls. In complex studies, the use of analysis of variance is necessary to establish whether variables are really interacting and which ones are. In addition, the technique yields probability statements about the effects of the main variables.

Let us look at some examples of research strategies and of appropriate and inappropriate conclusions that might be drawn from research findings. A child development researcher wants to determine what effects the age of weaning has on the development of conscience, or on some other characteristic assessed at a later age. There are two research strategies he might adopt. (1) He may look for differences in conscience (or whatever variable he is concerned with) between two (or more) groups that differ in the age at which they were weaned. He would categorize all of his subjects into two or more groups according to the age of weaning (early vs. late, or early, average, and late). He would then measure a later behavior (amount of guilt at age twelve, say) by some specified technique. Then he would compare the amount of guilt shown by his groups and determine whether the difference (or differences) is significant. (2) Instead of looking for differences between groups, he may look for the *degree of relationship* between the variable age of weaning and the variable amount of guilt. Age is, of course, almost automatically quantified. The data on guilt must also be expressed in quantitative form (scores, perhaps). Then the correlation between the two can be determined and the degree of relationship thus assessed. In case 1, the finding might be that there is a significant *difference* between a group weaned early and one weaned late. In case 2, a significant *degree of relationship* between age of weaning and amount of guilt may be found. The actual magnitude (or size) of the difference or relationship may be large or small. If small yet statistically significant, it may be of importance for psychological theory. In such an event, the author of the study should not be misinterpreted as having shown that guilt at age twelve (or whenever) is determined in any close or direct fashion by age of weaning taken by itself. Even if a strong degree of relationship were found between two such variables, it does not necessarily mean that one causes the other. Each might be the result of a third, unstudied factor. An example of a possible finding of this nature follows.

The number of pots and pans in home kitchens might prove to be correlated with the political preferences of the householders, with more utensils in the kitchens of Republicans. Such a finding should not be used to argue that Republicans are fonder of food, are more "oral" in their personality tendencies, or dislike eating in restaurants. It would probably be because, on the average, persons with more money have tended both to buy more pots and pans and to vote for the party with the more conservative monetary policies. Thus, the correlation of both Republicanism and possession of kitchen utensils with a third factor, income, would give rise to the finding. Republicanism per se would not be a cause of utensil purchases! (Or vice versa.)

In addition to calling attention to the fact that significant relationships may be so small as to be of more theoretical than practical importance, we must call attention to the many which are large or important enough to have great practical utility for group prediction, but which are nevertheless not very useful for individual prediction. During World War II, for example, millions of dollars were saved by using psychological tests to screen candidates for pilot training. Predictions of success were far more accurate than those that could be obtained by coin-flipping or other arbitrary procedures. As a group, the trainees chosen by this means were more likely to succeed. Nevertheless, a number of those who underwent training did not succeed. Conversely, there is evidence for believing that many of those rejected for training would have succeeded. In short, the tests were good for group prediction, but imperfect for individual prediction.[4] Readers of psychological literature who understand this distinction between group and individual prediction and who bear in mind the other qualifications cited about the meanings of statistical results will be able to avoid the most common misinterpretations of investigators' findings.

[4] For a good elementary discussion related to this point, see Brown and Gilhousen, *College Psychology* (Prentice-Hall, 1950), Chapter 18, "Measuring Individuals," pp. 459–477.

I

GENERAL INTRODUCTION

This section does not deal with a "cause of behavior" or any other specific topic. The articles span a wide variety of issues and viewpoints. We hope that they will serve as stimuli to thinking and give readers perspective on important issues in child psychology. Such perspective should help in organizing students' thoughts so that they are less confused by the heterogeneity they will find in the rest of the book, in modern psychology, and in the behavioral sciences generally.

1

Freud and the Image of Man [1]

Jerome S. Bruner

Bruner assesses the theoretical and practical impact of Freudian ideas in this paper, which takes cognizance of people's increasing psychological sophistication during the past half century. Bruner's 1965 presidential address to the American Psychological Association ("The Growth of Mind") is included in Section XI. Long a professor of psychology at Harvard University and director of its Center for Cognitive Studies, he is now Watts Professor of Psychology at Oxford University in England.

By the dawn of the sixth century before Christ, the Greek physicist-philosophers had formulated a conception of the physical world as a unitary material phenomenon. The Ionics had set forth a conception of matter as fundamental substance, transformation of which accounted for the myriad forms and substances of the physical world. Anaximander was subtle enough to recognize that matter must be viewed as a generalized substance, free of any particular sensuous properties. Air, iron, water, or bone were only elaborated forms, derived from a more general stuff. Since that time, the phenomena of the physical world have been conceived as

continuous and monistic, as governed by the common laws of matter. The view was a bold one, bold in the sense of running counter to the immediate testimony of the senses. It has served as an axiomatic basis of physics for more than two millennia. The bold view eventually became the obvious view, and it gave shape to our common understanding of the physical world. Even the alchemists rested their case upon this doctrine of material continuity and, indeed, had they known about neutron bombardment, they might even have hit upon the proper philosopher's stone.

The good fortune of the physicist—and these matters are always relative, for the material monism of physics may have impeded nineteenth century thinking and delayed insights into the nature of complementarity in modern physical theory—this early good fortune or happy insight has no counterpart in the sciences of man. Lawful continuity between man and the animal kingdom, between dreams and unreason on one side and waking rationality on the other, between madness and sanity, between consciousness and unconsciousness, between the mind of the child and the adult mind, between primitive and civilized man—each of these has been a cherished discontinuity preserved in doctrinal canons. There were voices in each generation, to be sure, urging the exploration of continuities. Anaximander had a passing good approximation to a theory of evolution based on natural selection; Cornelius Agrippa offered a plausible theory of the continuity of mental health and disease in terms of bottled-up sexuality. But Anaximander did not prevail against Greek conceptions of man's creation nor Cornelius Agrippa against the demonopathy of the *Malleus Maleficarum.* Neither in establishing the continuity between the varied states of man nor in pursuing the continuity between man and animal was there conspicuous success until the nineteenth century.

I need not insist upon the social, ethical, and political significance of this image, for it is patent that the view one takes of man affects profoundly one's standard of the humanly possible. And it is in the light of such a standard that we establish our laws, set our aspirations for learning, and judge the fitness of men's acts. It is no surprise, then, that those who govern must perforce be jealous guardians of man's ideas about man, for the structure of government rests upon an uneasy consensus about human nature and human wants. The idea of man is of the order of *res publica,* and by virtue of its public status, it is an idea that is not subject to change without public debate. The behavioral

---

[1] This article also appeared in the July 1956 *Partisan Review* and was read earlier in the year at the Conference on Science and the Modern World View under the auspices of the American Academy of Arts and Science.

Jerome S. Bruner, "Freud and the image of man," *American Psychologist,* 1956, *11,* 463–466. Reprinted by permission.

scientist, as some nowadays insist on calling him, may propose, but it is the society at large that disposes. Nor is it simply a matter of public concern. For man as individual has a deep and emotional investment in his image of himself. If we have learned anything in the last half-century of psychology, it is that man has powerful and exquisite capacities for defending himself against violations of his cherished self-image. This is not to say that Western man has not persistently asked: "What is man that thou art mindful of him?" It is only that the question, when pressed, brings us to the edge of anxiety where inquiry is no longer free.

Two figures stand out massively as the architects of our present-day conception of man: Darwin and Freud. Freud's was the more daring, the more revolutionary, and in a deep sense, the more poetic insight. But Freud is inconceivable without Darwin. It is both timely and perhaps historically just to center our inquiry on Freud's contribution to the modern image of man. Darwin I shall treat as a necessary condition for Freud and for his success, recognizing, of course, that this is a form of psychological license. Not only is it the centenary of Freud's birth; it is also a year in which the current of popular thought expressed in commemoration of the date quickens one's awareness of Freud's impact on our times.

Rear-guard fundamentalism did not require a Darwin to slay it in an age of technology. He helped, but this contribution was trivial in comparison with another. What Darwin had done was to propose a set of principles unified around the conception that all organic species had their origins and took their form from a common set of circumstances—the requirements of biological survival. All living creatures were on a common footing. When the post-Darwin era of exaggeration had passed and religious literalism had abated into a new nominalism, what remained was a broad, orderly, and unitary conception of organic nature, a vast continuity from the monocellular protozoans to man. Biology had at last found its unifying principle in the doctrine of evolution. Man was not unique but the inheritor of an organic legacy.

As the summit of an evolutionary process, man could still view himself with smug satisfaction, indeed proclaim that God or Nature had shown a persistent wisdom in its effort to produce a final, perfect product. It remained for Freud to present the image of man as the unfinished product of nature: struggling against unreason, impelled by driving inner vicissitudes and urges that had to be contained if man were to live in society, host alike to seeds of madness and majesty, never fully free from an infancy anything but innocent. What Freud

was proposing was that man at best and man at worst is subject to a common set of explanations: good and evil grow from a common process.

Freud was strangely yet appropriately fitted for his role as architect of a new conception of man. We must pause to examine his qualifications, for the image of man that he created was in no small measure founded on his painfully achieved image of himself and of his times. We are concerned not so much with his psychodynamics, but with the intellectual traditions he embodies. A child of his century's materialism, he was wedded to the determinism and the classical physicalism of 19th-century physiology so boldly represented by Helmholtz. Indeed, the young Freud's devotion to the exploration of anatomical structures was a measure of the strength of this inheritance. But at the same time, as both Lionel Trilling and W. H. Auden have recognized with much sensitivity, there was a deep current of romanticism in Freud—a sense of the role of impulse, of the drama of life, of the power of symbolism, of ways of knowing that were more poetic than rational in spirit, of the poet's cultural alienation. It was perhaps this romantic's sense of drama that led to his gullibility about parental seduction and to his generous susceptibility to the fallacy of the dramatic instance.

Freud also embodies two traditions almost as antithetical as romanticism and nineteenth century scientism. He was profoundly a Jew, not in a doctrinal sense but in his conception of morality, in his love of the skeptical play of reason, in his distrust of illusion, in the form of his prophetic talent, even in his conception of mature eroticism. His prophetic talent was antithetic to a Utopianism either of innocence or of social control. Nor did it lead to a counsel of renunciation. Free oneself of illusion, of neurotic infantilism, and "the soft voice of intellect" would prevail. Wisdom for Freud was neither doctrine nor formula, but the achievement of maturity. The patient who is cured is the one who is now free enough of neurosis to decide intelligently about his own destiny. As for his conception of mature love, it has always seemed to me that its blend of tenderness and sensuality combined the uxorious imagery of the Chassidic tradition and the sensual quality of the Song of Songs. And might it not have been Freud rather than a commentator of the Haftorahs who said, "In children, it was taught, God gives humanity a chance to make good its mistakes." For the modern trend of permissiveness toward children is surely a feature of the Freudian legacy. [*In actuality, the respects in which Freudian writers have advocated indulgence of children are balanced by others in which they have urged parental firmness. If Freud-*

ian pronouncements gave rise to excessive leniency it is generally because they were misinterpreted.—Editor]

But for all the Hebraic quality, Freud is also in the classical tradition—combining the Stoics and the great Greek dramatists. For Freud as for the Stoics, there is no possibility of man disobeying the laws of nature. And yet, it is in this lawlessness that for him the human drama inheres. His love for Greek drama and his use of it in his formulation are patent. The sense of the human tragedy, the inevitable working out of the human plight—these are the hallmarks of Freud's case histories. When Freud, the tragic dramatist, becomes a therapist, it is not to intervene as a directive authority. The therapist enters the drama of the patient's life, makes possible a play within a play, the transference,* and when the patient has "worked through" and understood the drama, he has achieved the wisdom necessary for freedom. Again, like the Stoics, it is in the recognition of one's own nature and in the acceptance of the laws that govern it that the good life is to be found.

Freud's contribution lies in the continuities of which he made us aware. The first of these is the continuity of organic lawfulness. Accident in human affairs was no more to be brooked as "explanation" than accident in nature. The basis for accepting such an "obvious" proposition had, of course, been well prepared by a burgeoning 19th-century scientific naturalism. It remained for Freud to extend naturalistic explanation to the heart of human affairs. The *Psychopathology of Everyday Life* is not one of Freud's deeper works, but "the Freudian slip" has contributed more to the common acceptance of lawfulness in human behavior than perhaps any of the more rigorous and academic formulations from Wundt to the present. The forgotten lunch engagement, the slip of the tongue, the barked shin could no longer be dismissed as accident. Why Freud should have succeeded where novelists,

philosophers, and academic psychologists had failed we will consider in a moment.

Freud's extension of Darwinian doctrine beyond Haeckel's theorem that ontogeny recapitulates phylogeny is another contribution to continuity. It is the conception that in the human mind, the primitive, infantile, and archaic exist side by side with the civilized and evolved.

Where animals are concerned we hold the view that the most highly developed have arisen from the lowest. . . . In the realm of mind, on the other hand, the primitive type is so commonly preserved alongside the transformations which have developed out of it that it is superfluous to give instances in proof of it. When this happens, it is usually the result of a bifurcation in development. One quantitative part of an attitude or an impulse has survived unchanged while another has undergone further development. This brings us very close to the more general problem of conservation in the mind. . . . Since the time when we recognized the error of supposing that ordinary forgetting signified destruction or annihilation of the memory-trace, we have been inclined to the opposite view that nothing once formed in the mind could ever perish, that everything survives in some way or other, and is capable under certain conditions of being brought to light again. . . . (Freud, *Civilization and Its Discontents*, pp. 14–15).

What has now come to be common sense is that in everyman there is the potentiality for criminality, and that these are neither accidents nor visitations of degeneracy, but products of a delicate balance of forces that, under different circumstances, might have produced normality or even saintliness. Good and evil, in short, grow from a common root.

Freud's genius was in his resolution of polarities. The distinction of child and adult was one such: It did not suffice to reiterate that the child was father to the man. The theory of infantile sexuality and the stages of psychosexual development were an effort to fill the gap, the latter clumsy, the former elegant. Though the alleged progression of sexual expression from oral, to anal, to phallic, to genital has not found a secure place either in common sense or in general psychology, the developmental continuity of sexuality has been recognized by both. Common sense honors the continuity in the baby-books and in the permissiveness with which young parents of today resolve their doubts. And the research of Beach and others has shown the profound effects of infantile experience on adult sexual behavior—even in lower organisms.

If today people are reluctant to report their dreams with the innocence once attached to such recitals, it is again because Freud brought into

---

* Transference. Misinterpretations of a therapist's statements or actions, or other misperceptions of the therapist on the part of a psychotherapeutic patient, arising from the tendency to react to the therapist as though he were some other person important in the patient's emotional life. The study by therapist and patient of these perceptual distortions is one of the ways in which patients undergoing some kinds of psychotherapy are helped to understand and control their proclivities to perceive certain people inaccurately and to behave inappropriately. The corresponding term "counter-transference" refers to distortions of the therapist about the patient. For instance, a therapist may at times respond emotionally to a female patient as though she were his daughter, sister, or mother. The well-trained therapist has become adept at noticing his own tendencies to distort. As a result, the intrusion of his personal needs upon his professional work can be minimal.—EDITOR.

common question the discontinuity between the rational purposefulness of waking life and the seemingly irrational purposelessness of fantasy and dream. While the crude symbolism of Freud's early efforts at dream interpretation has come increasingly to be abandoned, the conception of the dream as representing disguised wishes and fears has become common coin. And Freud's recognition of deep unconscious processes in the creative act has gone far toward enriching our understanding of the kinship between the artist, the humanist, and the man of science.

It is our heritage from Freud that the all-or-none distinction between mental illness and mental health has been replaced by a more humane conception of the continuity of these states. The view that neurosis is a severe reaction to human trouble is as revolutionary in its implications for social practice as it is daring in formulation. The "bad seed" theories, and nosologies of the 19th century, the demonologies and doctrines of divine punishment—none of these provided a basis for comparison toward human suffering comparable to that of our time.

One may argue, finally, that Freud's sense of the continuity of human conditions, of the likeness of the human plight, has made possible a deeper sense of the brotherhood of man. It has in any case tempered the spirit of punitiveness toward what once we took as evil and what we now see as sick. We have not yet resolved the dilemma posed by these two ways of viewing. Its resolution is one of the great moral challenges of our age.

Why, after such initial resistance, were Freud's views so phenomenally successful in transforming common conceptions of man?

One reason we have already considered: the readiness of the Western World to accept naturalistic explanation of organic phenomena and, concurrently, to be readier for such explanation in the mental sphere. There had been at least four centuries of uninterrupted scientific progress, recently capped by a theory of evolution that brought man into continuity with the rest of the animal kingdom. The rise of naturalism as a way of understanding nature and man saw a corresponding decline in the explanatory aspirations of religion. By the close of the 19th century, religion, to quote Morton White, "too often agreed to accept the role of a non-scientific spiritual grab-bag, or an ideological know-nothing." Elucidation of the human plight has been abandoned by religion and not yet adopted by science.

It was the inspired imagery, the proto-theory of Freud, that was to fill the gap. Success in transforming the common conception of man was not simply its recourse to the "cause-and-effect" discourse of science. Rather it is Freud's imagery, I think, that provides the clue to his ideological power. It is an imagery of necessity, if I may call it that, an imagery that combines the dramatic, the tragic, and the scientific views of necessity. It is here that Freud's intellectual heritage matters so deeply. Freud's is a theory or a proto-theory peopled with actors. The characters are from life: the blind, energic, pleasure-seeking id; the priggish and punitive superego; the ego, battling for its being by diverting the energy of the others to its own use. The drama has an economy and a terseness. The ego develops canny mechanisms for dealing with the threat of id impulses: denial, projection, and the rest. Balances are struck between the actors, and in the balance is character and neurosis. Freud was using the dramatic technique of decomposition, the play whose actors are parts of a single life—a technique that he himself had recognized in phantasies and dreams, one which is honored in his essay, "The Poet and the Daydream."

The imagery of the theory, moreover, has an immediate resonance with the dialectic of experience. True, it is not the stuff of superficial conscious experience. But it fits the human plight, its conflictedness, its private torment, its impulsiveness, its secret and frightening urges, its tragic quality.

In its scientific imagery, it is marked by the necessity of the classical mechanics. At times the imagery is hydraulic: suppress this stream of impulses, and it breaks out in a displacement elsewhere. The system is closed and mechanical, at times electrical, as when cathexes are formed and withdrawn like electrical charges. The way of thought fitted well the common-sense physics of its age.

Finally, the image of man presented was thoroughly secular; its ideal type was the mature man free of infantile neuroticism, capable of finding his own way. This freedom from both Utopianism and asceticism has earned Freud the contempt of ideological totalitarians of the Right and the Left. But the image has found a ready home in the rising, liberal intellectual middle class. For them, the Freudian ideal type has become a rallying point in the struggle against spiritual regimentation.

I have said virtually nothing about Freud's equation of sexuality and impulse. It was surely and still is a stimulus to resistance. But to say that Freud's success lay in forcing a reluctant Victorian world to accept the importance of sexuality is as empty as hailing Darwin for his victory over fundamentalism. Each had a far more profound effect.

Can Freud's contribution to the common understanding of man in the twentieth century be likened to the impact of such great physical and biological theories as Newtonian physics and Darwin's conception of evolution? The question is an empty one. Freud's mode of thought is not a theory in the conventional sense, it is a metaphor, an analogy, a way of conceiving man, a drama. I would propose that Anaximander is the proper parallel: his view of the connectedness of physical nature was also an analogy—and a powerful one. Freud is the ground from which theory will grow, and he has prepared the twentieth century to nurture the growth. But far more important, he has provided an image of man that has made him comprehensible without at the same time making him contemptible.

2

Psychological Models for Guidance

GORDON W. ALLPORT

Gordon Allport evaluates three alternative ways of looking at human behavior. The first of these is the typical stance of the "experimental" psychologist or "behaviorist" or "learning theorist." The second is that of most clinical psychologists, especially those who are psychoanalytically oriented (i.e., influenced heavily by Freud's writings). The third is just becoming popular. Allport calls it existential psychology. It is also referred to as humanistic psychology. Major proponents of this outlook include Carl Rogers and the late Abraham Maslow. We recommend reading Maslow's "Toward a Humanistic Biology" (American Psychologist, 1969, 24, 724–735).

Allport's article is a commentary not only upon the Freudian orientation described by Bruner (preceding selection), but also upon many of the articles in this book that reflect the work of behavioristic laboratories such as that of B. F. Skinner.

Until his death in 1967, Allport taught social psychology and personality at Harvard University. He was president of the American Psychological Association in 1939. In 1963 he received the Gold Medal of the American Psychological Foundation for his lifelong contributions to psychology.

However excellent his natural eyesight may be, a counselor always looks at his client through professional spectacles. It could not be otherwise. After all, he has invested time and money in his psychological training. Of what use is it unless it adds special prisms to his own unaided eyesight?

The lenses we wear are ground to the prescription of our textbooks and teachers. Even while we are undergraduates a certain image of the nature of man is fitted to our eyes. We grow accustomed to the image and when we become practitioners or teachers we may still take it for granted.

But every so often comes a time for optical re-examination. Perhaps the image we have is still the best fit we can get; perhaps it is not. We can tell only by examining alternative lenses. In particular I believe that three are worthy of special scrutiny:

1. MAN SEEN AS A REACTIVE BEING. Under this rubric I would include outlooks known as naturalism, positivism, behaviorism, operationism, physicalism; these are also sometimes called—mistakenly, I think—"scientific psychology."

2. MAN SEEN AS A REACTIVE BEING IN DEPTH. Here I include what is variously called psychoanalysis, psychodynamics, depth psychology.

3. MAN SEEN AS A BEING-IN-PROCESS-OF-BECOMING. This label covers recent trends known as holism, orthopsychology, personalistics, existential psychology.

These three images provide a focus not only for guidance practices, but for all other professional psychological activity whether it be teaching, research, counseling or therapy.

MAN: A REACTIVE BEING

One hundred years ago in his *Beiträge* Wilhelm Wundt mapped a program for the newly conceived science of psychology. His own view of the proper development of this science was broad and permissive, especially in the field of social psychology. But what has taken hold in the Anglo-American tradition is the experimental outlook of his *Physiologische Psychologie*. Fusing with Darwinism, Machian positivism, the quantitative outlook of Galton and his successors, as well as with techniques invented by Binet, Pavlov, Hull and others —this experimental outlook prevailed and has ground the lens that is fitted to the eyes of almost all undergraduate students of psychology. Many of us who continue in the profession feel no need for further correction in this image of man.

Gordon W. Allport, "Psychological models for guidance," *Harvard Educational Review,* 1962, *32* (4), 373–381. Reprinted by permission.

Seen through this lens man is no different in kind from any other living reactor; and therefore, like the paramecium or pigeon, may be studied biologically, behaviorally, mathematically. To be sure a few special concepts need to be devised to take care of the vast complexity of human behavior, but all these concepts—among them habit hierarchy, secondary reinforcement, input and output of information, and the like—are consistent with the postulates of physicalism and naturalism.

If we ask, "What does it mean to be a human being?" this school of thought replies, "Man is one more creature of nature; his behavior though complex is predictable in principle. His present state is determined by his past state. A man's consciousness is unreliable and must be distrusted, preferably disregarded altogether. We seek the general laws of nature, not personal uniqueness. We study man, not men; objective reality, not subjective."

In principle this broad positive tradition, which we all know so well, puts a desirable end to psychological naïveté. It cautions us not to believe every verbal report that comes to our ears; it warns us to be skeptical of our own naked eyesight; and from it we learn to check ourselves for observer reliability. It teaches us to use precise and repeatable methods. Because of its stress on reliable methods this favored tradition in psychology has become known as "scientific psychology." Its methods are indeed scientific; but its primary postulate—that man is simply a reactive organism—is no more scientific than any other postulate.

It is here that the counselor encounters his first difficulty. Trained in tests, statistics, and experimental design, he may think, quite mistakenly, that to employ these useful aids he must also view his client as a reactive being—an exclusive product of stimulus impact, homeostasis, drive-reduction and reinforcement learning. The term "scientific" has spread like a grease spot from method to theory. Just because most of our methods evolved through the positivistic tradition does not mean that the postulates of this tradition concerning the nature of man are the only acceptable postulates for scientific psychology.

A counselor whose theoretical spectacles disclose a merely reactive being, is likely to think of his client in terms of past conditioning and potential re-conditioning; in terms of reinforcements, in terms of environmental determinism. He will assume that his client's basic motives are drive-reduction or second-order conditionings which in some shadowy way are supposed to account for all his adult interests and vocational ambitions.

The vocabulary emanating from this type of postulate is replete with terms like *reaction, re-*

sponse, reinforcement, reflex, respondent, reintegration—all sorts of *re*-compounds. The reference is backward. What *has* been is more important than what *will* be. Terms such as *proaction, progress, program, production, problem-solving,* or *propriate* are characteristically lacking. One would think that the client seated opposite would *pro*test, for the language of response negates the subject's immediate certainty that his life lies in the future.

The positivistic view of man as a reactor has performed a good service, shaking us out of common sense naïveté, endowing us with useful methods, and correctly informing us that man is, in *some* aspects of his being, a simple respondent to simple pressures. Its postulates are, however, questionable. It sees reality as ordered but not as personal; it sees consciousness as a nuisance; it looks at man as reactive, not proactive.

It is probably true that no counselor fully follows this creed in his daily practice. Indeed he could not do so. It is too impoverished a view of real life. When a convinced positivist attempts to fit his image of man to concrete human situations, as B. F. Skinner has done in *Walden Two*, the result strikes many of us as threadbare, even pitiable.

Probably for this reason many behaviorists (starting even as far back as E. B. Holt in *The Freudian Wish and its Place in Ethics*) attempt to combine stimulus-response with psychoanalysis. Neal Miller and John Dollard in their *Personality and Psychotherapy* offer a good example. Man as a reactive being is combined with man as a reactive being in depth.

MAN: A REACTIVE BEING IN DEPTH

So influential is this image of man that we find it everywhere: dominant in literature, in social work, in guidance, in therapeutic practice, and in the market place. There is no need today to describe this image to any educated, or even semi-educated, American adult. Freudianism, like positivism, is our daily dish.

What I should like to do is to make clear that Freudianism (in spite of its less reliable methods) is a close kin of traditional positivism. The only change in the image of man lies in adding the depth dimension. To the long psychological vocabulary of *re*-compounds, depth psychology adds *repression, regression, resistance, abreaction, reaction formation,* and many others.

Like other simple naturalistic views of man, psychoanalysis puts its chief weight upon the press of pleasure and pain. This pressure produces in the organism a tendency to seek an equilibrium between the force of his drives and the circumstances of reality. The fact that Freud maximizes the role of sex and locates the whole constellation of reactive forces chiefly in the unconscious does not alter the essential similarity.

For Freud causation lies in the past history of the individual just as it does for the conditioned-response theorist. Both have a dismaying disregard for the person's phenomenology of the future, for his sense of personhood and sense of freedom. The ego is a reactive agent, having no energy of its own, but borrowing from the unsocialized Id.

Central to depth psychology, and important for guidance, is the doctrine of *recall* and *recovery* (two more *re*-compounds). Therapy, and presumably guidance, proceeds by disclosing to the client some buried motive, or a troublesome and repressed psychic trauma. The client's salvation, if indeed he has any, lies in this vital recall. A troublesome memory is brought to cognizable form. Presumably the result is helpful to the individual in solving his conflicts. The theory, however, does not allow for any interaction between the person and the recovered memory. Simple re-instatement is itself, as Freud says, the "pure gold" of psychoanalysis. What values a client should live by when once the re-instatement has taken place is not the "pure gold" of psychoanalysis. That all adult values are simply sublimated aim-inhibited wishes, is the central doctrine. Freud never allows for the individual's capacity to disregard his past or to reshape it freely. Indeed, since the structure of the Id never changes, the future can at best be a redirection, never a transformation, of one's purposes. What one becomes is essentially what one is, and what one was.

Among the valid portions of psychoanalysis of special use to all counselors, is the brilliant account given us by Freud and by his daughter Anna, of the defensive mechanisms of the ego. In dealing with our client we do well to follow the advice of psychoanalysis and watch for rationalizations, denials of reality through repression, and displacements of aggression. All these, and other, ego-defenses belong to the nature of man, and therefore must find a place in any theory of human personality.

But what perplexes me is why so many of the ego-processes described by psychoanalysis should be merely protective strategies. Are there no ego-processes that lead to a transformation of what is recovered? To a creative cognition? To a revised sense of personhood and a new phenomenology of the future? To Freud the person seems never to be truly proactive, seldom even active. Almost always he is seen as reactive to early fixations—perhaps to some castration threat that occurred years ago, or to some other unsocialized infant complex, especially to Oedipal fantasies. My difficulty with this image of man is summed up most tersely by the late satirist, Max Beerbohm, who said, "They were a tense and peculiar family—those Oedipuses."

There is, I am well aware, a large group of theories that derive from the psychodynamic tradition but at the same time deviate considerably from the orthodox view of reactivity-in-depth. All these theories, in my judgment, move in a desirable direction. Here I shall mention only some of the relevant authors: Adler, Jung, Hartmann, Horney, Erikson, Fromm. Still more deviant from Freud are Goldstein, Maslow, Rogers, and Robert White. These and other writers offer a type of theory that views man as a being in the process of becoming. Many of them ask the pivotal question differently from the reactivist schools of thought. And it makes a good deal of difference just how a question is asked.

A story is told about two priests. They were arguing whether it was proper to smoke and to pray at the same time. One said "Yes," the other "No." To settle the matter they decided that both should write to the Holy Father for his opinion. Sometime later they met and compared notes. Each claimed that the Holy Father had supported his view. They were perplexed. Finally one asked, "How did you phrase your question?" The other replied: "I asked whether it was proper to smoke while one is praying; and the Pope answered, 'Certainly not, praying is serious business and permits no distractions.' And how did you phrase your question?" "Well," said the other, "I asked if it were proper to pray while smoking, and the Pope answered, 'Certainly, prayer is always in order.'"

Instead of asking Aristotle's question, "What is the place of man in Nature?" many authors today are asking St. Augustine's question, "Who am I?" This question, rephrased in the 20th Century, has opened the floodgates to a new theorizing of the broad type often labeled *existentialist*.

MAN: BEING IN THE PROCESS OF BECOMING

Seelye Bixler, former president of Colby College, tells of a student who recently remarked, "I can't tell you how much satisfaction I take in my existential despair." In some student circles despair has always been popular. To label it "existentialist" makes it doubly attractive, in fact irresistible.

But overlooking the fashionable flavor of existentialism it is surely necessary for the modern counselor to take seriously the present-day anxieties of the younger generation. No longer can youth contemplate its future under the protection of the great social stabilizers of the past. No longer can one counsel within the framework of Victorian decorum, theological certainties, or the Pax Britannica. It is obvious to us all that some sort of shattering transformation is under way. The comfortable stabilities of culture, caste, the gold standard, and military supremacy are no longer ours.

Nor are the comfortable stabilities of traditional psychology adequate. Of what use is it to invoke an impersonal theory of learning, a biological theory of motivation, and a late Victorian formula for the unconscious, when youth's problems today are acutely conscious, intensely personal, and propelling him like an unguided astronaut into an unknown future? A counselor is not equipped for his job unless he can share in some degree the apprehensions of modern youth, and sense the swampy underpinning on which youth treads. Over his desk the counselor might well tack the wisdom of the Spanish writer Unamuno, "Suffering is the life blood that runs through us all and binds us together." While not every youth who comes to the counselor is at that moment a sufferer, it is a safe assumption that he comes for guidance that will fortify him for the inevitable suffering that he will encounter in his course of life.

TENTATIVENESS AND COMMITMENT

From the existential point of view the ideal counselor will strive to develop two attitudes in his client. Taken separately they seem antithetical; but fused into a world-view they provide strength for the future. One attitude is *tentativeness* of outlook. Since certainties are no longer certain, let all dogmas be fearlessly examined, especially those cultural idols that engender a false sense of security: dogmas of race supremacy, of naïve scientism, of unilinear evolutionary progress. Let one face the worst in oneself and in the world around him, so that one may correctly estimate the hazards.

Taken by itself such tentativeness, such insightfulness, might well lead to ontological despair. Yet acceptance of the worst does not prevent us from making the best of the worst. Up to now psychologists have not dealt with the remarkable ability of human beings to blend a tentative outlook with firm commitment to chosen values. The poet Tennyson perceived the point.

> There lives more faith in honest doubt,
> Believe me, than in half the creeds.

A commitment is, as Pascal has said, a wager. One may lose it, but one may also win. Cardinal Newman warned us that our religion can never be a matter of certainty. It is at best a subjective condition of certitude which he defined as "probability supported by faith and love." Yet a mature religion, thus defined, can be infinitely sustaining and heroically motivating. Existentialism, whether theistic or atheistic, makes the same point. We have the freedom to commit ourselves to great causes with courage, even though we lack certainty. We can be at one and the same time half-sure and whole-hearted.

William James, probably America's greatest thinker, tried to teach us this lesson, but fifty years ago we were not ready for it. It is surely noteworthy that, writing as he did in a period of social stability, James saw clearly how ultimately uncertain are our foundations of value. Wealth, he saw was a false god, leading us into a national disease that has recently been called "galloping consumption." The more we build up our material resources, the more we fear poverty. In religion, James knew, there was no certainty; yet, like Cardinal Newman, he recognized the constructive power of a mature religious commitment. Whatever ideal leads to long-range constructive consequences is psychologically sound. It is also pragmatically true. And who is to say that we have a test for truth more absolute than our own commitment in so far as it is validated by fruitful consequences?

Neither positivistic nor psychodynamic schools of thought allow for the fact that our psychological constitution permits both total tentativeness and total commitment. Such a paradox reminds us of the electron that is able to go in two opposite directions at the same time. Taken by itself tentativeness is disintegrative; commitment is integrative. Yet the blend seems to occur in personalities that we admire for their soundness and perspective. Presumably through teaching and guidance we may develop both attitudes in our youth.

Whenever the two attitudes coexist in a life we find important desirable by-products from the fusion. One is a deep sense of compassion for the lot of the human race in general and in each separate social encounter that marks our daily life. The other by-product is likewise graceful; it is the sense of humor. Humor requires the perspective of tentativeness, but also an underlying system of values that prevents laughter from souring into cynicism. As Meredith said, humor is a capacity to laugh at the things you love and still to love them.

RATIONALISM VS. IRRATIONALISM

The chief criticism made of existentialism is that it leads away from reason and exalts irrationalism.

While this charge may apply to certain literary and theological trends in the existential movement I doubt that it jeopardizes the future of scientific psychology. The attitudes of tentativeness and commitment of which I speak are perfectly sound concepts—call them "intervening variables" if you wish. Indeed in so far as they reflect important states in human personality, and thus lead to improvement in understanding, prediction, and direction of human behavior, they are sounder scientific concepts than many of those we have been using.

And just what is rationalism? We venerate the ancient Greeks for their exaltation of human reason; and as psychologists we venerate Aristotle for asking the question, "What is man's place in nature." But Greek rationalism was broader than the limited, method-centered, scientism into which it has degenerated. The Greeks themselves saw a place for tentativeness and commitment within the scope of reason. The case is beautifully stated in an ancient inscription found somewhere on the coast of Greece:

> A shipwrecked sailor buried on this coast
> Bids you set sail.
> Full many a bark, when we were lost,
> Weathered the gale.

The dead sailor urges us to make the wager, take the risk, although we cannot be sure of coming through to our destination.

IMPLICATIONS FOR THEORY

What does all this mean in terms of psychological theory, and in terms of guidance? First of all it means that in order to achieve a more realistic image of man and his potentialities, we need to revise our current theories of learning and growth, of motivation and personality structure. Elsewhere (in *Pattern and Growth in Personality*, 1961) I have discussed some of the needed changes in detail, and so shall say only a few words about each.

The trouble with our current theories of learning is not so much that they are wrong, but that they are partial. They fit best the learning of animals and young children. The concepts of conditioning, reinforcement, identification, seem a bit hollow when the counselor tries to apply them to his work. They are not very helpful, for example, in explaining how a youth may learn both tentativeness of outlook and firmness of commitment. Supplementary theories in terms of organizational, biographical, and propriate learning are needed.

Except in the sense of physical maturation the concept of *growth* scarcely exists in psychology at all. Nor will it have its proper place until we have agreed upon normative standards for the maturity of personality. Up to now normative problems, except in the sense of statistical norms, are much neglected.

As for motivation and personality structure psychologists are in a state of turmoil and disagreement. That the past stages of a life do not fully explain the motivational "go" of the present, I for one am firmly convinced. Therefore we need a concept (*functional autonomy*, I think will do) to represent that portion of a life that is oriented toward the future and not toward the past. Also we need a theory of personal structure (of *personal dispositions*) to represent the important cleavages and foci of a given, concrete personality. Such a theory will, I am convinced, carry us much further than a conception of uniform variables to which every client is forcibly ordered, whether we call these variables factors, needs, dimensions, or common traits.

Most of all we need to surrender the models that would compress human personality into the routine homeostatic situation that we find in quasi-closed systems. Human personality is a wide-open system, responsive to tangible and intangible culture, on the look-out for new ideas, and capable of asking an altogether new type of question—asked by no other creature in nature, viz., "Who am I?"

There are, I am glad to say, many psychologists who feel as strongly as I that these various types of improvement need to be made before the counselor will have a fully fashioned science of psychology to undergird his practice.

IMPLICATIONS FOR GUIDANCE

Guidance is not a matter of gimmicks, nor of rules of thumb. A guide, like a philosopher and friend, is a person who loves wisdom and loves his fellow men. True, he has skills to mark him off from the professional philosopher or the untrained friend. To some extent the counselor's present-day skills are useful. Standard tests and measurements are helpful; so too achievement records and focused interviews. Most of our devices come from researches conducted under the positivistic outlook, or (in the case of projective techniques) under the psychodynamic. While many of them are serviceable I look forward to the invention of new instruments still better suited to the study of the central or propriate aspects of single personalities.

Most important, of course, are the spectacles the counselor wears. The image should no longer be borrowed from the tradition of simple naïve reactivism. Just as centimeters, grams, seconds are outmoded in modern physics so too are simple stimulus-response connections in modern psychology. In psychology, even more than in physics, we need theory capable of dealing with fluid becoming.

The plain fact is that man is more than a reactive being, more even than a reactive being in depth. If he were comfortably fixed at these levels we could with confidence apply a uniform stencil in studying his nature. But the life process is no less paradoxical than the processes of modern physics. How can one deal with space that is both finite and unbounded, with light that is both wave and particle, with electrons that pass from orbit to orbit without traversing the space between? Similarly, a human person is both structure and process, a being both biological and noetic, a being who changes his identity even while he retains it. Small wonder that at the end of his life, the famous physicist, P. W. Bridgman, said, "The structure of nature may eventually be such that our processes of thought do not correspond to it sufficiently to permit us to think about it at all."

We need not, I think, be quite so pessimistic. Our first duty is to affirm a new and wider rationalism; that is to say, to redouble our efforts to find a more adequate image of man to guide us in fashioning a more suitable science of personality.

And what about our personal attitudes as guidance specialists or teachers? Should we not cultivate the same twin virtues that we recommend to client and student: tentativeness and commitment? We can hold our own present image of man on trial, reviewing our own past psychological training in critical perspective. At the same time we can embrace courageously our task of interpreting the wisdom of the past in such a way as to make it most available to the youthful personality who is facing an uncertain, but not uninviting, future. Tentativeness and commitment are twin ideals for both counselor and client. To my mind they lie at the heart and center of guidance, of teaching, and of living.

3

Continuity and Change in Personality[1]

Walter Mischel

Walter Mischel examines the question of the extent to which a person remains "himself" over the years and the extent to which he becomes a "different person" as he adapts to new circumstances. Mischel artfully sifts the sometimes confusing evidence on this topic and draws the implications for personality theories. A professor of psychology at Stanford University, Mischel is the author of Introduction to Personality *(New York: Holt, Rinehart & Winston, 1971).*

The question of continuity and change in personality has enduring importance, and the position that one takes on this topic profoundly influences one's approach to most other issues in personality psychology. Almost no psychologist, myself included, would argue with the basic and widely shared assumption that continuity does exist in personality development (e.g., Kagan, 1969). Indeed, few other phenomena seem to be so intuitively self-evident. The experience of subjective continuity in ourselves—of basic oneness

[1] This article is based on a paper presented at the symposium "Behavioral Continuity and Change with Development," held at the meeting of the Society for Research in Child Development, Santa Monica, California, March 27, 1969. Preparation of this paper was facilitated by Grant M-6830, from the National Institutes of Health, United States Public Health Service.

and durability in the self—is perhaps the most compelling and fundamental feature of personality. This experience of continuity seems to be an intrinsic feature of the mind, and the loss of a sense of felt consistency may be a chief characteristic of personality disorganization.

Clinically, it seems remarkable how each of us generally manages to reconcile his seemingly diverse behaviors into one self-consistent whole. A man may steal on one occasion, lie on another, donate generously to charity on a third, cheat on a fourth, and still construe himself readily as "basically honest and moral." Just like the personality theorist who studies them, our subjects also are skilled at transforming their seemingly discrepant behavior into a constructed continuity, making unified wholes out of almost anything.

It might be interesting to fantasize a situation in which the personality theorist and his subjects sat down together to examine each subject's data on behavioral consistency cross-situationally or over time. Actually it might not even be a bad idea for psychologists to enact such a fantasy. In inspecting these data the theorist would look for genotypic unities that he is sure must be there; his subject would look for genotypic unities and be even more convinced that they exist and would proceed to find his own, often emerging with unities unknown to the theorist. But the consistency data on the IBM sheets, even if they reached statistical significance, probably would account for only a trivial portion of the variance, as Hunt (1965) has pointed out. A correlation of .30 leaves us understanding less than 10% of the relevant variance. [The proportion of variation that is accounted for by a correlation is given by the square of the correlation coefficient: $.30 \times .30 = .09$ or 9% of the variation.—EDITOR] And even correlations of that magnitude are not very common and have come to be considered good in research on the consistency of any noncognitive dimension of personality.

How does one reconcile our shared perception of continuity with the equally impressive evidence that on virtually all of our dispositional measures of personality substantial changes occur in the characteristics of the individual longitudinally over time and, even more dramatically, across seemingly similar settings cross-sectionally? I had the occasion to broadly review the voluminous evidence available on this topic of consistency and specificity (Mischel, 1968). In my appraisal, the overall evidence from many sources (clinical, experimental, developmental, correlational) shows the human mind to function like an extraordinarily effective reducing valve that creates and maintains the perception of continuity even in the face of perpetual observed changes in actual behavior. Often this cognitive construction of continuity, while not arbitrary, is only very tenuously related to the phenomena that are construed.

To understand continuity properly it is necessary to be more specific and to talk about types of variations and the conditions that regulate them. In this regard it may be useful to distinguish between consistency in various types of human activity.

There is a great deal of evidence that our cognitive constructions about ourselves and the world—our personal theories about ourselves and those around us (both in our roles as persons and as psychologists)—often are extremely stable and highly resistant to change. Data from many sources converge to document this point. Studies of the self-concept, of impression formation in person perception and in clinical judgment, of cognitive sets guiding selective attention—all these phenomena and many more document the consistency and tenacious continuity of many human construction systems (Mischel, 1968). Often these construction systems are built quickly and on the basis of little information (e.g., Bruner, Olver, & Greenfield, 1966). But, once established, these theories, whether generated by our subjects or ourselves, become exceedingly difficult to disconfirm.

An impressive degree of continuity also has been shown for another aspect of cognition: These are the features of problem solving called cognitive styles. Significant continuity often has been demonstrated on many cognitive style dimensions (e.g., Kagan, 1969; Witkin, Goodenough, & Karp, 1967). The current prolific cognitive style explorations on this topic provide excellent evidence of developmental continuity. In this case the research also reveals a welcome continuity in our professional developmental history. Research into consistent individual differences in cognition has had deep roots and a long and distinguished history in experimental psychology. Simple cognitive measures like reaction time and response speed and duration have intrigued psychologists since the earliest laboratory work on mental measurement began more than 70 years ago. Individual differences on specific measures of problem solving, such as speed of reaction time and weight judgments, began to be explored in 1890 by James McKeen Cattell and others. Their studies of responses on specific cognitive and ability measures in the early laboratories were neglected when the development of practical intelligence testing started in this century. At that time, Binet and Henri shifted attention to the measurement of generalized intelligence by studying individual differences in more complex global tasks. Now it is refreshing to witness the reawakened interest in such enduringly important topics as reaction time and "conceptual tempo" and it is good to see sophisticated consistency evidence for it (Kagan, 1969). The generality and stability of behaviors assessed by these cognitive measures often have been found to be among the best available in personality research.

Some puzzling problems may arise, however, from the correlations found between some of the most promising new cognitive style measures and the traditional measures of generalized intelligence such as the performance IQ on the WISC. That is, correlations between measures of generalized intelligence and cognitive style such as Witkin's field dependence raise the question of the degree to which the consistency of cognitive styles may be due to their associations with intellectual abilities. The obtained generality and stability, as well as the external personality correlates, of at least some cognitive style measures thus may rest in part on their sizable correlations with indexes of more generalized intelligence and achievement behavior, as has been found in other studies (e.g., Crandall & Sinkeldam, 1964; Elliott, 1961). To illustrate, the Witkin measures of cognitive style are strongly related to performance IQ ability indexes. Indeed the relationship between the Witkin Embedded Figures Test and the Wechsler Intelligence Block Design subtest is so strong that Witkin (1965) has indicated he is willing to use Block Design scores when available as a substitute for other field-dependence measures. When such cognitive styles as field independence and such coping patterns as "intellectualization" are substantially correlated with IQ then the stability reported for them and their correlates (e.g., by Schimek, 1968) may partly reflect the stability of the IQ.

This issue might also constitute a problem in interpreting such cognitive styles as Kagan's conceptual tempo. To the extent that conceptual tempo involves reaction time, and fast reaction time is a determinant of generalized performance IQ, one would have to be alert to their interrelations, as has been pointed out by Campbell and Fiske (1959). It will be interesting to continue to explore exactly how conceptual tempo and other cognitive styles based on performance indexes such as response speed and accuracy take us beyond generalized ability measurement and into the domain of personality traits. Ultimately research on cognitive styles surely will provide a clearer analysis of intellective behavior. The implications of cognitive styles for the concept of general intelligence (as well as the reverse relation) should then become more explicit than they are now. In the course of these explorations the meaning of inter-correlations among diverse cognitive style measures —such as conceptual tempo, field dependence-independence, leveling-sharpening, and so on—will become clearer. At the same time our understanding of the interactions among cognitive and non-cognitive personality dimensions hopefully will improve.

When we turn away from cognitive and intellective dimensions to the domain of personality and interpersonal behavior, consistency evidence is generally much harder to establish, at least whenever we use conventional tactics and the correlation coefficient (e.g., Maccoby, 1969). On the basis of past literature on this topic, one should no longer be surprised when consistency correlations for social behavior patterns turn out to be quite low. Theoretically, in my view, one should not expect social behavior to be consistent unless the relevant social learning and cognitive conditions are arranged to maintain the behavior cross-situationally. On theoretical as well as on empirical grounds, much of the time there is no reason to expect great consistency in the social behaviors comprising most of our personality dimensions.

It is not possible to even begin to cite here the extensive evidence that I believe supports this point, namely, that noncognitive global personality dispositions are much less global than traditional psychodynamic and trait positions have assumed them to be (Mischel, 1968). A great deal of behavioral specificity has been found regularly on character traits such as rigidity, social conformity, aggression, on attitudes to authority, and on virtually any other nonintellective personality dimension (Mischel, 1968; Peterson, 1968; Vernon, 1964). Some of the data on delay of gratification with young children, emerging from our current studies at Stanford, are illustrative. In an ongoing longitudinal study on this problem we have obtained evidence that delay of gratification has some developmental consistency and increases with age, up to a point.[2] Much more impressive in my view, however, is our finding that within any child there exists tremendous variability on this dimension. Now we are studying how long preschool children will actually sit still alone in a chair waiting for a preferred but delayed outcome before they signal to terminate the waiting period and settle for

a less preferred but immediately available gratification. We are finding that the same $3\frac{1}{2}$-year-old child who on one occasion may terminate his waiting in less than half a minute may be capable of waiting by himself up to an hour on another occasion a few weeks earlier or later, *if* cognitive and attentional conditions are appropriately arranged. Our conclusion is that some significant predictions of length of voluntary delay of gratification certainly can be made from individual differences data; but the most powerful predictions by far come from knowledge of the cognitive and incentive conditions that prevail in the particular situation of interest.

These results are not at all atypical. A tribute to the interaction of person and environment is usually offered at the front of every elementary textbook in the form of Kurt Lewin's famous equation: Behavior is a function of person and environment. In spite of such lip service to the stimulus, most of our personality theories and methods still take no serious account of conditions in the regulation of behavior. Literally thousands of tests exist to measure dispositions, and virtually none is available to measure the psychological environment in which development and change occurs.

Evidence on observed instability and inconsistency in behavior often has been interpreted to reflect the imperfections of our tests and tools and the resulting unreliability and errors of our measurements, as due to the fallibility of the human clinical judge and his ratings, and as due to many other methodological problems. Undoubtedly all these sources contribute real problems. Some of these have been excellently conceptualized by Emmerich (1969). His emphasis on the need for considering rate and mean changes over age if one is to achieve a proper understanding of continuity, growth, and psychological differentiation is especially important. Likewise, his call for longitudinal, multimeasure, and multivariate studies needs to be heeded most seriously.

I am more and more convinced, however, hopefully by data as well as on theoretical grounds, that the observed inconsistency so regularly found in studies of noncognitive personality dimensions often reflects the state of nature and not merely the noise of measurement. Of course, that does not imply a capriciously haphazard world—only one in which personality consistencies seem greater than they are and in which behavioral complexities seem simpler than they are. This would, if true, be extremely functional. After all, if people tried to be radical behaviorists and to describe each other in operational terms they would soon run out of breath and expire. It is essential for the

---

[2] W. Mischel, E. B. Ebbesen, & A. Raskoff. In progress research report, Stanford University, entitled "Determinants of Delay of Gratification and Waiting Behavior in Preschool Children."

mind to be a reducing valve—if it were not it might literally blow itself!

Perhaps the most widely accepted argument for consistency in the face of seeming diversity is the one mentioned so often, the distinction between the phenotypic and the genotypic. Thus most theorizing on continuity seems to have been guided by a model that assumes a set of genotypic personality dispositions that endure, although their overt response forms may change. This model, of course, is the one shared by traditional trait and dynamic dispositional theories of personality. The model was well summarized in the example of how a child at age 12 may substitute excessive obedience to a parent for his earlier phobic reaction as a way of reducing anxiety over parental rejection (Kagan, 1969). At the level of physical analogy Kagan spoke of how the litre of water in the closed system is converted to steam and recondensed to liquid.

This type of hydraulic Freudian-derived personality model, while widely shared by personality theorists, is of course not the only one available and not the only one necessary to deal with phenomena of continuity and change. Indeed, in the opinion of many clinical psychologists the hydraulic phenotypic-genotypic model applied to personality dynamics, psychotherapy, and symptom substitution has turned out to be a conceptual trap leading to some tragic pragmatic mistakes in clinical treatment and diagnosis for the last 50 years (e.g., Mischel, 1968; Peterson, 1968). I am referring, of course, to the unjustified belief that seemingly diverse personality problems must constitute symptoms of an underlying generalized core disorder rather than being relatively discrete problems often under the control of relatively independent causes and maintaining conditions.

The analysis of diverse behaviors as if they were symptomatic surface manifestations of more unitary underlying dispositional forces also is prevalent in our theories of personality development (e.g., Kagan, 1969; Maddi, 1968). But while diverse behaviors often may be in the service of the same motive or disposition, often they are not. In accord with the genotype-phenotype distinction, if a child shows attachment and dependency in some contexts but not in others one would begin a search to separate phenotypes from genotypes. But it is also possible that seeming inconsistencies, rather than serving one underlying motive, actually may be under the control of relatively separate causal variables. The two behavior patterns may not reflect a phenotype in the service of a genotype but rather may reflect discrimination learning in the service of the total organism. Likewise, while a child's fears sometimes may be in the service of an underlying motive, most research on the topic would lead me to predict it is more likely that the fear would involve an organized response system with its own behavioral life, being evoked and maintained by its own set of regulating conditions (e.g., Bandura, 1969; Paul, 1967).

When we observe a woman who seems hostile and fiercely independent some of the time but passive, dependent, and feminine on other occasions, our reducing valve usually makes us choose between the two syndromes. We decide that one pattern is in the service of the other, or that both are in the service of a third motive. She must be a really castrating lady with a facade of passivity—or perhaps she is a warm, passive-dependent woman with a surface defense of aggressiveness. But perhaps nature is bigger than our concepts and it is possible for the lady to be a hostile, fiercely independent, passive, dependent, feminine, aggressive, warm, castrating person all-in-one. Of course which of these she is at any particular moment would not be random and capricious—it would depend on whom she is with, when, how, and much, much more. But each of these aspects of her self may be a quite genuine and real aspect of her total being. (Perhaps we need more adjectives and hyphens in our personality descriptions. That is what is meant, I think, by "moderator variables.")

I am skeptical about the utility of the genotype-phenotype distinction at the present level of behavioral analysis in personality psychology because I fear it grossly oversimplifies the complexity of organized behavior and its often nonlinear causes. The genotype-phenotype oversimplification may mask the complex relations between the behavior and the organism that generates it, the other behaviors available to the organism, the history of the behavior, and the current evoking and maintaining conditions that regulate its occurrence and its generalization.

The question of the nature of the similarity or dissimilarity among the diverse responses emitted by a person is one of the thorniest in psychology. Even when one response pattern is not in the service of another the two of course may still interact. No matter how seemingly separated the various branches of behavior may be, one can always construe some common origins for them and some current interactions. At the very least, all behavior from an organism, no matter how diverse, still has unity because it is all generated from the same source—from the same one person. At the other extreme, incidentally, few response patterns are ever phenotypically or physically identical: Their similarity always has to be grouped on some higher-order dimension of meaning. To make sense of bits of raw behavior one always has to group them into larger common categories. The interesting theoretical issue is just what the bases of these groupings should be. Dispositional theories try to categorize behaviors in terms of the hypothesized historical psychic forces that diverse behaviors supposedly serve; but it is also possible to categorize the behaviors in terms of the unifying evoking and maintaining conditions that they jointly share.

Moreover, few potent response patterns can occur without exerting radical consequences for the other alternatives available to the person. Thus an extremely "fast-tempo" child may be so active that, in addition to fatiguing his parents, he may as Kagan (1969) found, smile less. Perhaps that happens because he is too busy to smile. My comment about how fast-tempo children may be too busy to smile is not really facetious. One of the intriguing features of any strong response syndrome is that it soon prevents all kinds of other intrinsically incompatible behaviors. If a child darts about a lot and is fast there are all sorts of other things he automatically cannot do. His speed in living, his pace, not only automatically influences his other possible behavior, it also soon starts to shape his environment. I now expect my fast-tempo children to be fast tempo, and currently it takes almost no cues from them to convince me I am right about them.

It would have been relatively simple to assess and predict personality if it had turned out to consist mainly of stable highly generalized response patterns that occur regularly in relation to many diverse stimulus constellations. The degree and subtlety of discrimination shown in human behavior, however, is at least as impressive as is the variety and extensiveness of stimulus generalization. What people do in any situation may be altered radically even by seemingly minor variations in prior experiences or slight modifications in stimulus attributes or in the specific characteristics of the evoking situation. From my theoretical perspective this state of affairs—namely, the enormously subtle discriminations that people continuously make, and consequently the flexibility of behavior—is not a cause of gloom. Instead, the relative specificity of behavior, and its dependence on environmental supports, is the expected result of complex discrimination learning and subtle cognitive differentiation. When the eliciting and evoking conditions that maintain behavior change—as they generally do across settings—then behavior surely will change also. While the continuous interplay of person and condition may have been a surprise for faculty and trait psychology it should come as no upset for us now. If one pays more than verbal tribute to the dependency of behavior on conditions, and to the modification of behavior when situations change, then the so-called negative results of dispositional research on behavioral continuity appear attributable largely to the limitations of the assumptions that have guided the research. From the viewpoint of social behavior theory the findings of behavioral specificity, rather than primarily reflecting measurement errors, are actually congruent with results from experimental research on the determinants and modification of social behavior (Mischel, 1968). When response consequences and valences change so do actions; but when maintaining conditions remain stable so does behavior.

The last decade has seen an exciting growth of research on cognitive styles and many researchers have begun to study the person as an information-processing and problem-solving organism. Generally, however, these processes have been viewed in dimensional and dispositional terms and quickly translated back to fit the consistency assumptions of traditional global trait and psychodynamic theory. Individual differences on dimensions such as conceptual tempo, field dependence, leveling-sharpening, and so on, have been isolated with some promising results. Less progress has been made in applying the concepts and language of information processing and cognitive styles to forming a better theoretical conception of personality structure itself. It has become fashionable to speak of the organism as creating plans, generating rules, and, depending on his needs and situations, devising strategies. These tactics yield payoffs and consequences, and in light of these the person modifies his plans accordingly. But when contingencies change stably, what happens? For example, what happens when the mother-dependent child finds that his preschool peers now consistently have little patience for his whining, attention-getting bids, and instead respect independence and self-confidence? Generally the child's behavior changes in accord with the new contingencies, and if the contingencies shift so does the behavior—if the contingencies remain stable so does the new syndrome that the child now displays. Then what has happened to the child's dependency trait?

One might argue that the basic genotype remained but its manifestation phenotypically has altered. But is this just a "symptom" change leaving unaffected the psyche that generated it and the life space in which it unfolds? A vigorous "No!" to this question comes from much research on behavior change in the last few years (e.g., Bijou, 1965; Fairweather, 1967; Mischel, 1966; Patterson, Ray, & Shaw, 1969).

What would happen conceptually if we treated the organism as truly active and dynamic rather than as the carrier of a stable dispositional reservoir of motives and traits? Might one then more easily think of changes in the developing organism not as phenotypic overlays that mask genotypic unities but as genuinely new strategies in which many of the person's old plans are discarded and replaced by more appropriate ones in the course of development? (Perhaps Gordon Allport's idea of functional autonomy needs to be rethought.) Can the person even become involved in plans to change what he *is* as well as what he does? George Kelly and the existentialists in their search for human nature noted that existence precedes essence. According to that position, to find out what I *am* I need to know what I *do*. And if my actions change do they leave me (the "real me") behind? Or perhaps they just leave some of my discarded psychological genotypes behind?

A search for a personality psychology that has conceptual room for major variability and changes within the individual's dispositions can easily be misinterpreted as undermining the concept of personality itself. That would be an unfortunate misconstruction. Instead, we do need to recognize that discontinuities—real ones and not merely superficial or trivial veneer changes—are part of the genuine phenomena of personality. If one accepts that proposition, an adequate conceptualization of personality will have to go beyond the conventional definition of stable and broad enduring individual differences in behavioral dispositions. We may have to tolerate more dissonance than we like in our personality theory. To be more than nominally dynamic our personality theories will have to have as much room for human discrimination as for generalization, as much place for personality change as for stability, and as much concern for man's self-regulation as for his victimization by either enduring intrapsychic forces or by momentary environmental constraints.

REFERENCES

BANDURA, A. *Principles of behavior modification.* New York: Holt, Rinehart & Winston, 1969.

BIJOU, S. W. Experimental studies of child behavior, normal and deviant. In L. Krasner & L. P. Ullmann (Eds.), *Research in behavior modification.* New York: Holt, Rinehart & Winston, 1965.

BRUNER, J. S., OLVER, R. R., & GREENFIELD, P. M. *Studies in cognitive growth.* New York: Wiley, 1966.

CAMPBELL, D., & FISKE, D. Convergent and discriminant validation by the multitrait-multimethod matrix. *Psychological Bulletin,* 1959, *56,* 81–105.

CRANDALL, V. J., & SINKELDAM, C. Children's dependent and achievement behaviors in social situations and their perceptual field dependence. *Journal of Personality,* 1964, *32,* 1–22.

ELLIOTT, R. Interrelationships among measures of field dependence, ability, and personality traits. *Journal of Abnormal and Social Psychology,* 1961, *63,* 27–36.

EMMERICH, W. Models of continuity and change. Paper presented at the meeting of the Society for Research in Child Development, March 27, 1969, Santa Monica, California.

FAIRWEATHER, G. W. *Methods in experimental social innovation.* New York: Wiley, 1967.

HUNT, J. McV. Traditional personality theory in the light of recent evidence. *American Scientist,* 1965, *53,* 80–96.

KAGAN, J. Continuity in development. Paper presented at the meeting of the Society for Research in Child Development, March 27, 1969, Santa Monica, California.

MACCOBY, E. E. Tracing individuality within age-related change. Paper presented at the meeting of the Society for Research in Child Development, March 27, 1969, Santa Monica, California.

MADDI, S. R. *Personality theories: A comparative analysis.* Homewood, Ill.: Dorsey Press, 1968.

MISCHEL, W. A social learning view of sex differences in behavior. In E. E. Maccoby (ed.), *The development of sex differences.* Stanford: Stanford University Press, 1966.

MISCHEL, W. *Personality and assessment.* New York: Wiley, 1968.

PATTERSON, G. R., RAY, R. S., & SHAW, D. A. Direct intervention in families of deviant children. *Oregon Research Institute Bulletin,* 1969, *8*(9), 1–62.

PAUL, G. L. Insight versus desensitization in psychotherapy two years after termination. *Journal of Consulting Psychology,* 1967, *31,* 333–348.

PETERSON, D. *The clinical study of social behavior.* New York: Appleton-Century-Crofts, 1968.

SCHIMEK, J. G. Cognitive style and defenses: A longitudinal study of intellectualization and field independence. *Journal of Abnormal Psychology,* 1968, *73,* 575–580.

VERNON, P. S. *Personality assessment: A critical survey.* New York: Wiley, 1964.

WITKIN, H. Psychological differentiation and forms of pathology. *Journal of Abnormal Psychology,* 1965, *70,* 317–336.

WITKIN, H. A., GOODENOUGH, D. R., & KARP, S. A. Stability of cognitive style from childhood to young adulthood. *Journal of Personality and Social Psychology,* 1967, *7,* 291–300.

4

The Split-level American Family

Urie Bronfenbrenner

Influences upon children are not the same as they used to be. Urie Bronfenbrenner describes ways in which the lives of most American children today are drastically different from those of most American children of the past. The explanation of these differences is not simply technological changes such as the dishwashing machine and TV set. As Bronfenbrenner summarizes, the "conditions of life have changed."

Because the clock cannot be turned back, cures are needed for what ails the interpersonal environment of the nation's young. In 1970 Bronfenbrenner proposed that business create new work schedules to give men and women more time with their families. The Los Angeles Times *quoted him as follows:*

> *... although we like to think of America as a child-oriented society, a hard look at our way of life shows that the priorities of parents lie elsewhere. We put our children last, after everything else. . . . In today's world, parents find themselves at the mercy of a society which imposes pressures and priorities that allow neither time nor place for meaningful activities, and [which imposes] relations between children and adults which down-grade the role of parent and the functions of parenthood, and which prevent the parent from doing the things he wants to do as a guide, friend and companion to his children. . . .*

> *I don't know how long it will take us before we are able to turn this around. I am not a prophet, only a*

realist. But if we don't change things, we will go down the drain like Greece and Rome and other societies that fall apart.[1]

Dr. Bronfenbrenner has long been a professor at Cornell's Department of Child Development and Family Relations, one of the leading centers for the study of human development. The department is now a part of Cornell's College of Ecology.

Children used to be brought up by their parents.

It may seem presumptuous to put that statement in the past tense. Yet it belongs to the past. Why? Because *de facto* responsibility for upbringing has shifted away from the family to other settings in the society, where the task is not always recognized or accepted. While the family still has the primary moral and legal responsibility for developing character in children, the power or opportunity to do the job is often lacking in the home, primarily because parents and children no longer spend enough time together in those situations in which such training is possible. This is not because parents don't want to spend time with their children. It is simply that conditions of life have changed.

To begin with, families used to be bigger—not in terms of more children so much as more adults—grandparents, uncles, aunts, cousins. Those relatives who didn't live with you lived nearby. You often went to their houses. They came as often to yours, and stayed for dinner. You knew them all—the old folks, the middle-aged, the older cousins. And they knew you. This had its good side and its bad side.

On the good side, some of these relatives were interesting people, or so you thought at the time. Uncle Charlie had been to China. Aunt Sue made the best penuche fudge on the block. Cousin Bill could read people's minds (according to him). And all these relatives gave you Christmas presents.

But there was the other side. You had to give Christmas presents to all your relatives. And they all minded your business throughout the years. They wanted to know where you had been, where you were going, and why. If they didn't like your answers, they said so (particularly if you had told them the truth).

Not just your relatives minded your business. Everybody in the neighborhood did. Again this had its two sides.

If you walked on the railroad trestle, the phone would ring at your house. Your parents would know

[1] *Los Angeles Times,* Dec. 13, 1970.

what you had done before you got back home. People on the street would tell you to button your jacket, and ask why you weren't in church last Sunday.

But you also had the run of the neighborhood. You were allowed to play in the park. You could go into any store, whether you bought anything or not. They would let you go back of the store to watch them unpack the cartons and to hope that a carton would break. At the lumber yard, they let you pick up good scraps of wood. At the newspaper office, you could punch the linotype and burn your hand on the slugs of hot lead. And at the railroad station (they had railroad stations then), you could press the telegraph key and know that the telegraphers heard your dit-dah-dah all the way to Chicago.

These memories of a gone boyhood have been documented systematically in the research of Professor Herbert Wright and his associates at the University of Kansas. The Midwestern investigators have compared the daily life of children growing up in a small town with the lives of children living in a modern city or suburb. The contrast is sobering. Children in a small town get to know well a substantially greater number of adults in different walks of life and, in contrast to their urban and suburban agemates, are more likely to be active participants in the adult settings that they enter.

As the stable world of the small town has become absorbed into an ever-shifting suburbia, children are growing up in a different kind of environment. Urbanization has reduced the extended family to a nuclear one with only two adults, and the functioning neighborhood—where it has not decayed into an urban or rural slum—has withered to a small circle of friends, most of them accessible only by motor car or telephone. Whereas the world in which the child lived before consisted of a diversity of people in a diversity of settings, now for millions of American children the neighborhood is nothing but row upon row of buildings inhabited by strangers. One house, or apartment, is much like another, and so are the people. They all have about the same income, and the same way of life. And the child doesn't even see much of that, for all the adults in the neighborhood do is come home, have a drink, eat dinner, mow the lawn, watch TV, and sleep. Increasingly often, today's housing projects have no stores, no shops, no services, no adults at work or play. This is the sterile world in which many of our children grow, the "urban renewal" we offer to the families we would rescue from the slums.

Neighborhood experiences available to children are extremely limited nowadays. To do anything at all—go to a movie, get an ice cream cone, go swimming, or play ball—they have to travel by bus or private car. Rarely can a child watch adults working at their trades. Mechanics, tailors, or shopkeepers are either out of sight or unapproachable. A child cannot listen to gossip at the post office as he once did. And there are no abandoned houses, barns, or attics to break into. From a young point of view, it's a dull world.

Hardly any of this really matters, for children aren't home much, anyway. A child leaves the house early in the day, on a schoolbound bus, and it's almost suppertime when he gets back. There may not be anybody home when he gets there. If his mother isn't working, at least part-time (more than a third of all mothers are), she's out a lot—because of social obligations, not just friends—doing things for the community. The child's father leaves home in the morning before the child does. It takes the father an hour and a half to get to work. He's often away weekends, not to mention absences during the week.

If a child is not with his parents or other adults, with whom does he spend his time? With other kids, of course—in school, after school, over weekends, on holidays. In these relationships, he is further restricted to children of his own age and the same socioeconomic background. The pattern was set when the old neighborhood school was abandoned as inefficient. Consolidated schools brought homogeneous grouping by age, and the homogenizing process more recently has been extended to segregate children by levels of ability; consequently, from the preschool years onward the child is dealing principally with replicas of the stamp of his own environment. Whereas social invitations used to be extended to entire families on a neighborhood basis, the cocktail party of nowadays has its segregated equivalent for every age group down to the toddlers.

It doesn't take the children very long to learn the lesson adults teach: Latch onto your peers. But to latch he must contend with a practical problem. He must hitch a ride. Anyone going in the right direction can take him. But if no one is going in that direction just then, the child can't get there.

The child who can't go somewhere else stays home, and does what everybody else does at home. He watches TV. Studies indicate that American youngsters see more TV than children in any other country do. By the late 1950s, the TV-watching figure had risen to two hours a day for the average five-year-old, three hours a day during the watching peak age period of twelve to fourteen years.

In short, whereas American children used to spend much of their time with parents and other grownups, more and more waking hours are now lived in the world of peers and of the television screen.

What do we know about the influence of the peer group, or of television, on the lives of young children? Not much.

The prevailing view in American society (indeed in the West generally) holds that the child's psychological development, to the extent that it is susceptible to environmental influence, is determined almost entirely by the parents and within the first six years of life. Scientific investigators—who are, of course, products of their own culture, imbued with its tacit assumptions about human nature —have acted accordingly. Western studies of influences on personality development in childhood overwhelmingly take the form of research on parent-child relations, with the peer group, or other extraparental influences, scarcely being considered.

In other cultures, this is not always so. A year ago, at the International Congress of Psychology in Moscow, it was my privilege to chair a symposium on "Social Factors in Personality Development." Of a score of papers presented, about half were from the West (mostly American) and half from the Socialist countries (mostly Russian). Virtually without exception, the Western reports dealt with parent-child relationships; those from the Soviet Union and other East European countries focused equally exclusively on the influence of the peer group, or, as they call it, the children's collective.

Some relevant studies have been carried out in our own society. For example, I, with others, have done research on a sample of American adolescents from middle-class families. We have found that children who reported their parents away from home for long periods of time rated significantly lower on such characteristics as responsibility and leadership. Perhaps because it was more pronounced, absence of the father was more critical than that of the mother, particularly in its effect on boys. Similar results have been reported in studies of the effects of father absence among soldiers' families during World War II, in homes of Norwegian sailors and whalers, and in Negro households with missing fathers, both in the West Indies and the United States. In general, father absence contributes to low motivation for achievement, inability to defer immediate for later gratification, low self-esteem, susceptibility to group influence, and juvenile delinquency. All of these effects are much more marked for boys than for girls.

The fact that father-absence increases susceptibility to group influence leads us directly to the question of the impact of the peer group on the child's attitudes and behavior. The first—and as yet the only—comprehensive research on this question was carried out by two University of North Carolina sociologists, Charles Bowerman and John Kinch, in 1959. Working with a sample of several hundred students from the fourth to the tenth grades in the Seattle school system, these investigators studied age trends in the tendency of children to turn to parents versus peers for opinion, advice, or company in various activities. In general, there was a turning point at about the seventh grade. Before that, the majority looked mainly to their parents as models, companions, and guides to behavior; thereafter, the children's peers had equal or greater influence.

Though I can cite no documentation from similar investigations since then, I suspect the shift comes earlier now, and is more pronounced.

In the early 1960s, the power of the peer group was documented even more dramatically by James Coleman in his book *The Adolescent Society*. Coleman investigated the values and behaviors of teenagers in eight large American high schools. He reported that the aspirations and actions of American adolescents were primarily determined by the "leading crowd" in the school society. For boys in this leading crowd, the hallmark of success was glory in athletics; for girls, it was the popular date.

Intellectual achievement was, at best, a secondary value. The most intellectually able students were not those getting the best grades. The classroom wasn't where the action was. The students who did well were "not really those of highest intelligence, but only the ones who were willing to work hard at a relatively unrewarded activity."

The most comprehensive study relevant to the subject of our concern here was completed only a year ago by the same James Coleman. The data were obtained from more than 600,000 children in grades one to twelve in 4,000 schools carefully selected as representative of public education in the United States. An attempt was made to assess the relative contribution to the child's intellectual development (as measured by standardized intelligence and achievement tests) of the following factors: (1) family background (e.g., parents' education, family size, presence in the home of reading materials, records, etc.); (2) school characteristics (e.g., per pupil expenditure, classroom size, laboratory and library facilities, etc.); (3) teacher characteristics (e.g., background, training, years of experience, verbal skills, etc.); and (4) characteristics of other children in the same school (e.g., their background, academic achievement, career plans, etc.).

Of the many findings of the study, two were particularly impressive; the first was entirely expected, the second somewhat surprising. The expected finding was that home background was the most important element in determining how well the child did at school, more important than any of all aspects of the school which the child attended. This generalization, while especially true for Northern whites, applied to a lesser degree to Southern whites and Northern Negroes, and was actually reversed for Southern Negroes, for whom the characteristics of the school were more important than those of the home. The child apparently drew sustenance from wherever sustenance was most available. Where the home had most to offer, the home was the most determining; but where the school could provide more stimulation than the home, the school was the more influential factor.

The second major conclusion concerned the aspects of the school environment which contributed most to the child's intellectual achievement. Surprisingly enough, such items as per pupil expenditure, number of children per class, laboratory space, number of volumes in the school library, and the presence or absence of ability grouping were of negligible significance. Teacher qualifications accounted for some of the child's achievement. But by far the most important factor was the pattern of characteristics of the other children attending the same school. Specifically, if a lower-class child had schoolmates who came from advantaged homes, he did reasonably well; but if all the other children also came from deprived backgrounds, he did poorly.

What about the other side of the story? What happens to a middle-class child in a predominantly lower-class school? Is he pulled down by his classmates? According to Coleman's data, the answer is no; the performance of the advantaged children remains unaffected. It is as though good home background had immunized them against the possibility of contagion.

This is the picture so far as academic achievement is concerned. How about other aspects of psychological development? Specifically, how about social behavior—such qualities as responsibility, consideration for others, or, at the opposite pole, aggressiveness or delinquent behavior? How are these affected by the child's peer group?

The Coleman study obtained no data on this score. Some light has been shed on the problem, however, by an experiment which my Cornell colleagues and I recently carried out with school children in the United States and in the Soviet Union. Working with a sample of more than 150 sixth-graders (from six classrooms) in each country, we placed the children in situations in which we could test their readiness to engage in morally disapproved behavior such as cheating on a test, denying

responsibility for property damage, etc. The results indicated that American children were far more ready to take part in such actions.

The effect of the peer group (friends in school) was quite different in the two societies. When told that their friends would know of their actions, American children were even more willing to engage in misconduct. Soviet youngsters showed just the opposite tendency. In their case, the peer group operated to support the values of the adult society, at least at their age level.

We believe these contrasting results are explained in part by the differing role of the peer group in the two societies. In the Soviet Union, *vospitanie,* or character development, is regarded as an integral part of the process of education, and its principal agent—even more important than the family—is the child's collective in school and out. A major goal of the Soviet educational process, beginning in the nursery, is "to forge a healthy, self-sufficient collective" which, in turn, has the task of developing the child into a responsible, altruistic, and loyal member of a socialist society. In contrast, in the United States, the peer group is often an autonomous agent relatively free from adult control and uncommitted—if not outrightly opposed—to the values and codes of conduct approved by society at large. Witness the new phenomenon of American middle-class vandalism and juvenile delinquency, with crime rates increasing rapidly not only for teen-agers but for younger children as well.

How early in life are children susceptible to the effects of contagion? Professor Albert Bandura and his colleagues at Stanford University have conducted some experiments which suggest that the process is well developed at the preschool level. The basic experimental design involves the following elements. The child finds himself in a familiar playroom. As if by chance, in another corner of the room a person is playing with toys. Sometimes this person is an adult (teacher), sometimes another child. This other person behaves very aggressively. He strikes a large Bobo doll (a bouncing inflated figure), throws objects, and mutilates dolls and animal toys, with appropriate language to match. Later on, the experimental subject (*i.e.,* the child who "accidentally" observed the aggressive behavior) is tested by being allowed to play in a room containing a variety of toys, including some similar to those employed by the aggressive model. With no provocation, perfectly normal, well-adjusted preschoolers engage in aggressive acts, not only repeating what they had observed but elaborating on it. Moreover, the words and gestures accompanying the actions leave no doubt that the child is living through an emotional experience of aggressive expression.

It is inconvenient to use a live model every time. Thus it occurred to Bandura to make a film. In fact, he made two, one with a live model and a second film of a cartoon cat that said and did everything the live model had said and done. The films were presented on a TV set left on in a corner of the room, as if by accident. When the children were tested, the TV film turned out to be just as effective as real people. The cat aroused as much aggression as the human model.

As soon as Bandura's work was published, the television industry issued a statement calling his conclusions into question on the interesting ground that the children had been studied "in a highly artificial situation," since no parents were present either when the TV was on or when the aggressive behavior was observed. "What a child will do under normal conditions cannot be projected from his behavior when he is carefully isolated from normal conditions and the influences of society," the statement declared. Bandura was also criticized for using a Bobo doll (which, the TV people said, is "made to be struck") and for failing to follow up his subjects after they left the laboratory. Since then, Bandura has shown that only a ten-minute exposure to an aggressive model still differentiates children in the experimental group from their controls (children not subjected to the experiment) six months later.

Evidence for the relevance of Bandura's laboratory findings to "real life" comes from a subsequent field study by Dr. Leonard Eron, now at the University of Iowa. In a sample of more than 600 third-graders, Dr. Eron found that the children who were rated most aggressive by their classmates were those who watched TV programs involving a high degree of violence.

At what age do people become immune from contagion to violence on the screen? Professor Richard Walters of Waterloo University in Canada, and his associate, Dr. Llewellyn Thomas, showed two movie films to a group of thirty-four-year-old hospital attendants. Half of these adults were shown a knife fight between two teen-agers from the picture, *Rebel Without a Cause;* the other half saw a film depicting adolescents engaged in art work. Subsequently, all the attendants were asked to assist in carrying out an experiment on the effects of punishment in learning.

In the experiment, the attendants gave an unseen subject an electric shock every time the subject made an error. The lever for giving shocks had settings from zero to ten. To be sure the assistant understood what the shocks were like, he was given several, not exceeding the level of four, before the

experiment. Since nothing was said about the level of shocks to be administered, each assistant was left to make his own choice. The hospital attendants who had seen the knife-fight film gave significantly more severe shocks than those who had seen the art-work film. The same experiment was repeated with a group of twenty-year-old females. This time the sound track was turned off so that only visual cues were present. But neither the silence nor the difference in sex weakened the effect. The young women who had seen the aggressive film administered more painful shocks.

These results led designers of the experiment to wonder what would happen if no film were shown and no other deliberate incitement were introduced in the immediate setting of the experiment. Would the continuing emotional pressures of the everyday environment of adolescents—who see more movies and more TV and are called on to display virility through aggressive acts in teen-age gangs—provoke latent brutality comparable to that exhibited by the older people under direct stimulation of the movie of the knife fight?

Fifteen-year-old high school boys were used to test the answer to this question. Without the suggestive power of the aggressive film to step up their feelings, they pulled the shock lever to its highest intensities (levels eight to ten). A few of the boys made such remarks as "I bet I made that fellow jump."

Finally, utilizing a similar technique in a variant of what has come to be known as the "Eichmann experiment," Professor Stanley Milgram, then at Yale University, set up a situation in which the level of shock to be administered was determined by the lowest level proposed by any one of three "assistants," two of whom were confederates of Milgram and were instructed to call for increasingly higher shocks. Even though the true subjects (all adult males) could have kept the intensity to a minimum simply by stipulating mild shocks, they responded to the confederates' needling and increased the degree of pain they administered. [A more important criticism of all these studies is to be found in the work on the demand characteristics of experiments (Orne).—EDITOR]

All of these experiments point to one conclusion. At all age levels, pressure from peers to engage in aggressive behavior is extremely difficult to resist, at least in American society.

Now if the peer group can propel its members into antisocial acts, what about the opposite possibility? Can peers also be a force for inducing constructive behavior?

Evidence on this point is not so plentiful, but some relevant data exist. To begin with, experiments on conformity to group pressure have shown that the presence of a single dissenter—for example, one "assistant" who refuses to give a severe shock—can be enough to break the spell so that the subject no longer follows the majority. But the only research explicitly directed at producing moral conduct as a function of group experience is a study conducted by Muzafer Sherif and his colleagues at the University of Oklahoma and known as the "Robber's Cave Experiment." In the words of Elton B. McNeil:

War was declared at Robber's Cave, Oklahoma, in the summer of 1954 (Sherif *et al.,* 1961). Of course, if you have seen one war you have seen them all, but this was an interesting war, as wars go, because only the observers knew what the fighting was about. How, then, did this war differ from any other war? This one was caused, conducted, and concluded by behavioral scientists. After years of religious, political, and economic wars, this was, perhaps, the first scientific war. It wasn't the kind of war that an adventurer could join just for the thrill of it. To be eligible, ideally, you had to be an eleven-year-old, middle-class, American, Protestant, well-adjusted boy who was willing to go to an experimental camp.

Sherif and his associates wanted to demonstrate that within the space of a few weeks they could produce two contrasting patterns of behavior in this group of normal children. First, they could bring the group to a state of intense hostility, and then completely reverse the process by inducing a spirit of warm friendship and active cooperation. The success of their efforts can be gauged by the following two excerpts describing the behavior of the boys after each stage had been reached. After the first experimental treatment of the situation was introduced . . .

good feeling soon evaporated. The members of each group began to call their rivals "stinkers," "sneaks," and "cheaters." They refused to have anything more to do with individuals in the opposing groups. The boys . . . turned against buddies whom they had chosen as "best friends" when they first arrived at the camp. A large proportion of the boys in each group gave negative ratings to all the boys in the other. The rival groups made threatening posters and planned raids, collecting secret hoards of green apples for ammunition. To the Robber's Cave came the Eagles, after a defeat in a tournament game, and burned a banner left behind by the Rattlers; the next morning the Rattlers seized the Eagles' flag when they arrived on the athletic field. From that time on name-calling, scuffles, and raids were the rule of the day.
. . . In the dining-hall line they shoved each other aside, and the group that lost the contest for the head of the line shouted "Ladies first!" at the winner. They threw paper, food, and vile names at each other at the tables. An Eagle bumped by a Rattler was admonished by his fellow Eagles to brush "the dirt" off his clothes.

But after the second experimental treatment . . .

. . . The members of the two groups began to feel more friendly to each other. For example, a Rattler whom the Eagles disliked for his sharp tongue and skill in defeating them became a "good egg." The boys stopped shoving in the meal line. They no longer called each other names, and sat together at the table. New friendships developed between individuals in the two groups.
In the end the groups were actively seeking opportunities to mingle, to entertain and "treat" each other. They decided to hold a joint campfire. They took turns presenting skits and songs. Members of both groups requested that they go home together on the same bus, rather than on the separate buses in which they had come. On the way the bus stopped for refreshments. One group still had $5 which they had won as a prize in a contest. They decided to spend this sum on refreshments. On their own initiative they had invited their former rivals to be their guests for malted milks.

How were each of these effects achieved? Treatment One has a familiar ring:

. . . To produce friction between the groups of boys we arranged a tournament of games: baseball, touch football, a tug-of-war, a treasure hunt, and so on. The tournament started in a spirit of good sportsmanship. But as the play progressed good feeling soon evaporated.

How does one turn hatred into harmony? Before undertaking this task, Sherif wanted to demonstrate that, contrary to the views of some students of human conflict, mere interaction—pleasant social contact between antagonists—would not reduce hostility.

. . . we brought the hostile Rattlers and Eagles together for social events: going to the movies, eating in the same dining room, and so on. But far from reducing conflict, these situations only served as opportunities for the rival groups to berate and attack each other.

How was conflict finally dispelled? By a series of stratagems, of which the following is an example:

. . . Water came to our camp in pipes from a tank about a mile away. We arranged to interrupt it and then called the boys together to inform them of the crisis. Both groups promptly volunteered to search the water line for trouble. They worked together harmoniously, and before the end of the afternoon they had located and corrected the difficulty.

On another occasion, just when everyone was hungry and the camp truck was about to go to town for food, it developed that the engine wouldn't start, and the boys had to pull together to get the vehicle going.

To move from practice to principle, the critical element for achieving harmony in human relations, according to Sherif, is joint activity in behalf of a *superordinate goal*. "Hostility gives way when groups pull together to achieve overriding goals which are real and compelling for all concerned."

Here, then, is the solution for the problems posed by autonomous peer groups and rising rates of juvenile delinquency: Confront the youngsters with some superordinate goals, and everything will turn out fine.

What superordinate goals can we suggest? Washing dishes and emptying wastebaskets? Isn't it true that meaningful opportunities for children no longer exist?

This writer disagrees. Challenging activities for children can still be found; but their discovery requires breaking down the prevailing patterns of segregation identified earlier in this essay—segregation not merely by race (although this is part of the story) but to an almost equal degree by age, class, and ability. I am arguing for greater involvement of adults in the lives of children and, conversely, for greater involvement of children in the problems and tasks of the larger society.

We must begin by desegregating age groups, ability groups, social classes, and once again engaging children and adults in common activities. Here, as in Negro-white relations, integration is not enough. In line with Sherif's findings, contact between children and adults, or between advantaged and disadvantaged, will not of itself reduce hostility and evoke mutual affection and respect. What is needed in addition is involvement in a superordinate goal, common participation in a challenging job to be done.

Where is a job to be found that can involve children and adults across the dividing lines of race, ability, and social class?

Here is one possibility. Urbanization and industrialization have not done away with the need to care for the very young. To be sure, "progress" has brought us to the point where we seem to believe that only a person with a master's degree is truly qualified to care for young children. An exception is made for parents, and for babysitters, but these are concessions to practicality; we all know that professionals could do it better.

It is a strange doctrine. For if present-day knowledge of child development tells us anything at all, it tells us that the child develops psychologically as a function of reciprocal interaction with those who love him. This reciprocal interaction need be only of the most ordinary kind—caresses, looks, sounds, talking, singing, playing, reading stories—the things that parents, and everybody else, have done with children for generation after generation.

Contrary to the impression of many, our task in helping disadvantaged children through such programs as Head Start is not to have a "specialist" working with each child but to enable the child's parents, brothers, sisters, and all those around him to provide the kinds of stimulation which families ordinarily give children but which can fail to develop in the chaotic conditions of life in poverty. It is for this reason that Project Head Start places such heavy emphasis on the involvement of parents, not only in decision-making but in direct interaction with the children themselves, both at the center and (especially) at home. Not only parents but teenagers and older children are viewed as especially significant in work with the very young, for, in certain respects, older siblings can function more effectively than adults. The latter, no matter how warm and helpful they may be, are in an important sense in a world apart; their abilities, skills, and standards are so clearly superior to those of the child as to appear beyond childish grasp.

Here, then, is a context in which adults and children can pursue together a superordinate goal, for there is nothing so "real and compelling to all concerned" as the need of a young child for the care and attention of his elders. The difficulty is that we have not yet provided the opportunities—the institutional settings—which would make possible the recognition and pursuit of this superordinate goal.

The beginnings of such an opportunity structure, however, already exist in our society. As I have indicated, they are to be found in the poverty program, particularly those aspects of it dealing with children: Head Start, which involves parents, older children, and the whole community in the care of the very young; Follow Through, which extends Head Start into the elementary grades, thus breaking down the destructive wall between the school on the one hand and parents in the local community on the other; Parent and Child Centers, which provide a neighborhood center where all generations can meet to engage in common activities in behalf of children, etc.

The need for such programs is not restricted to the nation's poor. So far as alienation of children is concerned, the world of the disadvantaged simply reflects in more severe form a social disease that has infected the entire society. The cure for the society as a whole is the same as that for its sickest segment. Head Start, Follow Through, Parent and Child Centers are all needed by the middle class as much as by the economically less favored. Again, contrary to popular impression, the principal purpose of these programs is not remedial education but the giving to both children and their families of a sense of dignity, purpose, and meaningful activity without which children cannot develop capacities in any sphere of activity, including the intellectual.

Service to the very young is not the only superordinate goal potentially available to children in our society. The very old also need to be saved. In segregating them in their own housing projects and, indeed, in whole communities, we have deprived both them and the younger generations of an essential human experience. We need to find ways in which children once again can assist and comfort old people, and, in return, gain insight to character development that occurs through such experiences. [Swedish communities which earlier built separate accommodations for the elderly, later chose to integrate units for the elderly in general purpose housing.—EDITOR]

Participation in constructive activities on behalf of others will also reduce the growing tendency to aggressive and antisocial behavior in the young, if only by diversion from such actions and from the stimuli that instigate them. But so long as these stimuli continue to dominate the TV screen, those exposed to TV can be expected to react to the influence. Nor, as we have seen, is it likely that the TV industry will be responsive to the findings of research or the arguments of concerned parents and professionals. The only measure that is likely to be effective is pressure where it hurts most. The sponsor must be informed that his product will be boycotted until programing is changed.

My proposals for child rearing in the future may appear to some as a pipedream, but they need not be a dream. For just as autonomy and aggression have their roots in the American tradition, so have neighborliness, civic concern, and devotion to the young. By re-exploring these last, we can rediscover our moral identity as a society and as a nation.

II

BIOLOGICAL BASES FOR BEHAVIOR

The label "biological bases for behavior" avoids old and often sterile dichotomies, for example, heredity versus environment, or nature versus nurture. A more useful distinction is that between learned and non-learned attributes. Non-learned attributes include not only those that are genetically determined but also others such as the effects of disease and injury. Thus, birth injury is not hereditary but acquired, and it is a biological (in this case congenital [1]) and non-learned determinant of behavior.

When the theorist who emphasizes biological determinants of behavior and the unfolding of innate or congenital potentialities seeks to explain behavior, he is likely to ask the following kinds of questions: What species of organism is this? What are the characteristics of the species? Is it a particular strain of the species? Does that strain have particular characteristics? What is the specific genetic inheritance of this individual organism? What environmental events (other than opportunities for learning) have affected the organism?

Over the centuries, psychological thought has gone through periods when the predominant fashion was to consider heredity, constitution, or—more broadly—man's biological makeup as *the* all-important determinant of his behavior. This included his individual behavior, and not just those behaviors characteristic of his species. The swing of the pendulum came, and it became "unfashionable" to consider any influences other than environmental experiences, or individual life history, as important in determining the individual's behavior. These different emphases have not been unrelated to the political thinking of the times. Democracy, after all, de-emphasized hereditary position. It is an optimistic philosophy of government, and it produced men who could see more possibility for change and improvement through control of the environment than through control of biology or heredity. Recent work with such genetic diseases as phenylketonuria has shown that environmental action can alter the effects of some genetic "errors." In such an instance we see that acceptance of genetic determinism does not necessarily rule out optimism regarding the outcome.

At present, it is fair to say that most psychologists would defend some compromise position, not claiming all importance for one or the other side of the old dichotomy. There is general recognition that (in the words of the old song about "love and marriage") "you can't have one without the other." Nevertheless, one or the other set of determinants is emphasized by various workers.

As this edition is being completed, one of the most widely discussed issues in this area is what can only be labeled "the Jensen controversy." In order to cover the complexities of this controversy completely, we would have to print much too much material. We shall, however, try to summarize it and provide the interested reader with some of the basic references.

The Winter 1969 issue of *Harvard Educational Review* (vol. 39, no. 1) con-

---

[1] "Congenital"—acquired during development in the uterus or dating from birth; it is to be distinguished from "hereditary."

33

tained a 123-page article entitled "How Much Can We Boost IQ and Scholastic Achievement?" by Arthur R. Jensen, a nationally respected professor of educational psychology at the University of California at Berkeley. A substantial portion of this article dealt with the question of the "heritability" of intelligence, or the degree to which IQ is determined genetically. To grasp this aspect of the article you must understand the statistical procedures used to arrive at the estimates of "heritability." The article is, nevertheless, quite readable, and we encourage you to look it up. Another issue raised by Jensen is the effectiveness of compensatory education. Jensen's thesis is that compensatory education has failed, and many psychologists have taken issue with him on this aspect of the paper. Some have criticized his choice of data and his interpretation of those data. Others feel that we have never made a realistic test of compensatory education, thus it cannot be fairly evaluated at present. However, the controversy surrounding this aspect of Jensen's paper is nothing compared to that surrounding the ten or so pages he specifically devoted to race and IQ. (Since much of his discussion of SES* and IQ applies equally to race under current circumstances of overlap, ten pages may underestimate his emphasis on race.)

Under the heading "Genetic Aspects of Racial Differences" Jensen states:

> No one, to my knowledge, questions the role of environmental factors, including influences from past history, in determining at least some of the variance between racial groups in standard measures of intelligence, school performance, and occupational status.... I recently co-edited a book which is largely concerned with the environmental aspects of disadvantaged minorities (Deutsch, Katz, & Jensen, 1968). But the possible importance of genetic factors in racial behavioral differences has been greatly ignored, almost to the point of being a tabooed subject, just as were the topics of venereal disease and birth control a generation or so ago (pp. 79–80).

Jensen's charge is undoubtedly correct, and relatively few psychologists (though there are some) would argue that one should not be allowed to do research on the topic, or to analyze the existing data. At the same time, however, many psychologists have disputed his conclusions or his methods of arriving at them, and have opposed even more strongly the implications that seem so readily drawn from his presentation, despite his many disclaimers.

The Spring 1969 issue of the *Harvard Educational Review* presented seven solicited responses to his paper. The Summer 1969 issue (vol. 39, no. 3) presented a rebuttal by Jensen and four articles that had been triggered by his original article, including a paper by Deutsch (see above). The journal also devoted about 50 pages of correspondence to the issues raised. A thorough reading and comprehension of those papers and letters would make one a considerable expert in the field. Moreover, the material is instructive in relation to the problems faced by social and even biological science when these fields deal with complex issues that relate to public policies.

Jensen's original paper and the subsequent "Jensen controversy" were picked up by the mass media. As a result, many students may feel that they have sufficient acquaintance with the topic. However, we earnestly suggest that they go to the original sources cited here. In addition to the materials from the *Harvard Educational Review,* we recommend the following: "Intelligence and Race," by Bodmer and Cavalli-Sforza, in the October 1970 issue of *Scientific American* (vol. 223, no. 4), which presents a more popularized response by geneticists; and "Black Genes—White Environment," in the June 1969 issue of *Trans-Action,* which presents a popularized response by the psychologist J. McVicker Hunt.

---

* SES means socio-economic status.

Readers will want to keep in mind the issues posed in this biological determinants section when they read other parts of the book. The topics of Age or Developmental Stage (Sec. VII), Sex (Sec. VIII), and Cognition (Sec. IX) are all topics in which biological causes play an important role. In addition, biological causes are clearly germane to Group Memberships (Sec. VI), which includes both race and SES. Differences between the sexes in behavior and differences among people in intelligence are products, after all, of both biology and learning. Certain workers who have placed major emphasis on age or developmental stage have assumed the primacy of biological over experiential determinants. Much of the writing that takes its intellectual origin from either Freud or Jean Piaget is of this type. The cross-reference chart at the beginning of this book lists all the articles included that bear on biological determinants.

The student with little or no background in genetics might find it helpful to consult one or more of the following sources:

1. *Heredity and the Nature of Man* (Harcourt, Brace & World, 1964). By the important geneticist Theodosius Dobzhansky, this book is based on a lecture series given in the springs of 1963 and 1964.
2. *Behavior Genetics* (John Wiley and Sons, 1960, reprinted in 1967). This book is by two psychologists, John L. Fuller and William R. Thompson.
3. *The Future Man* (Basic Books, 1959). This book is based on a series of BBC lectures by the British Nobel Laureate geneticist Peter Medawar. Chapters 4 and 6 are of particular interest for the purposes of readers of this book.
4. *The Language of Life: An Introduction to the Science of Genetics* (Doubleday & Co., 1966). This book is by George and Muriel Beadle. He is a Nobel Prize winner in genetics and she is a well known author.* Chapters 13 through 21 and Chapter 24 are perhaps most interesting for the novice.
5. *The Code of Life* (Columbia University Press, 1965). By Ernest Borek, this book is intended for the educated layman. Chapter 23 of the Beadles' book above is also suitable for this level.

In addition to the books listed above, we would like to refer to two articles. "Should We Weaken or Strengthen Our Genetic Heritage?" (Daedalus, 1961, *90*, 432–450) is an abridgement by Hermann J. Muller of a longer and more technical article. He too is a Nobel Laureate. It would be of particular interest to contrast his views with those of Medawar (see above). In addition, some readers may be interested in the genetic code itself. An article on it for educated laymen appeared in *Scientific American* (1962, *207*, 66–74), written by F. H. C. Crick, another British Nobel Laureate in genetics.

Those who do not desire to go into genetics per se but would like to understand the issues raised by Jensen, might want to consult chapter 6 of Donald O. Hebb's *A Textbook of Psychology*. It is entitled "Heredity, Maturation, Early Learning." Those who would like to understand more about the mechanisms that mediate hereditary and environmental effects on behaviors, such as learning, should read Mark R. Rosenzweig's "Effects of Heredity and Environment on Brain Chemistry, Brain Anatomy, and Learning Ability in the Rat," published in *Kansas Studies in Education*, 1964, *14*, 3–15.

---

* Among her works is a book entitled *The Child's Mind: How Children Learn During the Critical Years from Birth to Age 5* (Doubleday & Co., 1970).

5

Constitutional Factors
in Behavior

SIDNEY L. BECK
AND JUDY F. ROSENBLITH

This paper was prepared for this volume to take into account the growing amount of work showing the importance of genetic factors and their mechanisms of operation. We had been unable to discover a single article that described a reasonable portion of this literature simply enough for those who are not biology students. While the introduction to this section has cited some of the literature on genetics that is valuable to students of child psychology, a partial survey seemed necessary here.

Dr. Beck is professor of biology at Wheaton College, where Judy Rosenblith is also located.

Biological contributions to behavioral parameters are many and varied. They can be classified into major groupings depending upon the period during ontogeny when they manifest themselves. Or, more precisely, one can distinguish between those biological determinants which are inherited in a truly genetic sense, or transmitted through the genome, and those which are congenital, or a consequence of developmental events and not transmitted through the genome. Finally there are those which manifest themselves only after birth but which nevertheless contribute to the biological constitution of the child. The latter may well be familial without being either genetic or congenital in origin.

Considering only the more easily ascertained category of abnormal behavior, genetic causes would include mutations of a single gene and chromosomal abnormalities. Non-genetic congenital defects would include those caused by drugs, bacterial or viral infections, and physical insults during gestation, as well as traumata occasioned by the birth process itself. Finally, post-natal defects may be occasioned by nutritional factors, disease processes, or physical damage.

Although we shall in the remainder of this paper deal primarily with those aspects of the biological endowment which are important in atypical behavior, it must be recognized that the constitution of the individual sets the limits within which all subsequent environmental events act. In a very fundamental sense it is specious to speak of "nature versus nurture." Rather, all behavior, indeed all characteristics, both behavioral and physical, represent a series of interactions between constitutional and environmental agencies. Thus one must always consider the role of nature *and* nurture in shaping the individual.

GENETIC FACTORS

While genetic contribution to normal behavioral attributes has been investigated using twin studies, the attributes studied are almost always controlled by a large number of genes each producing small additive effects. The best that can be determined from this is an estimate of heritability. The method of investigation of heritability involves a comparison of like-sexed dizygotic (DZ) twins and monozygotic (MZ) twins controlled for age, socioeconomic factors, etc. Since MZ twins have an identical genetic makeup, any variation between members of a pair of MZ twins for a given trait can be attributed to environmental factors. Variation between members of DZ twin pairs, on the other hand, includes both genetic and environmental factors. Therefore, if the amount of measurable variation between members of MZ twin-pairs is less than between DZ twin-pairs, the difference is due to differences in genetic factors among the DZ individuals. Such genetic variation (expressed as a fraction of the total variation which can be measured) gives an estimate of *heritability* for that trait. Twin studies do not reveal *how* genes operate, or even *what* genes are operating; only *whether* genetic factors are operating and roughly how much of the total variation observed is genetic in origin.

A number of identifiable genes are known to influence behavior in detectable ways. Some of these genes primarily affect sensory capacities, others physical appearance, physiological characteristics, or intellectual functioning. Behavioral effects may be secondary and socially conditioned. They include various forms of blindness, deafness, deafmutism, cretinism, albinism, chondrodystrophy, muscular dystrophy, Huntington's chorea, and palsy, to name but a few. For a detailed discussion the reader is referred to Stern (1960). Single gene effects on intellectual capacity include amaurotic idiocy (Tay-Sachs disease) and phenylketonuria. The last named is an intriguing example of how nurture can dramatically influence the expression of a severe behavioral disorder which is clearly inherited as a simple recessive gene. Phenylalanine is a normal constituent of most proteins taken in as food. It is made available for the synthesis of other products by digestion. The first step in the normal utilization of phenylalanine is its conversion to a different compound, tyrosine, by an enzyme produced in the liver. In phenylketonurics this enzyme is lacking and phenylalanine builds up to abnormally high concentrations. At these concentrations other pathways of utilization occur and some of the end products will cause severe mental retardation, especially between the ages of 4 months and 4 years. Indeed, in one study it was found that up to 1 percent of all patients in hospitals for the mentally deficient were phenylketonurics (Harris, 1966). One of the end products of phenylalanine metabolism, phenylpyruvic acid, is excreted in the urine of phenylketonurics. It is not excreted to any appreciable extent by normal individuals, and it is easily detected.* Since phenylalanine is an essential amino acid it cannot be completely eliminated from the diet, but it has been possible to prepare diets with a severely restricted phenylalanine content and when these are given to phenylketonurics at any age the blood levels of phenylalanine can be kept at normal levels. If this low-phenylalanine diet is exclusively fed to phenylketonurics up to four years of age, mental retardation can be prevented. After four years of age it appears that it may no longer be necessary to restrict phenylalanine, the sensitive period being then past.† There are other genetically determined metabolic diseases or "inborn errors of metabolism" which are receiving this type of biochemical analysis with its logically associated treatment possibilities (Stanbury et al., 1960). Such studies are still in early stages.

A great deal of excitement has been generated in recent years by improvements in methods of detecting other kinds of genetically determined defects involving abnormalities of larger genetic units, the chromosomes. It is now possible to take specimens from blood or smears from inside the mouth, or cells from sternal puncture and treat the cells in various ways to accurately separate each of the chromosomes one from another. These spread chromosomes can then be photographed, cut out of the photograph and arranged in order of size for subsequent analysis (Figure 1). This process, called karyotyping, revealed that the true number of chromosomes in man was 46, rather than the previously published number of 48 (Tjio and Levan, 1956). Since the establishment of karyotype analysis, progress in detecting abnormal variations at the chromosome level has been rapid and the information obtained has been so voluminous as to have required the establishment of a committee of investigators in this field to standardize nomenclature (Chicago Conference, 1966). The usefulness of karyotype analysis has been greatly enhanced by the recently developed technique of amniocentesis. In this process samples of the amniotic fluid which surrounds the fetus are taken using a hypodermic syringe. This is relatively free of hazard. The fluid removed contains cells that have been sloughed off by the fetus. Karyotyping of these cells permits detection of an ever growing list of abnormalities early in pregnancy. The advent of the computer has simplified the task of karyotyping considerably, making such determinations feasible for greater numbers of patients.

The normal complement of human chromosomes consists of twenty-two pairs of autosomes and a single pair of sex chromosomes. The sex chromosomes in females are both alike (XX) and in males are morphologically and functionally different (XY). The chromosomes are numbered consecutively according to size. When arranged by size (see Figure 1) they form seven groups. The members of a single group are difficult to distinguish from one another, but each group is clearly different from the others. Currently a technique involving treatment of the chromosomes with a fluorescent dye (quinocrine) (Caspersson et al., 1970) gives promise of allowing all 23 pairs to be unequivocally distinguished from one another.

In addition to size, the chromosomes also differ with respect to the location of the centromere, a structure which gives the chromosome a "waist." The centromere divides the chromosome into arms. Since the chromosomes are taken from dividing cells in which the chromosomes have doubled, each appears with four arms held together by the centromere. The short arm of a chromosome is labelled "p" and the long arm "q." Shortening or absence of an arm or of a chromosome is indicated with a minus sign; increase in length of an arm or the presence of an extra chromosome is indicated with a plus sign.

The first defect in man known to be attributable to a chromosomal abnormality was Mongolism,

---

* Tests immediately after birth are not conclusive, however.

† Currently, new findings have complicated this picture, but until the issues now raised are resolved, we accept this view.

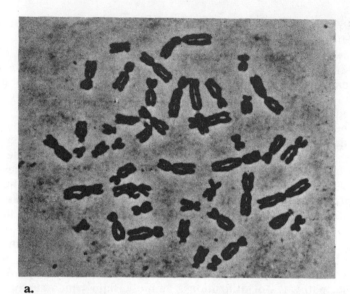

a.

b.

FIGURE 1. *Analysis of human chromosome complement. (a) Chromosome spread from leukocyte culture. (b) Arrangement of chromosomes into standard karyotype. (Furnished by Dr. J. J. Biesele.)* [*From* An Introduction to Human Genetics *by H. Eldon Sutton. Copyright © 1965 by Holt, Rinehart and Winston, Inc. Reprinted by permission of Holt, Rinehart and Winston, Inc.*]

or more properly, Down's syndrome. This disorder is due to the presence of an extra chromosome 21, and the abbreviation of the resultant karyotype is 47,XY,21+ in a male and 47,XX,21+ in a female. The syndrome was originally described by Down in 1866, and its association with an extra chromosome was suggested by Waardenburg in 1932. In 1959, three groups of investigators independently and nearly simultaneously established that the condition was due to the presence of an extra chromosome-21, or trisomy-21. Individuals with Down's syndrome are characterized by the presence of an epicanthic fold on the eyelid which, along with a yellowish cast to the skin, first led Down to apply the term "Mongolism." Other stigmata associated include abnormalities of the face, a somewhat enlarged tongue, the presence of a simian crease on the palmar surface of the hand as well as characteristic patterns of ridges on the fingers and palms, high susceptibility to infection, and a variable degree of mental retardation. This is a fairly common abnormality, with an overall incidence of about 0.15 percent in caucasian populations (Stern, 1960). There is a very striking effect of maternal age on likelihood of occurrence: women who are 35 years or older are 100 times more likely to produce a child with trisomy-21 than those mothers who are under 35. More than one in 40 children born to women over forty years of age will have Down's syndrome. This age-related difference in frequency of occurrence suggests that in the formation of the fertilized ovum the two chromosomes-21 fail to separate (non-disjunction), thus giving rise to the extra chromosome. Various explanations for this phenomenon have been proposed including aging effects on an ovum held so long in the ovary, aging effects on an ovum fertilized longer after its release,* viral infection of the ovum, etc., but the cause is not known. There is a variant form of the disorder, familial mongolism. In these cases there are but 46 chromosomes instead of a 47,XX,21+ or 47,XY,21+. Karyotype analysis reveals that there is indeed extra chromosome-21 material but that it is attached to another chromosome. Translocation of chromosomal material shows no effect due to age of mother, but will likely affect several members of a sibship. A young mother, not herself a carrier of translocation, who had an offspring suffering from trisomy-21 would not be more likely than any other mother to have this disorder occur in subsequent progeny, since primary trisomy-21 is a random non-disjunctional event. Women carrying a translocated chromosome-21 are themselves normal, but their karyotype is 45,XX,21−. About one in five of the progeny of such a carrier will have Down's syndrome; the others will appear and behave normally, but may be carriers of the disorder. Surviving individuals with trisomy of chromosomes 18 or 13 (see Nusbacher and Hirschhorn, 1968 for a review) and trisomies involving the sex chromosomes are also known. In general, however, trisomy is incompatible with life.

If trisomy is a result of non-disjunction of a chromosome during gamete formation, then there should be comparable classes of fetuses which are monosomic as well; that is, which contain only one of a pair of chromosomes. Monosomics are known involving the sex chromosomes (45,XO), but no other viable monosomic chromosome con-

stitutions are known. Indeed, except for those mentioned above, no other aneuploid chromosome patterns (i.e., other than complete sets) appear to be viable. Recent studies (see Inhorn 1967 for review) have shown, however, that chromosomal abnormalities account for a large proportion of "spontaneous" abortions. Some studies have shown that between 20 (Carr, 1967) and 65 percent (Boué et al., 1967) of fetuses aborted in the first trimester have abnormal chromosomal complements. Although trisomy-21 was the first major viable chromosomal abnormality to be studied, the most studied group of abnormal chromosome patterns are those involving the sex chromosomes. The presence of an extra X-chromosome (47,XXX or 47,XXY), an extra Y (47,XYY), or absence of an X (45,XO) are all known and are associated with behavioral derangement of varying degrees. One can easily detect an extra or absent X-chromosome because of the fact that each X-chromosome in excess of one is visible in the nuclei of non-dividing cells as a sex-chromatin mass (Barr and Bertram, 1949). Thus normal females (XX) show a single sex-chromatin mass at the periphery of nearly all of their cells, whereas normal males (XY) do not show this phenomenon. Disorders involving aneuploidy of the sex chromosomes are Turner's and Klinefelter's syndromes. Turner's syndrome affects females; they show reduced stature, poor mammary development, immature external genitalia, and failure to commence menstruation. The ovaries of these individuals are almost entirely absent and have no ova whatever (see McKusick, 1964 for additional details). These individuals have no sex chromatin, and karyotype analysis reveals a 45,XO constitution, or absence of the second X-chromosome. Klinefelter's syndrome affects males; they have immature and small testes, little body hair, and, frequently, female-like breast development. These individuals show sex chromatin and their karyotype is 47,XXY. Klinefelter's occurs with a frequency of one in 400–600 births; Turner's, one in 5,000.

Recently there has been considerable interest in another abnormality of the sex chromosomes, the presence of an extra Y. The 47,XYY karyotype was discovered to be present in a high proportion of males in prison populations and there is the suggestion from subsequent studies that the extra Y-chromosome may be associated with increased stature, an increased tendency towards aggressive and antisocial behavior, and crimes of violence (Marinello et al., 1969). A few examples of 47,XXX females are known, and while they may show some mental deficiency they tend not to be grossly abnormal.

While the presence of even a single extra auto-

---

* This may occur because the older woman is having less frequent intercourse.

some is usually incompatible with life, this does not seem to be the case with the sex chromosomes, and cases of 48,XXXY and 48XXXX are known. Individuals with five X-chromosomes have also been described. They often appear as exaggerated Klinefelter's types if a Y is also present. An explanation for the viability of the four-X and five-X karyotypes comes from the interesting observation that, with an increase in the number of X-chromosomes, there is an increase in the number of sex chromatin masses seen in the cells. This observation, plus the related observations that female humans and mice may be mosaic for a number of traits carried on the X-chromosome, led Mary Lyon (1961, 1966) to propose the theory that all of the X-chromosomes but one are inactivated early in embryonic development in mammals. This theory accounts for the fact that there are no differences in expression of X-linked genes in males and females, since, if the theory is true, only one X-chromosome would in fact be active in both men and women. It would also account for why such great variation in the number of X-chromosomes can be tolerated, whereas aneuploidy for most of the other chromosomes (except 13, 18, and 21) is inviable. That is, no matter how many X-chromosomes are present, only one is active.

Karyotype analysis has also revealed numerous cases of individuals who are mosaics with respect to chromosomal abnormalities. That is, some of their cells may be abnormal while others appear perfectly normal. Thus karyotypes from different cells of the same individual may show 45,XO and 46,XX patterns, or 47,XX,21+ and 46,XX, etc. These individuals are generally less severely affected and may even appear normal but, if the gamete-producing cells are affected as well, they may transmit the abnormality to progeny. The presence of mosaics can be explained by non-disjunction or loss from other causes during embryogenesis.

Not only may entire chromosomes be abnormally represented in an individual, but parts of a chromosome may be duplicated or lost. One striking example of this type of disorder was originally described as the "cri-du-chat" or cry of the cat syndrome (Nusbacher and Hirschhorn, 1968). This syndrome, so-named because afflicted individuals issue a peculiar cat-like cry, invariably involves mental retardation, and other abnormalities in differing proportions of cases. The defect is more common in females and was shown to be a result of reduction or absence of the short arm of chromosome-5 (46,XX,5p— or 46,XY,5p—). Deletions are also known involving chromosome-18. Other bizarre patterns have been reported including duplications, deletions, and formation of ring-shaped

chromosomes. Each has its own characteristic pattern of associated abnormalities almost invariably including mental retardation.

In summary, then, we have presented an overview of a variety of easily describable biological factors that influence behavior in predictable and measurable ways. While we have focused on those determinants concerned with abnormalities and abnormal behavioral patterns, it is equally clear that the coefficient of biological determination of any behavioral attribute is measurably greater than zero, and in no case can constitutional factors be ignored.

TERATOLOGICAL FACTORS

Increases in the number of man-made chemicals as a consequence of new technologies and modern medicine, and the changing epidemiological patterns of infectious disease as a consequence of freer travel, are not without hazard to man's biological endowment. Of particular interest in the present context are those birth defects attributable to non-genetic causes which have behavioral ramifications.

The relatively young discipline of teratology, or the study of abnormal development, gained momentum as a result of the production of thousands of malformed babies in parts of Europe and Japan following the introduction of the mild sedative Thalidomide prescribed as a relaxant for anxious pregnant women (Lenz, 1964). The characteristic disturbances associated with Thalidomide teratogenesis are gross malformations of the limbs, especially the arms. Typically the arms are "flipper-like" or almost totally absent. These children clearly pose serious problems to the physician and psychologist. Thalidomide is an example of a chemical teratogen. In the broadest sense, a teratogen is any agent, physical or chemical, which may act directly on the fetus or indirectly through the mother in such a way as to interfere with normal fetal development. Other drugs have been implicated as being teratogenic in man with greater or lesser degrees of certainty. These include the tranquilizer meclazine, the abortifacient aminopterin, the radiomimetic myleran, the steroid cortisone (Lenz, 1964, Smithells, 1966), and the antibiotic tetracycline (Carter and Wilson, 1963). Progestational compounds used to maintain pregnancy in women with histories of recurrent abortions can cause masculinization of female fetuses (Smithells, 1966). There are very clear data in experimental animals (Filippi, 1967) on the severe teratogenic effect of a variety of maternal vitamin deficiencies and antibiotic excesses which will lead to vitamin deficiencies.

Another important class of teratogenic situations

involves maternal viral infection during the first third of pregnancy. The best documented and most serious of these is infection with rubella, the German measles virus. The presence of rubella and other viruses in the fetus following maternal infection can be detected by means of amniocentesis. Rubella periodically reaches epidemic proportions and can cause a broad spectrum of defects in from 10 to more than 50 percent of the fetuses of infected mothers, depending on when during gestation the infection occurs (Desmond et al., 1970). The principal disorders produced are cataracts, deafness, heart defects, and a variety of behavioral disturbances, neuro-motor defects, autistic tendencies, and mental retardation. Other viruses have also been implicated as being teratogenic, and the suggestion has been made (Stoller, 1968) that infectious hepatitis, a presumed viral disease, is in part responsible for Down's syndrome, by being responsible for the maternal non-disjunction of chromosome-21.

X-irradiation has been described as a "universal teratogen" in animals, producing maldevelopment in all organ systems depending upon the time of administration and the dose. Not only are high acute doses damaging, but chronic low doses administered to rats and mice have resulted in reduced fertility and poor performance in a variety of learning situations. Radiation has been implicated in human teratogenesis as well, and is definitely known to cause chromosome breakage with a subsequent loss of parts of broken chromosomes. Data on the possible effects of radiation on behavioral parameters in man are lacking because the obvious physical danger has tended to limit his exposure (Hicks and D'Amato, 1966).

ADDITIONAL CONSIDERATIONS

The contributions of biological determinants to behavior do not cease with birth; culture simply intervenes and becomes a prominent factor. Not only do the constitutional characteristics of the child continue to operate, but new biological factors enter the picture. The effect, for example, of nutritional factors on intelligence is one basic concern about which much heat and little light has been generated. The data are clear in animal studies: malnutrition *in utero* can be teratogenic; malnutrition in early post-natal life can depress learning performance; malnutrition in both periods has the most drastic effects—greater than a simply additive mechanism would account for. The corresponding data for man are less clear. It is clear, however, that nutritional level does contribute to man's constitution and health (Scrimshaw and Gordon, 1968).

Implicit in much of the discussion of the preceding sections is the idea of variability in symptoms. Different individuals who have the same genetic (or constitutional) characteristic show great variation in the severity of their symptoms. This is true both with respect to physical stigmata and intellectual capacity. There is always interaction between environmental and biological factors in determining any behavioral attribute. In addition, there is always a continuum of directness-indirectness in the operation of constitutional factors on behavior. At one extreme, essential physical prerequisites for normal intellectual development may be lacking as a result of severe brain injury or of hereditary metabolic disorders. Here there is a very direct relation to the outcome.

A different level of determinism is shown in a disorder such as deafness. Whether it is due to heredity or to non-hereditary congenital factors (e.g., a result of some intrauterine factor such as rubella), it can lead to handicaps in communication and even retardation. However, these result from interference with language acquisition, poor social interaction, lack of schooling, etc. Adequate special instruction, especially at an early age, may act to reduce or eliminate the handicaps. The importance of starting such training early means that the child deaf at birth due to heredity may have a better chance to minimize the handicaps since he will be suspect and therefore more apt to be detected early and thus receive the appropriate training. Only if the mother is known to have had rubella during pregnancy are the chances of early detection as good for the non-hereditarily congenitally deaf child. This is especially true since we have no good ways of assessing hearing in the newborn period (Hardy, 1970 and Rosenblith, 1970). In summary, the effects of congenital deafness on communication and intelligence are not very direct and depend on the early environment to a very large degree.

A still less direct way in which heredity may influence behavior is through social stereotypes. The physical characteristics that serve to trigger such stereotypes may lead to either special restriction or to special opportunity, to enhanced or to enfeebled self-concept. As one proceeds along the continuum of indirectness which we have tried to indicate in these examples:

". . . the range of variation of possible outcomes of hereditary factors expands rapidly. At each step in the causal chain, there is fresh opportunity for interaction with other hereditary factors as well as with environmental factors. And since each interaction in turn determines the direction of subsequent interactions, there is an ever-widening network of possible outcomes" (Anastasi, p. 46, as reprinted in Rosenblith and Allinsmith, 2nd edition).

Again, as Anastasi (1958) has so clearly stated: "Hereditary influences—as well as environmental factors of an organic nature—vary along a 'continuum of indirectness.' The more indirect their connection with behavior, the wider will be the range of possible outcomes" (pp. 51–52).

It should now be clear that behavior in the psychological domain cannot be predicted from knowledge of genetic factors alone. At the same time there is much excitement over the new knowledge from genetics that helps us understand (and sometimes even treat) clinical syndromes. However, when we attempt to assess the biological contributions to normal behavior or behavior in congenitally normal individuals, the situation is much less clear. Here the environmental influences are easier for the psychologist to assess. Wide diversity of methods of study, psychological functions studied, and subjects studied is necessary if we are to arrive at a better understanding of the ways in which hereditary and environmental influences interact in the development of behavior.

The effects of early experience in relation to genetic variables is one important type of research needed. Recent work indicates that major revisions of research methodology and of interpretation of results may be needed (Henderson, 1968). Henderson's studies indicate that the rate of acquisition, the retention, and the extinction of conditioned fears are all heritable characteristics. However, the evidence points to their being inherited independently of each other. Additional evidence points to genetic independence of other heritable traits that appear to be involved in the effects of early experience. Henderson shows that different genotypes of mice are likely to react quite differently to varied early experiences such as "enrichment." *

Reasonable methods for estimating heritability have existed in agricultural research where the complexity of genotype-environment interactions are analogous to those in the behavioral sciences. These methods are beginning to be applied to behavioral research (Roberts, 1967). After even a cursory examination of the behavior-genetic studies using primarily sub-human animals (see Hirsch, 1967, e.g.), it becomes clear that one cannot generalize responses to identical stimuli across genotypes within a species (rats or mice). Therefore, we must certainly be very modest in our expectations of the ease with which we shall be able to understand the effects of early experience (for example,

enrichment) on children whose individual differences are as great as strain differences in mice.

Perhaps these new emphases on genetics and on other biological factors (including nutrition, viral diseases, drugs, etc., operating *in utero* to determine the constitution of the newborn) and on behavioral genetics may serve to enhance the concern of psychology with individuals or with individuality. Much of the life of psychology has seemingly been devoted to trying to control for individual differences in the hopes of finding general laws of development and behavior. In the process, concern has often been with the average differences between groups which are commonly very small compared to the differences within the groups (individual differences). The time may now be right for increasing concern with individual differences. A recent book written at a popular level by the biochemist Roger J. Williams (1967) is concerned with human individuality. In a chapter devoted to psychology and psychiatry he says: "We can in one sentence summarize the future of psychology and psychiatry in the new and different world where everyone is recognized as having a high degree of inborn individuality. Psychology and psychiatry will expand and become far more useful and expert through centering attention on real individuals. Insofar as psychology's interest has been in the average man, the tail has been wagging the dog. Eventually 'differential psychology' † with all of its ramifications will be the dog, wagging the rest of psychology as an appendage" (p. 177).

REFERENCES

ANASTASI, ANNE (1958). Heredity, environment and the question how. *Psychol. Rev.* 65: 197–208. (Reprinted in Rosenblith and Allinsmith, *The Causes of Behavior*, 2d ed.)

BARR, M. L., & E. G. BERTRAM (1949). A morphological distinction between neurones of the male and female and the behavior of the nucleolar satellite during accelerated nucleoprotein synthesis. *Nature 163:* 676–677.

BOUÉ, J. G., A. BOUÉ, & P. LAZAR (1967). Les aberrations chromosomiques dans les avortements. *Ann. Génétique 10:* 179–187.

CARR, D. H. (1967). Chromosome anomalies as a cause of spontaneous abortion. *Am. J. Obstet. Gynec. 97:* 283–293.

CARTER, M. P., & F. WILSON (1963). Antibiotics and congenital malformations. *Lancet* I, p. 1267.

CASPERSSON, T., L. ZECH, & C. JOHANSSON (1970). Analysis of human metaphase chromosome set by

---

* One should also note that the effects of early experience may vary not only according to genotype, but also according to early experiences of a previous generation (See Section II, Article 8).—EDITOR

---

† Differential psychology is the study of "individual differences," of the variations among people in whatever attributes are being investigated.—EDITOR

aid of DNA-binding fluorescent agents. *Exp. Cell Res. 62:* 490–492.

CHICAGO CONFERENCE (1966). Standardization in Human Cytogenetics. Birth defects, original article series, Vol II, No. 2, The National Foundation. New York.

DESMOND, M. M., G. S. WILSON, W. M. VERNIAUD, J. L. MELNICK, & W. E. RAWLS (1970). The early growth and development of infants with congenital rubella. *Adv. Teratol. 4:* 39–63.

DOWN, J. L. (1866). Observations on an ethnic classification of idiots. *Lond. Hosp. Rep. 3:* 259. (Cited in Penrose, 1966)

FILIPPI, B. (1967). Antibiotics and congenital malformations: Evaluation of the teratogenicity of antibiotics. *Adv. Teratol. 2:* 239–256.

HARDY, JANET B., WILLIAM G. HARDY, & MIRIAM P. HARDY (1970). Some problems in neonatal screening. *Trans. of the American Academy of Ophthalmology and Otolaryngology 74:* 1229–1235.

HARRIS, H. (1966). *Human Biochemical Genetics.* Cambridge University Press, Cambridge, England.

HENDERSON, N. D. (1968). The confounding effects of genetic variables in early experience research: Can we ignore them? *Developmental Psychobiology,* 1(2):146–152.

HICKS, S. P., & CONSTANCE D'AMATO (1966). Effects of ionizing radiations on mammalian development. In *Advances in Teratology*, D. H. M. Woollam, Ed., Academic Press, New York.

HIRSCH, J. (1967). *Behavior-Genetic Analysis.* McGraw-Hill, New York.

INHORN, S. L. (1967). Chromosomal studies of spontaneous human abortions. *Adv. Teratol. 2:* 37–99.

LENZ, W. (1964). Chemicals and malformations in man. *in Proc. II Int. Congress Cong. Malf.*, Int. Med. Congress, New York. pp. 263–276.

LYON, M. F. (1961). Gene action in the X-chromosome of the mouse (*Mus musculus* L.). *Nature 190:* 372–373.

LYON, M. F. (1966). X-chromosome inactivation in mammals. *Adv. Teratol. 1:* 25–54.

MARINELLO, M. J., R. A. BERKSON, J. A. EDWARDS, & R. M. BANNERMAN (1969). A study of the XYY syndrome in tall men and juvenile delinquents. *J. Amer. Med. Assoc. 208:* 321–325.

MCKUSICK, V. A. (1964). *Human Genetics.* Prentice-Hall, New Jersey.

NUSBACHER, J., & K. HIRSCHHORN (1968). Autosomal anomalies in man. *Adv. Teratol. 3:* 11–63.

PENROSE, L. S. (1966). The causes of Down's syndrome. *Adv. Teratol. 1:* 9–24.

ROBERTS, R. C. (1967). Some concepts and methods in quantitative genetics. *in Behavior-Genetic Analysis,* J. Hirsch, Ed., pp. 214–257.

ROSENBLITH, JUDY F. (1970). Our newborn auditory responses prognostic of deafness. *Trans. of the American Academy of Ophthalmology and Otolaryngology 74:* 1215–1228.

SCRIMSHAW, N. S., & I. E. GORDON (1968). *Malnutrition, Learning and Behavior.* MIT Press, Cambridge, Mass.

SMITHELLS, R. W. (1966). Drugs and human malformations. *Adv. Teratol. 1:* 251–278.

STANBURY, J. B., J. B. WYNGAARDEN, & D. S. FREDERICKSON (1960). *The Metabolic Basis of Inherited Disease.* McGraw-Hill, New York.

STERN, C. (1960). *Principles of Human Genetics,* 2nd Ed. Freeman, San Francisco.

STOLLER, A. (1968). Virus-chromosome interaction as a possible cause of cases of Down's syndrome (Mongolism) and other congenital anomalies. *Adv. Teratol. 3:* 97–126.

TJIO, J. H., & A. LEVAN (1956). The chromosome number of man. *Hereditas 42:* 1–6.

WAARDENBURG, P. J. (1932). Das menschliche Auge und seine Erbenlagen. *Nijhoff,* The Hague. (Cited by Penrose, 1966)

WILLIAMS, R. J. (1967). *You Are Extraordinary.* Random House, N. Y.

6

Prediction of Behavior from Birth to Maturity

MARJORIE P. HONZIK

(A Book Review of *Birth to Maturity:
A Study in Psychological Development,*
by JEROME KAGAN and HOWARD MOSS)

*Dr. Marjorie Honzik has long been connected with
Berkeley, one of the important centers for longitudinal studies. In this article she reviews a book
that is based on data from the longitudinal studies
at the Fels Research Institute. The book deals
with the stability of behavior from birth to maturity.*

*The review offers a cogent commentary on longi-
tudinal studies in general, and compares the results of other studies to those presented in the book
reviewed. If certain behaviors are indeed stable
from birth to maturity, one can present a strong
argument for their being biologically determined
(without ruling out the effects of interaction with
the environment).*

*Because the actual findings of the book empha-
size sex differences, the review could have been
placed in Section VIII instead of here.*

*Other aspects of continuity in behavior (over a
shorter span) have been studied by a research
group made up of two psychiatrists—Dr. Alexander
Thomas and his wife, Dr. Stella Chess—and
Dr. Herbert G. Birch, who is both a psychologist
and a pediatrician. Their article "The Origin of
Personality" (Scientific American, 1970, 223 (2),
102–109) is a highly readable account of their work.*

*The idea of such continuities in behavior has,
of course, been emphasized in earlier work. For
example, in 1948 Patricia (Neilon) Naka had*

*judges match personality sketches written about
children who had been studied in their first two
years with sketches made when they were seventeen years old.[1] The persons writing the later
sketches had no knowledge of the earlier sketches
or data. The judges had significant success; however, some individuals appeared to have been
much more stable over time than others. There
also appeared to be more stability in personality
characteristics than in some of the more physical
characteristics, for example, height. Thus, we
have a precursor of some of the researches in this
section. The greater stability of some individuals
than of others could, of course, be given either a
biological or an environmental interpretation. Unfortunately, Naka did not analyze her data for some
of the more obvious changes in the family situations of stable children as compared with less
stable children.*

From birth to maturity is a long time. It is not
surprising, therefore, that longitudinal research
covering the entire period of growth has been so
slow in yielding its findings. And it is with a feeling
of excitement that we approach the analysis of
stability and change in certain personality variables
for a group of young people who grew to maturity
between 1929 and 1958.

Few research centers had elected to study personality
development longitudinally around 1930. Notable exceptions were the Fels Research Institute's investigation
which Lester Sontag, M.D., initiated in 1929 and has
continued to direct for 35 years; the three independent
investigations, with differing purposes, launched by the
University of California's Institute of Child Welfare between 1928 and 1931—the Berkeley Growth Study, the
Guidance Study, and the Oakland Growth Study (Jones,
Macfarlane, and Eichorn, 1960); and the two-year investigation of Mary Shirley (1931) at the University of
Minnesota's Institute of Child Welfare with the follow-
up by Neilon in 1948. The children first described by
Escalona and Heider in their study of "Prediction and
Outcome" (1959) and later by Lois B. Murphy in "The
Widening World of Childhood" (1962) were born in the
1940's. This was also true of the children in the study by
Anderson et al. (1960) of the prediction of adjustment of
the school children of Nobles County over a seven-year
period. More recently an investigation specifically concerned with personality development in early childhood
was undertaken in this country (Chess, Thomas, Birch,

---

[1] *J. Genet. Psychol.*, "Shirley's Babies after Fifteen Years,"
1948, *73*, 175–186.

Marjorie P. Honzik, "Prediction of behavior from birth to maturity," a book review of *Birth to maturity: a study in psychological
development,* by Jerome Kagan and Howard Moss (New York: Wiley, 1962). *Merrill-Palmer Quarterly of Behavior and Development,* 1965, *11* (1), 77–88. Reprinted by permission.

and Hertzig, 1960); and a series of longitudinal growth studies have gotten under way in London (Moore, Hindley, and Falkner, 1954), Western Europe (Skard, 1960), and Africa (Geber, 1962) during the past decade. While this listing covers some of the major projects, it is well to keep in mind that the total number of individuals included in all longitudinal studies of personality development is an infinitesimal sampling of the world's peoples.

Investigations of mental growth have been more numerous than those of personality consistency and change and the results have been more definitive. It is reassuring to note that when the measuring instruments are as reliable as carefully administered intelligence tests, the results from the various centers and universities are remarkably similar (Bayley, 1949; Ebert et al., 1943; Honzik et al., 1948; Sontag et al., 1958). This fact encourages us to believe that if comparable care is used in defining and measuring behavior and personality, we may have in the next decade a verified body of facts leading to more encompassing theories of personality development.

The purpose of the Kagan and Moss investigation was, in their words, to find "the link between child and adult behavior . . . and to discover classes of stable response systems and the developmental periods during which they become manifest." They chose to look for continuity and change in "motive related behaviors, sources of anxiety, defensive behavior and modes of social interaction" rated at different age periods in childhood and in early adulthood. More specifically, they considered the stability of "passivity and dependence, aggression, fear of physical harm, achievement, sex typed activity, and spontaneity." The rationale for the choice of behavior variables was "the emphasis in current theory and research on four classes of variables: (a) behaviors aimed at attainment of culturally salient goals (i.e., motive related behaviors), (b) sources of anxiety and conflict, (c) defensive responses to anxiety arousing situations and conflicts, and (d) modes of interpersonal interaction."

We propose to examine in some detail the methodology, results, and interpretations of the Kagan and Moss investigation and to compare certain of their procedures and findings with those of other longitudinal studies. The reasons for this are twofold. The results are basic to personality theory, and decisions as to sampling of cases and behaviors and the nature of data analysis become magnified many times in importance when personality is considered in a time perspective. A decision to include or not to include certain individuals will color not one but all relationships. The decision to use a certain type of analysis will determine not one

but the many relationships at an age and through time. And, of course, the point of view or theoretical vantage point of the investigators determine not only what they look for, and at, but how the results are interpreted; and once a course of action is taken, it has to be maintained.

Kagan and Moss used a correlational analysis in looking for continuities of behavior. In this type of analysis, the size and nature of the available sample is crucial. Although the method of selecting the Fels longitudinal sample is not described, the parents' education approximates a normal distribution. However, the major difficulty in using the described group in a correlational analysis of consistency of behavior is that "the 89 children came from 63 different families, with 19 families supplying 45 of the children." Further, 44 families had one child in the study, 12 had two children, and 7 families had three children in the group. One of the three-child families had male triplets whose zygosity is not reported. After an initial clear statement of the sample composition, the authors make no further mention of the group other than to report that 71 of the 89 subjects participated in the adult assessment. Since Pearsonian correlation coefficients constitute the sole method of describing stability and change in behavior, the inclusion of siblings of some but not all children presents a major methodological difficulty in assessing the results. If the siblings, and especially the triplets, are more alike in their behaviors than randomly selected children, the correlation coefficients may be remarkably inflated. Not only learning theory but also recent studies of the "heritability of personality dimensions" (Cattell et al., 1957; Gottesman, 1963) support this hypothesis. It would be of considerable interest to know whether the relationships would be changed if only one child from each family were selected for study. A recomputing of these materials excluding siblings would seem feasible and desirable.

The longitudinal data available at the Fels Institute for rating were observational records of the children in the natural settings of the home (in semi-annual visits), at nursery school, and at later ages in day camps and public school. One of the authors, Moss, used this rich observational material to rate 29 dimensions of behavior at four successive age periods from birth to 14 years. The age range included in each period was: birth to 3 years, 3 to 6, 6 to 10, and 10 to 14 years. One could certainly wish that the first and last of these periods had been further divided into finer age groupings. Erikson (1963), who has proposed one of the few truly developmental personality theories,* divides the age period from birth to 3 years into the three stages—"basic trust," "autonomy," and "initiative"—while he finds five more stages adequate to

---

* Erikson's theory is presented in selection 38 of this book.— EDITOR

describe the remaining entire life span of the individual. Erikson's fourth stage, "industry vs. inferiority," coincides very nicely with Kagan and Moss's 6 to 10 year period. Of the age periods used by Kagan and Moss, the 6 to 10 year span is probably the most satisfactory.

On the other hand, giving one overall rating for years 10 to 14 for both boys and girls involves a certain discounting of the impact of puberty on behavior. There is evidence from another longitudinal investigation, the Guidance Study, that at least one of the dimensions rated by Moss, "dependence," fluctuates for girls during the age period when the largest proportion of the girls were in the pubertal cycle but does not do so during the same age span for boys (Macfarlane, Allen, and Honzik, 1954). Furthermore, it was observed that markedly dependent behavior showed a significant increase in incidence a year before menarche and declined to a much lower level at menarche. The perturbations of the dependence-independence dimension during the entire cycle of sexual maturation in girls was clear in the two independently studied groups of the Guidance Study, and it would certainly be of interest if this relationship also occurred in the Fels material.

This result is mentioned here because of its relevance to the age-period grouping and, as has been stated, the purpose of Kagan and Moss was not to portray every possible relationship but to present the continuities and discontinuities over the four specified age periods and adulthood.

One of the major strengths of this investigation is the complete independence of the adult and childhood material. Another strength lies in the fact that the senior author, Kagan, interviewed all the subjects as adults. The interviews were tape-recorded and the behavior dimensions rated by Kagan for all the subjects, and by a second psychologist for 32 subjects.

The age range of the subjects at the time of adult interview was 19 to 29 years. An effort was made to narrow this range by interviewing the older subjects first but, nevertheless, there was an age difference of approximately 10 years between the age of the oldest and youngest subject at the time of the adult interview. This means that the interviewer was a peer of the oldest subjects but would appear as a "professor" or older man to the youngest subjects. Seventy-one per cent of the women and 56 per cent of the men were married at the time of the adult interview. While this wide age-range at the time of the adult assessments is a real difficulty, it is one which could be evaluated at some later date by considering the relation of the rated dimensions to age, marital status, number of children, etc.

The actual scales used in rating behavior either during childhood or as adults are not described, but the authors report that 7-point scales were constructed and detailed behavioral referents for scale points 1, 4, and 7 provided. A word about the variables rated and their reliabilities is in order. The titles of the variables are reported but only one end of what must be a continuum is mentioned, e.g., passivity, independence. This emphasis on one end of each scale has led to some difficulties in interpretations which will be discussed later in this report. A second psychologist rated "samples of the behaviors." The reported inter-rater reliabilities are high, which is to be expected when two psychologists have access to the same narrative material in making their ratings.

In an earlier study of the constancy of personality assessments of the Oakland Growth Study sample from 14 to 33 years, Tuddenham (1959) reported inter-interviewer agreement of .61 on the average when the two interviewers differed in sex and discussed different topics. The median reliabilities reported by Kagan and Moss when the two raters were reading the same material varied from .68 for Period I (birth to 3 years) to .85 for Period IV (10 to 14 years). Kagan and Moss state that "the dissimilarity between the adolescent and adult rating situations and the low inter-rater reliabilities were two major sources of error in (Tuddenham's) study." Tuddenham perhaps erred in his emphasis on the limitations of an outstanding investigation. The expectancies of agreement should not be the same when (1) two judges rate the same material, and when (2) the ratings of two judges, or interviewers, who have each obtained different material in different contexts from the subjects, are compared. The latter condition is more akin to a validity coefficient.

Thousands of correlation coefficients were computed for the approximately 4,500 behavior ratings. These results are well organized into tables showing continuities between Periods I (birth to 3 years), II, III, and IV (10 to 14 years) and the relation of status at each of these age-periods with that at adulthood.

The number of cases for each r is not given and the effect of differences in variability on the correlations not discussed. These would seem to be sins of omission. But one superfluous result is reported and that is the relationship for the sexes combined. A good rule might be to give the findings for the sexes separately whenever the number of cases permits, only reporting results for sexes combined when the N is small or the sex differences not significant. These technical points might be thought irrelevant in a review—except that longitudinal investigations of stability and change are now coming forth with their results in increasing numbers, and comparative evaluations are going to be hard to make unless the results are fully presented, including sample size and heterogeneity.

Kagan and Moss report that the most dramatic and consistent finding in their study was that many of the behaviors exhibited by the child during Period III (6 to 10 years) and a few during Period II (3 to 6 years) were moderately good predictors of theoretically related behaviors in early adulthood. Among the adult variables which were related to analogous behaviors during the early school years were for women, "passive withdrawal from stressful situations" and "dependency on the family"; for men, "ease of anger arousal" and "sexual behavior"; and for both men and women, "involvement in intellectual mastery," "sex role identification," and "spontaneity."

Of these variables, the persistence of "spontaneity" is most impressive since it is stable and predictive for both males and females and is neither a "sex-typed" behavior nor is it an ability-related variable like achievement. Kagan and Moss consider "social interaction anxiety" to be at the opposite end of the spontaneity continuum; and they report that childhood ratings of spontaneity are predictive of spontaneity in adulthood (or "lack of adult social interaction anxiety"). They find consistency on this dimension in males from Period I (birth to 3 years) to adulthood, and in females from the 6 to 10 year period.

In at least three other longitudinal studies, investigators have reported a similar variable to be highly stable. Tuddenham (1959) reported the persistence of certain personality ratings for the young people in the Oakland Growth Study from approximately age 14 years to age 33 years, and concluded that "among the most stable variables for both sexes were several which connote spontaneity vs. inhibition." No two studies have used exactly the same variables, but in the Berkeley Growth Study a continuum which is probably highly correlated with spontaneity-inhibition is the dimension "active, extroverted vs. inactive, introverted." Bayley and Schaefer (1963) report this broad category of behavior to be the most stable and persistent of those they evaluated between birth and 18 years. In still another sample, the Berkeley Guidance Study, where the method of data collection was largely that of interviews with mothers and children over the age period 21 months to 18 years, the most consistent or stable variable of the approximately sixty considered was the dimension of "introversion vs. extroversion," and a second highly consistent dimension was "excessive reserve-spontaneity." Also in the Guidance Study sample, the most stable school behavior (according to the teachers' reports) was for boys "reserved-expressive" and for girls "somber-gay." Despite the great variation in variable description, findings of the different longitudinal studies suggest that this dimension of outgoing responsiveness versus a retractive, inward-looking response may be one of the truly stable personality dimensions. It will be of interest to all the investigators to look more carefully at the correlates of these ratings and possible determinants of this dimension over time.

The finding of Kagan and Moss that dependent behavior in girls shows a high degree of continuity is not an isolated result. In the Guidance Study (Honzik and Macfarlane, 1964) where the ratings are based on interviews with the parents and children, girls showed a greater consistency than boys on the dependent-independent continuum during the age period 4 to 16 years. Furthermore, when as 30-year-old women they checked themselves as "dependent," there was a high probability that they had been considered dependent during the middle years of childhood, and again at 15 and 16 years. What do these facts mean? Kagan and Moss believe that "congruence with traditional standards for sex-role characteristics accounts for the differential stability of behaviors of males and females." And they elaborate that "the individual's desire to mold his overt behavior in concordance with the culture's definition of sex appropriate responses is a major determinant of the patterns of continuity and discontinuity in his development."

A major flaw in this argument with respect to dependence is that the opposite end of this continuum, non-dependence or relative independence, is also predictive for the females in the Kagan and Moss study since the correlations are based on a continuum (7-point ratings). There is a correlation of .48 between passivity during the 6 to 10 years and withdrawal behavior as an adult. This means that girls with a rating of 6 or 7 on passivity in elementary school are likely to show withdrawal behavior as adults; but it also suggests that girls with ratings of 1 or 2 (very non-passive) were *not* showing withdrawal behavior as adults. This finding suggests that behavior along this continuum becomes stabilized early. The correlations do *not* show whether or not "the individual's desire to mold his overt behavior in concordance with the culture's definition of sex appropriate responses is a major determinant of the patterns of continuity and discontinuity in his development." Only if inspection of the correlation scatters showed that there is a shift toward passivity and dependence in the females and anger arousal in males, would we be justified in concluding that the boy and girl mold their behavior in concordance with the culture's definition of sex appropriate responses.

The significant question is why are these behavioral continua maintained, and differentially so, in males and females? One possibility is that these are chance findings since they are found in one but not both sexes. However, Tuddenham (1959) found drive *aggression* to be *the* most stable of 34 variables for men, from 14 to 33 years, in the Oakland Growth Study. Dependence and passivity were not rated in the Tuddenham investigations. But the dependence-independence continuum was rated, as has been mentioned, at twelve age levels, from 4 to 16 years, in the Guidance Study and was one of the more consistent behavioral dimensions for girls but not for boys—and a high degree of consistency occurred in spite of very low correlations during the 10 to 14 year age-period when the majority of girls were pubescent.

In summary, the finding that sex appropriate or inappropriate behaviors persist was not only replicated for certain variables by Kagan and Moss, but is cross-validated in other longitudinal studies. The explanation of this sex difference is not obvious. Among the possibilities are: (1) a sex difference in variability; (2) these behavioral dimensions are constitutionally or genetically determined; (3) the environmental milieu is continuously but differentially supporting of these behavioral continua; or (4) the impact of early experiences is so overwhelming that the child's learned mode of response is maintained or continued to adulthood. The first possibility may be easily checked by looking at the variance, but the relevance of constitutional and environmental factors requires the measurement of both early response patterns and continuous measurements of the milieu.

One of the most puzzling aspects of Kagan and Moss's conclusions and interpretations is the lack of coherence between some of the findings and the theory advanced to explain their findings. They place "the construct of sex-role identification in a central position in directing the selective adoption and maintenance of several behavior domains." And yet, it seems clear that correlations showing persistence and change in behaviors are only tangentially relevant to sex-role identification. There are, of course, a number of ways of investigating the changes the boy or girl makes in his behavior to conform with traditional sex-role standards. It would not be difficult, for example, to have judges rate the characteristics of the ideal male and female and then compare the changing behaviors of the boy or girl in relation to this ideal. Kagan and Moss discuss the "hypothetical ego ideal or idealized model that embodies the essential qualities of masculinity or femininity." And they add: "Each individual has a cognitive picture of the person he would like to be and the goal states he would like to command—an idealized model of himself. . . . It would appear that the desire to be an *ideal male* or *ideal female* (italics not ours), as

defined by the individual, comprises an essential component of everyman's model. Thus the position of a response on a cognitive dimension ranging from *highly masculine* to *highly feminine* is a primary determinant of its acceptability and, therefore, of its probability of occurrence."

This discussion, with italicized emphasis, of sex-role identification as "a governor of behavior" constitutes a major segment of the summary and conclusions which suggests its importance to the authors. But the extensive data were only analyzed to show "continuities or stability of behavior" over a number of age-periods and were not considered in relation to models. Nor is there any mention of mean changes in the direction of masculine or feminine behaviors among the boys and girls. There is clearly the possibility of further analysis of the 4,500 ratings to discover the extent of, or if, indeed, "sex-role identification *is* a governor of behavior."

The authors' second conclusion is that "the early school years are a critical period" in personality development. They report that "continuity between child and adult behavior generally became manifest during the first four school years (6 to 10)." This finding is in agreement with the conclusion of Schaefer and Bayley (1963) for the Berkeley Growth Study sample, that "more enduring behavioral traits are developed during the latency period." A corollary of this finding is that prediction from the two earlier periods (birth to 6 years) is not good for a number of variables. In some instances, prediction is actually better from the 6 to 10 year period than from the 10 to 14 year period. One example is the finding that aggression-anxiety in adult males tends to be better predicted by the 6 to 10 year ratings than by the 10 to 14 year ratings. Although the sample limitations preclude a too detailed analysis of changes in the predictive power from one age-period to another, it is likely that the turbulence of adolescence may temporarily disrupt certain attitudes and personality characteristics. It is also evident that some personality constellations observed in adolescence are more highly predictive of adult personality than are the early childhood ratings. "Aggressive retaliation" in adult men is one such variable. The correlation between the adult rating of "aggressive retaliation" and "aggression to mother" during the age-period birth to 3 years is .19, but by 10 to 14 years it is .47.

One of the impressive findings of longitudinal studies is the age change in relationships, and thus in prediction. This fact also points to the impossibility of assuming that predictions made from one age-period could necessarily be made from any other age-period. It may even be found that predictions vary within the adolescent period. McKee and Turner (1961) report that "drive" ratings made in adolescence are more predictive of CPI [California Personality Inventory.—EDITOR] scales in adulthood for females than males. They suggest that the basis for this difference is the later maturing of males than females. It may well be true that for some variables 12-year ratings of girls show a similar prediction to 14-year ratings of boys. In other words, biological as well as chronological age demands consideration.

The Fels data yielded many interesting sex differences in patterns of relationships. One of the most impressive sex differences occurred in the correlates of intellectual mastery: ". . . intellectually oriented men, in contrast to the intellectual women, were less competitive, more likely to withdraw to stress." This and other results lead the authors to the conclusion that "it may be unwise to pool data for males and females without first examining the data for sex differences." One of the interesting phenomena of growth data which these authors underscore is that frequently where there are no sex differences in means and standard deviations, there may be "sex differences in patterns of intercorrelations" either at an age-period or over time. (See Schaefer and Bayley, 1963, and Honzik, 1963, for comparable findings.)

One truly exciting finding in the Fels data is what Kagan and Moss have called the "sleeper effect." The authors appear to subsume two phenomena under this heading: first, the effects on later development of specific early experiences; and second, discontinuities in personality development such that behaviors manifested in infancy or early childhood may be more predictive of comparable adult behaviors than later childhood assessments of the behavior.

An example of the first type of sleeper effect is the finding that the "maternal protection of a daughter during age 0 to 3 predicted adult withdrawal from stress ($r = .52$, $p < .01$), whereas maternal protection during ages 3 to 6 or 6 to 10 showed no relation to adult withdrawal. . . ." There is a possibility that this specific result is a chance one. However, judging by reports from other longitudinal studies, as well as the Fels investigation and the observations of perceptive persons from the beginning of time, it is more than likely that certain experiences of early childhood have far-reaching effects and that these effects may not become manifest until maturity or even later adult life. Harlow's findings for monkeys (1962) support this hypothesis. One of the rewarding research projects of the future will be the documenting more specifically of the origins of significant behaviors from the cumulative records of the various growth studies.

An example of the second type of sleeper effect—i.e., a period of discontinuity—is the finding that certain behaviors such as passivity and fear of bodily harm for the age-period birth to 3 years were more predictive of "love object dependency" in adult men than later assessments of these childhood variables. This predictive discontinuity has its counterpart in physical growth. During puberty, prediction of adult height is not as good as during the age-periods immediately preceding the age span when a large proportion of the youngsters are pubescent (Tuddenham, 1954). The fact of perturbations in the inter-age correlation matrices may suggest not only the periods of greater and less prediction but may also suggest the factors contributing to the continuities and discontinuities. An example of this was obtained in the Guidance Study materials, where it was noted that the age-period of lowered prediction of physical measurements in girls coincided with a period of lowered prediction in the dependence-independence continuum. This finding suggests that either the physiological changes affect the girl's behavior directly, or that the changing status of the girl approaching sexual maturity leads to a change in her dependency behavior.

In summary, there will never be a longitudinal study in which there are no methodological limitations. The investigation by Kagan and Moss has its share, some of which can still be evaluated (for example, the effect of including siblings in the correlation coefficients, and the 10-year span of the adult data). On the other hand, this developmental investigation has many strengths, including the richness of the childhood materials, high reliability of the ratings, independence of adult evaluations, and good organization of a large body of interrelationships. The results of this investigation will be discussed for a long time and compared with those of other growth studies until the ingredients of a more adequate theory of personality growth are found. Although the behaviors rated by Kagan and Moss were derived from current theory, hypotheses were not always supported and the articulation of findings and theory is not one of the strong points of this book.

The inter-age correlations show certain continuities of behavior, some of which are cross-validated in other growth studies. One such variable is "spontaneity," which is highly persistent and may be related to an introversion-extroversion dimension which Gottesman (1963) finds "most heavily influenced by genetic factors." It is clear that behaviors which are more salient in boys such as the aggression–non-aggression continuum, and those more salient in girls, such as dependency–non-dependency, are more likely to persist. This is a significant finding in our culture where sex appropriate behavior is so valued, but these results do not provide a clue as to *why* a child's status on sex relevant continua are likely to be maintained. Do these results mean that within sex constitutional factors are determining this continuity, or that sex appropriate or inappropriate behaviors are learned early?

In conclusion, a correlational analysis of consistency and change in relevant variables is an excellent first step—but it is just that. Having now found the areas and age-periods of continuity and change, the next steps will be more difficult but also more rewarding—the looking again at the individuals to see just when and under what conditions consistency and change take place. And when, with more knowledge and greater understanding, the picture becomes clearer, we may be led to more enlightened personality theory than is now available.

REFERENCES

ANDERSON, J. E. The prediction of adjustment over time. In I. Iscoe and H. Stevenson (Eds.), *Personality development in children*. Austin: Univer. Texas Press, 1960.

BAYLEY, NANCY. Consistency and variability in the growth of intelligence from birth to eighteen years. *J. genet. Psychol.*, 1949, *75*, 165–196.

BAYLEY, NANCY, & SCHAEFER, E. S. Consistency of maternal and child behavior in the Berkeley Growth Study. Symposium on personality consistency and change. *Amer. Psychologist*, 1963, *18*, No. 7.

CATTELL, R. B., BLEWETT, D. B., & BELOFF, J. R. The inheritance of personality. *Amer. J. hum. Genet.*, 1955, *7*, 122–146.

CHESS, STELLA, THOMAS, A., BIRCH, H. G., & HERTZIG, MARGARET. Implications of a longitudinal study of child development for child psychiatry. *Amer. J. Psychiat.*, 1960, *117*, 434–441.

EBERT, ELIZABETH, & SIMMONS, KATHERINE. The Brush Foundation study of child growth and development. *Soc. Res. Child Develpm. Monogr.*, 1943, *8*, No. 2.

ERIKSON, E. H. *Childhood and society*. (2nd ed.) New York: Norton, 1963.

ESCALONA, SIBYLLE, & HEIDER, GRACE M. *Prediction and outcome*. New York: Basic Books, 1959.

GEBER, MARCELLE. Longitudinal study and psychomotor development among Baganda children. In G. S. Nielsen (Ed.), *Child and education*. Copenhagen: Munksgaard, 1962.

GOTTESMAN, I. Heritability of personality: a demonstration. *Psychol. Monogr.*, 1963, *77*, No. 9 (Whole No. 572).

HARLOW, H. The heterosexual affectional system in monkeys. *Amer. Psychologist*, 1962, *17*, 1–9.

HONZIK, MARJORIE P. A sex difference in the age of onset of the parent-child resemblance in intelligence. *J. educ. Psychol.*, 1963, *54*, 231–237.

HONZIK, MARJORIE P., MACFARLANE, JEAN W., & ALLEN, LUCILE. The stability of mental test performance between two and eighteen years. *J. exp. Educ.*, 1948, *17*, 309–324.

HONZIK, MARJORIE P., & MACFARLANE, JEAN W. Prediction of specific behaviors and personality characteristics from 21 months to 30 years. (MS)

JONES, H. E., MACFARLANE, JEAN W., & EICHORN, DOROTHY H. A progress report on growth studies at the University of California. *Vita Humana*, 1960, *3*, 17–31.

MACFARLANE, JEAN W., ALLEN, LUCILE, & HONZIK, MARJORIE P. A developmental study of the behavior problems of normal children between 21 months and 14 years. *Univer. Calif. Publ. in Child Develpm.*, 1954, Vol. 2

MCKEE, J. P., & TURNER, W. S. The relation of "drive" ratings in adolescence to CPI and EPPS scores in adulthood. *Vita Humana*, 1961, *4*, 1–14.

MOORE, T., HINDLEY, C. B., & FALKNER, F. A longitudinal research in child development and some of its problems. *Brit. Med. J.*, 1954, *II*, 1132–1137.

MURPHY, LOIS B. *The widening world of childhood*. New York: Basic Books, 1962.

NEILON, PATRICIA. Shirley's babies after fifteen years: a personality study. *J. genet. Psychol.*, 1948, *73*, 175–186.

SCHAEFER, E. S., & BAYLEY, NANCY. Maternal behavior, child behavior, and their intercorrelations from infancy through adolescence. *Soc. Res. Child Develpm. Monogr.*, 1963, *28*, No. 3.

SHIRLEY, MARY M. *The first two years: a study of twenty-five babies*. Vol. 3. *Personality manifestations*. Minneapolis: Univer. Minn. Press, 1933.

SKARD, ASE. Longitudinal observations of changing family relations. In G. S. Nielsen (Ed.), *Child and education*. Copenhagen: Munksgaard, 1962.

SONTAG, L. W., BAKER, C. T., & NELSON, VIRGINIA L. Mental growth and personality development: a longitudinal study. *Soc. Res. Child Develpm. Monogr.*, 1958, *23*, No. 2.

TUDDENHAM, R. D. The constancy of personality ratings over two decades. *Genet. Psychol. Monogr.*, 1959, *60*, 3–29.

TUDDENHAM, R. D., & SNYDER, MARGARET M. Physical growth of California boys and girls from birth to 18 years. *Univer. Calif. Publ. in Child Develpm.*, 1954, Vol. 1, No. 2.

7

Constitutional and Environmental Interactions in Rearing of Four Breeds of Dogs

D. G. FREEDMAN

If one thoroughly understood all of the data in this paper, one would have a good grasp of the interaction between heredity (breed) and experience. We are reprinting it again in our third edition because we cannot find a more cogent and succinct illustration of the points made. Freedman is now with the Committee on Human Development of the University of Chicago. His current research frequently brings biological and ethnological concepts to bear on psychological problems. He is actively pursuing research on the characteristics of newborns in many parts of the world, thus assuring greater genetic variability in the infants studied.

The initial intention of the present study was to determine the relative effects of "indulgent" and "disciplinary" modes of rearing in dogs, with particular emphasis on how each method affects the obedience of the animal at maturity. The work derived from the extensive observations of children made by D. M. Levy (1), who has shown that over-indulgent rearing may lead to psychopathy, a syndrome which involves an abnormal inability to inhibit one's impulses. The study described in this report was an attempt to deal experimentally with Levy's concept. As will be seen, the results are of interest aside from their reflection on this initial hypothesis.

Eight litters of four pups each were used. These included two litters each of Shetland sheep dogs, basenjis, wire-haired fox terriers, and beagles. Following weaning at 3 weeks of age, each litter of four was divided into two pairs equated as closely as possible on the basis of sex, weight, activity, vocalizations, maturation of eyes and ears, and reactivity to a startling stimulus. Each member of one pair was thereafter indulged, and each member of the other pair was disciplined, during two daily 15-minute periods from their third to their eighth week of age.

Indulgence consisted of encouraging a pup in any activity it initiated, such as play, aggression, and climbing on the supine handler. These pups were never punished. By contrast, the disciplined pups were at first restrained in the experimenter's lap and were later taught to sit, to stay, and to come upon command. When still older they were trained to follow on a leash. The pups were handled and tested individually by a single experimenter throughout the study. They lived in pairs in isolation boxes the remainder of the time, where members of indulged and disciplined pairs received identical treatment. The results were as follows:

At 8 weeks of age each pup was subjected to the following test: Each time a pup ate meat from a bowl placed in the center of a room, he was punished with a swat on the rump and a shout of "no!" After three minutes the experimenter left the room and, observing through a one-way glass, recorded the time that elapsed before the pup again ate. The results over 8 days of testing are summarized in Fig. 1. Basenjis tended to eat soon after the experimenter left, the method of rearing having no statistically significant effect. Shetland sheep dogs tended to refuse the food over the entire 8 days of testing. Again, the fashion of rearing had no significant effect. Beagles and wire-haired fox terriers, however, differentiated into two significantly disparate groups, depending on the condition of rearing. The Friedman non-parametric analysis of variance (2) indicates that the indulged pups took significantly longer to return to the food than did the disciplined pups ($p = 0.001$). Thus, as measured in this test, essentially the same differences in treatment had a decisive effect upon only two breeds.

Can characteristics of the breeds explain the differences in performance on this test? It was clear that, during training, beagles and wire-haired terriers were strongly oriented to the experimenter and sought contact with him continuously. Basenjis, by contrast, were interested in all phases

D. G. Freedman, "Constitutional and environmental interactions in rearing of four breeds of dogs," *Science,* 1958, *127* (3298), March 14, 585–586. Reprinted by permission.

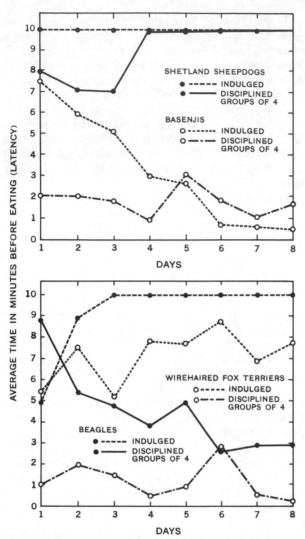

FIGURE 1. *Performance of 8-week-old puppies on the "inhibition-to-eating" test (see text for details of procedure).*

of the environment and often ignored the experimenter in favor of inanimate objects. Shetland sheep dogs showed yet another pattern; all became fearful of physical contact with the experimenter and tended to maintain distance from him. We see, then, that the two breeds that were highly attracted to the experimenter differentiated as a result of the mode of rearing, whereas the breeds that exhibited aloofness (basenjis) and excessive timidity (Shetland sheep dogs) did not. Apparently it was the strong (constitutional) attraction in interaction with indulgent treatment that enhanced the effectiveness of later punishment. It should be noted that basenjis and Shetland sheep dogs were not entirely unaffected by the differential treatment. The scores of *all* indulged animals were significantly different from those of their disciplined counterparts on five of ten tests administered. In general,

these tests indicated that the indulged pups were more active, more vocal, less timid (although more easily inhibited with punishment) than the disciplined pups.

A test of individual reactions to veterinary treatment based on vocalizations and the degree of activity during routine injections indicates that indulged pups were more vocal and active than disciplined pups in their protest ($p = 0.02$, Mann-Whitney) and that basenjis were more vocal and active than the other three breeds ($p = 0.01$, Friedman analysis of variance). It has been found at our laboratory that basenjis generally gain higher scores on this test than other breeds; hence these data suggest that similar behavior may be due in one instance to constitution (as in the basenjis) and in other instances to the conditions of rearing.

A test of the level of activity, in which the pups were observed from a hidden vantage point for 10 minutes, was administered. The testing area was 10 by 20 ft. and was demarcated into eight squares of 5 by 5 ft. each. In this setting, *disciplined* Shetland sheep dogs showed significantly less activity than any other animals ($p = 0.001$, Friedman analysis of variance). In another test the experimenter sat silently in a room for 10 minutes and recorded the amount of time the pups spent in contact with him. In this test the *indulged* Shetland sheep dogs differed significantly from all other dogs in that they rarely approached the experimenter ($p = 0.001$, Friedman analysis of variance). From these results it is clear that a specific test for a specific breed may facilitate expression of the effects of early rearing.

The conditions of rearing were continued over a second period, when the pups were 11 to 15 weeks of age, and all tests were readministered, with essentially the same results.

In the follow-up observations and tests, the indulged beagles, in contrast to all other animals, underwent dramatic changes, in time, although all animals were maintained under standard conditions. On a weekly test in which the time taken to catch each animal was recorded, these animals became exceedingly shy and wary of being caught when approached by various human beings, including the experimenter ($p = 0.05$, t test). Thus, it appears that changes in the behavior of certain animals may occur that are seemingly independent of the current environment and belatedly dependent, instead, upon the mediation of past experiences.

REFERENCES

LEVY, D. M., *Maternal Overprotection.* (Columbia Univ. Press, New York, 1943).

SIEGEL, S. *Non-parametric Statistics.* (McGraw-Hill, New York, 1956).

8

Nongenetic Transmission
of Information

VICTOR H. DENENBERG
AND KENNETH M. ROSENBERG

This paper supplements the previous ones because it points out that genetic factors are not the only ones that may act over more than one generation. The effects of experience are also important over more than one generation. The paper demonstrates that both a physical and a "temperamental" characteristic of rats (if one can use the word "temperament" when talking about rats) are affected by the handling experiences of their grandmothers. This finding tempts one to speculate about comparable effects in humans. Our understanding of human development is complicated by the addition of cultural effects to the apparently biological or biologically mediated effects shown in the rat. Efforts to compare different cultural groups, whose handling experiences, diet, medical status, etc. may differ markedly, become extremely complex. It is thus difficult to decide between the genetic and the experiential in assessing the causation of differences found between human cultural groups.

Dr. Denenberg is chairman of the Department of Biobehavioral Sciences at the University of Connecticut, where Dr. Rosenberg is also located. The existence of such a new department is, in itself, further demonstration of the current active concern with problems of relating biology to behavior. This is only one of several such laboratories and departments in the United States.

We have shown that one significant determinant of the rat's behaviour is the handling experience of the mother while she was an infant.[1] This experience was profound enough to modify her offspring's weaning weight and open field performance in adulthood. Thus the experience of one generation was visited on the next generation. Such a finding would appear to have broad implications for the evolution of behaviour. In this context a relevant question is: How far into the future can such effects extend? We have investigated this question by determining whether the experiences of female rats during their infancy would significantly affect the behaviour of their grandpups.

Again within an evolutionary framework, the habitat in which the animal is born and reared is known to affect profoundly his subsequent performance. We have shown that rats which are born and reared in a complex free environment between birth and weaning, or which are given free environment experience after weaning, differ along a number of behavioural dimensions from rats which are reared in standard cages during infancy and after weaning.[2-5] Thus for the laboratory rat, cages and free environments may be thought of as two different habitats. We investigated the effects of these habitats on the offspring's behaviour in this experiment.

The grandmothers' experience was as follows. At birth, litters of Purdue–Wistar rats were reduced to eight pups. Whole litters were randomly assigned to groups to be handled or not handled. Handling consisted of removing the pups from the maternity cage, leaving the mother in the cage, and placing each one into a tin can partially filled with shavings. The pups remained in the cans for 3 min and were then returned to their home cage. This procedure was followed once a day from day 1 until day 20. Non-handled controls were not disturbed between day 1 and 21, when all litters were weaned. The handled and non-handled females from these litters were the grandmothers of the animals used in this study. They were bred when

[1] Denenberg, V. H., and Whimbey, A. E., *Science 142*, 1192 (1963).

[2] Denenberg, V. H., and Morton, J. R. C., *J. Comp. Physiol. Psychol., 55*, 242 (1962).

[3] Denenberg, V. H., and Morton, J. R. C., *Anim. Behav., 12*, 11 (1964).

[4] Denenberg, V. H., Morton, J. R. C., and Haltmeyer, G. C., *Anim. Behav. 12*, 205 (1964).

[5] Whimbey, A. E., and Denenberg, V. H., *Multivar. Behav. Res., 1*, 279 (1966).

Victor H. Denenberg and Kenneth M. Rosenberg, "Nongenetic transmission of information," *Nature*, 1967, *216*, 549–550. Reprinted by permission.

about 100 days old. When pregnant, the females were assigned randomly to one of two housing conditions, to be described later.

The mothers' experiences were as follows. The females were placed either into stainless steel maternity cages (15 in. × 10 in. × 7·5 in.) or into free environment boxes. These boxes were triangular compartments formed by placing a diagonal insert into a 34 in.² box. Food was scattered on the floor, water was supplied by an externally mounted bottle, and "toys" (wooden block, can, ramp. running disk) were placed into each environment. At birth, litters were cut back to eight subjects consisting of four to six females.

When weaned on day 21, the females from each litter were randomly split into two groups, one going into a stainless steel laboratory cage (11 in. × 8·25 in. × 7·5 in.), and the other into a free environment. The free environments were the same as previously described except that the diagonal partition was removed. Two or three females were placed in each laboratory cage, while ten to twelve pups shared each free environment. On day 50 the females from the free environment were placed in the same type of laboratory cages as those described above.

These females were the parents of the animals used in this study. When approximately 150 days old, one female from each litter was bred to a randomly chosen colony male. All pregnant animals were placed in stainless steel maternity cages. At birth, litters were reduced to eight pups consisting, when possible, of four males and four females. No litter contained less than four pups. The pups remained undisturbed until they were 21 days old. At this time they were placed into a 32 in.² open field consisting of sixty-four squares. An activity count was recorded each time a pup made contact with a different square. Each pup was given one 3 min test, and after this was weighed.

Table 1 presents the experimental design, the mean activity score, the mean body weight, the number of pups and the number of litters for each of the eight treatment combinations. In the statistical analysis of these data the litter was used as the unit of measurement with a sub-classification for the sex of the pup. For example, the activity scores of all males within a litter were combined and a mean was obtained; the same procedure was applied to the females. These litter sex scores were subjected to a split plot unweighted means analysis of variance.[6] All F tests were based on 1/47 degrees of freedom.

ACTIVITY

The interaction of grandmother handling × mother preweaning housing was significant at the 0·01 level (F, 7·68): descendants of non-handled grandmothers were more active than descendants of handled grandmothers if their mothers had been reared in a maternity cage between birth and weaning. Exactly the opposite pattern was obtained if their mothers had been reared in a free environment during infancy. The grandmother handling × mother postweaning housing interaction was significant (F, 5·04; $P < 0·05$): the pattern was just the opposite to that described for the previous interaction. In addition, the preweaning housing × postweaning housing interaction was significant at the 0·05 level (F, 5·77). Offspring of mothers reared in two different environments during early life (that is, cage and free environment, or free environment and cage) were more active than the offspring of mothers which had been reared only in cages or only in free environments for the first 50 days of life.

The grandmother handling × sex interaction was significant at the 0·01 level (F, 21·44). Male wean-

[6] Winer, B. J., *Statistical Principles in Experimental Design* (McGraw-Hill, New York, 1962).

TABLE 1
SUMMARY OF MEANS FOR ALL EXPERIMENTAL CONDITIONS

Handling experience of grandmothers of experimental subjects	Preweaning housing of mothers of experimental subjects	Postweaning housing of mothers of experimental subjects	No. of litters	No. of subjects	Open-field activity		Weaning weight (g)	
					Male	Female	Male	Female
Non-handled	Maternity cage	Laboratory cage	17	123	17·00	15·02	50·00	47·05
		Free environment	17	133	23·60	20·70	48·43	46·26
	Free environment	Laboratory cage	11	82	13·08	9·31	51·45	50·32
		Free environment	11	85	15·48	11·58	45·63	44·29
Handled	Maternity cage	Laboratory cage	12	90	11·39	18·30	49·73	48·35
		Free environment	12	86	16·32	19·17	47·07	44·76
	Free environment	Laboratory cage	11	84	25·55	24·29	44·76	42·93
		Free environment	11	86	11·35	17·46	48·76	46·91

lings were only slightly affected by the handling experience their grandmothers had received, while the females were markedly affected, with grand-pups of handled females being significantly more active than grandpups of non-handled females. Finally, the preweaning housing × postweaning × sex interaction was significant at the 0·05 level (*F*, 4·55).

WEANING WEIGHT

The two main effects of grandmother handling and mother postweaning housing were both significant at the 0·05 level (*F*s of 4·55 and 5·20, respectively), while the interaction of these two factors was significant at the 0·01 level (*F*, 8·49). All three of these effects were brought about by one cell: those weanlings whose grandmothers were not handled in infancy and whose mothers were reared in laboratory cages after weaning weighed significantly more than the other three groups making up this interaction. Such groups did not differ among themselves. In addition, the grandmother handling × preweaning housing × postweaning housing interaction was significant (*F*, 18·80; *P* < 0·01), and sex was significant (*F*, 87·99; *P* < 0·01) with male weanlings weighing more than females.

These data for activity and weaning weight reveal that handling females in infancy can have an effect two generations further on; that the nature of the mother's living quarters during her early life will affect her offspring, and that these variables act in a non-additive interactive manner. The interactive nature of the variables should be emphasized: if we had merely taken the female offspring of handled and non-handled grandmothers and maintained them in standard laboratory caging conditions from birth until adulthood (first and fifth groups listed in Table 1) most of the significant findings would have disappeared. Thus the occurrence of free environment experience some

time during the mother's early ontogeny was necessary for the effects of the grandmother's handling experience to express itself in the grand-pups.

Others have reported findings extending into the next generation. Ginsburg and Hovda[7] reduced the incidence of death from audiogenic seizures in *dba* mice by transplanting fertilized *dba* eggs into *C57Bl* foster mothers shortly after fertilization, and Ressler[8] has shown that the strain of foster grandparent rearing young mice will influence the operant response rate of the offspring of those mice. As far as we know, the present experiment is the first documentation that the experiences which an animal has in early life will influence her unborn descendants two generations away by nongenetic mechanisms.

The nature of the mechanisms underlying these effects is not known. Both handling and free environment experience have behavioural and biological effects on the stimulated organisms.[2–5,9–12] These effects could act through changes in grand-maternal or maternal behaviour or through physiological changes which would affect the developing foetus or modify the milk supply of the grandmother or mother.

This work was supported, in part, by grants from the National Institute of Child Health and Human Development and the National Institute of Mental Health, U.S. Public Health Service.

[7] Ginsburg, B. E., and Hovda, R. B., *Anat. Rec.*, *99*, 621 (1947).

[8] Ressler, R. H., *J. Comp. Physiol. Psychol.*, *61*, 264 (1966).

[9] Denenberg, V. H., Brumaghim, J. T., Haltmeyer, G. C., and Zarrow, M. N. *Endocrinology* (in the press, 1967).

[10] Levine, S., Haltmeyer, G. C., Karas, G. G., and Denenberg, V. H., *Physiol. Behav.*, *2*, 55 (1967).

[11] Krech, D., Rosenzweig, M. R., and Bennett, E. J., *J. Comp. Physiol. Psychol.*, *53*, 509 (1960).

[12] Rosenzweig, M. R., *Amer. Psychol.*, *21*, 321 (1966).

"stress." Our usual ways of thinking about stress do not encourage us to consider such possibilities. Indeed, were it not for the animal data, such a hypothesis might never have been examined.

John W. M. Whiting is professor of social anthropology at Harvard University. His work has earned him recognition as a psychologist as well as an anthropologist. Thomas Landauer is currently a research worker at the Bell Telephone Laboratories after having taught at Stanford and at Dartmouth.

9

Infantile Immunization
and Adult Stature

JOHN W. M. WHITING,
THOMAS K. LANDAUER,
AND THOMAS M. JONES

This article uses data from the Berkeley and Fels studies (referred to in Honzik's paper) to examine the hypothesis that apparently stressful infant-care practices result in greater stature in adulthood. This hypothesis was generated in good part from the work of Levine and others using rats. (See the bibliography of the paper for references.) That work suggested the existence of beneficial effects (including increased size) from early physiological stress. Earlier, Whiting and his co-workers had looked at this hypothesis using cross-cultural data.

The present study provides further support for the hypothesis. In addition, it shows ways in which one can try to rule out certain explanations for the relations found, even when one cannot gain experimental control over the variables involved. An intriguing aspect of the paper is the apparent contradiction involved in finding "good" effects of

We are very grateful to Lester Sontag, director of the Fels Research Institute, and to Stanley Garn as member of the staff responsible for the materials on physical growth; to Millah Ayoub for overseeing the abstracting of materials from the Fels Institute files; to Jean Macfarlane and Marjorie Honzik of the Berkeley Guidance Study for providing us with the opportunity to use their excellent data as the basis of the study reported here; to Lincoln Moses and R. S. Srivastava for help in the statistical analyses; and to Henry Harpending who served as research assistant.

There is substantial evidence that unusually stimulating events during early infancy can cause acceleration of growth in rats (see Landauer & Whiting, 1964; Levine, 1960, for reviews of this evidence). It has been postulated (Levine, 1960) that the acceleration of growth results from an alteration in endocrine balance which is brought about by the occurrence of a physiological stress reaction at an early, perhaps critical, period. Whether or not this is the proper explanation of the phenomenon, it is nevertheless empirically clear that apparently stressful experiences in early life lead to increased size at maturity in rats.

In looking for a parallel effect in humans, Landauer and Whiting (1964) studied the relation between apparently stressful infant-care practices and the adult stature of males in two independent cross-cultural samples. They found that adult males in societies in which scarification, circumcision, inoculation, or repeated molding and shaping of the limbs or cranium was practiced before the age of 2 years were a statistically significant $2\frac{1}{2}$ inches taller, on the average, than adult males in societies without such practices. The relation between infant experience and adult stature was independent of cross-cultural measures of diet, race, and several geographical factors.

There are other data which may also be interpreted as suggesting an effect of stimulation on growth in humans parallel to that observed in lower animals. Gunders (1961), in a cross-cultural study, investigated the effect on growth of separation of an infant from its mother in the first days of life, which she interprets as a stressor. She found such separation to be significantly associated with greater stature in adults. Gunders and Whiting (1964) studied the relation between hospital birth and growth. Their assumption was that hospital deliveries ordinarily involve many of the same features as do the mother-separation practices of Gunders' cross-cultural study; notably, the child

John W. M. Whiting, Thomas K. Landauer, and Thomas M. Jones, "Infantile immunization and adult stature," *Child Development*, 1968, *39*, 59–67. Reprinted by permission. © 1968 by the Society for Research in Child Development, Inc.

is removed from the warm bed of his mother and may not be fed for 24 hours or so. They studied children born in a relocation camp in Israel in which the distribution of which individuals were born in the hospital and which at home seemed to be primarily determined by how far the family's assigned tent was from the camp hospital at the time of birth. Those children born in the hospital were found to be significantly heavier at ages 3 and 4 than those born at home.

Graham et al. (Graham, 1966; Graham, Ernhart, Thurston, & Craft, 1962) found that infants who suffered anoxia at birth showed a significant faster rate of growth than a normal control group. Many of the same children were studied again at age 7. Those who had suffered perinatal anoxia were significantly ($p < .01$) taller and heavier than normals (Corah, Anthony, Painter, Stern, & Thurston, 1965). Again, it is possible to interpret anoxia at birth as a stressful stimulus which might lead to the same changes which underlie the growth-accelerating effects of early stress in animals.

While none of these data can be taken as clear evidence of a causal relation between early stress and increased growth in humans, they may all be so interpreted; and the considerable variation among them, with the exception of the commonality of their probable stressfulness to the infant, suggests that the stress-growth hypothesis is worthy of further study. In an effort in this direction, we have reanalyzed data from two longitudinal-growth studies carried out in the United States: the Fels Study (Garn, 1962; Kagan, 1964), and the Berkeley Guidance Study (Macfarlane, 1938). We have searched the medical records of the cases from these studies for the occurrence of stressful events during early life. As suggested by the results of the earlier cross-cultural work, the age of 2 years was taken as an empirical cutoff point between early and later childhood. This cutoff is used as a matter of convenience only, based on our previous results, but with the possibility held open that examination of new data will lead to its modification.

Of the various infant-care practices which were associated with increased adult stature in the cross-cultural study, in the longitudinal study samples only inoculation was found in the necessary intermediate frequency which would allow a comparison of those who had been exposed to it with those who had not been so exposed. Inoculation may be presumed to be stressful on several counts. First of all it involves a pain at the time of occurrence, but this is probably the least significant of its stressful effects. An infant who has been inoculated for smallpox ordinarily shows symptoms of distress up to 2 or 3 weeks thereafter (Spock, 1957).

In addition, recent evidence (Marshall, 1966) indicates that smallpox and other inoculations are associated with the formation of bone lines, which have often been thought to be associated with stress (Tanner, 1962, p. 130).

It is important to enter a caveat to our argument at this point. It is obvious that early inoculations in the U.S. population may be associated with many other things. Those parents who have their children inoculated early almost certainly differ in many ways from those who do not. For example there may be an association between this medical procedure and other forms of medical care. We by no means reject the possibility that the association with growth which we have observed and will report below is due to these other factors rather than to stress per se. However, we feel it is important, as a first step, to see whether inoculation, which was associated with increased stature in a cross-cultural sample of primitive societies, is similarly associated with increased stature among members of our own society. Once this empirical question has been answered, a discussion of its interpretation will become more fruitful.

While we did not present cross-cultural data separately for inoculation as compared to other forms of stress in the original report (Landauer & Whiting, 1964), a significant relation between inoculation and stature existed in those data, as indicated by the following reanalysis. There were 5 societies in the sample of 65 that were reported to systematically inoculate children before the age of 2 years. The mean stature of the adult males in these five societies was 66.8 inches as compared to 64.2 inches for the remainder of the sample, and 63.0 for those societies in which no stress before the age of 2 was reported. Each case is a society in which at least 25 individuals were measured and their heights recorded in ethnographic literature and for which detailed data on child rearing were available. The ratings on the child-care practice and stature were done by independent (blind) raters. The differences are statistically significant (for inoculated vs. not inoculated $t = 2.61$, $df = 63$, $p < .02$ two-tailed; for inoculated vs. not stressed in any way $t = 4.46$, $df = 32$, $p < .001$ two-tailed).

METHOD

MATERIALS

From the Fels study we obtained inoculation and vaccination histories, and stature measurements made at age 18 for 77 boys and 69 girls born between 1928 and 1944 in or near Yellow Springs, Ohio. From the Berkeley Guidance Study we obtained inoculation, vaccination, and summary medical histories as well as yearly stature measurements up to maturity, from 80 boys and 90 girls, all born in 1927–29 in Berkeley, California. The two samples are roughly comparable with respect to socio-economic and racial factors. However, the Fels sample contains a much larger number of children from poor and rural backgrounds, while the Berkeley sample is almost entirely urban. We also obtained adult height data, most from actual measurements, some from report, for the mothers and fathers of all children in both samples.

In an attempt to control for parental stature, and factors which might operate through association with parental stature, a statistical correction for height of mother and father was used. For these data, it was found that the sum of mother's and father's height gave the most efficient prediction of the child's terminal stature, and this sum was used as the covariate control variable in all the comparisons to be reported below. A covariance technique was used in which the height of individuals was adjusted with respect to the best fit within-group linear regression of children's stature (separately for boys and girls and for the two samples) on sum of parental heights.

For each individual in both samples, the age at which the first immunological vaccination or inoculation of any kind occurred was determined. For over half of the cases, this procedure consisted of smallpox vaccination. Following the results of the cross-cultural study, we divided the samples into those individuals who did or did not receive one or more such treatments before the age of 2 years. The number of cases was too small to make the analysis of finer age ranges possible.

RESULTS

Table 1 gives the mean 18-year statures for boys and girls in the two samples separated according to whether or not they received an immunological vaccination or inoculation before the age of 2 years. The means presented have been adjusted for heights of mothers and

TABLE 1
MEAN 18-YEAR STATURE ADJUSTED FOR PARENTAL STATURE OF CHILDREN WITH AND WITHOUT EARLY IMMUNIZATION

Sample and Sex	Immuniza-tion Treatment before 24 Months	N	Adjusted (and Raw) Mean 18-Year Stature (Cm.)	F
Berkeley Guidance Study:				
Male	1 or more	38	180.31 (180.66)	1.073
	None	42	179.05 (178.74)	
Female	1 or more	48	166.61 (167.00)	2.116
	None	42	164.97 (164.52)	
Fels Growth Study:				
Male	1 or more	52	178.51 (178.73)	6.161
	None	25	175.99 (175.53)	
Female	1 or more	45	165.45 (166.35)	1.107
	None	25	164.08 (162.46)	

fathers. Separate analyses of covariance were performed for each of the four groups. The associated F ratios are given in Table 1. Only the difference for males in the Fels sample is significant by itself ($p < .04$), but the difference between the two treatment groups is in the same direction in all four groups, and the lack of significance is probably due to the rather small numbers in each. Combining the significance values for the four groups by a z transformation yields a probability of less than .02 for the full set of data. It thus appears reasonably clear that, on the average, the treated children exceeded the stature predicted from that of their parents to a greater extent than did those not treated.

INTERPRETATION

It remains to determine what interpretation may most reasonably be put on the finding that early immunization is associated with greater adult stature. One interpretation is that the relation is another instance of the growth-accelerating effect of early stress. But there are obviously other possibilities. One is that early immunization, through the protection afforded and/or through correlation with other forms of medical care, may result in less illness during the growth period and that a lack of illness contributes to adult stature. We were able to investigate the notion that illness during the growing period might be related to adult stature with the data from the Berkeley Guidance Study. Medical histories for each child were examined, abstracted, and rated by a person who did not have access to stature data for the same cases. The ratings were made in terms of the estimated number of days during which the individual had either an elevated temperature or elevated steroid hormone levels. Estimates of elevated temperature were made either from direct information given in the medical histories or from the usual course of a recorded illness, as described by standard pediatric texts. Estimates of elevated steroid levels had to be based on educated guesses, as direct evidence as to their usual course in common diseases and injuries is lacking.

Both illnesses and injuries were rated; such disparate items as severe allergic reactions, accidental ingestion of poison, rickets, infected ears, and mumps were all considered. The raters relied most heavily upon such signs as level and duration of fever, number of days of bed rest, descriptions of disability, and number of days of absence from school. When such information was only partially available, the raters relied on medical texts to determine the average course of a disease in order to make a rating. In general each illness or accident was given a rating in terms of presumed days of significantly heightened steroid levels. Each illness was given a duration rating and a severity rating. The severity ratings (1, 2, or 3) were generally "1." Ratings of "2" or "3" were reserved for definite indications of elevated steroid levels such as high fever. The total rating for each illness or accident was the product of the duration rating and the severity rating. Totals were tabulated for the years 0–2 and 2–18. A reliability coefficient of .88 was obtained between ratings on 36 separate 1-year records. While these ratings are obviously crude, they are probably sufficient for present purposes. There was an immense range—from 31 to 195 for summary ratings for 0–18 years among children in the sample—and it is thus quite clear that large differences in the amount of illness were being reflected. Certainly if gross amount of illness has an important influence on overall growth, children with such wide differences in rated illness histories should provide some evidence thereof.

To test the relation between illness and stature, we divided the groups at the median illness rating into those with much illness in their histories and those with little illness. The mean 18-year statures, adjusted for parental height, for those with much or little illness from birth to 2 years and from 2 to 18 years are given in Tables 2 and 3. It is clear that illness, as rated, bears no appreciable relation to stature. The F ratios obtained from analyses of covariance for these data are all insignificant. Moreover, the average illness ratings for those with and without early immunization also do not differ appreciably (mean illness ratings were 77.4 and 78.8 for those with and without early immunization, respectively: $F < 1$.). Thus, as far as we could determine, early immunization was not associated with less illness during the growing period, and differences in illness were not associated with 18-year stature. Thus it is implausible that the observed correlation between early immunization and adult stature could have been mediated by either direct or indirect

association of early immunization with decreased morbidity.

This is not to say, of course, that better medical or other care may not still be the mediator of the immunization-growth relation observed here. It is possible that early immunization is correlated, in these samples, with more frequent correlation of serious malnutrition, with supplementary vitamin therapy, with better diets, or with any one or more of a large number of potential growth-accelerating factors. The present data, unfortunately, provide no information on such matters. The present data cannot, therefore, be used to reject these many plausible alternatives. Other evidence is needed.

DISCUSSION

This seems an appropriate place to summarize the case to date concerning the hypothesis that infantile stress leads to increased growth in humans. No single definitive test of this hypothesis has been made, nor is one likely to appear in the future, because the experimental study of the effect of early stress is not possible with human subjects as it has been with laboratory animals. To explore the hypothesis with humans it is necessary to rely on correlational data with all its well-known pitfalls. Nonetheless, confidence in the likelihood of a particular interpretation may be gradually increased by the addition of new sources of confirmatory evidence in which various alternative interpretations are successively controlled. In the original cross-cultural study, it was possible to show that the association between early stress and adult stature was independent of race, geography, and diet. It was not possible to show that the causal relation might not be in the opposite direction, that is, that tall people stressed infants, with these data, however, since parental stature could not be controlled. Nor was it possible to assess the contribution of illness during growth since such information could not be obtained. In addition, these data left open the possibility of the effect being due to other cultural variables correlated with stressful infant-care practices. Perhaps most important, the cross-cultural evidence left open the possibility of selective differential mortality resulting from early stress.

In the present study, (a) culture was held relatively constant; (b) it was possible to control for parental stature by statistical means, making the directionality of the effect, from treatment to stature rather than vice versa, more plausible; (c) the possible contribution of decreased illness could be explored; and (d) there was essentially no mortality in the sample. But it was not possible, with the present data, to control for a variety of possible third-factor effects such as diet, which *were* controlled in the cross-cultural study.

TABLE 2

ADJUSTED MEAN 18-YEAR STATURE OF BERKELEY GUIDANCE STUDY SUBJECTS IN RELATION TO ILLNESS HISTORY DURING FIRST TWO YEARS

Sex and Amount of Illness	N	Adjusted Mean (and Raw) 18-Year Stature (Cm.)	F
Male:			
High	31	180.68 (179.48)	< 1
Low	33	179.32 (180.45)	
Female:			
High	33	166.03 (165.77)	< 1
Low	37	166.78 (167.02)	

TABLE 3

ADJUSTED MEAN 18-YEAR STATURE OF BERKELEY GUIDANCE STUDY SUBJECTS IN RELATION TO ILLNESS HISTORY BETWEEN THE AGES OF 2 AND 18

Sex and Amount of Illness	N	Adjusted Mean (and Raw) 18-Year Stature (Cm.)	F
Male:			
High	30	179.58 (179.22)	< 1
Low	34	180.33 (180.65)	
Female:			
High	33	167.21 (167.10)	1.328
Low	37	165.73 (165.83)	

In the same way, the assignment of treatment to individuals was probably anything but random in the present study. But in the Gunders study of hospital births (Gunders & Whiting, 1964), the initial treatment at least approached random assignment, the proximity of parents to the camp hospital being, apparently, the chief determinant of whether infants were born in the hospital or at home. Thus, self-selection of early stress by parents who might have other features contributory to growth, such as wealth and status, were controlled in Gunders' study, but in none of the others' to date, while in her study many of the other possibilities were not controlled.

Finally, in both the Gunders hospitalization study and the present investigation of immunization, the treatment was one generally thought to be benign, and thus some question of whether its stressful aspects were the crucial ones is raised. On the other hand, this is not true of many of the treatments considered in the cross-cultural studies, nor of the birth-anoxia effect reported by Corah et al. (1965), and by Graham (1966) and Graham et al. (1962).

In summary, there now exist a number of reports of enhanced growth associated with treatment in early infancy which have been interpreted as potential stressors. While no one of the studies controls for all possible artifacts, the following possible extraneous sources of the correlation have been at least partially controlled in at least one study: diet; race; geography, including sunlight and rain; parental stature; illness and selective mortality; self-selection of treatment by parents; and direct benign effects of the treatment.

What links all of these studies and leads to comparison of their results in the first place, of course, is the interpretation that they are all instances of infantile stimulation or stress. This assumption is for the most part made on insufficient evidence, and this is probably the weakest link in the case at present. What is needed is direct evidence of a common physiological effect of such growth-enhancing infant-care practices as mother separation, hospital birth, immunization, and birth anoxia, etc., and a real understanding of how such a physiological effect, if it exists, leads to acceleration of growth.

The lack of clear understanding of the mechanism, or of definitive evidence concerning the nature and site of action of infantile experiences on growth, should not, however, obscure the existence of a very real and important relationship. It is certain that there is an association between a variety of apparently stressful infant experiences and increased growth. Elucidation of the reason for this relation cannot help but shed significant light on the processes by which differences in growth rates are determined.

REFERENCES

CORAH, N. L., ANTHONY, E. J., PAINTER, P., STERN, J. A., & THURSTON, D. Effects of perinatal anoxia after seven years. *Psychological Monographs,* 1965, *79* (Whole No. 596).

GARN, S. M. Genetics of normal human growth. In L. Gedda (Ed.), *De genetica medica.* Rome: Gregor Mendel, 1962.

GRAHAM, F. Personal communication 1966.

GRAHAM, F., ERNHART, C. B., THURSTON, D. S., & CRAFT, M. Development three years after perinatal anoxia and other potentially damaging newborn experiences. *Psychological Monographs,* 1962, *76* (Whole No. 522).

GUNDERS, S. M. The effects of periodic separation from the mother during infancy upon growth and development. Unpublished doctoral dissertation, Harvard University, 1961.

GUNDERS, S. M., & WHITING, J. W. M. The effects of periodic separation from the mother during infancy upon growth and development. Paper presented at International Congress of Anthropological and Ethnological Science, Moscow, August, 1964.

KAGAN, J. American longitudinal research on psychological development. *Child Development,* 1964, *35,* 1–32.

LANDAUER, T. K., & WHITING, J. W. M. Infantile stimulation and adult stature of human males. *American Anthropologist,* 1964, *66,* 1007–1028.

LEVINE, S. J. Stimulation in infancy. *Scientific American,* 1960, *202,* 80–86.

MACFARLANE, J. Studies in child guidance. I. Methodology of data collection and organization. *Monographs of the Society for Research in Child Development,* 1938, *3,* No. 6 (Whole No. 19).

MARSHALL, W. Personal communication. 1966.

SPOCK, B. *Baby and child care.* New York: Pocket Books, Inc., 1957.

TANNER, J. N. *Growth at adolescence.* (2d ed.) Oxford: Blackwell Scientific, 1962.

III

LEARNING AS A DETERMINANT
OF BEHAVIOR

Because it is impossible to give adequate space in a book such as this to each of the schools of thought regarding the principles of learning, we have chosen one approach for major emphasis, that of reinforcement. A reinforcement theorist will seek to explain behavior by asking "What actions have been reinforced?" At times he will focus on asking "What is acting as the reinforcer for this behavior?" The latter question is particularly important when trying to eliminate undesired behaviors. At other times he will want to know what might be an effective reinforcer for the child.

We focus on reinforcement for two reasons: (1) Reinforcement theory has played a greater role than other conceptions of the learning process in stimulating and guiding research in child psychology. (2) To provide historical balance and recognize present trends in education. Since association theory with its emphasis on contiguity and practice dominated education in the past, our emphasis on reinforcement provides historical balance. Since much current work in education is strongly influenced by reinforcement, we are recognizing the present trend.

For surveys of various theoretical approaches to learning, the student might consult: (1) *Reward and Punishment* (Allyn and Bacon, Boston, 1965), by Frank A. Logan and Allen R. Wagner; (2) *Learning: A Survey of Psychological Interpretations* (Chandler, San Francisco, 1963), by Winfred F. Hill; and (3) *Cognitive Psychology* (Appleton-Century-Crofts, New York, 1967), by Ulric Neisser. Almost all introductory psychology texts would have one or more appropriate chapters. Chapter 11, Human Learning and Remembering, of *General Psychology* (Prentice-Hall, New Jersey, 1970), by William N. Dember and James J. Jenkins, is a recent example that has the advantage of focusing on human learning.

The section starts with a brief overview of theories of learning, shows the ways in which parents may be said to use learning theories (and with what results), and gives concrete examples of the application of reinforcement theory.

10

Theories of Learning and Behavior

JOHN W. M. WHITING

This first paper is by John W. M. Whiting, professor of social anthropology and curator of African ethnology at Harvard University. He was formerly director of Harvard's Laboratory of Human Development. Whiting, an anthropologist-psychologist, is a product of Yale University's Institute of Human Relations. Hull's exacting systematization of learning theory was spawned in that Institute. John Dollard, a clinical psychologist, and Neal Miller, an experimental psychologist, produced a book there that gave a concise version of Hullian theory and applied it to analysis of the therapeutic process.[1] A good deal of interdisciplinary work in psychology and anthropology also was undertaken at Yale. Indeed, Yale has markedly influenced contemporary behavioral science.

In this brief paper, Whiting presents an overview of different theories of learning in relation to behavior.

Research in the process of learning may be divided into three general areas of interest which may be referred to as *primary learning*, *secondary learning*, and *social learning*. Although my major interest is in the latter two, it is in the field of

---

[1] *Personality and Psychotherapy* (New York: McGraw-Hill, 1950).

primary learning that the basic principles and concepts have been developed—principles upon which secondary and social learning depend. It is necessary therefore to briefly review and summarize the various theories and concepts which have been developed in the field of primary learning.

PRIMARY LEARNING

Research in primary learning has been carried on in the laboratory under carefully controlled conditions with animals as subjects. Dogs, rats, cats and pigeons have been the species most generally used. Primary drives such as hunger, thirst or pain from electric shock have been characteristically employed for motivation; relatively simple stimuli such as buzzers or lights have been preferred to more complex ones and, similarly, relatively simple responses such as salivation, maze running, or pressing a bar.

Pavlov (5) was, of course, the father of learning theory and his experiments are so well known that they need not be described. It should be pointed out, however, that he viewed learning as essentially a process of stimulus substitution. A stimulus, which he called an unconditioned stimulus, was chosen which could be counted on to evoke a response. This was then paired repeatedly with a neutral or conditioned stimulus until the latter gained power to evoke the response. It should be noted that the stimulus situation was experimentally varied and the response controlled, and that contiguity between the unconditioned and the conditioned stimulus was considered to be the crucial event for learning.

In the United States quite a different view of learning was originally evolved by E. L. Thorndike (9), and developed by Hull (2), Skinner (7), N. E. Miller (3, 4), and Spence (8). This view, generally referred to as the reinforcement theory of learning, emphasizes motivation and reward. The experimental model which best expresses this view is provided by a hungry animal in a box learning to make some response (such as pressing a lever) to get a pellet of food. Rather than controlling the response and changing the stimulus as was the case in Pavlov's experimental design, the stimulus is held constant and the responses permitted to vary freely. This type of theory views learning as a process of response selection rather than stimulus substitution. Furthermore, reward following a correct performance is held to be crucial in this theory, mere contiguity between the conditioned and unconditioned stimulus is held to be insufficient.

John W. M. Whiting, "Theories of learning and behavior," in *The Causes of Behavior*, ed. Judy F. Rosenblith and Wesley Allinsmith (Boston: Allyn and Bacon, Inc., 1962). Reprinted by permission.

A third view of learning is the *S-R* contiguity theory of Guthrie (1). The basic postulate of this theory is that complete learning takes place whenever a response occurs in the presence of a stimulus. Neither the presence of an unconditioned stimulus nor a reward is required. Guthrie accounts for the fact that learning is often continuous rather than a sudden "all or none" process by the fact that an organism is not perceiving all the stimuli in a situation on any given trial and gradual improvement results from more and more stimuli getting associated with the response.

The application of gestalt psychology is best exemplified by Tolman (10). Learning in Tolman's view involves changes in cognition rather than the strengthening of *S-R* connections. Vivid or salient stimuli (events) which are repeatedly perceived by an organism to be in a consistent spatial or temporal relation to one another give rise to the belief that these events will be so related in the future. Improvement in performance thus depends upon the increasing adequacy and validity of the cognitive map which guides and directs the performance.

MOTIVATION AND PERFORMANCE

Since the consequences of learning can be measured only if the organism does something, a complete theory of learning must contain principles governing performance. That is, it must concern itself with factors such as motivation, generalization and response competition as well as with acquisition. Hull has been most explicit in this regard and has assumed that the amplitude, latency, resistance to extinction and probability of occurrence of any act is a joint function of learning and motivation.[2]

Generalization is another performance principle of considerable importance. This principle is concerned with the progressive decrement in the strength of a habit as the stimuli in test situations are made more dissimilar from those present during learning. It provides a basis for some of the complex problems involved in symbolic mediation. This principle has also been used by Miller, by Sears (6), and by Whiting and Child (11), to account for the Freudian mechanisms of displacement and projection.

Response competition or conflict between simultaneously evoked habits is a final performance principle which should be mentioned. Ambivalence, insecurity and anxiety may be defined as special cases of response competition.

SECONDARY LEARNING

As the term is being used here, secondary learning refers to the special principles which govern the so-called acquired drives and acquired rewards. That is, those motives and rewards which are learned rather than innate. Since these concepts are particularly relevant to the reinforcement theory of learning, it is the followers of Hull who have done most systematic work in this area.

Acquired drives may be divided into two classes which may be termed conditioned primary drives and purposive acquired drives. Fear provides a model for the conditioned primary drive. Neutral stimuli associated with pain become danger signals which come to evoke fear. When fear has been established, the organism will learn to avoid or to escape from the dangerous situation.

The concept of purposive acquired drives is derived from the assumption that a conflict between goal expectancies produces insecurity which will motivate an organism to solve the conflict. Dependency, aggression, and achievement are examples of acquired drives which have recently been accounted for in this manner.

Acquired rewards or token rewards are like acquired drives, learned rather than innate. It is generally held that the process of acquisition results from simple association of some neutral stimulus with some primary reward. Thus if a mother always smiles as she nurses the baby, her smile comes to be in itself rewarding. Tokens of value such as money gain their reward value in a somewhat more complicated manner, but presumably the process is not different in principle.

SOCIAL LEARNING

Culture and society provide some special circumstances or learning conditions which all children must face in growing up. Three factors in particular are important in this regard. First, rewards and punishments are administered by people, generally parents, who are perceived by the child to be similar to himself and whom he is generally taught to imitate. As a consequence, self-other discriminations, role adoption, projection, and the complicated process of identification and the internalization of values become central problems which any theory of social learning must face.

Secondly, the progressive maturation of the child from infancy to adulthood results in the child at first learning habits which he must later be forced to relinquish. For example, the child first learns to be dependent, then to be self-reliant and responsible. He may be permitted to have temper tantrums as an infant and then must learn to control his

---

[2] As he expresses it: $_sE_r = f(_sH_r) \times f(D)$ where $_sE_r$ is the term relating to performance, $_sH_r$ to accumulated learning, and D to current motivation.

aggression as an older child. These shifts in parental attitude produce conflicts which in many instances have enduring effects.

Thirdly, all human children are brought up into a society of people who speak a language. Theories of social learning have scarcely begun to account for the implications of this fact. The transmission of systems of belief and value by formal or informal and often unintended instruction, transfer or training by verbal mediation, and the learning of the cognitive structure involved in planning are only some of the problems deriving from the symbolic behavior of human beings which an adequate theory of social learning must account for.

Justice obviously cannot be done in such a brief review to the theories here presented. Many of the fine points have had to be omitted; others have no doubt been distorted by condensation. Furthermore, many important contributors to certain facets of the learning process have not been mentioned at all. It is hoped that this review will serve as a skeleton outline of the major viewpoints held by learning theorists and the problems which face investigators concerned with learning and behavior.

A brief bibliography of important works on learning and behavior.

1. GUTHRIE, E. R. *The Psychology of Learning.* New York: Harper, 1935.

2. HULL, C. L. *The Principles of Behavior.* New York: Appleton-Century, 1943.

3. MILLER, N. E., & DOLLARD, J. *Social Learning and Imitation.* New Haven: Yale University Press, 1941.

4. MILLER, N. E. Learnable drives and rewards. In S. S. Stevens (Ed.), *Handbook of Experimental Psychology.* New York: Wiley & Sons, 1951.

5. PAVLOV, I. P. *Conditioned Reflexes.* (Trans. by G. V. Anrep) London: Oxford Press, 1927.

6. SEARS, R. R., *et al.* Some child-rearing antecedents of aggression and dependency in young children. *Genet. Psychol. Monogr.,* 1953, *47,* 135–234.

7. SKINNER, B. F. *The Behavior of Organisms; an Experimental Analysis.* New York: Appleton-Century, 1938.

8. SPENCE, K. W. Theoretical interpretations of learning. In S. S. Stevens (Ed.), *Handbook of Experimental Psychology.* New York: Wiley & Sons, 1951.

9. THORNDIKE, E. L. *The Fundamentals of Learning.* New York: Teachers College, 1932.

10. TOLMAN, E. C. *Purposive Behavior in Animals and Men.* New York: Appleton-Century, 1932.

11. WHITING, J. W. M., & CHILD, I. L. *Child Training and Personality.* New Haven: Yale University Press, 1953.

11

Patterns of Parenthood as Theories of Learning [1]

JANE LOEVINGER

In this paper, Jane Loevinger looks at the ways in which parents implicitly follow one or another theory of learning in their child-rearing practices. The author points out the effects of the various parental theories on the actual behavior of the offspring. Loevinger, a psychologist at Washington University in St. Louis, is interested in ego development, psychometrics (or test theory), and psychoanalysis, and is the author of a test of ego development. She can be characterized as having a cognitive-developmental approach to socialization. Those concerned with ego development might want to read her paper "The Meaning and Measurement of Ego Development," in The American Psychologist *(1966, 21, 195–217).*

Gerhart Piers (in a talk which I quote from memory) has divided methods of learning into three types: learning by reinforcement, by insight, and by identification. All three types of learning unquestionably occur, and theories of learning espoused by professional psychologists must account for those facts, whatever they take as the prototype of all learning.

Any consistent method of child-rearing contains by implication a theory of how children function, particularly how they learn. One can easily set up a correspondence between well-known patterns of parenthood and the three types of learning. Corresponding to any pattern of child-rearing there is, then, a "theory of learning," emphasizing one type of learning at the expense of others. Theories of learning held by parents are, of course, far more naive and uncomplicated than similar theories held by psychologists. To avoid confusion, the term "parental theory" may be used to distinguish the implicit learning theory.

The disciplinarian parent apparently believes that any wrong thing a child does will be continued indefinitely if the parent does not see that it is punished. While psychological research has tended to emphasize rewards as more effective than punishments as reinforcing agents, disciplinarian parents emphasize punishments as reinforcers.

Apparently insight learning is assumed to predominate by those parents, once reputed to be numerous, who believe that every demand made on a child must be rationalized and explained.

Finally, the typical permissive parent must surely believe that the socialization of his child takes place by means of the child identifying himself with the well-socialized parent.

Consider the following situation. Five-year-old Johnny is beating on his two-year-old sister Sue. Mother comes in. Let us assume that every mother will want to prevent repetition of such behavior. What will she do?

Mother One believes that if Johnny does not feel pain, he will repeat the behavior at every coincidence of impulse and opportunity. She therefore punishes him sharply, thus demonstrating her adherence to a parental reinforcement theory of learning.

Mother Two believes that Johnny can be shown how wrong his conduct is and sets about to persuade him. She believes in a parental insight theory of learning.

Mother Three believes that Johnny wants to grow up to be like his parents. If she punishes him harshly, he will learn that it is all right for the bigger one to be mean to the littler one if he or she feels like it; so his behavior is less likely to be repeated if reprimanded gently than if dealt with harshly. She believes in a parental identification theory of learning.

There is one fallacy common to all parental learning theories. Kelly (1955) points out that we are not victims of our history but only of our con-

[1] Preparation of this note was supported by Research Grant M-1213 from the National Institute of Mental Health, Public Health Service.

Jane Loevinger, "Patterns of parenthood as theories of learning," *Journal of Abnormal and Social Psychology*, 1959, *59*, 148–150. Reprinted by permission.

struction of that history. Kelly finds in that fact hope for the psychotherapist. But just as it gives hope for the therapist, it generates despair for the parent. A parent can decide to beat his child, but he cannot decide how the child will construe the beating. Nor, if he abstains from punishing, can he decide how the child will construe the abstention.

Rules for rearing children are beyond the scope of this note, indeed, beyond the competence of the writer. But one superordinate rule can safely be stated: Whatever the parent's theory of learning, the child will in fact be learning by an alternative method. Thus the son of Mother One is probably identifying with a punitive, disciplinarian adult; for the son of Mother Two it is being stamped in that beating on sister has no painful consequences; while the son of Mother Three has probably discerned, "Aha! I can get away with it." The explanation of why a child shifts his mode of learning to escape his parent's vigilant efforts at socialization is not difficult. He is attempting to defend the gratification of his impulses, and in this respect he is not altogether different from his parents.

The foregoing formulation helps to solve two riddles. Why is the battle between the generations fought, generation after generation, with such vigor? And why is it that experts on child-rearing are not conspicuously more successful at the art than those less expert?

The failure of expertise in child-rearing was foreshadowed in 1909 with Freud's (1925) publication of *Analysis of a Phobia in a Five-Year-Old Boy,* for little Hans was the child of two of Freud's followers. One should not make too much of the fact. He was not necessarily the most neurotic child in Vienna, merely the one that Freud had opportunity to observe and indirectly to treat. Nonetheless, the occurrence of so severe a phobia in the child was a striking omen.

Reasons have been advanced for the failure of children of experts to be vastly superior to others in their adjustment. Without disputing or discounting those reasons, one can focus on a slightly different one. The experts know what other parents did wrong, and they avoid those errors. But while they avoid the errors of parents in other houses, their children contrive to defend their instinctual gratification against the parents in their own house. In current terms, a shift in parentmanship is countered by a shift in childmanship.

The battle between the generations is commonly accounted for by the fact that parents have need to socialize their children, and the children forever battle against the socializing process. This view is the one being elaborated here. But it is not quite the whole story. A useful way to test a theory is to see what happens in the most extreme cases.

Redl and Wineman (1957) have depicted extreme cases of "children who hate." Many of the sentiments of those children, such as "Grown-ups don't want kids to have any fun," are echoed occasionally in almost all homes. But the ferocity and implacability of the war with adults is entirely disproportionate to what takes place in an ordinary household. Were their parents, then, so rigorous in their attempts at socialization? On the contrary, the parents of those children presented a picture of impulsivity no less striking than that of the children. The abuses to which the children were subjected could hardly be called punishments; they did not appear to result from any theory of how children learn but rather were crude lashing out on impulse. The picture of parent-child relations in *The Aggressive Child* is a conspicuously undesirable one, both prima facie and in terms of outcome. It serves to demonstrate that not all parents are informed by a parental theory. The battle between the generations is never more vicious than when all pretense of representing the interests of society is dropped and it becomes the parent's impulsivity versus the child's.

A general theory of the battle between generations must account for all of the cases. It must therefore read that the child's impulse gratification conflicts with the needs of society, represented by parents, to socialize him, as well as with the parent's own impulse gratification. The normal parent, to be sure, satisfies many of his desires in and through his children. But moment by moment and day by day the needs which the children gratify are not always uppermost. The presence of an infant or child in the household necessarily imposes delay or surrender on many of the parents' wishes.

The conclusions of this discussion can be stated simply, though they do not exactly simplify life. Every consistent pattern of child-rearing embodies a theory of learning, and all those parental theories are substantially wrong. However, any parental theory is better than none.

Is it possible to base one's pattern of child-rearing on a more nearly realistic theory of learning? That is an intriguing question. In view of the adaptability of the normal child in shifting his tactics to match those of his parents, such a method would require constant reconsideration and change. Yet inconsistency, so the child-rearing experts tell us, is one of the worst faces a parent can turn to his child. Possibly, however, inconsistency got its bad name not from conscientious parents trying to outwit their children but from the label being applied to such parents as Redl and Wineman have sketched.

If, as the present discussion suggests, parental

theories are more wrong than right, how does it happen that it is better to have one than not? The chief value of a parental learning theory may well be in providing a model for the child of curbing one's own impulses out of regard for the future welfare of another. The very oversimplification of parental theories may serve to make accessible to the child that his parent is acting on principle rather than on impulse. To say this is to lay emphasis on learning by identification. But probably most psychologists, whatever their professional theories, act in relation to their own children as if they expect them to learn chiefly by identification.

"All I say is by way of discourse, and nothing by way of advice. . . . I should not speak so boldly, if it were my due to be believed" (de Montaigne, 1913, p. 283).

REFERENCES

DE MONTAIGNE, M. *The essays of Michel de Montaigne.* Vol. III. C. Cotton (Trans.); W. C. Hazlitt (Ed.) London: G. Bell, 1913.

FREUD, S. Analysis of a phobia in a five-year-old boy. In *Collected papers.* Vol. III. London: Hogarth, 1925. Pp. 149–289.

KELLY, G. A. *The psychology of personal constructs.* Vol. II. *Clinical diagnosis and psychotherapy.* New York: Norton, 1955.

REDL, F., and WINEMAN, D. *The aggressive child.* Glencoe, Ill.: Free Press, 1957.

A child is an act of faith about which one grows increasingly uncertain. An adult, it might follow, is a gambler in the process of losing. Still the perpetual motion is love, and within that motion every generation has tried to save what it has already lost by teaching the losing game to its children. This state of confusion is called, by general agreement, Parenthood.

—John Ciardi

12

Effects of Adult Social Reinforcement on Child Behavior *

FLORENCE R. HARRIS,
MONTROSE M. WOLF,
AND DONALD M. BAER

The Elimination of Tantrum Behavior by Extinction Procedures †

CARL D. WILLIAMS

The first paper demonstrates the principles of behavioral control through contingency management in the social setting of the nursery school. Several different behaviors are brought under control, including both desirable behaviors (which are strengthened) and undesirable ones (which are weakened). The authors of the paper, which was done at the University of Washington (Seattle) and its laboratory preschool, are Prof. Harris, director of the preschool, and Professors Baer and Wolf, now on the faculty at the University of Kansas.

The second, brief paper is an account by Carl D. Williams of the elimination of an undesirable behavior (bedtime tantrums). As in many studies of contingency of reinforcement, an individual child is the focus. Williams is a professor at the University of Miami, in Coral Gables, Florida.

There is general agreement among educators that one of the primary functions of a nursery school is to foster in each child social behaviors that contribute toward more pleasant and productive living for all. However, there is no similar consensus as to precisely how this objective is to be attained. Many writers subscribe to practices based on a combination of psychoanalytic theory and client-centered therapy principles, usually referred to as a mental hygiene approach. Yet there are considerable variation and vagueness in procedures recommended, particularly those dealing with such problem behaviors as the child's hitting people, breaking valuable things, or withdrawing from both people and things. Read (1955), for example, recommends accepting the child's feelings, verbalizing them for him, and draining them off through vigorous activities. Landreth (1942) advises keeping adult contacts with the child at a minimum based on his needs, backing up verbal suggestions by an implicit assumption that the suggestion will be carried out and, when in doubt, doing nothing unless the child's physical safety is involved. In addition to some of the above precepts, Taylor (1954) counsels parents and teachers to support both desirable and undesirable behaviors and to give nonemotional punishment. According to Standing (1959), Montessori advocates that teachers pursue a process of nonintervention, following careful preparation of a specified environment aimed at "canalizing the energy" and developing "inner command." Nonintervention does not preclude the "minimum dose" of instruction and correction.

Using some combination of such guidance precepts, teachers have reported success in helping some nursery school children who showed problem behaviors; but sometimes adherence to the same teaching principles has not been helpful in modifying the behavior of concern. Indeed, it is usually not at all clear what conditions and principles may or may not have been operative. All of these precepts have in common the adult behaviors

---

[1] These studies were supported in part by research grants from the National Institute of Mental Health (MH–02208–07) and the University of Washington Graduate School Research Fund (11–1873). The authors are also indebted to Sidney W. Bijou for his general counsel and assistance.

---

† Carl D. Williams, "The elimination of tantrum behavior by extinction procedures," *Journal of Abnormal and Social Psychology*, 1959, *59*, 269. Reprinted by permission.

of approaching and attending to a child. Therefore, it seemed to the staff of the Laboratory Preschool at the University of Washington that a first step in developing possible explicit criteria for judging when and when not to attend was to study the precise effects that adult attention can have on some problem behaviors.

This paper presents an account of the procedures and results of five such studies. Two groups of normal nursery school children provided the subjects studied. One group enrolled twelve three-year-olds and the other, sixteen four-year-olds. The two teachers of the younger group and the three teachers of the older group conducted the studies as they carried out their regular teaching duties. The general methodology of these studies was developed in the course of dealing with a particularly pressing problem behavior shown by one child at the beginning of the school year. It is worth considering this case before describing the procedures which evolved from it.

The study dealt with a three-year-old girl who had regressed to an excessive amount of crawling (Harris, Johnston, Kelley, and Wolf, 1964). By "excessive" is meant that after three weeks of school she was spending most of her morning crawling or in a crouched position with her face hidden. The parents reported that for some months the behavior had been occurring whenever they took her to visit or when friends came to their home. The teachers had used the conventional techniques, as outlined above, for building the child's "security."

Observations recorded in the third week at school showed, however, that more than 80% of the child's time was spent in off-feet positions. The records also showed that the crawling behavior frequently drew the attention of teachers. On-feet behaviors, such as standing and walking, which occurred infrequently, seldom drew such notice.

A program was instituted in which the teachers no longer attended to the child whenever she was crawling or crouching, but gave her continuous warm attention as long as she was engaging in behavior in which she was standing, running, or walking. Initially the only upright behaviors that the teachers were able to attend to occurred when the child pulled herself almost to her feet in order to hang up or take down her coat from her locker, and when she pulled herself up to wash her hands in the wash basin. Within a week of the initiation of the new attention-giving procedure, the child acquired a close-to-normal pattern of on-feet behavior.

In order to see whether the change from off- to on-feet behavior was related to the differential attention given by the teachers, they reversed their procedure, making attention once again contingent only upon crawling and other off-feet behavior.

They waited for occasions of such off-feet behavior to "reinforce" with attention, while not attending to any on-feet behavior. By the second day the child had reverted to her old pattern of play and locomotion. The observational records showed the child was off her feet 80% of the class session.

To see whether on-feet behavior could be re-established, the teachers again reversed their procedure, giving attention to the child only when she was engaging in behaviors involving upright positions. On-feet behavior rose markedly during the first session. By the fourth day, the child again spent about 62% of the time on her feet.

Once the child was not spending the greater portion of her day crawling about, she quickly became a well-integrated member of the group. Evidently she already had well-developed social play skills.

As a result of this demonstration that either walking or crawling could be maintained and that the child's responses depended largely upon the teachers' attending behaviors, the teachers began a series of further experimental analyses of the relationship between teacher attention and nursery school child behavior.

PROCEDURES

A specified set of procedures common to the next studies was followed. First, a child showing problem behavior was selected and records were secured. An observer recorded all of the child's behavior, the environmental conditions under which it occurred, and its immediate consequences under conventional teacher guidance. This was done throughout the 2½-hour school session, daily, and for several days. The records gave detailed pictures of the behavior under study. In each case, it became apparent that the problem behavior almost always succeeded in attracting adult attention.

As soon as these records, technically termed "baseline" records, of the typical behavior of the child and teachers were obtained, teachers instituted a program of systematically giving differential attention to the child. When the undesired behavior occurred, they did not in any way attend to him, but remained absorbed in one of the many necessary activities of teachers with other children or with equipment. If the behavior occurred while a teacher was attending to the child, she at once turned to another child or task in a matter-of-fact and nonrejecting manner. Concurrently, teachers gave immediate attention to other behaviors of the child which were considered to be more desirable than the problem behavior. The net effect of these procedures was that the child could gain a great deal of adult attention if he refrained from engaging in "problem behavior." If under this regime of differential attention the problem behavior diminished to a stable low level at which it was no longer considered a problem, a second procedure was inaugurated to check out the functional relationship between changes in the child's behavior and the guidance procedures followed.

The second procedure was simply to reverse the first procedure. That is, when the problem behavior occurred, the teacher went immediately to the child and gave him her full, solicitous attention. If the behavior stopped, she turned to other children and tasks, remaining thus occupied until the behavior recurred. In effect, one sure way for the child to secure adult attention was to exhibit the problem behavior. This procedure was used to secure reasonably reliable information on whether the teachers' special program had indeed brought about the changes noted in the child's behavior. If adult attention was the critical factor in maintaining the behavior, the problem behavior should recur in stable form under these conditions. If it did so, this was evidence that adult attention was, technically speaking, a positive social reinforcer for the child's behavior.

The final stage of the study was, of course, to return to procedures in which attention was given at once and continuously for behaviors considered desirable. Concurrently, adult attention was again withheld or withdrawn as an immediate consequence of the problem behavior. As the problem disappeared and appropriate behaviors increased, the intense program of differential adult attention was gradually diminished until the child was receiving attention at times and in amounts normal for the teachers in the group. However, attention was given only on occasions of desirable behavior, and never (or very seldom) for the undesirable behavior.

Crying and Whining

Following the above procedures, a study was conducted on a four-year-old boy who cried a great deal after mild frustrations (Hart, Allen, Buell, Harris, and Wolf, 1964). This child averaged about eight full-fledged crying episodes each school morning. The baseline observations showed that this crying behavior consistently brought attention from the teachers, in the form of going to him and showing solicitous concern. During the following days, this behavior was simply ignored. (The only exceptions to this were to have been incidents in which the child had hurt himself considerably and was judged to have genuine grounds for crying. Naturally, his hurts were to be attended to. Such incidents, however, did not occur.) Ten days of ignoring the outcries, but giving approving atten-

tion for verbal and self-help behaviors, produced a steady weakening of the crying response to a nearly zero level. In the final five days of the interval, only one crying response was recorded. The number of crying episodes on successive days is graphed in cumulative form in Fig. 1.

During the next ten days, crying was again reinforced whenever it occurred, the teachers attending to the boy on these occasions without fail. At first, it was necessary to give attention for mere grimaces that might follow a bump. The daily crying episodes quickly rose to a rate almost as high as formerly. A second ten-day period of ignoring the outcries again produced a quick weakening of the response to a near-zero level, as is apparent in the figure. Crying remained at this low level thereafter, according to the informal judgment of the teachers.

The same procedures were used in another study of "operant crying" of a four-year-old boy, with the same general results.

Isolate Play

Two studies involved children who exhibited markedly solitary play behavior. Extremely little of their morning at nursery school was spent in any interaction with other children. Instead, these children typically played alone in a quiet area of the school room or the play yard, or interacted only with the teachers. For present purposes, both of these response patterns will be called "isolate play." Sys-

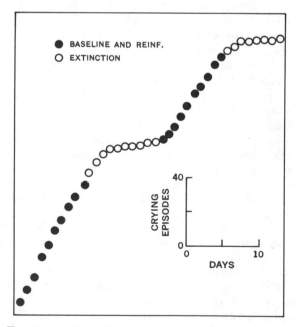

Figure 1. *Cumulative record of the daily number of crying episodes.*

tematic observation showed that isolate play usually attracted or maintained the attention of a teacher, whereas social play with other children did so comparatively seldom.

A plan was initiated in which the teacher was to attend regularly if the child approached other children and interacted with them. On the other hand, the teacher was not to attend to the child so long as he engaged in solitary play. To begin with, attention was given when the child merely stood nearby, watching other children; then, when he played beside another child; and finally, only when he interacted with the other child. Teachers had to take special precautions that their attending behaviors did not result in drawing the child away from children and into interaction solely with the teacher. Two techniques were found particularly effective. The teacher directed her looks and comments to the other child or children, including the subject only as a participant in the play project. For example, "That's a big building you three boys are making; Bill and Tom and Jim (subject) are all

working hard." Accessory materials were also kept at hand so that the teacher could bring a relevant item for the subject to add to the play: "Here's another plate for your tea party, Ann." In both isolate cases this new routine for giving adult attention produced the desired result: Isolate play declined markedly in strength while social play increased two- or threefold.

After about a week of the above procedure, the consequences of nonisolate and isolate play were reversed. The teachers no longer attended to the child's interactions with other children, but instead gave continuous attention to the child when he was alone. Within a week, or less, isolate play became the dominant form of activity in both cases.

The former contingencies were then reinstated: The teachers attended to social interactions by the child, and ignored isolate play as completely as they could. Again, isolate play declined sharply while social interaction increased as before. The results of one of these studies (Allen, Hart, Buell, Harris, and Wolf, 1964) are summarized in Fig. 2.

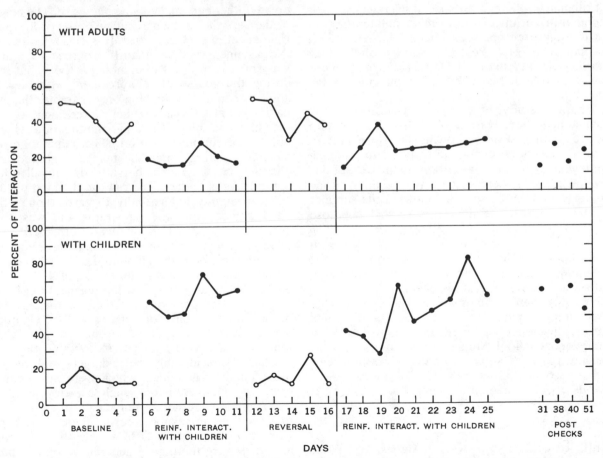

FIGURE 2. *Daily percentages of time spent in social interaction with adults and with children during approximately two hours of each morning session.*

Figure 2 shows the changes in behavior of a $4\frac{1}{2}$-year-old girl under the different guidance conditions. The graph shows the percentage of play time that she spent in interaction with other children and the percentage of time spent with an adult. The remainder of her time was spent alone. It is apparent that only about 15% of this child's play time was spent in social play as long as the teachers attended primarily to her solitary play. But interacting behaviors rose to about 60% of total play time when the teachers attended only to her social play. At the same time, her interactions solely with teachers, not being reinforced, fell from their usual 40% of the child's play time to about 20%. These were considered reasonable percentages for this nursery school child. During Days 17 through 25 the schedule of adult reinforcement of social play was gradually reduced to the usual amount of attention, given at the usual irregular intervals. Nevertheless, the social behavior maintained its strength, evidently becoming largely self-maintaining.

After Day 25, the teachers took care not to attend too often to the child when she was alone, but otherwise planned no special contingencies for attending. Four checks were made at later dates to see if the pattern of social behavior persisted. It is apparent (Fig. 2, Post Checks) that the change was durable, at least until Day 51. Further checks were not possible because of the termination of the school year.

A parallel study, of a three-year-old isolate boy (Johnston, Kelley, Harris, Wolf, and Baer, unpub.) yielded similar results showing the same pattern of rapid behavioral change in response to changing contingencies for adult attention. In the case of this boy, postchecks were made on three days during the early months of school following the summer vacation period. The data showed that on those days his interaction with children averaged 55% of his play time. Apparently his social play was well established. Teachers reported that throughout the remainder of the year he continued to develop ease and skills in playing with his peers.

The immediate shifts in these children's play behavior may be partly due to the fact that they had already developed skills readily adapted to play with peers at school. Similar studies in progress are showing that, for some children, development of social play behaviors may require much longer periods of reinforcement.

EXCESSIVE PASSIVITY

A fifth case (Johnston, Kelley, Harris, and Wolf, unpub.) involved a boy noted for his thorough-going lack of any sort of vigorous play activity. The teachers reported that this child consistently stood quietly about the play yard while other children ran, rode tricycles, and climbed on special climbing frames, trees, fences, and playhouses. Teachers also reported that they frequently attempted to encourage him, through suggestions or invitations, to engage in the more vigorous forms of play available. Teachers expressed concern over his apparent lack of strength and motor skills. It was decided to select a particular form of active play to attempt to strengthen. A wooden frame with ladders and platforms, called a climbing frame, was chosen as the vehicle for establishing this activity. The teachers attended at first to the child's mere proximity to the frame. As he came closer, they progressed to attending only to his touching it, climbing up a little, and finally to extensive climbing. Technically, this was reinforcement of successive approximations to climbing behavior. Fig. 3 shows the results of nine days of this procedure, compared to a baseline of the preceding nine days. In this figure, black bars represent climbing on the climbing frame, and white bars represent climbing on any other equipment in the play yard. The height of the bars shows the percentage of the child's play time spent in such activities. It is clear that during the baseline period less than 10% of the child's time was spent in any sort of climbing activity, but that during the course of reinforcement with pleased adult attention for climbing on the frame, this behavior greatly increased, finally exceeding 50% of the child's morning. (Climbing on other objects was not scored during this period.) There then followed five days during which the teachers ignored any climbing on the frame, but attended to all other appropriate activities. The rate of climbing on the frame promptly fell virtually to zero, though the child climbed on other apparatus and was consistently given attention for this. Another five days of reinforcement of use of the climbing frame immediately restored the climbing-frame behavior to a high stable level, always in excess of 40% of the boy's play time. After this, the teachers began an intermittent program of reinforcement for climbing on any other suitable objects, as well as vigorous active play of all sorts, in an effort to generalize the increased vigorous activity. Frame-climbing weakened considerably, being largely replaced by other climbing activities, which were now scored again as data. Activities such as tricycle-riding and running were not systematically recorded due to difficulties in reliably scoring them. It is clear from the data obtained, however, that climbing activities were thoroughly generalized by this final procedure. Checks made the following school year

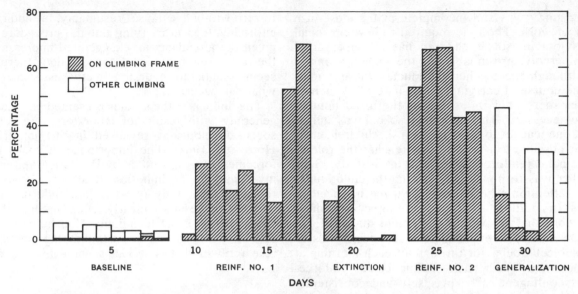

FIGURE 3. *Daily percentages of time spent in using a climbing-frame apparatus. Open bars indicate time spent in climbing on other equipment.*

in another play yard indicated that vigorous climbing had become a stable part of his behavior repertoire.

SUMMARY AND DISCUSSION

The above studies systematically examined effects of adult attention on some problem behaviors of normal preschool children. The findings in each case clearly indicated that for these children adult attention was a strong positive reinforcer. That is, the behavior which was immediately followed by a teacher's giving the child attention rose rapidly to a high rate, and the rate fell markedly when adult attention was withheld from that behavior and concurrently given to an incompatible behavior. While it seems reasonable that for most young children adult attention may be a positive reinforcer, it is also conceivable that for some children adult attention may be a negative reinforcer. That is, the rate of a behavior may decrease when it is immediately followed by the attention of an adult, and rise again as soon as the adult withdraws. Actually, for a few children observed at the preschool, it has been thought that adult attention was a negative reinforcer. This seemed to be true, for instance, in the case of the climbing-frame child. Before the study was initiated, the teachers spent several weeks attempting to make themselves positively reinforcing to the child. This they did by staying at a little distance from him and avoiding attending directly to him until he came to them for something. At first, his approaches were only for routine help, such as buttoning his coat. On each of these occa-

sions they took care to be smilingly friendly and helpful. In time, he began making approaches of other kinds, for instance, to show a toy. Finally, when a teacher approached him and commented with interest on what he was doing, he continued his play instead of stopping, hitting out, or running off. However, since his play remained lethargic and sedentary, it was decided that special measures were necessary to help him progress more rapidly. It was the use and effects of these special measures that constituted the study. Clearly, however, adult attention must be or become positively reinforcing to a child before it can be successfully used to help him achieve more desirably effective behaviors.

Studies such as those reported here seem to imply that teachers may help many children rapidly through systematic programming of their adult social reinforcements. However, further research in this area seems necessary. Some of our own studies now in progress suggest that guidance on the basis of reinforcement principles may perhaps bring rapidly into use only behaviors which are already available within the repertory of the child. If the desired behavior requires skills not yet in the child's repertory, then the process of developing those skills from such behaviors as the child has may require weeks or months. For example, a four-year-old child who could verbalize but who very rarely spoke was helped to speak freely within several days. On the other hand, a child of the same age who had never verbalized required a lengthy shaping process that involved reinforcing first any vocalization, and then gradually more appropriate sounds and combinations of sounds. The latter study was still incomplete at the close of a year of work. The time required to develop social behaviors in isolate children has likewise varied considerably, presumably for the same reasons.

Although the teachers conducted these studies in the course of carrying out their regular teaching duties, personnel in excess of the usual number were necessary. The laboratory school was staffed with one teacher to no more than six children, making it possible to assign to one teacher the role of principal "reinforcer teacher" in a study. This teacher was responsible for giving the child immediate attention whenever he behaved in specified ways. In addition, observers were hired and trained to record the behavior of each child studied. Each observer kept a record in ten-second intervals of his subject's behavior throughout each morning at school. Only with such staffing could reinforcement contingencies be precisely and consistently administered and their effects recorded.

Unless the effects are recorded, it is easy to make incorrect judgments about them. Two instances illustrate such fallibility. A boy in the laboratory preschool frequently pinched adults. Attempts by the teachers to ignore the behavior proved ineffective, since the pinches were hard enough to produce at least an involuntary startle. Teachers next decided to try to develop a substitute behavior. They selected patting as a logical substitute. Whenever the child reached toward a teacher, she attempted to forestall a pinch by saying, "Pat, Davey," sometimes adding, "Not pinch," and then strongly approving his patting, when it occurred. Patting behavior increased rapidly to a high level. The teachers agreed that they had indeed succeeded in reducing the pinching behavior through substituting patting. Then they were shown the recorded data. It showed clearly that although patting behavior was indeed high, pinching behavior continued at the previous level. Apparently, the teachers were so focused on the rise in patting behavior that, without the objective data, they would have erroneously concluded that development of a substitute behavior was in this case a successful technique. A second example illustrates a different, but equally undesirable, kind of erroneous assumption. A preschool child who had to wear glasses (Wolf, Risley, and Mees, 1964) developed a pattern of throwing them two or three times per day. Since this proved expensive, it was decided that the attendants should put him in his room for ten minutes following each glasses-throw. When the attendants were asked a few days later how the procedure was working, they said that the glasses-throwing had not diminished at all. A check of the records, however, showed that there was actually a marked decrease. The throwing dropped

to zero within five days. Presumably, the additional effort involved in carrying out the procedure had given the attendants an exaggerated impression of the rate of the behavior. Recorded data, therefore, seem essential to accurate objective assessments of what has occurred.

The findings in the studies presented here accord generally with results of laboratory research on social development reviewed in this journal by Horowitz (1963). The importance of social reinforcement was also noted by Bandura (1963) in his investigations of imitation. Gallwey (1964) has replicated the study of an isolate child discussed here, with results "clearly confirmatory of the effectiveness of the technique." Further studies in school situations that can combine the function of research with that of service seem highly desirable.

REFERENCES

ALLEN, K. EILEEN, HART, BETTY M., BUELL, JOAN S., HARRIS, FLORENCE R., & WOLF, M. M. Effects of social reinforcement on isolate behavior of a nursery school child. *Child. Develop.*, 1964, *35*, 511–518.

BANDURA, ALBERT. The role of imitation in personality development. *J. Nursery Ed.*, 1963, *18*, 207–215.

GALLWEY, MARY. Director of the Nursery School, Washington State University, Pullman, Wash., 1964. Personal communication.

HARRIS, FLORENCE R., JOHNSTON, MARGARET K., KELLEY, C. SUSAN, & WOLF, M. M. Effects of positive social reinforcement on regressed crawling of a nursery school child. *J. Ed. Psychol.*, 1964, *55*, 35–41.

HART, BETTY M., ALLEN, K. EILEEN, BUELL, JOAN S., HARRIS, FLORENCE R., & WOLF, M. M. Effects of social reinforcement on operant crying. *J. Exp. Child Psychol.* In press.

HOROWITZ, FRANCES DEGEN. Social reinforcement effects on child behavior. *J. Nursery Ed.*, 1963, *18*, 276–284.

JOHNSTON, MARGARET K., KELLEY, C. SUSAN, HARRIS, FLORENCE R., WOLF, M. M., & BAER, D. M. Effects of positive social reinforcement on isolate behavior of a nursery school child. Unpublished manuscript.

JOHNSTON, MARGARET K., KELLEY, C. SUSAN, HARRIS, FLORENCE R., & WOLF, M. M. An application of reinforcement principles to development of motor skills of a young child. Unpublished manuscript.

LANDRETH, CATHERINE. *Education of the Young Child.* New York: Wiley, 1942.

READ, KATHERINE H. *The Nursery School* (2nd ed.). Philadelphia: Saunders, 1955.

STANDING, E. M. *Maria Montessori, Her Life and Work.* Fresno: American Library Guild, 1959.

TAYLOR, KATHERINE W. *Parents Cooperative Nursery Schools.* New York: Teachers College, Columbia University, 1954.

WOLF, MONTROSE M., RISLEY, T. R., & MEES, H. L. Application of operant conditioning procedures to the behavior problems of an autistic child. *Behav. Res. Ther.*, 1964, *1*, 305–312.

(The Elimination of Tantrum Behavior by Extinction Procedures)

This paper reports the successful treatment of tyrant-like tantrum behavior in a male child by the removal of reinforcement. The subject *(S)* was approximately 21 months old. He had been seriously ill much of the first 18 months of his life. His health then improved considerably, and he gained weight and vigor.

S now demanded the special care and attention that had been given him over the many critical months. He enforced some of his wishes, especially at bedtime, by unleashing tantrum behavior to control the actions of his parents. [Readers are cautioned that some "tantrums" involve genuine loss of self-control rather than a manipulation of the parents. The causes and treatment of such tantrums differ from those of the "tyrant-like" tantrum behavior described in this article. A helpful discussion of tantrums may be found in *Emotional Problems of Living* by O. S. English and G. H. J. Pearson (New York, W. W. Norton and Co., 3rd Edition, 1963).—EDITOR]

The parents and an aunt took turns in putting him to bed both at night and for *S*'s afternoon nap. If the parent left the bedroom after putting *S* in his bed, *S* would scream and fuss until the parent returned to the room. As a result, the parent was unable to leave the bedroom until after *S* went to sleep. If the parent began to read while in the bedroom, *S* would cry until the reading material was put down. The parents felt that *S* enjoyed his control over them and that he fought off going to sleep as long as he could. In any event, a parent was spending from one-half to two hours each bedtime just waiting in the bedroom until *S* went to sleep.

Following medical reassurance regarding *S*'s physical condition, it was decided to remove the reinforcement of this tyrant-like tantrum behavior. Consistent with the learning principle that, in general, behavior that is not reinforced will be extinguished, a parent or the aunt put *S* to bed in a leisurely and relaxed fashion. After bedtime pleasantries, the parent left the bedroom and closed the door. *S* screamed and raged, but the parent did not re-enter the room. The duration of screaming and crying was obtained from the time the door was closed.

The results are shown in Fig. 1. It can be seen that *S* continued screaming for 45 min. the first time he was put to bed in the first extinction series. *S* did not cry at all the second time he was put to bed. This is perhaps attributable to his fatigue from the crying of Occasion 1. By the tenth occasion, *S* no longer whimpered, fussed, or cried when the parent left the room. Rather, he smiled as they left. The parents felt that he made happy sounds until he dropped off to sleep.

About a week later, *S* screamed and fussed after the aunt put him to bed, probably reflecting spontaneous recovery of the tantrum behavior. The aunt then reinforced the tantrum behavior by returning to *S*'s bedroom and remaining there until he went to sleep. It was then necessary to extinguish this behavior a second time.

Figure 1 shows that the second extinction curve is similar to the first. Both curves are generally similar to extinction curves obtained with subhuman subjects. The second extinction series reached zero by the ninth occasion. No further tantrums at bedtime were reported during the next two years.

It should be emphasized that the treatment in this case did not involve aversive punishment. All that was done was to remove the reinforcement. Extinction of the tyrant-like tantrum behavior then occurred.

No unfortunate side- or aftereffects of this treatment were observed. At three and three-quarters years of age, *S* appeared to be a friendly, expressive, outgoing child.

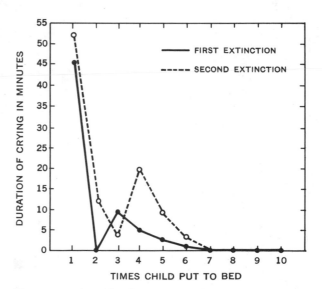

FIGURE 1. *Length of crying in two extinction series as a function of successive occasions of being put to bed.*

IV

INTERPERSONAL EXPERIENCES
AS DETERMINANTS OF BEHAVIOR

The nature of a person's expectations of others; his ways of gaining satisfaction, of expressing his feelings, and of resolving emotional conflicts (in mature or less mature ways); the content and fervor of his ideals; and the extent of his inhibitions and guilt feelings—*all* are formed in an interpersonal context. Those who emphasize interpersonal determinants are indebted to Sigmund Freud far more than to any other theorist, a debt Bruner made clear in an opening selection of this book. Although psychoanalytic theory today represents a gradual modification and differentiation of Freud's views, his recognition of the formative impact of emotional relationships in the family stands solidly as a cornerstone of today's conceptions of personality development.

The influence of the family is not limited to the tie with father and mother. A child's gratifications and deprivations, his loves and enmities in relation to figures other than the parents may be crucial. Which relationships are important depends upon the composition of the particular family group and the roles taken by the different members. In one family, a grandmother or an uncle may be a major source of influence; in another, the relationship with brother or sister vividly colors a child's life.

As the girl or boy grows, persons outside the family are likely to be involved in an increasing proportion of the youngster's experiences. In school, the association with a teacher may become significant. A rising responsiveness of many boys and girls to children in the neighborhood rapidly eclipses their earlier orientation to the parents. (Of course, children who have older siblings may have been more oriented to them than to their parents almost from birth.) Thus, one takes into account the "peer group," which, in practice, means not only age-mates of similar status, but also children older or younger who are in a position to be of importance in a given child's day-to-day existence.

Intense and prolonged hatreds or affectional bonds formed in childhood may be forgotten in adulthood. Yet, they may still affect one's perceptions of other people, especially in circumstances that arouse inner conflict. A man who has had chronic trouble with a brother, unmitigated by sufficient happy experiences, may have difficulties in a competitive situation with a peer at work. Such difficulties may lead not only to discomfort, but also to inappropriate behavior. Several types of alternative response are possible, ranging from overt hostility to over-submissiveness. The woman whose relation with her mother was unsatisfactory may have problems in getting along with an older woman who employs her. If the picture is further complicated by unresolved difficulties the older woman had with *her* younger sister, both the supervisor and employee may behave in such distorted ways that a total impasse is reached. In such ways, the cares of childhood may live on to burden adult associations in work, marriage, and parenthood.

The first approach to gaining knowledge about interpersonal determinants of behavior was the *clinical* one of Freud and his successors. This is still the approach most used by psychiatrists and social workers, as well as by some psychologists. In this approach, hypotheses are generated from a series of cases. Such cases usually concern patients undergoing treatment for emotional tensions or for bodily disorders that represent symptoms of inner conflict. The theories and hypotheses that have grown out of such clinical studies offer a fertile field to the empirical researcher who can make the controlled investigations needed in order to test, and enrich or correct, the hard-won theoretical formulations. All articles in this section present the results of empirical, rather than clinical, research. Yet, in many instances, it was clinical work that initially gave rise to the ideas now being pursued by empirical means, which allow replication of results and are therefore more suited to verification of hypotheses. At the present stage of the scientific study of human personality and behavior, clinical studies continue to be an indispensable counterpart to the empirical ones in providing guidelines for further work.

An example of a concept now being investigated by controlled research, although it was "invented" as a result of observing patients, is "identification." The formative effects of peers, parents, and siblings are often due to the rewards and punishments they administer either knowingly *or* unwittingly (see Section III for a discussion of Learning). But it appears that principles besides those of direct learning are necessary to give adequate recognition to ways in which some human behaviors seem to be acquired. "Identification" is the term most commonly applied to a process by which behavior is influenced without punishments or rewards except those from within (including inner self-exhortation, self-criticism, and self-praise). The educational implications of identificatory learning are implicit in the following statement by Edward Joseph Shoben, Jr.:

> Psychologically, it seems sound to argue that the essential curriculum for each school child at any given time is not what is on paper in the curriculum supervisor's office. It is much more likely to be the way he perceives his teacher. The curriculum, after all, is only a statement of what the pupil is to learn. His learning proceeds through the vital and basic mediation of the teacher. What he learns, therefore, is in significant degree a function of how he reacts to and interprets the mediating adult. . . .[1]

Included in this section are papers dealing with: (1) the nature of the infant's attachment to parent and the ways in which absence of mother or father may affect offspring; (2) child-rearing practices, especially disciplinary ones; (3) the extent to which children's characteristics may cause parental behaviors rather than vice versa; (4) identification and imitation; and (5) peer influence, including the effects of siblings as a special case in connection with which the impact of birth order is also considered.

Readers who are interested in pursuing the topic of interpersonal influences from the viewpoint of psychoanalytic psychiatry and psychology will enjoy spending an evening with Dorothy W. Baruch's book *One Little Boy* (Dell Publishing Co., 1964). Another book that is very well liked by many students is *Emotional Problems of Living,* by O. S. English and G. H. J. Pearson (Third Edition, Norton, 1963). Although written dogmatically—that is, as though psychoanalytic ideas are 100 per cent right and impervious to time and further investigation—their book conveys rich insights into the inner lives of children. It also deals with the ways in which such inner lives constitute a major component in determining children's and adults' behavior.

---

[1] The Shoben paper, called "Viewpoints from related disciplines: learning theory," is from an issue of *Teachers College Record* (1959, *60,* 272–282) devoted to the topic: "What Shall the Schools Teach?" Reprinted by permission.

Those desiring more exposure to the type of data and approach used in the Sears, Maccoby, and Levin material on aggression might well enjoy reading about other areas of parental and child behavior in their book *Patterns of Child Rearing* (Row, Peterson, 1957).

13

Maternal Deprivation: The Research and Its Implications

AASE GRUDA SKARD

This article summarizes materials that convey the ways in which having a mother is important and the conditions under which loss of the mother (or separation from her) can be detrimental or, in certain cases, beneficial.

Dr. Aase Gruda Skard, who teaches at the University of Oslo, has studied there, at the University of Paris, and at Harvard. She has been president of the Organization of Psychologists, the Organization for Early Childhood Education, and the World Organization for Early Childhood Education (1962–1968), as well as editor of the Norwegian Journal for Education *since 1935.*

In most Utopian societies, the principle has been, in theory or in practice, to raise all children in institutions. Would such an arrangement really be "utopian" for the new generation? In some preliterate societies, children are brought up by foster parents or the children are the "common property" of the society, so that all women function as mothers for all children. Although modern society arranges for each child to be brought up by his own parents, the society has always had to care for some children, those whose parents had died or were unable or unwilling to accept responsibility for their children. A system of children's homes, organizations

for adoption, and foster parents has been built up in conformity with the demands of society. This state and local control has steadily increased in scope with the growth of knowledge in this field and the extension of state responsibility to embrace such activities.

Fourteen years ago, all people concerned with children were made apprehensive by a report from the English child psychiatrist John Bowlby[1] about the damage to the child separated from his mother. The report, published by WHO, created new public demands regarding institutional care for children; and a storm of discussion arose about children's institutions, foster homes, women in professional life, etc. The demand that a woman should stay at home appeared with new strength; and changes were strongly called for in children's institutions, hospitals, and other related arenas.

Not everybody noted that Bowlby only wrote about small children. His observations were frequently applied to much larger groups of children than he had originally envisaged. Not all realized that he thought in terms of separations of months, and many used the same arguments for absences that lasted only a few hours. But many healthy changes were implemented, e.g., in children's institutions and in the rules and regulations concerning child welfare. During the years that have passed, the meaning of Bowlby's interpretations in his first report have become clearer; and he himself has arrived at viewpoints that have more nuances as he has continued to study the problem.[2] In addition, many new investigations throw light on the mother-child relationship and what it implies. These stress the importance of understanding the way children experience their surroundings and their daily life when the mother is not there, and how they can receive what they need from the surroundings, whether or not the mother is with them.

A great mass of recent literature in German, French, English, and other languages[3] attests that maternal deprivation is one of the problems in child psychology that has come most strongly to

[1] John Bowlby, *Maternal Care and Mental Health,* Geneva, Switzerland: World Health Organization Monograph Series, No. 2, 1951.

[2] John Bowlby, "The Nature of the Child's Tie to His Mother," *International Journal of Psychoanalysis,* 39 (1958), pp. 350–373.

[3] Cf. J. Svejcar, "Étude de l'influence de la mère sur le développement psychique de l'enfant," *Courrier,* 12 (1962), pp. 469–473; and S. Lebovici, *The Concept of Maternal Deprivation: A Review of Research,* Geneva, Switzerland: World Health Organization, 1962, pp. 75–95.

Aase Gruda Skard, "Maternal deprivation: The research and its implications," *Journal of Marriage and the Family,* 1965, 27, 333–343. Reprinted by permission.

the forefront during the last ten to 12 years. It has been approached from many different angles, and many different methods have been used.

The early investigations on which Bowlby based his conclusions were in many ways good and served the purpose of at least directing the attention of psychologists and psychiatrists to the problem, making it possible to develop a rudimentary theory of the effects of the many and different factors in the mother-child relationship. But the first investigations were groping and included, as a rule, far too many factors that were not properly distinguished. Later research has tried to isolate the factors involved and to investigate the effects of each of them. But the more the problem has received attention, the more involved it has seemed, and the more difficult to reach definite conclusions. It is impossible to experiment with children in all the ways that a research scheme would demand. One may not arrange situations that might cause serious damage to the children.

To facilitate a more focused approach to the problem, psychologists have tried to use animals of different kinds with which they could experiment freely. Other psychologists have investigated cultural groups with the same racial background who treated their children in different ways, and where there were definite differences in the amount of time the child stayed with the mother. And at the same time, many psychologists continued to study children in different kinds of institutions—hospitals, day-nurseries, kindergartens, and so forth—where children come at different age levels and stay for varying periods. In this type of investigation, they have been studying the effects of different conditions, not only while the children were in the institution or had just left it, but over a long period.

POSSIBLE CORRELATES WITH MATERNAL DEPRIVATION EFFECT

Very important factors are age and developmental level: Are there any special developmental levels at which children or young animals are particularly sensitive to separation from their mother, to moving from one place to another, to meeting new people? Will they become more or less sensitive to such influences as time passes, or are there special stages when the effect is particularly strong?

What is the effect of the different forms of contact with the mother and the different amounts of contact on a child at different developmental levels? Can there be too much of mother at some stage? What does the child need in addition to the mother as it grows? What will happen if the mother and child are not separated enough, or not early enough?

When the time period during which a child is separated from his mother varies, how long can the period be that would be without effect on each developmental stage? And how long will the effect last after a shorter or longer period of separation?

Will some factors in the surroundings increase or decrease the effect: for example, will a child who has been to a great extent satisfied in his need for mother contact suffer more or suffer less than one who has not received so much from the mother? What will the effect be if the milieu into which the child comes is of a different character?

What difference does it make if the mother leaves the child or the child is moved from the mother? In other words, if the child stays in the same home without the mother, or if he is moved to another home? And what influence will it have if the mother visits the child frequently or rarely in his new surroundings?

What will the effect be of the acute separation process itself? And what effect would it have on the child to stay without the mother for a long period? Does the child adjust to life without mother, and if so, how? What can the surroundings contribute to help children adjust themselves? Are there great differences here in children at different age levels, and also in individual children? Are some children tougher or more adjustable than others? Will new changes make the child more used to adapting himself to new people and relationships, or is the effect cumulative for each change of environment?

What is it that the mother gives to the child at each development stage and which the child finds so necessary? Is it breast-feeding, body warmth, an innate biological connection carried over from pregnancy or blood ties, or what? Is it right to speak about *maternal* deprivation, or is the deprivation which the child experiences something which really has nothing to do with the personal mother, such as missing the rocking or the small talk? Is it the mother love itself which is most important, or certain forms of behavior which others may learn and use in relationship in a child?

There are a host of questions, many more than Bowlby first thought. We have no answers to most of them. But we have some results from investigations, and these may throw some light on the problem.

THE FINDINGS OF ANIMAL PSYCHOLOGY

Everybody thinks that it is a matter of course that young mammals follow their mothers. They get their food from her and thus are able to stay alive. But it is not only because of the food that they seek the mother. Young apes cling to the fur of the mother from the time they are newly born, holding on to her belly or her back. Young kittens creep next to the mother's body, not only to suck, but also to sleep. And many other animals than mammals are strongly tied to their mothers or their parents—of course, the question can be raised if it is the young ones who stay close to the adults or vice versa. Many small birds stay in the nest, and the parents feed them until they are big enough to fly. How strong the tie is after this stage, and whether the young ones attempt to follow the parents or to follow the flock of birds, is not easy to ascertain.

Some young birds are large enough to move around as soon as they leave the egg, such as chickens, which follow the hen for a longer period while they grow. Is it to find their food, or is there something else about her that makes them follow her? Is it only the hen which has laid the egg that the chickens will follow, or the one that has been breeding them? Since it is the brood hen which becomes the mother when it comes to making the chickens follow, there can be no "blood tie." But will the chickens and others necessarily follow the brood hen?

During the last few years, birds such as hens, ducks, and geese, and mammals such as monkeys and apes have been the objects of research experiments that have provided increased insight into the mother-child relationship in these animals.

The German biologist Konrad Z. Lorenz,[4] the American Eckhard H. Hess,[5] and others have each performed a series of experiments with different kinds of birds. They have found that chickens do not necessarily follow "the mother" who has brooded them, but follow something that moves and gives certain sounds in front of them during the period when they have just left the egg. If a box is moved in front of the newly brooded chickens, they will follow the box; and if they are allowed to continue to follow it for some hours, they will only follow boxes and care nothing about the clucking mother. Lorenz, who was the first to work on this phenomenon, called the process "Prägung," or "imprinting."

Imprinting is a process whereby some impressions of early life have a lasting effect on the individual, marking the whole of his total social development. Lorenz pointed out that imprinting must happen at a critical period, at a certain developmental stage in each kind of animal, this usually lasting only for a short time. During this period, the animal is tied to a living or inanimate object which happens to be close by. The animal is thus lastingly imprinted not only by this object but also by all others of the same kind as that; only later will the animal learn to differentiate individual traits and follow a specific object.

The critical period for such imprinting, which makes the chicken follow the hen, a box, or a human being, has been studied particularly by Hess.[6] He finds that in ducklings, the tendency to follow gradually increases during the first hours after the brooding, up to 13 to 16 hours, and then decreases quickly. When the ducklings are around 24 hours old, the critical period is over, and they have lost their ability to be imprinted by something and to follow a certain figure.

Certain conditions in the situation can result in a quicker and more effective imprinting in ducklings, chickens, and others. If the young ones must work hard to follow, the imprinting appears more quickly and is more effective than if they are able to follow easily. If they must walk up a hill in order to follow the box, the imprinting will be more effective and accomplished much sooner than if the road is flat and easy to walk. Difficulties that must be overcome, such as the pain of an electric shock, which the young undergo when following something, will also make imprinting quicker and more effective.

From daily life, most people have some experience of such imprinting. Puppies must live with certain human beings during the age of three-and-a-half through nine to 13 weeks if they are to become "man's best friend," and the age of seven weeks seems to be the culmination point of the critical period for social development and imprinting.[7] If no human being touches or cares for kittens from the time that their eyes are opened until they are weaned, they will stay somewhat wild and fearful of people.[8] Continuing in the biological rank order, the question arises whether there are such critical periods for imprinting in all species where there are parent-young relationships, including the human child, and whether there are times when children are particularly approachable and particularly sensitive to human ties, which enables them to develop love for an adult.

Animals are not only tied to a thing or a person which may be close to them. They also become scared of the unknown and show flight tendencies

[4] Konrad J. Lorenz, "Comparative Behaviourology," in *Discussions on Child Development,* ed. by I. J. Tanner and B. Inhelder, London, 1956, Vol. I, pp. 108–131.

[5] Eckhard H. Hess, "Ethnology," in *New Directions in Psychology,* ed. by I. Brown *et al.,* New York, 1962, pp. 159–266.

[6] *Ibid.*

[7] J. P. Scott, "Critical Periods in the Development of Social Behavior in Puppies," *Psychosomatic Medicine,* 20 (1958), pp. 42–54.

[8] Hess, *op. cit.*

when faced with certain kinds of influences. Hess has observed that, as a rule, this tendency to run away needs a certain period for maturing.[9] Certain ducklings will follow anything during the first 24 hours after they have left the egg; after that period, however, they are scared of many kinds of creatures which they were earlier willing to follow but by which they were not imprinted at that time. It seems that animals must reach a certain stage of maturation before the reaction of fear appears. But this is not the whole story, because some experiments indicate that early experiences play a role also. In some kinds of animals (chickens, dogs, apes), the flight tendency will only appear if the young ones have been imprinted by something at an early stage and are happily tied to somebody from the critical period. This indicates that a positive tie is a precondition for the opposite reaction, namely, flight from the unknown or the threatening. Here observations relating to human children are interesting. The well-known child psychiatrist R. A. Spitz maintains, for example, that babies who are strongly tied to their mothers or their parents will be more afraid of strange people than those children who have not had the same kind of tie to their parents.[10] Imprinting should on one hand tie young animals to something or somebody and, on the other hand, make them particularly aware of dangers from the unknown.

It seems that it is not only the need for food that makes the young animals stay by their mothers. This aspect of the problem has been studied particularly by H. F. Harlow.[11] He works with animals who are close to the human being in the developmental rank order, namely, rhesus monkeys. Many animal observers have pointed out how the newborn young monkey takes hold of the mother's fur purely as a reflex. The hands will close around anything that touches the palm, and the grasp is nearly impossible to loosen again, similar to behavior observed in a newborn baby. The young monkey will hang in the mother's fur until it gets hold of the nipples, and through the operation of the sucking reflex, it begins to get milk. Harlow thought that there must be two different characteristics in the mother that the young would seek, the fur and the milk.[12] But what was the more important? Were

they tied to and did they grow to love their mother because she gave them food, or because she had fur that they could snuggle into?

Harlow started his experiments by isolating the maternal characteristics in artificial mothers, with which the young monkeys could grow up from the moment they were born.[13] He made one artificial mother out of netting and with bottles from which the monkeys could suck their milk, and another of fur and wool so that she was warm and soft but without milk. The small monkeys went to the milk-mother when they were hungry, but otherwise they kept always to the wool-mother. If they were scared or felt unwell, they went without exception to the soft wool-mother, not to the milk-mother. This indicates that the soft and warm fur has as great value for the young monkeys as the milk. They cannot live without food, but they also need something to take hold of, something soft around them that touches their skin, and it is this that gives them the feeling of protection and security when they for one reason or another feel threatened.

Are the characteristics that the monkey mother has fur and that she has food for her young ones enough for her to fulfill her task as a mother? Newer investigations have led Harlow to answer that more is needed than fur and food.[14] He followed the development in the young monkeys that he had taken away from their living mothers and left with the two artificial mothers. They grew up as usual monkeys, were healthy and strong and apparently normal. But when they were sexually mature, it turned out that they were not normal. They showed no sexual behavior, and they refused to copulate. When Harlow placed the young female monkeys from the artificial mothers together with usual mother-educated male monkeys, these males wanted to copulate with the females, but the females steadily refused. They tried to get away from the males, and threatened and hit out at them. Copulation was accomplished with only four of these female monkeys, and then only through the "patience, persistence, knowledgeability and motor skill of the breeding males," Harlow says.

These four artificially educated females had their babies. But they did not want to care for them. The young ones would hang in their fur and snuggle up to them just like normal young monkeys. But the mother only shook them off herself, pushed them away, and showed no sign of maternal behavior. There must have been something wrong in these mothers' development, something that led to their

---

[9] *Ibid.*

[10] R. A. Spitz and Katherine Wolf, "Anaclitic Depression," *Psychoanalytic Studies of Childhood*, 2 (1946), pp. 313–342.

[11] Harry F. Harlow, "The Nature of Love," *American Psychologist*, 13 (1958), pp. 673–685; and "The Development of Affectional Patterns in Infant Monkeys," in *Determinants of Infant Behavior*, ed. by B. M. Foss, London, 1961, Vol. I, pp. 75–88.

[12] Harlow, "The Development of Affectional Patterns . . . ," *Ibid.*

[13] Harlow, "The Nature of Love," *op. cit.*

[14] Harry F. Harlow and Margaret K. Harlow, "The Effect of Rearing Conditions on Behavior," *Bulletin of the Menninger Clinic*, 26 (1962), pp. 213–224.

not being sexually developed and maternal like other female monkeys. And the same was true for the males; they never managed to copulate properly, even with normal females who presented themselves to them. What could have been missing in the lives of these monkeys that enables usual monkeys to be normal in sexual and maternal behavior, but which evidently the artificial mothers could not give?

Harlow thinks that there are two important forms of behavior which can be observed in normal female monkeys, but that do not enter into the picture of the milk-mother and child. One is active play between mother and child. The other is the fact that the mother at a certain developmental stage begins to push the young ones away and only lets the young ones come close to her at intervals. In this way, the young monkeys have to turn to each other, to play with other young monkeys. Harlow wants to experiment with these characteristics also, but until his work is completed, other observations throw some light on the problem.

Female baboons have been closely observed by De Vore and by Jay,[15] who point out that there is a certain developmental sequence in the maternal behavior: First, the baboon mother keeps the young one tightly by her body and is only interested in this baby. During the first eight to ten days after delivery, the mother is busy licking her baby, plucking and picking him, pouting her mouth to him, sniffing him, and allowing him to suck. During this first period, the young ones will hold on to the nipples almost all of the time, or will hold on to the mother's fur while she is walking around and following the group to some other place. From the age of three weeks or so, the young one will begin to sit between the mother's legs without holding on to her, but as soon as she is ready to walk somewhere, she grasps the young one and presses him to her body until he has a firm hold of her fur and can hold himself while she is walking. When the young one is about one month old, he may take one or two steps away from the mother. From now on, he begins to notice the other young monkeys in the group when the female monkeys sit together; and the young ones in this way get close to each other. Gradually, mother and child fall into a kind of oscillation: the young one walks a little bit away from the mother, but returns—he will sometimes be picked up by other female monkeys and he tolerates this, but he tumbles back to his own mother afterwards, or the mother gets hold of him

and draws him to her body again. Other young monkeys which are a little older now begin to try to get the younger ones to join in their games. From the age of three months, the baboon is big enough to play with other young ones for a greater length of time than he spends with his mother, but still he runs back to her regularly and cuddles into her arms. At this time, the young baboon will also become increasingly interested in the other adult monkeys, crawling over the adult male monkeys which enjoy playing with the young ones, and on the whole becoming more and more remote from the mother and seeking the company of the group. From the age of six months, the young one begins to get other food in addition to his mother's milk, but still he will sleep in his mother's arms every night.

During the nine- to ten-month period, the mother begins to push the young one away. She pushes him away from the nipples if he wants to suck, and she shakes him down from her back when he wants to ride her. At about this time, the mother begins to experience a new period of heat and seeks the company of the male monkeys. But occasionally she still takes her young one in her arms. When the young one comes to the mother, he will then experience that she sometimes takes him into her arms, sometimes pushes him away. She never takes the initiative to get the young one to come to her; it is the young one which seeks the mother, with uncertain results. She will still come to his help if other monkeys attack her young one, but if he has other kinds of difficulties and cries, she does not care any more. Some young apes get easily through this period, but others are evidently out of balance, grieve, and try hard to keep up their relationship with the mother. Instead of the relationship with the mother, the young ones now play to an increasing extent with the group of young apes of about the same age, and the relationship to this group becomes more important. When a young ape is around one-and-one-half years old, he spends so little time with his mother that it is impossible for an observer to find out which young one belongs to any particular female monkey. Only if there is a big fight in the group, the young monkeys rush each to his own mother to help her or to stay with her, or the mothers throw themselves into the fight to protect their young ones. But at the age of two years, the young ones are wholly independent of their mother, and the two have forgotten each other. The tie to the mother is replaced by the tie to the peer group.

Other kinds of monkeys show the same development: 1. Mother and child hang tightly together. 2. The young one oscillates to and from the mother and seeks steadily to return to her, and the mother

---

[15] Irven De Vore, "Mother-Infant Relations in Free-Ranging Baboons," in *Maternal Behavior in Mammals,* ed. by Harriet L. Rheingold, New York, 1963, pp. 305–355; and Phyllis Jay, "Mother-Infant Relations in Langurs," in *Ibid.,* pp. 282–304.

always draws the young one to her. 3. The mother becomes neutral, she tolerates the fact that the young one seeks her, but she makes no effort to get hold of him. 4. The mother shakes the young one off herself and pushes him away toward life with the other young monkeys. During the different periods, different forms for play occur between the mother and the young one: hugging and plucking, pushing and playing, the mother running after the young one to get hold of him, etc.

Of course, these observations of animals can only give suggestions about what to look for in human children. The similarity in mother-child relationship between monkeys and human beings is probably greatest when the child is very small. Gradually, the particularly human characteristics come into play: more intelligent behavior and deeper, more lasting emotions than a monkey will ever have. Still, Harlow considers it important that besides getting food, other important factors exist in the monkey mother-child relationship, such as touching, protection, playing, and pushing away at the right time. Although human beings do not follow the exact pattern of monkeys, elements in the monkey mother-child relationship may be compared for the degree to which they exist in the human mother-child relationship. Where similarities exist, it may be asked at which stage in human development it is natural and healthy to find these different elements and to what degree they are present.

Harlow maintains that both monkey and human mothers "have the obligation of gradually dissolving the intense physical bonds which characterize the early mother-child relationship."[16] For the monkey mother, it is easier and more natural than for a woman, he says, because when the young one is so big that he becomes bothersome, the monkey mother pushes him away and punishes him, and the young one withdraws for a while so that she may rest; then she may be kind to him for a while when he returns. In this way, the young one becomes independent gradually. This will not happen with the wool-mother, which never gets tired of the young one, never pushes him away, never forces him over to the peer group, and in this way somehow resembles the overprotecting mothers among human beings who hold on to their children for too long and so prevent healthy ties to the peer group.

THE FINDINGS OF RESEARCH ON HUMAN MOTHER-CHILD RELATIONSHIPS

Many of the first investigations into the effect of living in a children's institution compared children from institutions with other children, but with no information about the age when they had arrived in the institution, why they had come there, what inheritance they carried with them, what they had experienced before they came, what the institution was like, or if they perhaps had been moved around from one institution to another. Newer research takes such factors into consideration.[17] The present paper compares observations of children with observations and experiments with young animals.

First of all, it is apparently extremely important at which developmental stage the child is separated from his mother,[18] and that the mother will have a different meaning to the child at different stages. On the basis of this, one may draw certain practical conclusions concerning the time when the mother and child may be separated, how often and for how long the child tolerates being without his mother, and how one may find a good substitute for the mother.

THE FIRST HALF YEAR

Apparently what may be called the "awakening of the senses" plays a great role during the first half year, perhaps most of all at the three- to six-months stage. Not all the senses are awake, and therefore not all can be used at the same time. Sight is evidently the sense that develops latest. Therefore the children cannot differentiate between different adults until they are somewhere between three and six months old. Only then will they begin to recognize mother and other people they know and differentiate them from the unknown. It is possible that they earlier have recognized the way the mother will hold them, her smell, the taste of the nipple, etc. But very little proof exists for this. Only a few children seem to suffer from being separated from their mother when they are less than three months old; and even in the age group three to six months, disturbances seem relatively slight.[19] If they suffer from being separated from their mother at this time, it may not be the mother as a person they miss, but rather something that she usually will give them and which they do not get to the same degree in a new milieu.

Now, what does a mother usually give a child at this time? Food, opportunity to suck, warmth from her body, fondling and rocking, small talk, and humming. All these things together will be

---

[16] Harlow and Harlow, *op. cit.*

[17] For closer survey and analysis of available research, see L. J. Yarrow, "Maternal Deprivation: Toward an Empirical and Conceptual Re-evaluation," *Psychological Bulletin*, 58 (1961), pp. 459–490.

[18] L. J. Yarrow, "Research in Dimensions of Early Maternal Care," *Merrill-Palmer Quarterly*, 9 (1963), pp. 101–114.

[19] *Ibid.*

called "mothering." Is there something in all this that is particularly important, more important than anything else?

The Harlow experiments with young monkeys show that they especially seek warmth and the soft skin of the mother. Other experiments with animals show that they suffer very much if they do not get any sense stimuli at all.[20] It is probable that something comparable may occur with human beings: they need sense stimuli, stimulation of the right kind. If they are moved during the first half year, it is likely that it is deprivation in general that makes them suffer rather than any special maternal deprivation.[21]

They are bored in children's institutions rather than being homesick for a personal mother. It appears that during this period one can separate mother and child if one takes care that the child gets the necessary mothering, i.e., that it gets the chance to experience body warmth from another human being; rocking and patting; and perhaps also to have something colorful to look at; to get food and something to suck; to be carried around; to have something moving around it; and to listen to voices, singing, and talking. But who stimulates the child in this manner is probably not important. The child may be said to be "care-oriented," not yet "person-oriented."[22]

FROM SIX MONTHS TO THREE
OR THREE-AND-ONE-HALF YEARS

During the second half year, the situation will be more complicated. And through the following years, much is happening to the child that makes it more difficult to move him.

The child begins to recognize the person or persons who tend to him, he begins to love and be tied to one or a few adults, and he begins to recognize things around him. From the age of five to seven months, it will be important for the child that one particular adult return again and again. The child needs real personal contact.

What happens in the mother-child relationship when the child [is] around seven months old is quite similar to the phenomenon of imprinting which Lorenz and others found in several animals. Observations of babies in hospitals[23] show that chil-

dren under seven and over seven ·months old are strikingly different, and that the difference is so evident that it may seem as if there is a jump in the development from one way of reacting to a completely new reaction from this stage on. Children of less than seven months made little or no protest if they only had kind nurses who would tend to them in a pleasant way and mother them. They adjusted rather easily to the new situation in the hospital. But children over seven months old were brought totally out of balance, they cried and turned away from the adults, they did not want to eat or they reacted in other ways, showing that they were not adjusted. Other investigations indicate that the warmer the child's relationship to his mother, the harder it will be for him to be separated from her when they have reached this new developmental stage.[24]

From around six to seven months or so, the baby evidently will become tied to the one or more adults who take care of it, and this process is a quick process, like imprinting in the animal young ones. When the children have more adults around, as for example, in the Israeli kibbutzim or in societies where all grown women care for and act as mothers for all babies, it seems as if each child has one main person to whom it is more tied than to the others. But in addition to this one, the child may also be tied to other adults without damage to his personality.[25]

When the child is becoming tied to one or more of the adults who are steadily around, he also begins to be shy and fearful of unknown people. This phenomenon may have its parallel in the flight tendency which animal young show in comparable situations. Child psychologists have already earlier noticed the so-called eight-months anxiety in the child, anxiety for new adults, but this has not been related to the process of becoming tied to a familiar figure. There is some reason to believe that this anxiety for the unknown has a close connection with the love for the familiar figure, which is just growing at this time. The tie with a few grown-ups is important for the development of basic trust which E. H. Erikson[26] regards as an extremely important process during the first year of life.

The situation for children at this age level should preferably be characterized by a few adults for a very few children. Children's institutions now rightly begin to organize the environment in such a way that there are only a few children in each

---

[20] Donald O. Hebb, *A Textbook of Psychology*, Philadelphia, 1958.

[21] H. R. Schaffer and W. M. Callender, "Psychological Effects of Hospitalization in Infancy," *Pediatrics*, 24 (1959), p. 538 ff.

[22] H. R. Schaffer, "Some Issues for Research in the Study of Attachment Behavior," in *Determinants of Infant Behavior*, ed. by B. M. Foss, London, 1963, Vol. II, pp. 179–196.

[23] Schaffer and Callender, *op. cit.*

[24] Spitz and Wolf, *op. cit.*

[25] Yarrow, "Maternal Deprivation . . . ," *op. cit.*

[26] Erik H. Erikson, "Growth Crises of the Healthy Personality," in *Symposium on the Healthy Personality*, New York, 1950, pp. 91–146.

children's home, and frequently children of different ages are present. This enables the smallest child to have his or her own substitute mother. Children experience daily and regular impressions, both in these institutions and when a mother takes care of her own child at home, and also variations in the mood of this one person, who may at one time be in one kind of mood, sometimes in another, and who is subjective and emotional, not only objective and monotonous. This period is particularly marked by development in emotional life and in the relationship to adults. In this respect, the children need nourishment and regular, rich experiences.

If persons who are very different take care of the child in this period, this will mean a particular stress for the child because so much will be unexpected and different from what he has been used to. One adult comforts a crying child by giving it something to eat or to suck, another may pick it up and pat it, a third one will rock it, a fourth will perhaps sing or talk to the baby. In these cases, crying will not produce consistent treatment; and even if some variation may be desirable, there may be too much of a good thing.

The anatomic-physiological development in the fetus has shown that structure and organs that are in the process of rapid development are particularly vulnerable. Therefore, rubella (German measles) is particularly dangerous for the fetus if the mother contracts this illness in a definite limited time period (second or third month) of the pregnancy when certain areas of the brain and the sense organs are in rapid development. In a parallel way, psychologists are trying to formulate hypotheses about vulnerability in the mental field: that functions and processes in rapid development are particularly vulnerable. According to such hypotheses, at the stage of development when a child is about to tie his emotions to one single or some very few adults, he would also be particularly vulnerable to separation from those to whom he was tied, and this is just the case. As pointed out by Bowlby, Spitz, and others, small children (from six to seven months upward) have great difficulties when they are separated from their mother for a long period, i.e., during several weeks continuously, especially if they have no substitute mother on whom they can fix their emotions. It may give additional security to a child to feel that he can rely upon more than one person for protection and care[27] and that he has more than one person whom he can trust.[28]

As the months and the years pass, the need for activity increases in the child. He needs freedom to move, to kick and roll around, to creep and walk, to grasp, handle things, throw, roll, wave, and hit out with things, crawl up the stairs, jump, run. But at the same time, he needs somebody to whom he may return, he needs the oscillation which was observed in the young monkeys. The mother's lap, the father's safe arms must be present. But the child needs also to leave the lap and the arms, to go out to play and use muscles, to be active and experiment.

Perhaps this is a period when the child needs to play with adults, as Harlow mentioned, to play peekaboo and show himself again, to pretend that the adults run hard to get hold of the child, on the whole the kind of game which creates distance and new contact.

Not all private homes can satisfy this need for activity in children. Not all small modern apartments can give enough space for play and enough toys of the right kind. Here, gradually, other institutions must come in to supplement the home: the nursery school, the park supervisor, etc. Frequently a transitional period is necessary when the child simultaneously needs both the mother and these new surroundings. Children's homes may, if they are good, give in this respect practically equally good conditions for this type of development where the need for activity can be satisfied while the same mother figure continues to be there for the child to return to.

FROM THREE OR THREE-AND-ONE-HALF
YEARS TO SEVEN YEARS

At preschool age, a relationship with a few adults seems to be important for the child. It will be less of a strain to be separated from the mother now, but it is still a strain. The child begins in this period to identify with adults, to take over the roles, attitudes, norms, and language of adults. The child learns his or her own sex role, learns what it means in his or her society to be a boy or a girl. Conscientiousness begins to develop as he acquires a feeling that it is wrong to go against the rules and the norms.

Observations of children who have grown up in large children's institutions with few adults tend to show that if the children cannot have such permanent adults with whom they can identify themselves, they begin to identify themselves with each other. One may find unusually strong coherence in groups of children and unusually deep love among them, but children are not carriers of ethical norms and values. Identification with one or more other children cannot give to each child a definite feeling

---

[27] Margaret Mead, "A Cultural Anthropologist's Approach to Maternal Deprivation," in *Deprivation of Maternal Care*, Geneva, Switzerland: World Health Organization, 1962, pp. 45–62.

[28] Barbara Wootton, "A Social Scientist's Approach to Maternal Deprivation," in *Ibid.*, pp. 63–73.

of right and wrong, nor an appreciation of the value of laws and rules, of work and industry.

On the other hand, social interest and the need for social relationships with other children are increasing in this period. A good relationship to parents seems to be a good base for a good relationship to the peer group also. In addition to one or more adults, the children now need human beings of the same size as themselves. Children's homes and institutions, kibbutzim, etc., may give to the children values which a private home with only one child can provide only with difficulty, but still the ties to the few adults are more important. And the children need adults of both sexes, both "mother" and "father." In this period, both "maternal" and "paternal deprivation" may cause them to experience stress.[29] But the memory is now so much better developed that parents may stay away from the children for a longer time, even for several months, so long as they return. And in the same way, it will take the child a shorter period of time to make up for the strain of the deprivation than it did in the earlier period.

From school age onward, and particularly during puberty and adolescence, the ties with adults will steadily loosen, and the child will gain independence and adult ability to fend for himself.

CHILDREN OF WORKING MOTHERS

The problem "children of working mothers" turns out to be difficult and complicated. It cannot be evaluated only from the child's viewpoint, or from the viewpoint of healthy development as a human being. A woman is more than just a milieu for her child or her children—she has her own value as a human being, and the problem must also be considered for what may serve her interests and development.

That women wish to do something different and to do more than just take care of their children is not something new that only contemporary women have begun to demand. Women in earlier times also lived for more than just their functions as mothers. They had richer and more varied work in and around their home, they baked bread, they spun and wove, they made the clothes for everybody in the family, they participated in the slaughtering of the farm animals, they had their domestic animals to care for, etc. And as a rule, many women co-operated in these functions. Today women are not so different from what they were in earlier generations, but now they live in a different situation, the work and the social milieus are different. At least

in the cities, the women very often carry out their domestic work in a lonely place, where during their work they have no contact with other human beings. The field of work in the home is much reduced because so many functions have moved out of the home, and others are made easier by modern labor-saving devices. In Oslo, where the author and her colleagues have been studying certain families for some years, it has been observed that mothers were happy to stop their professional work when they expected their first baby. But when the child reached the age of three or four, many mothers felt isolated and deserted. They wanted to have a job, not so much in order to earn money as to get to a place where they could meet others, where they had work companions. But most of them wanted a job only part of the day. They wanted to be professional workers, but not only professional workers. They wanted to be mothers, but not only mothers.

For most women, it still is important that what they want might hurt their babies, and in such cases they will give up their own demands. But is it necessary to give up outside work if they like and want such work? Will it hurt the children?

It is not easy to answer these questions, because life may be arranged so differently for the children concerned: (a) They may stay in the home with a grandmother, a nanny, etc.; or the father and the mother may have different times of work so that the father takes care of the child while the mother is away at work, at least part of this time. (b) They may be placed under supervision in a park, day nursery, or kindergarten, this depending on the length of time the mother will spend in her work. (c) They can live in a children's institution with the parents visiting them at certain times of the day, such as in the arrangement made at the Israeli kibbutzim.

On the other hand, there may be important variations in the mother's work and in her emotional experiences with regard to her job: (a) She may have regular work or only occasional jobs. (b) She may take on the job in order to get a larger income for the family, or she may take it on because she likes that particular work. (c) She may be happy or not happy in her domestic work.

Third and not least important, it makes a great difference how old the children are, and how many of them there are in the family.

And finally, it makes a great difference how the mate and the rest of the family react to the mother's work. The husband may think it is fine that the wife has a job, he may experience her as superior to him when she earns money, he may demand the same services from her around the house as from a woman working at home, the neighbors may

---

[29] Cf. R. G. Andry, "Paternal and Maternal Roles and Delinquency," in *Ibid.*, pp. 31–44.

wonder why she goes out to work. The attitudes the working mother encounters everywhere in her surroundings affect her position.

The problems concern not only employed women, but equally so women working in the home: How much do they take care of the children and to what extent do they send the children out—and to what? What is most important for the mother, the children's needs for play and activity, or order and cleanliness in the house? Does a woman working at home inhibit the children in their need to be independent? May the woman working at home inhibit the relationship between father and child, or does she make it easier for the father to spend time with the children? Is the husband happy to be the only financial supporter of the family, or is he ·discontented because the wife does not earn money outside the house?

Very little research has been done on all these relationships, but that which has shows that part of what people usually believe is not correct.

It is often said that "key children," the children who carry the key to the apartment on a string around their neck, easily become delinquents. In general, this is not correct. On the other hand, children of women who have occasional jobs, of women who take a job on some occasions and at other times work in the home, in many cases run into difficulties.[30] The reasons for this are varied: Perhaps nothing regular is arranged for these children since the mother is not permanently engaged in her work. Perhaps such occasional work is an expression of something moody and irregular in the mother's personality, and the same characteristics will be found also in her treatment of the children. Perhaps the mother takes a job to earn money once in a while but is not pleased with this state of affairs, and her unhappiness spreads to the rest of the home.

Strangely enough, research indicates that employed women are frequently together with their children more than the women who remain at home, and that the working mothers strive harder to participate in activities in which the children are particularly interested.[31] The domestic women seem more content to leave the children to play alone outdoors, and then perhaps to take them on errands or to other activities that interest the mother herself. The employed women show their children more tenderness, perhaps because they love their work and on the whole have a surplus of joy to share with the children. Or perhaps because

they have a bad conscience about leaving the children and try to make up for it by excessive cuddling.

Looking at the different age groups of children, it may be said that for the babies, it is good to have mother with them. But it is still more important that she return daily and regularly at specific times. For some children, it seems to be better if their mothers have always been employed, since the actual transition from having a domestic mother to a working mother is the most difficult for them.

In the preschool age, much depends on how life is organized for the children.[32] It may be difficult for active preschool children to stay at home in a small modern apartment with a mother who emphasizes cleanliness and order all the time. It may be healthy for them to have some hours daily in another milieu where life is organized in a different way. Like the young monkeys, they need to be pushed away to play with other children. They get a richer life in this way and become less rigid. But they need at the same time a mother and a father as something permanent in life. Preschool children seem to become more anxious when mother goes to work once in a while than when she goes regularly. In kibbutzim, the children at this age will be more firmly tied to their parents than to their substitute mother with whom they live, though they only see the parents for some hours daily. The love they encounter, and the feeling of being with persons who are "my mother" and "my father," evidently make them experience these ties.

School-age children of employed women on the whole are more independent than other children and manage better with their school subjects. But they have greater difficulties when first starting school than children from homes where the mothers do not go out to work. It is uncertain why this is so; perhaps these initial starting difficulties may have the same origin as that for mother's work, family difficulties in the home. Not enough is known about this problem so far.

Many investigations have had as their object the comparison of children of nonworking and working women. On the whole, these investigations show few or no differences. But greater differences are found if the mothers are grouped in another way, namely, in one group, those who love their outside work and those who love their domestic work,[33] and in a different group, those who are discontented with staying at home and those who are discontented in their outside work. More well-adjusted, happy children are found in the first group than in the second.

---

[30] Sheldon Glueck and Eleanor T. Glueck, *Unraveling Juvenile Delinquency*, Boston, 1950.

[31] Marian Radke Yarrow, "Maternal Employment and Child Rearing," *Children*, 8 (1961), pp. 223–228.

---

[32] Eleanor E. Maccoby, "Children and Working Mothers," *Children*, 5 (1958), pp. 83–89.

[33] M. R. Yarrow, *op. cit.*

The provisional conclusion from these investigations is that for some women the best thing is to go out to work, for others it is best to stay in the home. But it seems important that the mother have a permanent arrangement. Children develop best and most harmoniously when the mother herself is happy and gay. Whether she has work outside the home or not seems rather unimportant from the child's viewpoint. But in addition to this rather general conclusion, the whole question of the motives that drive a woman to one or the other form of life must be considered. Her own experience of the situation may play a greater role than the actual situation. More important than any other single factor, however, is the developmental stage of the child and his changing needs from one age level to another.

14

Adult Status of Children with Contrasting Early Life Experiences: A Follow-up Study

Harold M. Skeels

Is there a risk that some types of orphanage can blight the lives of children placed there? Is there any hope for boys or girls who have been labeled mentally retarded? These are among the questions answered by Skeels in this dramatic account of the follow-up nearly forty years later of orphanage children who had been placed in the care of high-level mental retardates. Comparison is made with other orphanage children. The work of Rosalyn Saltz on foster grand-parents* raises some important questions that serve to make more general those posed by Skeels's paper. If mothering by institutionalized retardates (Skeels)˙ and by foster grand-parents (Saltz) can improve IQ and social-emotional adequacy, we might well consider the advantages of relocating some of our institutions so that they can relate to each other in new ways suggested by these researches. Such interrelationship might be of benefit to those in each type of institution and save money for society in both the short run and the long run.

---

* Rosalyn Saltz, "Counteracting the effects of stress in young institutionalized children, in *Explorations in the Psychology of Stress and Anxiety*, B. P. Rourke (Ed.), Longmans, 1969; and Rosalyn Saltz, "Effects of part-time 'mothering' on IQ and SQ in institutionalized children," *Child Development*, in press.

I. Introduction

A follow-up study that covers a span of some 30 years will inevitably bracket changes in psychological concepts and practices. In the early 1930's when the subjects of this report were identified as infants, the prevailing concept of intelligence held by psychologists, social workers, and educators was that intelligence is a fixed individual characteristic. It was believed to be related to parental genetic traits that were inferred from the parents' occupational and educational achievements, to show little fluctuation from early childhood to maturity, and to be relatively uninfluenced by the impact of environment. Assessment of the intelligence of young children, while difficult, was regarded as not impossible. It was believed that knowing a child's mental level facilitated planning for his future, since the developmental quotient was considered to be an acceptably stable predictor of his future development. In the absence of reliable measures for an infant, for example, the parents' educational achievement, occupational classification, and general sociocultural status were considered to be predictive of the child's potentialities.

In developing plans for dependent children, social workers in the more sophisticated agencies placed considerable emphasis on details of family history. The resulting assessment of potential was used as a basis for matching children and prospective adoptive parents or for making other plans for the child. When such information was not available, or was unfavorable, the child was held for observation until his development could be assessed. For some children this meant several years of observation. Since foster homes were relatively scarce, most children in this category were detained in orphanages during the observation period.

At the same time, some agencies were not influenced by the prevailing, academically accepted concepts of intelligence and of prediction of future development. In these agencies, a variety of practices was found ranging from indiscriminate placements in adoptive homes to early diagnosis of retardation.

The validity of what were then regarded as desirable practices had never been empirically tested, nor was there evidence to contradict them. Conducting planned and carefully designed research in the area was out of the question for both financial and humanitarian reasons. However, the possibility of observing and studying the results of existing

Harold M. Skeels, "Adult status of children with contrasting early life experiences: A follow-up study," *Monographs of the Society for Research in Child Development*, Serial No. 105, 1966, vol. 31, no. 3. Reprinted by permission. Copyright 1966 by The Society for Research in Child Development, Inc.

practices was completely feasible. The natural-history approach of observing, measuring, recording, and interpreting data without intervention in the practices that produced them was basic to the initial reports in the so-called Iowa Studies. Included among them were the follow-up studies of the mental development of children who had been placed in adoptive homes in infancy and in later childhood (Skeels, 1936; 1938; Skodak, 1939; Skodak & Skeels, 1945; 1949), and the study of the mental growth of children who had been in inadequate homes for varying periods (Skeels & Fillmore, 1937). Later, studies were made of the effects of specific intervention, such as the influence of language training (Dawe, 1942) and the effect of a nursery-school program (Skeels, Updegraff, Wellman, & Williams, 1938; Wellman, 1938).

The present study is a report on the status as adults of two groups of children originally encountered in the Iowa institutions. One group experienced what was then regarded as the normal course of events in a child-caring institution, while the other experienced a specifically designed and implemented intervention program. Reports on the development of these children have appeared in two previous publications. The first (Skeels & Dye, 1939) described the original experimental period, and the second (Skeels, 1942) reported a follow-up some two years later. The study was not planned nor the data gathered in a way to form the basis for studies of personality structure in depth. The findings reported here, therefore, are concerned with the question of whether and for how long a time mental development is affected by major changes in early environment and, specifically, with the factors significantly associated with deflections in mental development. It is hoped that these findings will contribute to the growing body of evidence on the effects of deprivation and poverty on the young child's ability to learn.

Mention may be made that this report summarizes one unit of a series of studies that were the center of much controversy over the years. In addition to its historical interest, it is hoped that it will have contemporary value and support for workers in the applied fields of child development. Comparisons with the growing body of literature on early childhood development and on the impact of environment on children are left to the reader.

II. The Original Study

All the children in this study had become wards of the orphanage through established court procedures after no next of kin was found able to provide either support or suitable guardianship. Of the 25 children, 20 were illegitimate and the remainder had been separated from their parents because of evidence of severe neglect and/or abuse. Then as now, the courts were reluctant to sever the ties between child and parents and did so only when clearly presented with no other alternative. All the children were white and of north-European background.

The orphanage in which the children were placed occupied, with a few exceptions, buildings that had first served as a hospital and barracks during the Civil War. The institution was overcrowded and understaffed. By present standards, diet, sanitation, general care, and basic philosophy of operation were censurable. At the time of the study, however, the discrepancies between conditions in the institution and in the general community were not so great and were not always to the disadvantage of the institution. Over the past 30 years, administrative and physical changes have occurred that reflect the economic and social gains of our society. The description of conditions in the institution in the 1930's, therefore, does not apply to the present.

At the time the original study was begun, infants up to the age of 2 years were housed in the hospital, then a relatively new building. Until about 6 months, they were cared for in the infant nursery. The babies were kept in standard hospital cribs that often had protective sheeting on the sides, thus effectively limiting visual stimulation; no toys or other objects were hung in the infants' line of vision. Human interactions were limited to busy nurses who, with the speed born of practice and necessity, changed diapers or bedding, bathed and medicated the infants, and fed them efficiently with propped bottles.

Older infants, from about 6 to 24 months, were moved into small dormitories containing two to five large cribs. This arrangement permitted the infants to move about a little and to interact somewhat with those in neighboring cribs. The children were cared for by two nurses with some assistance from one or two girls, 10 to 15 years old, who regarded the assignment as an unwelcome chore. The children had good physical and medical care, but little can be said beyond this. Interactions with adults were largely limited to feeding, dressing, and toilet details. Few play materials were available, and there was little time for the teaching of play techniques. Most of the children had a brief play period on the floor; a few toys were available at the beginning of such periods, but if any rolled out of reach there was no one to retrieve it. Except for short walks out of doors, the children were seldom out of the nursery room.

At 2 years of age these children were graduated to the cottages, which had been built around 1860. A rather complete description of "cottage" life is reported by Skeels et al. (1938) from which the following excerpts are taken:

> Overcrowding of living facilities was characteristic. Too many children had to be accommodated in the available space and there were too few adults to guide them. . . . Thirty to thirty-five children of the same sex under six years of age lived in a "cottage" in charge of one matron and three or four entirely untrained and often reluctant girls of thirteen to fifteen years of age. The waking and sleeping hours of these children were spent (except during meal times and a little time on a grass plot) in an average-sized room (approximately fifteen feet square), a sunporch of similar size, a cloakroom, . . . and a single dormitory. The latter was occupied only during sleeping hours. The meals for all children in the orphanage were served in a central building in a single large dining room. . . .
>
> The duties falling to the lot of the matron were not only those involved in the care of the children but those related to clothing and cottage maintenance, in other words, cleaning, mending, and so forth. . . . With so much responsibility centered in one adult the result was a necessary regimentation. The children sat down, stood up, and did many things in rows and in unison. They spent considerable time sitting on chairs, for in addition to the number of children and the matron's limited time there was the misfortune of inadequate equipment. . . .
>
> No child had any property which belonged exclusively to him except, perhaps, his tooth brush. Even his clothing, including shoes, was selected and put on him according to size [pp. 10–11].

After a child reached the age of 6 years, he began school. His associates were his cottage mates and the children of the same age and opposite sex who lived on the other side of the institution grounds. Although the curriculum was ostensibly the same as that in the local public school, it was generally agreed that the standards were adjusted to the capabilities of the orphanage children. Few of those who had their entire elementary-school experience in the institution's school were able to make the transition to the public junior high school.

The orphanage was designed for mentally normal children. It was perpetually overcrowded, although every opportunity to relieve this pressure was exploited. One such relief occurred periodically when new buildings were opened at other institutions, such as at the schools for the mentally retarded. It was not uncommon for a busload of children to be transferred on such occasions. A valued contribution of the psychologists was the maintenance of lists of children who, on the basis of test scores and observable behavior, were regarded as eligible for transfers.

The environmental conditions in the two state institutions for the mentally retarded were not identical but they had many things in common. Patient-inmates were grouped by sex, age, and general ability. Within any one ward, the patients were highly similar. The youngest children tended to be the most severely disabled and were frequently "hospital" patients. The older, more competent inmates had work assignments throughout the institution and constituted a somewhat self-conscious elite with recognized status.

Personnel at that time included no resident social workers or psychologists. Physicians were resident at the schools for the mentally retarded and were on call at the orphanage. Administrative and matron and caretaking staffs were essentially untrained and nonprofessional. Psychological services were introduced in the orphanage in 1932 when the author, on the staff of the Iowa Child Welfare Research Station, State University of Iowa, became the first psychologist to be employed by the Iowa Board of Control of State Institutions. Over the years this proved to be a happy marriage of service and research related to the care of dependent children.

IDENTIFICATION OF CASES

Early in the service aspects of the program, two baby girls, neglected by their feebleminded mothers, ignored by their inadequate relatives, malnourished and frail, were legally committed to the orphanage. The youngsters were pitiful little creatures. They were tearful, had runny noses, and sparse, stringy, and colorless hair; they were emaciated, undersized, and lacked muscle tonus or responsiveness. Sad and inactive, the two spent their days rocking and whining.

The psychological examinations showed developmental levels of 6 and 7 months, respectively, for the two girls, although they were then 13 and 16 months old chronologically. This serious delay in mental growth was confirmed by observations of their behavior in the nursery and by reports of the superintendent of nurses, as well as by the pediatrician's examination. There was no evidence of physiological or organic defect, or of birth injury or glandular dysfunction.

The two children were considered unplaceable, and transfer to a school for the mentally retarded was recommended with a high degree of confidence. Accordingly, they were transferred to an institution for the mentally retarded at the next available vacancy, when they were aged 15 and 18 months, respectively.

In the meantime, the author's professional responsibilities had been increased to include itinerant psychological services to the two state institutions for the mentally retarded. Six months after the transfer of the two children, he was visiting the wards at an institution for the mentally retarded and noticed two outstanding little girls. They were alert, smiling, running about, responding to the playful attention of adults, and generally behaving and looking like any other toddlers. He scarcely recognized them as the two little girls with the hopeless prognosis, and thereupon tested them again. Although the results indicated that the two were approaching normal mental development for age, the author was skeptical of the validity or permanence of the improvement and no change was instituted in the lives of the children. Twelve months later they were re-examined, and then again when they were 40 and 43 months old. Each examination gave unmistakable evidence of mental development well within the normal range for age.

There was no question that the initial evaluations gave a true picture of the children's functioning level at the time they were tested. It appeared equally evident that later appraisals showed normal mental growth accompanied by parallel changes in social growth, emotional maturity, communication skills, and general behavior. In order to find a possible explanation for the changes that had occurred, the nature of the children's life space was reviewed.

The two girls had been placed on one of the wards of older, brighter girls and women, ranging in age from 18 to 50 years and in mental age from 5 to 9 years, where they were the only children of preschool age, except for a few hopeless bed patients with gross physical defects. An older girl on the ward had "adopted" each of the two girls, and other older girls served as adoring aunts. Attendants and nurses also showed affection to the two, spending time with them, taking them along on their days off for automobile rides and shopping excursions, and purchasing toys, picture books, and play materials for them in great abundance. The setting seemed to be a homelike one, abundant in affection, rich in wholesome and interesting experiences, and geared to a preschool level of development.

It was recognized that as the children grew older their developmental needs would be less adequately met in the institution for the mentally retarded. Furthermore, they were now normal and the need for care in such an institution no longer existed. Consequently, they were transferred back to the orphanage and shortly thereafter were placed in adoptive homes.

At this point, evidence on the effects of environment on intelligence had been accumulated from a number of studies. Skeels and Fillmore (1937) had found that older children who came from inadequate non-nurturant homes were mentally retarded or borderline but that their younger siblings were generally of normal ability, which suggested that longer residence in such homes had a cumulatively depressing effect on intelligence. Children also became retarded if they remained for long periods in an institution (1930-style) supposedly designed for normal children (Skeels, 1940). However, if children were placed in adoptive homes as infants, or even as young preschoolers, their development surpassed expectations, and improvement continued for long periods following placement (Skodak, 1939). In even more extreme cases, seriously retarded children were able to attain normal levels of functioning when placed in a setting officially designed for the mentally retarded (Skeels & Dye, 1939). The consistent element seemed to be the existence of a one-to-one relationship with an adult who was generous with love and affection, together with an abundance of attention and experiential stimulation from many sources. Children who had little of these did not show progress; those who had a great deal, did.

Since study homes or temporary care homes were not available to the state agency at that time, the choice for children who were not suitable for immediate placement in adoptive homes was between, on the one hand, an unstimulating, large nursery with predictable mental retardation or, on the other hand, a radical, iconoclastic solution, that is, placement in institutions for the mentally retarded in a bold experiment to see whether retardation in infancy was reversible.

By the time these observations were organized into a meaningful whole and their implications were recognized, individual psychological tests were available for all children in the orphanage. As part of a continuing program of observation and evaluation, all infants over 3 months of age were given the then available tests (Kuhlmann-Binet and Iowa Tests for Young Children), and were retested as often as changes seemed to occur. Retests at bimonthly intervals were not uncommon. Older preschoolers were re-examined at 6- to 12-month intervals; school-aged children, annually or biennially. Children who were showing marked delay in development were kept under special observation.

Children whose development was so delayed that adoptive placement was out of the question remained in the orphanage. The only foreseeable alternative for them was eventual transfer to an institution for the mentally retarded. In the light of the experiences with the two little girls, the possibility was raised that early transfer to such an institution might have therapeutic effects. If not all, then at least some of the children might be able to attain normal mental functioning. In the event they did not, no significant change in life pattern would have occurred, and the child would remain in the situation for which he would have been destined in any case.

This radical proposal was accepted with understandable misgivings by the administrators involved. It was finally agreed that, in order to avoid the stigma of commitment to a state school for the retarded, children would be accepted as "house guests" in such institutions but would remain on the official roster of the orphanage. Periodic re-evaluations were built into the plan; if no improvement was observed in the child, commitment would follow. Insofar as possible, the children were to be placed on wards as "only" children.

In the course of time, in addition to the two little girls who have been described and another transferred to the second of the two institutions at about the same time, 10 more children became "house guests." The transfers were spaced over a year's span in groups of 3, 3, and 4. All went to one institution for the mentally handicapped, the Glenwood State School. Unfortunately, the number of "house guests" exceeded the number of "elite" wards of older girls and necessitated the use of some environments that were less desirable. Consequently, in some wards there were more children, or fewer capable older girls, or less oppor-

tunity for extra stimulation, with a resulting variation in developmental patterns.

Experimental Group. . . . All were under 3 years of age at the time of transfer. Their development had been reliably established as seriously retarded by tests and observation before transfer was considered. . . .

The experimental group consisted of 10 girls and 3 boys, none with gross physical handicaps. Prior to their placement as "house guests," the examinations were routinely administered to them without any indication that they would or would not be involved in the unusual experience.

At the time of transfer, the mean chronological age of the group was 19.4 months (SD 7.4) and the median was 17.1 months, with a range of from 7.1 to 35.9 months. The range of IQ's was from 35 to 89 with a mean of 64.3 (SD 16.4) and a median of 65.0. Additional tests were made of 11 of the 13 children shortly before or in conjunction with the pretransfer tests reported in Table 1, using the Kuhlmann-Binet again or the Iowa Test for Young Children, and the results corroborated the reported scores.

The children were considered unsuitable for adoption because of evident mental retardation.

TABLE 1

EXPERIMENTAL GROUP: MENTAL DEVELOPMENT OF CHILDREN AS MEASURED BY KUHLMANN-BINET INTELLIGENCE TESTS BEFORE AND AFTER TRANSFER

Case Number[a]	Sex	Before Transfer Test 1		Chronological Age, Months, at Transfer	After Transfer — Test							Length of Experimental Period, Months	Change in IQ, First to Last Test
					2		3		Last			
		Chronological Age, Months	IQ		Chronological Age, Months	IQ	Chronological Age, Months	IQ	Chronological Age, Months	IQ		
1.........	M	7.0	89	7.1	12.8	113	...	...	12.8	113	5.7	+24
2.........	F	12.7	57	13.1	20.5	94	29.4	83	36.8	77	23.7	+20
3.........	F	12.7	85	13.3	25.2	107	...	...	25.2	107	11.9	+22
4.........	F	14.7	73	15.0	23.1	100	...	...	23.1	100	8.1	+27
5.........	F	13.4	46	15.2	21.7	77	32.9	100	40.0	95[b]	24.8	+49
6.........	F	15.5	77	15.6	21.3	96	30.1	100	30.1	100	14.5	+23
7.........	F	16.6	65	17.1	27.5	104	...	...	27.5	104	10.4	+39
8.........	F	16.6	35	18.4	24.8	87	36.0	88	43.0	93	24.6	+58
9.........	F	21.8	61	22.0	34.3	80	...	...	34.3	80	12.3	+19
10.........	M	23.3	72	23.4	29.1	88	37.9	71	45.4	79	22.0	+ 7
11.........	M	25.7	75	27.4	42.5	78	51.0	82[b]	51.0	82[b]	23.6	+ 7
12.........	F	27.9	65	28.4	40.4	82	...	...	40.4	82	12.0	+17
13.........	F	30.0	36	35.9	51.7	70	81.0	74[b]	89.0	81[b]	52.1	+45

[a] Arranged according to age at time of transfer.
[b] Stanford-Binet IQ.
Source: Adapted from H. M. Skeels & H. B. Dye (1939, Table 1).

For example, in Case 1, although the IQ was 89, it was felt that actual retardation was much greater, as the child at 7 months could scarcely hold up his head without support and showed little general bodily activity in comparison with other infants of the same age. In Case 3, at 12 months, very little activity was observed, and the child was very unsteady when sitting up without support. She could not pull herself to a standing position and did not creep. Case 11 was not only retarded but showed perseverative patterns of behavior, particularly incessant rocking back and forth. Cases 5, 8, and 13 were classified at the imbecile level. In present-day terms, they would have been labeled "trainable mentally retarded children."

Table 1 lists for each child the pretransfer test findings and ages at time of transfer; also shown are posttransfer test results, length of experimental period, and changes in IQ from first to last test.

Contrast Group. Since the original purpose of the experiment was to rescue for normalcy, if possible, those children showing delayed or retarded development, no plans had been made for a control or comparison group. It was only after the data had been analyzed that it was found that such a contrast group was available because of the tests that were routinely given to all children in the orphanage. To select such a contrast group, therefore, records were scrutinized for children who met the following criteria:

1. Had been given intelligence tests under 2 years of age.
2. Were still in residence in the orphanage at approximately 4 years of age.
3. Were in the control group of the orphanage preschool study (Skeels et al., 1938).
4. Had not attended preschool.

The Skeels et al. (1938) study had included two groups of children matched in chronological age, mental age, IQ, and length of residence in the institution, of which one group had the advantages of the more stimulating environment of preschool attendance while the other group, the controls, experienced the less stimulating environment of cottage life. Since the purpose of the contrast group in the present study was to provide data on children in a relatively nonstimulating environment, those who had attended preschool were not included. Such limitations, however, did not constitute a selective factor as far as the characteristics of the children were concerned.

A total of 12 children were selected on the basis of the criteria and became the contrast group. The mean chronological age of the group at the time of first examination was 16.6 months (SD 2.9), with a median at 16.3 months. The range was from 11.9 to 21.8 months. The mean IQ of the group was 86.7 (SD 14.3) and the median IQ was 90. With the exception of two cases (16 and 24) the children had IQ's ranging from 81 to 103; the IQ's for the two exceptions were 71 and 50, respectively. When the children were examined, it was not known that they were or would become members of any study group. The re-examinations were merely routine retests that were given to all children.

At the ages when adoptive placement usually occurred, nine of the children in the contrast group had been considered normal in mental development. All 12 were not placed, however, because of different circumstances: 5 were withheld from placement simply because of poor family histories, 2 because of improper commitments, 2 because of luetic conditions, 2 because of other health problems, and one because of possible mental retardation.

The subsequent progress of the children in both the experimental and the contrast groups was influenced by individual circumstances. The groups were never identified as such in the resident institution; the members of each group were considered together only in a statistical sense. A child in the experimental group remained in the institution for the mentally retarded until it was felt that he had attained the maximum benefit from residence there. At that point, he was placed directly into an adoptive home or returned to the orphanage in transit to an adoptive home. If he did not attain a level of intelligence that warranted adoptive plans, he remained in the institution for the mentally retarded.

The contrast-group members remained in the orphanage until placement. One was returned to relatives, but in most instances the children were eventually transferred to an institution for the mentally retarded as long-term protected residents. A few of the contrast group had been briefly approved for adoptive placement, and two had been placed for short periods. None was successful, however, and the children's decline in mental level removed them from the list of those eligible for adoption.

Table 2 lists the chronological ages and test findings for the children in the contrast group over the experimental period and the changes in IQ that occurred.

DESCRIPTION OF EXPERIMENTAL AND CONTRAST GROUPS

Birth Histories. The birth histories of the two groups were not significantly different. Prematurity

TABLE 2
CONTRAST GROUP: MENTAL DEVELOPMENT OF CHILDREN AS MEASURED BY REPEATED KUHLMANN-BINET
INTELLIGENCE TESTS OVER AN AVERAGE EXPERIMENTAL PERIOD OF TWO AND ONE-HALF YEARS

| | | Test | | | | | | | | Length of Experimental Period, Months | Change in IQ, First to Last Test |
| | | 1 | | 2 | | 3 | | Last | | | |
Case Number[a]	Sex	Chrono-logical Age, Months	IQ	Chrono-logical Age, Months	IQ	Chrono-logical Age, Months	IQ	Chrono-logical Age, Months	IQ		
14	F	11.9	91	24.8	73	37.5	65	55.0	62	43.1	−29
15	F	13.0	92	20.1	54	38.3	56	38.3	56	25.3	−36
16	F	13.6	71	20.6	76	40.9	56	40.9	56	27.3	−15
17	M	13.8	96	37.2	58	53.2	54	53.2	54	39.4	−42
18	M	14.5	99	21.6	67	41.9	54	41.9	54	27.4	−45
19	M	15.2	87	22.5	80	35.5	74	44.5	67	29.3	−20
20	M	17.3	81	43.0	77	52.9	83[b]	52.9	83[b]	35.6	+ 2
21	M	17.5	103	26.8	72	38.0	63	50.3	60	32.8	−43
22	M	18.3	98	24.8	93	30.7	80	39.7	61	21.4	−37
23	F	20.2	89	27.0	71	39.4	66	48.4	71	28.2	−18
24	M	21.5	50	34.9	57	51.6	42	51.6	42	30.1	− 8
25	M	21.8	83	28.7	75	37.8	63	50.1	60	28.3	−23

[a] Arranged according to age at first test.
[b] Stanford-Binet IQ.
Source: Adapted from H. M. Skeels & H. B. Dye (1939, Table 2).

was of particular interest in relation to the initial tests of intelligence, as a somewhat slower rate of mental and motor development or possible brain damage or retardation may be associated with it. . . .*

Medical Histories. In evaluating the medical histories of both the experimental and contrast groups, little of significance was found in the relation between illnesses and rate of mental growth. . . .

Family Backgrounds. Social histories of the children revealed that all in both the experimental and contrast groups came from homes in which the social, economic, occupational, and intellectual levels were low. The family backgrounds are comparable to those reported by Skeels and Fillmore (1937), in their study of the mental development of children from underprivileged homes, and in Skodak's study (1939) of younger siblings placed in adoptive homes at ages 2 to 5.

Mothers. Information relating to education was available for 11 of the 13 mothers in the experimental group and for 10 of the 12 mothers in the contrast group. The mean grade completed by mothers of children in the experimental group was 7.8, with a median at grade 8. Only two had any

high-school work; one completed grade 11 and one grade 10 (Cases 3 and 6). In one case, it was doubtful if the second grade had been completed (Case 8). Two (Cases 1 and 5) had dropped out of grade 8 at the age of 16.

In the contrast group, the mean grade completed was 7.3, with a median at 7.5. One mother (Case 19) had completed high school and one had an equivalent of ninth-grade education. . . .

Intelligence tests[1] had been obtained on five of the mothers in the experimental group and on nine of the mothers in the contrast group. The mean IQ for the five mothers of the experimental group was 70.4, with a median at 66. Four mothers had IQ's below 70, and one was classified as normal with an IQ of 100. One additional mother, although not tested, was considered feeble-minded and had gone only as far as the second grade. Of the nine mothers tested in the contrast group, only two had IQ's above 70: one, 79 and the other, 84. The other scores ranged from 36 to 66. The mean IQ was 63, with a median at 62.

Fathers. Little information was available on the fathers, and in fact, in many cases paternity was doubtful. Ten of the children in each group were illegitimate. . . .

* There were 3 premature infants among the experimentals and only one among the contrast group. This difference would not bias the findings in favor of the experimental group, but would, if anything, work against the findings.—EDITOR.

[1] Stanford-Binet (1916) intelligence tests. Most of the tests were given by psychologists either at the Psychopathic Hospital or at the University Hospital of the State University of Iowa. Maximum chronological age used was 16 years.

A qualitative analysis of social histories seems to justify the conclusion that within . . . educational and occupational classifications, the parents represented the lower levels in such groups. Most of the fathers and mothers had dropped out of school because they had reached the limits of achievement and were not, in any sense of the word, average for their grade placements. The same may be said about occupational status.

DESCRIPTION OF THE ENVIRONMENTS

Experimental Group. Children in the experimental group were transferred from the orphanage nursery to the Glenwood State School, an institution for mentally retarded, and were placed on wards with older, brighter inmate girls. The wards were in a large cottage that contained eight wards with a matron and an assistant matron in charge and with one attendant for each ward. Approximately 30 patients, girls ranging in age from 18 to 50 years, were on each ward. On two wards (2 and 3), the residents had mental ages of from 9 to 12 years. On two other wards (4 and 5), the mental levels were from 7 to 10 years, and on another (ward 7), the mental ages were from 5 to 8 years. With the exception of ward 7, the wards housed few or no younger children other than the experimental "house guests." It was planned to place one, or at the most two, children from the experimental group on a given ward.

As with the first two children, who, by chance, were the first participants in the experiment, the attendants and the older girls became very fond of the children placed on their wards and took great pride in them. In fact, there was considerable competition among wards to see which one would have its "baby" walking or talking first. Not only the girls, but the attendants spent a great deal of time with "their children," playing, talking, and training them in every way. The children received constant attention and were the recipients of gifts; they were taken on excursions and were exposed to special opportunities of all kinds. For example, it was the policy of the matron in charge of the girls' school division to single out certain children who she felt were in need of special individualization and to permit them to spend some time each day visiting her office. This furnished new experiences, such as being singled out, receiving special attention and affection, new play materials, additional language stimulation, and meeting other office callers.

The spacious living rooms of the wards furnished ample space for indoor play and activity. Whenever weather permitted, the children spent some time each day on the playground under the supervision of one or more older girls. Here they were able to interact with other children of similar ages. Outdoor play equipment included tricycles, swings, slides, sand boxes, etc. The children also began to attend the school kindergarten as soon as they could walk. Toddlers remained for only half the morning and 4- or 5-year olds, the entire morning. Activities carried on in the kindergarten resembled preschool rather than the more formal type of kindergarten.

As part of the school program, the children attended daily 15-minute exercises in the chapel, which included group singing and music by the orchestra. The children also attended the dances, school programs, moving pictures, and Sunday chapel services.

In considering this enriched environment from a dynamic point of view, it must be pointed out that in the case of almost every child, some one adult (older girl or attendant) became particularly attached to him and figuratively "adopted" him. As a consequence, an intense one-to-one adult-child relationship developed, which was supplemented by the less intense but frequent interactions with the other adults in the environment. Each child had some one person with whom he was identified and who was particularly interested in him and his achievements. This highly stimulating emotional impact was observed to be the unique characteristic and one of the main contributions of the experimental setting.

The meager, even desolate environment in the orphanage has been described. The contrast between the richly stimulating, individually oriented experience of the children in the experimental group and the depersonalizing, mass handling, and affectionless existence in the children's home can hardly be emphasized enough.

MENTAL DEVELOPMENT

The mental development of individual children in the experimental group from the beginning to the end of the experimental periods is presented in Table 1. The 1922 Kuhlmann Revision of the Binet was used as the standard measure of intelligence, except for two or three tests on children who were 4 years of age or more for whom Stanford-Binet (1916) was used. All examinations were made by trained and experienced psychologists. Test one was the measure of intelligence just prior to transfer. Tests two, three, and the last were given at varying intervals of time following transfer. The last test was given at the end of the experimental period and was the second, third, or fourth, depending on the number of tests available at representative time intervals for a given child. Similar data showing the mental growth of the individual children in the contrast group over the 2½-year period are presented in Table 2.

. . . Using the *t* test, the difference for the experimental group between the means of first and last tests was statistically significant at the .001 level. Every child showed a gain of from 7 to 58 points. Three children made gains of 45 points or more, and all but two children gained more than 15 points (Table 1).

Length of the experimental period was from 5.7 months to 52.1 months. The period was not constant for all children as it depended upon the individual child's rate of development. As soon as a child showed normal mental development, as measured by intelligence tests and substantiated by qualitative observations, the experimental period was considered completed and the child's visit to the school for mentally retarded was terminated. Either he was placed in an adoptive home or returned to the orphanage.

These results are directly comparable with those reported by Kirk (1958) for his community experimental and contrast groups. After preschool experience, his experimental group made significant gains in IQ whereas the contrast group did not.

The mental-growth pattern for children in the contrast group was quite opposite that of the experimental group. Using the *t* test, the difference between the means of first and last tests was statistically significant ($p < .001$) but with the exception of one child who gained 2 points in IQ from first to last test, all children showed losses of from 9 to 45 points. Ten of the 12 children lost 15 or more points in IQ over the period of the study.

In the experimental group, children who were initially at the lower levels tended to make the greater gains. The three children classified at the imbecile level on the first examination made gains of 58, 49, and 45 IQ points. Also, the greatest losses in the contrast group were associated with the highest initial levels. Six children with original IQ's above 90 lost from 29 to 45 points in IQ. While this shift may be partially due to regression, there must have been other factors operating to bring about such a large and consistent change.*

These results, although more marked, are comparable to the findings reported in the orphanage preschool study by Skeels et al. (1938). In that study, children of the preschool group who were initially at the lower levels made the greatest gains following a period of preschool attendance, and children in the control group who were originally at the higher levels showed the greatest losses.

Family History and Children's Mental Development. No clear relation between family-history information and the mental-growth pattern of the children could be identified. Since the number of cases was small, examination of the data, rather than statistical treatment, was advisable.

In the experimental group, children whose mothers were classified as mentally retarded showed gains as marked as those children whose mothers were at a higher mental level. . . .

That the gains in intelligence evidenced by the children of the experimental group were true gains and not the results of vagaries in testing, seems validated. Improvement was noted independently by members of the medical staff, attendants and matrons, and school teachers. Practice effects could not have been a contributing factor to these gains, as the children in the contrast group, who showed continual losses in IQ, actually had more frequent tests than the children in the experimental group.

Parent Surrogates and Children's Mental Development. A close bond of love and affection between a given child and one or two adults who assume a very personal parental role appears to be a dynamic factor of great importance. Nine of the 13 children in the experimental group were involved in such relationships. The four other children (Cases 2, 9, 10, and 11) tended to be less individualized on the wards; their relationships with adults were more general, less intense, and did not involve any individual adult. It is significant that the children who experienced the more intense personal relationships made greater gains than those who were limited to more general interactions. The 9 children in the "personal" group made gains in IQ ranging from 17 to 58 points, with an average gain of 33.8 points. The 4 children in the more "general" group made gains of from 7 to 20 points, with an average of 14.

Two children (Cases 10 and 11) showed little progress on ward 7 over a period of 1½ years. This ward differed significantly from the others in that it housed 8 to 12 children of younger ages (3 to 8 years), and the older girls were of a lower mental level. The attendant on the ward was especially fine with young children but was unable to give much individual attention because of the large number of young children. At one time it was feared that the two children would continue to be hopelessly retarded. However, they were subsequently placed as singletons on wards with brighter girls and, after a period of six months with the more individualized attention, showed marked gains in intelligence.

---

* The statistical concept of regression refers to the tendency for scores, upon retesting, to be less toward the extreme than previously.—EDITOR

FIRST FOLLOW-UP

The experiment ended for each child in the experimental group when the decision was made that he had attained the maximum benefit from his "house-guest" experience. Of the 13, one remained in the institution until adulthood, 5 went directly into adoptive homes from the host institution, 6 had brief periods in the orphanage in transit to adoptive homes, and one was returned to the orphanage for some years and then was committed to the institution for the retarded.

As part of the pre-adoptive procedures and the planned follow-up evaluations, all the children were given individual intelligence tests approximately 2½ years after the close of the experimental period. Thus, the 11 adopted children were tested after approximately 2½ years of living in a family home, and the two children remaining in the institutions, after a similar period of continuing residential care. The mean length of the post-experimental period was 33 months (SD 8.0) and the median 29.8 months, with a range of 21 to 53 months.

The children in the contrast group were still wards of the state institutions and were given routine re-examinations. Those tests that most nearly coincided with the 2½-year-interval testing for the experimental group were used for comparison purposes in this study.

For the contrast group, the mean interval between the follow-up test and the last experimental-period test was 36.0 months (SD 12.2), with a median of 34.2 months. The 1916 Stanford-Binet was used as the standard measure of intelligence since all the children were past 4 years of age. . . .

Mental Development of the Experimental Group. The mean IQ of the 13 children in the experimental group on the follow-up examination was 95.9 (SD 16.3), and the median was 94.0. For the 11 children who had been placed in adoptive homes after the experimental period, the mean IQ at the time of the follow-up study was 101.4; the range of IQ's was from 90 to 118. Changes in IQ for the 11 children ranged from +16 points to −5 points. The greatest gain (16 points) was made by a child (Case 4) who had been placed in a superior adoptive home; the child (Case 5) showing the only loss was in a home considered to be far below the average of the other adoptive homes.

Losses of 17 and 9 points, respectively, were shown by the two children (Cases 9 and 2) who were not placed in adoptive homes. Case 9 had been returned to the orphanage although it was felt that the move was premature.[2] It was true that she

---

[2] The return followed a change in administration rather than psychological readiness.

became lost in the orphanage group and received very little, if any, individual attention, but whether her development would have been influenced by a different environment is speculative. Case 2, whose IQ was 77 at the close of the experimental period, had remained in the institution for the mentally retarded and, at the time of the follow-up, was expected to require continuing residential care.

Mental Development of the Contrast Group. To facilitate comparisons between the experimental and contrast groups, the time interval between the examinations during the experimental period and the time of examinations for follow-up purposes were kept as nearly the same as possible. For individual children, the test intervals ranged from 20.1 months to 57.6 months. The mean IQ of the 12 children in the contrast group was 66.1 (SD 16.5), a mean gain of 5.6 points over the last test of the experimental period. Despite this small average gain, 8 of the 12 children showed marked mental deterioration between the initial test and the follow-up test. During the three years following the close of the experimental period, a number of changes were made in the group's living situation. Two children (Cases 15 and 16) were transferred to the Glenwood State School, where they experienced essentially the same type of environment as that of the experimental group, but beginning at an older age. The two were 41 months of age at time of transfer. Thirty-four months following this transfer, Case 16 was examined and obtained an IQ of 80, showing a gain of 24 points. She was returned to the orphanage, therefore, as continued residence in the institution for mentally retarded seemed unwarranted. Case 15, on the other hand, failed to show any gain after 34 months. An examination six months later resulted in an IQ of 52, a 4 point loss.

Six of the contrast children were transferred to the Woodward State Hospital and School following the close of the experimental period. This transfer was made on a permanent basis, inasmuch as mental retardation and lack of development and adjustment made continued residence in the orphanage seem inadvisable. Four of the children (Cases 14, 17, 18, and 21) were transferred within three months after the close of the experimental period, and the other two (Cases 22 and 24) were transferred 16 months after the close of the experimental period.

The children sent to Woodward experienced a different environment from that of the experimental children who had been "house guests" at Glenwood. The children sent to Woodward were much older at the time of transfer and received, in general, less individual attention and had fewer interactions with adults. They interacted primarily with children of a similar or slightly older chronological age who were mentally more retarded.

Over a period ranging from two to three years, 2 of the 6 transferred children experienced further losses in IQ (Cases 18 and 21), 2 remained relatively constant (Cases 14 and 17), and 2 showed gains (Cases 22 and 24). None attained a level higher than that of borderline intelligence.

The two children who showed marked gains in intelligence had experienced enriched environments. Case 22 was quite the favorite from the time of his transfer. After a year he was placed in the primary group in school. His teacher was especially fond of him and took a great interest in his achievements. The psychologist reported, "Because he was a likable boy with possibilities for improvement under training, he has been given much special attention. His reports show that though he appears quiet and unassuming he has an active imagination and curiosity and often shows initiative." At 6 years of age he surpassed all members of his class in reading skills and in identifying flash cards.

Case 24 was the only one of this transfer group not placed in the nursery ward. He was placed on a ward with older, brighter boys, where his adjustment was consistently satisfactory. Since he was one of the younger boys on the ward, he received additional individual attention from attendants and older boys.

The three contrast children who remained in the orphanage after the close of the original study subsequently also experienced a change of environment. Case 20 did not attend preschool but entered kindergarten at 68 months of age, and he had just completed the year in kindergarten when the follow-up examination was given. Case 23 attended preschool one year, kindergarten one year, first grade one year (with a D average in grades), and, at the time of the follow-up examination, was 9 years of age and in the second grade.

Of the three children who remained in the orphanage, Case 19 had the most enriched and varied experience during the follow-up period and showed by far the greatest gain (22 points) in IQ. Beginning at 5 years of age, he spent one year in preschool and one year in kindergarten. During the year in kindergarten, he was also included in a special mental-growth stimulation study, which was carried on by a research assistant from the State University of Iowa (Dawe, 1942), that included an intensified, individualized program of experimental instruction and frequent trips away from the institution. He was the only child from the contrast group included in this special study.

The last of the contrast children to be accounted for (Case 25) was paroled to his grandparents immediately following the close of the experimental period. The home was a very marginal one, and the family had been on relief for years. At the time of the follow-up examination at 8 years of age, the boy was still in the first grade, doing failing work, and was continually "picked on" by other children. A recommendation was made to transfer the boy to an institution for the mentally retarded.

III. THE FOLLOW-UP STUDY OF ADULT ACHIEVEMENT

The purpose of this follow-up study was to obtain answers to a few very simple questions: What happened to the two groups of children when they became adults? How were the differences in mental growth in childhood reflected in adult achievement and adjustment? Were the two divergent pathways maintained or did they converge over the years? Were there significant changes indicating improvement or regression within and between groups? Was there a relation between adult status and such factors as social history, health history, or environmental experiences? . . . The two groups had maintained their divergent patterns of competency into adulthood. All 13 children in the experimental group were self-supporting, and none was a ward of any institution, public or private. In the contrast group of 12 children, one had died in adolescence following continued residence in a state institution for the mentally retarded, and 4 were still wards of institutions, one in a mental hospital, and the other 3 in institutions for the mentally retarded.

In education, disparity between the two groups was striking. The contrast group completed a median of less than the third grade. The experimental group completed a median of the twelfth grade. Four of the subjects had one or more years of college work, one received a B.A. degree and took some graduate training.

Marked differences in occupational levels were seen in the two groups [see Table 5]. In the experimental group all were self-supporting or married and functioning as housewives. The range was from professional and business occupations to domestic service, the latter the occupations of two girls who had never been placed in adoptive homes. In the contrast group, four (36%) of the subjects were institutionalized and unemployed. Those who were employed, with one exception (Case 19), were characterized as "hewers of wood and drawers of water." Using the *t* test, the difference between the status means of the two groups (based on the Warner Index of Status Characteristics applied to heads of households) was statistically significant ($p < .01$).

TABLE 5
EXPERIMENTAL AND CONTRAST GROUPS: OCCUPATIONS OF SUBJECTS AND SPOUSES

Case No.	Subject's Occupation	Spouse's Occupation	Female Subject's Occupation Previous to Marriage
Experimental Group:			
1[a]	Staff sergeant	Dental technician	....
2	Housewife	Laborer	Nurses' aide
3	Housewife	Mechanic	Elementary school teacher
4	Nursing instructor	Unemployed	Registered nurse
5	Housewife	Semi-skilled laborer	No work history
6	Waitress	Mechanic, semi-skilled	Beauty operator
7	Housewife	Flight engineer	Dining room hostess
8	Housewife	Foreman, construction	No work history
9	Domestic service	Unmarried	....
10[a]	Real estate sales	Housewife	....
11[a]	Vocational counselor	Advertising copy writer[b]	....
12	Gift shop sales[c]	Unmarried	....
13	Housewife	Pressman-printer	Office-clerical
Contrast Group:			
14	Institutional inmate	Unmarried	....
15	Dishwasher	Unmarried	....
16	Deceased	....	....
17[a]	Dishwasher	Unmarried	....
18[a]	Institutional inmate	Unmarried	....
19[a]	Compositor and typesetter	Housewife	....
20[a]	Institutional inmate	Unmarried	....
21[a]	Dishwasher	Unmarried	....
22[a]	Floater	Divorced	....
23	Cafeteria (part time)	Unmarried	....
24[a]	Institutional gardener's assistant	Unmarried	....
25[a]	Institutional inmate	Unmarried	....

[a] Male.
[b] B.A. degree.
[c] Previously had worked as a licensed practical nurse.

Educational and occupational achievement and income [see Table 9] for the 11 adopted subjects in the experimental group compared favorably with the 1960 U.S. Census figures for Iowa and for the United States in general. Their adult status was equivalent to what might have been expected of children living with natural parents in homes of comparable sociocultural levels....

Eleven of the 13 subjects in the experimental group had married, and one of the 11 had been divorced. The spouses came from the same type of middle-class working-class families as the adoptive homes of the experimental subjects, which is indicated by the comparable level of education in each pair and was corroborated during the interviews with parents and subjects.

TABLE 9
EXPERIMENTAL AND CONTRAST GROUPS: COMPARISON OF INCOME WITH EMPLOYED MALES
IN IOWA AND NORTH CENTRAL REGION

	Median Income 1959		Group	
	Iowa[a]	North Central Region[b]	Experimental	Contrast
All males 14 and older	$4,182	$4,525	$4,224[c]	$1,200[c]
White males, 25–34 years	4,782	5,174	4,800[d]	1,200[c]

[a] U.S. Bureau of the Census, 1963b.
[b] U.S. Bureau of the Census, 1963c.
[c] All wage earners.
[d] Males only.

As far as could be observed in the interviews, the marriages gave every indication of stability and permanence. The one divorce was secured by the husband of an experimental subject who alleged that his wife had been unfaithful and neglected the children. Custody of the five children was awarded to him. His wife had spent some time in a facility for delinquent girls during her adolescence.

Nine of the families had children of their own. Making up this second generation at the time of the study were 28 children ranging in age from 1 to 10½ years; 18 were boys and 10, girls.

Arrangements were made for individual intelligence tests to be given these children (Schenke & Skeels, 1965). The Stanford-Binet, form L-M, was given to 22 children, the Stanford-Binet, form L, to one, and the Wechsler Intelligence Scale for Children to 2. The Cattell Infant Intelligence Scale was administered to the three children under 2 years of age.

... The 28 children had a mean IQ of 103.9 and a median of 104. The range of IQ's was from 86 to 125, and no child tested below the dull-normal level. Only about half of the children had reached school age, but among those who had, grade achievement was commensurate with age. ... In no instance was there any indication that a child would have to repeat a grade. While specific achievement scores were not obtained, reports of parents indicated that at least in these early grades, achievement was at levels commensurate with intelligence-test results and sociocultural levels of the homes.

Examiners were impressed by the fact that none of the children showed any sign of abnormality or organic pathology, and, as a group, were attractive and physically well developed. Personality development and adjustment were considered well within the normal range. In one or two instances, there was some evidence of feelings of insecurity or lack of self-confidence.

In the contrast group, only two men of the 11 living subjects had married, Cases 22 and 19. Case 22 had one child, a boy, and subsequently was divorced. He was living in a modest apartment some distance from his family. The boy was examined in the home of his mother at the age of 6 years, 8 months, on the Stanford-Binet, form L-M. An estimated IQ of 66 was obtained. In the examination, the child evidenced signs of possible brain damage of unknown etiology. The mother indicated that she and the boy's father had maintained no permanent address and had traveled about the country a great deal; as a result the child had been cared for by various persons, including the mother's sister and mother, and other persons. The wife stated that her husband had been quite abusive to the boy, frequently striking him during

fits of rage. She attributed the child's retarded physical and mental development to the mistreatment he had received in the past. The mother had remarried, and she indicated that her current husband was kind to the child and showed him much consideration.

Case 19 is the subject that consistently was the exception within the contrast group. He was married, had four children, and maintained a comfortable home in a very attractive middle-class residential area. His four children were physically well developed, of average size for age, and were very attractive and nicely adjusted. The oldest child, a boy 5 years, 11 months of age, was doing satisfactory work in the first grade and had an IQ of 107 on the Stanford-Binet, form L. The three younger children were girls; when tested the 4½-year-old had an IQ of 117 and the 2½-year-old, 119, on form L, and the 9-month-old infant had an IQ of 103 on the Cattell Infant Test.

None of the four girls in the contrast group had married. Two had been sterilized in late adolescence prior to work placement in the community.

In neither experimental nor contrast group was there illegitimacy or indication of serious promiscuity. ...

It would be useful in many kinds of planning if the developmental course of progeny could be predicted. Information about family histories has been seen as providing the basis for such predictions. By inference, educational attainment, vocational success, and general social conformity have been accepted as indications of genetic differences. The unreliability of these indicators can be judged by inspecting, for example, the differences in average educational level between 1930 and 1960, and the differences in educational attainment between contrasting geographic areas of the United States. Delinquency rates, dependence on community agencies, and "general social adequacy" are influenced by many factors other than individual genetic constitution.

Even if the family history data were predictive, the significant items were frequently missing from the case records. The problem of base-line information was further complicated by the fact that 10 of the 13 experimental and 10 of the 12 contrast children were illegitimate. In several instances, in both groups, the identity of the alleged father was speculative. History material on the adopting parents, while not quite as meager, also had omissions, since the adoption agency worker's decision that the petitioners did or did not qualify as adoptive parents was frequently based on a global impression. Such details as school grade completed were likely to be interpreted in the light of the worker's own value system. ...

With the small numbers of cases involved and the

frequency of entries such as "no information" or "unknown," any statistical analysis of these data is not possible. From long experience in evaluating social histories, an inspection of the available information suggests that even if all the missing data were known the total picture for the experimental and contrast groups would not be materially changed.

The sociocultural levels of the biological parents in both the experimental and contrast groups were similar and represented the lower class in American society. Even within this category they represented a lower selection: Many were unemployed, had been known to welfare agencies over the years, or were cited for law infringements.

Adoptive parents of the 11 children in the experimental group could be characterized as coming from the lower middle class. Within this class, in contrast to the biological parents, they represented an upper selection, in that approval for adoptive placement demanded that they be good, solid, substantial citizens in their respective communities and that they be financially capable of supporting a child in the home. The level of these adoptive homes, while representing a marked selection upward in comparison to the natural parents, nevertheless was rated as somewhat below the average level of the adoptive homes in the Skodak-Skeels longitudinal study of 100 adopted children (Skodak, 1939; Skodak & Skeels, 1945; 1949). The selection of relatively modest levels of adoptive homes for the experimental children had been purposeful, and the subsequent development and achievements of the children were similar to or exceeded those that would have been anticipated for natural children in such homes. The question can be raised whether the attainments might have been even higher had the children been placed in homes of higher aspirations and stimulation levels. Conceivably, such placement might have resulted in higher achievement. It is equally possible, on the other hand, that excessive demands and pressures might have resulted in lower achievement.

With such small numbers of subjects and with gaps in information, it is impossible to identify relations between achievement of the subjects and specific characteristics of either the adoptive or natural parents. . . .

The cost to the state for the contrast group, for whom intervention was essentially limited to custodial care, was approximately five times that of the cost for the experimental group. It seems safe to predict that for at least four of the cases in the contrast group costs to the state will continue at a rate in excess of $200.00 per month each for another 20 to 40 years.

IMPLICATIONS OF STUDY

At the beginning of the study, the [13] children in the experimental group evidenced marked mental retardation. The developmental trend was reversed through planned intervention during the experimental period. The program of nurturance and cognitive stimulation was followed by placement in adoptive homes that provided love and affection and normal life experiences. The normal, average intellectual level attained by the subjects in early or middle childhood was maintained into adulthood.

It can be postulated that if the children in the contrast group had been placed in suitable adoptive homes or given some other appropriate equivalent in early infancy, most or all of them would have achieved within the normal range of development, as did the experimental subjects.

It seems obvious that under present-day conditions there are still countless infants born with sound biological constitutions and potentialities for development well within the normal range who will become mentally retarded and noncontributing members of society unless appropriate intervention occurs. It is suggested by the findings of this study and others published in the past 20 years that sufficient knowledge is available to design programs of intervention to counteract the devastating effects of poverty, sociocultural deprivation, and maternal deprivation.

Since the study was a pioneering and descriptive one involving only a small number of cases, it would be presumptuous to attempt to identify the specific influences that produced the changes observed. However, the contrasting outcome between children who experienced enriched environmental opportunities and close emotional relationships with affectionate adults, on the one hand, and those children who were in deprived, indifferent, and unresponsive environments, on the other, leaves little doubt that the area is a fruitful one for further study.

It has become increasingly evident that the prediction of later intelligence cannot be based on the child's first observed developmental status. Account must be taken of his experiences between test and retest. Hunt (1964, p. 212) has succinctly stated that,

. . . In fact, trying to predict what the IQ of an individual child will be at age 18 from a D.Q. obtained during his first or second year is much like trying to predict how fast a feather might fall in a hurricane. The law of falling bodies holds only under the specified and controlled conditions of a vacuum. Similarly, any laws concerning the rate of intellectual growth must take into account the series of environmental encounters which constitute the conditions of that growth.

The divergence in mental-growth patterns between children in the experimental and contrast groups is a striking illustration of this concept.

The right of every child to be well born, well nurtured, well brought up, and well educated was enunciated in the Children's Charter of the 1930 White House Conference on Child Health and Protection (White House Conference, 1931). Though society strives to insure this right, for many years to come there will be children to whom it has been denied and for whom society must provide both intervention and restitution. There is need for further research to determine the optimum modes of such intervention and the most appropriate ages and techniques for initiating them. The present study suggests, but by no means delimits, either the nature of the intervention or the degree of change that can be induced.

The planning of future studies should recognize that the child interacts with his environment and does not merely passively absorb its impact. More precise and significant information on the constitutional, emotional, and response-style characteristics of the child is needed so that those environmental experiences that are most pertinent to his needs can be identified and offered in optimum sequence.

The unanswered questions of this study could form the basis for many lifelong research projects. If the tragic fate of [most of the] contrast-group children provokes even a single crucial study that will help prevent such a fate for others, their lives will not have been in vain.

REFERENCES

DAWE, HELEN C. A study of the effect of an educational program upon language development and related mental functions in young children. *Journal of Experimental Education*, 1942, *11*, 200–209.

HUNT, J. McV. The psychological basis for using preschool enrichment as an antidote for cultural deprivation. *Merrill-Palmer Quarterly of Behavior and Development*, 1964, *10*, 209–248.

KIRK, S. A. *Early education of the mentally retarded.* Chicago: Univer. of Ill. Pr., 1958.

SCHENKE, L. W., & SKEELS, H. M. An adult follow-up of children with inferior social histories placed in adoptive homes in early childhood. Study in Progress, 1965.

SKEELS, H. M. The mental development of children in foster homes. *Pedagogical Seminar & Journal of Genetic Psychology.* 1936, *49*, 91–106.

SKEELS, H. M. Mental development of children in foster homes. *Journal of Consulting Psychology*, 1938, *2*, 33–43.

SKEELS, H. M. Some Iowa studies of the mental growth of children in relation to differentials of the environment: a summary. In *Intelligence: its nature and nurture*. 39th Yearbook, Part II. National Society for the Study of Education, 1940. Pp. 281–308.

SKEELS, H. M. A study of the effects of differential stimulation on mentally retarded children: a follow-up report. *American Journal of Mental Deficiency*, 1942, *46*, 340–350.

SKEELS, H. M., & DYE, H. B. A study of the effects of differential stimulation on mentally retarded children. *Proceedings & Addresses of the American Association on Mental Deficiency*, 1939, *44*, 114–136.

SKEELS, H. M., & FILLMORE, EVA A. The mental development of children from underprivileged homes. *Journal of Genetic Psychology*, 1937, *50*, 427–439.

SKEELS, H. M., UPDEGRAFF, RUTH, WELLMAN, BETH L., & WILLIAMS, H. M. A study of environmental stimulation: an orphanage preschool project. *University of Iowa Studies in Child Welfare*, 1938, *15*, No. 4.

SKODAK, MARIE. Children in foster homes: a study of mental development. *University of Iowa Studies in Child Welfare*, 1939, *16*, No. 1.

SKODAK, MARIE, & SKEELS, H. M. A follow-up study of children in adoptive homes. *Journal of Genetic Psychology*, 1945, *66*, 21–58.

SKODAK, MARIE, & SKEELS, H. M. A final follow-up study of one hundred adopted children. *Journal of Genetic Psychology*, 1949, *75*, 85–125.

WELLMAN, BETH L. Our changing concept of intelligence. *Journal of Consulting Psychology*, 1938, *2*, 97–107.

White House Conference on Child Health and Protection. *Addresses and Abstracts of Committee Reports, 1930.* New York: Appleton-Century, 1931.

15

The Father in Contemporary Culture and Current Psychological Literature *

JOHN NASH

The Effect of Limited Father Absence on Cognitive Development †

F. LANDY, B. G. ROSENBERG,
AND B. SUTTON-SMITH

Having dealt with the effects of mothers or mothering, we now present an article dealing with fatherhood, a topic that psychologists have tended to neglect in the past. The topic of father-absence has become prominent in recent years because of national concern about the plight of fatherless families among the lower class, especially the black lower class, where there are high proportions of fatherless families. The assumption has often been made that boys from homes without fathers are more likely to be delinquent than those from homes where the father is present. In their review of literature on the point, Elizabeth Herzog and Cecelia Sudia found the evidence to be insufficient (Boys in Fatherless Families, Office of Child Development, Children's Bureau, U.S. Department of Health, Education, and Welfare, 1970). Nevertheless, absence of the father (or neglect by him) is likely to have deleterious effects in other ways.

The first paper of this double selection is the summary of an article reviewing our knowledge of the role of the father. The original paper has an extensive bibliography which those interested in pursuing this topic would do well to consult. The author, John Nash, is currently in the Department of Psychology at the University of Hong Kong.

The other paper deals with the effect of partial absence of fathers on the quantitative abilities of their daughters. Rosenberg is a professor of psychology at Bowling Green State University, while Landy is at Pennsylvania State University. Professor Sutton-Smith is at Teachers College, Columbia University.

(The Father in Contemporary Culture and Current Psychological Literature)

The aim of this review is to examine present day thought on the relationships between fathers and their children, and to consider the adequacy of present assumptions.

Much of the scientific literature in this field is sociological rather than psychological in content. While relatively few scientists write about the father, of those that do sociologists and anthropologists form a sizeable proportion. Much of the literature is observational rather than experimental in character and, indeed, experimental studies meeting reasonable standards of methodological sophistication, including such refinements as control groups, are scarce; but this is a difficult area in which to practice sound method. Since the primary aim of this review is to survey the field as it is, some assertions that may or may not stand up to critical examination in the future will be cited....

SUMMARY

From an over-all view of the literature on fathers and their place in child-rearing, it appears that:

1. In the opinion of some sociologists, American society in particular, and probably Western industrial society in general, can be epitomized as "mother-centered" in its philosophy of child care.

2. This is in contrast to certain primitive societies with a family cooperative economy, which have typically a way of child-rearing which em-

* John Nash, "The father in contemporary culture and current psychological literature," *Child Development, 36,* 1965, 261–293. Reprinted with abridgement by permission. Copyright 1965 by The Society for Research in Child Development, Inc.

† F. Landy, B. G. Rosenberg, and B. Sutton-Smith, "The effect of limited father absence on cognitive development," *Child Development,* 1969, *40,* 941–944. Reprinted by permission. © 1969 by The Society for Research in Child Development, Inc.

phasizes father-son and mother-daughter relationships.

3. The difference can be explained by the economic history of our industrial civilization, in which the primitive family cooperative economy has been supplanted by one in which the father is usually the sole support of the family. While engaged in this economic activity, he delegates his place in child-rearing to his wife.

4. Psychologists have adopted this cultural philosophy of child care, perhaps uncritically, and many appear to have assumed that it is both the only and the most desirable pattern of child care. In consequence, the majority of psychologists have not perceived the father as important in child-rearing, and this is reflected in their writings. Some psychologists have adopted the cultural assumption so thoroughly as to ignore the father entirely or even to deny him a position of any significance.

5. This culturally determined concept of child care has further removed the father by enhancing the assumption that the rearing of children is a specifically feminine duty.

6. Clinical studies and investigations of delinquents suggest that father-child relationships, and especially those between father and son, may be of considerable etiological importance to both social and psychological abnormality.

7. Psychosexual difficulties, such as homosexuality, apparently result when a child's major identification is with the parent of the opposite sex. If this is the case, a mother-centered system is peculiarly unsuited to the needs of the boy, for while he is under cultural pressure to act as a male, he is reared predominantly by women from whom he is likely to acquire a feminine pattern.

8. Identification of child with parent is significant in sex-role and psychosexual development, and can be understood in terms of learning theory: warm, affectionate relationships and prolonged associations (in contrast to the veiled hostility of the oepidal theory) are probably among the more vital requirements to successful identifications.

9. Though as yet little understood, critical periods may be found in human development, as they almost certainly are important in the acquisition of some animal behavior.

10. There is some evidence from the few available studies of early paternal deprivation that there is a critical period during which the kind of affectional relationship with the father necessary to identification can be built up. This critical period appears to be early, and has tentatively been described as lasting from the time of weaning to entering school.

11. The role of the peer culture as a factor in

sex-role development has been discussed, and its possible limitations because of its immaturity.

(The Effect of Limited Father Absence on Cognitive Development [1])

In an earlier paper the present authors contrasted the effects of father absence or presence on families of varying sibling composition (Sutton-Smith, Rosenberg, & Landy 1968). It was found that the effects of father absence varied with the size of the family and the sibling composition. While contrasts were made between the lengths of the fathers' absences and the children's ages at the time they were absent, no further examination of the character of that "absence" was presented. In the study that follows, the "absence" variable is further explored through an analysis of the effects of father shift work on children's performances. It is proposed that, when a man works on the night shift for long periods of time, his children will manifest behavioral patterns similar to those discovered in families where the father has been totally absent for a number of years, but to a lesser degree, since limited father absence is expected to have a less profound effect.

The dependent variable in this, as in the previous study, was performance on a college-entrance test, and the prediction derived from that previous study was that girls whose fathers were on shift work for long periods when the girls were between the ages of 5 and 10 years would show a depressed performance on tests of quantitative ability.

METHOD

The sample was composed of female students enrolled in a developmental psychology course who were predominantly sophomores with a median age of 19 years.

The Ss were categorized into five groups on two related dimensions of father absence: (1) the *period* in the S's life when the father worked the night shift—consecutively, no night-shift work, night shift from ages birth to 4 years, 5–9, 10 or older, and a final group whose fathers had been totally absent from the home for 10 or more years; (2) the absolute *number* of years that a father worked on the night shift—consecutively, no night-shift work, 1–5 years, 6–10 years, 11 or more years, and again a total father-absent group. It was necessary to use two different year-grouping criteria for the two absence dimensions in order to insure sufficient cell sizes. The first and last groups of each dimension were included to

[1] This study was assisted in part by grant MH 07994–05 from the National Institute of Mental Health.

provide limits within which the influence of shift work should fall. There were 20 Ss in each group. The night shift was defined as 8 consecutive hours of work with the major portion of the time falling between the hours of 8:00 P.M. and 8:00 A.M. All night-shift jobs as well as father-present jobs were of a manual nature, in an attempt to minimize socioeconomic differences between groups. Manual work was defined as factory work below the level of foreman. Forms were sent home to the father of each S to check on the accuracy of the S's report of length of absence and period of absence. The correlation coefficient between the number of years absent as reported by the subject and that reported by her father was +.98. The product-moment coefficient calculated to determine the agreement in relation to the reported period of absence was +.92.

The American College Entrance Examination (ACE) scores (Berdie, Dressel, & Kelson 1951) taken by all entering freshmen at the university were obtained from the University Counseling Center. Only the Q (quantitative) scores on the ACE were presented in the present study. For statistical purposes, all ACE scores (reported in percentiles) were converted to standard scores, and t tests were employed in the analysis. Nevertheless, median scores are also presented in the tables, as they communicate more directly than do standard scores.

RESULTS

Table 1 presents median ACE Q scores for the entire sample on the dimension of number of years of father absence. A simple analysis of variance to examine the effect of number of years of father absence (shift work) on Q scores proved to be significant ($F = 3.00$, df 4/95, $p < .05$). Multiple comparisons were undertaken employing the Newman-Keuls method (Winer 1962). The only significant difference found was between the father-present group and the total father-absent group ($p < .01$); although, directionally, scores on Q tend to decrease with the degree of father absence.

Table 2 presents median ACE Q scores for the entire sample on the dimension of age of S when father was

absent. A simple analysis of variance to examine the effect of age of S when father was absent on Q scores yielded significance ($F = 3.18$, df 4/95, $p < .05$). Further analysis by Newman-Keuls revealed that, in addition to a father-present–total father-absent difference, total father-absent girls obtained significantly lower Q scores than girls whose fathers worked the night shift after they had reached the age of 10 ($p < .05$). Again, the trend for the shift-work groups indicates that the later in life father was absent on shift work, the less on Q scores.

In order to assess whether any trends were evident in the linguistic (L) portion of the ACE, a median test of the L scores was performed on the dimensions of length of father absence and period of father absence. The χ^2 values derived from both of these tests yielded probability statements in excess of .30, indicating no systematic relations between either length or period of father absence and linguistic ability.

DISCUSSION

Even though the overall F was significant for the absolute number of years of shift work, this can be accounted for almost entirely by the difference between the total father-absent group and the father-present group. The fact that the predicted depressant effect was found only in the extreme father-absent group suggests that the degree of partial father-absence becomes a relevant variable only as it approaches its upper limits.

More interesting findings emerge when Q scores are considered in terms of the *period* of father absence. The Ss whose father had worked the night shift after they had reached the age of 10 had significantly higher Q scores than the total father-absent group. This finding, coupled with the lack of difference between the total father-absent group and the 0–4 and 5–9 groups, would seem to indicate that the years from 1 to 9 compose a critical

TABLE 1
SUMMARY SCORES ON ACE FOR LENGTH OF FATHER ABSENCE

	Father Present	1–5	6–10	11+	Father Absent
ACE median scores	78.00	62.00	58.00	51.00	43.00
Z Scores	0.67	0.38	0.36	0.10	−0.12

NOTE.—$N = 20$ per category.

TABLE 2
SUMMARY SCORES ON THE ACE FOR PERIOD OF FATHER ABSENCE

	Father Present	1–4	5–9	10+	Father Absent
ACE median scores	78.00	55.00	62.00	70.00	43.00
Z Scores	0.67	0.30	0.40	0.65	−0.12

NOTE.—$N = 20$ per category.

period for the development of quantitative skills in girls, a finding also demonstrated in a previous study (Sutton-Smith et al. 1968). Thus, the important dimension to be considered in the relation of partial father absence to cognitive abilities would seem to be the period of absence.

The results of the present study show that it is feasible to treat long-term night-shift work by the father on a father-presence-absence continuum. Furthermore, as fathers who are completely absent have similar effects to fathers who are partially absent when girls are under the age of 9 years, then it is possible to define *absence* in a slightly more refined way than was previously the case. It seems now less likely that the various absence effects described in the earlier article were due to the compensatory behavior of the mother without a husband. It appears more likely that the absence effects are due simply to the decreased amount of interaction between father and child.

References

Berdie, R.; Dressel, K.; & Kelson, P. Relative validity of the *Q* and *L* scores on the ACE Psychological Examination. *Educational and Psychological Measurement,* 1951, *11,* 803–812.

Sutton-Smith, B.; Rosenberg, B. G.; & Landy, F. Father absence effects on cognitive ability in families of different sibling composition. *Child Development,* 1968, *39,* 1213–1222.

Winer, B., *Statistical principles in experimental design.* New York: McGraw-Hill, 1962.

16

Authoritarian vs. Authoritative Parental Control[1]

DIANA BAUMRIND

In this paper, Diana Baumrind of the University of California at Berkeley summarizes her work about parents' approaches to the discipline of their children. She discusses whether permissiveness is the only alternative to authoritarianism, bringing in the relevant views of such workers as Montessori, Piaget, and A. S. Neill, the author of Summerhill. *The final portions of the paper deal with the special problems of parental control of adolescents. Here she acknowledges the dilemma that confronts today's youth.*

Social protest against our political institutions, national policy, and cultural mores is so vigorous in its expression, and fundamental in its rejection of constituted authority, that it should provoke a thoughtful inquiry not only into the issues raised, but also into the conditions which legitimate authority and into those which render authority illegitimate or ineffectual.

Three years ago I wrote an article entitled *Effects of Authoritative Parental Control on Child Behavior* (2). In that article I contrasted three modes of parental control—permissive, authoritarian, and authoritative—in order to show that relevant arguments against the use of authoritarian parental control did not apply to authoritative parental control. I shall repeat some of those arguments because I think that they are still cogent.

However, the analysis which I made at that time is most relevant to what Dubin and Dubin (5) call the Authority Inception Period which ends at about 6 years. It deals very little with the conditions which legitimate authority in late childhood and adolescence, a matter of considerable social importance today. I will use the feminine gender to refer to the parent and the masculine gender to refer to the child.

There are a number of arguments[2] against the use of certain disciplinary techniques which are made in support of permissive childrearing which I would like to discuss briefly after defining the *permissive parent.*

As I understand the values of the permissive parent, she attempts to behave in a nonpunitive, acceptant, and affirmative manner toward the child's impulse, desires, and actions. She consults with him about policy decisions and gives explanations for family rules. She makes few demands for household responsibility and orderly behavior. She presents herself to the child as a resource for him to use as he wishes, not as an active agent responsible for shaping or altering his ongoing or future behavior. She allows the child to regulate his own activities as much as possible, avoids the exercise of control, and does not encourage him to obey externally defined standards. She attempts to use reason but not overt power to accomplish her ends.

The alternative to adult control, according to Neill, is to permit the child to be self-regulated, free of restraint, and unconcerned about expression of impulse or the effects of his carelessness.

To quote Neill:

Self-regulation means the right of a baby to live freely, without outside authority in things psychic and somatic. It means that the baby feeds when it is hungry; that it becomes clean in habits only when it wants to; that it is never stormed at nor spanked; that it is always loved and protected (14, p. 105, italics Neill's).

I believe that to impose anything by authority is wrong. The child should not do anything until he comes to the opinion—that it should be done (14, p. 114, italics Neill's).

Every child has the right to wear clothes of such a kind that it does not matter a brass farthing if they get messy or not (14, p. 115).

[1] This is a revised version of a talk delivered at San Jose State College Workshop, Conflict and Adolescence, June 21, 1968, San Jose, Calif. This talk was in part supported by research grant HD0228 from the National Institute of Child Health and Development.

[2] For a more detailed treatment of the validity of such arguments, see (2).

Diana Baumrind, "Authoritarian versus authoritative parental control," *Adolescence, 3,* 1968, 255–272. Reprinted by permission.

110

Furniture to a child is practically nonexistent. So at Summerhill we buy old car seats and old bus seats. And in a month or two they look like wrecks. Every now and again at mealtime, some youngster waiting for his second helping will while away the time by twisting his fork almost into knots (14, p. 138).

Really, any man or woman who tries to give children freedom should be a millionaire, for it is not fair that the natural carelessness of children should always be in conflict with the economic factor (14, p. 139).

Arguments given against the use of certain disciplinary techniques:

1. It has been argued by clinically trained advocates of permissive childrearing, such as Lawrence Frank (7) or the early Spock, that *punishment has inevitable negative side effects, and is an ineffective means of controlling behavior.* However, the experimental or clinical evidence for this contention is by no means convincing. Clinical studies have tended to confuse punitive, rejecting attitudes in parents with the effects of punishment *per se* and to attribute the known negative effects of punitive and rejecting attitudes to the use of aversive stimuli, i.e., punishment, as well. Severe, unjust, and ill-timed punishment administered by an unloving parent is probably harmful as well as ineffective. However, there are some theoretical grounds to suppose that the milder forms of punishment, unlike traumatic rejection or beatings may have, like other forthright uses of power, beneficial side effects, such as the following:

a. more rapid re-establishment of affectional involvement on both sides following emotional release;
b. high resistance to similar deviation by siblings who vicariously experience punishment;
c. emulation of the aggressive parent resulting in prosocial assertive behavior;
d. lessening of guilt reactions to transgression; and
e. an increased ability of the child to endure punishment in the service of a desired end.

In addition, the proposition that punishment is an *ineffective* means of controlling human behavior may indeed be a "legend" as Solomon (20) and Walters, Parke, & Crane (21) suggest. Under conditions prevailing in the home setting, punishment may be quite effective in helping to accomplish particular objectives.

2. Another argument against the exercise of parental control is *that close supervision, high demands, and other manifestations of parental authority provoke rebelliousness* in children.

In fact, Bandura and Walters (1), Glueck and Glueck (9), and McCord, McCord, and Howard (12) found that higher demands were made by the parents of the least hostile or delinquent children. Finney (6) found that, while parental rigidity was associated with covert hostility in children, firm control was associated with conscience development.

In my own study of middle class parents of preschool children (3, 4), those parents who demanded that their children be orderly and assume household responsibilities provided more enriched and orderly surroundings, and involved themselves more conscientiously with their welfare. Perhaps that is why such demands were viewed by the child as reasonable, and did not tend to provoke rebellion.

A distinction must be made between the effects on the child of unjust, restrictive, subjective authority, when compared to rational, warm, and issue-oriented authority. There is considerable evidence that arbitrary authority but not rational authority is associated in the child with negative affect, disaffiliativeness, and rebelliousness.

3. A third argument against the imposition of authority is that *firm parental control generates passivity and dependence.* However, Hoffman's (11) results indicate that parental assertiveness, and submissiveness in the child are negatively correlated. Sears' (18) findings on early socialization and later aggression suggest that high punishment for aggression, like "reactive unqualified power assertion," does not lead to submissive behavior. My own results were that parents of the most self-reliant and approach-oriented group of children were rated highest in firm control and reactive power assertion.

4. It has been argued in support of permissive childrearing that *permissiveness frees the child from the presence and authority of the parent.* However, rather than having no effect upon him, the noninterference of an adult who is present when the child is misbehaving seems to signify approval of his behavior, not neutrality, and actually tends to increase rather than leave unaffected the incidence of that behavior. For example, Siegel and Kohn (19) demonstrated that the presence of a permissive adult increased the incidence of aggression shown by nursery school boys to somewhat younger boys. To quote Siegel and Kohn:

Two-thirds of the *S*s in the adult-present sessions were more aggressive in the second than in the first session, and all the *S*s in the adult-absent sessions were less aggressive in the second than in the first session. This finding is in confirmation of the hypothesis which was drawn from a consideration of the nature and the effects of adult permissiveness with children, and of the nature of young children's controls for aggression (19, pp. 140–141).

5. It has also been argued that *controlling parents are motivated by the Authoritarian Personal-*

ity Syndrome. Fromm used the term authoritarian personality to refer to the syndrome in which enactment of the role of inhibiting authority characterizes the individual's interpersonal relations in order to defensively protect a weak ego from any possible assault.

While parents motivated by the authoritarian personality syndrome are controlling, it does not follow that the converse is true. Some subgroups of controlling parents permit high autonomy in many areas of the child's life. Lois Hoffman et al. (10) described a subgroup of parents who were perceived by their children as both coercive and permissive of high autonomy.

I found that, whereas the parents of relatively alienated pre-school children tended to use inhibiting control, the parents of exceptionally mature children exerted even firmer control, used reason to explain their directives, and encouraged independent expression. This latter group of parents certainly did not exhibit the authoritarian personality syndrome. They were open and receptive although highly authoritative in their requirement for compliance. Thus, several investigators have identified subgroups of controlling parents who are not restrictive of children's autonomy or motivated by the authoritarian personality syndrome and have shown that children react differently to inhibiting and rational control.

It seems likely that:

Authoritarian control and permissive noncontrol may both shield the child from the opportunity to engage in vigorous interaction with people. Demands which cannot be met or no demands, suppression of conflict or sidestepping of conflict, refusal to help or too much help, unrealistically high or low standards, all may curb or understimulate the child so that he fails to achieve the knowledge and experience which could realistically reduce his dependence upon the outside world. The authoritarian and the permissive parent may both create, in different ways, a climate in which the child is not desensitized to the anxiety associated with nonconformity. Both models minimize dissent, the former by suppression and the latter by diversion or indulgence. To learn how to dissent, the child may need a strongly held position from which to diverge and then be allowed under some circumstances to pay the price for nonconformity by being punished. Spirited give and take within the home, if accompanied by respect and warmth, may teach the child how to express aggression in self-serving and prosocial causes and to accept the partially unpleasant consequences of such actions (2, p. 904).

AUTHORITARIAN VS. AUTHORITATIVE

I would like to *contrast the prototype authoritarian parent with the prototype authoritative parent.*

The *authoritarian parent* as she is generally described in the literature attempts to shape, control,

and evaluate the behavior and attitudes of the child in accordance with a set standard of conduct, usually an absolute standard, theologically motivated and formulated by a higher authority. She values obedience as a virtue and favors punitive, forceful measures to curb self-will at points where the child's actions or beliefs conflict with what she thinks is right conduct. She believes in inculcating such instrumental values as respect of authority, respect for work and respect for the preservation of order and traditional structure. She does not encourage verbal give or take, believing that the child should accept her word for what is right.

The *authoritative parent* as she appears in my studies also attempts to direct the child's activities but in a rational, issue-oriented manner. She encourages verbal give and take, and shares with the child the reasoning behind her policy. She values both expressive and instrumental attributes, both autonomous self-will and disciplined conformity. Therefore, she exerts firm control at points of parent-child divergence, but does not hem the child in with restrictions. She recognizes her own special rights as an adult, but also the child's individual interests and special ways. The authoritative parent affirms the child's present qualities, but also sets standards for future conduct. She uses reason as well as power to achieve her objectives. She does not base her decisions on group consensus or the individual child's desires; but also, does not regard herself as infallible or divinely inspired.

Some quotations from Rambusch, in describing the Montessori method, illustrate the way in which authoritative control is used to resolve the antithesis between pleasure and duty, and between freedom and responsibility.

The discipline resides in three areas in a Montessori classroom: It resides in the environment itself which is controlled; in the teacher herself who is controlled and is ready to assume an authoritarian role if it is necessary; and from the very beginning it resides in the children. It is a three-way arrangement, as opposed to certain types of American education in which all of the authority is vested in the teacher, or where, in the caricature of permissive education, all of the authority is vested in the children.

When a child has finished his work he is free to put it away, he is free to initiate new work or, in certain instances, he is free to not work. But he is not free to disturb or destroy what others are doing. If the day is arranged in such a way that at a certain time the teacher must demand of the children that they arbitrarily finish what they are doing—if it is lunchtime, or recess or whatever—the child must accommodate himself to the demand of the group. It is largely a question of balance. In a Montessori class the teacher does not delude herself into believing that her manipulation of the children represents their consensus of what they would like to do. If she is manipulating them insofar as she is determining arbitrarily that this must be done at this time, she is cognizant of what she is doing, which the child may or may not be.

The importance of the responsibility in selecting matter for the child to learn is placed in the hands of those adults who are aware of what the culture will demand of the child and who are able to "program" learning in such a way that what is suitable for the child's age and stage of development is also learnable and pleasurable to him. Both Dewey and Montessori feel that interest and discipline are connected and not opposed. Dewey himself decried unrestrained freedom of action in speech, in manners, and lack of manners. He was, in fact, critical of all those progressive schools that carried the thing they call freedom nearly to the point of anarchy (17, p. 63).

The body of findings which I reviewed in the article cited, and certainly the results of my own research, support the position that authoritative control can achieve responsible conformity with group standards without loss of individual autonomy or self-assertiveness.

As Dubin and Dubin (5) point out, by the imposition of parental authority, the child in his first six years learns to express his social individuality, within the confines of what the culture will accept. He finds that there are ranges of acceptable behavior in most situations of action. By having orderly experiences with available behavioral choices, the child learns to distinguish between conforming and deviant behavior. Later when he is capable of moral judgments, he may choose to engage in deviant behavior, but he will do so prepared to endure the punishment which may follow. Hopefully he will have learned the value to him of authoritative behavior and know how to play the role behavior which is reciprocal. He will also have had his parent as a model for the role of a rational authority, a role he can himself assume at a later age.

Use of Power in Childhood and Adolescence

I believe then that the imposition of authority even against the child's will is useful to the child during the Authority Inception Period. During those early years exercise of power is a legitimate right of the parents. Indeed, power serves to legitimate authority in the mind of the child.

During childhood, power is asymmetrical in the family unit. That is, the parent's ability to exercise control over the child and to restrict his autonomy exceeds that of the child, in reciprocal interaction with his parent. The parent by virtue of her physical size, experience, and control over the sources of supply can, in most instances where there is a divergence, carry out her wishes despite the re-

sistance of the child, and the child cannot do likewise. Parents vary of course in the extent to which they acknowledge the asymmetry of their power, or are effectively able to use power.

The major way in which parents exercise power is by manipulating the stimuli which affect the child —rewarding with positive reinforcers and punishing with aversive stimuli. The main factor which makes a parent a successful reinforcing agent or an attractive model for her child to imitate is her effective power to give the child what he needs— i.e., her control over resources which the child desires, and her willingness and ability to provide the child with these resources in such a manner and at such a time that the child will be most gratified. Both morally and practically, gratification of the child's needs is a precondition for the effective imposition of parental authority.

Piaget's analysis of the development of the idea of justice (15) suggests that the child's organization of a moral order is based upon power in the early years. In the mind of the young child, power legitimates the parent's right to exercise authority. The parent's ability to gratify the child and to withhold gratification legitimates her authority. The child has not yet reached the level of cognitive development where he can legitimate authority, or object to its imposition, on a principled basis.

The parent can accelerate the child's cognitive development both by requiring the child to accommodate at the top limit of his ability to do so, and by using reason to support her directives. Even though the specific reason may not be understood by the child, he learns that authority must ultimately be legitimated on a principled basis. By using reason, the authoritative parent teaches the child to seek the reasons behind directives and eventually to exercise his option either to conform, or to deviate and to cope with the consequences. Reason does not really legitimate authority for the young child, in the same way as power does, or in the same way as it will at adolescence.

Punishment has an informational role for the parent and the child. By setting a price on negatively sanctioned behavior, both the parent and the child can determine how important it is to the child that he perform an act which he knows will be punished at a given level of intensity. When a child repeats an act knowingly for which he has been punished moderately severely, the parent has grounds to question the legitimacy of her rejection of that act. Punishment and other manifestations of power then are an important part of the feedback which advance the parent's understanding of the child and his level of cognitive and moral development.

By early adolescence, however, power cannot

and should not be used to legitimate authority. The young person is now capable of formal operational thought. He can formulate principles of choice by which to judge his own actions and the actions of others. He has the conceptual ability to be critical even though he may lack the wisdom to moderate his criticism. He can see clearly many alternatives to parental directives; and the parent must be prepared to defend rationally, as she would to an adult, a directive with which the adolescent disagrees. Moreover, the asymmetry of power which characterizes childhood no longer exists at adolescence. The adolescent cannot be forced physically to obey over any period of time.

When a young child refuses to obey, his parent can persist until he does obey, giving him a reason based upon a principle which he may not understand, or a reason based upon the asymmetry of power, which he is sure to understand. She can say, "you must do it because I say so;" and the child will accept such a parental maneuver as legitimate even if he continues to have objections on hedonistic grounds, because he is not yet capable of principled objections.

An adolescent, on the other hand, is capable of principled objections. When an adolescent refuses to do as his parent wishes, it is more congruent with his construction of reality for the parent simply to ask him "Why not?" Through the dialogue which ensues, the parent may learn that her directive was unjust; or the adolescent may learn that his parent's directive could be legitimated. In any case, a head-on confrontation is avoided. While head-on confrontation serves to strengthen authority in the Authority Inception Period, it undermines authority during adolescence.

This does not mean that the parent relinquishes her authoritative role. It does mean that she enacts her role in a different way, one suited to the level of development of the older child. She makes limited use of power to settle parent-child divergences, and then primarily to guard her personal interests or to break a stalemate when the adolescent's objection is based, not on principle, but on pique. The adolescent can understand and be held to a contractual agreement. The adolescent, egocentric as he is, can recognize the egocentric needs of parents. More often than is admitted, a parent-child divergence involves a simple conflict of interests. The parent requires quiet and the young person wants to play loud music; if the adolescent were to come in late, his parent would lose sleep; if the working parent is to rest after dinner, the children must do the dishes. Children recognize the legitimacy of demands based on personal rights, provided that parents represent the matter as it is, and the balance of giving is well in favor of the children,

as indeed it must be if parents are to have any special rights.

The authority of the parent at adolescence stands or falls on the parent's past performance, and what she is at present, in relation to what the adolescent needs her to be. The adolescent needs a parent who has something to say that is worth listening to, and who is fully receptive to what he has to say. The adolescent needs to have someone to argue with in order to develop his own position. His parents can play this role of friendly adversary. The adolescent needs a strongly stated thesis to relate his own thinking to. A convincing antithesis requires a well-formulated thesis. The authoritative parent can state and defend her own thesis vigorously, and yet not limit the freedom of the adolescent to express and argue for his antithesis. The parent must not expect the resultant synthesis to be merely a restatement of her own thesis. By receiving the antithesis presented to her by her adolescent, the parent gains knowledge of that with which she is authorized to deal.

Receptivity does not mean listening in order to achieve conformity after talk. It does mean that an antithetical position which may threaten the stability of the system is encouraged to interact with that system. Only in that way can the system continue to perform its function. A system which cannot absorb dissent cannot survive. Revolutionary fervor is nourished by the refusal of constituted authority to receive antithesis, to be renewed by dissent. If constituted authority were as successful in absorbing dissent as Marcuse thinks it is, there would be no basis for the revolutionary fervor he advocates.

Under normal conditions, adolescents do not rebel against all authority by any means. They differentiate quite accurately between authoritarian and authoritative parental control. Pikas (16), in his survey of 656 Swedish adolescents, showed that significant differences occurred in their acceptance of parental authority, depending upon the reason for the directive. Authority which was based on rational concern for the child's welfare was accepted well by the child, while authority which was based on the adult's desire to dominate or exploit the child was rejected. The former, which he calls rational authority, is similar to "authoritative control," and the latter, which he calls inhibiting authority, is similar to "authoritarian control," as these terms are used in this discussion. Pikas' results are supported by Middleton and Snell (13) who found that parental discipline regarded by the child as either very strict or very permissive was associated with lack of closeness between parent and child and with rebellion against the parents' political viewpoints.

THE MAJOR CHALLENGE TO AUTHORITY TODAY

The major challenge to authority today is not that the young have no respect for authority, but that they have little reason to have respect for authority. Both youth and their parents are disaffected with their social institutions—with their schools, churches and their government. The mythology of affluence has been exploded. The credibility gap on issues of poverty and war has made extension of trust unfeasible, and open rebellion morally feasible. It is very difficult today for constituted authorities, even rational authorities, to have respect for themselves. Rational authorities have cause to question the legitimacy of their authority. Until relatively recently, parents could believe that by maintaining order within the family, they were upholding a higher order to which they too submitted —this higher order was defined by religious mandate, cultural tradition, or national way. Think of the basis upon which Susannah Wesley, mother of the founder of Methodism, legitimated her authority in the 18th century. These are her words:

As self-will is the root of all sin and misery, so whatever cherishes this in children insures their after-wretchedness and irreligion; whatever checks and mortifies it promotes their future happiness and piety. This is still more evident, if we further consider, that religion is nothing else than doing the will of God, and not our own: that the one grand impediment to our temporal and eternal happiness being this self-will, no indulgences of it can be trivial, no denial unprofitable. Heaven or hell depends on this alone. So that the parent who studies to subdue it in his child, works together with God in the renewing and saving a soul. The parent who indulges it does the devil's work, makes religion impracticable, salvation unattainable; and does all that in him lies to damn his child, soul and body forever (8, pp. 30–31).

Since the impediment to temporal and eternal happiness was thought to be self-will, the parent behaved in authoritarian ways because she cared for the child, not because she was weak or punitive.

While Mrs. Wesley believed that the mores of her society were divinely inspired, many parents not only know these mores are not divinely inspired, but find them in no sense inspirational. Concerning our social structure, many parents agree with their adolescents, when they in the words of Mario Savio find the operation of the machines so odious and vile as to require of them that they put their bodies on the gears and upon the wheels and upon the levers to prevent these wheels from working at all. To be more specific, these parents share the moral outrage of their adolescents at the atrocities of the Vietnam war, and the gross inequities in distribution of wealth in this country. Maintenance of structure and order is high in the hierarchy of values of authoritative parents, as we have defined these parents. What are they to do, they ask, when maintenance of structure and order conflicts with a higher value, such as killing to no just purpose. These parents feel responsible for the sins of their generation, and their faith in their own expertness is shaken. Their faith in the value of obedience, and in the possibility of constructive nonconformity is shaken. We have said that authoritative control can achieve responsible conformity with group standards without loss of individual autonomy and self-assertiveness. Conformity with group standards, if this means support of the Vietnam war, does not seem responsible to many parents today. How are they to rear their children to conform responsibly if they do not believe that it is responsible to conform? How are they to rear their children to constructively dissent if they do not believe that constructive dissent will be received by constituted authority?

In summary, I examined the criticisms directed by advocates of permissiveness against parental control and showed that to the extent that these criticisms were valid, in early childhood they were relevant to authoritarian control and not authoritative control. I contrasted the conditions and processes which legitimate authority in childhood with those which legitimate authority in adolescence. In particular, I argued that the imposition of authority by use of power is legitimate in childhood and not in adolescence, because the level of cognitive and moral development of the adolescent is such as to require that he be bound by social contract and moral principles rather than by power. Lastly, I discussed what I felt to be the fundamental challenge to authority today.

In closing, I would like to say that an increasingly larger segment of today's youth are rejecting the alternatives offered by established authority, not because they are rebellious neurotics, but because these alternatives are not morally acceptable. If their dissent is not received, and the system to which they object is not radically altered, we who are in a position of authority can expect to be confronted with what Marcuse calls the Great Refusal. We will be faced with an absolute rejection of the society and its institutions by many of our brightest and most competent youth. That absolute rejection will negate the distinction between rational and arbitrary authority, between authoritative and authoritarian adult control. If we cannot fully receive the message from the most dissenting of our youth, we may be faced with the complete withdrawal of legitimacy from rational as well as arbitrary authority by the very youth upon whom we count for cultural continuity.

REFERENCES

1. BANDURA, A., & WALTERS, R. H. *Adolescent Aggression.* New York: Ronald, 1959.
2. BAUMRIND, D. "Effects of Authoritative Parental Control on Child Behavior," *Child Development,* 1966, *37-4,* 887–907.
3. BAUMRIND, D. "Child Care Practices Anteceding Three Patterns of Preschool Behavior," *Genetic Psychology Monographs,* 1967, *75,* 43–88.
4. BAUMRIND, D., & BLACK, A. E. "Socialization Practices Associated with Dimensions of Competence in Preschool Boys and Girls," *Child Development,* 1967, *38-2,* 291–327.
5. DUBIN, E. R., & DUBIN, R. "The Authority Inception Period in Socialization," *Child Development,* 1964, *34,* 885–898.
6. FINNEY, J. C. "Some Maternal Influences on Children's Personality and Character," *Genetic Psychology Monographs,* 1961, *63,* 199–278.
7. FRANK, L. K. "Freedom for the Personality." *Psychiatry,* 140, *3,* 341–349.
8. GESELL, A. *The Guidance of Mental Growth in Infant and Child,* New York: Macmillan, 1930.
9. GLUECK, S., & GLUECK, E. *Unraveling Juvenile Delinquency.* New York: Commonwealth Fund, 1950.
10. HOFFMAN, L. ROSEN, S., & LIPPITT, R. "Parental Coerciveness, Child Autonomy, and Child's Role at School," *Sociometry,* 1960, *23,* 15–22.
11. HOFFMAN, M. L. "Power Assertion by The Parent and Its Impact on the Child," *Child Development,* 1960, *31,* 129–143.
12. MCCORD, J., & HOWARD, A. "Familial Correlates of Aggression in Non-delinquent Male Children," *J. Abnorm. Soc. Psychol.,* 1961, *62,* 79–93.
13. MIDDLETON, R., & SNELL, P. "Political Expression of Adolescent Rebellion," *Amer. J. Sociol.,* 1963, *68,* 527–535.
14. NEILL, A. S. *Summerhill.* New York: Hart, 1964.
15. PIAGET, J. *The Moral Judgment of the Child.* New York: Free Press, 1965.
16. PIKAS, A. "Children's Attitudes Toward Rational Versus Inhibiting Parental Authority," *J. Abnorm. Soc. Psychol.,* 1961, *62,* 315–321.
17. RAMBUSCH, N. M. *Learning How to Learn: An American Approach to Montessori.* Baltimore: Helicon, 1962.
18. SEARS, R. R. "Relation of Early Socialization Experiences to Aggression in Middle Childhood," *J. Abnorm. Soc. Psychol.,* 1961, *63,* 466–492.
19. SIEGEL, A. E., & KOHN, L. G. "Permissiveness, Permission, and Aggression: The Effects of Adult Presence or Absence on Aggression in Children's Play," *Child Development,* 1959, *30,* 131–141.
20. SOLOMON, R. L. "Punishment," *Amer. Psychologist,* 1964, *19,* 239–253.
21. WALTERS, R. H., PARKE, R. D., & CANE, V. A. "Timing of Punishment and Observation of Consequences to Others as Determinants of Response Inhibition," *J. Exp. Child Psychol.,* 1965, *2,* 10–30.

17

The Socialization of Aggression

Robert R. Sears,
Eleanor E. Maccoby,
and Harry Levin

This is a report of the ways in which parents deal with children's aggressiveness. It is taken from a study done at the Harvard Laboratory of Human Development when all three authors were there and Sears was the director of the Laboratory. Sears later became head of Stanford University's Psychology Department and then Dean of its School of Humanities and Science. Maccoby too is a psychology professor at Stanford. Harry Levin is chairman of the Department of Psychology at Cornell University.

The type of investigation reported here has frequently been criticized because it relies on mothers' memories and their self-reports. Such criticism is vitiated by the success of studies that have reported consistent findings about the same children in later years. Thus, the child-rearing data obtained through the mother interviews continues to have predictive value with respect to the behavior of the offspring. Confidence in the data is also bolstered by the theoretical sense the findings make. Nevertheless, retrospective reports are recognized as a fallible source of data, as Sears, Maccoby, and Levin would agree.

An even more basic question is raised by all correlational research of this type. One can never interpret the direction of cause and effect with assurance. The introduction to the next paper comments further on this topic.

Aggression, as the term is commonly used, means behavior that is intended to hurt or injure someone. Most human adults have quite a repertory of acts that fit this definition. Some of these are bold and violent, others sly and attenuated. Some are accompanied by rage or annoyance; others are done coldly and seemingly, to the perpetrator, without emotion. The complexity and subtlety of adult aggression is the end product of two or three decades of socialization by the individual's parents and peers, however, and bears little resemblance to the primitive quality of the infant's action patterns, from which it developed.

To understand the problem of aggression in child rearing, one does well to remind himself firmly that man is a mammal, and that there are certain kinds of behavior which characterize all mammals. The two that are most relevant to the problem of aggression are *fighting* and the *expression of rage*.

From the lowest quadruped to the highest biped, physical attack is used for defense. Techniques vary, depending on the sharpness of hooves, the strength of jaws, and the presence of specialized weapons like antlers. Man, being the most intelligent and inventive of all, makes use of many of the other species' techniques and adds a host of new ones that, happily, no other animal has ever dreamed of. He can bite like a dog, claw like a cat, kick like a stallion, trade insults like a howling monkey, squeeze like a gorilla; and he constructs his own clubs, blow-pipes, knives, and guns to make up for his lack of antlers and horns. The evolutionary continuity becomes crystal clear in any TV wrestling match.

In spite of this ingenuity, however, physical fighting is not the commonest form of human aggression. *Injury* is a broad term, and the socialization process develops many motives that can be thwarted. Interference with any of these motives causes pain or anguish, and if this was the intention, the interfering act was truly aggressive.

Defensive fighting is usually accompanied by expressions of rage. The older child or adult, who can report his feelings, may recognize his desire to hurt, and be very aware of his angry emotion. But this quality of aggression is attenuated, too, in the process of socialization, and there are many forms of hurt that an adult inflicts with little emotional arousal.

In a civilized society adults are rarely beaten or knifed or lashed. More often, they are hurt by attacks on their pride or status, their desire for social approval, or their feelings of affection for their families and friends. These kinds of hurt can be far more serious and more prolonged than most physical hurts. The withholding of affection by a loved spouse, for example, can have the meaning of pain that goes far beyond that from broken legs or crushed fingers. Nor do injuries that come through sheer accident, the vagaries of nature, hurt like injuries to self-esteem. Contrast them with the gratuitous insult from an admired and intimate friend, or the malicious gossip that one is "slipping" at his job, or the suggestion by a neighbor that one has been a failure in child rearing, or the rejection of a young girl seeking membership in a college sorority. And it is a strong and seasoned old man who can recall without pain his first failure as a lover—and his mistress's amusement.

Not all injuries are so great as these, of course. There are tongue-lashings that do not hurt—much —and insults that are shrugged off. There are the little obstinacies in one's friends, and the noncooperative indifferences of one's working associates. There are the irritants of family living—a tired and sassy child, a grumpy and complaining husband, a daughter who dawdles. Since all these cause discomfort, they can be forms of aggression. Whether they are in fact, however, depends on whether the discomfort they engender was *designed* by the perpetrator to hurt someone else.

Not all acts that hurt are intended to do so. Even sophisticated and sensitive adults sometimes fail to anticipate the effects of what they do. The unanswered letter can seem a slight; the unasked question can be interpreted as indifference. With children, the problem is especially noticeable in the manipulation of physical forces. A child's innocently swinging stick only too easily turns into a painful club, the experimental bombing into a brother's broken toys.

Since these hurts are obviously unintentional, they do not qualify as *aggression* in the technical sense of the word. There are certain borderline examples, however, that are hard to be sure about. There are acts that sometimes are and sometimes are not aggressive. Most mothers consider obedience of some importance, for they use much verbal guidance in instructing and controlling their children. The children know their mothers want compliance with directions, and hence willful disobedience is widely recognized as a form of aggression. Now if a child has been told to pick up his clothes a dozen times, and if he has remembered to do this the last half-dozen times, his mother may look suspiciously at his motives if he forgets the thirteenth time. Did he just forget? Or was he angry and disobedient? People differ considerably in the degree to which they perceive an aggressive intent in the behavior of others, and what one mother calls carelessness another will call disobedience.

If we disregard borderline cases and accidents, however, there is still a great deal of human behavior that is designed to hurt. Such activity develops early in life and is a disrupting influence on family living. Later it becomes a problem for the peer group. . . .

All human societies, even all colony-living subhuman primates, have rules to limit the kinds and direction of aggression that may be expressed. The most fundamental of these is the high degree of prohibition on in-group fighting. The closer together people live, the more interdependent they are, the less they dare be aggressive toward one another. Free fighting and antagonism within the household—whether it be a nomad's hut or a suburbanite's four-bedrooms-and-two-baths—could only lead to wreckage of the family unit. Hence, all societies require that only very attenuated forms of aggression be expressed among family members, and that, within the parent-child relationship, aggression be expressed only downward. One mother described this principle with great clarity:

I. How do you handle it (if he strikes you)?
M. I don't allow it. I slap him and punish him for it, and explained that he was never to raise his hand to anyone older than himself, that he must respect older people—his mother and father especially. Never! But they do attempt it, of course; but I do think it should be checked right away.
I. How did you handle this?
M. I would just put him right in his room. Just take hold of him right at the moment and put him right in his room, and say "You mustn't do that! You never should hit your mother and father, ever; they're always right." I always make a big issue out of it.
I. That your mother and father are always right?
M. Always right; "You must never raise your hand to your mother or father."

Not all mothers felt as strongly as this one did, and different societies have different degrees of tolerance for in-family aggression, but the prohibition exists in some degree in all known societies.

Outside the family, limitations are less severe in most societies. As will be seen later, the mothers in this present study were less concerned—more permissive—about fighting between their own children and neighbor youngsters than about sibling quarreling. There were a number of instances in which mothers felt children must be encouraged to fight, to protect their own interests. Even so, there is still a good deal of necessary restriction on the more severe forms of aggression, no matter toward whom they are directed.

To insure the firm establishment of these rules, many mothers feel they must begin the control of aggression very early in the child's life. A newborn infant is not particularly dangerous, even to himself, but he represents a potential threat nevertheless. The family, indeed the whole society, has a delicate balance; the forces of aggression are being kept in check, and co-operation and love are out-weighing non-co-operation and hate. The baby is an alien who does not know all the rules. He lacks knowledge of when to hit and when not to. He has no skill at securing compliance by a *little* hurting. He cannot be counted on to channelize, to displace, or to attenuate his aggressions. He must be taught them if he is to be an acceptable member of society. . . .

PUNISHMENT AND ANXIETY

The mother's almost automatic aggressive response to her child's aggression creates a special problem in child-rearing tactics that does not seem to arise nearly so seriously in connection with other areas of child behavior. Unless a mother is busy, or annoyed to start with, dependency is likely to elicit nurturance from her, and an expression of affection will evoke its like. But aggression, being a frustration to its object, has a strong tendency to evoke counter-aggression or punishment. After all, the mother was once a child herself and learned the same ways of reacting that her child is now learning.

This built-in relationship between the aggressor and his victim has an important consequence. It means that every child grows up with the experience of being punished in some degree for his aggressive behavior. The extent and severity of such punishment differs greatly from one child to another, of course, depending on the tolerance of his parents and siblings. It is our impression, however, that the average child in our sample received more actual *punishment* (as distinguished from *non-reward*) for aggressive behavior than for any other kind of changeworthy action.

One significant effect of punishment is the production of anxiety. If the punishment is repeated many, many times through early childhood, situations that provoke aggressive feelings gradually come to arouse anxiety, too—anxiety over the danger of being punished for aggression. Eventually, the aggression itself, or the accompanying feeling of being angry, becomes sufficient to arouse anxiety. In such cases the anxiety may properly be called aggression-anxiety.

The formation of such a reaction has two kinds of consequences that are relevant to the socialization process. One is the uneasiness and discomfort that become connected with the arousal of aggressive impulses. By and large, adults in our culture do not tolerate aggression comfortably, neither their own nor that displayed by others. It evokes too much anxiety; this may be reflected in feelings of worry, dislike, avoidance, guilt, or moral disapproval. They cannot feel fully comfortable when they are angry. They are in conflict—ambivalent—about their own impulses. The carrying through of an aggressive act is often followed not simply by the catharsis or satisfaction that one would expect from a successful action (assuming the action accomplished the intended results), but also by feelings that arise from the undercurrent anxiety. These may be shame, embarrassment, guilt, regret, self-deprecation, or even just plain fear of retaliation. A mother's uneasiness and conflict often make difficult a calm use of reason in deciding how to handle a child's aggressive actions.

A second consequence of punishment and its ensuing anxiety is the development, by the child, of techniques for avoiding punishment. The child who is consistently punished for swearing is likely to cease the practice in his parent's presence. This does not necessarily mean he will stop swearing, for punishment seems usually to have a rather localized inhibiting effect. The impulse to be aggressive is not reduced, but only the overt aggressive act that was punished. The total impulse to aggression is made stronger than ever, for the punishment is itself an additional frustration. . . .

We can turn now to the findings from our interviews. In this chapter we will describe first the ways in which the mothers handled aggression, with respect to both permissiveness and punishment. It will be seen that there was some consistency in individual mothers' attitudes, and we will indicate what some of the other personality characteristics were that were commonly associated with gentle or severe handling. Finally, we will examine the relation between these child-rearing practices and the mothers' own reports of their children's aggressiveness to discover what procedures seemed to influence such behavior. . . .

THE MOTHERS' PERMISSIVENESS FOR AGGRESSION

In the discussion so far we have talked of aggression as a changeworthy form of behavior, particularly that directed toward the parents. This is a generalization, however, that hides a multitude of individual differences among the mothers. As might easily be predicted from what has been said of aggression-anxiety, parents differ greatly from one another in the amount of aggression they can tolerate. Some set great store by a completely non-aggressive child; others accept the inevitability of a certain amount of aggression even as late as age five; a few believe aggression is such a natural quality of early childhood behavior that they simply ignore all but the most violent episodes. . . .

In our interviews, the mothers described the ways in which children got on adult nerves, found ingenious devices for expressing annoyance or getting revenge, and in general created the social and emotional havoc that goes with anger. They also expressed their own attitudes toward their children's aggression, and gave descriptions of how this changeworthy behavior was handled. With respect to aggression of children toward their parents, the mothers were asked:

Sometimes a child will get angry at his parents and hit them and kick them or shout angry things at them. How much of this sort of thing do you think parents ought to allow in a child of (his, her) age? How do you handle it when (child's name) acts like this?

[* CASE A

M. I think he's at the age right now where you're apt to get quite a lot of it. I think as they get a little bit older, you can stop and reason with them, but right now I think that they get pretty angry at times and they do say things. And afterwards they're sorry for it, so I let him say it and it's over with, and afterwards I might say, "You weren't very nice to Mummy," and he'll generally admit it.

CASE B

I. In what ways do you get on each other's nerves?

M. I think our mutual tempers, as much as anything, as he has one, and so have I. I attempt to control it, so for instance I can understand things that he does. He gets very angry and he goes upstairs and throws things, and I can understand that perfectly. I don't know whether I was ever allowed to or whether I ever did throw things, but I wanted to, so that heaving things into the closet, I can easily understand; so that kind of thing doesn't aggravate me the way it would somebody else, and the same way with getting very angry at me. I never mind that as much, because I also get angry at him, and if I am going to, he has got to be allowed that privilege also.

CASE C

M. Well, she'll say, "I don't like you." She seldom says, "I hate you," or "I don't like you anymore," or something like that. I have let her go up to now because I feel she's just getting it out of her system. If it isn't too loud, or if she isn't too angry about it, I just let it go. If it's something that I can't turn my back on, if it's something that she's so angry about that she won't stop, then I speak to her. Otherwise she'll say, "Well, I don't like you." And I say, "Well, that's all right," or something like that. I don't pay too much attention to it because I know that she doesn't actually mean it. She means it because she isn't getting what she wants, and she doesn't mean it actually.

---

*The material in brackets, ending on page 121, is an edited version taken from Maccoby, Newcomb, and Hartley (eds.), *Readings in Social Psychology* (Holt, 1958).—EDITOR

If she kicked me or if she slapped me, I'd slap her back. I just told her that it doesn't feel good to get slapped. If she didn't want to get slapped herself, not to slap other people. The reaction would be the same in anyone that got slapped—they wouldn't like it.

CASE D

M. They never should allow him to hit them back. If he hits them, they should hit him right back. If you let him get away with it once he will always want to get away with it.

I. How do you handle it when he acts like this?

M. If he hits me I hit him back twice as hard, and if he does it again, I just get my paddle I have, and I give it to him again, and then he stops.

I. How do you handle it if he is deliberately disobedient?

M. I take off his clothes and he's in for the day and he's not to play with anything—not even his toys or anything that belongs to him—he's not to touch anything—he's to leave things alone and stay in bed.

CASE E

M. That is something I will not tolerate—my child has never done it. I mean, they have done it once in a while, both of them, but I would absolutely not tolerate it.

I. How did you teach them not to do this?

M. I don't know—I guess I just told them once, in no uncertain terms, that it was something that was never done, and I have never had any trouble with it; and if I did, I don't know just how I would cope with it, because I wouldn't stand for it.

I. How much of this sort of thing do you think a parent ought to allow?

M. I don't think they should allow it at all. I think a child should be allowed to express himself, and all that, but I don't think there is ever an exception for a child to hit his parents.

Responses of these kinds, together with much other relevant material elsewhere in the interview, enabled us to rate each mother on two dimensions: (1) her *permissiveness* for aggression, directed by the child toward herself and (2) the amount (and severity) of *punishment* she had administered to the child for such aggression. Under the heading of permissiveness we included not only the mother's stated values as to whether aggression should be allowed but also her behavior toward the child, *i.e.*, whether she actually *did* allow it or whether she always tried to take measures to prevent or stop it.

As might be expected, the two scales were correlated. That is, the mothers who were permissive about aggression, tended to use little punishment, while the nonpermissive mothers used quite a bit. But the correlation was only −.46, a low enough value to warrant considering the two dimensions separately. The two scales did not correlate more closely because there were a number of mothers who did not permit aggression from their children, but stopped it by other means than punishment.

Surprisingly, there were also a number whom we rated both quite permissive and highly punishing. In this latter group were some mothers who felt they *should* allow their children to display aggression; but they could restrain their own impulses to suppress the child's aggression only so long, and then they would blow up. When the punishment came, it was likely to be severe.

In this sample of 379 normal mothers, we found that a majority were most accurately rated at the *nonpermissive* end of our permissiveness scale. The social norm prevailing in these families was one of little tolerance about parent-directed aggression from children, although there was considerable variation in the severity with which this value was enforced.

It is of some interest to note that parents allowed somewhat more aggression from their sons than from their daughters, and that working-class parents were less permissive about aggression than parents at the middle-class level.

EFFECTS ON CHILDREN'S AGGRESSION

We turn now to a consideration of the child's aggressiveness, and will then address ourselves to the question: Does the amount of overt aggression a child displays at home have any relation to the values parents hold about aggression and the techniques they have employed in dealing with the child's aggression?]

THE SOURCES OF AGGRESSION IN THE HOME

What makes a child aggressive and quarrelsome? Among these youngsters, there were a few whose mothers could recall almost no angry behavior around home, but this was not the case for most of them. In spite of the general aura of prohibition, the majority of the youngsters had displayed many varieties and combinations of angry emotional response. Some children were more aggressive toward one parent than the other, some quarreled mainly with siblings and were pleasant toward the parents, some expressed themselves openly, and some relied chiefly on non-co-operation for their expression.

Nearly all the mothers gave fairly detailed reports of the typical forms of aggression their children displayed. It was thus possible to make a rating of *amount of aggression exhibited in the home* (excluding that toward siblings). . . .

These ratings can be compared with the mothers' reports of child-rearing practices to discover what characteristics of the latter were associated with high or low degree of reported aggression by the child.

The measures of the mothers' practices and the children's reactions were not independent. Both came from the mother herself. We cannot be certain in any particular case, therefore, that we have secured an unbiased report of the child's actual behavior. It is possible that some quality in a given mother—for instance, a sense of despair about her effectiveness as a child rearer—might lead her to give an exaggerated report about her child's aggressiveness. If we find, as we do, that mothers who felt little confidence in themselves had more (reportedly) aggressive children, we cannot tell whether this finding results from exaggerated reports by these mothers, or whether there was actually something about their behavior toward children that evoked more child aggressiveness. It would not be surprising if both were true, for the same qualities of her personality that influence her perception of the child may also induce a characteristic set of responses in him. . . .

Permissiveness and punishment. There is a constant tug of war in a child's behavior between the instigation and the inhibition of aggression. On one hand there are frustrations, threats, or other stimulating situations that tend to evoke aggressive action; on the other, there are warnings that inhibit aggression, and there are instigators to competing responses that the mother finds more desirable than aggression. One of the major research problems in the investigation of the socialization process is the discovery of just what kinds of maternal behavior fall into these classifications. What does the mother do that excites aggression in her child? What does she do that inhibits it?

The two scales of *permissiveness for aggression* and *severity of punishment for aggression* are the most obviously relevant dimensions to examine first. What should we expect of their relation to the reported amount of aggression the child shows in the home? Permissiveness, by definition, is an expression of the mother's willingness to have the child perform such acts. A simple and straightforward prediction is that children with permissive mothers will be more aggressive than children with non-permissive mothers. Similarly with punishment: if we assume that this method of discipline establishes in the child a fear of behaving aggressively then the more punitive the mother is, the more the child should avoid being aggressive. These two predictions fit together nicely. The scales for *permissiveness* and *punishment* are correlated $-.46$; that is, to some degree the more permissive mothers tended to be less severe in their punishment.

In point of fact, however, one of the predictions is right and the other is wrong. It is true that high *permissiveness* is associated with high aggression.

The correlation is +.23. But *punishment* works just the other way: the more severe the punishment, the more aggression the child showed. The correlation is +.16. Both these correlations are small, but they are significant, and they are artificially reduced by the negative correlation between the permissiveness and punitiveness scales. Their true importance is substantially greater, as will be seen in the next section.

We interpret these findings in this way. When a mother adopts a permissive point of view about aggression, she is saying to her child, in effect, "Go ahead and express your angry emotions; don't worry about me." She gives few signals in advance that would lead the child to fear to be aggressive. On the contrary, her attitude is one of expectancy that he *will* be, and that such behavior is acceptable. It is scarcely surprising that the child tends to fulfill her expectations. The non-permissive mother, however, does something quite different. She has an attitude that aggression is wrong, that it is not to be tolerated, and an expectancy (often very subtly expressed) that the child will not behave in such undesirable ways. When he is aggressive, she does something to try to stop it—sometimes by punishment, sometimes by other means. He, also, fulfills his mother's expectations. This dimension of permissiveness, then, is a measure of the extent to which the mother prevents or stops aggression, the non-permissive extreme being the most common.

Punishment is apparently a somewhat different matter. It is a kind of maternal behavior that occurs *after* the child's aggression has been displayed. The child has already enjoyed the satisfaction of hurting or of expressing anger—and so has had a reinforcement for aggressive action. But then he gets hurt in turn. He suffers further frustration. This should, and on the average does, incite him to more aggression. If the punishment is very severe, he may gradually learn to fear the consequences of his own actions, and the particular acts

that get most repeatedly punished may be inhibited. But the total frustration is increased, and hence the total amount of aggression displayed in the home is higher. The dimension called *severity of punishment for aggression toward parents,* then, is one measure of the amount of painful frustration that is imposed on the child without direct guidance as to what would be a more acceptable form of behavior.

It is evident from this analysis that the mothers who were most permissive but also most severely punitive would have the most aggressive children; those who were most non-permissive but least punitive would have the least aggressive ones. As may be seen in Table VII:8, this was the case for both sexes. The children of mothers in the other two groups were in between.

These findings are similar to those of an earlier study (Sears *et al.,* 1953) in one respect. In that research, 40 children were observed in nursery school. The amount of aggression they showed there was compared with their mothers' reports of the severity of punishment for aggression that they suffered at home. In that study, too, high aggression was found to be associated with severe punishment, especially in the boys. There was some indication that the most severely punished girls had become quite passive and inhibited. They displayed little activity of any kind, including aggression. When activity level was taken into consideration, they tended to be more like the boys, i.e., the more severely punished girls were *relatively* more aggressive than the less severely punished. It is interesting to note the similarity between the present findings and the earlier study, because in that research the measure of child aggression was entirely independent of the measures of child-rearing practices.

A word of caution must be said here about the interpretation of our results. We have shown that the mothers who punished their children most severely for aggression tended to report that their

TABLE VII:8

PERCENTAGE OF HIGHLY AGGRESSIVE CHILDREN IN SUBGROUPS DIVIDED ACCORDING TO WHETHER MOTHER WAS IN UPPER OR LOWER HALF OF THE DISTRIBUTION ON PERMISSIVENESS AND SEVERITY OF PUNISHMENT FOR AGGRESSION TOWARD PARENTS

| | *Highly Aggressive* * | | | |
| | *Boys* | | *Girls* | |
Subgroup	*Per Cent*	*N* †	*Per Cent*	*N*
Low permissiveness and low punishment	3.7	27	13.3	30
Low permissiveness and high punishment	20.4	51	19.1	47
High permissiveness and low punishment	25.3	81	20.6	63
High permissiveness and high punishment	41.7	36	38.1	22

* By "highly aggressive" is meant that the child was rated by one or both raters as being in one of the two highest levels of aggression. . . .
† Number of cases.

children displayed more than the average amount of aggression toward their parents. We have implied in our discussion that the maternal behavior *caused* the child behavior. It is entirely possible, of course, that the correlation could be explained as a parental response to the child's pre-existing temperament. That is, some children may have been born with a higher level of aggressive impulses than others, and the more aggressive the child naturally was, the more his parents were forced to punish him for aggression. We have chosen to interpret the matter the other way around: that punishment by the mother bred counter-aggression in the child. Our reason is that permissiveness was also associated with aggression, and we cannot see why aggression in the child should elicit permissiveness in the mother.

Our interpretation must be tentative, however, for the other explanation of the results cannot be ruled out without further research. It is quite possible, of course, that a circular process develops: the parent's punishment makes the child aggressive, this aggression leads to further punishment, and so on. Which came first, to set the whole thing in motion, is a problem we cannot solve with our existing information. . . .

Our findings suggest that the way for parents to produce a non-aggressive child is to make abundantly clear that aggression is frowned upon, and to stop aggression when it occurs, but to avoid punishing the child for his aggression. Punishment seems to have complex effects. While undoubtedly it often stops a particular form of aggression, at least momentarily, it appears to generate more hostility in the child and lead to further aggressive outbursts at some other time or place. Furthermore, when the parents punish—particularly when they employ physical punishment—they are providing a living example of the use of aggression at the very moment they are trying to teach the child not to be aggressive. The child, who copies his parents in many ways, is likely to learn as much from this example of successful aggression on his parents' part as he is from the pain of punishment. Thus, the most peaceful home is one in which the mother believes aggression is not desirable and under no circumstances is ever to be expressed toward her, but who relies mainly on non-punitive forms of control. The homes where the children show angry, aggressive outbursts frequently are likely to be homes in which the mother has a relatively tolerant (or careless!) attitude toward such behavior, or where she administers severe punishment for it, or both.

These conclusions will certainly not astonish anyone who has worked professionally with children and their parents. Social workers, psychologists, teachers, psychiatrists, and probation officers have seen the twin effects of permissiveness and punishment many times in their own experience. What is important in the present report is the demonstration with this group of families. When one works with a few cases, particularly when most of them are quite deviant from the general population, one often has some uncertainty as to whether the relationships he sees would apply to a more normal group. Here is as normal a group of American mothers and their children as one could want for these purposes. The principles hold good.

There is another aspect to the matter worth emphasizing, however. The effects of these two aspects of control may already be known by professionals, but, even with a demonstration of this sort, they will not find ready acceptance by many others. There are two reasons.

First, *punishment is satisfying* to the parent. When a child aggresses toward his mother, he angers her, interferes with what she is doing, with her peace of mind, with her dignity and self-respect. Aggression hurts. It is meant to. And it produces in the mother the appropriate stimulation to retaliate in kind. Combined with her sense of obligation to rear her child properly, this retaliation comes out in a way she thinks of as "punishment"— that is, a form of aggression designed to have a good *training* effect on its recipient. As will be seen in a later chapter, many mothers have developed strong beliefs that punishment is a helpful method of control. (Sometimes it is, too.) These beliefs are essential to the peace of mind of such mothers. Without the conviction that "punishment is *good* for my child," these mothers would be forced to view their own behavior as retaliatory, aggressive, childish— in short, contemptible. This would not long provide a tolerable self-image. It is to be expected, then, that our demonstration of the deleterious effect of severe punishment of aggression will not be an easy finding for many people to swallow.

A second matter has to do with permissiveness. The difficulty grows out of the problem of punishment. During the last three decades there has developed, among the more literate and sensitive part of the American people, an uneasy recognition that punishment sometimes eliminates a few specific responses, but leaves a strongly hostile drive bottled up within the child. There is evidence to support this belief. With this consideration in mind, and an urgent desire to provide better mental hygiene for their children, not a few parents have developed what almost amounts to a cult of being permissive about aggression. Their aim is to avoid repression, to permit the child easier and freer expression of his impulses, and thus to prevent the development of aggression-anxiety, with its accompanying displacements, projections, and sometimes uncontrollable fantasies.

This aim is good, both for the children and the society they will compose, but whether it can be achieved by a high degree of permissiveness for expression of aggression toward the parents is a question. Does a permissive attitude, with the consequent freer expression of aggression, decrease the strength of projective fantasies? There is no indication in our own data that it does. Each of the children in the present study was tested with two 20-minute sessions of doll play. The children of the more non-permissive half of the group of mothers showed little if any more fantasy aggression under these circumstances than the children of the more permissive half. This finding is in sharp contrast to that with respect to punishment; the children of the more severely punishing mothers displayed quite significantly more fantasy aggression than the children of the less severely punishing ones (Levin and Sears, 1956). Permissiveness does not seem to decrease fantasy indications of aggressive impulses.

Permissiveness does increase the amount of aggression in the home, however, and it is worth considering what this does to the child himself. An angry child is not usually a happy child, nor is he one who receives affection and willing companionship from others. He is a source of discomfort to family and peers, and probably receives a certain amount of retaliation. He upsets his siblings, raises the level of frustration imposed on his parents, and inevitably has an increase, to some extent, of his own aggression-anxiety. There seems little advantage in all this, either to the child himself or to his parents.

These comments may seem to encourage a con-

clusion that parents will find it to their advantage to be somewhat non-permissive of aggression that is directed toward themselves. This can be a dangerous conclusion if the kind of permissiveness we mean is not clearly understood.

Therefore, let us be as clear as possible about the aspect of permissiveness we have in mind. A child is more likely to be non-aggressive if his parents hold the value that aggression is undesirable and should not occur. He is more likely to be non-aggressive if his parents prevent or stop the occurrence of aggressive outbursts instead of passively letting them go on, but prevent them by other means than punishment or threats of retaliation. If the parents' non-permissiveness takes the form of punishing the child (and thus leading the child to *expect* punishment) for aggressive behavior, then non-permissiveness will not have the effect of reducing the child's aggression. On the contrary, the instant that punishment enters, all the consequences of punishment that have been discussed earlier may be anticipated, including that of increasing the child's level of aggression.

One cautionary point: we are not suggesting that parents should band together in omnipotent suppression of every justifiable angry response the child makes. The right to be angry without fear or guilt is as inalienable as any other, and more important than some. But since anger interferes with constructive action in the face of many, if not most, problem situations that the child and his family face, parents are understandably anxious to keep it within reasonable bounds; and our interest has been in showing what parental actions are likely to have the desired effects and what actions are likely to have undesired side-effects.

18

A Reinterpretation of the Direction of Effects in Studies of Socialization

RICHARD Q. BELL

When research unearths associations between parental tactics of child control and children's behaviors, the usual response of psychologists has been to "explain" the children's behaviors as resulting from the parents' techniques. To what extent is it plausible to reason in reverse fashion? Could one assert that the parents' choice of one rather than another disciplinary approach is a consequence of the child's behavior rather than a cause of it? Does the severely punished child act aggressively because he has been severely punished? Or was he severely punished because of his highly aggressive behavior?

Richard Bell of the Child Research Branch, National Institute of Mental Health, takes up this question in the following paper. Readers who wish to delve further into this theme may consult the article by Lawrence V. Harper, "The Young as a Source of Stimuli Controlling Caretaker Behavior," (Developmental Psychology, 1971, 4, 73–88) or the article by Bell in the same journal (pp. 63–72), "Stimulus Control of Parent or Caretaker Behavior by Offspring."

It is not too surprising to find that most research on parent-child interaction has been directed to the question of effects of parents on children. The historian Palmer (1964) maintains that our political and social philosophy emerged in a period when there were many revolutionary or protorevolutionary movements ranging from the Carolinas to Sweden, movements directed not just against monarchical absolutism but against all constituted bodies such as parliaments, councils, assemblies, and magistracies. These institutions tended to be hereditary, either in theory or through firmly established practice. In taking a strong stand against hereditary determination of position in our society we have also stressed the malleability and susceptibility to improvement of the child. Although scientific research on parents and children is a fairly recent phenomenon, it still shows the primary influence of this broad social philosophy by emphasizing parents and educational institutions as determinants of human development.

Until recent years there have been very few findings which would indicate that this is not a fruitful approach. The prolonged helplessness of the human infant, in comparison to the early competence of some other animal infants, fits in with the picture of an organism designed to be taught and modified by the parent in the early years. It seems eminently plausible to visualize the human parent as the vehicle for the transmission of culture and the infant as simply the object of an acculturation process. The parent is the initial agent of culture, the child the object.

Because of this general view, it is often overlooked that even John Locke, to whom we are indebted for the concept of the infant as a tabula rasa, placed great emphasis in his advice to parents on early observation of congenital characteristics (Kessen, 1965, p. 67). Locke questioned the existence of innate ideas, not all innate characteristics. Currently, at least one major work on the socialization of the child has acknowledged that there are probably constitutional differences between children which affect behavior (Sears, Maccoby, & Levin, 1957, 454–455), and that the model of a unidirectional effect from parent to child is overdrawn, a fiction of convenience rather than belief (Sears et al., 1957, p. 141). The model was adopted in order to proceed with research, leaving the validity of the approach to be judged by the results.

This paper summarizes data indicating that a unidirectional approach is too imprecise and that another formulation is possible which would accommodate our social philosophy as well as new data from studies of man and other animals. Before proceeding, usage of two terms must be explained. Individual behavior sequences cannot be

Richard Q. Bell, "A reinterpretation of the direction of effects in studies of socialization," *Psychological Review, 75,* 1968, 81–95. Reprinted by permission.

referred to as exclusively genetically or experientially determined. It is possible, however, to employ experimental operations in such a way that a *difference* between two groups or between two conditions applied to the same subjects can be attributed to genetic or experiential differences. Thus the terms *genetically, congenitally,* or *experientially determined* are abstractions derived from experimental operations. For brevity, a *congenital effect* will refer to both genetic and congenital determination.

The same consideration applies to the question of whether parent and child effects can be separated. In the ordinary interaction of any parent and child we can speak only of an event sequence. However, by experimental operations we can isolate parent effects and child effects. In the remainder of this paper a child or parent effect will refer to such a derivative of an experimental operation. No implication about origin of the behavior need be drawn in this case since such studies can take as their starting point any behavior which is available at the time in the repertoire of parent or child.

We must also keep in mind that demonstration of a child effect indicates only that it plays *some* role in parent behavior. The development of the parent behavior is not explained by such a demonstration. In the same vein, Epstein (1964) has pointed out relative to studies of learning that evidence of the modifiability of a response provides no explanation of its origin.

RECENT DATA DISCORDANT WITH PARENT-EFFECT MODEL

Discordant data at the human level are still meager. This is because most research efforts have been directed to the task of testing parent effects and have not always been designed so as to permit clear interpretation of "negative" results. It will be necessary to rely upon informal observations and data generated unintentionally.

Rheingold (1966, pp. 12–13) has pointed to a compelling fact observable under ordinary circumstances in any human group containing an infant. "The amount of attention and the number of responses directed to the infant are enormous—out of all proportion to his age, size, and accomplishments." The effect of the appearance of helplessness and the powerful stimulus of distress cries were also noted. "So aversive, especially to humans, is the crying of the infant that there is almost no effort we will not expend, no device we will not employ, to change a crying baby into a smiling one —or just a quiet one."

Studies of variations in parental behavior with different children provide one other kind of data discordant with a parent-effect model. A mother of identical schizophrenic quadruplets was found to be uniformly extreme in restrictiveness with her daughters but not uniform in affection when rated against a theoretical normal group (Schaefer, 1963). Yarrow (1963, pp. 109–110) has reported that . . . [foster mothers] showed differences in behavior with infants assigned to [them] at different times. In one particularly dramatic case extreme differences in maternal care existed for two infants of the same sex and age assigned to a foster mother at the same time. Characteristics of the infants appeared to have evoked very different behavior in this foster mother and in other members of her family.

Reports of lack of uniformity of behavior of parents towards their children are not confined to intensive case studies. Stott (1941) reported a correlation of only .22 between sibling reports of a positive or negative home environment. Lasko (1954, p. 111) correlated maternal characteristics across 44 sibling pairs and found that mothers were not consistent in affection but were in restrictiveness, a finding which is in agreement with the report on the quadruplets. In a parent-effect model, it is easy to explain differences between the behavior of two parents with the same child, but awkward to accommodate a difference in the behavior of one parent toward two children. The latter difficulty is due to the fact that the parent-effect model assumes a fixed and invariantly applied repertoire. The usual method of explaining differences in behavior of a parent with different children is to postulate effects associated with ordinal position or sex of siblings. The reports on infants in foster homes could not be explained this way.

Levy (1958, p. 8) was unable to find consistency in maternal greeting behavior when the infant was brought from the nursery for a feeding, until it was noted that this behavior was a function of the state of the infant. The present author carried out separate chi-square analyses of Levy's data for each of three successive observations. There were no differences on the initial observation, but for the second and third observations it was found that infants awake or awakening were greeted, whereas those asleep were not ($p < .01$; $p < .05$, respectively). Other data in the same volume support Levy's contention that specific maternal behavior could be accounted for more by the infant's behavior than by the mother's general "maternal attitude," whether the latter was estimated from interview material or from actual observation of her behavior. Another finding with a similar implication was reported by Hillenbrand (1965). The amount the infant consumed in breastfeeding during the newborn period was highly correlated with the number of weeks the mother continued feeding at the breast, whereas the latter measure showed no correlation with personality characteristics of the mother.

One other study at the human level is best accommodated by a bidirectional model (Bell, 1964). Scores on one parent-attitude scale have been found consistently higher in mothers of children with congenital defects than in mothers of normals. Differences between groups of parents were ascribed to the effects on parents of a limitation in coping ability associated with the congenital disorder in affected children.

Research on lower animals provides stronger evidence of the stimulating and selective effect of the young. A volume edited by Rheingold (1963) covers maternal behavior from the deer mouse to the baboon and provides a number of observations on the importance of the young in shaping interactions. An example is the report of two instances in which the clinging of rhesus infants fostered with nonlactating females induced maternal responsiveness and biochemically normal lactation (pp. 268–269). In other studies offspring effects have been manipulated experimentally. Lactation in the rat has been maintained for long periods by supplying new litters of pups; number and age of pups were effective parameters (Bruce, 1961). Licking and nest-building occurred when 1-day-old pups were presented to female mice without previous [maternal] experience; short-term stimulus-specific decrements in the maternal response followed repeated presentation of 1-day-old pups, but recovery of response was shown to an older pup (Noirot, 1965). This study is the most recent in a series supporting the hypothesis that changes in the interest of the female mouse in the litter from birth to weaning depend mainly upon changes in stimuli coming from the young.

It has been shown by cross-fostering that pups from one strain of mice induced more retrieving and licking behavior than pups from another strain (Ressler, 1962). The open-field behavior of rat foster mothers has shown effects of the experience of rearing pups subjected to direct treatments such as shock (Denenberg, 1963), or indirect treatments such as subjecting their true mothers to premating and gestational stress (Joffe, 1965).

In a classic study, Beach and Jaynes (1956) manipulated appearance and behavior of offspring so as to identify specific classes of stimuli controlling parent behavior. Visual, olfactory, tactile, thermal, and movement cues from rat pups were shown to be capable of inducing maternal retrieving, being effective individually and in combination.

It is evident from the foregoing brief review that students of animal behavior have been much more aware of offspring effects on parents than investigators of human parent-child interaction; this more comprehensive view of parent-offspring interaction may be a simple consequence of availability; all phases of development are accessible to direct observation and manipulation. It is also possible that our political and social philosophy has limited scientific outlook at the human more than the animal level. The animal mother is not seen as an agent of socialization, nor her offspring as a tabula rasa.

There are many implications of this research on animal behavior. For the present purpose two are most salient. If variations in offspring behavior affect animal parents from which we expect fairly rigid patterns, even greater effects would be expected on human parental behavior, which is presumably more plastic and susceptible to all classes of influence. The other point is brought out by the variety of offspring stimulus parameters being opened up by animal studies; it should not be difficult to accept the notion of offspring effects if we consider the fact that offspring are at least sources of stimuli. Some stimulus control of human parental behavior should be expected since we take for granted the general likelihood of finding stimulus control over behavior in general.[1]

MODIFIERS OF PARENT RESPONSE

CONGENITAL DETERMINANTS

Three propositions concerning congenital determinants of later behavior will be advanced in this section. Some studies of human subjects will be cited which provide relatively clear evidence. Only reasonable inferences can be made from others. All in all, these studies suggest but by no means document the propositions which are advanced concerning child effects. The present objective is to take the first steps toward developing an alternative to existing socialization theory. A limited scheme which is merely plausible and parsimonious will serve the purpose. Provisional acceptance of this scheme will make it possible to provide concrete illustrations of how some recent findings in the research literature may be reinterpreted.

It will first be assumed that there are congenital contributors to human assertiveness, which will be taken to mean maintenance of goal-directed behavior of high magnitude in the face of barriers. Reasoning, threat of withdrawal of love, and appeals to personal and social motives can all be used

---

[1] The author is indebted to Leon J. Yarrow for suggesting this point.

to arrest ongoing child behavior in excess of parental standards, providing the child is not extreme in assertiveness. With a child who is strongly assertive a parent may more often fall back on quick tangible reinforcement or nonreinforcement. At times when the child, the parent, or both are stressed, the parent falls back further to distraction, holding, frightening verbalization, and physical punishment. The foregoing effects on parent behavior also are considerèd likely to issue from the behavior of hyperactive, erratic, and unpredictable children, and it is assumed that there are congenital determinants of this kind of behavior as well.

It is further assumed that a different kind of behavior is shown by parents of children congenitally low in assertiveness, activity, or sensory-motor capability. Drawing attention to stimuli, rewarding an increase in behavior, urging, prompting, and demanding are examples of parent response to these child characteristics.

It is also assumed that there are congenital contributors to differences in person orientation. Children high in person orientation attend to the behavior of their parents and reinforce social responses emanating from them. Children low in person orientation induce less nurturance from parents, and their behavior is controlled less by variations in social response of parents. They are interested in physical activity and inanimate objects. Their stimulus characteristics primarily mobilize those elements in the parent nurturance repertoires pertaining to providing and withholding physical objects and activities. Since love-oriented control techniques are less useful with these children and material reinforcers cannot always be flexibly applied, their parents more frequently show further recourse to physical punishment.

Support for a congenital contribution to assertive behavior is seen in the finding that sex differences in socialization training are pronounced in primitive cultures in which large animals are hunted (Barry, Bacon, & Child, 1957).* Furthermore, in all of the 224 primitive cultures surveyed by Murdock (1937), males were accorded roles involving fighting. Greater skeletal muscle development in males is probably an important factor, since even newborn males possess more muscle tissue, females more fat, relative to total body weight (Garn, 1958). It appears reasonable that some potential for use of muscles in physically assertive behavior can also be assumed. We would not expect the exclusive allocation of the fighting role to males if they possessed only greater skeletal muscle mass with no accompanying potential for use, or if there were equal distribution of potential between the

sexes. Males in our advanced societies do not carry spears, but it is improbable that our congenital dispositions have changed as rapidly as our cultural evolution. Even theoretical systems committed to the study of parent effects have acknowledged the probable existence of constitutional bases for sex differences in overt aggressiveness (Sears et al., 1957, p. 484).

One other line of evidence is from twin studies. Direct observation of monozygotic and dizygotic twins each month during the first year of life has shown significant heritability for an item from the Bayley Infant Behavior Profile labeled "goal directedness," which denotes absorption with a task until it is complete (Freedman, 1965). Vandenberg (1962) has pointed out that such twin contrasts in early infancy are more likely to detect genetic contributions than studies of children and adults because later social functioning shapes behavior in ways remote from the circumstances under which genetic selection took place. However, even in studies of school-age children which use the admittedly insensitive self-report questionnaires, significant heritability has been shown for groups of items interpreted as reflecting vigor (Vandenberg, 1962) and dominance (Gottesman, 1965).

Stronger evidence exists for a congenital contribution to person orientation; not only in the twin studies just cited but in several others summarized by Scarr (1965), heritability has been shown for social responsiveness or sociability, the findings cutting across age, sex, social class, and even cultural differences.

Some specific ways in which congenital factors may affect person orientation can be suggested on the basis of data from other studies. Schaffer and Emerson (1964) concluded that avoidance by some infants of being held, carried on the lap, stroked, or kissed was not accounted for by propensities of the mothers, but was due to the infant's restlessness and negative response to the restraint involved in these contacts. Infants who avoided contact showed lower intensity in later social contacts, though neither timing nor breadth of contacts was affected. There was a nonsignificant tendency for those who avoided early contacts to be males. The study is suggestive rather than conclusive because the sample of infants who avoided contacts was small.

Moss (1967) reports from day-long naturalistic observations in the home at 3 and 12 weeks that male infants were more irritable (crying, fussing), and slept less than females. This would mean that, on the average, the mother-son interaction was more one of physical caretaking, the mother being engaged in a variety of efforts to soothe males. Walters and Parke (1965) summarize evidence

---

* The article is in Section VIII of this book.—EDITOR

that the development of social response is relatively independent of the primary-drive reduction which might be expected to follow from such physical acts of caretaking. In fact, there are many reasons for expecting that greater irritability in the males would not favor development of social responses positively valued by parents (i.e., smiling, visual regard, noncrying vocalizations): *(a)* appearance of the mother at the time of crying could lead to an increase in the rate of crying, as reported for institutional infants by Etzel and Gewirtz (1967); *(b)* ministrations which follow the mother's appearance would necessarily contain some stimulation of an aversive nature, as in diaper changing or efforts to release ingested air, a point made by Rheingold (1966, p. 11); *(c)* nonaversing reinforcing elements in caretaking would be less likely to reinforce the infant's positively valued social responses since an irritable infant probably emits less of this behavior; *(d)* the mother would have less time available for purely social stimulation, and might simply wish to avoid the infant when he is quiet.

These possibilities are all consistent with Moss' (1967) finding that by the 12th week, mothers provided less stimulation of an interactional-social nature (imitation) for male than for female infants. It might also be argued that mothers imitated female infants more because of the earlier maturation of social responsiveness in females, an alternative explanation in congenital terms. Mothers could have begun differential sex-role training in social responsiveness sometime in the intervening period, but a ready explanation for initiating such training in just this period is not available. The data do not permit decisions on these different explanations, but the one selected for the present thesis seems at least as defensible as the others: Greater irritability in males led to less stimulation from mothers of the kind which should produce positively valued social responsiveness. This, in turn, may be extended developmentally using data from Bayley and Schaefer (1964, p. 44): Males were rated as less responsive to persons during 11 out of 12 developmental examinations between 10 and 36 months. Goodenough's (1957) report of sex differences in object and person orientation is typical of many other reports in the literature which indicate that males show less social orientation by the preschool period.

The research of Pasamanick, Robers, and Lilienfeld (1956) provides evidence that complications of pregnancy and delivery are associated with later behavior, and that males are more frequently affected. The foregoing studies permit an inference that there is a congenital contributor to early response to social reinforcement. If hyperactive or restless infants do not respond as well as other infants to some of the early social reinforcers, it would be reasonable to expect that their later behavior would be controlled less adequately by use of love-oriented techniques which depend for their efficacy on the strength of the social bond. It could also be inferred that they would be less person-oriented, as a consequence of the less intense primary social bond.

Stechler (1964) lists a number of recent prospective studies which confirm the general validity of Pasamanick's approach, and reports his own finding that neonatal apnea was associated with low developmental quotients in the first 2 years of life. Higher irritability or crying during the newborn period and lower developmental quotients later in infancy have been reported for infants whose mothers reported fears or anxiety during pregnancy (Davids, Holden, & Gray, 1963; Ferreira, 1960; Ottinger & Simmons, 1964). We have already mentioned a study of congenital handicaps which limit sensory-motor development (Bell, 1964). Reports of congenital contributors to sensory-motor development are not limited to populations showing pathology. Kagan and Garn (1963) have reported that chest width measured from roentgenographic films of parents or their children is positively correlated with the children's perceptual-motor and language development in the preschool years.

To summarize, there is direct evidence of congenital factors contributing to two classes of child behavior which are likely to have very different effects on parents: impaired sensory-motor development, and behavior disorders involving hyperactivity. From twin studies there is evidence of a congenital contributor to person orientation and to facets of behavior which appear related to assertiveness. On the other hand, the evidence for congenital contributors to sex differences in person orientation and assertive behavior is mostly inferential. This is particularly true for assertive behavior: No relevant data on early development of sex differences could be located in the literature. In view of this, the arguments relative to assertiveness are merely advanced to indicate that congenital determination is at least reasonable. If we accept this, albeit provisionally, we can further assume that variation within the sexes on congenital grounds could also occur. Polygenetic rather than simple all-or-none determination would be favored by modern genetic theory.

DIFFERENTIATION OF PARENT RESPONSE

Parents do not have fixed techniques for socializing children. They have a repertoire of actions to accomplish each objective. Furthermore, activation of elements in the repertoire requires both cultural pressures and stimulation from the object of acculturation. Characteristics that most infants and children share, such as helplessness, evoke responses.

Another major effect of the child is shown in the parent's selective performance of elements from the caretaking repertoire. It is assumed that there are hierarchies of actions, that different children induce responses from different parts of these hierarchies. Others escalate the actions of their parents so that at one time or another, or in sequence, the entire hierarchy relevant to a certain class of child behavior may be elicited. The child in turn reinforces or fails to reinforce the parent behavior which is evoked. The repertoire changes as a function of cultural demands and also as a result of stimulation and reinforcement received from the child.

Two types of parent control repertoires must be differentiated. *Upper-limit control behavior* reduces and redirects behavior of the child which exceeds parental standards of intensity, frequency, and competence for the child's age. *Lower-limit control behavior* stimulates child behavior which is below parental standards. In other words, parent control behavior, in a sense, is homeostatic relative to child behavior. To predict interaction in particular parent-child pairs it is necessary to know the behavior characteristics of the child, the cultural demands on the parent, and the parents' own individual assimilation of these demands into a set of expectations for the child. Nonetheless, for purposes of illustration we might say that the average parent would show an increase in upper-limit control behavior in response to excessive crying in the infant, or in response to impulsive, hyperactive, or overly competent or assertive behavior in the young child. These widely different behaviors are only considered similar with respect to their effect on upper-limit control. Parental lower-limit control behavior would be stimulated by lethargy in the infant, by low activity, overly inhibited behavior, and lack of competence in the young child. Again, these are different behaviors but are assumed to be similar in effect.

It is customary to observe or rate parental behavior without reference to stimulation provided by the young. When this is done, a parent showing extreme upper-limit behavior in several areas is likely to be described as "punitive," or "restrictive," one showing extreme lower-limit behavior as "intrusive," or "demanding." Both could be considered "controlling," but according to the present conceptual scheme designed to accommodate child effects, the history of preceding interaction sequences could be quite different. The need for differentiating these two types of control

is indicated not only by the present theoretical considerations but also by the empirical findings that punitive and strict behavior is not correlated with intrusive and demanding behavior in parents of young children (Schaefer, 1959, p. 228).

REINTERPRETATION OF RECENT LITERATURE

The child-effect system of explanation which has just been developed states that parent behavior is organized hierarchically within repertoires in the areas of social response and control. Reasonable bases exist for assuming that there are congenital contributors to child behaviors which (*a*) activate these repertoires, (*b*) affect the level of response within hierarchies, and (*c*) differentially reinforce parent behavior which has been evoked.

This system will be applied next to current findings in several major areas in which parent and experiential family effects on children have been given almost exclusive consideration. The findings in most cases are from recent studies which replicate or are consistent with previous studies, or in which results are more defensible than usual because of careful attention to sampling, procedural controls, and measurement. In most cases the authors of these papers were careful not to claim that causes and effects could be clearly differentiated. The question of direction of effects may be raised nonetheless, to ascertain whether the findings are relevant to the theory which motivated the research.

Though in the discussion which follows, the evidence is organized to support the validity of a child-to-parent effect, this should not be taken to mean that an "either-or" approach to the study of parent and child effects is preferred to an interactional view. This reinterpretation is only an expedient considered necessary to direct attention to the possibility of child effects. If this possibility is admitted we can then begin the task of thinking of parent *and* child effects. The primary goal of an expanded model of the socialization process is to uncover interactions of child and parent effects as well as main effects attributable to either source.

Lefkowitz, Walder, and Eron (1963) found in 8-year-olds that peer ratings of aggression were highest and parent reports of the child's use of confession lowest where use of physical punishment was reported by the parents. Bandura and Walters (1959) reported more physical punishment used in a group of male 15- to 16-year-old repeated offenders than in nondelinquents. One theory being tested in each case was that use of punishment in the home produces frustration and conflict or affords a model of aggression which in turn produces aggressive behavior in the child.

An alternative explanation is that these children were congenitally assertive. Congenital assertiveness activated upper-limit control repertoires in parents and techniques within the repertoire were escalated toward physical punishment. Congenital hyperactivity could produce similar results.

Reviewing the area of moral development, Hoffman (1963) found consistent results in studies dealing with reaction to transgression. His interpretation was that an internalized moral orientation, indicated by confession, guilt, or reparation efforts, was fostered by an affectionate relation between the parent and child, in combination with disciplinary techniques which utilized this relation by appealing to the child's personal and social motives. One alternative explanation is that the children showing little internalization of a moral orientation were congenitally low in person orientation. Because of this their mothers were less affectionate and did not appeal to the child's personal or social values.

A study of sex-role development by Mussen and Rutherford (1963) reports findings which replicated those in a previous study. Boys 5–6 years old scoring high in masculinity on the IT test, in comparison with lows, revealed high father nurturance, punishment, and power in doll play. A high power score indicated that father figures were both highly rewarding and punishing. These findings generously supported all major contending theories: developmental identification, defensive identification, and role-theory. A congenital explanation would be that the highs were more masculine in the sense that they showed lower person orientation and higher assertiveness. The father responded with affection because the son's assertiveness and interests in physical activity and toys were sex appropriate, reinforcing his own identification vicariously through his boy. Much as he felt affectionate toward his masculine boy he found he retreated to punishment frequently because the child, being assertive and less responsive to social stimuli, could not be controlled readily by love-oriented techniques.

In the area of intelligence, Bing (1963) found that mothers of children who showed higher verbal than spatial or numerical ability had a more close and demanding relation with their children both in interviews and observation situations than did mothers of children who showed discrepant non-verbal abilities. These findings confirmed the hypothesis that discrepant verbal ability is fostered by a close relation with a demanding and somewhat intrusive mother, discrepant nonverbal abilities being enhanced by allowing the child a considerable degree of freedom. An alternative explanation would be that the high-verbal children were high in person orientation and low in assertiveness.

This is a reasonable combination of characteristics if one assumes that congenital determinants of assertiveness and person orientation are independent or at least not highly positively correlated. These children reinforced their mothers' social responses and elicited nurturant behavior. The resultant interaction intensified verbal expression because this is the primary channel of communication. The fact that these children were low in assertiveness led to lower-limit control behavior reflected in the mother's demanding and intrusive behavior.

Schaefer's (1959) summary of his own work and that of others indicates that a major portion of the variance in parent behavior can be accounted for under two dimensions described as love-hostility and autonomy-control. This is a useful finding, offering the possibility of descriptive parsimony, regardless of the question of direction of effects. However, the two-dimensional model might represent a system of effects of children on parents. The hostility extreme of the love-hostility dimension (strictness, punishment, perceiving the child as a burden) could be characterized as a parent upper-limit control pattern in response to overly assertive, unpredictable, or hyperactive behavior. The love extreme could reflect positive evaluation of children showing more modal behavior but not behavior extreme in the opposite direction.

In support of this we find in longitudinal data from the Berkeley Growth Study (Schaefer & Bayley, 1963) that calm children were evaluated positively by their mothers during the first 3 years. Children who were rapid and active were perceived as a burden during the first 15 months. The next set of measurements available for both mothers and children covered the period when the child was between 9 and 12 years. Mothers of children rated as rapid at this time were themselves rated as irritable and perceiving the child as a burden. No rating of calmness was available. A rating of the child's inactivity in this same period could not be considered a simple inverse of the activity rating made in the first 3 years, either from the standpoint of wording or correlation pattern across the sexes. If we assume that it primarily differentiated degree of inactivity running from the highly inactive to modal levels of activity, this rating becomes relevant to the autonomy versus control dimension.

The autonomy extreme of the autonomy-control dimension might reflect parents' granting autonomy to children who conform to parental expectations of capability and assertiveness. The control extreme (intrusiveness, anxiety, achievement demand, anxiety relative to the child's behavior and health) would be considered parental lower-limit control behavior in response to children low in assertiveness or sensory-motor capability. In support of this we find that mothers of male and female inactive children during the period 9–14 years were rated as intrusive and as high in achievement demand, but low in granting autonomy to the child. All relations cited from this study (Schaefer & Bayley, 1963) were consistent for both sexes and significant beyond the .05 level for combined male and female samples according to the present author's analysis of tabular material on pages 109–110 and 121–122. Data from earlier age periods could not be brought to bear on a child-effect interpretation of the autonomy-control dimension because of very differing relations between maternal and child behavior in mother-son versus mother-daughter pairs.

Social class differences in parent behavior may also be interpreted as influenced by child effects. According to Bronfenbrenner's (1958) analysis, middle-class parents show less use of physical punishment and more use of love-oriented techniques than lower-class parents. There was no clear evidence of a change in this finding in the period from 1932 to 1952, as there was for other child-rearing techniques. Complications of pregnancy and delivery are more frequent in the lower classes (Pasamanick & Knobloch, 1960), and on this basis we could expect more hyperactivity in children from lower-class samples. From the earlier discussions relative to hyperactivity we would expect to find in lower-class parents more upper-limit control behavior, of which physical punishment is a salient example, and less use of love-oriented techniques. It is clear that studies of social-class differences in the future should control for complications of pregnancy and delivery. Some class differences may be reduced in magnitude or altered qualitatively when the samples are made comparable with respect to complications of pregnancy and delivery.

Another area receiving considerable attention in the research literature is that of family structure effects such as birth order, sex of siblings, and family size and density. Data from several studies would support the assumption that differences in parent behavior with different children in the family may be primarily due to increased experience and change in availability to children as the family grows (Conners, 1963; Lasko, 1954; Waldrop & Bell, 1964). However, this does not make it possible to dismiss the possibility of child effects. Second- or later-born neonates show higher skin conductance than firstborn (Weller & Bell, 1965). There is collateral evidence that this indicates heightened arousal and greater maturity in this early period, though there is no information available on later development. Another paper summarizes data indicating that the physiology of pregnancy

and delivery is quite different for the mother with her first versus later births (Bell, 1963), raising the possibility that some differences in parent behavior with first- versus later-born children may be a response to congenital differences in the child.

A similar child effect could be operative with increases in family size and density. Since greater dependency was found in preschool children coming from large families with short intervals between siblings it was assumed that these children were simply more deprived of maternal attention (Waldrop & Bell, 1964). While this may have been true in part, further study revealed that newborns from large dense families were more lethargic (Waldrop & Bell, 1966). In this case information on later development was available and the finding was that measures of lethargy in the newborn period were correlated with later dependency. In short, there may be congenital factors operating in determining family structure effects, and credence cannot be given to an interpretation solely in terms of experiential factors until influences identifiable in pregnancy, delivery, and the newborn period are isolated.

Examples of Studies Difficult to Reinterpret

In contrast to these studies, there are others yielding data which could not be reinterpreted as a function of congenital effects contributed by the child. For example, there are studies which substitute experimenters for parents and assign children at random to experimental groups in which different "parental" treatment is administered. In one study, experimenters played the role of parents who did or did not control access to food and toy resources in familylike interactions with preschool children (Bandura, Ross, & Ross, 1963): Children imitated parents who controlled resources.* In a study of moral development, experimenters behaved with different groups of children in such a way as to create differences in the child's control over punishment and in the cognitive clarity of a task which preceded a contrived transgression (Aronfreed, 1963). Self-critical and reparative responses following transgression were maximized by prior cognitive clarity and child control. These studies used a flexible approach which can be applied to a wide variety of parent-effect parameters very rapidly. One limitation is that we do not obtain data on the cumulative effects of parents on children. The other problem is that of ownness. It is encouraging

---

* See Bandura, Ross, and Ross, "A Comparative Test of the Status Envy, Social Power, and Secondary Reinforcement Theories of Identificatory Learning," reprinted later in this section.—Editor

in this respect that Stevenson, Keen, and Knights (1963) in studies of social reinforcement with 4- and 5-year-olds, found effects common to fathers and male experimenters, and effects common to mothers and female experimenters. This reassures us that at least with young children it may be possible to produce results with experimenters similar to effects parents have on their own children.

One other approach involves experimental manipulation of the behavior of parents and measurement of the effects on children. This is an approach that is only slightly less flexible than the foregoing and can be carried out very rapidly. Merrill (1946) manipulated parent behavior by providing mothers in two matched groups with different feedback relative to the behavior of their children. As in the previous approach which substituted experimenters for parents, the possibility of pseudo-parent effects being produced by latent child effects is minimal where the children are assigned to experimental groups at random, or on the basis of some relevant matching variable. On the other hand, since the parent is present in the interaction, the child may respond in terms of past expectancies rather than to the manipulated behavior of the parent as such. This operates against obtaining differences in child behavior in different treatments, but where differences are obtained they can be interpreted as free of child effects.

Offspring effects can also be isolated. An example is provided in a summary of a series of studies carried out by Siegel (1963). Retardates aged 10 and 15 were classified into high- and low-verbal ability groups. Children in each group were then placed in brief interaction situations with adults who had had no previous contact with them. The adults were to assist children in learning how to assemble a puzzle. Generally, adult responses and questions with low-verbal children were more frequent but shorter and more redundant. Labeling children of similar verbal ability as high or low had no effect on the adult behavior. Support was provided for the hypothesis that linguistic level of children exerts a control over adult verbal behavior.

A second variant of the first design is suggested by the research of Yarrow (1963), already discussed, which took advantage of the assignment of young infants to foster mothers for temporary care while adoption procedures were pending. It is necessary only to measure infant characteristics prior to assignment to foster mothers and then make the assignment systematically so that each foster mother's behavior with at least two different kinds of infants could be measured.

One other approach would make it possible to obtain effects with natural parents. Clinicians frequently report that successful medication of children who are hyperactive and impulsive produces pronounced reactive changes in parent and even total family behavior. Addition of pre- and post-medication measures of parent-child and family interaction to a well-controlled study of drug effects should make it possible to evaluate this and other possible child effects.[2]

Other approaches have been mentioned in the introductory section of this paper (Bell, 1964; Levy, 1958). A detailed discussion of all possible research designs is beyond the scope of this paper, which is primarily concerned with a substantive question of how studies of socialization may be interpreted. This brief recapitulation of designs is to serve the purpose of emphasizing the fact that offspring and parent effects can be separately identified and experimentally manipulated. This will require less reliance on correlation studies of parent and child behavior upon which theories of socialization have been largely based up to the present. Even correlations obtained between parent and child behaviors from longitudinal studies offer no means of ascertaining the direction of effects, unless specially designed for the purpose. Kagan and Moss (1962) have pointed out that the problem of whether maternal hostility is a reaction to child aggression or vice versa is not solved by the demonstration of long-term relations between these maternal and child behaviors in follow-up studies.

REFERENCES

ARONFREED, J. M. The effects of experimental socialization paradigms upon two moral responses to transgression. *Journal of Abnormal and Social Psychology,* 1963, *66,* 437–448.

BANDURA, A., ROSS, D., & ROSS, S. A. A comparative test of the status envy, social power, and secondary reinforcement theories of identificatory learning. *Journal of Abnormal and Social Psychology,* 1963, *67,* 527–534.

BANDURA, A., & WALTERS, R. H. *Adolescent aggression.* New York: Ronald Press, 1959.

BARRY, H., III, BACON, M. K., & CHILD, I. L. A cross-cultural survey of some sex differences in socialization. *Journal of Abnormal and Social Psychology,* 1957, *55,* 327–332.

BAYLEY, N., & SCHAEFER, E. S. Correlations of maternal and child behaviors with the development of mental abilities: Data from the Berkeley Growth Study. *Monographs of the Society for Research in Child Development,* 1964, *29*(6, Whole No. 97).

BEACH, F. A., & JAYNES, J. Studies of maternal retrieving in rats. III. Sensory cues involved in the lactating females' response to her young. *Behaviour,* 1956, *10,* 104–125.

---

[2] This adaptation of drug studies was suggested by Paul H. Wender.

BELL, R. Q. Some factors to be controlled in studies of behavior of newborns. *Biologia Neonatorum,* 1963, *5,* 200–214.

BELL, R. Q. The effect on the family of a limitation in coping ability in a child: A research approach and a finding. *Merrill-Palmer Quarterly,* 1964, *10,* 129–142.

BING, E. Effect of childrearing practices on development of differential cognitive abilities. *Child Development,* 1963, *34,* 631–648.

BRONFENBRENNER, U. Socialization and social class through time and space. In E. E. Maccoby, T. M. Newcomb, & E. L. Hartley (Eds.), *Readings in social psychology.* New York: Holt, Rinehart & Winston, 1958. Pp. 400–425.

BRUCE, H. M. Observations on the suckling stimulus and lactation in the rat. *Journal of Reproduction and Fertility,* 1961, *2,* 17–34.

CONNERS, C. K. Birth order and needs for affiliation. *Journal of Personality,* 1963, *31,* 408–416.

DAVIDS, A., HOLDEN, R. H., & GRAY, G. B. Maternal anxiety during pregnancy and adequacy of mother and child adjustment eight months following childbirth. *Child Development,* 1963, *34,* 993–1002.

DENENBERG, V. H. Early experience and emotional development. *Scientific American,* 1963, *208,* 138–146.

EPSTEIN, W. Experimental investigations of the genesis of visual space perception. *Psychological Bulletin,* 1964, *61,* 115–128.

ETZEL, B., & GEWIRTZ, J. Experimental modification of caretaker-maintained high rate operant crying in a 6- and a 20-week-old infant *(Infans Tyrannotearus). Journal of Experimental Child Psychology,* 1967, *5,* 303–317.

FERREIRA, A. J. The pregnant woman's emotional attitude and its reflection on the newborn. *American Journal of Orthopsychiatry,* 1960, *30,* 553–561.

FREEDMAN, D. G. Hereditary control of early social behavior. In B. M. Foss (Ed.), *Determinants of infant behaviour III.* New York: Wiley, 1965. Pp. 149–159.

GARN, S. M. Fat, body size, and growth in the newborn. *Human Biology,* 1958, *30,* 265–280.

GOODENOUGH, F. W. Interest in persons as an aspect of sex difference in early years. *Genetic Psychology Monographs,* 1957, *55,* 287–323.

GOTTESMAN, I. I. Genetic variance in adaptive personality traits. Paper presented at the 73rd annual convention of the American Psychological Association, September 1965, Chicago, Illinois.

HILLENBRAND, E. D. The relationship of psychological, medical, and feeding variables to breast feeding. Unpublished master's thesis, George Washington University, 1965.

HOFFMAN, M. L. Childrearing practices and moral development: Generalizations from empirical research. *Child Development,* 1963, *34,* 295–318.

JOFFE, J. M. Genotype and prenatal and premating stress interact to affect adult behavior in rats. *Science,* 1965, *150,* 1844–1845.

KAGAN, J., & GARN, S. M. A constitutional correlate of early intellectual functioning. *Journal of Genetic Psychology,* 1963, *102,* 83–89.

KAGAN, J., & MOSS, H. A. *Birth to maturity.* New York: Wiley, 1962.

KESSEN, W. (Ed.) *The child.* New York: Wiley, 1965.

LASKO, J. K. Parent behavior toward first and second children. *Genetic Psychology Monographs,* 1954, *49,* 97–137.

LEFKOWITZ, M. M., WALTER, L. O., & ERON, L. D. Punishment, identification and aggression. *Merrill-Palmer Quarterly,* 1963, *9,* 159–174.

LEVY, D. M. *Behavioral analysis: Analysis of clinical observations of behavior as applied to mother-newborn relationships.* New York: Thomas, 1958.

MERRILL, B. A measurement of mother-child interaction. *Journal of Abnormal and Social Psychology,* 1946, *41,* 37–49.

MOSS, H. A. Sex, age, and state as determinants of mother-infant interaction. *Merrill-Palmer Quarterly,* 1967, *13,* 19–36.

MURDOCK, G. P. Comparative data on the division of labor by sex. *Social Forces,* 1937, *15,* 551–553.

MUSSEN, P., & RUTHERFORD, E. Parent-child relations and parental personality in relation to young children's sex-role preferences. *Child Development,* 1963, *34,* 589–607.

NOIROT, E. Changes in responsiveness to young in the adult mouse. III. The effect of immediately preceding performances. *Behavior,* 1965, *24,* 318–325.

OTTINGER, D. R., & SIMMONS, J. E. Behavior of human neonates and prenatal maternal anxiety. *Psychological Reports,* 1964, *14,* 391–394.

PALMER, R. R. *The age of the democratic revolution:* Vol. II. *The struggle.* Princeton: Princeton University Press, 1964.

PASAMANICK, B., & KNOBLOCH, H. Brain damage and reproductive casualty. *American Journal of Orthopsychiatry,* 1960, *30,* 298–305.

PASAMANICK, B., ROBERS, M. E., & LILIENFELD, A. M. Pregnancy experience and the development of behavior disorders in children. *American Journal of Psychiatry,* 1956, *112,* 613–618.

RESSLER, R. H. Parental handling in two strains of mice reared by foster parents. *Science,* 1962, *137,* 129–130.

RHEINGOLD, H. L., (Ed.) *Maternal behavior in mammals.* New York: Wiley, 1963.

RHEINGOLD, H. L. The development of social behavior in the human infant. In H. W. Stevenson (Ed.), Concept of development: A report of a conference commemorating the fortieth anniversary of the Institute of Child Development, University of Minnesota. *Monographs of the Society for Research in Child Development,* 1966, *31*(5, Whole No. 197).

SCARR, S. The inheritance of sociability. *American Psychologist,* 1965, *20,* 524. (Abstract)

SCHAEFER, E. A circumplex model for maternal behavior. *Journal of Abnormal and Social Psychology,* 1959, *59,* 226–235.

SCHAEFER, E. Parent-child interaction patterns and parental attitudes. In D. Rosenthal (Ed.), *The Genain quadruplets.* New York: Basic Books, 1963. Pp. 398–430.

SCHAEFER, E., & BAYLEY, N. Maternal behavior, child behavior, and their intercorrelations from infancy through adolescence. *Monographs of the Society for Research in Child Development,* 1963, *28*(3, Whole No. 87).

SCHAFFER, H. R., & EMERSON, P. E. Patterns of response to physical contact in early human development. *Journal of Child Psychology and Psychiatry,* 1964, *5,* 1–13.

SEARS, R. R., MACCOBY, E. E., & LEVIN, H. *Patterns of child rearing.* Evanston, Ill.: Row, Peterson, 1957.

SIEGEL, G. M. Adult verbal behavior with retarded children labeled as "high" or "low" in verbal ability. *American Journal of Mental Deficiency,* 1963, *68,* 417–424.

STECHLER, G. A longitudinal follow-up of neonatal apnea. *Child Development,* 1964, *35,* 333–348.

STEVENSON, H. W., KEEN, R., & KNIGHTS, R. M. Parents and strangers as reinforcing agents for children's performance. *Journal of Abnormal and Social Psychology,* 1963, *67,* 183–186.

STOTT, L. H. Parent-adolescent adjustment: Its measurement and significance. *Character and Personality,* 1941, *10,* 140–150.

VANDENBERG, S. G. The hereditary abilities study: Hereditary components in a psychological test battery. *American Journal of Human Genetics,* 1962, *14,* 220–237.

WALDROP, M., & BELL, R. Q. Relation of preschool dependency behavior to family size and density. *Child Development,* 1964, *35,* 1187–1195.

WALDROP, M., & BELL, R. Q. Effects of family size and density on newborn characteristics. *American Journal of Orthopsychiatry,* 1966, *36,* 544–550.

WALTERS, R. H., & PARKE, R. D. The role of the distance receptors in the development of social responsiveness. In L. P. Lipsitt & C. C. Spiker (Eds.), *Advances in child development and behavior.* Vol. 2. New York: Academic Press, 1965. Pp. 59–96.

WELLER, G. M., & BELL, R. Q. Basal skin conductance and neonatal state. *Child Development,* 1965, *36,* 647–657.

YARROW, L. J. Research in dimensions of early maternal care. *Merrill-Palmer Quarterly,* 1963, *9,* 101–114.

Art Buchwald at Home

THE GROWN-UP PROBLEM

There has been so much discussion lately about teen-age problems that the grown-up problem is practically being ignored. And yet if you pick up a newspaper, you realize grown-ups are responsible for some of the most serious problems this country has ever faced.

For example, 60 per cent of all crime in the United States is committed by grown-ups.

The birth rate among grown-up women is four times that of teen-agers.

The divorce rate is double.

The purchasing power of grown-ups almost exceeds that of teen-agers.

Grown-ups are responsible for more daytime accidents than any other age group.

The source of these statistics is sociology Prof. Heinrich Applebaum, B.A., M.S., LL.D., Y.E.H., Y.E.H., Y.E.H., who told me in an exclusive interview that his studies showed grown-ups were drifting farther away from society all the time.

"The average grown-up," Prof. Applebaum said, "feels his children don't understand him. The more time he spends with them the less they communicate with him. So the adult feels isolated, insecure, and misunderstood. In defense he seeks out other grown-ups who feel the same way he does. Pretty soon they form gangs, go to the theater together, hold cocktail parties and dances, and before you know it you have a complete breakdown of the family."

"Why do you think grown-ups are constantly rebelling against their children, Professor?"

"I guess it's an age-old old-age problem. You have parents wanting to break away and yet not having the nerve to cut the ties completely. Grown-ups are afraid to stand up to their children, so they rebel against society instead."

"Do you think teen-agers could in some way be responsible for the behavior of their parents?"

"I definitely do," the Professor said. "Grown-ups try to emulate teen-agers. They want to do exactly what teen-agers do, which is to drink, smoke, and drive fast cars. If teen-agers didn't do these things, their parents wouldn't. For every bad adult in America, I'm sure you'll find a bad teen-ager somewhere in the background."

"Where do you think the trouble starts?"

"In the home. Teen-agers are too rough on their parents. They're always criticizing them for listening to Frank Sinatra records and reading Holiday magazine. Teen-agers don't have any patience with their mothers and fathers. They can't understand why their parents like Doris Day and Rock Hudson movies or what they see in Cary Grant. If teen-agers spent more time with grown-ups and tried to understand them, I don't think you'd have half the trouble that you have in the United States today."

"Do you mean teen-agers should spend more time at home with their parents?"

"Of course. Grown-ups need security. They want to know where their children are. They want the feeling they belong. Only teen-agers can give grown-ups this feeling."

"Professor, have you found any homes where grown-ups are leading healthy, normal, secure lives, thanks to the attention they've received from their loving teen-age children?"

"We haven't yet. But we've been looking only a year. These surveys take time."

19

A Comparative Test
of the Status Envy, Social
Power, and Secondary
Reinforcement Theories
of Identificatory Learning [1]

ALBERT BANDURA, DOROTHEA ROSS,[2]
AND SHEILA A. ROSS

This article is well described by its title. We might add that the test was done using three-person groups that were prototypes of those found in families. Imitation was the behavior studied. In addition to the data of the report, the student will find good brief summaries of the three theories. The senior author, Albert Bandura, is a professor of psychology at Stanford University, and one of the more prolific writers in the field of psychology.

Although it is generally assumed that social behavior is learned and modified through direct reward and punishment of instrumental responses, informal observation and laboratory study of the social learning process reveal that new responses may be rapidly acquired and existing behavioral repertoires may be considerably changed as a func-

[1] This investigation was supported by Research Grant M-5162 from the National Institutes of Health, United States Public Health Service.

The authors are indebted to Beverly Busching, Malka Yaari, Nancy Wiggins, and John Steinbruner, who assisted in collecting the data.

[2] This research was carried out while the junior author was the recipient of an American Association of University Women International Fellowship for postdoctoral research.

tion of observing the behavior and attitudes exhibited by models (Bandura, 1962).

The latter type of learning is generally labeled "imitation" in behavior theory, and "identification" in most theories of personality. These concepts, however, are treated in the present paper as synonymous since both encompass the same behavioral phenomenon, i.e., the tendency for a person to match the behavior, attitudes, or emotional reactions as exhibited by actual or symbolized models. While the defining properties of identification are essentially the same in different personality theories, a host of divergent learning conditions have been proposed as the necessary antecedent variables for matching or identificatory behavior (Bronfenbrenner, 1960; Freud, 1946; Freud, 1924, 1948; Kagan, 1958; Klein, 1949; Maccoby, 1959; Mowrer, 1950; Parsons, 1955; Sears, 1957; Whiting, 1960).

In the experiment reported in this paper predictions were derived from three of the more prominent theories of learning by identification, and tested in three-person groups representing prototypes of the nuclear family. In one condition of the experiment an adult assumed the role of controller of resources and positive reinforcers. Another adult was the consumer or recipient of these resources, while the child, a participant observer in the triad, was essentially ignored. In a second treatment condition, one adult controlled the resources; the child, however, was the recipient of the positive reinforcers and the other adult was assigned a subordinate and powerless role. An adult male and female served as models in each of the triads. For half the boys and girls in each condition the male model controlled and dispensed the rewarding resources, simulating the husband dominant family; for the remaining children, the female model mediated the positive resources as in the wife dominant home. Following the experimental social interactions the two adult models exhibited divergent patterns of behavior in the presence of the child, and a measure was obtained of the degree to which the child subsequently patterned his behavior after that of the models.

According to the *status envy theory* of identification recently proposed by Whiting (1959, 1960), where a child competes unsuccessfully with an adult for affection, attention, food, and care, the child will envy the consumer adult and consequently identify with him. Whiting's theory represents an extension of the Freudian defensive identification hypothesis that identificatory be-

Albert Bandura, Dorothea Ross, and Sheila A. Ross, "A comparative test of the status envy, social power, and secondary reinforcement theories of identificatory learning," *Journal of Abnormal and Social Psychology*, 1963, *67*, 527–534. Reprinted by permission.

havior is the outcome of rivalrous interaction between the child and the parent who occupies an envied consumer status. While Freud presents the child as in competition with the father primarily for the mother's sexual and affectional attention, Whiting regards any forms of reward, material and social, as valued resources around which rivalry may develop. The status envy theory thus predicts that the highest degree of imitation by the child will occur in the experimental condition in which the rivalrous adult consumes the resources desired by the child, with the consumer adult serving as the primary object of imitation.

In contrast to the envy theory, other writers (Maccoby, 1959; Mussen & Distler, 1959; Parsons, 1955) assume that the controller, rather than the consumer, of resources is the main source of imitative behavior. The *power theory* of social influence has received considerable attention in experimental social psychology, though not generally in the context of identification theories.

Social power is typically defined as the ability of a person to influence the behavior of others by controlling or mediating their positive and negative reinforcements. French and Raven (1959) have distinguished five types of power based on expertness, attractiveness, legitimacy, coerciveness, and rewarding power, each of which is believed to have somewhat differential effects on the social influence process. For example, the use of threat or coercion, in which the controller derives power from his ability to administer punishments, not only develops avoidance behavior toward the controller but also decreases his attractiveness and hence his effectiveness in altering the behavior of others beyond the immediate social influence setting (French, Morrison, & Levinger, 1960; Zipf, 1960). The use of reward power, in contrast, both fosters approach responses toward the power figure and increases his attractiveness or secondary reward value through the repeated association of his attributes with positive reinforcement. Attractiveness is assumed to extend the controller's power over a wide range of behavior (French & Raven, 1959).

In the present investigation power based upon the ability to dispense rewards was manipulated experimentally. In accordance with the social power theory of identification, but contrasting with the status envy hypothesis, one would predict that children will reproduce more of the behavior of the adult who controls positive reinforcers, than that of the powerless adult model, and that power inversions on the part of the male and female models will produce cross-sex imitation.

The *secondary reinforcement theory* of identification, which has been alluded to in the discussion of social power through attractiveness, has been elaborated in greatest detail by Mowrer (1950, 1958). According to this view, as a model mediates the child's biological and social rewards, the behavioral attributes of the model are paired repeatedly with positive reinforcement and thus acquire secondary reward value. On the basis of stimulus generalization, responses which match those of the model attain reinforcing value for the child in proportion to their similarity to those made by the model. Consequently, the child can administer positively conditioned reinforcers to himself simply by reproducing as closely as possible the model's positively valenced behavior. This theory predicts that the experimental condition in which the child was the recipient of positive reinforcements will yield the highest imitation scores with the model who dispensed the rewards serving as the primary source of imitative behavior.

METHOD

SUBJECTS

The subjects were 36 boys and 36 girls enrolled in the Stanford University Nursery School. They ranged in age from 33 to 65 months, although the variability was relatively small with most of the ages falling around the mean of 51 months.

An adult male and female served as models in the triads so as to reproduce possible power structures encountered in different types of family constellations. A female experimenter conducted the study for all 72 children.

DESIGN AND PROCEDURE

The subjects were assigned randomly to two experimental groups and one control group of 24 subjects each. Half the subjects in each group were males, and half were females.

High rewarding power was induced experimentally through the manipulation of material and social reinforcements, and the use of verbal structuring techniques. While accompanying the child to the experimental room, for example, the experimenter informed the child that the adult who assumed the role of controller owned the nursery school "surprise room," as well as a fabulous collection of play materials. After introducing the child to the controller, the experimenter asked whether the child may play in the surprise room. The controller explained that he was on his way to his car to fetch some of his most attractive toys, but the experimenter and the child could proceed to the room where he would join them shortly. As the controller left, the experimenter commented on how lucky they were to have access to the controller's play materials.

On the way to the experimental room they met the other adult who insisted on joining them but the experimenter informed her that she would have to obtain permission from the controller since he owned the room, and it was doubtful whether sufficient play materials were available for both the adult and the child. This brief encounter with the other adult was designed primarily to create the set that rewards were available to one person only and thereby to induce rivalrous feelings over the controller's resources.

As soon as the experimenter and the child arrived in the experimental room, they sat down at a small table and played with the few Lincoln Logs and two small cars that were provided. A short time later the other adult appeared and announced that the controller also granted her permission to play in the room.

The controller then entered carrying two large toy boxes containing a variety of highly attractive masculine and feminine toys, a colorful juice dispensing fountain, and an ample supply of cookies. As soon as the controller appeared on the scene, the experimenter departed.

For children in the Adult Consumer condition, the adult who assumed the role of consumer requested permission to play with the articles and the controller replied that, since the child appeared to be occupied at his table, the consumer was free to use the play materials. This monopolistic move by the consumer adult left the child stranded at a table with two relatively uninteresting toys.

During the 20-minute play session, the controller offered the consumer, among other things, miniature pinball machines, mechanical sparkling toys, kaleidoscopes, dolls, and actively participated with the consumer in dart games and other activities. To add to the credibility of the situation, both the controller and consumer devoted most of their attention to articles, such as the pinball machine and dart game, which could be used in adult appropriate activities. Throughout the interaction the controller was most helpful, supportive, and generous in dispensing social reinforcers in the form of praise, approval, and positive attention. The consumer, in turn, commented frequently on the controller's highly attractive resources so as to further enhance the controller's rewarding status. The consumer also verbalized considerable positive affect characteristic of a person experiencing positive reinforcements.

Approximately half way through the session, the controller remarked, "Say, you look hungry. I have just the thing for you." He then brought forth the soda fountain dispenser, poured colorful fruit juices into paper cups and served them to the consumer along with a generous supply of cookies. While the consumer was enjoying his snack, the controller turned on a "TV-radio" that played a nursery melody while a revolving dial displayed a series of storybook scenes.

Toward the end of the session, the controller informed the consumer that he will be leaving on a shopping trip to San Francisco that afternoon, and asked the consumer if there was anything special she would like him to buy for her. The consumer requested a super two-wheel bicycle, a high status object among the nursery school children. The controller promised to purchase the bicycle along with any other items the consumer might think of before the controller departed for the city.

The procedure for the Child Consumer condition was identical with that described above except the child was the recipient of the material rewards and the social reinforcement. During the session the other adult sat at the opposite end of the room engrossed in a book, and was totally ignored by the controller. In discussing the prospective San Francisco shopping trip, the controller mentioned to the child that he was planning to visit some toy stores in the city that afternoon, and asked for suggestions of attractive toys he might purchase for future play sessions with children.

For half the boys and girls in each treatment condition the male model controlled and dispensed the resources, simulating the husband dominant family; for the remaining children the female model mediated the positive resources as in the wife dominant home.

At the completion of the social interaction session the controller announced that he had a surprise game in his car that the three of them could play together. The controller then asked the other adult to fetch the experimenter to assist them with the game, and as soon as the adult departed, the controller removed the toys and assembled the imitation task apparatus.

IMITATION TASK

The imitation task was essentially the same two-choice discrimination problem utilized in an earlier experiment (Bandura & Huston, 1961), except the response repertoires exhibited by the models were considerably extended, and the procedure used in the acquisition trials was somewhat modified.

The apparatus consisted of two small boxes with hinged lids, identical in color and size. The boxes were placed on stools approximately 4 feet apart and 8 feet from the starting point. On the lid of each box was a rubber doll.

As soon as the other adult returned with the experimenter, the controller asked both the child and the experimenter to be seated in the chairs along the side of the room, and the other adult to stand at the starting point, while the controller described the game they were about to play. The controller then explained that the experimenter would hide a picture sticker in one of the two boxes and the object of the game was to guess which box contained the sticker. The adults would have the first set of turns, following which the child would play the guessing game.

The discrimination problem was employed simply as a cover task that occupied the children's attention while at the same time permitting observation of the models as they performed divergent patterns of behavior during the discrimination trials in the absence of any set to attend to or learn the responses exhibited by the models.

Before commencing the trials, the controller invited the other participants to join him in selecting a "thinking cap" from hat racks containing two identical sets of four caps, each of which had a different colored feather. The controller selected the green feathered hat, remarked, "Feather in the front" and wore the hat with the feather facing forward. The other model selected the yellow feathered hat, commented, "Feather in the back," and placed the hat on her head with the feather facing backward. The child then made his choice from the four hats in the lower rack and it was noted whether he matched the color preference, hat placement, and the verbal responses of the one or the other model.

The models then went to the starting point, the child returned to his seat, and the experimenter loaded both boxes with sticker pictures for the models' trials.

During the execution of each trial, each model exhibited a different set of relatively novel verbal and motor responses that were totally irrelevant to the discrimination problem to which the child's attention was directed. At the starting point the controller stood with his arms crossed, but at the experimenter's warning not to look, the controller placed his hands over his eyes, faced sideways, and asked, "Ready?" The other model stood with his arms on his hips, then squatted with his back turned to the boxes, and asked, "Now?"

As soon as the experimenter gave the signal for the first trial, the controller remarked, "Forward march" and began marching slowly toward the designated box repeating, "March, march, march." When he reached the box he said, "Sock him," hit the doll aggressively off the box, opened the lid and yelled, "Bingo," as he reached down for the sticker. He then remarked, "Lickit-sticket," as he pressed on the picture sticker with his thumb in the upper-right quadrant of a 24×24 inch sheet of plain white paper that hung on the wall immediately behind the boxes. The controller terminated the trial by replacing the doll facing sideways on the container with the comment, "Look in the mirror," and made a final verbal response, "There."

The other model then took her turn and performed a different set of imitative acts but equated with the controller's responses in terms of number, types of response classes represented, structural properties, and interest value. At the starting point, for example, she remarked, "Get set, go" and walked stiffly toward the boxes repeating "Left, right, left, right." When she reached the container she said, "Down and up," as she lay the doll down on the lid and opened the box. She then exclaimed, "A stickeroo," repeated, "Weto-smacko," and slapped on the sticker with the open hand in the lower-left quadrant of the sheet of paper. In terminating the trial, the model lay the doll on the lid of the container with the remark, "Lie down," and returned with her hands behind her back, and emitted the closing remark, "That's it."

The two sets of responses were counterbalanced by having the models display each pattern with half the subjects in each of the three groups.

The models performed alternately for four trials. At the conclusion of the fourth trial the controller explained that he had to check some materials in his car and while he and the other model were away the child may take his turns. Before they departed, however, the experimenter administered a picture preference test in which the models were asked to select their preferred picture from six different stickers pasted on a 5×8 inch card, after which the child was presented a similar card containing an identical set of stickers and requested to indicate his preference.

In addition to the introductory block of four trials by the models, the child's 15 total test trials were interspersed with three two-trial blocks by the models. The models were always absent from the room during the child's test series. This procedure was adopted in order to remove any imagined situational restraints against, or coercion for, the child to reproduce the models' responses. Moreover, demonstrations of delayed imitation in the absence of the model provide more decisive evidence for learning by means of imitation.

The models always selected different boxes, the right-left position varying from trial to trial in a fixed irregular order, and the controller always took the first turn. Although the models received stickers on each trial, the child was nonrewarded on one third of the trial in order to maintain his interest in the cover task.

At the beginning of each of the blocks of subjects' trials, the experimenter administered the picture preference test and the selection of stickers that matched the models' choices was recorded. In addition, on the eighth trial the models removed their hats and hung them in different locations in the room. If the child removed his hat during the session and placed it along side one or the other of the model's hats, this imitative act was also scored.

At the completion of the imitation phase of the experiment, the children were interviewed by the experimenter in order to determine whom they considered to be the controller of resources, and to assess their model preferences. The latter data were used as an index of attraction to the models. In addition, for the children in the adult consumer condition, the session was concluded by providing them the same lavish treatment accorded their adult rival.

Children in the control group had no prior social interaction with the models but participated with them in the imitative learning phase of the study. The experimenter assumed complete charge of the procedures and treated the models as though they were naive subjects. The control group was included primarily to determine the models' relative effectiveness as modeling stimuli. In addition, the models alternated between subjects in the order in which they executed the trials so as to test for the possibility of a primacy or a recency of exposure effect on imitative behavior.

IMITATION SCORES

The imitation scores were obtained by summing the frequency of occurrence of the postural, verbal, and motor responses described in the preceding section, and the hat, color, and picture preferences that matched the selections of each of the two models.

The children's performances were scored by three raters who observed the experimental sessions through a one-way mirror from an adjoining observation room. The raters were provided with a separate check list of responses exhibited by each of the two models, and the scoring procedure simply involved checking the imitative responses performed by the children on each trial. In order to provide an estimate of interscorer reliability, the performances of 30% of the children were recorded simultaneously but independently by two observers. The raters were in perfect agreement on 95% of the specific imitative responses that they scored.

RESULTS

The control group data revealed that the two models were equally effective in eliciting imitative responses, the mean values being 17.83 and 20.46 for the male and female model, respectively; nor did the children display differential imitation of same-sex ($M = 20.30$) and opposite-sex ($M = 17.92$) models. Although children in the control group tended to imitate the second model ($M = 22.21$) to a somewhat greater extent than the one who performed first ($M = 16.08$) on each trial, suggesting a recency of exposure effect, the difference was not of statistically significant magnitude ($t = 1.60$).

Table 1 presents the mean imitation scores for children in each of the two experimental triads. A $2 \times 2 \times 2 \times 2$ mixed factorial analysis of variance was computed on these data in which the four factors in the design were sex of child, sex of the model who controlled the resources, adult versus child consumer, and the controller versus the other model as the source of imitative behavior.[3] As shown in Table 2, the findings of this study clearly support the social power theory of imitation. In both experimental treatments, regardless of whether the rival adult or the children themselves were the recipients of the rewarding resources, the model who possessed rewarding power was imitated to a greater degree than was the rival or the ignored model ($F = 40.61$, $p < .001$). Nor did the condition combining resource ownership with direct reinforcement of the child yield the highest imitation of the model who controlled and dispensed the positive rewards. The latter finding is particularly surprising since an earlier experiment based on two-person groups (Bandura & Huston, 1961), demonstrated that pairing of model with positive reinforcement substantially enhanced the occurrence of imitative behavior. An examination of the remaining significant interaction effects together with the postexperimental interview data suggest a possible explanation for the discrepant results.

The differential in the controller-other model imitation was most pronounced when the male model was the con-

TABLE 2
SUMMARY OF THE ANALYSIS OF VARIANCE OF THE IMITATION SCORES

Source	df	MS	F
Between subjects	47	310.17	
Sex of subjects (A)	1	283.59	< 1
Sex of controller model (B)	1	128.34	< 1
Adult versus child consumer (C)	1	518.01	1.61
A × B	1	23.01	< 1
A × C	1	1.76	< 1
B × C	1	742.59	2.31
A × B × C	1	21.10	< 1
Error (b)	40	321.49	
Within subjects	48	113.24	
Controller versus other model (D)	1	2,025.84	40.61***
A × D	1	297.51	5.96*
B × D	1	237.51	4.76*
C × D	1	396.09	7.94**
A × B × D	1	256.76	5.15*
A × C × D	1	19.52	< 1
B × C × D	1	23.02	< 1
A × B × C × D	1	184.00	3.69
Error (w)	40	49.88	

* $p < .05$.
** $p < .01$.
*** $p < .001$.

troller of resources ($F = 4.76$, $p < .05$), particularly for boys. In fact, boys who were the recipients of rewarding resources mediated by the female model tended to favor the ignored male as their object of imitation. In the postexperiment interview a number of boys in this condition spontaneously expressed sympathy for the ignored male and mild criticism of the controller for not being more charitable with her bountiful resources (for example, "She doesn't share much. John played bravely even though she didn't even share. . . . She's a bit greedy.").

As a partial check on whether this factor would tend to diminish the differential imitation of the two models, six children—three boys and three girls—participated in a modified Child Consumer treatment in which, halfway through the social interaction session, the ignored adult was informed that he too may have access to the playthings. He replied that he was quite content to read his book. This modified procedure, which removed the rivalry and the exclusion of the model, yielded four times as much imitation of the controller relative to the model who was ignored by choice.

The significant triple interaction effect indicates that the differential in the controller-other model imitation was greatest when the same-sex model mediated the positive reinforcers, and this effect was more pronounced for boys than for girls.

The data presented so far demonstrate that manipulation of rewarding power had produced differential imitation of the behavior exhibited by the two models. In order to assess whether the dispensing of positive reinforcers in the prior social interaction influenced the

TABLE 1
MEAN NUMBER OF IMITATIVE RESPONSES PERFORMED BY SUBGROUPS OF CHILDREN IN THE EXPERIMENTAL TRIADS

Subjects	Objects of Imitation			
	Male	*Female*	*Female*	*Male*
	Controller	Consumer	Controller	Consumer
Girls	29.00	9.67	26.00	10.00
Boys	30.17	18.67	22.33	16.17
Total	29.59	14.17	24.17	13.09
	Controller	Ignored	Controller	Ignored
Girls	22.00	16.17	31.84	22.17
Boys	29.17	16.67	26.83	34.50
Total	25.59	16.42	29.34	28.34

[3] The assistance of Eleanor Willemsen with the statistical computations is gratefully acknowledged.

overall level of matching responses, the imitation scores in each of the three groups were summed across models and analyzed using a Sex × Treatment design.

The mean total imitative responses for children in the Child Consumer, Adult Consumer, and the Control group were 50.21, 40.58, and 37.88, respectively. Analysis of variance of these data reveals a significant treatment effect ($F = 3.37$, $.025 < p < .05$). Further comparisons of pairs of means by the t test, show that children in the child rewarded condition displayed significantly more imitative behavior than did children both in the Adult Consumer treatment ($t = 2.19$, $p < .05$), and those in the Control group ($t = 2.48$, $p < .02$). The Adult Consumer and Control groups, however, did not differ from each other in this respect ($t = .54$).

The model preference patterns were identical for children in the two experimental conditions and consequently, the data were combined for the statistical analysis. Of the 48 children, 32 selected the model who possessed rewarding power as the more attractive, while 15 preferred the noncontrolling adult. The greater attractiveness of the rewarding model was significant beyond the .05 level ($x^2 = 5.34$). The experimental triad in which boys were the recipients of positive reinforcers while the male model was ignored, and the female consumer–girl ignored subgroup, contributed the highest preference for the non-controlling adult.

In addition to the experimental groups discussed in the preceding section, data are available for 9 children in the Adult Consumer condition, and for 11 children in the Child Consumer treatment who revealed, in their postexperiment interviews, that they had actually attributed rewarding power to the ignored or the consumer adult despite the elaborate experimental manipulations designed to establish differential power status. A number of these children were firmly convinced that only a male can possess resources and, therefore, the female dispensing the rewards was only an intermediary for the male model (for example, "He's the man and it's all his because he's a daddy. Mommy never really has things belong to her. . . . He's the daddy so it's his but he shares nice with the mommy. . . . He's the man and the man always really has the money and he lets ladies play too. John's good and polite and he has very good manners.") This view of resource ownership within the family constellation was often directly reinforced by the mothers (for example, "My mommy told me and Joan that the daddy really buys all the things, but the mommy looks after things."). Children who attributed the resource ownership to the consumer or ignored female model had considerable difficulty in explaining their selection (for example, "I just knowed it does. . . . I could tell, that's how."), perhaps, because the power structure they depicted is at variance with the widely accepted cultural norm.

As shown in Table 3, models who were attributed rewarding power elicited approximately twice as many matching responses than models who were perceived by the children as possessing no control over the rewarding resources. Because of the small and unequal number of cases in each cell, these data were not evaluated statistically. The differences, however, are marked and quite

TABLE 3

IMITATION AS A FUNCTION OF ATTRIBUTED
REWARDING POWER TO THE MODELS

Treatment Condition	Objects of Imitation			
	Female Controller	Male Noncontroller	Male Controller	Female Noncontroller
Adult consumer	24.0	12.3	29.8	14.6
Child consumer	18.2	6.7	35.5	16.2

in accord with those produced by the experimentally manipulated variations in power status.

DISCUSSION

To the extent that the imitative behavior elicited in the present experiment may be considered an elementary prototype of identification within a nuclear family group, the data fail to support the interpretation of identificatory learning as the outcome of a rivalrous interaction between the child and the adult who occupies an envied status in respect to the consumption of highly desired resources. Children clearly identified with the source of rewarding power rather than with the competitor for these rewards. Moreover, power inversions on the part of the male and female models produced cross-sex imitation, particularly in girls. The differential readiness of boys and girls to imitate behavior exhibited by an opposite-sex model are consistent with findings reported by Brown (1956, 1958) that boys show a decided preference for the masculine role, whereas, ambivalence and masculine role preference are widespread among girls. These findings probably reflect both the differential cultural tolerance for cross-sex behavior displayed by males and females, and the privileged status and relatively greater positive reinforcement of masculine role behavior in our society.

Failure to develop sex appropriate behavior has received considerable attention in the clinical literature and has customarily been assumed to be established and maintained by psycho-sexual threat and anxiety reducing mechanisms. Our findings strongly suggest, however, that external social learning variables, such as the distribution of rewarding power within the family constellation, may be highly influential in the formation of inverted sex role behavior.

Theories of identificatory learning have generally assumed that within the family setting the child's initial identification is confined to his mother, and that during early childhood boys must turn from the mother as the primary model to the father as the main source of imitative behavior. However, throughout the course of development children are provided with ample opportunities to observe the behavior of both parents. The results of the present experiment reveal that when children are exposed to multiple models they may select one or more of them as the primary source of behavior, but rarely reproduce all the elements of a single model's repertoire or confine their imitation to that model. Although the children adopted many of the characteristics of the model who possessed rewarding power, they also reproduced some of the elements of behavior exhibited by the model who occupied the subordinate role. Consequently, the children were not simply junior-size replicas of one or the other model; rather, they exhibited a relatively novel pattern of behavior representing an amalgam of elements from both models. Moreover, the specific admixture of behavioral elements varied from child to child. These findings provide considerable evidence for the seemingly paradoxical conclusion that imitation can in fact produce innovation of social behavior, and that within the same family even same-sex siblings may exhibit quite different response patterns, owing to their having selected for imitation different elements of their parents' response repertoires.

The association of a model with noncontingent positive reinforcement tends to increase the incidence of imitative behavior in two person groups (Bandura & Huston, 1961), whereas the addition of a same-sex third person who is denied access to desired rewards may provoke in children negative evaluations of the rewarding model and thereby decreases his potency as a modeling stimulus. These two sets of data demonstrate how learning principles based on an individual behavior model may be subject to strict limitations, since the introduction of additional social variables into the stimulus complex can produce significant changes in the functional relationships between relevant variables.

SUMMARY

Predictions derived from 3 prominent theories of identificatory learning were tested in 3-person groups representing prototypes of the nuclear family. In 1 condition an adult assumed the role of controller of positive reinforcers. Another adult was the consumer of these resources, while the child, a participant observer in the triad, was essentially ignored. In a 2nd treatment condition, one adult controlled the rewarding resources; the child, however, was the recipient of the positive reinforcers, while the other adult was assigned a subordinate and powerless role. Following the experimental social interactions the 2 adult models exhibited divergent patterns of behavior in the presence of the child, and a measure was obtained of the degree to which the child subsequently patterned his behavior after that of the models. Children imitated primarily the model who possessed rewarding power rather than the competitor for the rewards. Moreover, power inversions on the part of the male and female models produced cross-sex imitation, particularly in girls.

REFERENCES

BANDURA, A. Social learning through imitation. In M. R. Jones (Ed.), *Nebraska symposium on motivation: 1962.* Lincoln: Univer. Nebraska Press, 1962.

BANDURA, A., & HUSTON, ALETHA C. Identification as a process of incidental learning. *J. abnorm. soc. Psychol.,* 1961, *63,* 311–318.

BRONFENBRENNER, U. Freudian theories of identification and their derivatives. *Child Develpm.,* 1960, *31,* 15–40.

BROWN, D. G. Sex-role preference in young children. *Psychol. Monogr.,* 1956, *70* (14, Whole No. 421).

BROWN, D. G. Sex-role development in a changing culture. *Psychol. Bull.,* 1958, *55,* 232–242.

FRENCH, J. R. P., JR., MORRISON, H. W., & LEVINGER, G. Coercive power and forces affecting conformity. *J. abnorm. soc. Psychol.,* 1960, *61,* 93–101.

FRENCH, J. R. P., JR., & RAVEN, B. The bases of social power. In D. Cartwright (Ed.), *Studies in social power.* Ann Arbor, Mich.: Institute for Social Research, 1959. Pp. 150–167.

FREUD, ANNA. *The ego and the mechanisms of defense.* New York: International Univer. Press, 1946.

FREUD, S. The passing of the Oedipus-complex. In, *Collected papers.* Vol. 2. London: Hogarth Press, 1924. Pp. 269–282.

FREUD, S. *Group psychology and the analysis of the ego.* London: Hogarth Press, 1948.

KAGAN, J. The concept of identification. *Psychol. Rev.,* 1958, *65,* 296–305.

KLEIN, MELANIE. *The psycho-analysis of children.* London: Hogarth Press, 1949.

MACCOBY, ELEANOR E. Role-taking in childhood and its consequences for social learning. *Child Develpm.,* 1959, *30,* 239–252.

MOWRER, O. H. Identification: A link between learning theory and psychotherapy. In, *Learning theory and personality dynamics.* New York: Ronald Press, 1950. Pp. 69–94.

MOWRER, O. H. Hearing and speaking: An analysis of language learning. *J. speech hear. Disord.,* 1958, *23,* 143–152.

MUSSEN, P., & DISTLER, L. Masculinity, identification, and father-son relationship. *J. abnorm. soc. Psychol.,* 1959, *59,* 350–356.

PARSONS, T. Family structure and the socialization of the child. In T. Parsons & R. F. Bales (Eds.), *Family, socialization, and interaction process.* Glencoe, Ill.: Free Press, 1955, Pp. 35–131.

SEARS, R. R. Identification as a form of behavioral development. In D. B. Harris (Ed.), *The concept of development.* Minneapolis: Univer. Minnesota Press, 1957. Pp. 149–161.

WHITING, J. W. M. Sorcery, sin, and the superego: A cross-cultural study of some mechanisms of social control. In M. R. Jones (Ed.). *Nebraska symposium on motivation: 1959.* Lincoln: Univer. Nebraska Press, 1959. Pp. 174–195.

WHITING, J. W. M. Resource mediation and learning by identification. In I. Iscoe & H. W. Stevenson (Eds.), *Personality development in children.* Austin: Univer. Texas Press, 1960, Pp. 112–126.

ZIPF, SHEILA G. Resistance and conformity under reward and punishment. *J. abnorm. soc. Psychol.,* 1960, *61,* 102–109.

20

Learning by Imitation
in Kindergarten Children [1]

This article on imitation is also relevant to identification, which was discussed in the preceding papers. The dependent variable discussed in this paper is the amount of learning of the mazes on an imitative basis. Another part of the study examined the influence of the same independent variables on a different kind of imitative behavior (or dependent variable), the degree to which the children chose the same color of pencil as the adult to work the mazes with. That color-matching aspect of the study was reprinted in the first edition of this book. The effects of the experimental manipulations on the two types of imitation are different despite the fact that the same Ss are engaging in both behaviors.

This study was done when the author, one of the editors of this book, was at Harvard's Laboratory of Human Development. Judy Rosenblith is professor of psychology at Wheaton College and a member of the Institute of Life Sciences at Brown University. Her research there examines the relations between assessments of newborn behavior and later development.

[1] This paper is based on a dissertation submitted to Harvard University in partial fulfillment of the requirements for the Ph.D. The author would like to express gratitude to Dr. Wesley Allinsmith for his encouragement and counsel. This research was aided by a grant to the Laboratory of Human Development from the Public Health Service.

This study asks four main questions: (a) Does having a model lead to significantly greater improvement in learning than additional experience only? (b) Is the extent of a child's learning by copying an adult "leader" or model affected by the sex of that leader (considered, especially, in relation to the child's sex)? (c) Does the way in which the leader treats the child immediately before the copying session affect learning? (d) Is there an interaction between the "sex" and "treatment" variables?

The problem of imitation examined in an experimental framework has received its most extensive treatment in Miller and Dollard's book *Social Learning and Imitation* (4). They demonstrated that the tendency to imitate is acquired in rats and children, and that the operations of reinforcement are necessary for the establishment of imitative tendencies.

Schein (8) attempted to test the assertions of Miller and Dollard with adult *S*s. Studying the effect of reward on adult imitative behavior, he found that a significant number of *S*s "learned" to imitate a model when such imitation was rewarded. He also found that the imitative response generalized to a similar but new situation. Since the absolute level of imitation was not high, Schein speculated about motives (e.g., "imitation is equivalent to cheating") which might have been operative to demand that his adult *S*s not imitate. Such motives all appeared less apt to be present in young children than in adults. Also, Schwartz (9) found more imitation in 9- and 10-year-olds than in 15- and 16-year-olds, suggesting that more imitation might be expected in kindergarten *S*s.

Miller and Dollard classified imitation into three categories of behavior: *same* behavior, *matched-dependent* behavior, and *copying*. They asserted that all three behaviors are learned via the principles of instrumental conditioning. Learning by imitation is linked to their concept of copying in which one person learns to model his behavior on that of another. They further asserted that all three kinds of imitative learning respond to the same conditions.

In this study there was no attempt to teach the child to copy. There was reliance on the child's having learned to make imitative responses as a result of past experience in the processes of socialization. Generalization of this established learning to imitate is what was looked for. As Miller and Dollard have said: "An analysis in terms of learning principles indicated that the factor of generalization should play an important role in the proc-

Judy F. Rosenblith, "Learning by imitation in kindergarten children," *Child Development,* 1959, *30,* 69–80. Reprinted by permission of the Society for Research in Child Development.

esses determining the degree to which any leader will be reacted to as a prestigeful model" (4, p. 166). Thus, generalization to a male model from significant males in the child's life was expected, and similarly for a female model. Since the child has very little contact with the particular adults who serve as models, it was assumed that the degree to which the model is effective does stem from such generalization. Nevertheless, rewards were not excluded from the situation. The leader to be imitated or copied was not only prestigeful by virtue of age and size, but the leader's skill was emphasized by verbally rewarding his correct performance. The child was also verbally rewarded when his performance was a sufficiently close copy of the leader's (i.e., was correct).

This problem can also be examined in the theoretical framework of identification theory. Doing so poses the question of whether an adult leader of the same sex as the child might not be a more effective model for imitative behavior for 5-year-old children.

Miller and Dollard, in commenting that sex-typing may belong to a list of social conditions that may enhance or inhibit imitation or the tendency to imitate, do not tell at which age level this factor should become important. It is, however, not unreasonable to assume that at kindergarten age most children have had more reinforcement for imitating a female and hence that a female model should be more effective for both sexes. Such a view would be congruent with that expressed by Miller and Dollard or by contiguity theorists with regard to the secondary reward value which people acquire.

Most identification theories, on the other hand, would lead one to expect that a good deal of identification has taken place by the kindergarten age. Thus, one would expect that a leader of the same sex as the child should be the most effective, with considerable individual fluctuation due to differences in the stage of identification that has been reached.

Another aspect of identification theories leads to a consideration of the role of threat in the formation of identification (Freud, castration threat; Fromm, threat from authoritarian father). Mowrer (5) posits two kinds of identification. The first is developmental, it is with the mother for both sexes, threat does not play a role in it, and it is related to the learning of skills. The second kind of identification is a later form. It is with the parent of the same sex and threat may play a role. Mowrer calls this kind defensive identification, and says that it is related to character learning and is well under way by kindergarten age. In line with these considerations one might expect differences in the amount

of identification shown or generalized (hence in the effectiveness of the adult as a model for copying) according to the presence or absence of an implied threat in the adult-child relation. The contingency or uncertainty-reduction theory of effectiveness of secondary rewards would lead to the same set of expectations.

These considerations led to the following experimental manipulations: (a) the adult leader was attentive to the child for the entire period prior to the copying session for some Ss, and (b) the adult withdrew attention from the child after half of the period and stayed withdrawn for the remainder of the period prior to the copying session for other Ss. Such withdrawal presumably constitutes a mild threat to the child's relation to the adult.

The present study was not intended to provide an *experimentum crucis* for deciding the merits of the above theories, but only to shed light on these problems.

PROCEDURE

The Ss were 120 kindergarten children from two public schools in a Boston suburb composed of middle and upper-middle class residents. Each child was brought individually from the classroom to the experimental room by the E in order to "play a game." In this initial session the child was tested using the Porteus Maze Test (6); this test was administered with slight modifications in the instructions and procedure to make it more suitable to the age of the children.[2] The Porteus Test contains one maze for each year from 3 through 11. Two trials were allowed on each of these as in the Porteus Test. There are also mazes for 12- and 14-year-olds and adults. Porteus allows four trials for each of these mazes. In this experiment only two trials were allowed since the 5-year-old Ss who reached the 12-year-old level or above were apt to be frustrated by four trials on such difficult mazes and want to quit the "game." The Porteus criteria for discontinuing testing were used, i.e., failure on two consecutive or on two out of three consecutive age levels.

On the basis of level of performance in this initial session children were assigned to one of four groups. Group 1 consisted of those who passed only the first two mazes, (i.e., the 3- and 4-year mazes). Group 2 consisted of those who passed a total of three or four of the mazes. Group 3 passed five mazes, and Group 4 passed six or more of the mazes. Children from each group were then assigned to each of the treatments.

One to three weeks after this initial session the

---

[2] Copies of the exact procedure may be seen in (7).

child was brought from his room by E to "have a second turn at the game." This will be referred to as the copying session. Just before arriving at the experimental room, E said to each child who was not in a control group: "You know what? I have someone else here to play the game with us." E and child then entered the room and E introduced the child to the other adult by first names. E then explained to the child that she had something to do for a while and invited the child and the other adult to go to another table in the room and play with the toys on it until E was ready to play the game.[3] The child was seated facing the table of toys and the adult at the adjacent side facing the child and/or table.

It should be noted that E essentially was treating the other adult in the same manner as the child. E did nothing to enhance the adultness or maleness (or femaleness) of the leaders except to reward their proficiency. They were not called Mr. or Mrs. and not described as fathers or mothers. However, they were adult and they were proficient at the task. During the play period the leader behaved as an adult interested in the play of the child and not as another child playing.

The experiment was first run using a male for a leader. The treatments or conditions were: (I) Male leader with a child of the same sex, leader attentive to child throughout the 10-minute period that preceded the copying session proper. (II) Male leader with a child of the same sex, leader attentive to the child for 5 minutes, then leader said: "I'm sorry, I can't play with you any more, I have to read a book." Leader then turned his chair so his back was toward the child and read a book for 5 minutes. (III) Control Ss, males, who were brought to the room by E and who immediately received two additional trials at each maze previously failed, until the criterion for discontinuing testing was reached. (IV) Male leader with a child of the opposite sex, attentive throughout (as in I). (V) Male leader with a child of the opposite sex, withdrew attention after 5 minutes (as in II). (VI) Control Ss, females, tested in the same fashion (as in III). The entire design was then repeated using a female leader.

In treatments I, II, IV, and V, at the end of the 10-minute period E said: "I'm ready to play the game now." Adult leader and child moved to the E's table. They took adjacent seats at the table on the side opposite E and facing her with the adult to the right of the child. E then said to the child: "You've played this game with me before. —— (adult) wasn't here when we played then, so how would it be if you take turns and give —— (adult) the first turn?" (We might note here that no child ever argued with the suggestion of taking turns.) The adult was then given the first maze which the child failed previously and the same instructions that the child had received. The leader did the maze correctly at a rather slow pace and with pauses at choice points accompanied by some visual search. The child watched during this period and then was given a turn at the same maze. To ensure that the child was watching the entire performance, the adult paused when he was not and only continued when the child had again turned his attention to the maze. There were two such trials on each maze failed initially (unless the child passed it correctly on the first trial, in which case there was only one), until the criterion for discontinuing testing was reached. This yields a design in which there are six treatments (including controls) and four replications (by initial level of performance). The part of the study using the male leader was started at one school and completed at the second. The repetition with the female leader was started at the second school and completed at the first.

The number of Ss decided on for each cell was based on the distribution of passes obtained by the children in the first school. Since the second school had a different distribution of passes (fewer children with a high number of passes), the number of children from groups 3 & 4 of initial performance level in each cell was decreased from 3 to 2, thus dropping the total N from an anticipated 132 to 120 (*see* Table 1).

The data to be analyzed here, in investigating the amount of learning by imitation, are the number of new mazes passed ("new passes") in the second or copying session.

RESULTS

Since the distribution of the number of new passes is not normal, and since the number of mazes passed forms only an ordinal scale, the results will be examined using nonparametric statistics.

The data in Table 2 refer to the over-all experimental design, i.e., to both the male and female leader experiments. If one applies Friedman's $\chi^2 r$ (9) to these data, one finds the p values[4] shown in Table 3. The differences found justify separate examination of pairs of treatments.

---

[3] The toys on the table were chosen for their masculine and feminine identification potential. E was actually recording the child's behavior as the child played with the toys. Ratings of these protocols for masculine and feminine identification will be examined later. The toys included shaving set and make-up kit, carpenter tools and kitchen utensils, and a family of dolls, among others.

[4] All p values reported in this paper are for a two-tailed test.

TABLE 1
EXPERIMENTAL DESIGN (NUMBER OF *S*s IN EACH CELL IS SHOWN)

Initial Performance Groups	Male *S*s			Female *S*s			
	A†(I)	*WA†(II)*	*C†(III)*	*A(IV)*	*WA(V)*	*C(VI)*	
Male Leader *							
1	3	3	3	3	3	3	18
2	3	3	3	3	3	3	18
3	2	2	2	2	2	2	12
4	2	2	2	2	2	2	12
	10	10	10	10	10	10	60

* The entire design is repeated with a female leader.

† A stands for leader attentive throughout, WA, for withdraws attention for last half of period, and C, for controls in this and all subsequent tables.

TABLE 2
NUMBER OF NEW PASSES OBTAINED BY *S*s IN THE VARIOUS CELLS

Initial Performance Groups	Male *S*s			Female *S*s		
	A(I)	*WA(II)*	*C(III)*	*A(IV)*	*WA(V)*	*C(VI)*
Male Leader						
1	7	6	5	5	4	2
2	9	12	8	9	6	6
3	4	6	1	4	4	2
4	6	7	1	4	5	2
Total	26	31	15	22	19	12
Female Leader						
1	6	2	4	4	1	1
2	10	4	6	6	3	4
3	8	4	2	3	3	4
4	6	4	1	3	5	3
Total	30	14	13	16	12	12
Total	56	45	28	38	31	24

Before doing so, it is interesting to examine the data according to the sex of *S*s and of leaders. Table 3 shows the *p* values of X^2r calculated for the various combinations of sex of *S*s and of leader. Male leader and male *S*s show more influence of these manipulations.

Examination of pairs of treatments by a method described by Wilcoxon (11) shows that boys and girls who are control *S*s do not differ significantly, although there is a tendency for the control boys to improve more than the control girls. This tendency is close to the .05 level for those whose initial performance placed them in level 1. The remaining results of these comparisons are presented in Table 4. In summary it can be seen that: (a) having a model is more effective than merely having additional trials; (b) girls seem less sensitive to the experimental manipulations than are boys; (c) the female leader was less effective than the male leader; (d) attention is more effective than withdrawal of attention.

Certain qualifications of these general statements are found in the detailed results. The finding concerning the effectiveness of the male and female leaders cannot be labeled a sex difference without further replication since it is possible that individual characteristics of the leaders rather than their immediately perceptible sex characteristics were responsible. In any event, these rather major effects of sex (of both leader and child) which operate in a way that cuts across the original experimental design make the next step of analysis less apt to yield significant results.

The next step was to examine the two experiments together. Since the *S*s were not randomly assigned to treatments across both sexes of leader, some justification for combining the data is probably needed. Both leaders did have *S*s from both schools, though not equal proportions of *S*s from each. The control *S*s in both replications showed no significant difference; in fact, the rank totals are 412 for the first group and 408 for the second. It

TABLE 3
COMPARISON OF TREATMENTS EXAMINED BY THE FRIEDMAN X^2r

	p Values	
Treatments Compared	Male Leader	Female Leader
Total Table (Conditions I through VI)	.01	.09
Treatments—controls not included (Conditions I, II, IV, V)	.06	.052
Conditions involving male Ss (Conditions I, II and III)	.04	.05
Conditions involving female Ss (Conditions IV, V and VI)	.15	.80

TABLE 4
COMPARISONS OF PAIRS OF TREATMENTS USING THE WILCOXON RANKING METHOD

	p Values *			
	Male Leader		Female Leader	
Comparison †	Male Ss	Female Ss	Male Ss	Female Ss
A plus WA vs C	.01 (A&WA)	.01 (A&WA)	ns (A&WA)	ns (A&WA)
A vs C	.10 (A)	$.05 > p > .02$ (A)	.10 (A)	ns (A)
WA vs C	.05 (WA)	$.10 > p > .05$ (WA)	ns (WA)	ns (WA)
A vs WA	ns (WA)	ns (A)	ns (A)	ns (A)
A plus WA vs C (by initial performance groups)				
Group 1	ns (A&WA)	.05 (A&WA)	ns (C)	ns (C)
Group 2	.05 (A&WA)	ns (A&WA)	ns (C)	ns (A&WA)
Group 3 and 4	$.05 > p > .02$ (A&WA)	ns (A&WA)	.01 (A&WA)	ns (A&WA)

* Exact p values or p values larger than the .10 level are not available in the published tables. "ns" is used to indicate that p is greater than .10, i.e., is *not significant*.

† The abbreviations in the parentheses indicate which side of the comparison gave the superior performance.

thus seems reasonable to conclude that the two populations are similar enough to justify combining them for comparisons.

Analyzing the data in this way, the design yields five conditions: opposite sex attentive, opposite sex withdraws attention, same sex attentive, same sex withdraws attention, and controls. If these treatments are examined over the four replications provided by initial level groups, the X^2r is 8.85, which (with 4 *df*) has a p value between .06 and .07. As in the earlier analysis, the boys show a significant effect of treatments (p is .02) and the girls do not (p is .15). An extension of the Kruskal-Wallis technique [5] yields an analysis of variance the results of which are shown in Table 5.

DISCUSSION

The difference between the results for the male leader and the female leader are striking, as are the differences between the results for boys and girls. The fact that the boys tended to show more improvement than the girls may provide more ceiling

for finding differences between treatments for the boys. However, such differences between boys and girls remain puzzling since they had been equated for pretest performance. Although there was no significant difference between boys and girls as controls, the consistent superiority of all Ss with a male leader is noted ($p < .05$ that they differ from controls by chance, but $p < .10$ that Ss with the female leader do). Hartup (3) found that boys learned a concept formation task more quickly than girls. He speculated that the blocks involved were more salient for boys than for girls. (Note: The mazes used as a subtest on WISC correlate most highly

TABLE 5
KRUSKAL-WALLIS ANALYSIS OF VARIANCE
AS EXPANDED BY HYMAN

Source of Variation	H	df	Approximate p
Among subcells	36.6	39	ns (.5)
Treatments	7.87	4	.10
Levels of initial performance	7.13	3	.07
Sex of Ss	3.00	1	.09
Sex × Levels	.72	3	ns (.85)
Levels × Treatments	8.4	12	ns (.75)
Sex × Treatments	7.43	4	.11
Sex × Treatments × Levels	2.05	12	ns (.99)

[5] This extension of the Kruskal-Wallis analysis of variance was suggested to the author by Dr. R. Hyman of the Department of Social Relations at Harvard.

with block design and object assembly, about .48). Publications on the Porteus Test fail to give any information on sex differences that sheds any light on this problem.

One should also note that the level of performance on the pretest is a significant source of variation. Thus, it is wise to control for level of pretest performance in a study such as the present one. The fact that levels did not enter into any significant interaction term mitigates this conclusion. It does, however, seem (*see* Table 4) more profitable to look for certain effects of treatments at particular levels rather than in a random population or a representative one.

Now one can turn to the questions raised at the beginning of the paper.

1. Does having a model have a significant effect on the amount of improvement? The answer to this question is yes.

2. Is one sex of leader more effective in evoking learning by imitation? In particular the question raised was whether a female leader or a leader of the same sex as the child would be more effective. Actually the male leader was more effective for both sexes, though only significantly so for the girls. One possible explanation for this finding might lie in the fact that an adult male is more unusual in the school setting, hence has more reward value. Gewirtz and Baer (2), in studying the effectiveness of a social reinforcer (approval) in conjunction with social deprivation, found that the effectiveness of the isolation was qualified by an interaction which indicated that the woman was less effective relative to the man under the condition where *S*s were tested immediately on removal from the play group than the condition where *S*s were tested after a 20-minute period of total isolation. Our situation would seem to be closer to the former condition. Perhaps the whole school setting is one of social deprivation in respect to adult males who play a role in the life of kindergarten children. In summary, there is an effect of sex of leader, but it is not the effect anticipated from either of our theoretical approaches.

3. Does an implied threat to the relation between the child and the adult operate to enhance identification and thus enhance learning by imitation? For boys there was a tendency for those from whom the male leader withdrew attention to do better than boys with an attentive male leader; but they were better than controls at the .05 level, while the male leader attentive group were better than controls at only the .10 level. For girls, however, the effectiveness of the leader of the same sex withdrawing attention does not appear. With the female leader, as with the male, girls tend to do better when they have attention throughout.

The failure to find a relation between implied threat and better learning for girls with a female leader is particularly puzzling in view of Hartup's findings (3). In his study he found that 4-year-old girls learned a simple concept formation task twice as fast when the woman for whom they were doing it had been very nurturant for 5 minutes and then had sat "busy" at her desk for 5 minutes. This quicker learning was not shown for the 4-year-old boys in general. There are a number of differences that could account for the discrepancy: (a) He used 4- instead of 5-year-olds. (b) His task was presented by the person who withdrew instead of by a third person. (c) There were differences in the task (his *S*s learned the concept that determined which of four blocks is the "right" one, ours the way to do a maze). (d) Our results also might be idiosyncratic to our female leader.[6] Hartup used two females and found no significant differences between them. (e) The nurturance which his leaders interrupted was of a more active kind (getting down on the floor and playing with the child). The possible effects of the last four differences are very difficult to speculate about. There is, however, an interesting question we might raise concerning the first point. There are reasons to expect on the basis of Freudian thinking that a girl changes her primary object from mother to father at about age 4. If that is the case, the girl may be particularly sensitive to threat from females at that age. Boys presumably do not change until resolution of the Oedipus complex, well into the fifth year on the average. In that case, 5-year-old boys might be particularly sensitive to threat from males. This interpretation would be congruent with both Hartup's and our findings. Very general support for this idea may be found by examining the data for all girls and boys in the sample who are under 5 years, 3 months, in comparison with all those who are over 5 years, 7 months. We find that the older boys improve significantly more than the younger ($p = .02$), while the older girls do not improve significantly more than the younger ($p > .10$). Unfortunately, there are too few cases to enable us to look at the operation of the attention and withdrawal of attention variables within these age subgroups.

In summary, there is equivocal evidence for threat having the effect of enhancing performance where boys with the male leader are concerned, but in no other case.

4. Is there an interaction between the sex and

---

[6] We did a spot check using another female leader for 4 children (2 boys and 2 girls, all at the same initial level of performance). It is suggestive that there was no apparent difference between results for these 4 children and a comparable 4 from our female leader experiment.

treatment variables? Yes. This answer must be qualified by saying that we cannot be certain whether it is the sex of the leaders or other personal characteristics which account for some of the interactions. Further replications are needed to settle this issue. However, one should bear in mind that generalization from adults significant in the child's life was expected to be more important than the personal characteristics of the leaders to whom the Ss were exposed for only a brief span of time. Also, Hartup's failure to find differences between two female adults in their effect on the children, and the lack of differences in our own small check are signs which indicate that this is a reasonable view.[7]

On the basis of the data, boys and girls both respond better to attention from the opposite sexed leader than to withdrawal. Boys, and not girls, tend to do better after withdrawal of attention from the leader of the same sex. As indicated above, the differential functioning of threat may be, in part at least, a function of the age of the Ss. The rank orders of effectiveness of treatments for the over-all design is given in Table 6.

SUMMARY

The effectiveness of learning by imitation was studied in a context which permitted examination of a number of variables relevant to learning and identification theories. These were: (a) the effectiveness of having a leader or model as contrasted with experience in the absence of a model; (b) the effectiveness of the sex of the leader and of the leader's sex in relation to that of the child; (c) the effectiveness of the adult leader who gives attention to the child for the entire period preceding the imitation, as contrasted with the adult who pays attention to the child for half the time and withdraws attention for the remaining half.

In general, having a model was more effective than merely having additional trials. There were important differences between the effectiveness of the male leader and the female leader. The male leader was, in general, more effective. There were also important differences between boys and girls. Boys showed more improvement. Girls seemed less sensitive to the experimental manipulations. There was a tendency for attention to be more effective than withdrawal of attention except in the case of boys with a male leader. The specific findings were examined in detail and their relation to current theories discussed. Analysis of variance on the male and female leader parts of the study combined showed effects of: (a) treatments, (b) sex of Ss, (c) initial or pretest level of Ss' performance on the mazes, and (d) interaction between the sex of Ss and the treatments.

REFERENCES

1. BISHOP, BARBARA M. Mother-child interaction and the social behavior of children. *Psychol. Monogr.*, 1951, *65*, No. 328.
2. GEWIRTZ, J. L., & BAER, D. M. Does brief social "deprivation" enhance the effectiveness of a social reinforcer ("approval")? *Amer. Psychol.*, 1956, *11*, 428–429.
3. HARTUP, W. W. Nurturance and nurturance-withdrawal in relation to the dependency behavior of preschool children. *Child Develpm.*, 1958, *29*, 191–201.
4. MILLER, N. E., & DOLLARD, J. *Social learning and imitation.* New Haven: Yale Univer. Press, 1941.
5. MOWRER, O. H. *Learning theory and personality dynamics.* New York: Ronald, 1950.
6. PORTEUS, S. D. *The Porteus Maze Test and intelligence.* Palo Alto: Pacific Books, 1950.
7. ROSENBLITH, JUDY F. Imitation in kindergarten children. Unpublished doctoral dissertation, Radcliffe College, 1958.

---

[7] Additional evidence of this kind is provided by Bishop (1), who found that when children were brought into a play room situation with a neutral adult (female) they reacted in the same way they had earlier reacted to their mothers with respect to aggressive stimuli, cooperation, noncooperation and resistance.

TABLE 6
RANK ORDERS OF AMOUNT OF IMPROVEMENT

	SS-A	SS-WA	OS-A	OS-WA	C
Boys	3 (26)	1 (31)	2 (30)	5 (14)	4 (15)
Girls	3 (17)	4 (12)	1 (21)	2 (19)	5 (11)

NOTE.—SS-A stands for leader of same sex—attentive throughout;
SS-WA stands for leader of same sex—withdraws attention;
OS-A stands for leader of opposite sex—attentive throughout;
OS-WA stands for leader of opposite sex—withdraws attention;
C stands for controls, additional experience with no leader.
Figures in parentheses represent the number of new passes obtained by all subjects in that cell.

8. SCHEIN, E. H. The effect of reward on adult imitative behavior. *J. abnorm. soc. Psychol.*, 1954, *49*, 389–395.

9. SCHWARTZ, N. An experimental study of imitation. The effects of reward and age. Senior honors thesis, Radcliffe College, 1953.

10. SIEGEL, S. *Nonparametric statistics for the behavioral sciences.* New York: McGraw-Hill, 1956.

11. WILCOXON, F. Individual comparisons by ranking methods. *Biometrics Bull.*, 1945, *1*, 80–83.

21

Teaching Styles of Four-Year-Olds and Their Mothers

Norma D. Feshbach

This article by Norma D. Feshbach offers a bridge between the topic of parental influences and the topic of peers as factors in the child's socialization. Feshbach, who teaches at the University of California at Los Angeles, reports her findings about mothers' attempts to teach their children. She also shows the methods that each of the children in her study used to teach a younger child of the same sex, race, and social class. Since the findings relate to social status and race, the paper might also have been placed in Section VI rather than here.

It has long been recognized that social class and intellectual performance are related. Children from economically disadvantaged homes have, in general, more depressed scores on achievement, learning, and intelligence measures than children from more advantaged backgrounds (Deutch et al., 1968; Jensen, 1969). In addition, a research literature exists documenting different behavior patterns and socialization practices in parents of different social classes (Becker, 1964; Bronfenbrenner, 1958;

Kohn, 1963; Miller and Swanson, 1960; Sears, Maccoby, & Levin, 1957). However, only within the last decade have there been efforts to directly link specific patterns of the mother's behavior to the child's level and type of cognitive skills.

The theorizing of Bernstein (1961), emphasizing the importance of maternal speech as a reflection of social structure shaping the child's cognitive development, provided the impetus to the study of mechanisms mediating the effects of social class membership upon the child's cognitive performance. Hess and Shipman (1965, 1968), like Bernstein (1962), provided evidence of two modes of linguistic style, the elaborate formal code being more characteristic of the middle-class parent and the restricted code, manifested in a rigid and limited grammatical usage, being more typical of the lower-class parent. In addition, Hess and Shipman (1967, 1968) related maternal linguistic codes and maternal teaching strategies to the child's level of cognitive functioning.

The results of a recent study by Bee and her co-workers (1969) support Bernstein's formulations regarding maternal language modes and social class and are also consistent with the Hess and Shipman findings relating maternal teaching strategies to social class. Of particular relevance to the present study is the evidence they report indicating that lower-class mothers are more restrictive and negative than middle-class mothers in their interactions with their children.

This tendency of lower-class mothers to make more negative responses is compatible with the results of a recent study by Feshbach and Devor (1969), which demonstrated that as early as age four, children display very different reinforcement patterns as a function of their race and social-class background. Middle-class white four-year-olds used substantially more positive reinforcement when "instructing" a younger peer than did the middle class black, lower-class white, or lower-class black groups. It seems reasonable to assume that these social class and race differences in children's use of reinforcement are a reflection of social class and race differences in parental reinforcement style. Since reinforcement is a significant factor in the learning process, having both motivational and information functions, variations in reinforcement style may be another factor mediating the relationship between social-class membership and the child's cognitive performance.

The purpose of the present investigation is to assess social-class and race differences in mothers' and children's use of reinforcement. The general

This research was supported in part by Contract 4-6-061646-1909, from the Office of Education, HEW, to the Research and Development Center, School of Education, University of California, Los Angeles.

Norma D. Feshbach, "Teaching styles of four-year-olds and their mothers." Paper presented at the 1970 Annual Meeting of the Western Psychological Association, Los Angeles, California. Reprinted by permission.

153

hypothesis underlying this approach is the expectation of a functional similarity between social class and race effects on children's and on mothers' use of reinforcement.

METHOD

SUBJECTS

The subjects were 109 four-year-old boys and girls, their mothers, and a corresponding number of three-year-olds. There were four groups of subjects based on social class and race: middle class-white (MCW), lower class-white (LCW), middle class-black (MCB), and lower class-black (LCB). Assignment to class was determined by father's occupation and area of residence. The participating sample of mothers and children were drawn from 11 different parent-education pre-school centers in Los Angeles.

PROCEDURE

There were two instructional interaction situations. During the first session the four-year-old child was paired with a randomly selected three-year-old child of the same sex, social class, and ethnic background. The four-year-olds acted as "teachers" while the three-year-olds acted as "pupils." There were 57 male and 52 female pairs.

Prior to the first experimental situation the four-year-old was taken to the experimental room where the experimenter carefully described the details of a simple wooden puzzle. The child was then given three trials to assemble it. During the first trial, the experimenter actively helped the child. For the second trial the experimenter made one positive verbal remark ("that's very good") and one critical remark ("that's not right") concerning the child's performance. For the third trial the four-year-old completed the puzzle alone while the experimenter left to get the three-year-old.

After being provided appropriate instructions the four-year-old teacher-child proceeded to teach the puzzle to the younger child. All comments made by the teacher-child pertaining to the "pupil's" performance were recorded verbatim and subsequently categorized as either positive or negative reinforcement. The positive category included statements of praise, encouragement, and affirmation such as "That's right," "There you go," "That's it," while the negative category included criticism, negations, and derogatory comments such as "That doesn't go there," "No, not that way," "Uh uh." To determine the reliability of this dichotomous classification, 60 randomly selected statements of reinforcement were scored by two independent raters. There were only two instances in which the raters disagreed. The total number of positive and total number of negative statements were determined for each child and constituted the reinforcement measures. In addition, the number of errors and time taken to complete the puzzle were calculated for the younger children.

The second instructional sequence was scheduled one hour after the initial situation. During this second session each mother was asked to teach her own four-year-old child a puzzle. The study had been initially represented to the parents as one which focused on how children behaved in various learning situations and the mothers understood that this task represented one of these situations. The same procedures used in analyzing the child-child interaction were applied to the mother-child interaction. The reliability of scoring for the categorization of reinforcement was again very high, there being only one disagreement for 60 randomly selected statements of reinforcement.

RESULTS

The experimental findings will be presented in the following order:

1. The types of reinforcements used by the four-year-old teacher-child in his instruction of the three-year-old "pupil."
2. The types of reinforcements used by the mothers when instructing their four-year-old children.
3. The relationships between the reinforcements used by the four-year-olds and those used by their mothers.

The mean frequency of positive reinforcements displayed by the four-year-olds in each of the experimental sub-groups is presented in Table 1. The pattern of these data, with the exception of the relatively high number of positive reinforcements employed by lower-class white boys, is similar to that observed in the earlier Feshbach and Devor (1969) study. White children made significantly greater use of positive reinforcements than black children, with the middle-class blacks again using fewer positive reinforcements than any other group. The variance in this group was also lower than that in the other groups and, in view of the divided opinion concerning the influence of heterogeneity upon the analysis of variance, a log transformation of the data was carried out. An analysis of variance applied to these transformed data yielded an even stronger race effect than that indicated in Table 1, with an F of 7.6 for the race variable significant at the .01 level.

The mean frequency of negative reinforcements used by the children in each sub-group is presented in Table 2. Although the earlier Feshbach and Devor (1969) study had not yielded any significant ethnic differences in the frequency of negative reinforcements, the present data indicate that white children tend to make greater use than black children of negative as well as positive rein-

TABLE 1
POSITIVE REINFORCEMENTS USED BY FOUR-YEAR-OLD
TEACHER CHILDREN AS A FUNCTION OF SOCIAL CLASS,
RACE AND SEX

| | Mean Frequencies | | | |
| | Boys | | Girls | |
	White	Black	White	Black
Middle Class	3.3	0.1	1.1	.05
Lower Class	2.4	0.8	1.2	.09

TABLE 2

NEGATIVE REINFORCEMENTS USED BY FOUR-YEAR-OLD TEACHER-CHILDREN AS A FUNCTION OF SOCIAL CLASS, RACE AND SEX

	Mean Frequencies			
	Boys		Girls	
	White	Black	White	Black
Middle Class	3.3	.6	.94	0.0
Lower Class	3.6	1.9	1.3	1.3

TABLE 4

NEGATIVE REINFORCEMENTS ADMINISTERED TO FOUR-YEAR-OLD BOYS AND GIRLS BY THEIR MOTHERS AS A FUNCTION OF SOCIAL CLASS AND RACE

	Mean Frequencies			
	Boys		Girls	
	White	Black	White	Black
Middle Class	1.8	2.6	.8	.5
Lower Class	2.6	6.3	1.8	4.5

forcements. The effect of the race factor becomes significant at the .05 level, when an analysis of variance is applied to a log transformation of the data. Some insight into the functional significance of the greater utilization of positive and negative reinforcements by white as compared to black four-year-olds is provided by an examination of the performance of their three-year-old "pupils." The differences between the white and black three-year-olds in time taken to complete the puzzle and in number of errors made were small and statistically insignificant. However, pupil performance was not unimportant. For the white sample, there was a correlation of +.71 between the four-year-old teacher-child's negative reinforcement score and the number of errors made by his pupil, while the comparable correlation for the black teacher-child's behavior and the performance of his pupil was close to zero.

The analyses of the mother-child interaction, while consistent with the findings for the child-child interaction, reflect a somewhat different pattern. As Table 3 indicates, there are no significant race or class differences in the use of positive reinforcements by the mothers when instructing their four-year-old children. There is a tendency, significant at only the .10 level, for mothers to administer more positive reinforcements to boys than to girls.

Significant class and race differences emerge when the frequency of mothers' use of negative reinforcement is examined. These data are presented in Table 4. Lower-class mothers use many more negative reinforcements than middle-class mothers, and the number of negative reinforcements displayed by black mothers is considerably greater than that displayed by white mothers. The effects of race appear to be more pronounced for lower-class than middle-class mothers, the p value for the interaction falling just short of the .05 level.

Although no differences were found in the performance of the three-year-olds when administered the puzzle task by the four-year-olds, there are highly significant race differences in the error and time scores of the four-year-olds when they are instructed by their mothers. As Tables 5 and 6 indicate, both male and female black children, regardless of social class, took longer to complete the puzzle and made significantly more errors than white children. In this instance, the greater use of negative reinforcements by the black mothers could be a function of the child's performance since the frequency of negative reinforcements administered by the mother is significantly correlated with the number of errors made by the child.

TABLE 5

TIME OBTAINED BY FOUR-YEAR-OLDS AS "PUPILS"

	Mean Time (seconds)			
	Boys		Girls	
	White	Black	White	Black
Middle Class	146	211	133	174
Lower Class	145	222	152	178

TABLE 3

POSITIVE REINFORCEMENTS ADMINISTERED TO FOUR-YEAR-OLD BOYS AND GIRLS BY THEIR MOTHERS AS A FUNCTION OF SOCIAL CLASS AND RACE

	Mean Frequencies			
	Boys		Girls	
	White	Black	White	Black
Middle Class	7.3	5.4	5.3	3.3
Lower Class	4.7	5.6	4.6	4.0

TABLE 6

NUMBER OF ERRORS MADE BY FOUR-YEAR-OLDS AS "PUPILS"

	Mean Time			
	Boys		Girls	
	White	Black	White	Black
Middle Class	5.8	6.6	3.6	7.3
Lower Class	4.9	7.9	5.2	6.1

TABLE 7

INTERRELATIONSHIPS AMONG CHILD'S AND MOTHER'S USE
OF POSITIVE AND NEGATIVE REINFORCEMENTS

		Child's Use of Negative Reinforcement	Mother's Use of Positive Reinforcement	Mother's Use of Negative Reinforcement
Child's Use	MC-W	.31*	.13	.10
of Positive	LC-W	.79**	.29	.02
Reinforcement	MC-B	−.21	.25	−.10
	LC-B	.30	.24	.04
	Total	.57**	.22*	.04
Child's Use	MC-W		.28	.65**
of Negative	LC-W		.21	−.08
Reinforcement	MC-B		.02	.07
	LC-B		.15	.18
	Total		.23*	.16
Mother's Use	MC-W			.54**
of Positive	LC-W			.54**
Reinforcement	MC-B			.60*
	LC-B			.37
	Total			.37**

(MC-W) Middle-Class White (N = 40)
(LC-W) Lower-Class White (N = 38)
(MC-B) Middle-Class Black (N = 11)
(LC-B) Lower-Class White (N = 20)
Total (N = 109)
 *p < .05
**p < .01

The correlations between the types of reinforcements used by the mother and those used by her child are presented in Table 7. These correlations are presented separately for each class and race sub-groups and for the entire sample as well. For the total sample only, there is a small but statistically reliable correlation between the mothers' and children's use of positive reinforcement. Mother's frequency of positive reinforcement is also correlated with her child's use of negative reinforcement. The only other significant relationship obtained is the positive correlation of .65, significant at the .01 level, between middle-class white mothers' and their children's use of negative reinforcement.

DISCUSSION

These data reflect an interesting but complex set of correlations between the mother's and child's use of positive and negative reinforcement. In general, they can be interpreted in terms of modeling influences. However, the limited degree of association found overall, and the fact that a number of correlations were carried out, calls for cross-validation procedures.

More directly relevant to the purpose of the present study are the data relating social class and race to children's and mothers' patterns of rein-

forcement. The results for the child-child interaction are generally similar to those obtained in the earlier Feshbach and Devor study, while the mother-child interaction data are in accord with the findings reported by Hess and Shipman and by Bee and her colleagues. Although the experimental task may be a more contrived situation for the mothers than for the children, the systematic pattern of the obtained results and their consistency with other data strongly suggest that these findings are indicative of more general social class and race differences in maternal reinforcement styles.

One can infer from these findings that the lower-class black child received more negative reinforcements from his mother and less positive reinforcements from his peers than the middle-class white child. It would appear then that the learning environment for the lower-class black child is a less hospitable one than the environment experienced by his white advantaged counterpart and is potentially more disruptive of the learning process.

It remains for subsequent research efforts to establish the linkages between the parent's reinforcement style, the child's reinforcement style, and the child's cognitive performance so that methods can be developed for intervening in this chain when reinforcement experiences are not conducive to effective cognitive functioning.

REFERENCES

BECKER, W. C. Consequences of different kinds of parental discipline. In M. L. Hoffman & L. W. Hoffman (eds.), *Review of child development research.* New York: Russell Sage, 1964, pp. 169–208.

BEE, H. L.; EGEREN, L. F.; STREISAGUTH, A. P.; NYMAN, B. A.; & LECKIE, M. S. Social class differences in maternal teaching strategies and speech patterns. *Developmental Psychology, 1,* 1969.

BERNSTEIN, B. Social class and linguistic development: A theory of social learning. In A. H. Halsey, J. Floud, and C. A. Anderson, (eds.), Education, economy, and society. New York: Free Press, 1961.

BERNSTEIN, B. Social class, linguistic codes, and grammatical elements. *Language and Speech,* 1962, 5, 221–240.

BRONFENBRENNER, U. Socialization and social class through time and space. In E. E. Maccoby, T. M. Newcomb, & E. L. Hartley (eds.), *Readings in social psychology,* 1958.

DEUTSCH, M.; KATZ, I.; & JENSEN, A. *Social class, race and psychological development.* New York: Holt, Rinehart & Winston, 1968.

FESHBACH, N. & DEVOR, G. Teaching styles in four-year-olds. *Child Development,* 1969, 40, 183–190.

HESS, R. D., & SHIPMAN, V. Early experience and the socialization of cognitive modes in children. *Child Development,* 1965, 34, 869–886.

Hess, R. D., & Shipman, V. Cognitive elements in maternal behavior. In J. P. Hill (ed.), *Minnesota symposium on child psychology*, Vol. *1*. Minneapolis: University of Minnesota Press, 1967.

Hess, R. D., & Shipman, V. Maternal influences upon early learning: The cognitive environments of urban pre-school children. In R. D. Hess & R. M. Bear (eds.), *Early education*. Chicago: Aldine, 1968.

Jensen, A. How much can we boost IQ and scholastic achievement? *Harvard Educational Review*, 1969, *39*, 1–123.

Kohn, M. L. Social class and parent-child relationship: An interpretation. *American Journal of Sociology*, 1963, *68*, 471–480.

Sears, R. R.; Maccoby, E. E.; & Levin, H. *Patterns of child rearing*. Evanston, Illinois: Row, Peterson, 1957.

22

Imitation of a Peer as a Function of Reinforcement from the Peer Group and Rewardingness of the Model

WILLARD W. HARTUP
AND BRIAN COATES

This article shows that even those nursery school children who were not accustomed to having active social interchange with the peer group are susceptible to peer influence. However, there is a difference in which peers they are affected by compared to those with more social interaction.

Willard W. Hartup is a professor at the University of Minnesota. Previously, he was associated with Iowa's Child Welfare Research Station. Brian Coates is now at the University of North Carolina at Chapel Hill.

Considerable research has been generated by the hypothesis that rewarding models are imitated to a greater extent than nonrewarding models. This hypothesis figures prominently in several general theories of identification, including the theory of anaclitic identification developed by Freud (1914), the secondary reinforcement interpretation of imitation by Mowrer (1950; 1960), and the extension

This study was completed with the assistance of a stipend awarded to Brian Coates from grant 5–T01–MHO–6668, National Institute of Mental Health. The authors are particularly grateful to Rosalind Charlesworth for her help and to the collaborating nursery school teachers.

of these theories formulated by Sears (1957) and Sears, Rau, and Alpert (1965).

The formulation developed by Mowrer is particularly specific concerning the mechanisms underlying imitation. Mowrer suggested that rewards given to S by a model increase the secondary reinforcing value (for S) of behaviors manifested by the model. When S reproduces these behaviors, the proprioceptive feedback from the imitative acts is presumed, as a consequence of stimulus generalization, to be secondarily reinforcing. This secondary reinforcement predisposes S to reproduce the behavior of the model. Although Mowrer originally provided this theory as an explanation for the imitation of verbal behavior, the theory has since been extended to account for all imitative acts (Mowrer, 1960; Sears, 1957).

Both differential and experimental strategies have been used to test the prediction that rewarding models produce more imitation in children than nonrewarding models. One kind of evidence is provided by studies of the relation between parental affection and nurturance, on the one hand, and identification-related behaviors in children, on the other. Sears (1953) reported that boys with warm, affectionate fathers employed the father doll more frequently in doll play than boys of colder, less affectionate fathers. Mussen and Distler (1960) reported that fathers of highly masculine kindergarten boys were more affectionate than fathers of less masculine subjects, and, in a series of other studies by Mussen and his associates (Mussen & Distler, 1959; Mussen, 1961; Mussen & Rutherford, 1963), highly masculine boys were found to perceive their fathers as more rewarding and nurturant (as well as strong and powerful) than less masculine boys. The results of a recent study by Sears et al. (1965), however, failed to support the hypothesis that warmth and nurturance are related to identification in either girls or boys.

Experimental evidence concerning this hypothesis has been provided by Bandura and Huston (1961), who found that preschool Ss who had received social rewards from the model during two 15-minute play periods reproduced "incidental" verbal and motor responses displayed by the model to a greater extent than Ss experiencing nonrewarding interaction. These two groups, however, did not differ significantly in duplicating the model's choices in a discrimination task. Next, Bandura, Ross, and Ross (1963) reported that nursery school children more frequently imitated models from whom they received social and material rewards

Willard W. Hartup and Brian Coates, "Imitation of a peer as a function of reinforcement from the peer group and rewardingness of the model," *Child Development*, 1967, *38*, 1003–1016. Reprinted by permission. Copyright 1967 by The Society for Research in Child Development, Inc.

than models with whom they competed for such rewards. Mischel and Grusec (1966) found that the rewardingness of the model facilitated imitation, but this effect depended on the type of behavior being modeled ("aversive" or "neutral") and whether imitation was measured in terms of "rehearsal" or "transmission." More recently, Grusec (1966) reported that the model's rewardingness influenced children's imitation of self-criticism, depending on whether the model had previously used withdrawal of love, as opposed to withdrawal of material rewards.

Other evidence pertinent to the secondary reinforcement theory of imitation is provided by Rosenblith (1959), who reported that the attentiveness of the experimenter-model, as compared to attention withdrawal, enhanced imitation, but only in girls. Rosenhan and White (1967) reported no effect of the prior relation existing between S and model on the imitation of altruistic behavior, except that boys whose relations with the model were "negative" showed greater continuity in amount of imitation from model-present to model-absent conditions than boys whose relations with the model were positive or boys who had no prior relations with the model.

Stein and Wright (1964) reported that nurturance by an adult model affected imitation in preschool children, depending on the extent of change in the manifestation of dependency by the child during the experimental session. The Ss who responded to withdrawal of nurturance or to isolation with *increased* dependency and Ss who responded to continuous nurturance from E with *decreased* dependency imitated the model to a greater extent than Ss whose changes in dependency were in directions opposite to those mentioned. Lastly, Kobasigawa (1965) reported that adult models who had previously dispensed social rewards and were then observed to undergo a frustration experience elicited no greater emotionality in first-grade boys than models not dispensing social reinforcement.

Many of the findings reviewed above support the secondary reinforcement theory of imitation. Simultaneously, they suggest that situational and individual differences modify the effect of reward from the model on imitation. Sex of S, personality characteristics, and type of response being imitated are examples of such modifiers. But what antecedents are responsible for these interaction effects? What, for example, are the antecedents of sex differences in the impact of rewarding models on imitation? Differences in the socialization history of boys and girls are probably responsible, but which?

The main purpose of this experiment was to study one likely source of variation in the effect of the model's rewardingness on imitation—S's general history of reinforcement from persons resembling the model. The study was based on the hypothesis that the effects of exposure to a rewarding model, as compared to a nonrewarding model, depend on the nature of S's previous experience with people who are like the model. Peers were selected as the class of models to be used. Nursery school children were believed to be appropriate Ss because, even in nursery school groups, the range of reward frequencies exchanged among them is large.

The study was guided by the dimensional prediction stated above. Directional predictions were partially formulated prior to the experiment. For example, it was expected that rewarding peer models would produce more imitation than nonrewarding models for children with a history of frequent reinforcement from their peers. The results for children with histories of infrequent peer reinforcement were more difficult to predict because low frequencies of reinforcement from peers are often characteristic of children who are actively rejected or who are fearful in social situations. Solely on the basis of Mowrer's hypothesis, it would be expected that the rewarding-model effect would be diminished for such Ss. To the extent that such Ss are socially anxious, however, it is possible that nonrewarding peers may exert greater imitative influence than peers who, in the past, have been sources of reassurance and support.

The behaviors modeled in the experiment consisted of an altruistic response plus a group of verbal and motoric actions "incidental" to the altruistic act. Since the study involved peers as models and altruistic behavior as the major dependent variable, it accomplishes two secondary purposes: *(a)* it contributes to the slowly growing literature concerning the influence of peer models on the socialization of the child (e.g., Bandura & Kupers, 1964; Clark, 1965; Grosser, Polansky, & Lippitt, 1951; Hicks, 1965), and *(b)* it adds to the sparse evidence concerning imitation as a determinant of altruism (Rosenhan & White, 1967).

METHOD

Subjects

The pool from which Ss were drawn consisted of 64 children enrolled in four groups at the Laboratory Nursery School of the University of Minnesota. This pool included all children enrolled both at the time observations were conducted in the peer group and during a later experimental period. The Ss were 56 children from this pool. Excluded were two children who were receiving psychotherapy, two children who refused to participate, two children whose models failed to carry out the prescribed procedure, and two who were dropped to yield equal cell frequencies. These Ss ranged in age from 3–9 through 5–4, with a mean age of 4–6.

EXPERIMENTAL DESIGN

The experimental design consisted of the following groups:

Frequent reinforcement from peers (FR):
   Rewarding peer model (RM) ($N = 12$)
   Nonrewarding peer model (NRM) ($N = 12$)
Infrequent reinforcement from peers (IR):
   Rewarding peer model (RM) ($N = 12$)
   Nonrewarding peer model (NRM) ($N = 12$)
No model (control) ($N = 8$)

ASSIGNMENT OF SUBJECTS

The initial step in the assignment of Ss was the measurement of reinforcement frequencies occurring in the nursery school peer group. For this purpose, observations were conducted extending over a 5-week period.[1] Briefly, the observations produced 12 3-minute samples of each child's behavior, recorded in running account form by observers stationed in the nursery school. These records contained information concerning the child's activity, persons in his vicinity, and accounts of the interaction occurring between the child and other persons.

The 3-minute protocols were then rated by two judges. The records were screened for instances in which the child dispensed or received "generalized social reinforcers" (Skinner, 1953). Four types of positive social reinforcers were tabulated: (*a*) attention and approval (e.g., attending, offering praise, smiling and laughing, offering guidance or suggestions); (*b*) affection and personal acceptance (both physical and verbal); (*c*) submission (e.g., passive acceptance of another child's demands, sharing, compromise); (*d*) tokens (tangible objects).

A total of 161 protocols were rated by both raters. The ratio of agreements concerning the occurrence of social reinforcement divided by agreements plus disagreements was .77.

It was possible to compute the total number of reinforcements dispensed by each child to his peers and the number received. The latter score was assumed to be an index of the total frequency of positive reinforcement the child received from the peer group.[2] It was on the basis of these scores, which ranged from 0 to 55, that the children were divided into two groups: those above the median, for their own nursery school class, in number of

reinforcements received (frequent reinforcement group) and those below (infrequent reinforcement group). The mean number of reinforcers received from peers in the FR group was 24.9, while the mean for the IR group was 9.0.

The children in each of the two reinforcement groups were then randomly assigned to model conditions: rewarding peer model (RM) or nonrewarding peer model (NRM). The observational records for each S assigned to group RM were searched for the name of the like-sex peer who had given S the most frequent reinforcement during the observations. This peer was designated as S's model. The RM Ss had received a mean of 5.4 reinforcements from their models during the 36 minutes of observation. Next, a list was prepared for each S in group NRM consisting of all like-sex children in the class who had never been observed to furnish S with reinforcement. One child, randomly selected from this list, was designated as S's model. The mean reinforcements given to the NRM Ss by their models had, of course, been zero.

The final preliminary step consisted of establishing a testing sequence permitting all the available children to serve as Ss. Some children participated only as Ss; others, who were designated as models, participated first as Ss, then were trained and served as models during subsequent sessions (not more than two for any child).

One boy and one girl from each preschool class were required to start the testing by serving as "first" models. These children were randomly selected. If this selection did not make it possible to test all of the children in that preschool class in sequence, substitute first models were picked. Those children designated as first models completed the experimental task prior to being trained as models. This group of eight children (two from each preschool class) thus comprised a no-model control group (C).

PROCEDURE

No-Model Condition

The S was brought to a laboratory room which contained three hats (maroon, green, and yellow) hung on pegs, three feathers (white, yellow, and orange) placed on a chair, three pencils (black, brown, and green) also hung on pegs, and a table containing a stack of dittoed mazes (simple one-turn puzzles) and three bowls. One bowl, placed in front of the child, was a receptacle for trinkets released by a dispensing device. The other bowls were placed to S's left and right (counterbalanced across Ss); one was designated as belonging to a preschool child (not known to S) whose picture was attached, the other was designated as S's bowl. The following instructions were given:

> We have a game for you today. It is a puzzle game and these are the puzzles. (E displays puzzles.) The way you play this game is to draw a line from one flower to another flower, like this. (E demonstrates.) Now you can do some. (S was helped to complete two or three of the puzzles.) There is one other thing that I want to tell you about the

---

[1] A detailed description of the observational procedure can be found in Charlesworth and Hartup (1967).

[2] The extent to which the total number of positive reinforcements received serves as an index of total social interaction is not known. It was possible to compute correlations between receipt of positive and receipt of negative reinforcements for Ss in two of the preschool groups. These correlations were .43 ($p < .10$) and .51 ($p < .05$). Incidents of nonreinforcing contacts among peers were numerous but were not tabulated.

game. Whenever you are doing a good job on the puzzle, some little cats will come out of the machine back there. They will come down this chute and fall into this bowl. Whenever some cats come down the chute I want you to put them in one of these other bowls. Either put them over here in Alec's bowl (Kathy's for female Ss) or over here in your bowl. Alec is another boy in the nursery school. Now remember, whenever you are doing a good job on the puzzle, some little cats will come out of the machine into this bowl here and you are to put them in one of these two bowls, either in Alec's bowl or your bowl, your bowl or Alec's bowl. Do you understand? I have to do some work so I will sit in here."

Nothing further was said concerning whether S could keep the trinkets in his bowl at the conclusion of the session. The E then went into an adjoining room, left the door ajar, and seated himself out of sight. S was told to proceed, and after each maze was completed six trinkets were ejected through the chute. The session consisted of ten mazes, each followed by the dispensing and allocation of six trinkets. If S failed to pick up the trinkets, E urged him to do so by saying, "Put the cats in the bowls; in Alec's bowl or your bowl, your bowl or Alec's bowl."

Model Conditions

Training the model. Each child designated as a model was brought to the laboratory several days after he had participated as S. He was reminded of the earlier session, given an opportunity to complete two mazes, and asked to help E by demonstrating the game for another child from his class. The E stressed that it was necessary to play the game in a particular way. First, M was told that he should go to the hats, pick out the green one (color alternated across Ss), attach the white feather (also alternated) to the hole in the hat, and put the hat on his head. Next, he was told to select the black pencil (color also alternated), to seat himself at the table, and begin work on the puzzles. Then M was instructed to pick up the six trinkets ejected after each maze, place them in a row on the table, and pick them up one at a time, placing all but the last one in Alec's (or Kathy's) bowl. The M was also instructed to repeat the words "One for Alec" each time a trinket was placed in "Alec's bowl." The E stressed that only the last trinket should be placed in M's own bowl. This procedure was practiced, with E coaching and sometimes demonstrating, until M was able to perform the task with consistent accuracy. The M accompanied E to the nursery school for the purpose of inviting S to play the game.

Experimental session. When the children arrived in the laboratory, E described the game using the instructions given above. He also explained that the children would take turns and that M would be first. The S was seated so as to face M at a 90° angle and was told that he should try not to bother M. The E entered the adjoining room, leaving the door partly open. Then M was told to proceed. If M failed to respond or engaged in distract-

ing behavior, E prompted him from the other room. In no case, however, were mistakes in allocating trinkets corrected. Such mistakes were made by only two Ms whose Ss were subsequently excluded from the experiment.

After ten mazes, the children were told it was time for S to play the game. The M was invited to wait in the adjoining room with E, and the instructions were repeated briefly to S. When everyone had reached his appropriate spot, S was told to begin.

RESPONSE MEASURES

The following information was recorded by E (observing through a small one-way window): (a) whether or not S chose a hat, a feather, and/or a pencil and the colors of these objects; (b) whether or not S lined up the trinkets and whether the trinkets were placed in the bowls one at a time or in groups; (c) frequency with which S reproduced the verbalization of M; and (d) the particular bowl chosen for allocation of each trinket.

The response measures derived from these records included: (a) presence-absence of imitative hat, feather, and pencil choices; (b) presence-absence of "line up" behavior on each trial (ranging from 0 to 10 over entire session); (c) presence-absence of imitative verbalization (ranging from 0 to 6 on each trial); (d) number of trinkets placed in the "other's" bowl (ranging from 0 to 6 on each trial); (e) latency of the first nonaltruistic choice—the number of trinkets placed in "other's" bowl before placement of the first trinket in S's own bowl (ranging from 0 to 7 on each trial).

RESULTS

Intercorrelations among four of the dependent measures are shown in Table 1. All of these measures represent components of the response sequence used in allocating the trinkets. The correlations, which were computed only for S's who observed a model, are all significantly positive, but five are relatively small. It should be noted that the two altruism scores (frequency of "giving to other" and latency of "giving to self") are highly correlated. This relation is artifactual. Consequently, "giving to other" was used alone as the altruism index in the data analysis.

Where possible, subsequent analyses were completed with scores divided into two five-trial blocks. Inspection revealed that the treatment effects varied over time.

EFFECT OF MODEL

To assess the effects of observing a model on altruistic behavior, a one-way analysis of variance was conducted on the data for all five of the groups in the experiment. "Giving to other" scores were analyzed separately for the first and second blocks of five trials. The treatments effect was significant in all instances. For the first trial block, $F = 7.49$, $df = 4/51$, $p. < 005$; second trial block, $F = 3.39$, $df = 4/51$, $p < .02$.

Contrasts between the amount of "giving to other" in group C and in each of the model groups (t tests) revealed significant differences for each contrast in both trial

TABLE 1
INTERCORRELATIONS AMONG FOUR IMITATION SCORES
(N = 48)

Score	Giving to Other (Total)	Latency of Giving to Self (Total)	Verbali- zation (Total)	Line Up (Total)
Giving to other..	...	...	...	...
Latency of giving to self..............................	.92**	...	...	...
Verbalization...	.28*	.32*	...	...
Line up	.32*	.36*	.54**	...

* p < .05.
** p < .01.

blocks. Thus, observation of the model produced significantly more altruism than occurred when no opportunity to observe a model was provided (see Table 2).

Observing the model also affected the frequency of "incidental" behaviors. Statistical analysis was not performed, but it can be seen in Table 3 that no verbalization or "line up" behavior occurred in group C, although appreciable amounts were displayed by Ss who had observed a model.

EFFECTS OF PEER REINFORCEMENT AND REWARDINGNESS OF MODEL

The "giving to other" scores for Ss who observed models were subjected to mixed-design analysis of variance. The between-Ss factors were reinforcement from peers (FR vs. IR) and type of peer model (RM vs. NRM). The within-Ss factor consisted of trial blocks (first vs. second five trials). Mean scores for each subgroup may be seen in Table 2.

The analysis revealed a significant effect of trial blocks ($F = 7.80$, $df = 1/44$, $p < .01$), indicating that fewer altruistic responses were made during the second block of five trials than during the first. In addition, the interaction between reinforcement from peers and type of model was significant ($F = 4.59$, $df = 1/44$, $p < .05$), as was the interaction between reinforcement from peers, type of model, and trial blocks ($F = 7.80$, $df = 1/44$, $p < .01$). Further analysis revealed that the treatments effects were

TABLE 2
MEAN "GIVING TO OTHER" SCORES IN BLOCKS OF FIVE TRIALS BY REINFORCEMENT CONDITION AND TYPE OF PEER MODEL

Group	Trial Block 1	Trial Block 2
Frequent reinforcement:		
Rewarding model	21.00	19.25
Nonrewarding model	13.42	13.83
Infrequent reinforcement:		
Rewarding model	17.50	17.08
Nonrewarding model	22.83	18.58
No model	5.63	3.75

TABLE 3
MEAN NUMBER OF "INCIDENTAL" BEHAVIORS ACCORDING TO REINFORCEMENT CONDITION AND TYPE OF PEER MODEL

Group	Verbalization (Total)	Line-Up Responses (Total)
Frequent reinforcement:		
Rewarding model	36.83	4.50
Nonrewarding model	7.58	1.67
Infrequent reinforcement:		
Rewarding model	21.08	3.92
Nonrewarding model	18.00	3.92
No model	0.00	0.00

confined principally to the first five trials. There was a significant interaction between reinforcement from peers and type of model in the data for the first five trials ($F = 8.44$, $df = 1/44$, $p < .01$), but not for the second. During the first trials, Ss who had received frequent reinforcement from their peers imitated a rewarding peer model more frequently than a nonrewarding model ($t = 3.17$, $p < .01$). On the other hand, Ss who were observed to receive infrequent peer reinforcement imitated a nonrewarding model more frequently than a rewarding model ($t = 2.61$, $p < .02$). Additional contrasts made on the data for the first five trials revealed: (a) among Ss who observed a rewarding model, those with a history of frequent peer reinforcement did not differ significantly from those with a history of infrequent reinforcement ($t = 1.41$, $p < .20$); (b) among those who observed a nonrewarding model, Ss who had received infrequent reinforcement from the peer group imitated significantly more than those who had received frequent peer reinforcement ($t = 4.88$, $p < .01$).

Analysis of imitative verbalization scores was conducted as described for the preceding measure. None of the interactions was significant. Rather, a significant main effect of type of model was obtained ($F = 5.39$, $df = 1/44$, $p < .02$). As can be seen from Table 3, Ss who observed a rewarding model reproduced the model's verbal behaviors more frequently than Ss who observed nonrewarding models. This trend is less clear for IR Ss than for FR Ss, and the interaction between reinforcement from peers and type of model approached significance ($F = 3.53$, $df = 1/44$, $p < .10$).

"Line up" scores were collapsed over all ten trials prior to analysis because this score consisted of presence-absence on single trials. None of the main or interaction effects was significant.

The data concerning the child's behavior with the hats, feathers, and pencils were analyzed by means of χ^2. All possible contrasts between pairs of experimental groups were completed. The only significant difference to emerge from these analyses showed that FR–RM *S*s reproduced the pencil choices of the model more frequently than IR–NRM *S*s ($\chi^2 = 4.45$, $p < .05$).* This single finding may be attributed to chance. With respect to these particular incidental behaviors, then, the experimental conditions failed to influence differentially the child's imitative behavior.

DISCUSSION

EFFECTS OF MODEL

Observation of altruistic models increased the frequency of altruistic behavior of the *S*s, a finding which confirms the results of Rosenhan and White (1967). Since frequency of altruism was highly correlated with the latency of nonaltruistic behavior, the evidence suggests that two parameters of altruism were imitated. As pointed out earlier, however, the most conservative description of the results is in terms of one altruism index, not both.

Can it be assumed that the behavior displayed by the model was construed by *S* as "altruism"? It is true that *S* was not told explicitly that he would be able to keep the trinkets in his own bowl and that those in the other child's bowl were to be given away. Nevertheless, in postsession interviews with ten *S*s, all ten thought they could keep the trinkets in their own bowl, and seven thought the trinkets in the second bowl would be given to the child whose picture was attached to the bowl. Consequently, the assumption that the experiment involved imitative effects on altruism is tenable.

Among *S*s who observed a model, those showing imitative altruism tended to imitate other components of the altruistic response sequence. Most of the intercorrelations among response measures were low, however, indicating that the effects of observing a model were not highly pervasive. The experimental findings are consistent with the intercorrelations. The peer reinforcement history tended

---

* These findings are congruent with those of Rosenblith in an aspect of the study reprinted here (Section IV, article 20). In analyzing a task-irrelevant behavior (choice of color of pencil) she found that children with an attention (rewarding?) model chose the same color as the adult more than those whose adult model had withdrawn attention.—EDITOR

to have significant effects on behavior which was central in the altruistic response sequence (frequency of "giving to other"). Borderline effects of peer reinforcement were found with respect to imitative verbalization, and no effects were obtained with respect to less central actions ("lining up" behavior or choices of hat, feather, and pencil). This failure of the treatment effects to generalize to all measures could simply have been a function of "response centrality." It is also possible that the treatment effects did not generalize to "lining up" scores and hat, feather, and pencil choices because these behaviors occurred much less frequently than trinket sorting or verbalization.

EFFECTS OF PEER REINFORCEMENT

The relation between rewardingness of the peer model and imitative altruism was positive when *S* was reinforced frequently by the peer group but negative when reinforcement was infrequent. It is known that peer reinforcement is correlated with social acceptance (e.g., Hartup, Glazer, & Charlesworth, 1967; Marshall & McCandless, 1957). Therefore, the four experimental groups were contrasted with respect to the social acceptance of the models, the acceptance of the *S*s, and the friendliness existing between the models and their respective *S*s. Data from a picture sociometric test were used for this purpose. First, no significant differences were found in the frequency with which the models in the four groups were chosen by their peers as "liked," as "disliked," or in total times mentioned. Similarly, the social acceptance of the *S*s themselves did not differ significantly among the four groups. Finally, children in group FR–RM were significantly more friendly toward their models, as revealed by the frequency with which the model was included among *S*'s sociometric choices, than were the children in the other three groups. However, *S*s in group IR–NRM, which imitated as much as group FR–RM, were less friendly toward their models than *S*s in the latter group. Thus, overall, status differences among the groups do not account for the observed differences in imitation.

It is concluded that the results support Mowrer's secondary reinforcement theory of imitation when *S*'s history includes relatively frequent reinforcement from persons resembling the model. For infrequently reinforced *S*s, the influence of model rewardingness did not diminish; rather, nonrewarding models proved to be more efficacious than rewarding ones.

One explanation for these results is based on the assumption that children who receive little reinforcement are also anxious when placed in contact with other children. For them, exposure to a nonrewarding model may arouse discomfort or anxiety, adding motivation to perform the actions which the situation elicits (including, in the present instance, imitation). Exposure of such children to a rewarding model, however, could result in anxiety reduction, thereby lowering S's motivation for imitative behavior.

This argument implies a dual theory of peer imitation: *(a)* when reinforcement from peers is frequent, matching the behavior of a rewarding model has greater incentive value than matching a nonrewarding model (the Mowrer hypothesis); *(b)* when peer reinforcement is not frequent, a nonrewarding model sustains or increases anxiety, whereas the presence of a rewarding model reduces such motivation for imitation. This theory is similar to the hypothesis advanced by Hill (1967) concerning the role of anxiety in task performance under social reinforcement and, in some respects, parallels the dualism in psychoanalytic theories of identification. For example, it could by hypothesized that *(a)* nurturant models are emulated (anaclitic identification) when reinforcement from persons like the model has been frequent, and *(b)* when reinforcement has been infrequent, the model who elicits anxiety (or who does not behave in such a way as to reduce it) is defensively emulated. Thus, the present speculations contain interesting implications for predicting the conditions under which anaclitic and defensive identification operate.

It is also possible to consider the present results in terms of perceived similarity. It is known that, in the peer group, the correlation between "giving reinforcement to others" and "getting reinforcement from others" is positive and high (Charlesworth & Hartup, 1967). Thus, it is possible that FR–RM Ss perceive themselves to be similar to the model (both give as well as receive frequent reinforcements) as do IR–NRM Ss (both receive and give few reinforcements). On the other hand, perceived similarity would not be great in the other two experimental groups, FR–NRM and IR–RM. Earlier studies have shown that if S perceives himself as similar to M, conformity is enhanced (e.g., Stotland & Patchen, 1961) as well as imitation (Maccoby, 1959; Rosekrans, 1967). The perceived similarity (or reduced dissimilarity) existing for frequently reinforced Ss with rewarding models and for infrequently reinforced Ss with nonrewarding models would thus account for the greater amounts of imitation shown by these two groups than by the other groups in the experiment.

The present study helps to clarify the influence of the model's rewardingness on imitation. The generality of the results needs to be assessed in further research and theoretical implications explored. It appears, however, that the child's so-

cialization history contributes importantly to the effects on imitation of rewards from the model.

REFERENCES

BANDURA, A., & HUSTON, ALETHA C. Identification as a process of incidental learning. *Journal of abnormal and social Psychology,* 1961, *63,* 311–318.

BANDURA, A., & KUPERS, CAROL J. Transmission of patterns of self-reinforcement through modelling. *Journal of abnormal and social Psychology,* 1964, *69,* 1–9.

BANDURA, A., ROSS, DOROTHEA, & ROSS, SHEILA A. A comparative test of the status envy, social power, and secondary reinforcement theories of identificatory learning. *Journal of abnormal and social Psychology,* 1963, *67,* 527–534.

CHARLESWORTH, ROSALIND, & HARTUP, W. W. Positive social reinforcement in the nursery school peer group. *Child Development,* 1967, *38,* 993–1002.

CLARK, BARBARA S. The acquisition and extinction of peer imitation in children. *Psychonomic Science,* 1965, *2,* 147–148.

FREUD, S. On narcissism: an introduction (1914). In J. D. Sutherland (Ed.), *Collected papers of Sigmund Freud.* Vol. 4. London: Hogarth, 1957. Pp. 30–60.

GROSSER, D., POLANSKY, N., & LIPPITT, R. A laboratory study of behavioral contagion. *Human Relations,* 1951, *4,* 115–142.

GRUSEC, JOAN. Some antecedents of self-criticism. *Journal of Personality and social Psychology,* 1966, *4,* 244–253.

HARTUP, W. W., GLAZER, JANE, & CHARLESWORTH, ROSALIND. Peer reinforcement and sociometric status. *Child Development,* 1967, *38,* 1017–1024.

HICKS, D. J. Imitation and retention of film-mediated aggressive peer and adult models. *Journal of Personality and social Psychology,* 1965, *2,* 97–100.

HILL, K. T. Social reinforcement as a function of test anxiety and success-failure experiences. *Child Development,* 1967, *38,* 723–737.

KOBASIGAWA, A. Observation of failure in another person as a determinant of amplitude and speed of a simple motor response. *Journal of Personality and social Psychology,* 165, *1,* 626–631.

MACCOBY, ELEANOR E. Role-taking in childhood and its consequences for social learning. *Child Development,* 1959, *30,* 239–252.

MARSHALL, HELEN R., & McCANDLESS, B. R. A study in prediction of social behavior of preschool children. *Child Development,* 1957, *28,* 149–159.

MISCHEL, W., & GRUSEC, JOAN. Determinants of the rehearsal and transmission of neutral and aversive behaviors. *Journal of Personality and social Psychology,* 1966, *3,* 197–206.

MOWRER, O. H. Identification: a link between learning theory and psychotherapy. In *Learning theory and personality dynamics.* New York: Ronald Press, 1950. Pp. 69–94.

MOWRER, O. H. *Learning theory and the symbolic process.* New York: Wiley, 1960.

MUSSEN, P. H. Some antecedents and consequents of masculine sex-typing in adolescent boys. *Psychological Monographs,* 1961, *75* (Whole No. 506).

MUSSEN, P. H., & DISTLER, L. Masculinity, identification, and father-son relationships. *Journal of abnormal and social Psychology,* 1959, *59,* 350–356.

MUSSEN, P. H., & DISTLER, L. Child-rearing antecedents of masculine identification in kindergarten boys. *Child Development,* 1960, *31,* 89–100.

MUSSEN, P. H., & RUTHERFORD, E. Parent-child relations and parental personality in relation to young children's sex-role preferences. *Child Development,* 1963, *34,* 589–607.

ROSEKRANS, MARY A. Imitation in children as a function of perceived similarity to a social model and vicarious reinforcement. *Journal of Personality and social Psychology,* 1967, in press.

ROSENBLITH, JUDY F. Learning by imitation in kindergarten children. *Child Development,* 1959, *30,* 69–80.

ROSENHAN, D., & WHITE, G. M. Observation and rehearsal as determinants of pro-social behavior. *Journal of Personality and social Psychology,* 1967, *5,* 424–431.

SEARS, PAULINE S. Child rearing factors related to the playing of sex-typed roles. *American Psychologist,* 1953, *8,* 431. (Abstract)

SEARS, R. R. Identification as a form of behavior development. In D. B. Harris (Ed.), *The concept of development.* Minneapolis: University of Minnesota Press, 1957. Pp. 149–161.

SEARS, R. R., RAU, LUCY, & ALPERT, R. *Identification and child rearing.* Stanford, Calif.: Stanford University Press, 1965.

SKINNER, B. F. *Science and human behavior.* New York: Macmillan, 1953.

STEIN, ALETHA H., & WRIGHT, J. C. Imitation learning under conditions of nurturance and nurturance withdrawal. *Child Development,* 1964, *35,* 927–937.

STOTLAND, E., and PATCHEN, M. Identification and change in prejudice and in authoritarianism. *Journal of abnormal and social Psychology,* 1961, *62,* 254–274.

23

Birth Order Effects

ROBERT HELMREICH

Helmreich introduces the final theme of this section. What does it mean to be an only child or first-born as compared to having one or more older siblings? The earlier articles on peer influence are followed by these on siblings. For the majority of children born into a family in which there are older children, the topic of "ordinal position," or birth order, is largely a case of peer influence. The new-comer finds himself in an environment where the liveliest, noisiest members are the older sibs. In such surroundings, many a baby late in the order will soon be taking his cues from the older children more than from the mother.

In this paper Helmreich, who teaches psychology at the University of Texas, summarizes ways that first-born children have been found to differ from later-borns. He concentrates on those differences that are in response to hazardous situations.

Investigations of the effects of birth order have a long, if not altogether reputable, history in psychology. The relationship between birth order and the attainment of intellectual eminence was first noted by Sir Francis Galton in 1874.[1] By using such criteria as being a Fellow of the Royal Society, Galton concluded that oldest and only children

were more likely to achieve eminence than younger children. A generation later, Havelock Ellis found the same relationship between birth order and eminence.[2]

Despite these and other similar findings, the topic has been in ill repute for several reasons. Although a large number of studies have found significant differences between first- or only-borns and later-borns on a wide range of variables, much of this data is inconsistent and contradictory. Also, most researchers have considered that an individual's ordinal position has less psychological meaning than other factors, such as intelligence, extroversion, or anxiety level. As a result, interest in birth order phenomena has languished for a number of years. Recently, however, beginning with research being conducted by Stanley Schachter at Columbia University, concern with the phenomena has revived.[3]

Schachter conducted a series of experimental studies on gregariousness. In particular, he investigated the hypothesis that people have an increased need for the company of others while under high stress. In his laboratory studies, subjects waiting for either mild or extremely painful electric shocks were offered the chance to wait alone or in the company of others. Schachter found, in support of his hypothesis, that stress does increase gregariousness—but primarily for first- and only-borns. Numerous subsequent studies have confirmed that first- and only-borns respond to stress by showing a greater desire for affiliation with others than do later-borns. Since much of the current research on birth order effects centers around reactions to stress, this will be the primary focus in the article. First, however, a brief review of other relatively stable findings concerning ordinal position is in order.

Galton's early finding that first- and only-borns achieve more than later-borns has been reaffirmed in present-day American society. Objective indices of accomplishment such as *Who's Who* and rosters of scientists include an overproportionate number of first- and only-borns. Also, data show that eldest offspring are [on the average] more intelligent than younger children and that enrollments in the more "elite" colleges have higher percentages of first- and only-borns.[4] Although some of this over-

[1] Galton, F., *English Men of Science,* London: McMillan & Co., 1874.

[2] Ellis, H., *A Study of British Genius,* Boston: Houghton Mifflin, 1926, new revised edition.

[3] Schachter, S., *The Psychology of Affiliation,* Stanford: Stanford University Press, 1959.

[4] Altus, W. D., "Birth order and its sequelae." *Science, 151,* 44–48, 1966.

Robert Helmreich, "Birth order effects," *Naval Research Reviews, 21* (February 1968). Reprinted by permission.

representation may be due to the fact that the eldest son typically has the greatest opportunity for advancement, the findings are so stable that it is warranted to conclude that order of birth has a strong effect on motivation and performance. First- and only-borns are also more likely to volunteer for special tasks ranging from events as prosaic as laboratory psychological experiments to experiences as hazardous as space flight.

Although attempts to isolate ordinal position differences in personality (as measured by standard personality tests) have generally produced contradictory results, two relatively stable findings have emerged. One is that first- and only-borns probably have a higher motivation for achievement than later-borns. This means that oldest and only children tend to show more need to achieve in competitive situations as measured by various psychological and behavioral tests. The second finding is that first- and only-borns exhibit greater dependency than do later-borns. This has been demonstrated primarily in research with children where first- and only-borns make more approaches to adults and are less independent in their behavior.

One additional and more tenuous birth order effect proposed is that first- and only-borns have a lower level of self-esteem than later-borns. This effect has been measured primarily by psychological tests which indicate that oldest and only children have less confidence in their own ability and less certainty about their proficiency in various skills.

The apparent superiority of first- and only-borns in achieving academic and professional eminence stands in marked contrast to the evidence concerning performance under stressful conditions. Schachter, in his original study, reanalyzed data on the performance of fighter pilots during the Korean War.[5] He found that under the stressful conditions of combat, first- and only-borns were inferior in performance when judged on the criterion of number of Migs shot down; *i.e.*, later-borns were significantly more likely to achieve "Ace" ranking as pilots.

More recently, the author collaborated with Dr. Roland Radloff of the Naval Medical Research Institute in studying the performance and psychological reactions of divers on Project Sealab II.[6] In the Sealab situation, an excellent, objective criterion of performance was available—the amount of time spent by each diver working in the extremely stressful underwater environment outside the Sealab capsule. The average diving time per day over the 15 days spent underwater by each team ranged from 13 minutes to 72 minutes, with an overall average of 48 minutes for the three ten-man teams. Using this measure, the performance of later-borns was significantly better than that of first- and only-borns. The later-borns had an average of more than 56 minutes of diving per day while the first- and only-borns logged slightly less than 43 minutes per day.

Another measure employed in Sealab was a questionnaire which was designed to assess the individual's level of fear while underwater. This test, given every other day for an average of seven times per man during the dive, indicated that first- and only-borns reported themselves as significantly more frightened than later-borns throughout their sojourn underwater.

The fact that eldest and only children volunteer disproportionately more than their later-born counterparts for both stressful and nonstressful undertakings seems paradoxical in light of the provocative finding that first- and only-borns do not perform as well under stressful conditions. It seems strange that they would expose themselves selectively to situations in which their performance tends to be of a lower caliber than that of later-borns. Yet, data on selective volunteering and acceptance for hazardous and stressful experiences seem unequivocal. All seven of the original Mercury astronauts were first-born or eldest in their family. Twelve of 15 candidates for the Gemini program were the oldest or only male offspring.[7] Sixteen of the 28 Sealab aquanauts were eldest or only children. In a study currently being conducted by the author, 55 percent of a large sample of Army helicopter pilot trainees are eldest children, a finding which is in marked contrast to a non-volunteer sample of male University of Texas students of the same age which includes slightly less than 40 percent first-borns. Thus, for those concerned with both the nature of volunteer populations and the selection of candidates for hazardous duty, birth order appears to be a meaningful bit of information.

THEORETICAL INTERPRETATIONS OF
BIRTH ORDER EFFECTS

The most likely theoretical explanations for birth order effects seem to center on differences in the behavior of parents and in the home environment. Research findings typically show that parents instill

[5] Schachter, S., *op. cit.*

[6] Radloff, R., and Helmreich, R., *Groups Under Stress: Psychological Research in Sealab II*. New York: Appleton-Century-Crofts, in press.

[7] Perry, C. J. G., "Psychiatric selection of candidates for space missions." *Journal of the American Medical Association*, 1965, 194, 841–844.

high achievement standards in their first- and only-born children. This parental characteristic could account for much of the difference in accomplishment between first- and later-borns and for differences in volunteering for achievement-oriented tasks. It is probably also true that first- and only-borns are more consistently rewarded for attending to and being oriented toward others—perhaps because the oldest and only children, being first in line, will be most rewarded for seeking out the attention of parents. Even more important may be the fact that the absence of slightly older siblings to serve as behavioral guides doubtless forces the first- and only-borns to employ parents and other adults as their social models during early childhood, an act that can have profound effects on the individual. Since parents are widely discrepant in both age and ability, they are models whom the child cannot hope to emulate successfully. His failure to master the same tasks as the model may well result in a lowered opinion of his own ability. This argument is supported by the studies which have reported lower self-esteem among first- and only-borns. It follows that, if first- and only-borns lack peer models with whom they can favorably compare their own reactions and abilities, they should be less certain of the quality and appropriateness of their reactions in novel or stressful situations. The result of this uncertainty may be a greater need for social and emotional comparison of one's self with peers in anxiety-provoking situations, which in turn would account for the increased gregariousness of first- and only-borns under stress. The uncertainty of first- and only-borns about their reactions or abilities could also result in greater anxiety under trying circumstances. Considerable research evidence indicates that high levels of anxiety interfere with performance, a finding which could account for inferior performance of first- and only-borns under high stress.

On the other hand, the child with a slightly older sibling can contrast his abilities and reactions with someone much closer in physical, social, intellectual, and sexual development than a parent. Such an individual should have a more accurate conception of his own abilities and of the appropriateness of his responses to novel situations. This could account for less anxiety and less need to affiliate under stressful conditions. It would appear that the differences between first- or only-borns and later-borns should be strongest in situations where the individual is uncertain about what he should feel, think, or how he should behave or perform.

One crucial test of the accuracy of some of these formulations is to look at the reactions of later-born children who are much younger than their older siblings. Such individuals should have less accurate social models than later-borns who are closer in age to their older brothers and sisters. If the theory is correct, these later-borns with a large gap separating them from their older siblings should behave more like first- or only-borns than like later-borns without such an age gap. Recent research supports this theory. In one study, the behavior of first-borns, later-borns less than two years younger than their next older sibling, and last-borns more than five years younger than their next oldest sibling were contrasted under stressful conditions.[8] The results showed that first-borns and large age-gap last-borns were highly similar in their reactions; and that both groups were significantly different from small age-gap later-borns, thus supporting the social comparison hypothesis.

It seems that the most parsimonious explanations for widely observed birth order phenomena are based on different experiences in childhood. Greater motivation for achievement and more pressing needs for social comparison seem to account for many of the observed differences between first- or only-borns and later-borns. At present, though, any theories concerning this phenomena must be evaluated as *not proved*. The importance of birth order effects and the increasing amount of research that shows consistent results give reason to hope that order and coherence can be brought to this perplexing area.

Investigation of the effects of birth order forms part of a research area aimed at utilizing biographical information in the screening, selection and placement of men. While it is obvious that experiences forming the life history are relevant to success or failure in subsequent endeavors, particularly in stressful environments, psychologists are only beginning to understand and appreciate the important variables and their specific relevance. In order to utilize this type of information with maximum effectiveness, understanding of the conceptual and theoretical importance of relevant variables in the life history and in adjustment to a variety of environments is necessary. The basic aim of psychology is to specify with increasing precision the lawful nature of individual and group behavior. The effects of birth order on later behavior and adjustment appear at this time to have potentially profound implications for our understanding of human behavior.

[8] Miller, N., and Zimbardo, P. G., "Motives for fear-induced affiliation: emotional comparison or interpersonal similarity." *Journal of Personality*, 1966, *34*, 481–503.

24

Social and Play Responses of First-born and Later-born Infants in an Unfamiliar Situation

ROBERTA R. COLLARD

Roberta R. Collard, of the Department of Human Development at the University of Massachusetts in Amherst, illustrates the point we made in the introduction to the previous paper. When there are older sibs fairly close in age to a baby, he is likely to behave differently from when there are not. Attentiveness to sibs lessens the focus on parents, whose influence on the socialization of the later-born is apt to be diminished. As Bragg and Allen mention in their article "Ordinal Position and Conformity: A Role Theory Analysis" (Sociometry, 1970, 33, 371–381):

> *. . . first- and later-born children use a different family member as a standard for behavioral comparison. The first-born child acquires sex-role expectations primarily through interaction with parents (simply because siblings are not present). Thus, the first-born should be oriented toward adults—as several studies have shown. . . . During acquisition of sex-role expectations, the later-born child interacts with an older brother or sister. Because of the later child's greater similarity to his elder sibling, rather than to his parents, he will tend to employ the elder sibling, rather than a parent, as a behavioral referent.*

The data in this study were collected as part of a larger study on "Age and Sex Differences in the Exploratory and Social Behavior of Infants" which was supported by the University of California Agricultural Experiment Station. Appreciation is due to Dr. Dorothy Eichorn for her valuable suggestions and criticisms.

Consequently, the later-born should be oriented towards peers. . . .

Note that in mentioning housing and life-style patterns, which have effects analogous to those of sibs, Collard calls attention to an aspect of settings (Section V) as a related determinant of the behaviors under examination.

During the past 2 years, while collecting data on the exploratory behavior of infants 9 to 13 months old, the writer was impressed by the difference in readiness of first-borns and later-borns to accept the first toy presented by the E who was a stranger to them. First-born infants seemed to pause much longer before picking up the toy and to take a much longer time to warm up in the testing situation than did infants with one or more siblings. First-borns also seemed to cry more and to show fewer positive social responses such as smiling at or initiating play with the E.

Differences in social responsiveness and sensitivity of first-borns compared to later-borns have been noted before by others. In a study on preschool children by Dean (1947), mothers rated their first-borns as more excitable, fearful, and sensitive than second-borns. Lasko found mothers to be more protective and restrictive of their first-born children (1952) and to be more anxious about their care (1954). Koch (1955) concluded that "the first-born is not toughened so early as later-borns by interaction with his peers" and is thus apt to be more sensitive. The teachers of the 5- and 6-year-olds in her study rated first-borns as more intense emotionally than later-borns. Several workers have found adult first-borns to show a greater reaction to stress than later-borns (Warren, 1966). Others have found first-borns to be more dependent on their mothers (Sears, 1950) and to score higher on need affiliation than do the latter (Warren, 1966).

Bayley (1932), Gesell and Thompson (1934), and Spitz (1950) all observed sobering or crying in the presence of strangers to be typical of home-reared infants during the second half of the first year, although Gesell never found such indications of fear of strangers to occur in more than 50 per cent of the babies he studied at any age.

The number of persons involved in the care of infants appears to make a difference in their reactions to strangers. Rheingold (1956) did not observe fear of strangers to occur by 8 months of age in institutional babies cared for by an average of 13 persons a day. The critical period for the de-

Roberta R. Collard, "Social and play responses of first-born and later-born infants in an unfamiliar situation," *Child Development*, 1968, *39*, 325–334. Reprinted by permission. © 1968 by The Society for Research in Child Development, Inc.

velopment of this fear probably occurs before 6 months of age, because Rheingold also found that institutional infants cared for from 6 to 8 months of age predominately by one person did not develop fear of strangers during this period. The writer (1962) observed that 9- to 13-month-old babies in the same institution hesitated a significantly shorter time before picking up a toy presented by a stranger than did a group of home-reared babies.

Studies by Caldwell (1963) and Schaffer and Emerson (1964) indicate that infants cared for by mother alone are more intensely attached to their mothers than are infants cared for by several persons. In the latter study, intensity of attachment was found to be positively (but not significantly) related to degree of fear of strangers. Schaffer and Emerson also make the important point that in addition to caretakers, infants often become attached to persons who play with them, such as siblings, grandparents, and friends of the family.

The above studies make it appear likely that an infant's readiness to accept strangers depends largely upon his opportunities to have experienced adaptation to a certain number or range of different persons during a certain period of development. These studies would lead one to predict that infants over 6 months old who have not had a chance to interact with many persons would show more indications of fear of strangers than would those used to many persons. First-born infants as a group would probably show more fear of strangers than would infants who have had a chance to adapt to older siblings. However, this should be true only of first-borns who have been cared for most of the time by their mothers in relative social isolation and not true of infants who have often been around many other persons, for example, in an extended family. Infants with an age-spacing of 6 years or more between them and next-older sibling should also be expected to show more fear of strangers than other later-borns if the older siblings of the former have not been involved in their care and are not at home as often as preschool siblings usually are.

Method

In the present study, the social, exploratory, and play responses of matched groups of first-born and later-born infants were measured in the presence of a stranger in an unfamiliar room. A baby was considered to be more fearful than his matched partner if he showed a longer response latency before picking up a novel toy and if he made fewer exploratory and play responses to the toy during a test period immediately following. Exploratory responses included such behaviors as looking at,

mouthing, and poking the toy; play responses included banging, waving, dropping or casting the toy, or handing it to the *E*. Negative social responses such as sobering, fussing, crying, and restlessness during the test were also assumed to indicate fear. Restlessness consisted of extreme wriggling about in the absence of play. A baby was considered to be less fearful than his matched partner if he made more positive social responses such as smiling, laughing, or initiating play with the stranger than the latter did. A difference between the two groups was assumed to be significant if the probability of its occurrence by chance was less than .05 on the Wilcoxon Test for Matched Samples, one-tailed test.

Subjects

The *Ss* were 36 infants 38 to 56 weeks of age. Twelve first-borns were matched to 12 later-borns whose next-older sibling was under 6 years of age, and 6 infants with an age-spacing of 6 years or more between them and next-older sibling were matched to later-borns less widely spaced (see Table 1). Infants were matched in age, sex, and socioeconomic status of parents. They were from white, native-American, upper-middle-class families and were cared for most of the time by their mothers. Babies living in isolated nuclear families and cared for by one or two sitters once a month or less were classified as having been exposed to few persons. Babies cared for by one or two family members other than mother and father were categorized as having been exposed to several persons, and those who were exposed to many visitors or who lived in crowded student housing and had been cared for by three or more sitters two or three times a month were classified as having been around many persons.

Apparatus and procedure

During the experiment, the infant was held on the mother's lap at a testing table with the *E* sitting opposite them. On the table from the beginning was a pink soap box which was the "warm-up" toy. During the first 5 minutes, the *E* did not talk to or approach the infant in any way but talked to the mother, explaining the procedures of the tests to be given.

After 5 minutes, the mother was asked to remove the soap box from the baby's hand, and the *E* placed the test toy in the center of the table in front of the infant. This toy was made up of four wooden beads about an inch in diameter (one green, two orange, and one purple) and a bell strung together on a key chain. It was assumed to have moderate novelty and stimulus value because of its unusual colors (for infants) and its heterogeneity, while in other aspects it was similar to many infant toys. It had been found to be accepted readily (within 3 seconds) by institutional infants (Collard, 1962).

The baby's response latency was measured from the time the *E* released the test toy on the table until the baby picked it up. The infant's interception of the toy from the *E*'s hand was counted as a zero latency of response, and if he had not picked it up by 3 minutes the mother was asked to place it in his hand. Thus, the range in latencies of response was from 0 to 180 seconds. After the baby picked up the toy, his responses to the toy and his social responses were recorded sequentially by minute for 6 minutes. Interobserver reliability using this method was previously found to be between 85 and 90 per cent on two consecutive trials (see Collard, 1962, for description of recording method). The mother and *E* did not talk to or initiate play with the infant during the test. If the infant smiled they smiled in response, and if he handed them the toy they handed it back.

Observer bias in recording was minimal because the data in the present study were originally collected for use in another study; therefore the *E* did not ask in advance about the baby's position in the family. In most cases it was not known until after the test was given whether a particular *S* was a first-born or later-born infant. After the baby was tested, the mother was questioned about the baby's siblings, the other persons caring for him, and the kind of housing the family had. In two instances it was known beforehand that the *Ss* were later-borns because the mother requested baby-sitting services for an older sibling while the baby was being tested. At the time the records of the babies' social and play responses were made, the writer did not plan to use them in the present study; the original plan was to use only the differences in the infants' response latencies to the test toy as evidence of differences in fear of strangers between first- and later-borns.

RESULTS

From Table 1 it can be seen that the first-born infants tended to pause much longer before picking up the test toy than did later-borns. The mean response latencies were 55.3 seconds for first-borns and 7.9 seconds for later-borns. The probability that this difference was due to chance was

TABLE 1
CHARACTERISTICS OF SUBJECTS AND RESPONSES TO NOVEL TOY

Sex	Age in Weeks		Persons Around Baby (First-Born and Widely Spaced)	Number of Siblings		Age-Spacing to Next Sibling in Years		Latency of Response in Seconds		Responses to Toy During 6 Minutes	
	First-Born and Widely Spaced	Later-Born		Widely Spaced	Later-Born	Widely Spaced	Later-Born	First-Born and Widely Spaced	Later-Born	First-Born and Widely Spaced	Later-Born
Boy.....	45	46	Few	...	2	...	4.5	180	1	60	96
Girl.....	48	49	Few	...	1	...	2	180	0	...[a]	63
Girl.....	51	53	Few	...	4	...	2	145	10	57	63
Boy.....	43	44	Few	...	1	...	2	40	15	58	77
Boy.....	54	53	Few	...	4	...	3	31	0	64	78
Girl.....	50	52	Few	...	3	...	4	31	20	63	71
Girl.....	41	40	Several	...	1	...	4	24	5	80	70
Boy.....	55	56	Many	...	2	...	3	13	10	55	52
Girl.....	47	46	Many	...	1	...	2.5	9	16	52	98
Girl.....	45	43	Many	...	2	...	3	6	10	98	69
Girl.....	39	38	Many	...	5	...	1	4	0	71	51
Girl.....	51	51	Many	...	1	...	1	0	8	56	...[b]
Mean.....	47.4	47.6	...	...	2.3	...	2.7	55.3	7.9	64.9	71.6
Boy.....	51	51	Several	1	3	6	4	110	2	70	83
Boy.....	38	38	Few	3	1	15	2	43	2	62	74
Boy.....	51	51	Few	1	1	7	1.5	35	20	33	...[c]
Boy.....	48	48	Few	2	1	7	2	35	14	61	93
Boy.....	50	50	Several	3	4	8	2	23	1	88	109
Girl.....	44	42	Many	4	2	9	2	0	5	86	104
Mean.....	47.0	46.7	...	2.3	2.0	8.7	2.3	41.0	7.3	66.7	92.6

[a] Infant "froze" and refused to play.
[b] Infant fought and cried to get down from mother's lap.
[c] Not recorded.

TABLE 2
SOCIAL RESPONSES OF SUBJECTS DURING A 6-MINUTE PERIOD

Social Responses	Number of Responses		Number of Babies Showing Response		Number of Responses		Number of Babies Showing Response	
	First-Born	Later-Born	First-Born	Later-Born	First-Born and Widely Spaced	Later-Born	First-Born and Widely Spaced	Later-Born
	Positive							
Smiling or laughing:								
Smiling	17	34	5	8	34	45	9	13
Laughing	3*	40*	2	7	6*	50*	5	9
Smiling at *E*	15	31	6	9	28	40	11	12
Smiling at mother	3	4	2	2	6	6	4	4
Total	38*	109*	7	9	74*	141*	12	14
Social play with toy:								
Play with *E*	2	42	1	4	6	49	2	6
Play with mother	8	16	5	6	16	19	8	8
Dropping or casting toy	29	79	7	6	47*	120*	10	9
Total	39*	137*	10	9	69*	188*	13	13
	Negative							
Fussing or crying	15*	1*	6	1	21*	4*	8	2
Sobering	2	0	2	0	3	1	3	1
Restlessness	13	3	4	3	16	3	5	3
Total	30*	4*	9	3	40*	8*	12	5

* Difference between the groups is significant at < .05 level on the Wilcoxon Test for Matched Samples, one-tailed test.

less than .025 on the Wilcoxon Test ($p = .017$). The variability of the response latencies of the first-born infants was very great; the standard deviation of their scores was 69.8 compared to a value of 6.9 of the later-borns. If the latencies of response of the widely spaced infants and their matched partners are included in the data, the level of significance of the difference is less than 1 per cent ($p = .0012$).

The first-born and widely spaced infants made significantly fewer responses to the toy than did the later-borns matched to them ($p = .033$ on the Wilcoxon). Interestingly, the first-born babies who made more responses to the toy than their matched partners also showed relatively short response latencies to the toy, and all were infants who had been around many or several persons rather than few.

First-born and widely spaced infants made significantly more negative social responses such as fussing and crying than later-born infants did (see Table 2).

The only first-born girl in the present study who refused to play "froze" when the test toy was presented and would not hold the toy when it was handed to her. She poked it several times and withdrew her hand as if the toy were hot. The later-born girl who cried and did not play was a hyperactive early walker who picked up the toy after 8 seconds, but then fought and cried to get down from her mother's lap. Three other girls (two first-born and one later-born) who cried and would not play with the toy could not be included in the present study, because they were tested before the writer had become aware of the possible implications of their behavior, and their complete records were not retained.

Later-borns laughed and smiled significantly more often than did first-borns. Although 9 out of 12 later-borns matched to the first-born *S*s smiled at the *E* earlier in the testing period than did first-borns, half of the latter eventually smiled at her. Nine of the later-borns smiled during the first minute, while only two first-borns did this. If the first-born and widely-spaced infants are combined, about the same number of babies in each group smiled at the *E*, but the former tended to smile later and less often than did the later-borns matched to them. More later-borns initiated play with the *E*, and they also showed many more of these social responses with the toy than the first-borns did. Both groups of infants initiated play with the mother about the same amount, and both groups smiled at her equally often. Later-borns dropped or cast the toy more often, however, and these behaviors were usually in relation to the mother. Their exuberance in these activities was also evidence of less inhibition of play. First-born infants mouthed the toy more often than did later-borns, possibly because the latter were more often engaged in active play with it.

DISCUSSION AND CONCLUSIONS

In general, it can be concluded from this study that infants receiving social stimulation from few persons will tend to show more fear of strangers than will infants receiving stimulation from a variety of persons. Compared to later-borns with preschool s blings, first-born and widely spaced infants tended to make fewer exploratory and play responses to a novel toy and to respond more slowly to the strange person and toy. A decrease in exploration and play has been found to be associated with fear in young chimpanzees (Mason, 1965) and in rats (Montgomery & Monkman, 1955). First-born and widely spaced infants also responded to the unfamiliar testing situation with more signs of distress such as crying and fewer signs of being at ease such as laughing and playing with the *E*. Waldrop and Bell (1966) observed newborn infants from small families or from families in which the siblings were widely spaced to cry more than did infants from large families or those from families with smaller age-spacing between sibs.

Variability among infants in degree of acceptance of strangers is probably determined by a number of factors, including (*a*) the number of persons the infant is exposed to and their variety in terms of appearance and behavior, (*b*) the frequency and duration of exposure to different persons, and (*c*) the infant's developmental level at the time of exposure to others. Another variable may lie in individual differences in sensitivity (or increase in arousal level) on being exposed to novel social stimuli. Thomas, Chess, Birch, Hertzig, and Korn (1963) in their work on behavioral individuality discuss this factor as a "tendency to approach or withdraw from new stimuli." Still another factor in a child's acceptance of strangers could be based on how rewarding his previous contacts have been with the persons he knows.

In this study, the extreme variability among first-born infants in their readiness to accept a toy from a stranger can be explained largely in terms of their degree of exposure to persons in the past. The five first-born infants who showed the lowest response latencies lived in densely populated housing areas where much visiting and exchange of baby-sitter services occurred among the mothers. The mothers of the six first-born infants with the longest response latencies lived out in the larger community or in a rural area and reported that their infants had not been around many persons. The infant girl who "froze" during the test had been taken care of by sitters only two times in 11 months. The seventh girl was cared for often by her father and grandmother but had few sitters. In the group in which there was a wide age spacing to next-older sibling, the only infant showing a low response latency was the youngest member of a large family where many persons visited. The mother reported that this infant was often cared for by two older sisters and was played with by two brothers. Many of the mothers with several preschool children reported that the siblings played with the babies more than they did because the children had more time. Several of the mothers of first-borns said they did not leave their babies with sitters often because they did not trust anyone else to take care of them.

The previously cited findings by Lasko and Dean that mothers tend to be more anxious about and protective of their first-borns than of later-borns may imply that mothers often shield their first-borns from close contact with others. In addition to lack of exposure to siblings, first-born babies may not be given as much opportunity as later-borns to adapt to a variety of other persons, and this might also lead the former to show more fear of strangers.

REFERENCES

BAYLEY, N. A study of the crying of infants during mental and physical tests. *Journal of Genetic Psychology*, 1932, *40*, 306–329.

CALDWELL, B. M. Mother-infant interaction in monomatric and polymatric families. *American Journal of Orthopsychiatry*, 1963, *33*, 653–664.

COLLARD, R. R. *A study of curiosity in infants.* Unpublished doctoral dissertation, University of Chicago, 1962.

DEAN, D. A. *The relation of ordinal position to personality in young children.* Unpublished master's thesis, State University of Iowa, 1947.

GESELL, A., & THOMPSON, H. *Infant behavior: its genesis and growth.* New York: McGraw-Hill, 1934.

KOCH, H. L. Some personality correlates of sex, sibling position, and sex of sibling among five- and six-year-old children. *Genetic Psychology Monographs*, 1955, *52*, 3–50.

LASKO, J. K. Parent-child relationships: report from the Fels Research Institute. *American Journal of Orthopsychiatry*, 1952, *22*, 300–304.

LASKO, J. K. Parent behavior toward first and second children. *Genetic Psychology Monographs*, 1954, *49*, 97–137.

MASON, W. A. Determinants of social behavior in young chimpanzees. In A. M. Schrier, H. F. Harlow, & F. Stollnitz (Eds.), *Behavior of nonhuman primates.* Vol. *2.* New York: Academic Press, 1965. Pp. 335–364.

MONTGOMERY, K. C., & MONKMAN, J. A. The relation between fear and exploratory behavior. *Journal of Comparative and Physiological Psychology,* 1955, *48,* 132–136.

RHEINGOLD, H. L. The modification of social responsiveness in institutional babies. *Monographs of the Society for Research in Child Development,* 1956, *21,* (2, Serial No. 63).

SCHAFFER, H. R., & EMERSON, P. E. The development of social attachments in infancy. *Monographs of the Society for Research in Child Development,* 1964, *29,* (3, Serial No. 94).

SEARS, R. R. Ordinal position in the family as a psychological variable. *American Sociological Review,* 1950, *15,* 397–401.

SITZ, R. A. Anxiety in infancy: a study of its manifestations in the first year of life. *International Journal of Psycho-Analysis,* 1950, *21,* 138–143.

THOMAS, A., CHESS, S., BIRCH, H. G., HERTZIG, M. E., & KORN, S. *Behavioral individuality in early childhood.* New York: New York University Press, 1963.

WALDROP, M. F., & BELL, R. Q. Effects of family size and density on newborn characteristics. *American Journal of Orthopsychiatry,* 1966, *36,* 544–550.

WARREN, J. R. Birth order and social behavior. *Psychological Bulletin,* 1966, *65,* 38–49.

25

Birth Order, Personality Development, and the Choice of Law as a Profession[1]

PHILIP S. VERY
AND RICHARD W. PRULL

This short article, relating birth order to career choice, shows that an interesting study can be conducted in a very uncomplicated way. Students could readily carry out this sort of investigation, especially if they used fellow students as subjects and studied anticipated career rather than actual career. The senior author, Very, is at Rhode Island College in the Department of Psychology.

A. INTRODUCTION

The basis of this study is the belief that birth order is a factor which influences personality development and that personality, in turn, is an important factor in the vocational choice of an individual.

Alfred Adler's studies of the rivalry between the firstborn child and successive siblings was a pioneer effort in the area of birth order and personality research. He believed that these siblings were attempting to overcome feelings of inferiority; however, Adler practiced in Vienna during the Victorian Period and saw a clientele consisting of a considerable number of highly repressed, sometimes persecuted, ambitious people. America pre-

sents a more liberal environment to the newborn, certainly one in which the laws of primogeniture are not as significant as they were in Europe during the past half-century.

Nevertheless, personality differences corresponding to birth-order rank do appear to exist. An excellent review of the literature on birth order and its results has been presented by Altus (1). His text contains summaries of studies by Galton, Ellis, Clarke, Apperly, Jones, and Roe, who all found that there was a significantly greater number of firstborns in eminent positions.

Karl König, in his book *Brothers and Sisters* (3), states that there is a definite relationship between personality and birth order. He asserts that there are four basic sibling positions: only child, firstborn, second born, and third born. The first, second, and third positions repeat themselves in a triadic pattern for successive siblings (i.e., fourth = first, fifth = second, etc.). The firstborn is described as being ambitious, aggressive, independent, a leader and defender of the family's attitudes. The second born is more casual, leisurely, and harmonious. His personality style does not contain the attributes one expects a leader or a defender to possess. The third born is described as overly sensitive, withdrawn, reflective, and often being the one who feels lonely and segregated. The only child is a combination of first- and third-born personality traits.

In a study of 64 children from large families, Bossard and Boll (2) list eight personality types. Their research corroborates König's birth-order theory for the first and second born. The third born was not isolated in the study, but two of the roles found therein could be descriptive of König's third-born personality. The remaining four roles could be considered more specific descriptions of the basic three birth orders described by König.

Recent research by Very (5, 6) has demonstrated that birth order is a significant factor in effecting vocational choice. His prediction that the personality of second borns would predispose them toward a career, such as a beautician, was upheld. Another article by Very demonstrated that König's birth order theory applies to personality development in twins as well.

The personality traits of lawyers, as described by a prominent New England attorney, seem to correspond very closely to those of firstborns. "A lawyer is a person who can't sit still and wait for clients to come to him. He must be a hustler, a pusher, a doer, a joiner, and a leader." The purpose of this study was to ascertain whether the observed

[1] The authors are grateful to Audrey Demener and Marjorie Waterman for their help in obtaining a portion of the data and in its further analysis.

Philip S. Very and Richard W. Prull, "Birth order, personality development, and the choice of law as a profession," *The Journal of Genetic Psychology*, 1970, *116*, 219–221. Reprinted by permission.

frequency of firstborn lawyers in a random sample was actually greater than that expected by chance.

B. METHOD AND RESULTS

The sample consisted of 100 lawyers from the Greater Boston area whose age and birth order were determined by telephone. With the use of König's birth-order categorizations of the 100 lawyers sampled, 66 were firstborn, 23 were second born, eight were third born, and three were only children. In order to obtain an expected proportion of firstborns that would be appropriate, the data on firstborns born in the period from 1913–1942 according to the United States Bureau of Vital Statistics (4) was utilized.

Since size of family is affected by such external and environmental factors as depressions, wars, and the like, it was decided to compute what may be called a weighted average of the census percentages for firstborns. Ordinary averages over five-year periods from 1913–1942 were computed; then these averages were weighted by the numbers in the actual sample shown in these five-year periods in order to arrive at an appropriate expected percentage of firstborns for theoretical comparisons. The final weighted average expected value for firstborns was 37.2 percent.

The possible significance of the larger number of firstborns in the sample was tested by using the significance of the difference of the sample proportion from a theoretical value. This yielded a σ of 4.8 percent; therefore, 66 percent is six σ or above the expected value of 37.2 percent and is thus significant at the one percent level.

C. DISCUSSION

The results obtained tend to support the theory that there is a relationship between birth order and personality traits. The personality characteristics of lawyers appear to parallel those of firstborn individuals, and the results have shown that with respect to the sample studied a significantly greater number of lawyers are in fact firstborn. The personality traits characteristic of the birth orders are of course subject to the differing environmental situations. Parents, by their attitudes and expectations, lead the children to accept different roles. The added feelings of responsibility and desire for success the parents attempt to impart to the oldest child have a great tendency to make him develop characteristics of leadership and independence. When an individual becomes an adult, the profession of a lawyer is one of the roles suited to this type of personality. In this light it is understandable why a great number of firstborns with the ability would choose law as a vocation.

D. SUMMARY AND CONCLUSION

The birth orders of 100 lawyers were obtained and compared with the expected frequencies of birth order based on data from the United States Bureau of Vital Statistics. It was found as hypothesized that the observed frequency of firstborn lawyers was significantly greater than that expected by chance. It appears that there is a relationship between birth order and personality development and that personality, in turn, is a factor in the vocational choice of an individual.

REFERENCES

1. ALTUS, W. D. Birth order and its sequelae. *Science,* 1966, *151,* 44–48.
2. BOSSARD, J. H. S., & BOLL, E. S. Personality roles in the large family. *Child Devel.,* 1955, *26,* 71–78.
3. KÖNIG, K. Brothers and Sisters. New York: St. George Press, 1963.
4. NATIONAL OFFICE OF VITAL STATISTICS. Vital Statistics—Special Reports, National Summaries. November 17, September 14, 1959, *50.*
5. VERY, P., & VAN HINES, N. Personality patterns and order of birth in 30 sets of twins. *J. Genet. Psychol.,* 1969, *114,* 93–95.
6. VERY, P., & ZANNINI, J. Birth order and being a beautician. *J. Appl. Psychol.,* in press.

V

Settings and Specific Stimuli as Determinants of Behavior

In this class of determinant we incorporate various situational influences. Immediate *instigations* such as another person's act with reference to oneself are only one part of a stimulus situation. A second aspect is the *setting:* "Where did it happen?" People act differently in differing contexts; the gymnasium evokes orders of response seldom seen in the classroom, the parlor, or the church. It is not just that basketball is played in a gym rather than a classroom, but that in the gym, additional behaviors appear; for example, boisterousness, joking, or—in some individuals—unaccustomed restraint and shyness. Such shyness might not be suspected to be part of the person's repertoire if he were seen only in other settings.

Setting is not a question solely of location; a setting can change even when the place remains the same. A classroom is not likely to remain psychologically the same environment when the teacher is out of the room for a long time. Indeed, change in the amount of structure—either in the clarity of expected behavior or in the extent of external control—often causes marked alterations in response. (For instance, some persons who are free of anxiety during the week suffer from "weekend neurosis" when deprived of the routine of their workday lives.) Research on classroom atmosphere attempts to study the effects of different emotional climates in one type of setting.

Still another influence is the impact of the various *face-to-face groups* with which an individual deals personally—his recreational cronies; his employees, employers, and competitors at work; his family at home.[1] These groups comprise a series of social systems, changes in any of which can broadly affect a person's behavior. A man's troubles in the office or a boy's anxieties in school are betrayed by actions at home. Conversely, conflict at home may damage scholastic performance. A worsening state of affairs at home may heighten the importance, to man or boy, of his boon companions outside the family. Improvements at school (for instance, a new teacher generous with praise for a girl responsive to praise) may reduce the rate of outbursts at home. It is these kinds of face-to-face relations that are dealt with in this section. The wider social systems, involving cultural and institutional memberships, are discussed under Section VI, Group Memberships.

Kurt Lewin's application of a gestalt viewpoint to understanding human social behavior stands as a landmark in the history of psychological thought. The research on group dynamics that he spawned continues to push back conceptual horizons. More recently such authors as Roger Barker and Herbert Wright have been demonstrating the alterations in behavior that accompany changes in setting. Now leading psychiatrists such as Erich Lindemann have been studying the effects of face-to-face social systems on the eruption of mental illness, especially when an "emotional hazard" such as a point of *role transition* (see introduction

---

[1] The latter was partly covered under Interpersonal Experiences in Section IV, but here we deal with the immediate relationships rather than home social learnings of the past.

to Article 42) occurs in a social system that puts undue stress on a particular individual or fails to support him in accustomed ways. Some people will show neurotic responses in any setting, but others become disturbed solely because the role relationships in which they are involved are organized in ways "unhealthful" for them. In such cases, the most appropriate treatment may be to try to change *the social system* without necessarily treating the patient directly.

Another type of stimulus that may influence behavior is the mass media. The effects of comics, movies, and TV on children have long been debated. Some psychologists, as well as laymen, assume that the depiction of violence or sex on television or in comic books will encourage children to misbehave. Others argue that experiencing a behavior such as aggression vicariously through drama may have a cathartic effect, reducing the likelihood of expression in overt behavior.

In Section V of the second edition of *The Causes of Behavior* we printed Wilbur Schramm's review of a British study on the effects of television, as well as a study by W. Paul Blakely on the effects of comic books. Both investigations failed to show the bad effects that many people had expected. Since then Bandura, his students, and others have reported an increase in subjects' aggressive behaviors after exposure to aggressive models (in person or via movie or TV). The aggressive behaviors studied have primarily been directed at inanimate objects rather than at people.

A recent study by Donald P. Hartman, "Influence of Symbolically Modeled Instrumental Aggression and Pain Cues on Aggressive Behavior" (*Journal of Personality and Social Psychology,* 1969, *11,* 280–288), contradicts the catharsis hypothesis. However, his work used delinquents as subjects. Hence, one cannot draw sound conclusions about the effects of the stimuli on normal viewers. An even more recent study on the effects of TV on aggression in the naturalistic social behavior of preschool children was reported by Aletha Huston Stein and her collaborator, Friedrich, at the 1971 meetings of the Society for Research in Child Development. They found an increase in aggressive behavior after viewing aggressive TV programs, *but* only for those *S*s whose initial level of aggression was high. This study escapes one of the criticisms that can be made of much of the work on this topic, for it looked at aggressive behavior in the normal nursery school setting, not in the laboratory. The laboratory study of such behaviors always raises a question as to the extent to which the subject may perceive that he is in a respectable scientific laboratory (in the hands of powerful and wise adults) and consequently nothing really bad would be allowed to happen. Hence, any available behaviors are "safe."

Because of the disparate findings and conclusions in this field, we are not trying to cover it beyond our acknowledgment of the issues. The articles in this section, then, deal with the effects that are obtained from exposing children to particular types of influence other than those of the media. The effects of specific stimuli, settings, and face-to-face social systems are explored.

26

Changes in Attitudes Toward Negroes of White Elementary School Students After Use of Multiethnic Readers

JOHN H. LITCHER AND
DAVID W. JOHNSON

This article describes the effects produced by using one type of stimulus instead of another. The stimuli in this case were textbooks. Half of the pupils the authors studied, all of them white, read a conventional textbook in which the illustrations consisted solely of white people; the other half read almost identical books in which some characters were nonwhites. The experiment tested whether attitudes toward blacks were affected.

The data show that exposing white children to images of blacks who are behaving like middle-class whites does have an effect. This suggests that the recent portrayal on network television of blacks in responsible positions such as nurse, detective, or physician will have some degree of ameliorative influence upon racial prejudice among white viewers. Credit one social gain to TV!

The research was conducted at the University of Minnesota, where Dr. Johnson is a member of the faculty.

Changing racial attitudes on a wide scale basis is one of the most important social-psychological problems of our society. It is evident that from a very early age white children are prejudiced against Negroes (Blake & Dennis, 1943; Goodman, 1948; Gregor & McPherson, 1966; Horowitz, 1936, 1939; Katz & Braly, 1933; Landreth & Johnson, 1953; Radke & Trager, 1950; Radke, Trager, & Hadassah, 1949). There is some empirical evidence which indicates that under certain conditions (which have not been adequately researched) the attitudes of whites toward Negroes may be changed through direct experience. Singer (1967), for example, in a recent study of the effects of integrated classrooms upon the racial attitudes of fifth-grade children, found that white children in integrated schools, compared with white children in segregated schools, are more accepting of Negroes and more familiar with Negro celebrities. The more intelligent the white child in the integrated school, the more favorable are his attitudes toward Negroes.

It is not possible, however, to provide every white child with direct experiences with Negroes. In Minnesota and North Dakota, for example, the Negro population is so small that such direct experiences are impossible. One alternative to direct experience with Negroes is exposure to materials which portray Negroes in a positive way, contradicting prevailing prejudices and stereotypes. Research in social perception (Allport & Postman, 1945; Bartlett, 1932) and in the learning of controversial material (Edwards, 1941; Jones & Aneshansel, 1956; Levine & Murphy, 1943) suggests that materials portraying Negroes positively would be either distorted in various ways to support the prevailing stereotypes and prejudices or ignored and quickly forgotten. Research in counter-conditioning (Bandura & Walters, 1963), however, would predict that such an approach would be effective. If, for example, the stimulus "Negro" (which elicits a negative response) is repeatedly paired with the cluster of stimuli characteristic of "middle class" (which elicits a positive response), the stimulus "Negro" will elicit the positive response associated with "middle class"—if the stimulus "Negro" does not elicit a more powerful response than the response elicited by the stimuli characteristic of "middle class."

An exploratory study was conducted contrasting the social perception, social learning, and the counter-conditioning hypotheses by investigating the effect of multiethnic readers upon the racial attitudes of white elementary students. Multi-ethnic readers are readers which contain characters from several different racial and ethnic groups. In the readers used, Negroes are portrayed as having

John H. Litcher and David W. Johnson, "Changes in attitudes toward negroes of white elementary school students after use of multiethnic readers," *Journal of Educational Psychology, 60,* 1969, 148–152. Copyright 1969 by the American Psychological Association and reproduced by permission.

middle-class characteristics (works hard, dresses nicely, is clean, etc.) in integrated situations.*

METHOD

This study employed a pretest-posttest control group design. Experimental groups used a multiethnic reader for 4 months while control groups used the traditional reader. Both groups were interviewed before and after the experimental treatment. The study was conducted from February 1967 through May of the same year. Sixty-eight white, middle-class children were studied, 34 classified by their teachers as upper group readers and 34 classified as middle group readers. Both the multi-ethnic and the regular second-grade readers were used by each teacher in each classroom. Eight reading groups in four second-grade classrooms in two public elementary schools participated in the study. Through random assignment, two classrooms (one in each school) used the multiethnic reader in their upper reading group and the regular reader in their middle reading group. The other two classrooms (one in each school) used the regular reader in their upper reading group and the multiethnic reader in their middle reading group.

The four teachers who participated in the study were randomly selected from volunteers within the school system. The teachers' interest in this study was prompted by the opportunity it offered them to participate in research. They were generally informed as to the nature of the study and asked to teach the experimental and control groups as similarly as possible. Since the basal approach to reading instruction was followed, the teaching included the development of word recognition skills, comprehension skills, reading skills in other content areas, oral and silent reading, and emphasis on a personal reading program. A record of any discussion relating to race relations was requested. According to their reports, the teachers did not at any time initiate a discussion of the fact that many of the characters in the multiethnic reader were nonwhite. Neither did they encourage student discussion of the racial differences of the characters in the reader while the study was in progress. The students commented very little on the differences in race of the characters about whom they were reading. The multi-ethnic readers were the only multiethnic materials in the classroom.

The Scott-Foresman multiethnic (Robinson, Monroe, & Artley, 1965) and regular (Robinson, Monroe, & Artley, 1963) second grade readers were used in the study. These readers are identical except for the pictures (some of the characters in the pictures in the multiethnic reader are nonwhite) and the names used to represent the characters of the racial and ethnic groups found in the readers.

For both the pretest and the posttest each child was interviewed individually. Four tests were presented in random order and all were given in one sitting. On the average it took 9 minutes to administer the tests. All

questions were asked of each child, but answers were not made compulsory.

During the 4 months of the experimental treatment three children, all in the experimental group, moved out of the school district. They were, therefore, not available for the posttest.

The study was conducted in a Midwestern city of 50,000 inhabitants. The total Negro population in this city is less than 100. Of the 6,181 children attending the city's elementary schools, 10 are Negroes. No Negro children attended the two elementary schools studied.

The instruments used in this study were a variation of the Clark Doll Test (Gregor & McPherson, 1966), the Horowitz and Horowitz (1938) "Show Me" and Categories tests, and a Direct Comparison test (Blake & Dennis, 1943). In the Clark Doll Test the children were presented with two dolls which differed only in skin color (one white, one dark brown). The children were asked to point to one doll as a response to the following questions: Show me the doll that (a) you would like to play with, (b) you like best, (c) is a nice doll, (d) has a nice color, (e) looks bad, (f) looks like a white child, (g) looks like a colored child, (h) looks like a Negro child, and (i) looks like you.

The "Show Me" test developed by Horowitz and Horowitz (1938) consists of 12 portraits (3 white boys, 3 white girls, 3 Negro boys, and 3 Negro girls) placed randomly on a large sheet of paper. The following questions were asked of the children: Please show me the one that (a) you'd like to sit next to at school, (b) you'd want to play with, (c) comes from a poor home, (d) you do not want in your school, (e) you'd like to have as your cousin, (f) doesn't look very smart, (g) you would want to come to your house for a long visit, and (h) you do not like.

In the Categories test (Horowitz & Horowitz, 1938) five pictures mounted on a page were presented to each child. The children were asked to reject one picture as not belonging to the group. Categories of race versus sex and race versus age were used. For example, one page might contain five pictures, three white boys, one white girl, and one Negro boy. If the Negro boy was selected as not belonging, race is a more salient category than sex for that child. If the white girl was selected, sex could be considered as the more salient category. The test was designed to analyze the strength of race, sex, and age categories for the children.

The Direct Comparison test (Blake & Dennis, 1943) required the children to make direct comparisons between Negroes and whites in regard to 18 traits. The children were asked to indicate whether the trait was more characteristic of whites or Negroes or to respond "no difference" or "don't know." Examples of the traits used are: cheerful, honest, lazy, forgetful, neat, clean, lies.

RESULTS

As part of the pretest each child was asked to respond to several questions dealing with racial identification. From Table 1 it may be seen that with the exception of one child, all the children correctly identified the dolls used in the Clark Doll Test with

---

* It should be noted that readers that do this may be inappropriate for use in integrated (or non-integrated) ghetto settings—EDITOR

TABLE 1
FREQUENCY OF RESPONSES OF WHITE SECOND-GRADE CHILDREN TO ITEMS OF RACE IDENTIFICATION ON THE CLARK DOLL TEST—PRETEST

Which doll	Multiethnic reader group[a]		Regular reader group[b]	
	Negro doll	White doll	Negro doll	White doll
Looks like a white child	1	30	—	34
Looks like a colored child	31	—	34	—
Looks like a Negro child	31	—	34	—
Looks like you	1	30	—	34

[a] N = 31.
[b] N = 34.

their appropriate racial group. From these data it may be concluded that with one possible exception, all the children studied were able to respond to questions dealing with racial membership.

Each child studied responded to four tests of racial attitudes. Since the investigators were interested only in general changes in racial attitudes resulting from the use of multiethnic readers and not in responses to the specific questions of each test a general score of favorableness of attitudes toward Negroes was derived for each child for each test. A child was given one point for each response which indicated favorable attitudes toward Negroes. For the Clark Doll Test the range of possible scores was 0–5, for the "Show Me" test the range of possible scores was 0–8, and for the Categories test, 0–6. For the Direct Comparison test the proportion of responses favorable to Negroes was used, the possible range of scores being from 0–100%.

TABLE 2
CORRELATIONS BETWEEN TESTS OF RACIAL ATTITUDES—PRETEST AND POSTTEST

Racial attitude tests correlated	Pretest	Posttest
Clark Doll and Show Me Test	.19	.25
Clark Doll and Categories Test	.13	.08
Clark Doll and Direct Comparison Test	.12	.35
Show Me and Categories Test	−.08	.22
Show Me and Direct Comparison Test	.22	.26
Categories and Direct Comparison Test	.17	.18

Note.—N = 65.

In order to see if the tests were independent of each other the responses of the children to the four tests were correlated. From Table 2 it may be seen that the tests were only slightly correlated and, therefore, the data for each were analyzed separately.

On all tests there were no significant differences between the experimental and control group on the pretests. In order to control for slight differences between the groups, however, an analysis of covariance was used in analyzing the results of the posttest. The data in Table 3 indicate that on all four [posttests] the children using multiethnic readers responded significantly more favorably toward Negroes than the children using the regular readers.

DISCUSSION

The results of this study dramatically indicate that the use of multiethnic readers in an elementary school will result in more favorable attitudes toward Negroes. The data from the Clark Doll Test indicate that the use of the multiethnic reader decreased the preference for one's own racial group over the other. While the control group expressed marked preferences for the white rather than the Negro doll, the experimental group Ss were far less unanimous about their preferences.

In a recent study on the Clark Doll Test, Greenwald and Oppenheim (1967) report that 19% of the white children they interviewed (taking their more conservative figure) identified the Negro doll in re-

TABLE 3
COMPARISON OF ATTITUDES TOWARD NEGROES OF WHITE SECOND-GRADE CHILDREN—POSTTEST

Test	Multiethnic reader group[a]	Regular reader group[b]	Significance
Clark Doll Test (Range: 0–5)	1.39	0.44	$F = 15.90$; $p < .0002$
Show Me Test (Range: 0–8)	2.58	1.47	$F = 8.71$; $p < .005$
Categories Test (Range: 0–6)	4.42	3.44	$F = 4.38$; $p < .04$
Direct Comparison Test	51%	24%	$F = 14.94$; $p < .0003$

Note.—The higher the score the more favorable the attitudes toward Negroes. An analysis of covariance was used in analyzing the data.
[a] N = 31.
[b] N = 34.

sponse to the question, "Show me the doll that looks like you." In an earlier study Morland (1963) found that 14% of the white children interviewed responded similarly. Greenwald and Oppenheim (1967) concluded on the basis of these findings that the amount of Negro misidentification found in the Clark and Clark (1940) and other similar studies is misleading as they did not have a control group of white children. The present study (1.5% white misidentification) and the study of Gregor and Mc-Pherson (1966; 0% white misidentification) give no support to their findings or their conclusion.

On the "Show Me" test, the use of the multi-ethnic reader resulted in a reduction of the amount of social distance placed between the white and Negro racial groups. On the Categories test, the children in the experimental group were less likely to exclude a child on the basis of race than were the controls. The data for the Direct Comparisons test, furthermore, indicate that the experimental Ss were less likely to attribute negative traits to Negroes and positive traits to whites than were the control Ss. Examination of the individual items revealed that the experimental group basically became equalitarian in their response. Johnson (1967) found that Negro children who were taught Negro history in a Freedom School became much more convinced that Negroes and whites are equal. Thus, the use of the multiethnic reader had much the same effect on white children as learning Negro history had upon Negro children.

The evidence is quite clear. Through the use of a multiethnic reader, white children developed markedly more favorable attitudes toward Negroes. Under the conditions of this experiment, this finding supports the counter-conditioning hypothesis and does not support the social-perception and social-learning hypothesis. The implications of this finding hardly need elaboration. While it is not possible, due to lack of material resources and the distribution of the Negro population in the United States, for every white child to have direct experiences with Negroes (although the investigators believe it is desirable), it is possible to increase the visibility of the Negro in the curriculum materials of the schools. Such an action should, through the reduction of prejudice, increase racial harmony.

A limitation on the generalization of the results of this study should be noted. The Negro population in the city in which this study was conducted is quite small (Negroes make up less than .2% of the total population of the city). The probability is very high that the children participating in the study had no direct experience with Negroes and that the Negro community does not represent an economic or social threat to the white community. The racial attitudes of the children studied, therefore, are probably not firmly rooted in direct experiences or reference group norms.

REFERENCES

ALLPORT, G. W., & POSTMAN, L. J. The basic psychology of rumor. *Transactions of the New York Academy of Sciences*, Series II, 1945, *8*, 61–81.

BANDURA, A., & WALTERS, H. *Social learning and personality development.* New York: Holt, Rinehart & Winston, 1963.

BARTLETT, F. C. *Remembering.* Cambridge, England: Cambridge University Press, 1932.

BLAKE, R., & DENNIS, W. The development of stereotypes concerning the Negro. *Journal of Abnormal and Social Psychology*, 1943, *38*, 525–531.

CLARK, H. B., & CLARK, M. K. Skin color as a factor in racial identification of Negro preschool children. *Journal of Social Psychology*, 1940, *11*, 160.

EDWARDS, A. L. Political frames of reference as a factor influencing recognition. *Journal of Abnormal and Social Psychology*, 1941, *36*, 34–50.

GOODMAN, M. E. Evidence concerning the genesis of interracial attitudes. *American Anthropologist*, 1946, *48*, 624–630.

GREENWALD, H. J., & OPPENHEIM, D. B. Reported magnitude of self-misidentification among Negro children—artifact? *Journal of Personality and Social Psychology*, 1968, *8*, 49–52.

GREGOR, A. J., & MCPHERSON, D. A. Racial attitudes among white and Negro children in a deep-South standard metropolitan area. *The Journal of Social Psychology*, 1966, *68*, 95–106.

HOROWITZ, E. The development of attitude toward the Negro. *Archives of Psychology*, 1936, *194*, 5–47.

HOROWITZ, R. E. Racial aspects of self-identification in nursery school children. *Journal of Psychology*, 1939, *7*, 91–99.

HOROWITZ, L., & HOROWITZ, R. E. Development of social attitudes in children. *Sociometry*, 1938, *1*, 301–339.

JOHNSON, D. W. The effects of a freedom school on its students. In R. Dentler, B. Mackler, & M. E. Warshauer (Eds.), *The urban R's: Race relations as the problem in urban education.* New York: Praeger, 1967.

JONES, E. E., & ANESHANSEL, J. The learning and utilization of contravaluant material. *Journal of Abnormal and Social Psychology*, 1956, *53*, 27–33.

KATZ, D., & BRALY, K. W. Racial stereotypes of one hundred college students. *Journal of Abnormal and Social Psychology*, 1939, *28*, 280–290.

LANDRETH, C., & JOHNSON, B. C. Young childrens' responses to a picture and insert test designed to reveal reactions to persons of different skin color. *Child Development*, 1953, *24*, 63–80.

LEVINE, J. M., & MURPHY, G. The learning and forgetting of controversial material. *Journal of Abnormal and Social Psychology*, 1943, *38*, 507–517.

MORLAND, J. K. Racial self-identification: a study of nursery school children. *American Catholic Sociological Review*, 1963, *24*, 231–242.

RADKE, M. J., & TRAGER, H. G. Children's perception of the social roles of Negroes. *Journal of Psychology*, 1950, *29*, 3–33.

RADKE, M. J., TRAGER, H. G., & HADASSAH, D. Social perceptions and attitudes of children. *Genetic Psychology Monograph*, 1949, *40*, 327–447.

ROBINSON, H. M., MONROE, M., & ARTLEY, A. S. *New more friends and neighbors 2-2* and *New friends and neighbors 2-1*, Chicago: Scott, Foresman, 1963.

ROBINSON, H. M., MONROE, M., & ARTLEY, A. S. *More friends old and new 2-2* and *Friends old and new 2-1*, Chicago: Scott, Foresman, 1965.

SINGER, D. The influence of intelligence and an interracial classroom on social attitudes. In R. Dentler, B. Mackler, & M. E. Warshauer (Eds.), *The urban R's: Race relations as the problem in urban education.* New York: Praeger, 1967.

27

A Child in Distress:
The Effect of Focusing
Responsibility on Children
on Their Attempts to Help

ERVIN STAUB

A specific stimulus in the form of verbal instruction can make a great deal of difference in the ways that subjects respond. That fact is succinctly illustrated in this brief report by Ervin Staub of the Department of Social Relations at Harvard. Staub played a recording of a child's cries of distress in order to study the conditions under which another child, in an adjoining room, will go to help when he hears the cries.

This is one of a series of studies by Staub of the pro-social behavior of helping a child in distress. The studies are trying to isolate the conditions that influence such helping responses. See, for example, "A Child in Distress: The Influence of Age and Number of Witnesses on Children's Attempts to Help" (Journal of Personality and Social Psychology, 1970, 14, 130–140) or "Helping a Person in Distress: The Influence of Implicit and Explicit 'Rules' of Conduct on Children and Adults" (same journal, 1971, 17, 137–144).

Children may learn that one should help others by adults focusing responsibility on them externally or indicating to them that they are expected to respond to another person's need. In this study the effects of indirectly focusing responsibility on children on their subsequent attempts to help another child in distress were investigated.

The subjects were 42 kindergarten and 42 first-grade boys and girls. A female experimenter asked the subject to make a drawing, but "discovered" that she had no crayon. Before she left to get crayons she went into an adjoining room ostensibly to "check on a girl who is in there." When the experimenter returned she said casually: "She's fine. I hope she doesn't climb on that chair again." This procedure aimed to communicate that there was a child alone in the adjoining room, and to suggest an explanation for the distress sounds the subject would subsequently hear. In the distress group, the experimenter then left. In the distress-responsibility group, the experimenter said: "I will leave you in charge of things, O.K.?" After the subject acknowledged this in some manner the experimenter added: "If anything happens you will take care of it." Then the experimenter left. About a minute and a half after the experimenter left the subjects heard a crash from the adjoining room, followed by sounds of distress consisting of severe crying and sobbing, which lasted 70 seconds. In a third group, the distress-help group, the procedure was the same as in the distress group, but the subjects heard sounds of distress that included calls for help. The experimenter, observing from behind a one-way mirror, recorded the subjects' behavior as active help if they went into the adjoining room or went in search of the experimenter, as volunteering information if they reported what happened on the experimenter's return to the room a minute after the distress sounds ceased, and as no help if they did neither. Scores of 3, 2, and 1 were assigned to these responses, respectively. In the case of no help, the experimenter asked questions in order to elicit a report of the distress sounds. If the subjects said in response to the most direct question that they heard nothing this was recorded as denial. All subjects were carefully debriefed.*

---

* Dr. Staub has provided the following description of the debriefing procedure.

"The debriefing that followed attempted to assure in two ways that the procedure would have no negative consequences for children and would leave no feelings of guilt and resentment: (a) by reassuring them that no one was suffering and that nothing was amiss and (b) by continuing the session with pleasant activities during which the experimenter behaved in a warm and nurturant manner, which was expected to further indicate to children that everything was all right and to result in an overall pleasant experience. In all cases, permission was obtained from parents for their child's participation in the experiment; neither parents nor teachers reported any adverse consequences resulting from the procedure, suggesting the success of debriefing. To minimize confusion for younger subjects, kindergarten children who did not go into the adjoining room were not told that they heard a tape recording. The experimenter told these sub-

---

An analysis of variance of helping scores showed a significant treatment effect ($F = 4.78$, $df = 1/72$, $p < .02$). The subjects in the distress-responsibility group helped significantly more than those in the distress group ($t = 3.07$, $df = 72$, $p < .01$) and marginally significantly more than those in the distress-help group ($t = 1.87$, $df = 72$, $p < .07$). The differences between groups in first grade were of the same magnitude as in the total sample, while they were insignificant in kindergarten. A number of children who did not help denied that they had heard any noise. Denial was more frequent in kindergarten than in first grade ($\chi^2 = 6.80$, $df = 1$, $p < .01$) and within kindergarten slightly greater in the distress-responsibility group than in the other two groups combined ($\chi^2 = 3.60$, $df = 1$, $p < .10$).

Thus, assignment of responsibility enhanced helping behavior, particularly in first grade. Learning to take responsibility for others' welfare may often begin through assignment of responsibility to children by socializing agents. Whiting and Whiting (1969) found that children in cultures in which mothers report that they assign important tasks to them, such as baby tending, behave more altruistically, as measured by offers of help, support, and responsible suggestions, than children in cultures in which they are assigned fewer or less responsible tasks. Denial was probably due to children's fear of disapproval for not attempting to help, which was enhanced in the group where responsibility was focused on them.

jects that the other child was all right now and that on her way back she saw her returning to her classroom. In addition, the experimenter went into the adjoining room and returned, saying that the room was empty now, and repeating that the other child has returned to her classroom. First graders and children who helped by going into the adjoining room were debriefed by the experimenter's telling them that they had heard a tape recording because the experimenter wanted them to draw a picture of what they thought happened when they heard the sounds. All subjects then drew a picture of either what they thought had happened, or one of their choice. Afterwards all Ss played a game, and were asked about things they liked to do, in order to end the session on a positive note."—EDITOR

REFERENCE

WHITING, J. M. W., & WHITING, B. Children in six cultures. Unpublished manuscript, Harvard University, 1969.

28

Social Influence as a Function of Stimulus Ambiguity at Three Age Levels[1]

KENNETH L. HOVING, NORMAN HAMM, AND PAULA GALVIN

This study deals with a type of conformity: the responsiveness of children and adolescents to peer group standards or beliefs. We assign the article to Section V because it deals with influence of the face-to-face group of classmates, even though the classmates were not physically present when the children took their turns as research Ss.

Social influence studies on perceptual judgments have a long history in social psychology. The studies of Muzafir Sherif reported in The Psychology of Social Norms *(Harper, 1936) are cited in most introductory texts. These studies utilized a situation where the ambiguity was maximal. The amount of perceived motion of a stationary dot of light was studied in relation to the judgments of others. Perceived motion is a normally present illusion (the autokinetic effect) in the circumstances used.*

The classic study in which non-ambiguous stimuli were used was done by Solomon Asch (1952). He, Richard Crutchfield, and others have done many similar studies since then. The work reported here is a departure from most in that the degree

of ambiguity is varied, as are the ages of the subjects.

Hoving is at Kent State University in Ohio, where the study was done. Hamm is now at the University of Nebraska at Omaha.

Several recent articles have reported a nonmonotonic relationship between conformity and age. [A monotonic relation is one in which there is an increase (or decrease) in one variable for every increase in the other variable. In simple terms then, a nonmonotonic relation is one in which there is not consistency in the direction of change in the one variable as the other changes.—Editor] Costanzo and Shaw (1966) found that conformity increased from ages 7–9 to ages 11–13 and then decreased. Iscoe, Williams, and Harvey (1963) also reported increasing conformity from ages 7 through 12 in both boys and girls. Girls then decreased in conformity by age 15, but conformity in boys increased at least through age 15.

These findings are in marked contrast to those reported by Berenda (1950), who found significantly less conformity in a group of 10- to 13-year-old children than in a group of 7- to 10-year-old children. Hoving (1964) also found more conformity in second-grade (age 7) than fourth-grade (age 9) children. Hoving, Hamm, and Roehl (1967) have suggested that differences in task ambiguity may be responsible for these conflicting results. The tasks used in these studies differed in terms of the clarity with which the incorrect alternative chosen by the group differed from the objectively correct alternative. When the group's choice is clearly incorrect the subject is placed in a conflict situation in which he must either agree with the group and choose the same obviously false alternative or choose the objectively correct alternative and disagree with the group's choice. If, however, there is no objectively correct alternative and/or the subject does not perceive any difference between the group's choice and the objectively correct choice, no conflict is perceived. Thus, the subject's choice behavior should differ as a function of whether or not he perceives a conflict between objective reality and the group's choice. When conflict is perceived by the subject, it is assumed that there is an increasing tendency to choose the objectively correct alternative with increasing age. Thus, conformity should be negatively related to age on tasks that produce conflict for the subject. However, if no conflict or only minimal conflict is produced by the task (because of its high am-

[1] P. Galvin was supported under Grant NSF GY–2485 from the National Science Foundation. The authors wish to thank the administrators, teachers, and students of the Ravenna, Ohio, school system for their assistance and participation in this study.

Kenneth L. Hoving, Norman Hamm, and Paula Galvin, "Social influence as a function of stimulus ambiguity at three age levels," *Developmental Psychology*, 1969, *1*, 631–636. Reprinted by permission.

biguity), the subject may be increasingly influenced by the group's choice. Thus, conformity should be positively related to age on tasks that produce little or no conflict.

The tasks employed by Costanzo and Shaw (1966) and Iscoe et al. (1963) seem to be at least partially ambiguous and hence involved only minimal conflict for the subject. The tasks employed by Berenda (1950) and Hoving (1964) were, by contrast, clearly unambiguous and hence presented a clear-cut conflict situation to the subject. This difference in the amount of conflict produced may account for the apparent contradiction in the results of these studies.

The present study attempted to test the hypothesis that conformity behavior increases with age on tasks that produce minimal conflict, whereas conformity behavior decreases with age on tasks that produce conflict. Three levels of task ambiguity were employed at three grade levels in an attempt to evaluate this hypothesis. It was assumed that task stimuli that were maximally ambiguous would reveal the positive relationship between conformity and age, whereas the unambiguous stimuli would show the negative relationship between conformity and age.

METHOD

SUBJECTS

Subjects were 108 public school children from Grades 2, 5, and 8, equally divided as to sex and grade level. In addition, 173 subjects were used in the preexperimental procedure to empirically assess task difficulty. The subjects were drawn from a semiurban community that is largely lower middle class in terms of socioeconomic status. All of the subjects present in the classes during the period of data collecting who were at appropriate grade level for age were used.

APPARATUS

All equipment was housed in an 8 × 19 foot mobile trailer. A partition with a one-way mirror divided the trailer into an experimental and a control room. A modification of the Crutchfield procedure was employed. Three individual cubicles, a projection screen, and earphones were located in the experimental room. The control room contained a slide projector, electronic timers, a master control panel, and a two-way sound system and tape recorder.

Each subject's cubicle included a control box with a large green light, and a set of six small lamps arranged in three rows and two columns. A button was located beneath each column that when depressed, activated the light immediately above it and a corresponding light on the master response panel in the control room. The experimenter controlled the lights in the other two rows, although the procedure was such that the subject believed these reflected the responses of the two other subjects.

PREEXPERIMENTAL PROCEDURE

In order to objectively determine the ambiguity of a given stimulus, preexperimental sessions were conducted in classrooms located at the elementary and junior high schools from which the subjects were drawn. Preexperimental groups, of about 30 subjects each, were required to make judgments on 4 training and 44 experimental slides. Subjects were asked to determine which of two sides of a slide contained the greater number of dots. Each slide contained a varying number of white dots superimposed on a black field and was divided by a thin white line into two parts labeled Side One and Side Two. Answers were recorded on IBM answer sheets by the fifth and eighth graders; second-grade subjects circled the number of their choice on a mimeographed sheet.

Stimulus ambiguity was defined in terms of the percentage of error that the preexperimental group made when judging each of the 44 experimental slides. The unambiguous stimulus was selected on the basis of the extremely low error rate made by subjects at each grade level in the preexperimental session. More than 98% of the judgments were correct on this stimulus under noninfluence conditions. The partially ambiguous stimulus was correctly judged 80% of the time. The totally ambiguous stimulus was one in which both judgments available to the subject were equally correct, since both parts of the slide contained 15 dots. The preexperimental groups chose each side of this stimulus approximately equally in the three grade levels employed. The incorrect side contained 7 dots in the unambiguous condition and 16 in the partially ambiguous condition. One side of each slide always contained 15 dots.

PROCEDURE

In the experiment proper each of the three levels of stimulus ambiguity was presented eight times, with the side with the greater number of dots located on the right four times and on the left four times in the unambiguous and partially ambiguous series to correct for position effects. Twelve of these 24 slides, 4 at each level, were designated as test or influence slides in which the subject answered last. The subject was presented lights that indicated that the other subjects present had picked the objectively incorrect alternative on the unambiguous and partially ambiguous series and one of the equally correct alternatives on the ambiguous series. The remaining 12 slides were termed controls and were identical to the influence slides with the exception that on these trials the subject answered first. In addition, 6 slides containing other dot combinations were included. It was hoped that these slides would increase the overall credibility of the task. The slide sequence consisted of 4 training and 30 experimental slides. All subjects received the same randomly ordered sequence of slides. Each stimulus was presented for 4 seconds for each trial to reduce the subject's tendency to count the dots.

Three children of the same sex were escorted by the experimenter from their classroom to the trailer and seated in individual cubicles. A set of standardized instructions was read concurrently with the showing of four training slides. The slides were projected onto a screen located on the forward wall of the experimental room. The instructions given following the training sequence were as follows:

> On all the following pictures I want you to press the button of the side that has the most dots—button #1 if side one has the most or button #2 if side two has the most. From now on you will be able to see which choices your classmates made. If you look on your boxes, you will see three rows of lights. The bottom row belongs to each of you because it lights up when you press a button. Now let's talk for a minute about the top two rows of lights on your boxes. [The experimenter labels the top two rows with the names of the other two children present. He then explains to each subject individually that he will be able to tell how his other classmates answered by observing which light is on. The subject is then questioned with examples to determine if he understands the procedure.]
>
> So on all the rest of the pictures you will be able to see how the others have answered. Remember to wait for your green light before you answer. The green light tells you that it is your turn to answer. Watch the screen very carefully because you will see each picture for only a few seconds.
>
> Before we begin I would like you to put on the earphones that are setting in front of you. Make sure they fit comfortably. Now everyone look up at the screen.

During the experiment, a masking sound was fed through the earphones to minimize apparatus noise and subject collaboration. The experimenter manipulated the apparent choices of each peer with a master control panel; the panel also permitted the experimenter to monitor the subject's answer on each trial.

RESULTS

Two measures of social influence and an error rate measure were computed for each subject for each level of ambiguity. One measure of social influence was determined by totaling the frequency with which the subject's judgments were the same as the reference group on the influence trials. This measure of social influence is artificially inflated as it reflects errors in judgment as well as social influence. The relationship of this measure of social influence to age is graphically shown in Figure 1. The identifying numbers on the figure legends refer to the number of dots on each side of the slides used to measure social influence. The data were subjected to an analysis of variance procedure that revealed that the magnitude of social influence varied with the ambiguity of the task ($F = 235.59$, $df = 2/204$, $p < .01$), and that the magnitude of social influence at the different levels of ambiguity depended in part on the age of the subjects ($F = 11.78$, $df = 4/204$, $p < .01$). A Newman-

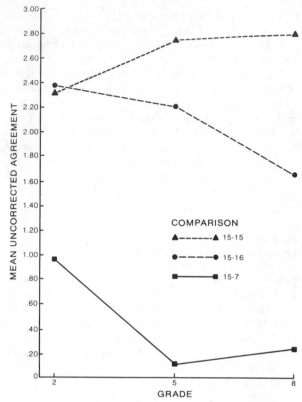

FIGURE 1. *Children's mean uncorrected agreement scores on tasks of varying ambiguity.*

Keuls test (Winer, 1962, p. 309) was computed on the differences in conformity on the ambiguous trials as a function of grade level. These tests revealed that the difference between the second and eighth grade was significant ($q = 4.81$, $r = 3/204$, $p < .01$) as was the difference between the second and fifth grade ($q = 3.63$, $r = 2/204$, $p < .05$). The difference between the fifth and eighth grade, however, was not significant.

Iscoe et al. (1963) have shown that the apparent relationship of social influence to age can be markedly distorted if error rate is not considered. Error rate was defined in the present study as the frequency with which the subject picked the side of the slide with fewer rather than more dots on the unambiguous (15–7) slide and the partially ambiguous (15–16) slide on noninfluence trials. Error rate is obviously much more difficult to define for the maximally ambiguous task (15–15). Errors were arbitrarily determined on these trials by tabulating the frequency with which the subject picked the same side under noninfluence conditions as the group chose in the influence condition. For example, on the 15–15 slide, if the group chose side one under influence conditions, an error on the slide was tabulated if the subject picked this same side when the same control 15–15 slide was shown.

Quite clearly this is a severe error measure. An analysis of variance of error rate data revealed that error rates differed as a function of ambiguity ($F = 211.59$, $df = 2/204$, $p < .01$) as well as age ($F = 5.138$, $df = 2/202$, $p < .01$). Error rate decreased with age at two levels of ambiguity as is shown in Figure 2. This figure also reveals that the greatest frequency of errors occurred on the most ambiguous slides with fewest occurring on the unambiguous slides.

A measure of social influence adjusted for error rate was also calculated. The number of errors made by each subject, calculated in the manner just described, was subtracted from his uncorrected conformity score for each level of stimulus ambiguity. This measure permits the assessment of peer influence with the differential error rate for the different difficulty levels at each age taken into account. The relationship of this measure of influence to ambiguity across age is portrayed in Figure 3. The analysis of variance of these data reveals that the magnitude of social influence differs significantly ($F = 21.9$, $df = 2/204$, $p < .01$) with the ambiguity of the task. The significant interaction of Ambiguity × Age ($F = 6.68$, $df = 4/204$, $p < .01$) indicates that children of different ages are differentially influenced by their peers depending on the ambiguity of the task.

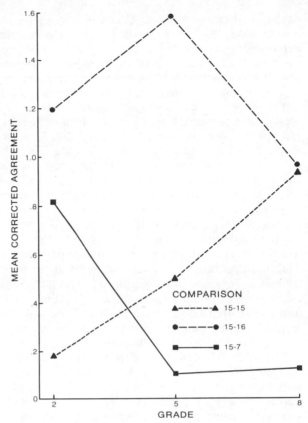

FIGURE 3. *Children's mean corrected agreement scores on tasks of varying ambiguity.*

To test the significance of the functions summarized graphically in Figure 3, a Newman-Keuls test on the corrected scores was computed. In the unambiguous condition, differences between the second and fifth grades ($q = 3.96$, $r = 3/204$, $p < .05$) and between the second and eighth grades ($q = 3.66$, $r = 2/204$, $p < .01$) were statistically significant. No difference was found between the fifth and eighth grades. In the partially ambiguous condition, only the difference between the fifth and eighth grade ($q = 3.35$, $r = 3/204$, $p < .05$) was significant. Neither the second and eighth grades nor the second and fifth grades differed significantly. In the totally ambiguous condition, the difference in conformity between the second and eighth grades was significant ($q = 4.73$, $r = 3/204$, $p < .01$), but the differences between the second and fifth and fifth and eighth grades were not significant.

DISCUSSION

The results clearly support the primary hypothesis of the present study. Conformity behavior decreases with age on tasks when the alternative chosen by the group clearly differs from the objec-

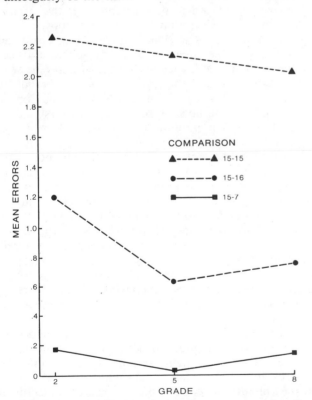

FIGURE 2. *Children's mean error rate on tasks of varying ambiguity under noninfluence conditions.*

tively correct alternative. This was shown by the line labeled 15–7 in Figures 1 and 3. Conformity behavior on tasks that are ambiguous and hence produce little, if any, conflict increases in a positive fashion with age. This was graphically demonstrated by the line labeled 15–15 in Figures 1 and 3.

These results are reflected in both the uncorrected and corrected measures of social influence. However, a comparison of Figures 1 and 3 clearly reveals the necessity of carefully specifying the criterion measures employed. In the present case, the correction for errors markedly changed the relative position of the functions describing the relationship of social influence in ambiguous tasks across age. The relationship of conformity to age on the ambiguous trials was basically the same whether a correction for errors is applied or not. This is important as the correction used for these trials is severe and in part arbitrary. The method of calculating errors for the totally ambiguous condition is one that considers a choice of the same alternative in the noninfluence condition as is chosen by the group in the influence condition as an error.

The high frequency of conformity behavior on the partially ambiguous task, Slide 15–16, may in part be explained in terms of the method used to correct for errors. Subjects at all three grade levels showed greater corrected agreement with the incorrect choice of the reference group in the partially ambiguous task than in either the totally ambiguous or unambiguous tasks. When the correction for errors is not employed, as in Figure 1, we find the level of agreement with the reference group between that found in the totally ambiguous and unambiguous situations. Quite probably, it is the elevated error rate of the totally ambiguous condition, shown in Figure 2, that accounts for the higher corrected level of agreement found in the partially ambiguous condition.

The higher corrected agreement score on the partially ambiguous condition at Grade 5 poses some difficulties since the total agreement score portrayed in Figure 1 reveals no elevation of agreement at Grade 5. However, an inspection of the error rate portrayed in Figure 2 reveals a lower error rate at this grade than at either of the other grades. This may be due to the greater difficulty of the task for subjects at Grade 2 and boredom with the task at Grade 8. In either case, when the lower error rate at Grade 5 is subtracted from the overall agreement score, we find the elevated corrected agreement score obtained at Grade 5. It is also possible that this elevation at Grade 5 may be the result of sampling error.

The motivational base responsible for conformity is commonly accepted as being at least twofold.

Deutsch and Gerard (1955), for example, have proposed a distinction between normative and informational forms of social influence. The former is thought to be controlled primarily by a need or desire for group acceptance and/or a desire to avoid disapproval, whereas informational conformity is governed by a desire for information or a desire to be correct. The operation of these motivational systems is thought to vary with the ambiguity of the task and the age of the child. The interaction of these motivational changes with task ambiguity across age may be used to tentatively account for the present results.

The need to be correct and the need for peer approval are both thought to increase in strength with age. In addition, the kinds of behavior that produce peer approval change with age. Mere agreement may be sufficient to gain peer approval only when it is compatible with the demands of objective correctness. Moreover, with age, children are increasingly able to answer questions correctly and to determine if a correct answer is possible.

These factors, in combination, may be used to at least partially account for the findings of the present study. The negative relationship between conformity and age on unambiguous tasks may be explained in the following fashion: In unambiguous tasks, the subject's need to be correct and need for peer approval are placed in direct conflict. If the subject agrees with the group to gain peer approval, he fails to satisfy his need to be correct. In the younger subjects neither need is great but apparently peer approval can be gained at this age by agreeing with the group even if the group's choice is obviously incorrect. This, when coupled with minimal opposition from the need to be correct, results in relatively large amounts of conformity at younger age levels. In older subjects we find a much stronger need to be correct coupled with the subject's presumed inability to gain peer approval for agreement when the apparent choice of the group is obviously incorrect. Hence the minimal conformity at older ages on unambiguous tasks. It is important to note that it is the decrease in the ability of older subjects to gain peer approval for agreement when the group's choice is clearly wrong, plus the increased strength of the need to be correct, that is believed to be responsible for the decrease in conformity behavior with age on unambiguous items.

The positive relationship between age and conformity on ambiguous tasks is also thought to be due to the increasing need to be correct and to gain peer approval, which occurs with age. The child's past history of reinforcement is presumed to result in his agreeing with the choices of others when in doubt as to the correct answer. Optimal satisfaction of both motivational systems occurs if the subject agrees with the choices of others in ambiguous situations. This optimizes his chances of being correct and produces maximal peer approval. As both the normative and informational motivational systems increase in strength with age, we expect and indeed do find a positive relationship between conformity and age on tasks that produce minimal or no conflict.

The frequency of agreement with the nonveridical choice of the reference group in the partially ambiguous condition is probably a function of an intermediate level of conflict produced by this task. Agreement with the group choice in the partially ambiguous condition is compatible with the subject's need for peer approval, and yet the task is sufficiently ambiguous to reduce the potential negating influence of the need to be correct. The need to be correct may motivate high levels of conformity in ambiguous situations as the subject follows the group in the hopes of being correct, whereas it motivates minimal conformity in unambiguous situations, as here the subject is motivated to choose the objectively correct alternative.

REFERENCES

BERENDA, R. W. *The influence of the group on the judgments of children.* New York: Kings Crown Press, 1950.

COSTANZO, P. R., & SHAW, M. E. Conformity as a function of age level. *Child Development,* 1966, *37,* 967–975.

DEUTSCH, M., & GERARD, H. B. A study of normative and informational social influence upon individual judgment. *Journal of Abnormal and Social Psychology,* 1955, *51,* 629–636.

HOVING, K. L. Some parameters of yielding in children. Paper presented at the meeting of the Midwestern Psychological Association, St. Louis, April 1964.

HOVING, K. L., HAMM, N. H., & ROEHL, K. Conformity in children as a function of adult vs. peer influence, hypothetical vs. real models, and degree of perceptual ambiguity. Paper presented at the meeting of the Society for Research in Child Development, New York, March 1967.

ISCOE, I., WILLIAMS, M., & HARVEY, J. Modification of children's judgments by a simulated group technique: A normative developmental study. *Child Development,* 1963, *34,* 963–978.

WINER, B. J. *Statistical principles in experimental design.* New York: McGraw-Hill, 1962.

29

Innovating Classroom Practices to Support Achievement Motivation and Ego-Development

RONALD LIPPITT,
ROBERT FOX,
AND RICHARD SCHMUCK

This paper reflects the influence of the University of Michigan's Research Center for Group Dynamics. Kurt Lewin founded the center with Ronald Lippitt and others at MIT (The Massachusetts Institute of Technology). After Lewin's death it was moved to Michigan, where Lippitt was associated with it until he and Floyd Mann founded the Center for Research on Utilization of Scientific Knowledge. Both centers are part of Michigan's huge Institute for Social Research.

Dr. Fox directs the University School in Ann Arbor. Run by the University of Michigan for local children, the school is maintained for purposes of teacher training and research. Fox's experiences at the school are doubtless reflected in the paper's sensitivity to the complex situation the educator faces when desiring to try something new.

Dr. Schmuck is professor of educational psychology and member of the Center for the Advanced Study of Educational Administration, University of Oregon.

The reader who is interested in further material about the implications of group dynamics for education will want to consult the book Learning in Social Settings, *edited by Matthew W. Miles and W. W. Charters, Jr. (Allyn and Bacon, 1970).*

Utilizing the resources of the behavioral sciences to improve classroom teaching practices is an exciting challenge. At least four types of resources are available as are a variety of ways of using them: relevant research knowledge; concepts and conceptual frameworks; diagnostic tools and methods; and scientists themselves as consultants and collaborators.

These four types of resource can be mobilized to stimulate and support an improvement process in several ways. Such patterns of improvement can be roughly classified into two types. In one the needed resources of new knowledge and practice are "imported" into the classroom and the school system from outside. In the second type of pattern the needed knowledge and resources are developed and mobilized within the classroom itself and utilized to make desired improvements. Let us look briefly at examples of these two patterns.

"IMPORTING" THE NEEDED RESOURCES

Through reading or a course or a consultant, the teacher learns about research findings and theory. In order for the materials to be useful, the teacher must perceive the information as relevant to the teaching problems with which she is coping and must be able to derive from it realistic ideas about possible action. The process of making research findings meaningful to the person who teaches has been very poorly developed in the field of education, as contrasted to such more advanced fields of research utilization as agricultural practice, medical practice, and industrial practice. In another "importing" process new educational practices developed in one setting become visible, accessible, and are adopted or adapted by another teacher. This progress requires that innovations be identified by some scanning procedure, be evaluated to eliminate those not worthy of dissemination, and then be communicated in an appropriate way which makes it possible for other teachers to understand and to adapt a new practice in their own teaching situation. One of the tragedies of American education is that so many creative teaching practice inventions consistent with the best behavioral science knowledge remain invisible and unevaluated.

INTERNAL RESOURCE DEVELOPMENT

In the second pattern of improvement the teacher is helped to collect data about her own classroom situation, to interpret the findings as a diagnosis of needs and potentialities for change, and to derive designs for improvement from the diagnosis of her own classroom situation. In other words, instead of importing knowledge from outside, she is involved in creating knowledge and utilizing it for designing improvement in her practice. Typically, in this pattern, resources from outside are required to help in the process. These resources are either diagnostic tools, or a consulting scientist, or both.

The sections which follow contain the results of our experiences in using both of these patterns to help a group of elementary and secondary classroom teachers to stimulate achievement motivation and enhance the ego-development of pupils.

DIAGNOSING THE ACHIEVEMENT AND EGO-DEVELOPMENT NEEDS AND OPPORTUNITIES IN THE CLASSROOM

A pupil with high ego-strength can be characterized in two general ways. First, he has developed cognitive skills and intellectual coping mechanisms through successful classroom learning experiences. Such a pupil has mastered, without an overload of anxiety, most of the academic challenges presented to him. He is able to utilize effectively his intellectual capacities. When a child is not utilizing his academic potential in classroom performance, it is a poor situation for ego-development. In many such cases, energy is being drained off by excessive anxiety, worry, and hostile feelings, so that the pupil is not free to utilize his abilities. He is blocked or distracted or focusing on solving other types of problems.

A second characteristic of ego-strength is affective integration. Such a pupil has positive feelings about himself and others, emanating from personal feelings of strength and worthwhileness. He feels only moderate tension when relating with peers and teachers in the school setting and perceives the significant people in his life as being supportive and encouraging of his school performance and conduct.

These two aspects of ego-strength, the cognitive and the affective, are interrelated. For instance, if a pupil experiences anxiety in his relations with peers and teachers, we find that much of his attention and energy will be directed toward coping with fears and reducing tension. Such pupils often have negative feelings about themselves and perform more poorly in their school work than their intelligence levels indicate they are capable of. On the other hand, pupils who experience acceptance and support from peers and teachers often approach academic tasks with the same mobiliza-tion of energy, effort, and expectations of adequacy and success they have experienced in these relationships. Such pupils' positive views of themselves facilitate their academic learning and the development of cognitive skills.

Considerable classroom research indicates that a pupil's interpersonal relationships condition the development of these two facets of ego-strength. Specifically, the research indicates that pupils who relate successfully to their peers and who feel relaxed and comfortable in the presence of teachers, are more likely to utilize their intellectual and emotional resources in building a strong ego. Furthermore, our research suggests that we can identify, explain, and create classroom groups with atmospheres conducive to ego-building. Teachers will be able neither to influence their pupils constructively nor to teach them academic subject matter without considering the classroom processes that offer opportunity for ego-development and enhancement. Since such problems and issues of interpersonal relations in the classroom are basic to ego-development, a teacher needs to master a style of approaching and solving these problems. One purpose of this chapter is to illustrate ways of approaching such a challenge.

First, the teacher must work toward understanding the network of interpersonal relationships in her classroom. Children attribute to each of their classmates levels of social power or ability to influence others which vary from very high to very low. Moreover, being able to do things well at school and being liked often constitute important sources of social power. Pupils assess the status of their classmates on these variables quickly at the beginning of the school year, and they maintain their judgments with relatively little variation throughout the school year.

However, even though pupils show considerable agreement when rating their peers on liking, influence, and expertness, classroom groups do differ considerably one from the other on how much consensus there is about these dimensions. In some classrooms, for instance, interpersonal acceptance and rejection are narrowly focused. Such classrooms are characterized by a large number of pupils who agree in giving high status and acceptance to only a small cluster of their classmates on a sociometric test. Along with this narrow focus on a small number of pupils, many other pupils are neglected entirely. On the other hand, some classrooms are characterized by a wide range of positive and negative choices, that is, little or no focus of interpersonal acceptance and rejection upon a few members. Such groups are distinguished by a more equal distribution of sociometric choices, by no distinct subgroups whose members receive the large proportion of preferences, and by few entirely neglected pupils.

Our research shows that classroom peer groups characterized by a wide spread of liking relations among members have positive emotional climates and that both peer group liking structure and pupil involvement in the classroom group help to fashion a pupil's perception of himself in the group. Furthermore, the research shows that this pupil evaluation of self in relation to others is associated with his attitudes toward self and school in general and that a pupil's perception of his place in the peer group, high status or low, is related also to his utilization of his ability in academic learning.

Therefore, the teacher who hopes to enhance both the cognitive skills and the affective integration of his pupils will want to learn more about the interpersonal relationships in his classroom. He will ask such questions as: Can a rejected pupil be helped to develop skills of relating to his classmates so that he will be more accepted; so that he will be listened to when he has an idea to contribute; so that he will be given support rather than negative feedback? Can the intellectual capabilities of a bright child with low social power be channeled in such a way as to be seen by his peers as resources for the group?

Besides being interested in the problems of individual pupils, the teacher who is attempting to enhance the ego-strength of his pupils looks for ways in which the general atmosphere of the classroom can become more supportive of wholesome group interaction and learning. Can pupils be taught to seek out the resources of their classmates, to be sensitive to the needs of others who may be less well-endowed than they, and to understand the effects of their own behavior on others? If the classroom atmosphere takes on some of these characteristics, it becomes a supportive setting for ego-development of all pupils.

The teacher's first step in trying to enhance pupil ego-strength through improving interpersonal relations in the classroom involves sensitivity to the dynamics of pupil behavior. The sensitive teacher learns to become objective and analytic in observing pupil behavior in the classroom and on the playground. He perceives clues of pupil aggression, underlying hostility, and negative attitudes toward academic work. He is aware of the friendship patterns in the classroom, the cliques that are influencing pupil activity, and the feelings of ostracized pupils. Perhaps he perceives that although his pupils are controlled and orderly in his presence, they are uncontrolled and disorganized in the gym and on the playground. In any case, the astute teacher is diagnostic, always attending, as best he

can, to the dynamics of pupil behavior and classroom interaction. He knows that careful observations of pupil behavior are necessary for the planning of constructive classroom change.

A teacher often finds simple diagnostic tools helpful in getting an accurate picture of a pupil's level of ego-strength, his feelings, attitudes, interpersonal relations, and academic performance. In other words, she seeks to assess the state of affairs in her classroom by having the pupils answer questions, write down their ideas, and express their feelings. Thus, she supplements the general research knowledge gathered in the study of other classrooms. Teachers have found it helpful to use such objective diagnostic inventories as, sociometric tests, attitude questionnaires, self-ratings, and achievement tests. During this diagnosis, the teacher asks: "What is it I wish to know?" Considering the answer to this question, the teacher may employ diagnostic tools similar to the following examples.

AFFECTIVE EGO-STRENGTH

Questionnaires are used often to give the teacher information concerning a pupil's emotional or affective valuations of himself. There are several types of inventories for assessing self-feelings, including the attitude survey, the sentence completion test, and the so-called "pie technique."

An example of an attitude survey item regarding personal work habits is:

How hard would you say that you are working on school work. (Circle one)
   A. Very hard
   B. Pretty hard
   C. Not very hard
   D. Not hard at all

A sentence completion item of the same general character is:

When I am doing school work, I feel _____.

Or, in measuring different aspects of feelings about self:

I like myself sometimes because _____.
When I think about other boys and girls and then think about myself, I feel _____.

The "pie technique" has been used as follows:

The plus stands for aspects about yourself that you like, the minuses for things you don't like. Place a check under the circle that stands for how you are usually.

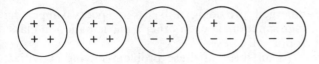

COGNITIVE EGO-STRENGTH

The teacher can assess the relationship between a child's classroom performance and his intelligence and in so doing, get one indication of his cognitive ego-strength. One procedure for doing this is as follows: the teacher first ranks all students according to their academic performance in her class. Then, she independently ranks them in order of their I.Q. score or some other measure of intelligence. The difference between positions on these rankings gives some indication of the child's utilization of intellectual potential. If a pupil ranks higher on intelligence than on achievement, he may be said to be underutilizing. If a pupil ranks higher on achievement than on intelligence, he is said to be more fully utilizing. If the class is made up of many underutilizers, the teacher should focus on improving the interpersonal atmosphere—at least as far as these underutilizers are concerned.

CLASSROOM SOCIAL RELATIONS

Sociometric questions are designed to give the teacher some indication of the social relationship among pupils in the class. He may ask pupils to select what peers they (1) like best, (2) like to work with, (3) like to play with, (4) think are smartest, (5) think like them about school, (6) like least, and so forth. In this manner, the teacher can see which pupils are friendly with one another and which are likely to make compatible work partners. In addition to getting information for grouping, she can sum and rank individual choices to find out who the peer leaders are, whether or not there are cliques, and what the general evaluation patterns are.

The major purpose of collecting such diagnostic information is to gain "leverage for thinking" creatively about the needs and potentialities of the unique teaching-learning situation of this particular classroom group.

MOVING FROM DIAGNOSIS TO ACTION

Using diagnostic information and interpretations to design a program of teaching action is a matter of disciplined professional skill. Actually the process of adopting or developing innovation in teaching practice is quite different from that in such professional fields as industry, medicine, and agriculture. A major difference is that the development or adopting of a new practice in teaching activity usually requires some re-orientation of values and attitudes as well as of behavioral skills. Such consideration of values and attitudes is not necessary in fields where the adoption of a new machine or a new fertilizer or new drug exerts no new requirements of value confrontation and skill development. Let us consider some illustrations of how a teacher can move from diagnosis to action in the classroom.

COPING WITH A COLLUSION OF IGNORANCE

A junior high teacher discovered from an analysis of his questionnaire data that the majority of the students in the classroom perceived that most of their fellow students looked down on enthusiastic participation in classroom discussion and the energetic accomplishment of homework assignments. The same questionnaire data indicated that a majority of the students would like to be more actively involved in classroom discussion and interaction with the teacher but perceived that their fellow students would be negative about this. As he reviewed these data, the teacher decided to share the information with the classroom group as a basis for discussion and mutual enlightenment as long as confidentiality was respected in the presentation of the data. He recognized, however, that there might be some embarrassment and resistance in getting into discussion. Therefore, he decided to consult with three or four of the class leaders about presenting the information and getting their collaboration in helping lead the discussion. He found them very interested in the data, ready to accept it as valid, and ready to help lead a discussion which would move the group toward a norm of enlightened participation rather than collusive withholding. With the leadership of the influential peers, the class discussion was interested, active, and enlightening. As a consequence, there were significant shifts in the pattern of group participation.

PASSIVE YOUNG LEARNERS

A second-grade teacher found that test data confirmed her observations that a significant portion of young learners who had a different racial and economic background from the majority of the class were uninterested in their work on the skills of reading. They were not openly rebellious but passive, distractable, and inattentive in the necessary drill work. The teacher and a consulting scientist discussed the data and decided that slightly older peers of the same race and background might be successful supporters and motivators of school work and might also impress upon the second graders the significance of putting energy into learning activity. With the help of the consultant, a program was designed utilizing volunteer sixth graders as teaching aides in the second grade. The sixth graders had a short seminar period each week on the techniques of being helpful. The response of the young learners was remarkable. They began to have fun working with the older peers, accepted their values about the importance of improving their achievement in reading, and began to relate more effectively to their teacher in other activities. The older peers also showed a significant upsurge in achievement motivation and in openness of collaboration with adults.

ANTI-LEARNING LEADERSHIP

From her diagnostic data collection, a fifth-grade teacher discovered that several of her high status figures in the classroom social structure were anti-schoolwork and anti-teacher in their orientation. It was clear that other members of the group were strongly influenced by this orientation. The teacher rejected several immediate derivations, such as the idea that she should try to downgrade such leadership status by direct confrontation which would have led her into a competitive struggle for leadership. After exploring a number of alternatives, she developed the plan of a classroom steering committee. She initiated the procedure by inviting four top status pupils, two of them pro-school and two anti-school, to meet with her for lunch to discuss the steering committee idea and to plan how it might work. This resulted in a classroom discussion led by the steering committee in which the question for discussion was "If a visitor came from Mars and knew nothing about classrooms and how they work, what might he see that would indicate whether we were or were not having a good day in this classroom?" Two large sheets of paper were put up in the front of the room and the steering committee recorded positive items on one and negative items on the other. Then each day one of the steering committee members served as observer and had the last few minutes of the day to state his observations on the positive and the negative list presented that day. At the end of the week, the steering committee led a discussion evaluating their week, making any revisions in the two lists, and projecting objectives for the next week. Every two weeks the steering committee rotated. Two types of things happened. Several of the negative high status figures changed their attitudes as it became clear to them what was sanctioned as desirable behavior by the classroom group. One or two of the negative high status leaders persisted in their original orientation and lost status with their peers as public group norms

emerged providing a basis for peers supporting and sanctioning each other's participation in classroom activities.

In all three of these problem-solving activities, the teacher went through several steps in the problem solving process. First of all she "brainstormed" by herself or with the help of others the possible implications of her findings and some of the alternative possibilities for action. Then there was a period of thinking out the consequences and potential "side effects" of the various courses of action. This was followed by the tentative decision to develop a particular line of action. Then she planned the line of action in detail and rehearsed her new pattern of performance. In all cases, the teacher also secured feedback from the pupils or students of response to the new classroom activity and attempted to guide and improve teaching performance in terms of an analysis of these responses.

It is time now to review some of the elements and conditions necessary for successful improvement of professional practice in the classroom. A desire to experiment is certainly important, but much creativity and enthusiasm has been lost because the professional discipline involved in the improvement of teaching practice has been ignored or neglected.

CONDITIONS FOR SUCCESSFUL CLASSROOM IMPROVEMENT ACTIONS

The creative efforts of classroom teachers to devise ways of building ego-strength in their pupils can become a major channel for improving classroom practice. However, although teachers have been exhorted to rise to their responsibilities as the key figures in effecting change in the learning environment, they are thwarted by rigid schedules, imposed curricula, lack of administrative support for changes that threaten the status quo, peer standards that discourage the seeking of advice from colleagues, lack of consultation resources, and the personal insecurity that effort to change accustomed procedures brings to the innovator. What are some of the conditions necessary to enable the teacher who has developed a plan of action such as those described in the preceding paragraphs to be successful in carrying it through the stages of initial trial, revision, further development, and evaluation? What contribution can the behavioral sciences make to the facilitation of the teacher's efforts?

Let us first look at the teacher, himself. Change in the classroom is most likely to occur if the teacher (1) is sensitive to the dynamics of the teacher-learning situation, (2) is concerned about this particular problem of building ego-strength in his pupils, (3) has some understanding of the forces which affect the development of ego-strength in children, (4) has access to resources and ideas that could be useful in bringing about change, (5) possesses the skills and tools for diagnosing the actual state of affairs within his classroom, (6) develops a strategy for altering the situation, (7) is supported by the principal and by colleagues in trying out the change plan, and (8) has professional consultation and training help available as needed, (9) has some means of evaluating the effectiveness of the change.

In exploring ways of providing for some of these conditions the University of Michigan projects have utilized a variety of techniques and procedures. For one thing, teachers have been given opportunity to experience and to examine some of the forces operating in group life and to become thoughtful about some of their own strengths and shortcomings. A technique used for this sensitivity training was the training group or "T-Group." Over a period of six weeks, within a summer workshop program, the teacher-participants came together for a series of two-hour sessions in which no agenda was provided and no leadership or rules of operation imposed. A staff member designated as "trainer" assisted the participants in focusing from time to time upon the interpersonal processes that occurred while the group engaged in interaction. It was possible to examine such aspects of group behavior as the development of group norms, friendships and influencing relationships, patterns of communication, relationships to authority and leadership, and giving and receiving feedback about the effects of our own behavior. The relevance and contribution of emotionality in group relations was also explored. These and other learnings, brought about through the opportunity to watch their own group behavior and then interpret it with the help of a skilled trainer, caused the participants to value the T-group highly among the workshop activities. They also found many occasions to explore the relevance of these new insights to pupil interaction in the classroom or to staff relationships within the school building.

Another in-service education technique was to assist teachers in learning and applying some of the concepts involving improvement of pupils' ego-strength that were described in the initial sections of this chapter.

A promising way to assist teachers in deciding upon appropriate targets for change in the classroom situation has been to help the teacher gain more information about the state of affairs in his classroom. We have seen how the teacher can learn through the use of diagnostic tools about the current peer standards toward academic work or toward the appropriateness of helping classmates.

The teacher can discover the kind of sociometric structure that exists, and can find out something of the forces from the pupil's life space or about his own self-concept. These data may give specificity to "hunches" the teacher has already had, or they may come as something of a shock. Whichever it is, the greater knowledge the teacher has about the conditions in his classroom, the better position he is in to develop an effective plan for change.

The involvement of others in the teacher's plan of action also appears to be of great significance. In some situations it was found that change efforts of teachers were best supported by teacher-administrator "change-agent" teams. In these cases, teachers who had been particularly innovative in improving their classroom practices and who were seen by other teachers as influential in the faculty power structure served with the building principal in planning ways for encouraging other teachers to consider some of the newer practices and for providing support for those who were attempting changes in their own classrooms.

Cross-building or cross-school system clinics of teachers engaged in similar types of change efforts have also proved effective. In many cases where the faculty peer standard within the school building has hampered free communication about classroom practices, teachers welcomed the opportunity to discuss plans for change and to get help on some of the obstacles faced by meeting with teachers from a distance.

Teachers have drawn upon another resource to help them bring about change—the pupils themselves. Pupil collaboration during a "try-out" phase can serve not only to build support and understanding of the change among those affected, but can also provide the teacher with useful feedback. Often the best information about the success of a plan, or about its shortcomings, can come from the pupils. Specific scales have been developed to help teachers get reaction from pupils.

It seems clear that creating the conditions for the continuous improvement of the quality of education and the development of social inventions in teaching practice is a mutual responsibility of school administrators, colleagues, the teacher herself, and also the students and their parents. The individual teacher, by herself, cannot be expected to utilize behavioral science resources creatively in an optimal way as she carries out her mission of high quality educational experience for children.

But we are very optimistic about the potentialities for the improvement of the educational experience because we have found administrators, teachers, and children usually open and eager to collaborate when they are helped to perceive new images of potentiality. Colleagues are hungry to achieve a deeper meaning from and a broader perspective on their teaching function and are ready to provide emotional support to each other. Moreover, children are ready to be invited to share in the responsibility for the adventure of learning if they are authentically and skillfully invited to do so.

The greatest stimulus to ego-development and the support of the motivation to achieve a high quality of learning activity derives from the sense of being invited into a meaningful classroom partnership. The gap between the generations must be coped with creatively in the classroom. To the degree that the adult teacher is ready to invite, listen to, and respond sensitively to the needs and influence attempts of her pupils, to that degree the child learners will be open and ready to receive and utilize the teaching efforts (that is, influence attempts) of the teacher. This respect and acceptance from the teacher is a basic ingredient of ego-development and motivation to learn. And motivating the pupils to learn is basic in the teacher's motivation to improve her teaching performance. The response of the learners is the greatest support for innovative teaching. The sharing by the teacher of power and responsibility for classroom management and learning activity is the greatest support for ego-development and motivation to learn. The growing resources of the behavioral sciences can now provide a school system, building faculty, classroom teacher, or classroom group with significant help in guiding and designing efficient group-learning experiences and effective personal growth opportunities. The challenge is to learn how to use these resources to achieve the big goal—helping children learn and grow.

REFERENCES

BARAKAT, HALIM K. *Alienation from the School System: Its Dynamics and Structure.* Ph.D. Thesis. Ann Arbor: University of Michigan, 1966.

CHESLER, MARK, RICHARD A. SCHMUCK, and RONALD O. LIPPITT. "The Principal's Role in Facilitating Innovation." *Theory into Practice, 2,* No. 5, Dec. 1963, 269–277.

CHESLER, MARK, ROBERT S. FOX, RONALD O. LIPPITT, et al. (Eds.) *The Innovation and Sharing of Teaching Practices: A Study of Professional Roles and Social Structures in Schools.* Final Report to the Office of Education, #OE 5-10-241. Ann Arbor: The Institute for Social Research (in preparation).

DENNERLL, DONALD, and MARK CHESLER. "Where Do New Teaching Practices Come From? . . . and Where Do They Go?" *Michigan Elementary Principal, 39,* No. 2, Nov.–Dec. 1964.

FOX, ROBERT S., MARGARET B. LUSZKI, and RICHARD A. SCHMUCK. *Diagnosing Classroom Learning Environments.* Chicago: Science Research Associates, Inc., 1966. (Teacher Resource Booklets on Classroom Social Relations and Learning)

FOX, ROBERT S. "In-Service Education for Innovation and Change." Paper presented to the Conference on Educational Change, Sponsored by the Illinois Demonstration Project for Gifted Youth, University of Illinois, Urbana. Feb. 28–March 2, 1966.

FOX, ROBERT S., RONALD O. LIPPITT, and RICHARD A. SCHMUCK. *Pupil-Teacher Adjustment and Mutual Adoption in Creating Classroom Learning Environments.* (mimeo)

FOX, ROBERT, RONALD O. LIPPITT, and associates, eds. *Developing Methods to Support the Creation and Spread of Innovative Teaching Practices.* Final Report to the Office of Education, #OE 4-10-197. Ann Arbor: The Institute for Social Research (in preparation).

JUNG, CHARLES, and RONALD O. LIPPITT. "The Study of Change as a Concept—in Research Utilization." *Theory into Practice, 1,* No. 1, Feb. 1966, 25–29.

LIPPITT, RONALD O. "Processes of Curriculum Change." Robert R. Leeper, ed. *Curriculum Change: Direction and Process.* Washington, D.C.: Association for Supervision and Curriculum Development, NEA, 1966, 43–59.

LIPPITT, RONALD O. "The Use of Social Research to Improve Social Practice." *American Journal of Orthopsychiatry, 35,* No. 4, July 1965.

SCHMUCK, RICHARD A., MARK CHESLER, and RONALD O. LIPPITT. *Problem Solving to Improve Classroom Learning.* Chicago: Science Research Associates, Inc., 1966. (Teacher Resource Booklets on Classroom Social Relations and Learning)

30

Introduction to "An Application of Psychoanalysis to Education"

LAWRENCE S. KUBIE

This is a brief passage by Lawrence Kubie, a prominent psychiatrist and psychoanalyst. In it he expresses his faith that a new kind of classroom climate can reduce neurotic interference with the learning process. (See Kubie's widely read book The Neurotic Distortion of the Creative Process *[New York: Farrar, Straus and Giroux, 1970].) A related paper that might have been placed in this section is that by Terry Borton included in Section XII.*

Throughout our educational system a realization is growing that both intellectual development and creativity will continue to be seriously hampered unless we find out how to make emotional maturation a part of education. Consequently educators are preoccupied increasingly with the difficult problems attendant on the attempt to introduce self-knowledge-in-depth into the main stream of formal education. They recognize that if this is to be done at all, it must start in the kindergarten and continue throughout the elementary grades, grammar school, high school, college and graduate years.

"Progressive education" was one of the early efforts in this direction. Originally, however, this involved a misapplication to education processes of techniques which are sometimes essential in formal psychotherapy. The predictable failures of these well-meant but inept efforts caused the climate of education to swing back temporarily to an opposite extreme, i.e., back to the old-fashioned techniques of drill and grill, and more drill and more grill.

A newer realization of the full complexity of these problems is now developing, i.e., that there is an incessant interaction between universal but subtly masked neurotic mechanisms and the educational process, and that as a result of this interplay education is blocked and distorted. The relationship between the two is evidently so close, that both must be solved if either is to be solved.

This does not, however, force us to the impossible conclusion that every teacher must be an analytically trained psychotherapist or that every school child must be psychoanalyzed. It brings us rather to conclude that all education should be conducted in an atmosphere in which the universal and recurrent emotional disturbances and repressive tendencies of childhood can be resolved as soon as they arise, and before they become chronic. The child's fifth freedom is the right to know what he feels; but this does not carry with it any right to act out his feelings blindly. This will require a new mores for our schools, one which will enable young people from early years to understand and feel and put into words all the hidden things which go on inside of them, thus ending the conspiracy of silence with which the development of the child is now distorted both at home and at school. If the conspiracy of silence is to be replaced by the fifth freedom, children must be encouraged and helped to attend to their forbidden thoughts, and to put them into words, i.e., to talk out loud about love and hate and jealousy and fear, about curiosity over the body, its products and its apertures; about what goes in and what comes out; about what happens inside and what happens outside; about their dim and confused feelings about sex itself; about the strained and stressful relationships within families, which are transplanted into schools. All of these are things about which school must help children to become articulate in the schoolroom.

Once any child becomes free in this sense then his great preconscious creative capacity will be freed from the retarding weight of pedestrian, literal, conscious processes, and at the same time from the distortions which arise out of neurotogenic and psychotogenic unconscious processes.

Lawrence S. Kubie, Introduction to Richard M. Jones, *An Application of Psychoanalysis to Education*, 1960, pp. vii–viii. Reprinted by permission of the authors and the publisher, Charles C. Thomas.

VI

GROUP MEMBERSHIPS
AS DETERMINANTS OF BEHAVIOR

The groups and institutions or organizations to which an individual belongs or with which he identifies himself are another important determinant of behavior. Face-to-face groups such as the family, whose impact is largely a matter of interpersonal influence (see Section IV), are not included here, nor do we refer to the classroom or playground groups, which were covered under settings and specific stimuli in Section V. Rather, we deal with (1) the society or culture in which a man is reared; (2) his connections with various organizations and societal institutions; (3) his economic and other role relations with his fellow men; and (4) the "reference groups" to which he belongs or with which he is identified (his membership in a caste, a social class, an ethnic or national group; political leanings; religious affiliation; and residence in a rural or urban area, etc.). Because sociology, social or cultural anthropology, and social psychology are in large part represented by this topic, the selections included here are merely illustrative of some realms of possible inquiry.[1] Such growing sub-disciplines as educational sociology and educational anthropology will increasingly demand study in their own right. In fact, W. W. Charters and N. L. Gage have produced a book entitled *Readings in the Social Psychology of Education* (Boston: Allyn and Bacon, 1963). The student especially interested in this area will find other useful papers in that collection.

Although some of the articles reprinted here and in other sections of the book do deal with socio-economic variables, it is hardly possible to give as much attention to *poverty* as a culture or subculture as a lot of contemporary writing does. Hence, we would like to direct your attention to several sources in this specific area. The poverty literature is important in relation to the extensive social action that is current or contemplated. Much of the social action to date has suffered from inadequate understanding of the psychological characteristics of persons toward whom the programs were directed. In the opinion of some, the fact that programs are directed toward a given group *by others* is one of the things that may be wrong. Vernon L. Allen has edited a book entitled *Psychological Factors in Poverty* (Markham Publishing Co., 1970). The papers in it represent a number of viewpoints. A very different attitude toward poverty can be found in the book *Blaming the Victim,* by William Ryan (Pantheon, 1971). That book attacks the often cherished idea, expressed sometimes subtly and sometimes not, that poor people are responsible for their own misfortune.

---

[1] It may be helpful to give a rough idea of the differing preoccupations of the principal disciplines mentioned. By and large, anthropologists are concerned with differences between societies, sociologists study differences between groups in the same society, and psychologists are interested in differences among individuals in the same group. Although there is increasing overlap of interests among all three fields, there are characteristic distinctions in viewpoint. The fact that most adult Americans use alarm clocks might be called to our attention by an anthropologist because of variations among peoples or cultures in technological development or in attitudes toward time and toward work. He might contrast behaviors of Americans with those of Italians or of Zulus. A sociologist might investigate attitudes toward time and work among religious or economic groups within a culture, comparing the groups to discover differences and seek explanations of them. Either psychologists or sociologists might investigate changes in such attitudes between the ages of 14 and 24 or differences between sorority members and non-members in their views and habits. Only psychologists would seek meaning in the fact that Suzie Snoozy neglects to set her alarm clock at night.

31

The Effect of Psychological Environment on Childbirth: Combined Cross-Cultural and Experimental Approach[1]

NILES NEWTON[2]

This imaginative paper looks at the impact of group membership on the birth process. Cultural attitudes toward the process of birth, and more broadly toward sex, appear to influence the speed and ease of labor. Hypotheses derived from this anthropological perspective were tested using laboratory mice. Despite what we assume to be the uncomplicated psyches of mice, we find analogous and even more dramatic effects of disturbances on the delivery of mice pups. This is not the first time that laboratory animals have been used to test the effects of "psychological" variables. The effects of stress (or "anxiety") during pregnancy on the later behavior of offspring were investigated earlier by Thompson. The fact that a number of workers failed to replicate Thompson's results led to the discovery that the effects found depended on the particular strain of rats used. There was an interaction between environmentally produced "anxiety" and the biological or genetic characteristics of the organisms being studied.

[1] Adapted from a paper presented at the XIX International Congress of Psychology in London, July 31, 1969, entitled "Impact of Collaborating with Margaret Mead." This work was supported in part by the John R. and Doris J. Haire Foundation.

[2] The author gratefully acknowledges the insights, guidance and training given her by Margaret Mead, Ph.D., in the use and interpretation of intercultural materials pertaining to childbearing in the course of their collaboration in writing a review of the cross-cultural literature in this area (Mead and Newton, 1967).

One might argue that the manipulations involved in influencing the birth process of the mice hardly make them members of a "group," unless it is of the defined experimental group. However, because the hypotheses are derived from consideration of group differences, the study is included in this section. One should note that such hypotheses based on group differences always direct our attention away from the fact that there are individual differences within the groups.

The author, Niles Newton, is at the Northwestern University Medical School. She is author of a number of monographs and chapters in books, and has written a book for parents (Family Book of Child Care, Harper & Row, 1957). She also teaches a course on the psychology of childbearing and reproduction.

The patterning of birth varies tremendously from culture to culture. This is particularly notable in studying data from contrasting preliterate cultures. Take, for instance, the example of the Cuna Indians of Central America (DeSmidt, 1948; Marshall, 1950; Stout, 1947) and the Siriono Indians of Bolivia, South America (Holmberg, 1950), groups that differ dramatically in their handling of birth.

Ideally, the Cuna girls did not learn of the existence of either coitus or childbirth until the final stages of the marriage ceremony. Pregnancy was seen by the Cuna as a time of anxiety and rising fear of childbirth. Each day the pregnant woman went to the house of the medicine man, who specialized in prenatal care and childbirth, for a cup of freshly brewed medicine tea. Labor, however, was too "hidden" for the medicine man to attend. Children and men, even husbands and medicine men, were excluded from the labor area. The midwives kept the medicine man informed of the progress of the labor. He chanted and supplied medications in response to the labor progress reports. Labor under these circumstances was frequently prolonged and so extreme that unconsciousness of the laboring woman occurred at times.

In contrast to this, the Siriono patterned birth as an easy, open process, in keeping with their relaxed sexual attitudes. Birth took place in a communal hut and was a public event freely witnessed by men as well as women. The mother labored in a hammock while groups of women gathered, gossiping about their own labors and wondering whether the coming baby would be a boy or a girl. No help, however, was given to the mother during the usual normal labor. She herself tied the child-

Niles Newton, "The effect of psychological environment on childbirth: Combined cross-cultural and experimental approach," *Journal of Cross-Cultural Psychology, 1,* 1970, 85–90. Reprinted by permission.

birth rope over her hammock to pull during contractions. She dug the earth under the hammock to cushion the baby's fall. The grunts and groans of labor did not appear to bother others within earshot. When the baby was born it slid over the edge of the hammock, dropping a few inches to the ground. This casual treatment of labor had an interesting accompaniment—extremely short labor durations. Seven of the eight labors observed by the recording anthropologist lasted only one to three hours. The eighth one, which took longer, resulted in the birth of twins.

From the psycho-physiological point of view [3] there is a marked difference—the Cuna girl in a culture which handled labor with frightening ritual tended to have an extreme experience in labor with unconsciousness and prolonged labor occurring at times. In contrast to this, the relaxed, casual Siriono had startlingly quick labors, far quicker not only than the Cuna appear to have had, but also far quicker than the labors of a typical woman in Western industrial cultures.

The rarity with which birth occurs at inconvenient times and places also becomes notable as one goes through anthropological accounts of birth in various cultures from many parts of the world (Mead & Newton, 1967). Of course, birth in a taxicab in the United States or by the roadside among agricultural and migrant people receive consideration and attention—perhaps only because they are actually so rare. The typical pattern of birth is that it usually takes place in an environment in which the mother feels safe, suggesting psychological as well as physiological triggering mechanisms.

If labor is really so markedly affected by environmental and cultural variations, this is indeed a fact of significance. It has important implications for the psychological management of women in labor—a problem met every day all over the world.

EXPERIMENTAL CONFIRMATION

Unfortunately, the nature of most anthropological material is such that it can suggest but not prove a point. Associative relationships cannot demonstrate cause and effect even when sufficient data are available to obtain significantly low probabilities. Experimental psychology can, however, take up insights gleaned from anthropological data and put them to controlled test. After developing hypotheses about birth based on the study of cross-cultural materials with Margaret Mead, they were tested experimentally in a series of experiments with mice.

The first experiment took up the problem of labor speed (Newton, Foshee, & Newton, 1966a). Since anthropological accounts seem to indicate that the swiftness of labor varies markedly from one society to another, mice were systematically disturbed (and presumably frightened) by subjecting them to complete olfactory, kinesthetic and visual change for one minute after the birth of their second pup. A laboratory assistant gently picked up the mouse and placed it in cupped hands, completely enclosing it for one minute. The control group was not disturbed. Two types of subjects were used: in Experiment A all the mice used had experienced only routine handling. Experiment B was identical to Experiment A except that all mice in both control and disturbed groups had been previously subjected to 15 periods of systematic human handling which included hand-cupping.

The undisturbed mice delivered their next pups in about 12 to 13 minutes (see Table 1). The disturbed mice were markedly slower in delivering the next pup. Labor after disturbance was significantly slower ($p < .05$) in both Experiment A and Experiment B. In each experiment the disturbed mice took over eight minutes longer than the controls to produce the next pup, a slowing of labor by about 65% to 72%.

The next anthropologically-based theory tested experimentally was that birth tends to be confined to more convenient or safe places, suggesting environmental as well as biochemical control of the labor mechanism (Newton, Foshee, & Newton, 1966b). Two environments for delivery were used. One was a glass fish bowl with a little bedding from cat cages to give it a strange odor; the other was a familiar cage complete with nesting box. Each expectant mouse at term was moved between these two environments at regular intervals.

During each time period the same number of

[3] Under some circumstances culturally determined variations in body mechanics during labor may influence its course. The experimental and cross-cultural data on this point have recently been extensively reviewed (Mead and Newton, 1967, 205–215). However, since both the Cuna and the Siriono deliver in hammocks it is unlikely that the differences in the difficulty of their labors can be chiefly attributable to variations in body position during delivery.

TABLE 1
EFFECTS OF DISTURBANCE ON LABOR SPEED

Groups	Minutes between birth of second and third pup (Means)	Parturient mice involved (N)
Experiment A:		
Controls	13.2	16
Disturbed	21.8	12
Experiment B:		
Controls	12.0	11
Disturbed	20.7	15

TABLE 2
RELATION OF ENVIRONMENT TO NUMBER OF PUPS DELIVERED

Groups	Number of pups born in familiar cage with shelter	Number of pups born in glass bowls with cat odor
First born pups of parturient females moved:		
Hourly	9	4
Every two hours	10	2
Total pups born to parturient females moved:		
Hourly	66	45
Every two hours	72	42

mice were in each type of cage. However, equal numbers of births did not occur in the two contrasting environments (see Table 2). Significantly more first born pups ($p < .01$) and total number of pups ($p < .05$) were born in familiar cages with nesting boxes than in the fish bowls. Only six first births took place in the glass fish bowl with cat odor as compared with 19 in the other cages. The mice under experimental conditions seemed to act like the women of many different cultural groups insofar as they appeared to avoid giving birth in a strange, open environment.

The third experiment (Newton, Peeler, & Newton, 1968) involved continuous disturbances during labor—a technique applied to laboring women in some societies. Mice were disturbed continuously by being moved every two hours from one glass bowl to another. The control group was alternated every two hours between one cage with shelter to a similar one (see Table 3). The mean elapsed time before the birth of the first pup was significantly longer for the continuously disturbed than for the control group mice ($p < .05$). The median delay in the appearance of the first pup was almost nine hours longer for the continuously disturbed group than for the controls, which is a considerable amount of time in view of the fact that the average mouse gestation in the strain used lasts only about 19 days.

Even more important, however, was what happened to offspring mortality rates (see Table 3). Significantly ($p = .036$) more dead pups were born to mice continuously disturbed than to the control group. The adverse psychological environment during parturition appears to have raised the mortality rate about 54%.

If *Homo sapiens* are as sensitive as mice to psychological environment during parturition, it is possible that preliterate cultures using patterned disturbance in labor actually have developed an indirect method of population control. In our so-

TABLE 3
EFFECT OF CONTINUOUS DISTURBANCE ON TIME OF
FIRST DELIVERY AND PUP MORTALITY

Group	Hours to first delivery		Total pups found	
	Mean	Median	Dead	Alive
Control	12.77	10.00	28	321
Experimental	17.10	18.50	43	306

ciety the effect of taking a poverty mother in labor away from her familiar environment and placing her in a hospital environment, which may be extremely strange to her, may be one factor contributing to the higher infant mortality rates of this group.

CONCLUSIONS

A series of psychological experiments were based on hypotheses suggested by anthropological data. Both cross-cultural and experimental data on mice suggest that equanimity may be conducive to more effective labors.

The gap between anthropological insight and experimental psychology is not too great to be bridged. Indeed, experimental psychologists can learn much from the breadth and variety of material available from anthropological sources.

REFERENCES

DESMIDT, L. S. *Among the San Blas Indians of Panama.* New York, the author, 1948.

HOLMBERG, A. R. *Nomads of the Long Bow: The Siriono of Eastern Bolivia.* Washington: Smithsonian Institution, Institute of Social Anthropology, Publication 10, 1950.

MARSHALL, D. S. *Cuna folk: conceptual scheme involving dynamic factors of culture, as applied to the Cuna*

Indians of Danien. Unpublished manuscript, Department of Anthropology, Harvard University, 1950.

MEAD, M., & NEWTON, N. Cultural patterning of perinatal behavior. *Childbearing: Its Social and Psychological Aspects.* Richardson, S. A., & Guttmacher, A. F. (Eds.), Baltimore: Williams & Wilkins, 1967.

NEWTON, N., FOSHEE, D., & NEWTON, M. Experimental inhibition of labor through environmental disturbance. *Obstetrics and Gynecology,* 1966a, *27,* 371–377.

NEWTON, N., FOSHEE, D., & NEWTON, M. Parturient mice: effects of environment on labor. *Science,* 1966b, *151,* 1560–1561.

NEWTON, N., PEELER, D., & NEWTON, M. Effect of disturbance on labor: an experiment using 100 mice with dated pregnancies. *American Journal of Obstetrics and Gynecology,* 1968, *101,* 1096–1102.

STOUT, D. B. *San Blas Cuna Acculturation: Introduction.* New York: Viking Fund Publications in Anthropology, No. 9, 1947.

32

The Child and the Parent-Child Relationship in Kibbutz Communities in Israel[*]

JOSEPH SHEPHER

Though very brief, this is a relatively comprehensive description of the kibbutz as a socializing agent. Membership in kibbutz groups in Israel determines much about the upbringing of children, although there are considerable differences among the kibbutzim (pl.) of the several political orientations. Such experiments with forms of group upbringing' are of great interest both theoretically and in terms of present day social concerns in our own society. The paper by Helen Faigin (Antonovsky) reprinted in the first two editions of The Causes of Behavior *should be read by those interested in a more detailed account of the treatment of young children in various kibbutzim (and of the behaviors that result). Other references to accounts of kibbutz life are given in that article.*

Those wishing to look into the socialization of the child and into parent-child relationships in a variety of cultures might want to consult the issue of Assignment Children *from which this selection was taken. The June 1969 issue of that UNICEF publication is devoted to this topic. For a more detailed comparison of children in different cultures see* Two worlds of Childhood: U.S. and U.S.S.R. *(Russell Sage Foundation, 1970) by Urie Bronfen-*

brenner. Professor Bronfenbrenner not only spent a full year in the Soviet Union (plus shorter visits), but went there with a command of the language.

Some of you may be interested in looking further into the issues of group care for children. Your interest may be oriented toward research, toward the benefits to mothers, or toward the hoped-for benefits for children (disadvantaged or other). You will find Chapter 9 by Meers and Marans in Early Child Care *(Laura L. Dittman, Ed., Atherton, 1968) a good starting place.*

The author of the paper reprinted here, Joseph Shepher, is a sociologist. He is a member of a kibbutz and a lecturer in sociology at Tel-Aviv University.

The kibbutz has been attracting the attention of Western scientists[1] for a variety of reasons. It is the most comprehensive collectivistic social structure known in modern society. The members of a kibbutz produce collectively and consume collectively. Private property is therefore limited to a few things of personal use and to a minimum annual budget for pocket money (about 3% of all the economic rewards distributed collectively) to use when the member is outside the kibbutz.

There is no differentiation of economic rewards and their distribution is based on equality when the supply of the reward is limited (e.g. clothing) or according to needs when the supply is on principle unlimited (e.g. health or educational services). The officers and functionaries of the kibbutz are elected by the general assembly of all the members and receive no special economic rewards. Most of the officers and functionaries do their public activity after the work day, in their leisure time. The political system is based on direct democracy, every member having the same active and passive political rights.

The most peculiar trait of the kibbutz system is probably the system of collective education.[2]

* I am very grateful to Professor Yehudi Cohen, Mr. Moshe Kerem, Mr. Yehuda Messinger and Miss Orah Kahanowitz who read the first draft of this paper, for their valuable remarks.

[1] The only bibliography known to me records more than 300 publications on sociological, psychological and political aspects of Kibbutz-life in the European languages. See Erik COHEN, Bibliography of the Kibbutz, Givat Haviva, 1964.

[2] See *i. a.*

GOLAN, Sh. "Collective Education in the Kibbutz," Collection of papers, Education Department of the Kibbutz Artzi, Merchavja 1961.
RAPAPORT, D. "The Study of Kibbutz Education and its Bearing on the Theory of Development," *American Journal of Ortopsychiatry*, 28, 1958, 587–597.
SPIRO, M. E. *Children of the Kibbutz*, Harvard University Press, Cambridge, Mass., 1958.

Joseph Shepher, "The child and the parent-child relationship in kibbutz communities in Israel," *Les Carnets de L'enfance (Assignment Children)*, United Nations Children's Fund, 1969, No. 10, 47–71. Reprinted by permission.

Kibbutz society, like every social experiment of far reaching innovation has emphasized education and has devoted to it maximum efforts in means and manpower because its ability to survive was dependent to a great extent on its success or failure in transmitting its values and norms to the second generation.

We shall try to describe this educational system by first presenting the social role of the child in the society, the age limit of this role, and the general attitude of the society towards childhood.

The Definition of Childhood and the Image of the Child

In the kibbutz the age limit of childhood in the broader sense, including adolescence, is 18, yet childhood is subdivided into 5 phases and socially each subdivision represents a separate social role with its expected rights and duties.

INFANCY

In most kibbutzim[3] the mother returning from hospital after delivery gives her child into the hands of a professional nurse at the babies' house. The mother sees her child in the nursing times (5 times a day) and even if she has no milk, she bottle feeds her child. Mother and father, even grandparents and siblings, may see the baby whenever they have time and want to.

Infancy is limited to one year and during this time the baby is entitled to uninterrupted attention on the part of the nurse and the mother; the former supporting and advising the latter, especially if she is a new mother. The babies are under constant medical supervision. During the night a special nightwatch (a woman) sits in the babies' house—ready to give the alarm to the nurse or the mother if anything is wrong with the baby.

The baby has no specified obligations. He is "expected" to develop properly, physically as well as psychologically, and to react favourably to the fondness and affection abounded on him by his environment.

TODDLERS

At about the age of 1 the babies are transferred to a new house with new equipment (larger beds, carpets for crawling, toys, etc.). In most cases the nurse remains with the group of toddlers until they enter kindergarten; in some cases the toddlers receive a new nurse. The social role of the toddler is more specified than that of the baby. He is expected to undergo successfully toilet-training, to be co-operative and friendly with his peers, to be active, docile and creative. The toddlers see their parents less (the mother begins to work full day about a year after delivery)—and make acquaintance with the kibbutz. They pay an occasional visit to the cowshed or the poultry; they take a walk in the orchards or in the fields of the kibbutz, observe the work in the workshops.

KINDERGARTEN

At about the age of 3, the children are transferred to the kindergarten, a multi-age educational unit comprising children from 3 to 6. In the kindergarten the children receive a more differentiated education. A specially trained kindergarten teacher is responsible for intellectual education, whereas a nurse cares for the physical well-being of the children. The child is expected at this age to master different skills in play and work. He gradually learns more and more creative play and at the end of the 3-year period he reaches a stage where through play he has absorbed the elements of reading, writing and simple arithmetic. He begins to help in simple household tasks, develops different skills such as drawing, day work, singing, dancing, etc.

Kindergarten children become more and more familiar with the everyday life of the kibbutz. In their daily walks they frequently visit the different work branches where every child can observe his parents working. Also, dependence on the parents diminishes. The parents' visits to the kindergarten become less frequent. On the other side, education towards a collective "esprit-de-corps" becomes more intensive.

ELEMENTARY SCHOOL

The transition to elementary school is gradual, and in most kibbutzim the first grade is achieved through play in the kindergarten. The children leaving the kindergarten pass to a "comprehensive house," a building which contains bed-rooms, a dining room, a class-room, and a play yard. The teacher and the nurse care jointly for the intellectual education and for the physical well-being, the division of labour being somewhat more explicit than in the kindergarten. The educational unit is homogeneous, the maximum age range being limited to one year. This unit receives a special name and forms a closely knit solidary collective.

The peer group, as a framework of the main socializatory activity, begins at the age of 2–3. Gradually it becomes more and more important and it serves as a channel of transition towards the

---

[3] In 1958 16 kibbutzim of the 226 used a different system. In these kibbutzim children slept in their parents' house. See: J. Shepher, "Familism and Social Structure; the Case of the Kibbutz," *Journal of Marriage and the Family*, 1969.

period of pre-adolescence and adolescence where the children's society becomes the main socializatory agency. This collective spirit is cultivated not only in every day activities but also in the classroom. Individual achievement is less emphasized than collective achievement. Academic achievement is not rewarded by marks, and no certificates are given. Every child passes to the higher grade whatever his academic performance may be. Only in exceptional cases of utter disability does the child receive remedial teaching in a special institution sponsored by the kibbutz federation.

The children participate in the household tasks of their house from the very beginning. They sweep the floor, wash the dishes, set the table, make the bed, etc.

School children gradually devote less time to their parents and more to their peers. Parents put children to bed in the evening until the age of 12–13.

SECONDARY SCHOOL AND THE CHILDREN'S SOCIETY

The Education Reform Bill,[4] which lowered the starting age of secondary school education to 12–13, was accepted in Israel only recently. Some of the kibbutzim, however, have been doing this for a long time and in at least one federation, children of the 7th grade formally joined the secondary school. Yet the transition to the new status is emphasized by entering the children's society rather than by the changes in the curriculum.

The children's society is the last phase of the long preparatory process towards adult social roles. The children organize their own life by establishing an organizational structure parallel to that of the kibbutz. They have their own General Assembly, committees and even their own economy. One or more young members of the kibbutz help the children in establishing the organization by giving advice but have no vote in their General Assembly and they try to render themselves gradually superfluous. In some kibbutzim the children's society is divided into two parts—the pre-adolescent age 12–14 and the adolescent age 15–18. Even if there is no formal division the pattern of activities and the leadership is different.

From the seventh grade children begin to work together with the adults in the different work branches of the kibbutz. They begin to work 1½ hours in the seventh grade, and in the twelfth grade they work 4 hours—during the school year. During vacations—and especially the summer vacation— children of the last two grades work 14 to 21 whole

work days. At this age their help in the kibbutz becomes considerable. During the Six Days' War and the antecedent period of tension and mobilization, youngsters of 16–18 maintained the whole kibbutz economy throughout the country.

Children of the last two grades are allowed to assist the General Assembly of the kibbutz. They may join all the forms of cultural activity of the kibbutz. By the age of eighteen the youngsters are generally ready to accept all the duties, responsibilities, as well as the rights of the adult members.[5] In most kibbutzim they are festively admitted to full membership before entering the army at the age of 18; in others, the membership is given to them only after demobilization at the age of 21.

Trying to summarize the general description of childhood, we can say that although the transition to adult roles is generally gradual, there are at every age some events which emphasize the transition from one phase to another. Changes of housing occur at least 3 times during 18 years: from the toddlers to the kindergarten, from kindergarten to the comprehensive house and from this house to the houses of the secondary school age. In parallel, at least 3 times there is change as well as differentiation of the socializators. Other marked changes are to be found in the sphere of normative requirements and dependence on adults, especially parents. Some *rites de passage*[6] dramatize the transition from childhood to adolescence as well as from adolescence to full membership.

THE GENERAL ATTITUDE OF THE KIBBUTZ TOWARD THE CHILD

The kibbutz is described by several authors as a child-centred society. This "child-centredness" is in fact an outcome of the general orientation of the kibbutz toward the future. One of the main aims of the kibbutz is to build a new form of living, and consequently most of its actions are probably more

---

[4] According to this law 12 years of study are divided into three phases: 1st–6th, elementary school; 7th—9th, transitory school phase (junior high school); and 10th—12th, high school.

[5] Eisenstadt and Bar-Yoseph are of different opinion. See: EISENSTADT, S. N. *Studies in Social Structure* (I-"Age Groups and Social Structure") Jerusalem, 1950; and BAR-YOSEPH, R. "The Pattern of Early Socialization in the Collective Settlements in Israel," *Human Relations, 12,* 1959. Critical observation of the activities of the children's society, the children's assistance in the general work assignment and in the general assembly does not give support to Eisenstadt's view of "role discontinuity." Kibbutz children are probably not entirely ready for adult roles from the point of view of some special occupational roles but these are only one component of the role cluster of a kibbutz member.

[6] Interestingly enough, the traditional Jewish "rite de passage," the Bar Mitzwah at the age of 13 is celebrated by all the kibbutzim in spite of the fact that 215 of 226 kibbutzim are not religious. Yet, from a sociological point of view the festive acceptance of the child in the children's society at the age of 12 seems more important.

future-oriented than in most modern societies. The successful socialization of the second generation is one of the crucial factors determining the ability of a society to survive. In the case of the kibbutz, a new social experiment, the peculiar attention devoted to almost everything connected with education is understandable. Kibbutz education is very expensive compared with education in alternative social forms in Israel. In cases of problems of priority (e.g. lack of manpower, of resources) educational tasks are almost always preferred.

The main goals of the education as formalized in a recent convention of the biggest kibbutz federation can be summarized as follows:

1. A personality that is capable of being immersed, absorbed and integrated into the collective.
2. A personality that internalizes and realizes the values of mutual help, fraternity and common efforts as a means for the achievement of collective goals.
3. A personality that emphasizes co-operation and friendship as the essence of inter-personal relationship.
4. A personality that internalizes the main human values of Jewish culture as well as general human values.
5. A personality that conceives of work not only as a means but as a value in itself.
6. A personality that accepts and realizes the main Zionist objectives as the building of a new Homeland for the Jews and rebuilding of the Jewish People.

7. A personality who accepts democracy as a form of life and fights every sort of autocracy.

This image of a new man reared in a collective society without differentiation of economic rewards, without legal social controls and coercive forces, is the ultimate goal of kibbutz education; and as far as the goal is achieved, it is the source of pride and satisfaction.

The Division of Labour Between and the Co-ordination of the Different Socializatory Agencies

Four agencies collaborate in the task of socialization of the kibbutz child.
— the educational institutions (nurses, teachers);
— the family;
— the children's society;
— the kibbutz community as a whole.

The division of labour between the different agencies changes with time. Through the continuity in time we can summarize the division of labour as follows [see figure below]:

As can readily be seen, the primary responsibility for the socialization is vested in the educational institutions. Until the age of 16 the institutions weigh more in the socializatory process than any of the other agencies, and only in the last two years does the influence of the children's society counter-

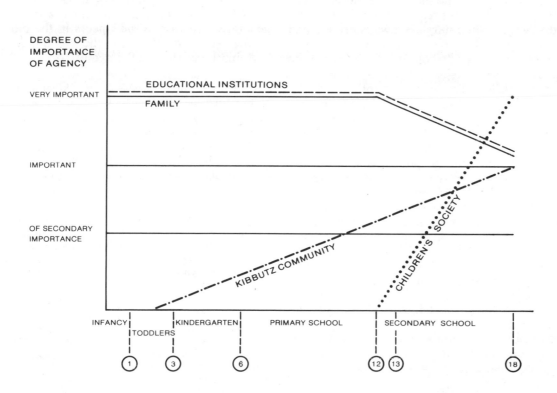

weigh their importance. Secondary to it is the importance of the family. The family is of primary importance in the stage of early childhood. Its importance declines in the stage of adolescence and its place is taken up again by the youth society. The youth society begins its socializatory task in the early adolescence phase, and its relative importance ascends quickly whereas the growth of the importance of the kibbutz community as a whole is more gradual through the different stages of the socializatory process. It reaches much importance only in the last two years, through its influence on the youngsters in the different working branches and through the General Assembly.

The graphic presentation also suggests the possible foci of co-ordination problems:

— between the educational institutions and the family especially during early childhood;
— between the educational institutions and the children's society during the last stage of adolescence;
— between the family and the children's society during adolescence;
— to a lesser extent between the work allocation committee of the kibbutz and the educational institutions and the family.

The main characteristic of the division of labour between the educational institutions and the family in the early phases of socialization can be described as follows. Two mother images appear before the infant: the mother and the nurse. The mother feeds the infant but she is not present except in the feeding-hours, whereas the nurse is always present and is ready to comfort the infant whenever he indicates a feeling of tension, or discomfort. Later, when the child enters the toddlers' house, the instrumentality of the nurse's role becomes more explicit.

The mother ceases to feed the child, and feeding becomes gradually less individual; the nurse gives food to the entire group of the children, helps them in eating skills, and encourages them to eat by themselves. At the same time the nurse teaches the children new norms of behaviour: training in personal hygiene, self-dressing, co-operation in play, etc. Although the nurse uses very permissive and liberal patterns of encouragement and conviction, she is ultimately the socializator of instrumental activity. Then too, the nurse always divides her attention between several children (4–6) inducing the child thereby to adjust itself to group-life, to learn that he has to acquiesce in the fact that he cannot be assured of the services of the nurse only for himself.

On the other hand, the parents devote their attention to the child almost exclusively during the time the child stays with them. The relationship between the child and the parents is very affective.

Nevertheless the orientation of the parents and nurses is not entirely polar. There is much affectivity in the child-nurse relationship (from both sides), as well as instrumental requirements of the parents toward the child.[7] The possible sources of tension reflect the ambivalence of the triangular social situation. The nurse sometimes accuses the parents of spoiling the child, whereas the parents may complain that the nurse is too disciplinary—she is like a "sergeant." On the other hand—if the nurse is affective as well as effective as a socializator she may arouse the jealousy of the parents. And again, if the parents refrain from being affective, they can be accused of neglecting their child.

In spite of the ambivalence of the situation, the tension may not appear at all if the basic values underlying the norms of behaviour of the parents and the nurse toward the child are common.

In other words, the situational factors are potential sources of tension and they become effective if —and only if—there is no value consensus. For instance, if the parents did not internalize the collective values and therefore they induce their child to be competitive and aggressive instead of co-operative, the potential tension might appear on the surface and be acute.

The fact that these situational factors are not detrimental to the development of the child's personality, is revealed by Rabin. He found in a comparative study that the emotional stability of the kibbutz infant is somewhat less than his counterpart of the moshav, yet this disadvantage quickly disappears and in later life kibbutz children are generally superior to their peers in the moshav in all the aspects dealt with in the Rabin inquiry.

Rabin finds[8] that, at the age of 10:

1. Kibbutz children surpass the non-kibbutz children as to intellectual development.
2. Concerning ego-strength, emotional and general maturity they are superior to non-kibbutz children.
3. Their Oedipal attachment is less and their identification with adult figures is more diffuse.
4. They show more positive attitudes toward the family unit and show less sibling rivalry than the non-kibbutz children.
5. There is some evidence of greater hostility of kibbutz children toward parental figures at a deeper unconscious level, yet the author wonders whether this hostility is not directed toward the nurse, the parent surrogate who is in charge of the toilet training.

---

[7] Contrary to Bar-Yoseph's observations. See BAR-YOSEPH, *op. cit.*

[8] See RABIN, A. I. *Growing up in the Kibbutz*, New York, 1965, p. 144.

The second focus of possible co-ordination problems appears during the age of adolescence. The children get involved in a strain of role conflict through the simultaneous expectations of the educational institutions and the children's society. The youngsters are expected by the educators to study hard, to work in the work branches of the kibbutz, to do housework in their house and at the same time they are required to be active in the committees of the children's society, to work in the children's economy, to participate in the different cultural and sportive activities. In cases of lack of co-ordination between the educational institutions and the children's society, the strain on the adolescent may be such that attempts at evading some of the legitimate duties are unavoidable.

Another possible strain evolves gradually between the parents and the children's society. This strain has two facets: the first is again a competition for the time of the adolescents. The youngsters gradually spend less time with the parents, and since most of the activities of the children's society are being carried out during the afternoon hours, which are customarily defined as the "parents' time," parents are more "jealous" of the children's society than any of the educational institutions. Then, too, insufficient identification with the kibbutz values may induce some parents to prefer school activities to the activities of the children's society.

As indicated above, youngsters of 17–18 contribute remarkably to the kibbutz economy by working in the various work branches. If the work-assignment committee does not take educational principles into consideration and its orientation is purely instrumental, an antagonistic situation may develop between it and the educational institution. Instrumental considerations require maximum possible exploitation of the economic resources stemming from the work of the youngsters, whereas educational considerations require an approach of making allowance for studying the work and of

considering the youngster's alternative commitments.

Conclusion

We have tried to describe briefly the collective educational system of the kibbutz, focusing on the problems of co-ordination between the different socializatory agencies. Analysing the socialization process we found that the parent-child relationship in this system is less central than in most known modern social systems. The success of the socialization is largely dependent on effective co-ordination between the different socializators.

The time has not yet come to sum up the results of socialization in the kibbutz. Yet there is at least some indication that the great majority of the second generation remains in the kibbutz and successfully enters upon adult tasks. Thus, after an existence of 60 years of the kibbutz, the second generation has already taken over the most important tasks in 52 kibbutzim.

In these kibbutzim the third generation has already reached the age limit of membership. In 80 more kibbutzim the second generation is in the process of taking over the management tasks. That means that in approximately 60% of the kibbutzim the second generation has succeeded in filling adult social roles.

The percentage of those second generation members who leave the kibbutz and join other forms of living is rather low, and does not exceed 25 percent even in the oldest kibbutzim. If we consider that the first sons and daughters born in the oldest kibbutzim reached adulthood in the late twenties, this would mean an average percentage of 1.6% leaving annually. As compared with utopian experiments in the past, this is a fact which gives rise to an optimistic view for the future of the kibbutz as a stable form of living rather than an ephemeral social experiment.

33

A Comparative Analysis of Fantasy Need Achievement among High and Low Achieving Male Hawaiian-Americans[1]

BARBARA B. SLOGGETT,
RONALD GALLIMORE,
AND EDWARD S. KUBANY

Sloggett, Gallimore, and Kubany focus on the ways in which culture may modify the relations between a variable such as need achievement and actual achievement. Although it can be considered a cross-cultural study, the cultures are found in the state of Hawaii. The authors are all affiliated with the University of Hawaii, where Gallimore has been involved in studies of indigenous Hawaiians and (to a lesser extent) other ethnic groups.

The degree to which need achievement as measured by fantasy productions can be studied in the same ways in different cultural groups is an interesting question in itself. The paper by Kubany, Gallimore and Buell in the same issue of the new publication Journal of Cross-Cultural Psychology *sheds further light on this question. We cannot reprint it in its entirety, but quote its concluding discussion as a good background for the paper by Sloggett et al.*

It is evident from the data that contemporaneous social factors may influence the manifestation of achievement-oriented activity, at least among Filipinos. Subjects

in the public condition, under the surveillance of the experimenter, selected a moderate risk on 75 out of 100 trials (chance equals 33/100), significantly more than subjects in the relatively anonymous, private condition. These results are consistent with the notion that Filipinos are highly concerned with social cues as guidelines for behavior. The glaring avoidance of easy risks by subjects in the public condition provides some further support for this conclusion. That is, in the face of public evaluation, acceptance of a moderate or difficult challenge might be construed as more socially desirable than taking the "easy" way out. Among Filipinos, striving for a "sense of accomplishment" may be considerably less important than the social consequences of such striving. The most obvious implication is that analysis of specific forms of achievement-oriented behavior among Filipinos should take into account the context in which such behavior does or does not occur; i.e., whether achievement-oriented behavior is considered as "competitive," "showing off," "expected," or "for the good name of the family."

Our principal intent was not to demonstrate the sensitivity of Filipinos to situational cues; that aspect is incidental. Rather, we have sought to illustrate in an isolated instance the danger of exporting American psychological methodologies and conceptions to non-Western groups. While the study was concerned with the behavior of a specific group, the findings reflect on some broader theoretical issues. Previous studies of achievement-oriented behavior have typically ignored the possible effects of extrinsic motives such as the desire for acceptance or social approval. Investigators have usually assumed that a subject may be concerned with cooperating with the experimenter's demands to perform a task, but that this concern does not systematically affect the degree of achievement-oriented behavior. However, the present findings and other recent experimental evidence (Atkinson & O'Connor, 1966; Gallimore, 1969; Klinger, 1967) suggest that under certain circumstances extrinsic factors may operate to enhance preference for moderately difficult tasks; for example, Gallimore (1969) reported that fantasy n Affiliation scores, but not resultant achievement motivation scores (TAT n Ach minus test anxiety scores), predicted intermediate risk taking among indigenous Hawaiians. Underscoring the potential effects of situational cues, Klinger (1967) recently found that subjects exposed to achievement-oriented models produced more fantasy achievement than subjects exposed to affiliative or neutral models. These findings raise doubts about the cross-cultural generality of the theory of achievement motivation (Atkinson & Feather, 1966) and draw attention to the potential importance of situational and social factors which have been neglected in most previous research on achievement motivation.[1]

[1] The research was supported by an NIMH research grant to the Bernice Pauahi Bishop Museum, Honolulu, and by the Social Science Research Institute, University of Hawaii. Alan Howard, Roland Tharp, and Anthony Marsella are due our appreciation for many contributions to this work.

[1] Kubany, Gallimore, and Buell, "The Effects of Extrinsic Factors on Achievement-Oriented Behavior: A Non-Western Case." Used by permission.

Barbara B. Sloggett, Ronald Gallimore, and Edward S. Kubany, "A comparative analysis of fantasy need achievement among high and low achieving male Hawaiian-Americans," *Journal of Cross-Cultural Psychology, 1,* 1970, 53–61. Reprinted by permission.

Investigating psychological motivation among ethnic minorities whose social problems are a matter of national concern is an endeavor of considerable importance. Most studies of *n* Ach (Barberio, 1967; McClelland, 1961; Mingione, 1965; Nuttall, 1964; Veroff, Atkinson, Feld, & Gurin, 1960) data have been collected in a fashion which has permitted only between group comparisons. Missing, in most cases, is analysis of within ethnic group relationships between *n* Ach and relevant indices, except for the abundant studies of Americans of Caucasian descent (Atkinson & Feather, 1966). For example, there are almost no studies comparing psychological motivation between academically successful and academically unsuccessful Afro-Americans. Nevertheless it has been generally assumed that the relationship between *n* Ach and achievement holds for ethnic groups of non-Western origins. Other writers, for example DeVos (1968), have seriously questioned this view, suggesting that *n* Ach, either theoretically or empirically need not be expected to relate to achievement within all cultural groups. The present study examined this question by comparing high and low achieving (HA and LA) indigenous Hawaiians on a fantasy measure of *n* Ach. The indigenous Hawaiians were drawn from two disparate populations. A low achieving (LA) Hawaiian group consisted of individuals living in a suburb of Honolulu which had been the focus of a year of participant observation and ethnographic analysis completed prior to the study reported here (Gallimore & Howard, 1968). The particular community and the majority of Hawaiians are plagued by educational problems confronting other impoverished American ethnic minorities. More particularly, the levels of educational achievement in this Hawaiian community were among the lowest in the entire State. The high achieving (HA) Hawaiian group was selected from a private school established in the last century specifically for Hawaiian children and which currently accepts, on a state-wide basis, only academically talented and accomplished Hawaiian youngsters. This group, in contrast to the LA group, was almost entirely from middle-class families with fathers in skilled or white-collar jobs; thus, for a variety of reasons, the LA Hawaiians should write fewer *n* Ach stories.

For purposes of contrast, small samples of Filipinos and Japanese were obtained.

METHOD

SUBJECTS

The *S*s, all males, included 31 LA Hawaiians—10th, 11th, and 12th graders from a high school in a low-income area. From the same school, 13 Japanese and 15 Filipinos from similar grades were also selected. The LA Hawaiians were living on lands leased by the Department of Hawaiian Homelands to individuals of at least 50 percent Hawaiian ancestry. The HA Hawaiian *S*s were 48 students attending a private school established for children of Hawaiian ancestry. Entrance to this school is based on academic ability and achievement, with the student population being selected on a state-wide basis. Average Hawaiian ancestry (self-report) was 49.50 and 43.45 percent for the LA and HA groups respectively.

English is spoken by almost all residents of Hawaii although, for some, particularly Hawaiians and Filipinos, a dialect of English, known as "pidgin," is the primary language.

MATERIALS

Merbaum (1961),[2] following an exacting psychometric procedure, developed a set of 12 TAT-like pictures in which racial cues were made deliberately ambiguous. That is, *S*s of any race or ethnic group could interpret the drawings as portraying people of any race they chose. The stimuli were line drawings representing school, work, or neutral scenes, such as a boy in a school hall, a boy standing on a street corner, etc. Of the original 12 pictures used by Merbaum (1961), six were eliminated from the Hawaii study because of the presence of cues not common to the Islands; e.g., a man on a farm tractor.

PROCEDURE

The picture stimuli were administered in a group setting at the respective schools; the instructions were identical to those employed by Merbaum (1961). Each of the pictures for which stories were to be written was reproduced on a separate page and accompanied by the four questions ordinarily used by *n* Ach researchers, including Merbaum (1961). Scoring followed the usual procedure; reliability of scoring was assessed by comparison of scores assigned by an experienced graduate student to stories scored by expert scorers as reported in Atkinson (1959). The degree of reliability was highly satisfactory, ranging from .80 to .94. The scorer had no knowledge of the samples or the purposes of the study.

Intelligence and achievement test scores were obtained from school records. The intelligence measure available was the total test score on the California Test of Mental Maturity (CTMM) and the achievement tests were the Scholastic Test of Educational Progress (STEP) in reading and math. Unfortunately, test data were not available for all *S*s.

RESULTS

Because of the multiplicity of possible comparisons and for simplicity of presentation, all statistical levels reported are two-tailed though some directional hypotheses were clearly suggested; e.g., Japanese were expected to have higher *n* Ach scores than the LA Hawaiians. For

---

[2] Merbaum's doctoral dissertation was published under her married name of Mingione (1965).

the same reasons, conservative *post hoc* comparisons of *n* Ach levels (Hays, 1963) were performed.

Table 1 presents the intelligence test scores for the four groups of boys. An analysis of variance yields a highly significant F of 17.07 (p < .01, *df* = 3/74). By *post hoc* analysis, the HA Hawaiians had significantly higher intelligence test scores than both the Filipinos and LA Hawaiians, who had the lowest scores, and were nonsignificantly higher than the Japanese. The Japanese also had significantly higher intelligence test scores than the LA Hawaiians.

Table 1 also presents the means and standard deviations among the groups in reading and math achievement. The overall analyses of variance for reading and math achievement were both highly significant. For reading achievement, F = 38.48 (p < .01, *df* = 3/78) and for math achievement, F = 23.91 (p < .01, *df* = 3/77). Consistent with the intelligence test scores, the data indicated that the HA Hawaiians had the highest achievement scores, both in math and reading. In math achievement, the HA Hawaiians scored significantly higher than both the Filipinos and LA Hawaiians and nonsignificantly higher than the Japanese, who also scored significantly higher than the Filipinos and LA

Hawaiians. The same relationships hold for reading achievement, with the single exception that the HA Hawaiians also had significantly higher reading achievement scores than the Japanese.

The classification of the two Hawaiian groups as LA and HA respectively was confirmed by the data, albeit on less than the entire *n* Ach sample. On each of the three measures, the HA Hawaiians were higher than the low achievers. The Japanese and Filipino boys, from groups less noted for academic problems, were generally intermediate to the two Hawaiian groups.

Table 2 presents the *n* Ach means and standard deviations for each of the four groups. Comparing the *n* Ach means for each of the four male groups, an overall analysis of variance was significant beyond the .01 level (F = 4.38, *df* = 3/103). All possible paired comparisons were made using the *post hoc* technique suggested by Hays (1963). Table 2 shows there was no significant difference in *n* Ach between the HA and LA Hawaiian groups. The one significant difference was between the Japanese and LA Hawaiians (p < .05) with the Japanese-HA Hawaiian difference marginally significant (p < .10). The Filipinos scored nonsignificantly intermediate to the Japanese and Hawaiian groups.

TABLE 1

MEANS, STANDARD DEVIATIONS, AND SIGNIFICANCE LEVELS FOR MALES IN ALL GROUPS ON ACHIEVEMENT AND INTELLIGENCE TESTS*

	California Test of Mental Maturity (CTMM)			
	HA Hawaiian	LA Hawaiian	Japanese	Filipino
N	39	19	8	12
X̄	113.87	90.58	105.13	100.00
SD	10.29	12.52	15.59	10.62
High Achieving Hawaiian	—		NS	.01
Low Achieving Hawaiian	.01	—	.01	NS
Japanese			—	
Filipino			NS	—

	STEP–Reading			
N	44	13	12	13
X̄	69.55	13.92	50.67	20.08
SD	19.73	11.42	28.17	17.49
High Achieving Hawaiian	—		.05	.01
Low Achieving Hawaiian	.01	—	.01	NS
Japanese			—	
Filipino			.05	—

	STEP–Math			
N	43	13	12	13
X̄	68.67	18.31	47.83	18.31
SD	24.83	17.25	32.45	16.06
High Achieving Hawaiian	—		NS	.01
Low Achieving Hawaiian	.01	—	.05	NS
Japanese			—	
Filipino			.05	—

* The variability in Ns reflects incomplete school records of some of the boys in the samples.

TABLE 2
MEANS, STANDARD DEVIATIONS, AND SIGNIFICANCE LEVELS FOR BOYS IN ALL GROUPS ON *n* ACHIEVEMENT

	HA Hawaiian	LA Hawaiian	Japanese	Filipino
N	48	31	13	15
$\overline{X}$	2.27	1.77	4.77	4.13
SD	2.86	2.23	3.92	4.12
High Achieving Hawaiian	—		.10	NS
Low Achieving Hawaiian	NS	—	.05	NS
Japanese			—	
Filipino			NS	—

The marked differences in variability reflected by the standard deviations shown in Table 2 prompted an additional form of analysis in terms of the percentage of subjects within each ethnic group who wrote at least one *n* Ach theme. The percentages of boys within each group who wrote from zero to three stories with an *n* Ach theme are presented in Table 3. The rank order of the various groups of boys in Table 3 is identical to the rank order shown in Table 2. It appears that the differences in Table 2 are not simply an artifact of the extreme variability reflected by the standard deviations. The *n* Ach differences among the Japanese and Hawaiian groups become more striking when viewed in this manner; it is evident that the Hawaiians produced an extremely small absolute amount of *n* Ach imagery. While 54 percent of the Japanese boys wrote *n* Ach themes in response to at least two cards, only 15 percent of the HA Hawaiians and only 3 percent of the LA Hawaiians wrote *n* Ach themes in response to more than one of the six pictures. For comparative purposes, it might be noted that 58 percent of the rural Caucasian males in Merbaum's (1961) study wrote *n* Ach themes in response to more than one of the same six pictures; thus, the Merbaum pictures had a stimulus value for the Japanese approximately equal to that observed for the rural Caucasians. Similarly, 24 percent of the Afro-Americans in Merbaum's study wrote *n* Ach themes to two or more pictures, compared to 33 percent of the Filipinos in the present study.

The Japanese wrote more *n* Ach themes than the LA Hawaiians and, as might be expected, also had higher intelligence and achievement test scores than the LA Hawaiians. However, the relationships between the HA Hawaiians and the other groups are not nearly so clear. For example, in spite of the fact that the HA Hawaiians had lower *n* Ach scores than the Japanese, they had nonsignificantly higher intelligence and math achievement test scores and significantly higher reading

achievement scores than the Japanese. Further, while the HA Hawaiians had substantially higher intelligence and achievement scores than the LA Hawaiians, there was no significant difference in *n* Ach between the HA and LA group. There was no *n* Ach difference in spite of the fact that the HA Hawaiian boys wrote longer stories ($\overline{X}$ number of words = 410, SD = 121), though not significantly longer, than the LA Hawaiians ($\overline{X}$ = 372, SD = 107).

To analyze the within ethnic group relationships between *n* Ach and actual accomplishment, Pearson product-moment correlations were computed between *n* Ach, intelligence, reading achievement and math achievement for each of the groups separately, and for all groups combined. These correlations are reported in Table 4. Among the Japanese, *n* Ach correlated significantly with intelligence and reading achievement and nonsignificantly with math achievement scores. However, among the Filipinos and both of the Hawaiian groups, there were no significant correlations between *n* Ach and intelligence nor between *n* Ach and achievement test scores. For all groups combined, however, *n* Ach correlated significantly with both reading and math achievement and intelligence; however, the magnitude of these correlations is small, ranging from .15 to .26. Of course, the attenuated distribution of *n* Ach scores, particularly in the LA Hawaiian group, substantially reduced the possibility of a significant correlation between *n* Ach and the achievement and intelligence tests.

DISCUSSION

In terms of experience, ability, achievement, and social status, there was every reason to believe that the HA Hawaiian boys ought to have written more *n* Ach themes than their LA counterparts. But they did not. In view of the performance of the Japanese and Filipinos, there appears to be no reason to attribute their performance to a lack of "pull" of the picture stimuli. These findings challenge the usefulness of the notion that Hawaiian boys do poorly in school because they lack *n* Ach.[3] As

TABLE 3
PERCENTAGE OF BOYS WRITING VARIOUS NUMBERS
OF *n* ACHIEVEMENT THEMES

	0	1	2	3	4	5	6
High Achieving Hawaiians	54%	31	13	2			
Low Achieving Hawaiians	56	41	3				
Japanese	31	15	54				
Filipinos	33	33	20	13			

[3] Comparable data for females yielded no differences in *n* Ach among Hawaiians, Japanese, and Filipinos; thus, the Discussion applies only to males. The female data were not reported, since there is a general lack of agreement about relationship of *n* Ach to female personality.

| *n Ach* | Hawaiians | | | | Japanese | | Filipino | | All Groups | |
| | High Achieving | | Low Achieving | | | | | | | |
	N	r	N	r	N	r	N	r	N	r
CTMM	79	.14	40	.19	21	.46**	18	.25	288	.15**
STEP–Reading	86	.05	30	−.14	27	.37*	21	−.02	309	.26***
STEP–Math	86	.08	30	−.07	27	.26	21	.35	309	.24

* *p* < .10
** *p* < .05
*** *p* < .01

previously indicated, the HA Hawaiian boys were students enrolled in a private school which selects pupils on the basis of ability and achievement. The LA Hawaiian sample, on the other hand, was drawn from a public high school and, as a group, was characterized by low levels of academic success, high truancy, dropout or push-out rates and other school behavior problems associated with impoverished areas.

The conclusion that Hawaiian males are poor scholars because they lack *n* Ach is a "deficiency" explanation (Gallimore, 1969); at best, it explains why Hawaiian children do not behave as middle-class Caucasian children do, but it does not explain what motivates those among the Hawaiian children who do achieve. Thus the issue becomes what motive, if not *n* Ach, is associated with achievement for Hawaiian males. One preliminary study (Gallimore, 1969) indicates that, for Hawaiian high school boys, fantasy *n* Affiliation and not *n* Ach, is correlated with achievement-oriented behavior in a risk taking task. This finding is consistent with the ethnographic data (Gallimore & Howard, 1968) which clearly reflected the importance attached by Hawaiians to affiliative rewards; thus, it is possible that among Hawaiians, both HA and LA, those individuals whose preferences for affiliative reinforcement are particularly strong may be motivated to work especially hard at achievement tasks in order to gain the approval of others. Consistent with this notion is the finding by Sloggett (1969) that affiliative reinforcers were more effective than individual rewards in a program designed to foster academic improvement among a group of male Hawaiian high school dropouts.

In general, the data suggest that attempts to explain the problems of American ethnic minorities in terms of psychological motives must first assess what is valued by the members of the respective groups. If there are variations across ethnic groups in the motivational antecedents of achievement, then attempts to foster higher achievement—for example, among Afro-American youngsters in ghetto schools—may fail if it is

assumed that *n* Ach is or can be a primary motive. It is likely that greater success could be achieved if the schools were organized to take advantage of the motives operative within particular ethnic groups.

REFERENCES

ATKINSON, J. W. (Ed.) *Motives in fantasy, action, and society.* Princeton: Van Nostrand, 1959.

ATKINSON, J. W., & FEATHER, N. T. *A theory of achievement motivation.* New York: Wiley, 1966.

BARBERIO, R. The relationship between achievement motivation and ethnicity in Anglo-American and Mexican-American junior high school students. *Psychological Record*, 1967, *17*(2), 263–266.

DEVOS, G. A. Achievement and innovation in culture and personality. In E. Norbeck, D. Price-Williams, & W. M. McCord (Eds.). *The study of personality: an interdisciplinary approach.* New York: Holt, Rinehart, & Winston, 1968.

GALLIMORE, R. Variations in the motivational antecedents of achievement among Hawaii's ethnic groups. Paper read at East-West Conference on Culture and Mental Health, Social Science Research Institute, Honolulu, Hawaii, 1969. (Proceedings in press.)

GALLIMORE, R., & HOWARD, A. (Eds.) *Studies in a Hawaiian Community: Na Makamaka O Nanakuli.* Pacific Anthropological Records No. 1. Honolulu: Department of Anthropology, B. P. Bishop Museum, 1968.

HAYS, W. L. *Statistics for psychologists.* New York: Holt, Rinehart, & Winston, 1963.

MCCLELLAND, D. C. *The achieving society.* Princeton: Van Nostrand, 1961.

MERBAUM, A. D. *Need for achievement in Negro and white children.* (Doctoral dissertation, University of North Carolina) Ann Arbor, Michigan: University Microfilms, 1961. No. 62-3140.

MINGIONE, A. D. Need for achievement in Negro and white children. *Journal of Consulting Psychology*, 1965, *29*(2), 108–111.

NUTTALL, R. L. Some correlates of high need for achievement among urban northern Negroes. *Journal of Abnormal and Social Psychology*, 1964, *68*, 593–608.

SLOGGETT, B. B. *Behavior modification of the underachieving rural Hawaiian: An experimental classroom*. Pacific Anthropological Records No. 5. Honolulu: Department of Anthropology, B. P. Bishop Museum, 1969.

VEROFF, J., ATKINSON, J. W., FELD, S. C., & GURIN, G. The use of thematic apperception to assess motivation in a nationwide interview study. *Psychological Monographs*, 1960, *74*(12), 32 pp.

34

Social Class Differences in Some Aspects of the Nonverbal Communication between Mother and Preschool Child [1]

TERRY HORE

The question of language development in different race and/or class groups will be dealt with in Section IX of this book. This paper, addressed to nonverbal aspects of communication, is placed here because social class is the crucial variable in the study. Nonverbal communication is getting increased attention currently in a variety of contexts, ranging from mother-infant interactions to encounter groups.

The following study was done in Canada, but its author, Dr. Terry Hore, is now at Monash University in Victoria, Australia.

Until recently, the study of communication has been regarded as synonymous with the study of language. Mead (1964) traced the roots of European and American linguistic research methodologies, and found that, whereas the meticulous analysis of written texts originates from Europe, the American tradition has developed from the observation of the language of non-literate peoples. This observation of people in the act of speaking has emphasized not only what people say, but also how they say it.

There is little doubt of the existence and im-

portance of the nonverbal aspects of the communication system in the life of the preverbal child; the child devises ways of telling what he wants. Church (1966a) has called this method "concrete enactment," and described a situation where a child who wants to be lifted up will hold out his arms. Neither can it be denied that these nonverbal methods of communicating are present when adults interact, for examples of such message transmission are seen frequently: the smile, the nod, the glance. But apart from observations of children's behaviour which have described nonverbal language incidentally (Church, 1966b), this method of communication has received little attention from child development researchers. Since 1925 there has been marked growth in interest in the linguistic aspect of communication, and developmental stages have been set for such variables as length of sentence, vocabulary and complex sentence types. Throughout these studies it has been a common finding that there is a marked positive relationship between socio-economic status (SES) of the family and the linguistic development of the child. The studies of Davis (1937) and McCarthy (1930) showed that middle class as opposed to working class children use more mature sentence forms and longer sentences at an earlier age. Deutsch (1963) showed that the differences which were present at Grade 1 were greater at Grade 5; an occurrence which Deutsch called the "cumulative deficit phenomenon." In addressing themselves to the question of why such SES differences exist researchers have become interested in the language environment, and the interaction of mothers with their pre-school child. The work of Hess & Shipman (1965, 1966) is an example of the latter. On the basis of the research cited previously, it can be assumed that there are differences in language "maturity" between mother-child samples taken from different SES levels. However, no experimental evidence was found to show differentiation in nonverbal language use by people from different SES groups. Robson (1967), for example, commenting on the role of eye-to-eye contact in maternal-infant attachment, suggested that early contingency experience may also determine the extent to which older children and adults rely upon and utilize nonverbal forms of communication. The majority of information on nonverbal behaviour has come from the study of adults in psychotherapy. Patients have unconsciously communicated information by bodily posture (Scheflen, 1964), physical contact (Spradlin, Rosenberg & Sanford, 1961) or glancing behaviour (Robson, 1967; Ruesch,

---

[1] This paper is based upon work carried out at the Department of Educational Psychology, University of Alberta, Canada.

Terry Hore, "Social class differences in some aspects of the nonverbal communication between mother and preschool child," *Australian Journal of Psychology, 22,* 1970, 21–26. Reprinted by permission.

1955). However, to this point, it is not known what relationship nonverbal language has to SES or what relationship it has to verbal communication.

There are some hints in the literature which may lead to the formulation of a tentative relationship from which testable hypotheses can be derived. For example, Ruesch (1955) saw the development of language as a transition from the nonverbal to the verbal. Szasz (1961) said something similar: "Since the use of iconic (body) signs is the simplest communicational device known to man, communication of this type varies inversely with knowledge and learning . . . conversations in this proto-language can occur only if the participants in the communication process do not readily speak a higher level of language (p. 121)." Within different SES groups Degerando (in Chamberlain, 1900) stated that rich children understood more words and less actions whereas poor children understood less words and more actions. More recently, Bernstein (1960) commented on the need for the "restricted code" user to employ nonverbal channels for the transmission of personal intent because he does not have the verbal facility enjoyed by the user of [an] "elaborated code." The foregoing comments seem to suggest that the relationships of nonverbal to verbal communication and of nonverbal communication to SES are both negative, that is, the more verbal facility one has, the less reliant one will be on the employment of the nonverbal channel.

Commencing from the assumption that the higher SES groups have greater verbal facility than a corresponding lower SES group, the general hypothesis was deduced that higher SES groups use nonverbal communication less than lower SES groups. More specifically, it was hypothesized that when mothers and children interact, high SES pairs show less (a) physical contact; (b) physical closeness; (c) mutual glances.

The Study

sample

The total group of non-working mothers with 5-year-old children was drawn from the census records of two areas of the City of Edmonton, Canada, which were representative of high and low income families.[2] The final sample of 15 high and 15 low income subjects was randomly drawn from the larger purposive sample. The children were matched for age and intelligence, as measured by the Peabody

Picture Vocabulary Test (PPVT). Apart from having no employment outside the home, the mothers were not matched. As expected, the high SES mothers used more complex[3] language than the low SES mothers (Practical Task, $t(28) = 2 \cdot 75$, $p < \cdot 05$, one-tailed test; Verbal Task, $t(28) = 3 \cdot 10$, $p < \cdot 05$, one-tailed test). There was no difference between the children of the two groups in the complexity of the language used during either task. The high SES group contained 7 boys and 8 girls, and there were 8 boys and 7 girls in the low SES group.

procedure

Recently, evidence has been accumulating regarding the significance of eye-to-eye contact or "glancing" behaviour in maternal-infant attachment (Robson, 1967). This behaviour is so fleeting that it requires recording equipment capable of freezing the action as well as providing for innumerable play-backs. Previous techniques to measure these variables have varied from an interval notation system (Merrill, 1946) to an elaborate shorthand (Birdwhistell, 1952), to the use of tape recordings (Hess & Shipman, 1965) and filmed sequences (Katz, 1964). The investigation described here made extensive use of videotaped recordings, to instruct the subjects and to record the interaction of the mother and child. An Interaction Timer was constructed to count and time the occurrence of each event, i.e., glance. The two other nonverbal variables measured were physical contact, and physical closeness without contact. Physical contact did not occur during the verbal task in any of the pilot studies and for this reason the discussion of this variable is restricted to its occurrence within the practical task only. In order to quantify physical closeness without contact, a grid was constructed to fit over the television monitor which divided the screen vertically into three parts. A tally was made each time the heads of mother and child appeared in the central portion simultaneously. Except for physical contact, measures were taken under two different task situations.

One task was largely manipulative and required the mother and child to work together with a toy,[4]

---

[2] The fathers of the high SES families earned over $10,000 (Canadian) per year. The fathers of the low SES families were manual workers earning less than $5,000 (Canadian) per year.

[3] Language complexity was operationally defined as "average number of words per communication unit." Loban (1963) outlined the division of spoken language called a communication unit, which approximates the more complex analysis of syntax; it requires a phonological division of the subjects' speech, without encompassing meaning, and a further subdivision into groups of words which cannot be divided further without the loss of essential meaning. These final groups of words are communication units.

[4] "Etch-a-sketch" No. 505, Peter Austin Mfg. Co. Ltd., Toronto, Canada.

the second task was mainly verbal, requiring the mother and child to tell each other stories based upon four cards from the supplement to the Children's Apperception Test. Since pilot studies had indicated that the presence of the investigator disturbed the mother-child interaction, this interaction was observed on a television monitor outside the testing area. The pilot studies had also enabled\ the investigator to construct the testing area in such a way as to obtain full profile shots of mother and child simultaneously from a concealed unattended camera. The mothers had been told that a recording would be made but the children were not aware that their reactions would be recorded.

Comparisons were made between the two SES groups by individual *t* tests on each pair of means for each nonverbal measure. (Parallel nonparametric tests, Welch's *t* prime for unequal variances and the Mann-Whitney *U* test, were carried out. The results were compatible with those from the parametric analyses.) A significance level of ·05 was adopted.

On completion of the home visits where the intelligence test was given and rapport established with mother and child, each mother brought her child to the television studio at the University of Alberta, where she was instructed, *via* two videotaped films, how to lead her child through the two tasks. The order of presentation of the tasks to the child was alternated for each half of each SES group, and each task was only presented when the child and mother had successfully completed an orientation task designed to overcome any uneasiness in the experimental situation.

RESULTS

The high and low SES groups did not differ on the cumulative time taken to complete either of the two tasks, so that the data which follow were based upon the total time spent working on each task.

Hypothesis (a). This hypothesis was supported by the data (see Table 1); the low SES mother-child pairs showed a greater amount of physical contact during the practical task than the high SES pairs.

Hypothesis (b). Table 2 summarizes the data which showed that there was no difference between the high and low SES groups, in terms of physical closeness, on the practical or the verbal task.

Hypothesis (c). The data presented in Table 3 did not support this hypothesis, in fact the direction was the reverse of the expectation. That is, the high SES pairs engaged in more, not less, mutual glances

TABLE 1
PHYSICAL CONTACT

| | Practical task | |
Measure	Low SES	High SES
Means	6·40	1·87
Standard deviations	9·27	2·50
No. of subjects	15	15
t (28)	1.76*	

* *p* < .05, one-tailed test.

than the low SES pairs. The implications of this result are discussed in the next section.

DISCUSSION

The groups did not differ in the amount of physical closeness in either task. This may have resulted from the crudeness of the measuring device which was not sensitive to small movements. Physical contact was found to discriminate between the groups: this contact was usually initiated by the mother and was seen as an indication of the tendency of the low SES mother to steer her child physically rather than verbally. The occurrence of this contact generally followed two or three verbal directives which were ignored, whereupon obedience was manually effected.

During the verbal task, visual interaction was more frequent in favour of the high SES pairs. On the practical task there was no difference between the SES groups when "mutual" glances were tallied and timed; it appeared that the task-oriented behaviour required by this task itself prevented this form of interaction from occurring.

Subsequent investigations of "unreciprocated" glancing behaviour during the verbal task revealed that the high SES mother spent more time looking at her child than the low SES mother. This had two results, first, the high SES child had fewer of his glances unreciprocated, hence the result of more "mutual" glances being recorded by this group; secondly, the low SES child who looked at his mother more often than the high SES child failed to receive the direct visual attention of his mother. Jensen (1967) considered that gesture and facial expression were parts of the differential reinforcement behaviour which he believed was more persistently carried out in the middle class homes (high SES in this study). It is suggested that "glancing" behaviour is part of this reinforcement behaviour and was differentially employed by the SES groups described here. Brown & Bellugi (1964) commented that the middle class child learns by feedback from his parents, who reduce or expand the child's expression to incorporate the correct grammatical

TABLE 2
PHYSICAL CLOSENESS

Measure	Practical task		Verbal task	
	Low SES	High SES	Low SES	High SES
Means	2·67	5·60	1·13	0·20
Standard deviations	4·45	8·12	2·73	0·75
No. of pairs	15	15	15	15
t (28)		1·19		1·23

TABLE 3
MUTUAL GLANCES

Measure	Practical task		Verbal task	
	Low SES	High SES	Low SES	High SES
Means	0·20	0·67	6·87	16·00
Standard deviations	0·40	1·07	4·94	11·27
No. of pairs	15	15	15	15
t (28)		−1·522 [a]		−2·778 [ab]

[a] Result was in reverse direction to expectation.
[b] For a two-tailed test, this result would have been significant, $p < .01$.

elements. The present study suggested that this feedback may not be singularly verbal, but may include concomitant nonverbal components, i.e., glances.

The results warn future investigators against treating nonverbal variables as homogeneous in their effect on the interaction process. It may be speculated that there is a continuum in nonverbal communication, parallel to the verbal, from less to more complex or mature. The results suggested that glancing behaviour is more "complex" than physical contact. In turn this could mean that culturally handicapped children are more than verbally handicapped by their environment; they may also be deficient in the nonverbal aspects of their exchanges with adults. Teachers should be alerted to the power of the nonverbal channels of communication as a means of influencing behaviour. Commenting on the effects of teacher expectations on teacher behaviour and pupil performance, Rosenthal & Jacobson (1968) suggested that teachers look more frequently at those children from whom they expected better performance. This is similar to the events recorded in this investigation, for at six years of age the children did not differ significantly in the number of times they looked at their mothers. What did differ was the number of times their mothers looked at them.

The study raises interesting questions for further research. Will it be possible to describe the nonverbal aspects of communication in such a way as to place them along a continuum? Such a description would facilitate research into the total communication process. Why did the high SES mothers look at their children more than the low SES mothers? Exline & Winters (1965) have demonstrated that there is a greater affective involvement, and willingness to relate to another, between individuals who participate in mutual glances; it may be important therefore to examine the affective components of the mothers' personality structure. The frequency with which a mother looks at her child may be one of the unconscious ways she "encourages excellence" (McClelland, 1961) but this awaits further investigation.

Although it has been a common finding that social class differences exist in the use of language, it is not known whether nonverbal communication is also used differentially by different SES groups. Videotaped recordings were made of the interactions between 2 divergent SES groups of 15 mothers and their preschool children in 2 situations. Data were analyzed with respect to three nonverbal variables. It was found that low SES mothers used more physical contact during a practical task; no difference existed between the SES groups on physical closeness during the tasks; the high SES mother-child pairs exchanged more mutual glances. The implications of these results for teachers are discussed.

REFERENCES

BERNSTEIN, B. Language and social class. *British Journal of Sociology*, 1960, *11*, 271–276.

BIRDWHISTELL, R. L. *Introduction to kinesics*. Louisville: University of Louisville Press, 1952.

BROWN, R. & BELLUGI, U. Three processes in the child's acquisition of syntax. *Harvard Educational Review*, 1964, *34*, 133–151.

CHAMBERLAIN, A. F. *The child: A study in the evolution of man*. London: Walter Scott, 1900.

CHURCH, J. *Language and the discovery of reality*. New York: Vintage, 1966. (a)

CHURCH, J. (Ed.) *Three babies: Biographies of cognitive development*. New York: Random House, 1966. (b)

DAVIS, E. A. The development of linguistic skill in twins, singletons with siblings and only children from age 5 to 10 years. *Institute of Child Welfare Monograph*, 1937, No. 14.

DEUTSCH, M. The disadvantaged child and the learning process. In A. H. Passow (Ed.), *Education in depressed areas*. New York: Teachers College, 1963. Pp. 163–180.

EXLINE, R. V. & WINTERS, L. C. Affective relations and mutual glances in dyads. In S. S. Tomkins & C. E. Izard (Eds.), *Affect, cognition and personality*. New York: Springer, 1965. Pp. 319–350.

HESS, R. D. & SHIPMAN, V. Early blocks to children's learning. *Children*, 1965, *12*, 189–194.

HESS, R. D. & SHIPMAN, V. Cognitive elements in maternal behaviour. Paper presented at the 1st Annual Minnesota Symposium on Child Psychology, May, 1966.

JENSEN, A. R. Social class and verbal learning. In J. P. de Cecco (Ed.), *The psychology of language, thought and instruction*. New York: Holt, Rinehart and Winston, 1967. Pp. 103–117.

KATZ, R. L. Body language: A study in unintentional communication. Unpublished doctoral dissertation, Harvard University, 1964.

LOBAN, W. D. *The language of elementary school children*. Champaign, Illinois: National Council of Teachers in English, 1963.

McCARTHY, D. M. Language development of the preschool child. *Institute of Child Welfare Monograph*, 1930, No. 4.

McCLELLAND, D. C. Encouraging excellence. *Daedalus*, 1961, *90*, 711–724.

MEAD, M. Vicissitudes of the study of the total communication process. In Sebeok, T. A., Hayes, A. S. and Bateson, M. C. *Approaches to semiotics*. The Hague: Mouton, 1964. Pp. 277–287.

MERRILL, B. A measurement of mother-child interaction. *Journal of Abnormal and Social Psychology*, 1946, *41*, 37–49.

ROBSON, K. S. The role of eye-to-eye contact in maternal-infant attachment. *Journal of Child Psychology and Psychiatry and Allied Disciplines*, 1967, *8*, 13–27.

ROSENTHAL, R. & JACOBSON, L. *Pygmalion in the classroom*. New York: Holt, Rinehart & Winston, 1968.

RUESCH, J. Nonverbal language and therapy. *Psychiatry*, 1955, *19*, 323–330.

SCHEFLEN, A. E. The significance of posture in communication systems. *Psychiatry*, 1964, *27*, 316–331.

SPRADLIN, J. E., ROSENBERG, S. & SANFORD, M. Interaction among retarded children as a function of their relative language skill. *American Psychologist*, 1961, *16*, 396. (Abstract).

SZASZ, T. S. *The myth of mental illness*. New York: Hoeber-Harper, 1961.

35

Race, Class, Family, and School Achievement[1]

STEVEN R. TULKIN

Steven Tulkin also looks at SES as an independent variable together with race and family. The dependent variable is school achievement. This study was published prior to the Jensen report referred to in the introduction to Section II on biological bases of behavior. It exemplifies a typical approach, but it is methodologically superior to many other studies because of the controls it was able to establish. The number of subjects used was also greater than in many other studies. Tulkin is in the department of psychology at the State University of New York at Buffalo.

[1] This report summarizes and expands certain aspects of an investigation conducted while the author was at the Department of Psychology, University of Maryland. Marvin G. Cline was very helpful in both planning the investigation and interpreting the results. The research was carried out as part of the Reading Ability and Outcome Study of the Mental Health Study Center (National Institute of Mental Health). J. R. Newbrough and Dee Norman Lloyd were especially helpful throughout the investigation. Grateful appreciation is also extended to Victor Rice, supervisor of testing and research of the Prince George's County (Maryland) Board of Education; Leo Walder, University of Maryland, and John Muller, Harvard University, for their help in obtaining and analyzing the present data; and to Thomas F. Pettigrew, J. R. Newbrough, and Jerome Kagan for their thoughtful comments on the present paper. Computer analyses were supported by the Computer Science Center of the University of Maryland and by a Field Foundation Grant to the Laboratory of Social Relations of Harvard University.

The debate surrounding heredity versus environmental influences on the development of intelligence is one of the oldest in the social sciences. The effects of characteristics such as social class have been acknowledged since Binet's work with intelligence testing (Binet & Simon, 1916). Although many social scientists interpret racial differences in tested intelligence and school achievement as resulting from social class differences, so-called "caste" differences, and various other environmental influences (Pettigrew, 1964, pp. 132–135), the advocates of the heredity view can still be heard (Burt, 1958; McGurk, 1959; Shuey, 1958, 1966). Still others have argued that the question has not been answered and insist that genetic differences be further investigated rather than assumed not to exist (Ingle, 1964).

The problem is a complex one, involving the interaction of race (caste), social class, family environments, and sex differences, as well as methodological questions such as random sampling and use of "culturally biased" tests. All of these problems must be considered when attempting to examine this complex question.

There have been many hypotheses about how these various factors influence intelligence. Some have related differential environmental experiences of Negroes and whites to differential academic performance. Deutsch (1960), for example, related racial differences on intelligence and achievement tests to the fact that the Negro student, not being a part of the majority culture, finds that identification with a set of majority culture symbols is not personally relevant. This "racial" difference is seen as existing all along the social class continuum, and, in fact, Deutsch and Brown (1964) reported that racial differences are greatest in the upper socioeconomic status (SES) groups. Similarly, Roen (1960) hypothesized that the psychological experiences of socioeconomic exclusion and generally more erratic family ties negatively influence the emerging personalities or self-perceptions of Negroes, especially as these relate to their intellectual potentials.

These authors, then, have suggested that Negro students—because of special environmental experiences associated with being Negro Americans —tend to be alienated from the majority culture, to have family backgrounds which are less conducive to the development of intellectual skills, and to have personality traits which themselves limit intellectual performance.

In contrast to the view that racial differences are found in each social class, Bloom, Whiteman, and

Steven R. Tulkin, "Race, class, family, and social achievement," *Journal of Personality and Social Psychology, 9,* 1968, 31–37.

Deutsch (1963) found that the relationships between social class and various family and environmental conditions are very similar in white and Negro samples. In fact, they reported that the association of environmental conditions with social class tends to be stronger than with race, and they tentatively concluded that "social class may be a more potent variable than race in predicting to environmental and attitudinal factors [p. 10]" which have been shown to be related to test scores on intelligence and achievement tests.

Sex has also been found to relate to measures of intelligence and school achievement. Kennedy Vande, and White (1963), for example, reported that although in the first grade there are no differences in the achievement scores of 1,800 Negro students, with each higher grade sex differences become greater. By Grade 6, achievement scores of the females are more than three-fourths of a grade level higher than the scores of the males. This is consistent with a report by Mingione (1965) that among Negroes the girls have a greater need for achievement than the boys, as would be expected, according to Veroff, Atkinson, Feld, and Gurin (1960), as a natural result of matriarchal Negro families.

This brief review serves to illustrate the complex interactions of race, social class, and sex, all of which may influence scores on tests of intelligence and school achievement. The majority of studies which have attempted to control these three factors have still found significant differences between racial groups, as is reported in both of Shuey's (1958, 1966) reviews of the literature. However, rather than conclude, as Shuey did, that the differences are caused by a genetic factor, one must ask whether, in fact, the groups studied were really equated. It has been shown that the more closely white and Negro groups are equated, the smaller are the differences that are found. McCord and Demerath (1958), for example, controlled for social class, father's occupation, nationality, generation of entry into America, and the "personality and emotional climate of the home." They found no significant differences among racial groups. However, in addition to the fact that this study has been criticized for its methodology (Shuey, 1966), the data were mostly on lower-middle- and lower-class subjects. The relationships among these factors in the middle and upper classes remain unstudied.

The present research is a study of a group of upper and lower SES Negroes and whites in which differences on intelligence and achievement tests are examined from the points of view of race, social class, family environments, and sex. Of particular interest is the extent to which environmental variables relate to differences between Negroes and whites on measures of intelligence and school achievement, and whether test-score differences are reduced as more of these environmental factors are controlled.

METHOD

The subjects were 389 fifth- and sixth-grade students from a suburban Maryland school system. They were divided into two SES groups (upper and lower), two racial groups (Negro and white), and two sexes, yielding eight groups (see Table 1). Background information was obtained from the students' permanent record cards. SES was determined by a modification of the Hollingshead (1957) Two-Factor Index of Social Position (occupation and education), with Levels 1 and 2 being used as upper SES and Level 5 as lower SES. Students from SES Levels 3 and 4 were not included in the sample. The Lorge-Thorndike Intelligence Test (Level Three) and the Iowa Tests of Basic Skills were administered by the local school system as a part of its regular testing program, and scores were obtained from the records.

A specially developed questionnaire consisting of items related to cultural participation, family participation, and family structure was also administered. The Cultural Participation Scale consists of four 1-point items (visit library, visit museum, attend concert, and read newspaper) and five items on which 1 point was given for each time an activity was performed (books read in previous 2 months, culturally related trips, etc.). The Family Participation Scale has two parts: time spent with parents (I), and verbal interaction between children and parents (II). In Section I, 1 point is given for each activity of the child in which one or both parents participate (Sunday activities, trips, visits to museums, libraries, etc.). In Section II, the student uses a scale from 0 to 3 to indicate how often he talks with parents about homework, personal problems, what to do on a rainy day, what he reads in the newspapers, and what is going on in school. These scores are summed and added to the total from Section I. Family-structure items include a crowdedness ratio (number of people living in the house divided by the number of rooms), data on maternal employment, marital status of parents, and number of siblings.

The questionnaire was developed in three stages: (a) testing of construct validity, (b) pretesting the instructions and vocabulary to improve clarity, and (c) obtaining sample distributions from pretest subjects on the Cultural Participation Scale, the Family Participation Scale, and the family-structure indexes.

TABLE 1
RACE, CLASS, AND SEX DISTRIBUTION OF
SAMPLE POPULATION

| SES | White | | Negro | | Total |
	Male	Female	Male	Female	
Upper	70	67	29	23	189
Lower	48	37	57	58	200
Total	118	104	86	81	389

Construct validity is based on a set of judgments by 10 members of the professional staff of the Mental Health Study Center (National Institute of Mental Health). Each of the judges rated all questions on the amount of relationship to the desired construct. Following this, the questionnaire was pretested with students from one white and one Negro classroom and administered by individual interview to two students representing each of the eight cells shown in Table 1. Questions which were ambiguous to the subjects or were not discriminating in the same direction as the total scale were modified or eliminated.

Analysis of the data consisted of two major phases. First, the data were analyzed on the basis of race and class only. Significance tests were computed on all variables, and an attempt was made to control further for environmental differences by use of a multivariate analysis of variance in which the environmental differences were statistically controlled through the use of covariate adjustors.[2] Correlations were also examined within each race-class group. In Phase 2, the data were examined to determine the importance of sex differences.

RESULTS

Table 2 presents race within class comparisons of the means, standard deviations, and significance levels of the test scores and home and family scales. Three-fourths of the tests yield significant differences in the upper SES group, while half of the differences are significant in the lower SES group. In the upper SES group, there are differences on both verbal and nonverbal tests, while differences in

the lower SES group are found only on nonverbal measures. On the family variables, there are racial differences on the crowdedness ratio in both SES groups, a difference in the number of siblings, and a difference on the Family Participation Scale in the lower SES group only.[3] (Univariate analyses of variance were done on each test separately and yielded identical significance levels.)

SES group differences were also tested within each race (upper white versus lower white and upper Negro versus lower Negro). On *every measure* presented in Table 2, social class differences are significant beyond the .001 level of confidence. Thus the breakdown into SES groups yields a greater number and larger differences than does the breakdown into racial groups.

In order to determine if other home and family differences existed among racial groups of similar SES background, comparisons were made on two other variables, broken homes and maternal employment. Tables 3 and 4 present these data. Again it appears that controlling for SES does not equate white and Negro samples. Broken homes are more common, proportionately, in the upper SES Negro group than in the upper SES white group. In fact, there is no significant difference between upper and lower SES Negro groups. Similarly, maternal employment seems to vary more along racial than SES lines.

---

[2] The program used was the Multivariate Analysis of Variance, General Linear Hypothesis Model, Biometric Laboratory, George Washington University.

[3] Since large racial differences were also found on "social desirability" questions that were asked in the questionnaire, and since "faking" was much easier on the Family Participation Scale, this latter difference may be largely attributable to social desirability.

TABLE 2

MEANS, STANDARD DEVIATIONS, AND SIGNIFICANCE LEVELS FOR STANDARD TESTS AND FAMILY SCALES

	Upper SES white		Upper SES Negro		Lower SES white		Lower SES Negro	
	M	SD	M	SD	M	SD	M	SD
Verbal IQ	114.48	14.56	109.15**	12.88	92.67	12.84	90.04	12.08
Nonverbal IQ	112.10	12.20	107.81*	11.79	95.41	13.57	91.01**	12.38
Vocabulary achievement[a]	6.22	1.38	5.88	1.18	4.40	.78	4.51	.65
Reading achievement	5.92	1.50	5.44*	1.38	4.12	.88	4.11	.92
Language achievement	6.42	1.44	6.16	1.38	4.48	.98	4.44	1.04
Work study achievement	5.80	1.00	5.42***	.74	4.48	.64	4.26*	.66
Arithmetic achievement	5.75	.83	5.33***	.76	4.74	.68	4.36****	.67
Total achievement	6.06	1.13	5.64***	.93	4.48	.72	4.36	.84
Crowdedness	.72	.25	.92***	.43	1.28	.54	1.73****	1.12
Cultural participation scale	13.89	3.98	13.60	3.83	7.82	3.79	8.44	4.27
Family participation scale	15.58	4.54	16.87	4.48	11.27	4.48	13.24***	5.46
No. siblings	2.47	1.60	2.08	1.36	3.34	2.00	4.97***	2.56

Note.—Significance levels represent difference between white and Negro means within each SES group.

[a] Achievement test scores are reported as "grade equivalents."

* $p = .05$.
** $p = .02$.
*** $p = .01$.
**** $p = .001$.

TABLE 3

INTACT AND BROKEN HOMES BY RACE AND CLASS

SES	White		Negro	
	Intact	Broken	Intact	Broken
Upper	126	11	42	10
Lower	66	19	91	24

Note.—Difference between upper and lower SES groups is significant for the white sample by chi-square analysis at $p < .01$. Difference between white and Negro upper SES groups is significant by chi-square analysis at $p < .05$.

In an attempt to further equate the groups in light of the environmental differences reported above, a multivariate analysis of variance was performed in which the environmental measures were used as covariate controls.[4] Table 5 presents this analysis both with and without the covariate controls. It can be seen that while the covariate controls reduce the size of the F for race in the upper SES group, they do not change the race effect in the lower SES group. Univariate analyses of variance on the individual tests also showed that individual F ratios in the upper SES group were all reduced by the introduction of the covariates, while none of the ratios were reduced in the lower SES group. The present measures, then, were unable to account for the test-score differences between the racial groups at the lower SES level.

More information about the above relationships can be seen in the correlations between total achievement and the other variables in each race-class group (Table 6). Two important relationships are evident. Significant SES differences are seen within each racial group in the correlations of verbal intelligence to total achievement. Verbal intelligence accounts for a much larger portion of the variance of total achievement in the upper SES groups. Since racial differences on these correlations are minimal, it appears that the extent to which a student achieves at a level which is correlated with his verbal intelligence tends to be more

TABLE 5

MULTIVARIATE ANALYSIS OF VARIANCE ON INTELLIGENCE AND ACHIEVEMENT TESTS WITH AND WITHOUT COVARIATE CONTROLS[a]

Effect	F			
	Upper SES		Lower SES	
	Without	With	Without	With
Race	2.34*	1.52	5.55**	5.57**
Sex	3.91**	3.55**	7.05**	7.88**
Race × Sex	0.86	0.98	1.12	1.12

[a] Covariate controls are intact home, maternal employment, and crowdedness ratio.
* $p = .05$.
** $p = .01$.

strongly related to SES than to race. Second, Table 6 shows that none of the home and family scales are significantly correlated with total achievement in the lower SES Negro group. This corroborates the previous assertion that factors other than those controlled in the present study are affecting the scores of the lower SES Negroes.

Since Table 5 has shown that the sex effect is highly significant in both SES groups, the data were also examined to determine if the racial differences discussed above are found in both males and females. Reanalysis of the racial differences controlling for sex showed that in the upper SES group all of the significant differences were attributable to racial differences between the male groups, while none of the differences between the female groups reached an acceptable level of significance. At the lower SES level, for the most part, the pattern was reversed, and differences were more often significant in the female group. Some sex differences in correlations were also obtained when the data presented in Table 6 were analyzed separately by sex groups.[5]

DISCUSSION

Shuey (1966) contended that racial differences in tested intelligence cannot be explained on the

[4] Since there are no reliable racial differences on the Cultural Participation Scale or the Family Participation Scale, these scales are not used as covariate controls.

[5] A more detailed presentation of the data on sex differences is available from the author.

TABLE 4

MATERNAL EMPLOYMENT BY RACE AND CLASS

SES	White			Negro		
	Employed full time	Employed part time	Not employed	Employed full time	Employed part time	Not employed
Upper	33	17	87	31	8	12
Lower	32	4	49	59	27	29

Note.—Difference between upper and lower SES groups is significant for the white sample by chi-square analysis at $p < .05$. Differences between white and Negro upper and lower SES groups are both significant by chi-square analysis at $p < .001$.

Variable	Upper SES white	Lower SES white	Upper SES Negro	Lower SES Negro
Verbal IQ	.81**	.64**	.81**	.62**
Nonverbal IQ	.63**	.54**	.57**	.43**
Cultural Participation Scale	.36**	.34**	.40**	.12
Family Participation Scale	.00	.26*	.21	−.01
Crowdedness	−.11	−.08	−.31*	−.10

Note.—For Verbal IQ, correlations in upper SES groups are significantly higher than correlations in lower SES groups.

* $p = .05$.

** $p = .01$

basis of environmental differences, and that research evidence points to the presence of some "native differences" in intelligence between white and Negro samples. One cannot deny that most studies previously reported have found racial differences, regardless of the controls that have been employed. It is possible from the present findings, however, to question whether all of these previous studies have adequately equated the racial groups. Equating experimental groups is difficult even when one draws samples from a relatively homogeneous population. Attempting to equate the environments and psychological experiences of individuals from different racial groups is a considerably more complex problem. It would seem that Shuey's argument is based largely on the weight of poorly controlled research. The present study demonstrates that controlling for SES (social class) alone does not equate white and Negro students on their home environments. When these family influences are controlled, the racial groups are certainly more similar, although still not "equated." Differences between these groups in the present study are minimal. No differences are found, in fact, between upper SES whites and Negroes when broken homes, maternal employment, and crowdedness of the home are controlled, and no differences are found between upper SES white and Negro females—even without the additional covariate controls. These results are contrary to the previous finding that racial differences are more pronounced in upper SES groups (Deutsch & Brown, 1964), although quite possibly this difference could be accounted for by the different measures of social class employed by the two investigations, or other uncontrolled characteristics of the populations studied.

The fact that the present analysis failed to eliminate racial differences among the lower SES students merits further discussion. First, it should

be pointed out that at the time of the study over 90% of the Negro students in the present sample attended all-Negro schools. Research has shown that this factor by itself is significant as a determinant of the level of school performance (United States Commission on Civil Rights, 1967). In addition, the present correlational analysis (Table 6) has shown that in the lower SES Negro group (compared with the lower SES whites), a larger amount of the variance of total achievement is not accounted for either by intelligence or by the home and family variables that were employed in the present investigation. This is perhaps where the "caste" analogy (Dreger & Miller, 1960) is most useful. Many lower SES Negroes seem to be at a distinct social class level, and, therefore, equating lower class groups appears to be particularly difficult, at least with the type of procedures used in the present study. Even on so-called "culture-fair" tests, significant differences are found. With the present subjects, for example, Tulkin and Newbrough (1968) found no significant differences on Raven's Progressive Matrices between upper SES groups, but did find a significant difference between the lower SES groups.

How can one explain a racial difference that is found among lower SES students and not among upper SES students? Pettigrew (1964) noted that the economic floor for lower class Negroes is "distinctively below" the floor of the whites. A recent review of economic trends among Negroes in the United States based on the 1960 census (Brimmer, 1966) supports this argument and further demonstrates that economic differences between the races are greatest at the lower income level. Furthermore, the difference between whites and nonwhites with incomes in the upper fifth group decreased since 1947, while the gap between white and nonwhite incomes in the bottom fifth group actually increased during that 13-year period. Brimmer (1966) concluded that within the Negro community "the middle and upper income groups are getting richer, while the lowest income group is getting poorer [p. 267]." The psychological feelings of hopelessness and helplessness resulting from this economic situation would be quite difficult to control statistically.

Another variable not usually considered when studying racial differences in academic performance is prematurity. Prematurity is related to intelligence (Kagan & Henker, 1966) and is more frequent in Negroes than in whites (Abramowicz & Kass, 1966). Here also, however, differences are greatest at the lower SES levels. Block, Lippsett, Redner, and Hirschl (1952), for example, found that the racial difference in the prematurity rates for the lower SES group is more than $2\frac{1}{2}$ times larger than the difference in the upper SES group.

These findings point to the need for multi-disciplinary studies to determine how the environment influences intellectual growth and behavior in general, and to determine the extent to which these environmental influences interact with "genetic predispositions." Poorly controlled research only adds confusion to the attempt to define the relationships between environmental backgrounds of students and their performance on tests of intelligence and achievement. Specifically, controls for race, class, sex, and home and family variables—including income—are prerequisites for meaningful results. The present study suggests that with adequate control measures it is possible to demonstrate that racial groups are not significantly different on measures of intelligence and school achievement. Although results are still inconclusive concerning the measures necessary to equate racial groups at the lower social class level, they do suggest that intellectual differences are not to be found between different racial groups with similar social class status and experiences.

Intelligence and achievement test scores and home and family information were collected from 389 5th- and 6th-grade students. Controlling for social class, racial differences were found on both test scores and family measures. When family differences were also statistically controlled, there were no significant racial differences on test scores in the upper socioeconomic group, although differences remained significant in the lower socioeconomic group. It was suggested that economic differences between the racial groups might be related to the present findings, and further research was suggested on environmental factors which could account for the racial difference among the lower socioeconomic groups.

REFERENCES

ABRAMOWICZ, M., & KASS, E. H. Pathogenesis and prognosis of prematurity. *New England Journal of Medicine*, 1966, *275*, 878.

BINET, A., & SIMON, T. *The development of intelligence in children.* (Trans. by E. S. Kite) Baltimore: Williams & Wilkins, 1916.

BLOCK, H., LIPPSETT, H., REDNER, B., & HIRSCHL, D. Reduction of mortality in the premature nursery: II. Incidence and causes of prematurity: Ethnic, socioeconomic and obstetric factors. *Journal of Pediatrics*, 1952, *41*, 300–304.

BLOOM, R., WHITEMAN, M., & DEUTSCH, M. Race and social class as separate factors related to social environment. Paper presented at the meeting of the

American Psychological Association, Philadelphia, September, 1963.

BRIMMER, A. F. The Negro in the national economy. In J. P. Davis (Ed.), *The American Negro reference book.* Englewood Cliffs, N.J.: Prentice-Hall, 1966.

BURT, C. The inheritance of mental ability. *American Psychologist*, 1958, *13*, 1–15.

DEUTSCH, M. Minority group and class status as related to social and personality factors in scholastic achievement. *Monographs of the Society for Applied Anthropology*, 1960, No. 2.

DEUTSCH, M., & BROWN, B. Some data on social influences in Negro-white intelligence differences. *Journal of Social Issues*, 1964, *20*, 24–35.

DREGER, R. M., & MILLER, K. S. Comparative studies of Negroes and whites in the United States. *Psychological Bulletin*, 1960, *57*, 361–402.

HOLLINGSHEAD, A. *The Two-Factor Index of Social Position.* New Haven, Conn.: Author, 1957.

INGLE, D. J. Racial differences and the future. *Science*, 1964, *146*, 375–379.

KAGAN, J., & HENKER, B. A. Developmental psychology. *Annual Review of Psychology*, 1966, *17*, 1–50.

KENNEDY, W. A., VANDE, R. V., & WHITE, J. C. Normative sample of intelligence and achievement of Negro elementary school children in the southeastern United States. *Monographs of the Society for Research in Child Development*, 1963, *28*(6).

McCORD, W. M., & DEMERATH, N. J., III. Negro versus white intelligence: A continuing controversy. *Harvard Educational Review*, 1958, *28*, 120–135.

McGURK, F. Negro versus white intelligence: An answer. *Harvard Educational Review*, 1959, *29*, 54–62.

MINGIONE, A. D. Need for achievement in Negro and white children. *Journal of Consulting Psychology*, 1965, *29*, 108–111.

PETTIGREW, T. F. *A profile of the Negro American.* Princeton, N.J.: Van Nostrand, 1964.

ROEN, S. R. Personality and Negro-white intelligence. *Journal of Abnormal and Social Psychology*, 1960, *61*, 148–150.

SHUEY, A. M. *The testing of Negro intelligence.* Lynchburg, Va.: Randolph-Macon Women's College, 1958.

SHUEY, A. M. *The testing of Negro intelligence.* (2nd ed.) New York: Social Science Press, 1966.

TULKIN, S. R., & NEWBROUGH, J. R. Social class, race, and sex differences on the Raven (1956) Standard Progressive Matrices. *Journal of Consulting and Clinical Psychology*, 1968, *32*, in press.

UNITED STATES COMMISSION ON CIVIL RIGHTS. *Racial isolation in the public schools.* Washington, D.C.: United States Government Printing Office, 1967.

VEROFF, J., ATKINSON, J. W., FELD, S., & GURIN, G. The use of thematic apperception to assess motivation in a nationwide interview study. *Psychological Monographs*, 1960, *74*(12, Whole Number 499).

36

Chaotic Reinforcement: A Socioeconomic Leveler [1]

JEAN L. BRESNAHAN
AND WILLIAM L. BLUM

This brief article examines the effects of reinforcement history (as provided in the laboratory) on the efficiency of learning. These variables might make it appear that the study should have been placed in Section III (Learning). However, the variables and their interrelations are examined within groups that differ in social class. The difference between the social classes in the effects of the experimental manipulation is of primary interest. Hence, the paper is included under Group Memberships.

The study was done at Emory University, where Jean Bresnahan, the senior author, received her Ph.D. and is now on the faculty.

Previous work (Bresnahan, 1966; Bresnahan, Ivey, & Shapiro, 1969) showed that low-socio-economic-level children do not adopt a win-stay lose-shift strategy in a concept-acquisition task. It was hypothesized from these data that low-socio-economic-level children perform less successfully on concept-attainment problems because of their inconsistent reinforcement histories. A study was planned, therefore, to investigate whether the in-troduction of chaotic reinforcement into the histories of high-socioeconomic-level children would lead to a comparable decrement in their performance.

Other researchers have taken another approach to this problem. They have used successive training procedures under which the performance of low-socioeconomic-level children improves. Since Harlow's (1949) paper on learning to learn, experimenters have hypothesized that with appropriate experience, the difference in the asymptotic behavior of originally discrepant groups can be attenuated or reduced to zero (e.g., Scholnick & Osler, 1969). However, learning not to learn is also a phenomenon which provides direct information regarding the establishment, if not the remediation, of low-socioeconomic-level performance.

The following experiment was designed to examine the effects of random (chaotic) reinforcement in a subsequent concept-acquisition task. Levine (1962) had demonstrated that the performance of college students on a concept-acquisition task was significantly lowered after random reinforcement. The effect was pronounced for even as few as four random reinforcement trials. In the usual concept-acquisition experiment, different values of the relevant stimulus dimension are consistently reinforced, for example, triangle is always correct and circle is always wrong. In the present design, the first n trials were randomly reinforced, that is, triangle was correct on one-half of the trials and circle was correct on one-half of the trials; after the n random trials, with no clues given to the subject, the actual concept-acquisition trials began and consistent reinforcement continued thereafter.

METHOD

SUBJECTS

The subjects were 60 first graders, with a mean age of 7.0 years, enrolled in the Cobb County, Georgia, school system. One-half of the subjects were from a high socioeconomic level and one-half from a low socioeconomic level; in each socioeconomic-level group one-half were boys and one-half girls. Considering socioeconomic level, sex, and experimental conditions, there were 12 independent groups of 5 subjects each.

Three indexes were used to determine socioeconomic level: residence, occupation of parents, and education of parents. All subjects were at the extreme ends of the Warner-Meeker-Eells scale (Warner, Meeker, & Eells, 1949); the high group corresponded to Categories 1 and 2, and the low group corresponded to Categories 6 and 7 on the scale. In the former group the parents were professionals, semiprofessionals, and proprietors of large

[1] This research was supported in part by Contract No. 6-062707-2127 from the Office of Education. The authors express their appreciation to the administrators and teachers of Cobb County, Georgia.

businesses; in the latter group the parents were craftsmen, semiskilled workers, and unskilled workers. In the high-socioeconomic-level group, most fathers were college graduates; in the low-socioeconomic-level group, most parents had a seventh- to tenth-grade education. The schools from which the subjects were chosen were either predominantly high or low in socioeconomic level, and the subjects were selected only if their socioeconomic level corresponded to the predominant socioeconomic level of the school.

APPARATUS

The apparatus used was a Lehigh Valley Electronics Company Human Intelligence Panel. Mounted on the panel were a dual multistimulus response key apparatus and a 1¢ reinforcement delivery system. The experimental procedure was controlled by automated electronic equipment and all responses and stimuli were recorded on a six-channel event recorder.

PROCEDURE

Each subject was individually seated in front of the Lehigh Valley console on which two different figures on two different colored backgrounds were presented on each trial. The subject's task was to choose between the two stimuli. A finger press against a stimulus activated a microswitch.

Each correct response was rewarded with a penny. The use of a correction procedure required the subject to press the correct key if his initial response did not result in a reward. No penny was given for a response correction.

The following instructions were given to each subject by the experimenter.

> We're going to play a little game. There will be lights in these two openings like this [the experimenter pointed to each one]. Do you see them? If you press the correct one both lights will go out, and a penny will drop here [the experimenter pointed to dispenser]. If you press the wrong one, then go ahead and press the correct one so you'll get another turn. Here's the way it works [the experimenter pressed the correct one]. See, that one was correct so both the lights went out and a penny dropped down here. [The experimenter then pressed the wrong one.] See, that one was wrong so I'll go ahead and press the correct one in order to get another turn. Do you understand how to play? Try to get as many correct as you can. Leave the pennies in here [the experimenter pointed to the dispenser] and after we're finished you can take them all home.

The subject was then told to wait for the lights to change before beginning to play the game. The subject was allowed to use only one hand and was corrected if he failed to do so. For the instructions, the subject was presented with stimuli different from those used for the test trials; in the left opening was a plus sign on a yellow background and in the right opening an X on a blue background. The test stimuli consisted of a triangle and a circle, one on a red background and the other on a green

background. The four permutations of form and color, GT–RC, RC–GT, GC–RT, RT–GC, appeared with equal frequency in an unsystematic order.

The 30 subjects in each socioeconomic-level group were divided into three subgroups of 10 subjects each. One-third of the subjects began immediately on the concept-acquisition task in which the triangle was always reinforced. One-third of the subjects had 6 trials on which the triangle and circle were randomly reinforced prior to the beginning of concept formation. One-third of the subjects had 12 trials on which triangle and circle were randomly reinforced prior to the beginning of concept formation. The red or green color and the positions of the circle and the triangle were never relevant stimuli. All subjects were run at least 42 trials. If a criterion of 12 correct responses in succession was not reached within the first 42 trials, the run was continued until the criterion was reached, up to a maximum of 120 trials.

RESULTS

Previous work with the same population (Bresnahan, 1966) had shown a significant difference between the IQs of the two socioeconomic-level groups, but no significant correlation between IQ and performance on the concept-acquisition task. Given the random distribution of IQs throughout the three experimental groups of each socioeconomic level, it is clear that even a true overall correlation between IQ and performance could not survive the significant experimental interaction to be reported in the following paragraphs.

The number of errors in the first 42 trials, divided into seven blocks of 6 trials each, can be seen in Table 1. An analysis of variance [was] calculated from these data . . . [is shown in Table 2.] Three main effects were significant: socioeconomic level, number of random reinforcements, and trials. The high-socioeconomic-level children made fewer errors than the low-socioeconomic-level children on all tasks combined, $F = 5.429$, $df = 1/48$, $p < .05$. Errors increased with an increase in the number of random reinforcements, $F = 9.065$, $df = 2/48$, $p < .001$. Errors decreased over the seven blocks of trials, $F = 6.300$, $df = 6/288$, $p < .001$. When the interaction of Socioeconomic Level × Number of Random Reinforcements was partitioned into two orthogonal comparisons, 12 and 6 versus 0, and 12 versus 6, only the former was significant, $F = 5.362$, $df = 1/48$, $p < .01$. This significant result can be explained by the fact that with 6 or 12 random reinforcements the high-socioeconomic-level subjects became progressively more similar to the low-socioeconomic-level subjects in performance (Figure 1). There were almost identical results from the high- and low-socioeconomic-level subjects run under 12 prior random reinforcements. The significant Socioeconomic Level × Trials interaction, $F = 2.867$, $df = 6/288$, $p < .05$, resulted from the fact that the high-socioeconomic-

TABLE 1
NUMBER OF ERRORS IN FIRST 42 TRIALS OF CONSISTENT REINFORCEMENT

No. of random reinforcements	Blocks of six trials							
	1	2	3	4	5	6	7	Total
High SEL								
12	33	31	20	19	24	24	28	179
6	29	26	26	18	17	23	12	151
0	18	13	13	6	2	3	1	56
Total	80	70	59	43	43	50	41	386
Low SEL								
12	31	27	24	30	22	24	22	180
6	25	28	25	25	25	16	25	172
0	24	16	25	22	22	16	20	145
Total	80	71	77	77	69	56	67	497
Grand total	160	141	136	120	112	106	108	883

level children improved more than the low-socio-economic-level children over trials (Table 1).

Nonparametric statistical tests computed on the data for number of trials to criterion in 120 trials yielded the same general results. Tests for independent samples (Wilcoxon, 1947) were used to compare the high-socioeconomic-level scores with the low-socioeconomic-level scores. After either 12 or 6 random reinforcements there was no significant difference between the two socioeconomic-level groups. After 0 random reinforcements, the number of trials to criterion was significantly different ($T = 76.5$, $p < .05$); the overall result combining the three Ts also yielded a significant difference between the high- and low-socioeconomic-level groups ($T = 255$, $p < .01$).

The number of errors for each of the six groups shown in Figure 1 was significantly superior to the chance level of 21 errors per subject; the smallest z value so obtained was 2.928.

DISCUSSION

This experiment demonstrated that the introduction of random reinforcement produces typically low-socioeconomic-level behavior in high-socioeconomic-level subjects. It was shown that this result was not a simple consequence of all concept acquisition degenerating to a chance level. Both number of errors and trials to criterion revealed that the high-socioeconomic-level performance progressively approached and ultimately equaled the ineffectual low-socioeconomic-level performance. The data add credibility to the hypothesis that the inferior performance of low-socioeconomic-level children is a function of their chaotic or inconsistent reinforcement histories.

REFERENCES

BRESNAHAN, J. L. The effect of task and incentive on concept acquisition with children from two socioeconomic levels. Unpublished doctoral dissertation, Emory University, 1966.

BRESNAHAN, J. L., IVEY, S. L., & SHAPIRO, M. M. Developmentally defined obviousness in concept formation tasks. *Developmental Psychology*, 1969, *1*, 383–388.

HARLOW, H. F. The formation of learning sets. *Psychological Review*, 1949, *56*, 51–65.

LEVINE, M. Cue neutralization: The effects of random reinforcements upon discrimination learning. *Journal of Experimental Psychology*, 1962, *63*, 438–443.

SCHOLNICK, E. K., & OSLER, S. F. Effect of pretest experiences on concept attainment in lower- and middle-class children. *Developmental Psychology*, 1969, *1*, 440–443.

WARNER, W. L., MEEKER, M., & EELLS, K. *Social class in America*. Chicago: Science Research Associates, 1949.

WILCOXON, F. Probability tables for individual comparisons by ranking methods. *Biometrics*, 1947, *3*, 119–122.

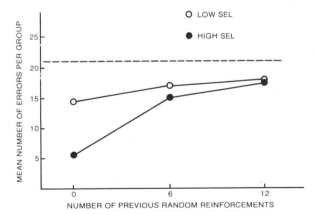

FIGURE 1. *Mean number of errors for each group of 10 subjects for 42 trials. (The broken line denotes chance level of performance; SEL = socioeconomic level.)*

37

A Note on the Relation of Reading Failure to Peer-Group Status in Urban Ghettos

WILLIAM LABOV AND CLARENCE ROBINS

This paper examines the relation of an out-of-school variable to an aspect of school performance. It is important to note, when we talk about the relation between the two variables, that we cannot talk about the direction of causation. That is, of course, true of all correlational studies. It is likely that the relations between the variables are complexly circular. This point does not in any way vitiate the suggestions the authors make for unusual use of para-professional helpers.

Implicitly, at least, the authors interpret their findings in terms of the school's failure to reach those students who have strong ties to the peer culture. Recently, there have been a number of charges made that the schools do not just passively fail to educate many of the students, but that they actively operate to prevent their education. For one example of such an approach, see "Student Social Class and Teacher Expectations: The Self-ful- filling Prophesy in Ghetto Education," by Ray C. Rist (Harvard Educational Review, 1970, 40, 411–451). Rist's longitudinal, observational study of children from kindergarten entry through second grade examines the relations between the "caste" systems of the classroom and of the society. An- other, and much more direct, indictment of the schools for seeking failure (even if unconsciously) is provided by Annie Stein, who has spent 35 years as a research analyst and has long been concerned with racial imbalance in various school systems.

Her article "Strategies of Failure" appeared in the May 1971 issue of the Harvard Educational Re- view.

The authors of the article reprinted here are William Labov and Clarence Robins. Professor Labov, the senior author, is professor of psy- chology at the University of Pennsylvania. Robins is a graduate student in sociology at Adelphi University.

For the past several years, we have been study- ing certain conflicts between the vernacular of the urban ghettos and schoolroom English, especially in relation to reading failure.[1] We work primarily with peer-groups of Negro boys within the culture of the street, since we believe that the major con- trols upon language are exerted by these groups rather than the school or the home. Our research has recently revealed a sharp and striking relation- ship between participation in this street culture and reading failure. The pattern is so clear and plainly so important in understanding the educational problems of ghetto areas, that we are sending this brief note to all those who have shown interest in our progress reports.

THE POPULATIONS CONCERNED

In the summer of 1965, we interviewed a sample of 75 Negro boys, age 10 to 12 years, in a geographi- cally random sample of "Vacation Day Camps" in Harlem. Boys had to be enrolled by their parents in these recreational programs, held in schoolyards and playgrounds, so that there was a bias of selec- tion for children from intact families with support for educational goals. Nevertheless, we found that the majority of these 10–12-year-olds had serious difficulty in reading aloud such second- and third- grade sentences as

Now I read and write better than Alfred does.
When I passed by, I read the sign.

---

[1] Data in this research note is the product of Cooperative Research Project 3288, "A Study of the Non-standard English of Negro and Puerto Rican Speakers in New York City," under OE-6-10-059. Preliminary linguistic findings of this research are published in "Some Sources of Reading Problems of Negro Speakers of Non-Standard English," in A. Frazier (Ed.), *New Directions in Elementary English* (Champaign, Ill.: N.C.T.E., 1967), pp. 140–167, and available in "Some Suggestions for Teaching Standard English to Speakers of Non-Standard Urban Dialects," submitted to the Bureau of Curriculum Research of the Board of Education of the City of New York.

William Labov and Clarence Robins, "A note on the relation of reading failure to peer-group status in urban ghettos," *The Record—Teachers College*, 1969, 70, 395–405. Reprinted by permission.

In August of 1965, we turned to the study of groups of boys in their natural associations on the streets of South Central Harlem. Our normal method of work was to interview a few individuals, locate their peer group and become acquainted with it; we then studied the language of the peer group in spontaneous interaction, and recorded the remaining individuals in face-to-face interviews. We used this approach first in studying two pre-adolescent groups in a low-income project, the "Thunderbirds" and the "Aces," against the general population of the project. We then began the study of the major adolescent groups that dominated the tenement areas from 110th Street to 118th Street between Sixth and Eighth Avenues. One of our staff members, Mr. John Lewis, acted as a participant-observer in the area. With his help, we followed two major adolescent groups, each composed of many subgroups, for two years. These groups were known as the "Cobras" and the "Jets." [2]

Our knowledge of the social structure, history, activities, and value systems of these groups is an essential aspect of the finding to be presented in this note. We traced the history of group relations and explored the value systems through individual face-to-face interviews, meetings with small groups of two or three close friends, and group sessions with six to twelve boys. In all these sessions, involving the most excited physical and verbal interaction, each person's statements and ideas were recorded on a separate track from a microphone several inches away from his mouth. We also studied group behavior in various field trips with the boys, and recorded their interaction en route. Most importantly, our participant-observer saw the boys every day on the streets, and met with them in their hang-outs and our "club-house." He was present at several moments of crisis when fighting was about to break out between the two major groups.

We also interviewed a number of isolated individuals in the same tenement areas, who were definitely not members of these groups, but who often knew about them. We are able then to assert that we reached all the major "named" groups in the area, although we did not have a representative sample of all adolescent boys. In the same areas we completed a stratified random sample of 100 adults, but only in the low-income projects did we

relate our groups quantitatively to the total population. [3]

THE STREET GROUPS

The larger associations which bear the names "Jets" or "Cobras" are known to the boys as "clubs." They are not to be confused with the groups which are organized within recreation centers by adults, which are also called "clubs" and sometimes overlap in membership. The groups we studied are initiated by the boys themselves, and are disapproved of by the adults in the neighborhood. [4]

The structure and value systems of these groups are partly inherited from the period of gang violence of the 1940's and 1950's. The frequency of group fighting, however, is comparatively low. These are not "gangs" in the sense of groups which frequently fight as a unit. Nevertheless, a major source of prestige for the leaders is skill in fighting, and individual fights are very common. The intergroup conflicts which do occur are the most important sources of group cohesion; they become a fixed part of the mythology and ideology of the group, and the obligation to support one's fellow members in a group fight is strongly felt by many members.

The general value systems of these groups conform to the lower class value pattern which has been described by Walter B. Miller. [5] The focal concerns of the groups are *toughness, smartness, trouble, excitement, autonomy,* and *fate.* Intelligence or smartness is used and valued as a means of manipulating others, rather than a means of obtaining information or solving abstract problems. The specific values of the Negro nationalist movement are reflected in some groups more than others. The members of the "Cobras," within the period that we worked with them, moved from a moderately nationalist position to deep involvement with the militant Muslim religion and its complex ideology. [6] This ideology involved the members in a strong interest in learning and abstract knowledge;

---

[2] The names "Cobras" and "Jets" are here used as cover symbols for a complex of formal groups which changes over time. The "Cobras," in particular, was originally a group formed by mergers of several groups which in turn underwent mergers with other groups under successive changes in nationalist orientation.

[3] See below for relative sizes of street groups and isolated population in one project.

[4] The "Thunderbirds" are a partial exception here, since the club was formed in a recreation center (and was successively re-formed with different names); however, the identity of the group was not confined to the center, and it contained members who had been banned from the center.

[5] "Lower Class Culture as a Generating Milieu of Juvenile Delinquency," *Journal of Social Issues, 14,* 1958, pp. 5–19.

[6] As noted above, the "Cobras" underwent a number of organizational transformations, with new officers, and merged with other groups as nationalist orientation increased.

but the general value systems of all the groups were such that school learning was seen as hostile, distant, and essentially irrelevant.

The groups have a formal structure which may include four officers: president, vice-president, prime minister and war-lord. Junior organizations are often formed by the appointment of a younger brother of an officer to a leading position among the 10-to-13-year-olds. However, this formal structure can be misleading. The day-to-day activities of the boys[7] are in smaller, informal hang-out groups, determined by geography and age; an individual's association with the larger group is often a matter of formal definition of his identity more than anything else.[8] Yet the ultimate sanction of the larger group and its fighting role is often referred to.

Sources of prestige within the group are physical size, toughness, courage and skill in fighting; skill with language in ritual insults, verbal routines with girls, singing, jokes and story-telling; knowledge of nationalist lore; skill and boldness in stealing; experience in reform schools; and connections with family members or others which provide reputation, money, hang-outs, marijuana, or other material goods. Success in school is irrelevant to prestige within the group, and reading is rarely if ever used outside of school.[9]

GROUP MEMBERSHIP

Full participation in the group consists of *endorsement* of this set of values, and *acceptance* of a set of personal obligations to others within the same environment and value system. The criterion of formal membership ("you are a Jet" or "you are not a Jet") is often disputed. A few individuals want to be members and are rejected; others could easily be members but do not care to. Full membership, as we define it, means that the individual is thoroughly involved with the values and activities of the group, and is defined as a member both by himself and by others. If some but not all of these criteria are fulfilled, we term the individual a "marginal member." The clearest evidence for full membership as against marginal status is provided by the symmetrical and asymmetrical relations in a socio-

metric diagram.[10] If an individual on the outskirts of the group wants to be a member, yet is prevented by the influence of other environments (family, school) and other value systems, he is classed with other non-members. In each area there are "social groups" which are strongly influenced by adult organizations: we do not include membership in such groups in the category of membership which we are studying.

It has been shown in many similar situations that group membership is a function of age.[11] Boys 8-to-9 years old are definitely outsiders for the groups we are studying, and they have only a vague knowledge of group activities. Membership is strongest in the 13-to-15-year-old range, and falls off rapidly in the later teens. A few 18-or-19-year-old boys act as seniors, especially if younger brothers are serving as officers, but as a rule older boys drift off into different activities.

It is difficult to estimate the percentage of boys who are full participants in the street culture. However, in the one 13-story low income project which we studied intensively,[12] there were 22 boys 10-to-12 years old. Their relationships to the major peer group, the "Thunderbirds," were as follows:

members	marginal members	non-members
12	3	7

Our general experience would indicate that 50 to 60 per cent of the boys in the age range 10-to-16 are full participants in the street culture we are studying here.

READING RECORDS

In all of our individual interviews, we used a number of special reading tests developed to yield specific information on the vernacular phonology and grammar.[13] However, the most direct evidence for reading performance in schools is obtained from the Metropolitan Achievement Test given every year in the New York City schools. With the help of the New York City Board of Education, we were able to study recently the academic records of 75 pre-adolescent and adolescent boys with whom we

---

[7] Major activities are flying pigeons, playing basketball, playing cards, petty theft, playing pool, smoking marijuana, hanging out . . . although not all members participate in all of these activities. The groups as formal wholes have relatively few activities.

[8] The problem of group identity, and the obligations which accompany membership, is not fully solved.

[9] As one indication of the importance of reading in the group, we may consider one pair of boys who were best friends and saw each other every day. One read extremely well, the other not at all: the other's performance was a total surprise to each.

[10] The most important data is derived from the question, "Who are the guys [cats] you hang out with?", supplemented with other questions on group leaders, best friends, and all other mentions of individuals in relevant roles.

[11] Cf. Peter Wilmott, *Adolescent Boys in East London*. London: 1966, p. 35. In answer to a question on main companions in spare time, 57 per cent of those 14–15 years old indicated a group of other males; 44 per cent of those 16–18 years old; and only 32 per cent of those 19–20 years old.

[12] The building studied here is 1390 Fifth Avenue.

[13] Gray's Oral Reading Test was also given to a section of the population for further calibration on school approaches to reading.

had worked in the years 1965 to 1967. The substance of this report is the correlation between the Metropolitan Achievement Reading Test and group membership.

Figure 1 shows the correlation between grade level and reading achievement for 32 boys we interviewed in the 110th-120th Street area who are not members of the street culture, or whose group status is unknown (from the Vacation Day Camp series). The horizontal axis is grade level at the time of the test; the vertical axis the Metropolitan Achievement Test score. Each individual's score and grade are indicated by the location of an *x*. The diagonal lines group together those who are reading on grade level [0], one to three years above grade level [+3 − +1], or one to six years behind grade level [−1 − −6]. As one would expect, there are a good many boys who are two years behind grade, which is average in New York City, but there are also quite a few on grade and some ahead of grade level. Eleven of the 32 boys are on grade or above. The general direction of the pattern is upward, indicating that learning is taking place.

Figure 2 shows the same relationships for 43 boys who are members or marginal members of street groups in South Central Harlem. Each indi-

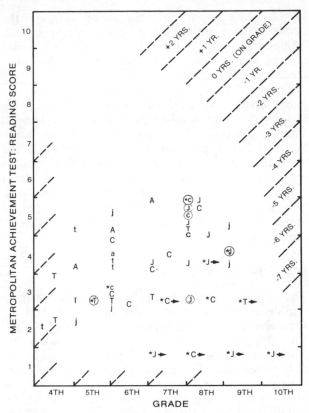

FIGURE 2. *Grade and reading achievement for 43 members of street groups in South Central Harlem, T,t = "Thunderbirds," A,a = "Aces," C,c = "Cobras," J,j = "Jets," other symbols: see text*

vidual is represented by a letter symbolizing the group of which he is a member or to which he is most closely related. Upper case letters are full members, and lower case marginal members. The over-all pattern is entirely different from Figure 1: no one is reading above grade, only one boy reading on grade, and the great majority are three or more years behind. Moreover, there are *no* boys who are reading above the fifth grade level, no matter what grade they are in. At each grade, the reading achievement for these boys forms a lower, more compact group than for the same grade in Figure 1. The close concentration of boys in the eighth grade below the fifth grade level shows a limitation on achievement which is quite striking. On the whole, Figure 2 shows very little learning as compared to Figure 1.[14]

The lower achievement of group members does not indicate over-all deficiency in verbal skills. Many of these boys are proficient at a wide range of

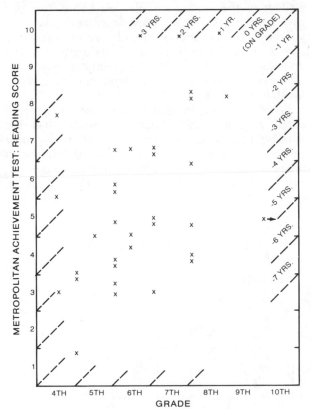

FIGURE 1. *Grade and reading achievement for 32 non-members of street groups in South Central Harlem*

---

[14] There is a close correlation between reading achievement and the Pintner-Cunningham IQ test (given in the early grades in New York City in former years) in Figure 1, and less markedly in Figure 2.

verbal skills appropriate for group activity: the verbal leaders are indicated by circles in Figure 2. While several are clustered near the highest point of achievement, there are other verbal leaders near the bottom of the diagram.

These findings are merely preliminary to our main body of correlations; we will shortly be able to provide more detailed data on a larger sample. There are a total of 170 boys whose reading abilities and language scores have been studied, and we will be able to correlate reading skill with many other factors besides membership in the street culture. However, the patterns revealed by Figures 1 and 2 are so striking that we thought all those interested in the problem should be aware of them as soon as possible.

What Is To Be Done?

The over-all view given by Figure 2 strongly reinforces our view that the major problem responsible for reading failure is a cultural conflict. The school environment and school values are plainly not influencing the boys firmly grounded in street culture. The group which does show learning contains a large percentage of boys who do not fit in with street culture—who reject it or are rejected by it. For the majority, Figure 2 confirms indirect evidence that teachers in the city schools have little ability to reward or punish members of the street culture, or to motivate learning by any means.

The usual statistics on reading achievement in urban ghettos are alarming, but they do not reveal the full extent of reading failure. Research inside the schools cannot discriminate membership in the street culture from non-membership, and educators are therefore not aware of the full extent of the cultural barrier between them and their students.

It should be understood that the educational goals of the adult Negro community are the same as that of our society as a whole. Our subjective evaluation tests, for example, show that adults in Harlem are almost unanimous in their norms of correct speech and the goals for language teaching in school. Many of the members of the street culture gradually break away and acquire these adult norms in their twenties. However, these norms are of little value for those who do not have the skills to put them into effect.

The reading failure that we have documented here is typical of other performance on the academic records. The pattern of failure is so widespread, in many urban areas, that one cannot hold responsible any one system, school or teacher. The majority of these boys have not learned to read well enough to use reading as a tool for further learning. For many of them, there is no realistic possibility of graduating from high school and acquiring the skills needed for the job market. In this particular note we are dealing only with the formal aspect of educational failure. In later publications, we will attempt to document the pessimism and despair with which these adolescents view their immediate future.

The absolute ceiling of Figure 2 is of course an artifact of the limited sample. We know from our own tests that there are group members who read very well, whose school records are not presently available. But even these rare individuals view the educational system with a profound cynicism. The majority of those who learn from the system are located in Figure 1.

We do not believe that the present college-educated teaching staff, Negro or white, has the specific knowledge of the street culture to solve this problem alone. Negro teachers raised in ghetto areas are not members of the *current* street culture. With a few rare exceptions, we find that success in

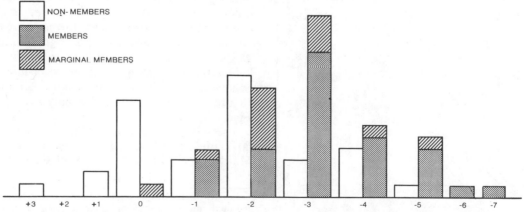

Figure 3. *Distribution of non-members, marginal members and members of street culture by years behind grade*

education removes the individual from his culture so effectively that his knowledge of it becomes quite marginal. The specific knowledge of the street culture which is needed is only available to those who are in constant interaction with the peer groups on the streets. Part of the reason is that the value system, though quite general, is intensely *local* in focus. The factors that control language behavior are often local and immediate: what happened last year, last month, or yesterday to that particular sub-group is the best stimulus for evoking spontaneous speech. And the general configurations of the culture change rapidly even though the value system remains intact: a teacher raised in Harlem in the 1950's, returning to the streets today, would find it difficult to understand how and why gang fighting is no longer in style.

We hope to elaborate on these problems of communication in later publications. Here we would like to indicate briefly the form of one proposal we believe will be effective in solving the problem of Figure 2.

We propose that a cultural intermediary be introduced into the classroom in the person of a young Negro man,[15] 16 to 25 years old, with high school

level reading skills, but not a college graduate. We propose the creation of a special license to allow this young man to carry out the following functions:

1. to acquaint the teacher with the specific interests of members of the class and help design reading materials centering on these interests.
2. to provide effective rewards and punishments that will motivate members of street culture for whom normal school sanctions are irrelevant.
3. to lead group discussion on topics of immediate concern to members of the class.
4. to lead boys in sports and other recreational activities in school time.
5. to maintain contact with boys outside of school, on the streets, and help organize extra-curricular activities.

We are well aware of the difficulties that any school system will have in absorbing such outside elements. The situation in most ghetto schools is plainly desperate enough so that many educators will be willing to endorse a proposal that may create such difficulties. We suggest that summer training schools be held for such special license teachers, in which regular teachers will participate, to develop jointly techniques for cross-cultural cooperation. At such training schools, it will also be possible to provide regular teachers and special license teachers with specific linguistic data of the type generated by our principal direction of research.

---

[15] We specifically designate a male for this role, in contrast to a number of proposals for "para-professionals" in the schools which utilize women from the community or from college training courses. We cannot elaborate on the importance of sex differentiation here, except to indicate that we believe it is a matter of prime importance.

VII

AGE OR DEVELOPMENTAL STAGE
AS A DETERMINANT OF BEHAVIOR

It is very likely that, when pressed, no theorist would maintain that chronological age per se is an important determinant of behavior. We can characterize as "maturationists" a number of authors who believe both that many psychological characteristics appear in a predictable sequence and that the absolute age for reaching a given stage of development varies among individuals. Despite their explicit statements on the importance of such individual variations in the age at which a stage is reached, some "authorities" have written in such a fashion that their readers have focused on absolute ages. The author may describe the "typical" behaviors for given ages (e.g., Gesell), or he may give age labels to the stages he discovers (e.g., Piaget). A more reasonable reading of these authors' materials would be to accept the ages stated as mere approximations while recognizing the assumption of such workers that the developmental stage reached is a crucial determinant of behavior.

Some of the most important workers whose thinking is (or was) dominated by a belief in the sequential orderliness of development are Jean Piaget[1] and the late Arnold Gesell, both mentioned above, and Myrtle McGraw and the late Heinz Werner. They have all tended to assume that the contrasts they find between younger and older human beings are found in the development of all individuals.

Psychoanalytic theory has a developmental aspect in its concept of psychosexual stages.[2] Although the stages themselves are considered to be biologically determined, life experiences are considered important in creating the behaviors held characteristic of each developmental stage. Inherited capacities appearing in accordance with chronological maturation interact with interpersonal influences to produce behavior. Consequently, a change in either the inherited capacities or the interpersonal experiences can alter the outcome of the interaction. Thus, individual differences, which have been of little interest to Piaget and Gesell, are accounted for in psychoanalytic theory by variations not only in hereditary tendencies, but also in emotional histories.

Some theorists stress the idea that certain ages or periods may be "critical." A period may be critical in two senses: (1) if certain experiences or learnings do not take place at that time, development cannot proceed properly; or (2) if certain experiences occur at that time, they may have more serious negative consequences than if they occurred either earlier or later. For example, it has been speculated that if the opportunity for language learning or for the development of social contacts and affectional bonds is not present at the proper time, later the child will not be able to speak properly or to form close attachments with others. Much of the germane work to date, however, has been based on rather loose

---

[1] For a detailed view of Piaget's contributions, see the book by John H. Flavell, *The Developmental Psychology of Jean Piaget,* D. Van Nostrand Co., Inc., Princeton, N.J., 1963.

[2] The term "psychosexual stages" refers to stages in the socialization of pleasure needs, and is not limited to "sexual" in the American use of the term.

analogies to ethological and embryological findings. The reader is referred to Bettye Caldwell's article "The Usefulness of the Critical Period Hypothesis in the Study of Filiative Behavior," which appeared in the *Merrill-Palmer Quarterly* (1962, *8*, 229–242) and was reprinted in the second edition of *The Causes of Behavior*.

We have not attempted to organize the selections in this section on exactly the lines dictated by these theoretical concerns. Instead, the section commences with two general papers that span a range of stages of development. Both of these owe much of their intellectual heritage to the psychoanalytic approach. Following these is a discussion of the rather astonishingly extensive capacities of the human infant to receive sensory stimulation and to learn. Then come three articles that focus on the period of adolescence.

The reader who is not acquainted with the writings of anthropologists on the topic of normality of adolescent difficulties may wish to refer to Margaret Mead's paper "Adolescence in Primitive and Modern Society," in Maccoby, Newcomb, Hartley (Eds.), *Readings in Social Psychology* (Henry Holt & Co., Inc., 1958). She reports the discovery of human societies in which adolescence is a period without turmoil and tension. A classic paper in a similar vein is Ruth Benedict's "Continuities and Discontinuities in Cultural Conditioning." It has been reprinted in at least two collections of readings (Martin and Stendler, *Readings in Child Development* [Harcourt, Brace & Co., 1954], pp. 142–148) and should be readily available to readers. A recent book by Daniel Offer, *The Psychological World of the Teen-ager* (Basic Books, Inc., 1969), presents a point of view contrary to the tenor of some of the articles presented in this section, that adolescence even in American society is by no means a time of surliness and rebellion, but rather is often a smooth and comfortable period.

Additional articles that relate to phases of development appear elsewhere in this book, for example, Baumrind's article in Section IV and Elkind's in Section IX.

38

A Healthy Personality
for Every Child

"A Healthy Personality for Every Child," adapted from the writings of Erik H. Erikson, was prepared for a White House conference. Erikson is a psychoanalyst noted for his clinical studies of children and for his theoretical work greatly enlarging upon and enriching Freudian developmental concepts. His book Childhood and Society *(New York: W. W. Norton & Co., Inc., 1950, rev. 1963) is a classic. Recently, Erikson has written noted books about Martin Luther* (Young Man Luther) *and Mahatma Gandhi* (Gandhi's Truth). *Erikson has been professor of human development at Harvard University since 1960. For many years before that he was at University of California in Berkeley.*

Many attempts have been made to describe the attributes of healthy personality. They have been put succinctly as the ability to love and the ability to work. A recent review of the literature suggests that the individual with a healthy personality is one who actively masters his environment, shows a unity of personality, and is able to perceive the world and himself correctly. Clearly, none of these criteria applies to a child. It seemed to us best, then, to present for the Conference's consideration an outline that has the merit of indicating at one and the same time the main course of personality development and the attributes of a healthy personality.

This developmental outline was worked out by Erik H. Erikson, a psychologist and practicing psychoanalyst who has made anthropological field studies and has had much experience with children. It is an analysis that derives from psychological theory, to which is added knowledge from the fields of child development and cultural anthropology. The whole is infused with the author's insight and personal philosophy.

In each stage of child development, the author says, there is a central problem that has to be solved, temporarily at least, if the child is to proceed with vigor and confidence to the next stage. These problems, these conflicts of feeling and desire, are never solved in entirety. Each shift in experience and environment presents them in a new form. It is held, however, that each type of conflict appears in its purest, most unequivocal form at a particular stage of child development, and that if the problem is well solved at that time the basis for progress to the next stage is well laid.

In a sense personality development follows biological principles. Biologists have found that everything that grows has a groundplan that is laid out at its start. Out of this groundplan the parts arise, each part having its time of special ascendancy. Together these parts form a functioning whole. If a part does not arise at its appointed time, it will never be able to form fully, since the moment for the rapid outgrowth of some other part will have arrived. Moreover, a part that misses its time of ascendancy or is severely damaged during its formative period is apt to doom, in turn, the whole hierarchy of organs. Proper rate and normal sequence is necessary if functional harmony is to be secured

Personality represents the most complicated functioning of the human organism and does not consist of parts in the organic sense. Instead of the development of organs, there is the development of locomotor, sensory, and social capacities and the development of individual modes of dealing with experience. Nevertheless, proper rate and proper sequence are as important here as in physical growth, and functional harmony is achieved only if development proceeds according to the groundplan.

In all this it is encouraging for parents and others who have children in charge to realize that in the sequence of his most personal experiences, just as in the sequence of organ formation, the child can be trusted to follow inner laws of development, and needs from adults chiefly love, encouragement, and guidance.

A Healthy Personality for Every Child: A digest of the Fact Finding Report to the Midcentury White House Conference on Children and Youth, 1951, 6–25.

The operation of biological laws is seen, also, in the fact that there is constant interplay between organism and environment and that problems of personality functioning are never solved once and for all. Each of the components of the healthy personality to be described below is present in some form from the beginning, and the struggle to maintain it continues throughout life.

For example, a baby may show something like "autonomy" or a will of his own in the way he angrily tries to free his head when he is tightly held. Nevertheless, it is not until the second year of life that he begins to experience the whole conflict between being an autonomous creature and a dependent one. It is not until then that he is ready for a decisive encounter with the people around him, and it is not until then that they feel called upon to train him or otherwise curb his free-questing spirit. The struggle goes on for months and finally, under favorable circumstances, some compromise between dependence and independence is reached that gives the child a sense of well-being.

The sense of autonomy thus achieved is not a permanent possession, however. There will be other challenges to that sense and other solutions more in keeping with later stages of development. Nevertheless, once established at two or three years of age, this early sense of autonomy will be a bulwark against later frustrations and will permit the emergence of the next developmental problem at a time that is most favorable for its solution.

So it is with all the personality components to be described. They appear in miniature early in life. The struggle to secure them against tendencies to act otherwise comes to a climax at a time determined by emergence of the necessary physical and mental abilities. There are, throughout life, other challenges and other responses but they are seldom so serious and seldom so decisive as those of the critical years.

In all this, it must be noted in addition, there is not the strict dichotomy that the analysis given below suggests. With each of the personality components to be described, it is not all or nothing: trust *or* mistrust, autonomy *or* doubt, and so on. Instead, each individual has some of each. His health of personality is determined by the preponderance of the favorable over the unfavorable, as well as by what manner of compensations he develops to cope with his disabilities.

THE SENSE OF TRUST

The component of the healthy personality that is the first to develop is the sense of trust. The crucial time for [its] emergence is the first year of life. As with the other personality components to be described, the sense of trust is not something that develops independent of other manifestations of growth. It is not that the infant learns how to use his body for purposeful movement, learns to recognize people and objects around him, and also develops a sense of trust. Rather, the concept "sense of trust" is a short-cut expression intended to convey the characteristic flavor of all the child's satisfying experiences at this early age. Or, to say it another way, this psychological formulation serves to condense, summarize, and synthesize the most important underlying changes that give meaning to the infant's concrete and diversified experience.

Trust can exist only in relation to something. Consequently a sense of trust cannot develop until the infant is old enough to be aware of objects and persons and to have some feeling that he is a separate individual. At about three months of age a baby is likely to smile if somebody comes close and talks to him. This shows that he is aware of the approach of the other person, that pleasurable sensations are aroused. If, however, the person moves too quickly or speaks too sharply the baby may look apprehensive or cry. He will not "trust" the unusual situation but will have a feeling of uneasiness, of mistrust, instead.

Experiences connected with feeding are a prime source for the development of trust. At around four months of age a hungry baby will grow quiet and show signs of pleasure at the sound of an approaching footstep, anticipating (trusting) that he will be held and fed. This repeated experience of being hungry, seeing food, receiving food, and feeling relieved and comforted assures the baby that the world is a dependable place.

Later experiences, starting at around five months of age, add another dimension to the sense of trust. Through endless repetitions of attempts to grasp for and hold objects, the baby is finally successful in controlling and adapting his movements in such a way as to reach his goal. Through these and other feats of muscular coordination the baby is gradually able to trust his own body to do his bidding.

The baby's trust-mistrust problem is symbolized in the game of peek-a-boo. In this game, which babies begin to like at about four months of age, an object disappears and then reappears. There is a slightly tense expression on the baby's face when the object goes away; its reappearance is greeted by wriggles and smiles. Only gradually does a baby learn that things continue to exist even though he does not see them, that there is order and stability in his universe. Peek-a-boo proves the point by playful repetition.

Studies of mentally ill individuals and observations of infants who have been grossly deprived of affection suggest that trust is an early-formed and important element in the healthy personality. Psychiatrists find again and again that the most serious illnesses occur in patients who have been sorely neglected or abused or otherwise deprived of love in infancy. Similarly, it is a common finding of psychological and social investigators that individuals diagnosed as a "psychopathic personality" were so unloved in infancy that they have no reason to trust the human race and, therefore, no sense of responsibility toward their fellow men.

Observations of infants brought up in emotionally unfavorable institutions or removed to hospitals with inadequate facilities for psychological care support these findings. A recent report says: "Infants under six months of age who have been in an institution for some time present a well-defined picture. The outstanding features are listlessness, emaciation and pallor, relative immobility, quietness, unresponsiveness to stimuli like a smile or a coo, indifferent appetite, failure to gain weight properly despite ingestion of diets which are entirely adequate, frequent stools, poor sleep, an appearance of unhappiness, proneness to febrile episodes, absence of sucking habits."[1]

Another investigation of children separated from their mothers at six to twelve months and not provided with an adequate substitute comes to much the same conclusion: "The emotional tone is one of apprehension and sadness, there is withdrawal from the environment amounting to rejection of it, there is no attempt to contact a stranger and no brightening if a stranger contacts him. Activities are retarded and the child often sits or lies inert in a dazed stupor. Insomnia is common and lack of appetite universal. Weight is lost, and the child becomes prone to current infections."[2]

Most significant for our present point, these reactions are most likely to occur in children who up to the time of separation at six to nine months of age had a happy relation with their mothers, while those whose relations were unhappy are relatively unaffected. It is at about this age that the struggle between trusting and mistrusting the world comes to a climax, for it is then that the child first perceives clearly that he and his environment are things apart. That at this time formerly happy infants should react so badly to separation suggests, indeed, that they had a faith which now was shattered. Happily, there is usually spectacular

change for the better when the maternal presence and love are restored.

It is probably unnecessary to describe the numerous ways in which stimuli from without and from within may cause an infant distress. Birth is believed by some experts to be a painful experience for the baby. Until fairly recently doctors were likely to advise that babies be fed on schedule and that little attention be paid to their cries of hunger at other times. Many infants spent many of the waking hours of the first four months doubled up with colic. All of them had to be bathed and dressed at stated times, whether they liked it or not. Add to these usual discomforts the fact that some infants are handled rather roughly by their parents, that others hear angry words and loud voices, and that a few are really mistreated, and it will not be difficult to understand why some infants may feel the world is a place that cannot be trusted.

In most primitive societies and in some sections of our own society the attention accorded infants is more in line with natural processes. In such societies separation from the mother is less abrupt, in that for some time after birth the baby is kept close to the warmth and comfort of its mother's body and at its least cry the breast is produced. Throughout infancy the baby is surrounded by people who are ready to feed it, fondle it, otherwise comfort it at a moment's notice. Moreover, these ministrations are given spontaneously, wholeheartedly, and without that element of nervous concern that may characterize the efforts of young mothers made self-conscious and insecure by our scientific age.

We must not exaggerate, however. Most infants in our society, too, find smiles and the comfort of mother's soft, warm body accompanying their intake of food, whether from breast or bottle. Coldness, wetness, pain, and boredom—for each misfortune there is prompt and comforting relief. As their own bodies come to be more dependable, there is added to the pleasures of increasing sensory response and motor control the pleasure of the mother's encouragement.

Moreover, babies are rather hardy creatures and are not to be discouraged by inexperienced mothers' mistakes. Even a mother cat has to learn, and the kittens endure gracefully her first clumsy efforts to carry them away from danger. Then, too, psychologists tell us that mothers create a sense of trust in their children not by the particular techniques they employ but by the sensitiveness with which they respond to the children's needs and by their over-all attitude.

For most infants, then, a sense of trust is not difficult to come by. It is the most important element in the personality. It emerges at the most

[1] Harry Bakwin, "Emotional Deprivation in Infants," *Journal of Pediatrics,* October, 1949, *35,* 512–529.

[2] John Bowlby, M.D., Summary of Dr. René Spitz's observations, unpublished manuscript.

vulnerable period of a child's life. Yet it is the least likely to suffer harm, perhaps because both nature and culture work toward making mothers most maternal at that time.

THE SENSE OF AUTONOMY

The sense of trust once firmly established, the struggle for the next component of the healthy personality begins. The child is now twelve to fifteen months old. Much of his energy for the next two years will center around asserting that he is a human being with a mind and will of his own. A list of some of the items discussed by Spock under the heading, "The One Year Old," will serve to remind us of the characteristics of that age and the problems they create for parents. "Feeling his oats." "The passion to explore." "He gets more dependent and more independent at the same time." "Arranging the house for the wandering baby." "Avoiding accidents." "How do you make him leave certain things alone?" "Droppings and throwing things." "Biting humans." "The small child who won't stay in bed at night."

What is at stake throughout the struggle of these years is the child's sense of autonomy, the sense that he is an independent human being and yet one who is able to use the help and guidance of others in important matters. This stage of development becomes decisive for the ratio between love and hate, between cooperation and wilfulness, for freedom of self-expression and its renunciation in the make-up of the individual. The favorable outcome is self-control without loss of self-esteem. The unfavorable outcome is doubt and shame.

Before the sense of autonomy can develop, the sense of trust must be reasonably well-established and must continue to pervade the child's feeling about himself and his world. Only so dare he respond with confidence to his new-felt desire to assert himself boldly, to appropriate demandingly, and to hurl away without let or hindrance.

As with the previous stage, there is a physiological basis for this characteristic behavior. This is the period of muscle-system maturation and the consequent ability (and doubly felt inability) to coordinate a number of highly conflicting action patterns, such as those of holding on and letting go, walking, talking, and manipulating objects in ever more complicated ways. With these abilities come pressing needs to use them: to handle, to explore, to seize and to drop, to withhold and to expel. And, with all, there is the dominant will, the insistent "Me do" that defies help and yet is so easily frustrated by the inabilities of the hands and feet.

For a child to develop this sense of self-reliance and adequacy that Erikson calls autonomy, it is

necessary that he experience over and over again that he is a person who is permitted to make choices. He has to have the right to choose, for example, whether to sit or whether to stand, whether to approach a visitor or to lean against his mother's knee, whether to accept offered food or whether to reject it, whether to use the toilet or to wet his pants. At the same time he must learn some of the boundaries of self-determination. He inevitably finds that there are walls he cannot climb, that there are objects out of reach, that, above all, there are innumerable commands enforced by powerful adults. His experience is much too small to enable him to know what he can and cannot do with respect to the physical environment, and it will take him years to discover the boundaries that mark off what is approved, what is tolerated, and what is forbidden by his elders whom he finds so hard to understand.

As problems of this period, some psychologists have concentrated particularly on bladder and bowel control. Emphasis is put upon the need for care in both timing and mode of training children in the performance of these functions. If parental control is too rigid or if training is started too early, the child is robbed of his opportunity to develop, by his own free choice, gradual control of the contradictory impulses of retention and elimination.

To others who study child development, this matter of toilet training is but a prototype of all the problems of this age-range. The sphincters are only part of the whole muscle system, with its general ambiguity of rigidity and relaxation, of flexion and extension. To hold and to relinquish refer to much more than the bowels. As the child acquires the ability to stand on his two feet and move around, he delineates his world as me and you. He can be astonishingly pliable once he has decided that he wants to do what he is supposed to do, but there is no reliable formula for assuring that he will relinquish when he wants to hold on.

The matter of mutual regulation between parent and child (for fathers have now entered the picture to an extent that was rare in the earlier stage) now faces its severest task. The task is indeed one to challenge the most resourceful and the most calm adult. Firmness is necessary, for the child must be protected against the potential anarchy of his as yet untrained sense of discrimination. Yet the adult must back him up in his wish to "stand on his own feet," lest he be overcome by shame that he has exposed himself foolishly and by doubt in his self-worth. Perhaps the most constructive rule a parent can follow is to forbid only what "really matters" and, in such forbidding, to be clear and consistent.

Shame and doubt are emotions that many primitive peoples and some of the less sophisticated individuals in our own society utilize in training children. Shaming exploits the child's sense of being small. Used to excess it misses its objective and may result in open shamelessness, or, at least, in the child's secret determination to do as he pleases when not observed. Such defiance is a normal, even healthy response to demands that a child consider himself, his body, his needs, or his wishes evil and dirty and that he regard those who pass judgment as infallible. Young delinquents may be produced by this means, and others who are oblivious to the opinion of society.

Those who would guide the growing child wisely, then, will avoid shaming him and avoid causing him to doubt that he is a person of worth. They will be firm and tolerant with him so that he can rejoice in being a person of independence and can grant independence to others. As to detailed procedures, it is impossible to prescribe, not only because we do not know and because every situation is different but also because the kind and degree of autonomy that parents are able to grant their small children depends on feelings about themselves that they derive from society. Just as the child's sense of trust is a reflection of the mother's sturdy and realistic faith, so the child's sense of autonomy is a reflection of the parents' personal dignity. Such appears to be the teaching of the comparative study of cultures.

Personal autonomy, independence of the individual, is an especially outstanding feature of the American way of life. American parents, accordingly, are in a particularly favorable position to transmit the sense of autonomy to their children. They themselves resent being bossed, being pushed around; they maintain that everybody has the right to express his opinion and to be in control of his affairs. More easily than people who live according to an authoritarian pattern, they can appreciate a little child's vigorous desire to assert his independence and they can give him the leeway he needs in order to grow up into the upstanding, look-you-in-the-eye kind of individual that Americans admire.

It is not only in early childhood, however, that this attitude toward growing children must be maintained. As was said at the outset, these components of the healthy personality cannot be established once and for all. The period of life in which they first come into being is the most crucial, it is true. But threats to their maintenance occur throughout life. Not only parents, then, but everybody who has significant contact with children and young people must respect their desire for self-assertion, help them hold it within bounds, and avoid treating them in ways that arouse shame or doubt.

This attitude toward children, toward all people, must be maintained in institutional arrangements as well. Great differences in educational and economic opportunity and in access to the law, discrimination of all kinds are threats to this ingredient of mental health. So, too, may be the over-mechanization of our society, the depersonalization of human relations that is likely to accompany large-scale endeavor of all kinds.

Parents, as well as children, are affected by these matters. In fact, parents' ability to grant children the kind of autonomy Americans think desirable depends in part on the way they are treated as employees and citizens. Throughout, the relation must be such as affirms personal dignity. Much of the shame and doubt aroused in children result from the indignity and uncertainty that are an expression of parents' frustrations in love and work. Special attention must be paid to all these matters, then, if we are to avoid destroying the autonomy that Americans have always set store by.

THE SENSE OF INITIATIVE

Having become sure, for the time being, that he is a person in his own right and having enjoyed that feeling for a year or so, the child of four or five wants to find out what kind of person he can be. To be any particular kind of person, he sees clearly, involves being able to do particular kinds of things. So he observes with keen attention what all manner of interesting adults do (his parents, the milkman, the truck driver, and so on), tries to imitate their behavior, and yearns for a share in their activities.

This is the period of enterprise and imagination, an ebullient, creative period when phantasy substitutes for literal execution of desires and the meagerest equipment provides material for high imaginings. It is a period of intrusive, vigorous learning, learning that leads away from the child's own limitations into future possibilities. There is intrusion into other people's bodies by physical attack, into other people's ears and minds by loud and aggressive talking. There is intrusion into space by vigorous locomotion and intrusion into the unknown by consuming curiosity.

By this age, too, conscience has developed. The child is no longer guided only by outsiders; there is installed within him a voice that comments on his deeds, and warns and threatens. Close attention to the remarks of any child of this age will confirm this statement. Less obvious, however, are experts' observations that children now begin to feel guilty for mere thoughts, for deeds that have been imagined but never executed. This, they say, is the explanation for the characteristic nightmares of this age period and for the over-reaction to slight punishment.

The problem to be worked out in this stage of

development, accordingly, is how to will without too great a sense of guilt. The fortunate outcome of the struggle is a sense of initiative. Failure to win through to that outcome leaves the personality overburdened, and possibly over-restricted by guilt.

It is easy to see how the child's developing sense of initiative may be discouraged. So many of the projects dreamed up at this age are of a kind which cannot be permitted that the child may come to feel he is faced by a universal "No." In addition he finds that many of the projects are impossible of execution and others, even if not forbidden, fail to win the approval of the adults whom he has come to love. Moreover, since he does not always distinguish clearly between actuality and phantasy, his over-zealous conscience may disapprove of even imaginary deeds.

It is very important, therefore, for healthy personality development that much leeway and encouragement be given to the child's show of enterprise and imagination and that punishment be kept at a minimum. Boys and girls at this stage are extraordinarily appreciative of any convincing promise that someday they will be able to do things as well, or maybe better, than father and mother. They enjoy competition (especially if they can win) and insistence on goal; they get great pleasure from conquest. They need numerous examples of the kinds of roles adults assume, and they need a chance to try them out in play.

The ability that is in the making is that of selecting social goals and persevering in the attempt to reach them.

If enterprise and imagination are too greatly curbed, if severe rebukes accompany the frequently necessary denial of permission to carry out desires, a personality may result that is over-constricted. Such a personality cannot live up to its inner capacities for imagination, feeling, or performance, though it may over-compensate by immense activity and find relaxation impossible.

Constriction of personality is a self-imposed constriction, an act of the child's over-zealous conscience. "If I may not do this, I will not even think it," says conscience, "for even thinking it is dangerous." Resentment and bitterness and a vindictive attitude toward the world that forces the restriction may accompany this decision, however, and become unconscious but functioning parts of the personality. Such, at least, is the warning of psychiatrists who have learned to know the inmost feelings of emotionally handicapped children and adults.

This developmental stage has great assets as well as great dangers. At no time in life is the individual more ready to learn avidly and quickly, to

become big in the sense of sharing obligation and performance. If during this preschool period the child can get some sense of the various roles and functions that he can perform as an adult, he will be ready to progress joyfully to the next stage, in which he will find pleasurable accomplishment in activities less fraught with phantasy and fear.

There is a lesson in this for later periods of personality development as well. As has been said before, these conflicts that come to a head at particular periods of a child's life are not settled once and for all. The sense of initiative, then, is one that must be continually fostered, and great care must be taken that youngsters and young people do not have to feel guilty for having dared to dream.

Just as we Americans prize autonomy, so too do we prize initiative; in fact, we regard it as the cornerstone of our economic system. There is much in the present industrial and political mode of life that may discourage initiative, that may make a young person think he had best pull in his horns. What these tendencies are and what they may do to youngsters and to their parents, who too must feel free if they are to cultivate the sense of initiative in their children, is a subject that warrants much serious discussion.

THE SENSE OF ACCOMPLISHMENT

The three stages so far described probably are the most important for personality development. With a sense of trust, a sense of autonomy, and a sense of initiative achieved, progress through the later stages is pretty well assured. Whether this is because children who have a good environment in their early years are likely to continue to be so favored, or whether it is because they have attained such strength of personality that they can successfully handle later difficulties, research has not yet made clear. We do know that nearly all children who get a good start continue to develop very well, and we know that some of those who start off poorly continue to be handicapped. Observations of this sort seem to support psychological theory in the conclusion that personality is pretty well set by about six years of age. Since, however, some children develop into psychologically healthy adults in spite of a bad start, and since some who start well run into difficulties later, it is clear that much research is needed before this conclusion can be accepted as wholly correct.

To return to the developmental analysis, the fourth stage, which begins somewhere around six years of age and extends over five or six years, has as its achievement what Erikson calls the sense of industry. Perhaps "sense of accomplishment" would make the meaning clearer. At any rate, this is the period in which preoccupation with phantasy subsides, and the child wants to be engaged in real tasks that he can carry through to completion. As with the other developmental stages, there are foreshadowings of this kind of interest long before six years of age. Moreover, in some societies and in some parts of our own society children are trained very early to perform socially useful tasks. The exact age is not the point at issue. What is to be pointed out is that children, after a period characterized by exuberant imagination, want to settle down to learning exactly how to do things and how to do them well.

In contrast to the preceding stages and to the succeeding ones, this stage does not consist of a swing from a violent inner upheaval to a new mastery. Under reasonably favorable circumstances this is a period of calm, steady growth, especially if the problems of the previous stages have been well worked through. Despite its unspectacular character, this is a very important period, for in it is laid a firm basis for responsible citizenship. It is during this period that children acquire not only knowledge and skills that make for good workmanship but also the ability to co-operate and play fair and otherwise follow the rules of the larger social game.

The chief danger of this period is the presence of conditions that may lead to the development of a sense of inadequacy and inferiority. This may be the outcome if the child has not yet achieved a sense of initiative, or if his experiences at home have not prepared him for entering school happily, or if he finds school a place where his previous accomplishments are disregarded or his latent abilities are not challenged. Even with a good start the child may later lapse into discouragement and lack of interest if at home or school his individual needs are overlooked—if too much is expected of him, or if he is made to feel that achievement is beyond his ability.

It is most important for health of personality, therefore, that schools be conducted well, that methods and courses of instruction be such as will give every child the feeling of successful accomplishment. Autobiographies of juvenile delinquents show time and again a boy who hated school—hated the fact that he was marked out as stupid or awkward, as one who was not as good as the rest. Some such boys find in jobs the sense of accomplishment they miss at school and consequently give up their delinquent ways. Others, however, are handicapped in job finding and keeping by the very fact that in school they did not develop the sense of industry; hence they have work failure added to their other insecurities. Nor is delinquency the only or the most likely outcome of lack of success in school. Many children respond in a quieter

way, by passive acceptance of their inferiority. Psychologically they are perhaps even more harmed.

Our Puritan tradition maintains that children will not work except under the spur of competition, so we tend to fear the suggestion that all should succeed. To help children develop a sense of accomplishment does not mean, however, merely giving all of them good marks and passing them on to the next grade. Children need and want real achievement. How to help them secure it, despite differences in native capacity and differences in emotional development, is one of the school's most serious challenges.

School, of course, is not the only place in which children at this stage of development can secure the sense of industry. In work at home there are many opportunities for a child to get a feeling of mastery and worthwhile endeavor. Rural youth groups and their urban counterparts cater to this need, and many recreation programs put as much emphasis on work as on play. School, however, is the legally constituted arrangement for giving instruction to the young, so it is upon teachers that the professional responsibility for helping all children achieve a sense of industry and accomplishment rests.

In addition to aiding personality development in this way, teachers have many opportunities for reconfirming their pupils' sense of trust, autonomy, and initiative or for encouraging its growth in children who have been somewhat hampered by previous life experiences. Teachers cannot work alone, of course, either in aiding a child in the development of new capacities or in strengthening old ones. Jointly with parents and others they can do much, not only for children of already healthy personality but also for many whose development has been handicapped.

THE SENSE OF IDENTITY

With the onset of adolescence another period of personality development begins. As is well known, adolescence is a period of storm and stress for many young people, a period in which previous certainties are questioned and previous continuities no longer relied upon. Physiological changes and rapid physical growth provide the somatic base for the turmoil and indecision. It may be that cultural factors also play a part, for it has been observed that adolescence is less upsetting in some societies than in others.

The central problem of the period is the establishment of a sense of identity. The identity the adolescent seeks to clarify is who he is, what his role in society is to be. Is he a child or is he an adult? Does he have it in him to be someday a husband and father? What is he to be as a worker and an earner of money? Can he feel self-confident in spite of the fact that his race or religion or national background makes him a person some people look down upon? Over all, will he be a success or a failure? By reason of these questions adolescents are sometimes morbidly preoccupied with how they appear in the eyes of others as compared with their own conception of themselves, and with how they can make the roles and skills learned earlier jibe with what is currently in style.

In primitive societies adolescents are perhaps spared these doubts and indecisions. Through initiation rites, often seemingly cruel in character, young people are tested out (and test themselves out) and are then welcomed into a socially recognized age category in which rights and duties and mode of living are clearly defined. In our society there are few rituals or ceremonies that mark the change in status from childhood to youth. For those who have religious affiliations, confirmation, joining the church, may serve this purpose in part, since the young people are thereby admitted, in this one segment of their lives at least, to the company of adults. Such ceremonies serve, in addition, to reaffirm to youth that the universe is trustworthy and stable and that a way of life is clearly laid out.

Graduation ceremonies might play a part in marking a new status were it not that, in present-day America, status is so ill defined. What rules of law and custom exist are too diverse to be of much help. For example, legal regulations governing age of "consent," age at which marriage is permitted, age for leaving school, for driving a car, for joining (or being required to join) the Army or Navy mark no logical progressions in rights and duties. As to custom, there is so much variation in what even families who live next door to each other expect or permit that adolescents, eager to be on their way, are practically forced into standardizing themselves in their search for status. In this they are ably abetted by advertisers and entertainers who seek their patronage, as well as by well-meaning magazine writers who describe in great detail the means by which uniformity can be achieved.

In this urge to find comfort through similarity, adolescents are likely to become stereotyped in behavior and ideals. They tend to form cliques for self-protection and fasten on petty similarities of dress and gesture to assure themselves that they are really somebody. In these cliques they may be intolerant and even cruel toward those they label as different. Unfortunate as such behavior is and not to be condoned, intolerance serves the important purpose of giving the group members at least the negative assurance that there is something they are not.

The danger of this developmental period is self-

diffusion. As Biff puts it in *The Death of a Salesman,* "I just can't take hold, Mom. I can't take hold of some kind of a life." A boy or girl can scarcely help feeling somewhat diffuse when the body changes in size and shape so rapidly, when genital maturity floods body and imagination with forbidden desires, when adult life lies ahead with such a diversity of conflicting possibilities and choices.

Whether this feeling of self-diffusion is fairly easily mastered or whether, in extreme, it leads to delinquency, neurosis or outright psychosis, depends to a considerable extent on what has gone before. If the course of personality development has been a healthy one, a feeling of self-esteem has accrued from the numerous experiences of succeeding in a task and sensing its cultural meaning. Along with this, the child has come to the conviction that he is moving toward an understandable future in which he will have a definite role to play. Adolescence may upset this assurance for a time or to a degree but fairly soon a new integration is achieved, and the boy or girl sees again (and with clearer vision) that he belongs and that he is on his way.

The course is not so easy for adolescents who have not had so fortunate a past or for those whose earlier security is broken by a sudden awareness that as members of minority groups their way of life sets them apart. The former, already unsure of themselves, find their earlier doubt and mistrust reactivated by the physiological and social changes that adolescence brings. The latter, once secure, may feel that they must disavow their past and try to develop an "American" personality.

Much has been learned and written about the adolescent problems of the boys and girls whose early personality development has been impaired. How they can be helped, if their disorders are not too severe, is also fairly well known. The full implications of these findings for parents, teachers, and others who would guide youth are still to be worked out but, even so, there is considerable information.

Less well understood are the difficulties and the ways of helping adolescents who grew up in cultures that are not of the usual run. These boys and girls may have been privileged in having had a childhood in which there was little inhibition of sensual pleasures, and in which development proceeded by easy, unself-conscious stages. For them, difficulties arise if their parents lose trust in themselves or if their teachers apply sudden correctives, or if they themselves reject their past and try to act like the others. The new role of middle-class adolescent if often too hard to play. Delinquency or bizarre behavior marks the failure.

How to reach these boys and girls, how to help

them attain their desire, is a matter not well understood. It is clear, however, that they should not be typed by pat diagnoses and social judgments, for they are ever ready to become the "bums" that they are called. Those who would guide them must understand both the psychology of adolescence and the cultural realities of the day. There is trust to be restored and doubt and guilt and feelings of inferiority to be overcome. The science of how to do this is still pretty much lacking, though here and there teachers, clergymen, probation officers and the like are highly successful in the task.

Hard though it be to achieve, the sense of identity is the individual's only safeguard against the lawlessness of his biological drives and the authority of an over-weening conscience. Loss of identity, loss of the sense that there is some continuity, sameness, and meaning to life, exposes the individual to his childhood conflicts and leads to emotional upsets. This outcome was observed time and again among men hard pressed by the dangers of war. It is clear, then, that if health of personality is to be preserved much attention must be given to assuring that America makes good on its promises to youth.

THE SENSE OF INTIMACY

After the sense of identity, to a greater or less extent, is achieved it becomes possible for the next component of the healthy personality to develop. This is the sense of intimacy, intimacy with persons of the same sex or of the opposite sex or with one's self. The youth who is not fairly sure of his identity shies away from interpersonal relations and is afraid of close communion with himself. The surer he becomes of himself, the more he seeks intimacy, in the form of friendship, love and inspiration.

In view of the early age at which boy and girl attachments are encouraged today, it may seem strange to put the critical period for the development of the sense of intimacy late in adolescence. The explanation is that, on the one hand, sexual intimacy is only one part of what is involved, and, on the other, boy-girl attachments of earlier age periods are likely to be of a somewhat different order. Regarding the latter point, it has been observed by those who know young people well that high-school age boys and girls often use each other's company for an endless verbal examination of what the other thinks, feels, and wants to do. In other words, these attachments are one means of defining one's identity.

In contrast to this use of friendship and companionship, boys and girls late in adolescence usually have need for a kind of fusion with the essence of other people and for a communion with their own inner resources. If, by reason of inadequacies in previous personality development, this sense of intimacy cannot be achieved, the youth may retire into psychological isolation and keep his relations with people on a formal, stereotyped level that is lacking in spontaneity and warmth or he may keep trying again and again to get close to others, only to meet with repeated failure. Under this compulsion he may even marry, but the role of mate is one he can rarely sustain, for the condition of true two-ness is that each individual must first become himself.

In this area of personality development as in the others, cultural factors play a part in sustaining or in discouraging the individual in his development. American culture is unusually successful in encouraging the development of the feelings of independence, initiative, industry, and identity. It is somewhat less successful in the area of intimacy, for the culture's ideal is the subordination of sexuality and sensuality to a life of work, duty, and worship.

Consequently, American adolescents are likely to be unsupported by their parents and to find little confirmation in story or song for their desire to sense intimately the full flavor of the personality of others. In many of them, then, the sense of intimacy does not develop highly and they have difficulty in finding in close personal relations the outlet for tension that they need.

There is some evidence that a change in conventions and customs in this respect is in the making, however. Too abrupt change in any such cultural matter is not to be urged, but it is to be hoped that gradual, frank discussion can bring about gradual alteration in attitude and overcome the dangers inherent in the traditional rigidity.

THE PARENTAL SENSE

"Parental sense" designates somewhat the same capacity as that implied in the words, creativity or productivity. The individual has normally come to adulthood before this sense can develop fully.

The parental sense is indicated most clearly by interest in producing and caring for children of one's own. It may also be exhibited in relation to other people's children or by a parental kind of responsibility toward the products of creative activity of other sorts. The mere desire for or possession of children does not indicate that this component of the healthy personality has developed. In fact, many parents who bring their children to child guidance clinics are found not to have reached this stage of personality development.

The essential element is the desire to nourish and nurture what has been produced. It is the ability to regard one's children as a trust of the community, rather than as extensions of one's own personality or merely as beings that one happens to live with.

Failure to develop this component of the healthy personality often results in a condition which has not been adequately categorized clinically. Although a true sense of intimacy has not developed, the individual may obsessively seek companionship. There is something of egotism in this as in his other activities, a kind of self-absorption. The individual is inclined to treat himself as a child and to be rivalrous with his children, if he has any. He indulges himself, expects to be indulged, and in general behaves in an infantile or immature manner.

There are both individual and social explanations of the failure to develop an adequate parental sense. Individually, the explanation may be found in the inadequate development of the personality components previously described. In some people this failure goes far back. Because of unfortunate experiences in childhood they did not arrive at a firm sense of trust, autonomy, and the rest. In others it is only inadequacies in later stages, especially in the development of the sense of intimacy, that are at fault.

Socially, as has been suggested throughout this analysis, healthy personality development depends upon the culture's ideals and upon the economic arrangements of the society. In order that most people may develop fully the sense of being a parent, the role of parent, both mother and father, must be a respected one in the society. Giving must rank higher than getting, and loving than being loved. The economy must be such that the future can be depended upon and each person can feel assured that he has a meaningful and respected part to play. Only so can most individuals afford to renounce selfish aims and derive much of their satisfaction from rearing children.

The Sense of Integrity

The final component of the healthy personality is the sense of integrity. In every culture the dominant ideals, honor, courage, faith, purity, grace, fairness, self-discipline, become at this stage the core of the healthy personality's integration. The individual, in Erikson's words, "becomes able to accept his individual life cycle and the people who have become significant to it as meaningful within the segment of history in which he lives."

To continue Erikson's description, "Integrity thus means a new and different love of one's parents, free of the wish that they should have been different, and an acceptance of the fact that one's life is one's own responsibility. It is a sense of comradeship with men and women of distant times and of different pursuits, who have created orders and objects and sayings conveying human dignity and love. Although aware of the relativity of all the various life styles that have given meaning to human striving, the possessor of integrity is ready to defend the dignity of his own life style against all physical and economic threats. For he knows that, for him, all human dignity stands or falls with the one style of integrity of which he partakes."

The adult who lacks integrity in this sense may wish that he could live life again. He feels that if at one time he had made a different decision he could have been a different person and his ventures would have been successful. He fears death and cannot accept his one and only life cycle as the ultimate of life. In the extreme, he experiences disgust and despair. Despair expresses the feeling that time is too short to try out new roads to integrity. Disgust is a means of hiding the despair, a chronic, contemptuous displeasure with the way life is run. As with the dangers and the solutions of previous periods, doubt and despair are not difficulties that are overcome once and for all, nor is integrity so achieved. Most people fluctuate between the two extremes. Most, also, at no point, either attain to the heights of unalloyed integrity or fall to the depths of complete disgust and despair.

Even in adulthood a reasonably healthy personality is sometimes secured in spite of previous misfortunes in the developmental sequence. New sources of trust may be found. Fortunate events and circumstances may aid the individual in his struggle to feel autonomous. Imagination and initiative may be spurred by new responsibilities, and feelings of inferiority be overcome by successful achievement. Even late in life an individual may arrive at a true sense of who he is and what he has to do and may be able to win through to a feeling of intimacy with others and to joy in producing and giving.

Evidence of such changes is found in the case records of psychiatrists and social workers. Common sense observation attests that similar changes in health of personality are sometimes accomplished without benefit of any form of psychotherapy. Much remains to be learned about this, however, especially about how life itself may serve as therapeusis.

For the healthy personality development of children and youth it is necessary that a large proportion of adults attain a sense of integrity to a considerable degree. Not only parents but all who deal with children have need of this quality if they are to help children maintain the feeling that the universe is dependable and trustworthy. Integrity is relatively easily attained and sustained when the culture itself gives support, when a meaning to life is clearly spelled out in tradition and ceremony, and roles are clearly defined. Our culture, with its rapidly changing technology and its diversity of value standards, leaves much for the individual to work out for himself. In the American dream, however, and the Judaeo-Christian tradition on which it is based there are values and ideals aplenty. In the interest of the welfare of children and youth, in order that a generation of happy individuals and responsible citizens be reared, it is highly important that these values and ideals be brought into prominence and that the promise of American life be kept.

39

Competence and the Psychosexual Stages of Development

Robert W. White

Robert W. White, Professor Emeritus at Harvard University, is the author of the widely used text The Abnormal Personality *(Ronald, 3rd ed., 1964). In the following classic article he comments on Erikson's elaboration of Freud's developmental stages. He suggests a new motivational dimension —competence—that he would add to the body of theory about ego psychology. Many lines of evidence have been brought to bear in support of this concept.*

The purpose of this paper is to reconsider a part of psychoanalytic theory, the part that deals with stages of emotional development. It will be necessary first, however, to show why I think it important to look again at a theory that has survived nearly half a century of critical onslaught and that enjoys enduring high esteem among clinicians. This will require a short exposition of the concept of competence and of certain related concepts which I have discussed at length elsewhere (1959). As you will see, my use of these concepts puts me at variance with theories that make drive the necessary condition for activity and learning; at variance, therefore, with Freud's theory of instincts. The concept of competence, moreover, leads to an idea of the ego that is different from the one we usually

find in discussions of psychosexual stages. Freud's theory of these stages undoubtedly occupies a secure historical position. It will stand in the history of thought as an astonishing first approximation to a theory of growth in its dynamic aspects. Nevertheless, I believe that the time has come when its continued use will only block further insights. The theory that illuminated us all as a first approximation may only hinder us in reaching those closer approximations that always mark the forward steps in a scientific pilgrimage.

In broadest outline, Freud's theory is that the most important features of childhood development, the ones that are fateful for emotional well-being and for the shape of personality, have their motive power in sexual energy or libido. Conceiving sexuality broadly to include the obtaining of pleasure from various zones of the body, he postulated a maturational sequence whereby first the mouth, then the anal zone, finally the genitals become the dominant source of libidinal gratification. Aggressive impulses, fused with libidinal ones, enter importantly during the anal stage and from then on, but the movement from one stage to another is determined biologically by the sequence of libidinal changes. The latency period * and the final genital stage likewise come into existence through developments strictly in the sphere of sexual energy. Thus it is possible to speak of psychosexual stages, and Freud intended the double adjective to be taken quite literally. It is libido, he said, that makes demands upon the mind, that calls forth psychic activity, that constitutes the motivating force behind the development of the mental apparatus (Freud, 1905, 1908, 1913, 1923).

The great virtue of this theory lies, of course, in its gathering and ordering of the confusingly diverse facts of development. For the first three and the last stages it provides us with a model or prototype of behavior: the infant at the breast, the child on the toilet, the phallic child concerned about genital impulses toward family members, the physically mature adult in the heterosexual relation. It tells us, moreover, that these prototypes are truly basic, that events in these situations are really the

---

* *Latency period*—The period of life corresponding roughly to the kindergarten and elementary school years when, in the psychoanalytic conception, children have gained control of—or are less preoccupied than formerly with—their body-pleasure needs and primitive impulsiveness. Oral, anal, and sexual interests are said to be less evident or more disguised, i.e., to be relatively "latent," remaining so until the resurgence of sexuality in adolescence.—EDITOR

---

most important things that happen, so that if we know just these aspects of a person's history we know all that counts. Each prototype involves not only libidinal and aggressive energies but also frustrations, anxieties, defenses, ego developments, and relations with other people. But all these other things are brought to pass by the instincts, and we are thus permitted to place them in a subordinate relation to the central libidinal events. The theory thus achieves a heroic simplification. Right or wrong, it rescued us historically from a tangled mass of facts and made it possible for the first time to think coherently about emotional development.

Freud's ideas on this subject were completed nearly forty years ago. His ideas concerning the libido itself, a highly mobile and general source of energy, look anything but plausible in the light of recent research on motivation. Many psychoanalysts, however, retain the libido model as a working tool, finding that it greatly helps them to understand their patients' problems. Other workers have proposed more or less extensive revisions in the theory of development. In the writings of Horney (1939), Thompson (1950), and Fromm (1947), for instance, emphasis is shifted sharply from instinctual roots to human relations, especially those between child and parents. These neo-Freudians treat motivation in an offhand, pluralistic way, with perhaps special accent on security and anxiety. Development really turns, they believe, on a series of crises in parent-child relations, crises which arise because the parents, acting both for themselves and for the culture, make successive demands upon the infant that put the relation under strain. The libido model is thus displaced in favor of an interpersonal model.

One might suppose that this change of model would sweep away the prototypes provided by psychosexual theory. But the fact is that only Sullivan (1953) has seriously attempted to revise the scheme of crises in strictly interpersonal terms. With most of the revisionists the oral, anal, phallic, and genital prototypes live on, either quite literally or in such guises as "neurotic trends" and "character orientations." The familiar stages, no longer libidinal, are still considered to be crucial. This situation is most clearly recognized by Silverberg (1952), who translates Freud's stages into *"areas of experience . . .* presented to the children of western civilization by parents performing the task of acculturating their offspring." Each area has its typical problem: deprivation in the oral area; obedience, conformity, and rebelliousness in the anal; rivalry and genitality in the phallic area. It is thus contended that the prototypes originally provided by libido theory are adequate models for the crucial events in the child's interpersonal develop-

ment. Feeding, toilet training, and the Oedipal triangle are still the fateful battlefields of growth.

The thesis of this paper can be set forth at this point in the form of two propositions. I shall contend, first, that *the child's emotional development cannot be adequately conceptualized by an exclusive libido model,* no matter how liberally we interpret this concept. Second, I shall try to show that *when the prototypes derived from libido theory are translated into interpersonal terms they still do not constitute adequate models for development.* The best of these prototypes is undoubtedly the feeding child of the oral stage, who cuts a prominent figure even in Sullivan's revision, but from then on the models simply miss part of the significant problems of growth. In particular they fail to embody the development of competence, and they tend to direct attention away from certain crises in the growth of the child's sense of competence. This weakness is attested most eloquently by the lack of a clear-cut model for the latency period, when competence is a central theme. What is needed, I shall argue, is a clearly conceived *competence model* that can be used throughout the stages. Sexual and interpersonal models will be needed too, but we can never do justice to emotional development until we work up a competence model to put beside them.

COMPETENCE AND SENSE OF COMPETENCE

By presenting my theme in this way I have placed a great burden on the word "competence," and I must now give this concept a fuller introduction. Let me say at the outset that it is not something I have invented. It has been distilled from the writings of a great many workers in animal psychology, child development, research on personality, and psychopathology—workers whose only common quality is a certain disenchantment with prevailing concepts of drive. It is a way of saying what I believe many voices have been saying, especially during the last twenty years. Among those who have moved in this direction, it seems to me, are Erikson, Hartmann, and other workers who are trying to carry psychoanalytic ego psychology forward from the point at which Freud left it. I am therefore not trying to promote a novel idea, but rather to find suitable expression for a concept which, suppressed for a time by the immensely popular drive theories, has lately begun to throw out restless derivatives in every direction.

Competence means fitness or ability. The competence of an organism means its fitness or ability to carry on those transactions with the environment which result in its maintaining itself, growing, and flourishing. Some parts of the environment must if possible be fought off, but other parts can safely be enjoyed, and still others can be ingested and transformed into materials for self-maintenance and growth. Some organisms are born more or less fully equipped with patterns of behavior that produce effective interactions with favorable surroundings. This is not the case with the higher animals, least of all with man, who has to learn almost everything that is useful in dealing with his world, yet who immeasurably surpasses all other living creatures in his ultimate ability to subdue and transform the environment to his own use. Man's prowess as a learner has long been an object of wonder. How does he do it, and when does he get it all done?

Theories in which drive is the central motivational concept deal quite simply with this problem. Drives arise from lacks and deficits. They are powerful and persistent internal stimuli which arouse the organism from homeostatic bliss and promote activities that ultimately eliminate the deficit, thus reducing the drive. Reduction of drive supplies the selective principle whereby patterns of behavior are retained or discarded. Our knowledge of the world and our competence in dealing with it are thus acquired in the course of satisfying our constantly recurring needs. We learn what helps us to reduce drives.

There have recently been some startling departures from this orthodoxy—not, as one might suppose, among soft-headed students of personality, but in the very heartland of hardheadedness, the animal laboratory. In a series of experiments Sheffield and others (1950, 1951, 1954) have shown that instrumental learning can take place without drive reduction, indeed under circumstances where one can suppose only that drive level is being increased. Olds and Milner (1954) have found a connection between reinforcement and the electrical stimulation of certain areas of the brain. A whole series of workers, including Harlow (1953), Butler (1958), Montgomery (1954), Berlyne (1950), and Myers and Miller (1954), have pointed out that animals show persistent tendencies toward activity, exploration, and manipulation even when all known primary drives have been satiated. Clearly the original drive model, based on hunger and other internal deficits, stands in need of extensive revision.

One way of accomplishing this revision is to postulate new drives not hitherto included in the list. In addition to hunger, sex, and the avoidance of pain we must attribute an exploratory drive and perhaps an activity drive to the higher animals, even a manipulative drive to those forms that have free use of the forelimbs. These new drives are like the older ones, it is argued, in that they provoke activity and lead to the reinforcement of instrumental learning. I find myself unable to climb aboard this drive bandwagon because I am so impressed by the differences between the old and new drives. Exploration and manipulation have nothing to do with deficits, they appear to arise in the nervous system without visceral stimulation, and they produce instrumental learning without any sign of consummatory response or drive reduction. Call them drives if you are fixated on that term, but remember that in doing so you have destroyed the original conception of drive, including Freud's conception of the instincts. Remember that you are separating drives from visceral deficits and somatic cravings, so that hunger and sex must be treated as special cases rather than as prototypes for the whole idea. But if you do remember these things, what good are you getting out of the concept of drive? I prefer to leave the word in its excellent original meaning so that we can look with a fresh eye at the adaptive significance of activity, manipulation, and exploration.

The theory that we learn what helps us to reduce our viscerogenic drives will not stand up if we stop to consider the whole range of what a child must learn in order to deal effectively with his surroundings. He has much to learn about visual forms, about grasping and letting go, about the coordination of hand and eye. He must work out the difficult problem of the constancy of objects. He must put together an increasingly varied repertory of skilled acts such as locomotion and the use of words. He must learn many facts about his world, building up a cognitive map that will afford guidance and structure for his behavior. It is not hard to see the biological advantage of an arrangement whereby these many learnings can get under way before they are needed as instruments for drive reduction or for safety. An animal that has thoroughly explored its environment stands a better chance of escaping from a sudden enemy or satisfying a gnawing hunger than one that merely dozes in the sun when its homeostatic crises are past. Seen in this light, the many hours that infants and children spend in play are by no means wasted or merely recuperative in nature. Play may be fun, but it is also a serious business in childhood. During these hours the child steadily builds up his competence in dealing with the environment.

Careful study of exploratory play, even in the first year of life, shows it to have the characteristics of directedness, selectivity, and persistence. Piaget's observations (1952) make it plain that the child seeks opportunities to investigate his surroundings and will go to no little trouble to find them. My proposal is that activity, manipulation, and exploration, which are all pretty much of a piece in the infant, be considered together as aspects of competence, and that for the present we assume that one general motivational principle lies behind them. The word I have suggested for this motive is *effectance* because its most characteristic feature is seen in the production of effects upon the environment. At first these effects may consist of any changes in sensory input that follow upon activity or exertion, but before long the child becomes able to intend particular changes and to be content only with these. The experience that goes with producing such changes I have designated as the *feeling of efficacy*. Effectance is to be conceived as a neurogenic motive, in contrast to a viscerogenic one. It can be informally described as what the sensori-neuromuscular system wants to do when it is not occupied with homeostatic business. Its adaptive significance lies in its promotion of spare-time behavior that leads to an extensive growth of competence, well beyond what could be learned in connection with drive reduction.

This, then, is the new motivational base from which I want to reconsider the stages of psychosexual development. But I must make it clear that my procedure will not consist merely of introducing a neglected motive and fighting for its recognition against the claims of sexuality and aggression. If the problem could be so easily solved, it would have been solved long ago. The difficulty is that effectance does not pursue a separate life. It does not typically come into sharp, decisive conflict with drives. It can be mobilized alone, as in the child's play or in the adult's fascination with puzzles, but it is often mobilized in close connection with other needs. The feeling of efficacy can be experienced alone, but it is often merged with other satisfactions, as when, for example, a campus Don Juan reduces his sexual drive while also congratulating himself on the success of his technique of seduction. Because of this high tendency toward fusion it is not profitable to carry on the analysis of later development in terms of effectance and feelings of efficacy. Competence is built up out of all kinds of interactions with the environment, including those due to effectance alone and those due to much more complex patterns of motives. Our interest from here on will be in *competence* and its very important subjective aspect, which I am calling *sense of competence*. And we shall not find it profitable to look for the sense of competence as if it were a separate thing in personality; rather, we must become aware of the *aspect of competence in a wide variety of actions and experiences*.

Sense of competence can be seen as the cumulative product of one's history of efficacies and inefficacies. It comes to operate in new behavior as a kind of set: we judge whether or not we can jump over a brook or carry out a proposed task. It also comes to be much cherished, so that we feel truly elated at new proofs of our ability and deeply humiliated when we cannot do something we supposed was within our power. The sense of competence thus has strong motivational backing, doubtless from a variety of sources. Its importance in personality will be more readily apparent if we bear in mind that it applies to interactions with people as well as to dealings with the inanimate environment. Just as the child explores his physical surroundings, finding out what he can do with objects and what they will do to him, so he investigates his human environment, learning what he can make people do and what he can expect of them. Sense of social competence may well be the more important of the two, though I think we should beware of the current fashion of discussing personality as if it grew in a physical vacuum where tumbles and bumps, victories of locomotion, and struggles with refractory objects are held to exist only insofar as they elicit social responses. We do not live exclusively in a social environment, but we live there importantly, and it is often harder to develop a stable sense of one's social competence than to know what one can accomplish with material objects.

COMPETENCE AND EGO PSYCHOLOGY

I should like now to indicate the relation between these ideas and some of the recent advances in psychoanalytic ego psychology. As you will see, there is a great deal of similarity when we talk on the level of general concepts. There are also many common implications for the psychosexual stages, though only Erikson has tried to reconsider these stages in a systematic way. . . .

[We omit here some material about writers other than Erikson.]

It is in the work of Erikson (1950, 1959) that one finds the most far-reaching attempt to extend the range of ego psychology. Erikson's eight stages in the development of the ego constitute, it seems to me, a major advance in psychoanalytic theory. For the first time the latency period is given a significance of its own. Likewise for the first time the problems of growth are seen as continuing beyond young adulthood when haply the goal of genital primacy has been achieved. But the most important step is the systematic relating of the child's unfolding capacities to his encounters with the social environment. Erikson sees early development as a process of mutual regulation between child and parents. The child's changing capacities and the parents' changing demands lead to a series of decisive encounters, the outcomes of which are fateful for future growth. Later on, these encounters involve the social environment more broadly conceived; in this way, Erikson achieves the social relatedness that is the virtue of neo-Freudian theories without falling into their vice of losing touch with the biological roots of behavior.

Erikson's description of development is remarkably inclusive. In his concept of zones he retains the essence of libido theory, though with a somewhat altered meaning. With the concept of mutual regulation he draws in the best features of the interpersonal model. With his idea of modes he introduces competence, describing at each stage the motor and cognitive capacities that determine the character of the crisis. Erikson's account therefore seems to have everything the heart could desire. But it has one thing I wish it did not have, namely, an implied close connection between zones and modes which I think can lead only to confusion.

In recasting libido theory Erikson undertakes to avoid the scientific crudeness of Freud's formulation by a generous broadening of the biological base. Zonal sensitivities are but part of the picture; the progression from oral to anal to phallic stages is determined by a general ripening of sensory-motor capacity as a whole. The concept of mode captures these broader possibilities. Thus the oral stage, called "oral-sensory," is dominated by the incorporative mode, which means that everything the infant does, even his visual and tactile exploration, has the character of a taking in of experience. The anal stage, renamed "muscular-anal," represents more advanced prowess in motor and manipulative control. It is dominated by the retentive and eliminative modes, which show themselves alike in bowel functions and in the familiar manipulative sequence characterized by grasping and a little later by letting go and throwing away. Likewise the "locomotor-genital" stage brings to full flower the intrusive mode, which includes "the intrusion into other bodies by physical attack; the intrusion into other people's ears and minds by aggressive talking; the intrusion into space by vigorous locomotion; the intrusion into the unknown by consuming curiosity" (Erikson, 1950, p. 83). Erogenous zones and neuromuscular competence are thus seen as strictly isomorphic, set in the same patterns of interaction with the environment.

My discontent with this idea comes from my belief that in trying to put the stages of development on a broader base Erikson has not sufficiently disengaged himself from the old libidinal prototypes. He wants to assign significance to the growth of competence, but he describes this growth in generalizations carried over directly from the original theory. Incorporation, retention, elimination, and

intrusion precisely describe the zonal impulses demanded by straight libido theory. Erikson then asks us to believe that these modes successively characterize virtually all the important things a young child does in the course of growth. This seems to me rather dubious, and I prefer a different strategy for finding out about it. It seems to me safer to treat visual exploration, manipulation, locomotion, and the many other aspects of competence as functions developing in their own right, more or less autonomously, without any presumed relation to zonal pleasures or presumed similarity to zonal impulses. By using the competence model in this way we can protect ourselves from unwarranted generalizations while yet leaving the facts free to tumble back into the old psychosexual stages if that is how they really look.

Let us proceed to re-examine the stages in the light of what I have said about effectance, feeling of efficacy, competence, and sense of competence, and let us see what happens. . . .

THE FINAL GENITAL STAGE

We come now to the last stage in psychosexual development, the stage at which newly strengthened sexual impulses bring about the possibility of genital primacy. In view of the great length of this paper you will be happy to hear that I shall have few words to say about the final stage. The plot is already clear. A prolonged fifth act would add little to whatever impact it may already have made. Obviously I would have words of praise for the more orthodox description of adolescence as given, for instance, by Anna Freud (1937, 1958), Bernfeld (1938), and Helene Deutsch (1944). Obviously there is great illumination in the treatment of this period as a time of increased instinctual drive and threat to established patterns of ego control. Certainly it is fruitful to look upon some aspects of adolescent behavior as a struggle to maintain and expand one's defenses. You would expect me also to mention some merit in the interpersonal model as developed, for instance, by Sullivan (1953), who described the task of late adolescence as that of establishing "a fully human or mature repertory of interpersonal relations." But then you would predict complaints on my part about the neglect of competence and the failure of the two models to capture whole ranges of behavior that are essential for full understanding. To spell out what you can so easily anticipate would be a bad anticlimax to anything as dramatic as adolescence and genital primacy.

Perhaps the one thing I should do is to indicate the kinds of behavior in adolescence that I consider important, well handled by a competence model, and neglected by libido and interpersonal models. Since the adolescent is reaching adult size, strength, and mental development, the behavior in question lies in the realm of serious accomplishment—serious in the terms either of the youth culture or of adult society. I am referring to the adolescent equivalent of what Erikson calls a *sense of industry* in the latency period, and I see this problem as continuing rather more strongly after puberty than seems to be implied in Erikson's account. No doubt I bring to this judgment an occupational bias different from that of a therapist. My professional life is spent among late adolescents whose sexual problems and social relations have for the most part not overwhelmed them. We talk together about their plans for study, their abilities and limitations, their struggles with materials to be learned and skills to be attained, their occupational leanings, career plans, and concerns about modern society as the scene of their future endeavors. We talk, in other words, mostly about their competence, and I do not believe that understanding is fostered by interpreting these concerns too much as displacements of instinctual drives, defense mechanisms, or interpersonal relations. They are real.

Adolescents today learn how to drive cars. Some of them learn to compete against adult records in sports, occasionally breaking them. Some of them become part of the football, band, and cheerleader complex that plays such an important part in community entertainment. Some of them try their hands at building workable radio sets, at scientific exploration, at editing newspapers, at writing stories and verse, at musical and dramatic performances, at political activity. Some of them with fewer opportunities or talents put their maturing bodies to heavy work or their maturing minds to white-collar office jobs. All this belongs in the sphere of work, and work, as Schilder (1942) so cogently argued, is importantly a phenomenon of competence. These happenings create many crises, many defeats, many victories for the sense of competence. Once again there are large spheres in which the adolescent can be suffering losses or making gains in ego strength. In theorizing about the subject we must not foreclose the possibility that these developments significantly affect what happens in the erotic and interpersonal realms.

I shall say no more about this stage of development except to launch my last complaint against the models bequeathed us by psychosexual theory. The model proffered by libido theory is that of heterosexual relations, and their ideal form is embodied in the concept of genital primacy. It is not argued, of course, that we all successfully become genital primates, but the ideal type serves to indicate the problems of the period. The sexual act itself plays a prominent part in genital primacy, reminding us that Freud's oft-mentioned broadened conception of sex sometimes touched base again in what no one has ever denied to be sexual. In libidinal terms, the regular discharge of genital tensions serves also to drain some of the energy from pregenital tensions, thus making the control and sublimation of the latter an easy problem for the ego. Erikson (1950) prefers "to put it more situationally: the total fact of finding, via the climactic turmoil of the orgasm, a supreme experience of the mutual regulation of two beings in some way breaks the point off the hostilities and potential rages caused by the oppositeness of male and female, of fact and fancy, of love and hate. Satisfactory sex relations thus make sex less obsessive, overcompensation less necessary, sadistic controls superfluous." Erikson's further account of what "the utopia of genitality" should include—mutual trust and a willingness to share lives in the interest of securing a happy development for the children—is something I commend to you all as an uncommonly beautiful statement of what we should aspire to in family life. It is an interpersonal statement as well as a libidinal one. I like it so well that I am sorry to point out that it has only the slightest relation to competence and to that other sphere of human concern—work.

Unfortunately the climactic turmoil of the orgasm is completely the wrong model for work. This is not to say that good sexual relations may not sometimes free a person from gnawing hates and doubts that have interfered with his capacity to work. But the emphasis of the idea of orgastic potency and mutuality is on an essential loss of ego, a drowning of all other considerations in the immense involuntary experience of the sexual relation. He who takes the ego to bed with him will never get a gold star for genital primacy. The orgastic model has virtue for certain human activities requiring a temporary submergence of self, such as inspiration, creative imagination, and thoroughly relaxed play. But it will never do for the serious, stable, lasting concerns of human life, the realm that I am trying to designate as work. This is the sphere in which the ego must always keep a firm hand on the helm.

Work requires a certain constancy of effort. There must be sustained endeavor with control of wayward impulses that distract from the requirements of external reality and social roles. There must be a capacity for persistent return to tasks, sometimes dull in themselves, that form part of the job requirement or that belong in a long-range plan to achieve remote goals. There must be a quality of reliability, so that one keeps promises and lives up to the obligations one has assumed. Even the fashion for being spontaneous and natural, even the bright vision of self-fulfilling work in Fromm's (1955) sane society, even Marcuse's (1955) fantasy of a nonrepressive civilization in which all work becomes libidinal pleasure cannot exorcize the true and somewhat stern nature of reality. And even Ernst Kris (1952), no enemy of psychoanalytic theory, reminded us that artistic creation required, in addition to a phase of inspiration, a second phase characterized by "the experience of purposeful organization and the intent to solve a problem." When we call an artist "merely competent" it is a weak form of praise, but if he were "merely inspired," without a certain rather high minimum of competency, we would never even see or hear his products.

I should like to close with a short coda on the words "merely competent." I particularly do not want to be misunderstood concerning the part to be assigned to competence and the sense of competence in human development. As a simple and sovereign concept it will never do. A person developed wholly along lines of competence, with no dimensions of passion, love, or friendliness, would never qualify for maturity. Competence is not intended to describe such experiences as enjoying food, immersing oneself in a sexual relation, loving children, cherishing friends, being moved by natural beauty or great works of art; nor is it designed to swallow up the problems created by aggression and anxiety. This is what I meant by saying that the competence model must always be used in conjunction with other models that do full justice to such things as hunger, sexuality, and aggression. It may hurt one's desire for logical simplicity to suppose that several models are needed to understand a problem. Yet I think no one can claim a probability that human nature was designed in the interests of logic.

It is my conviction, in short, that Freud's discoveries were of epoch-making importance, that psychoanalytic ego psychology has taken effective steps to fill out some of the undeveloped parts of Freud's theories, and that Erikson in particular has accomplished a synthesis that promises good things for future understanding of the growth of personality. But I also believe that our understanding cannot be rounded out by stretching Freud's concepts in a vain attempt to cover everything, or by calling everything interpersonal as if body and material world did not exist. We should add to the picture a meticulous consideration, at every level, of the growth of the child's capacity both for action and for understanding. We should try to be as shrewd in detecting the vicissitudes of the sense of competence as Freud was with sexuality, ag-

gression, and defense. It is to encourage such a development that I have had so much to say about the concept of competence.

Summary

Even an idea as monumental as Freud's theory of the psychosexual stages of development can come to have an adverse effect upon scientific progress if it is believed too literally too long. Libido theory provided a series of models for critical phases in emotional growth: feeding, toilet training, the Oedipus situation, latency, and the adult heterosexual relation. These models are largely preserved in revisions of Freud, though changed to interpersonal terms, and they continue to dominate the thinking of workers in psychoanalytic ego psychology. In this paper it is maintained that the models are in certain respects inadequate and misleading. In particular, they encourage us to neglect a range of facts which is ordered here under the concept of competence. If these facts are slighted, it is held, there can be little hope of further progress in psychoanalytic ego psychology or in closing the gap between this and other theories of development.

The concept of competence subsumes the whole realm of learned behavior whereby the child comes to deal effectively with his environment. It includes manipulation, locomotion, language, the building of cognitive maps and skilled actions, and the growth of effective behavior in relation to other people. These acquisitions are made by young animals and children partly through exploratory and manipulative play when drives such as hunger and sex are in abeyance. The directed persistence of such behavior warrants the assumption of a motivation independent of drives, here called effectance motivation, which has its immediate satisfaction in a feeling of efficacy and its adaptive significance in the growth of competence. Effectance motivation can be likened to independent ego energies in the psychoanalytic scheme. The child's actual competence and his sense of competence are built up from his history of efficacies and inefficacies, and sense of competence is held to be a crucial element in any psychology of the ego.

It is proposed that libidinal and interpersonal models for critical points in development be supplemented by a competence model. For the oral stage this means taking serious account of the growth of manipulative prowess and experimentation as seen both in the child's many hours of play and in his zeal for self-help in feeding. For the anal stage it means attributing importance to negativism in the sphere of giving and receiving commands, an early crisis in social competence, and to the enormous growth of motility with its constant influence upon self-esteem. Neither development is adequately implied in the anal-erotic model. For the phallic stage it means detecting the consequences of growth in locomotion, linguistic understanding, and imagination; it also means noticing the child's waxing ability to comprehend and try out various social roles, in many of which he receives encouragement. The Oedipus model, with its foreordained inexplicable defeat, cannot be considered typical for the period. During latency the chief developments are in the sphere of competence; this is clear in Erikson's account of the sense of industry and Sullivan's of competition and compromise. For the final genital stage the competence model invites us to take seriously the adolescent's continuing concern with sense of industry and with social competence, problems that confront him with new crises in their own right. The heterosexual relation does not provide an adequate model for all the serious concerns of this stage of life, nor can they be fully conceptualized in terms of instinctual drive and defense.

In short, the competence model is held to supplement in significant ways the models of development derived from psychoanalysis. By directing attention to action and its consequences and to the vicissitudes of the sense of competence, it should help to speed the construction of an adequate ego psychology.

REFERENCES *

BERLYNE, D. E. Novelty and curiosity as determinants of exploratory behavior. *Brit. J. Psychol.*, 1950, *41*, 68–80.

BERNFELD, S. Types of adolescence. *Psychoanal. Quart.*, 1938, *7*, 243–253.

BUTLER, R. A. Exploratory and related behavior: A new trend in animal research. *J. indiv. Psychol.*, 1958, *14*, 111–120.

DEUTSCH, HELENE. *The psychology of women,* Vol. I. New York: Grune & Stratton, 1944.

ERIKSON, E. H. *Childhood and society*. New York: Norton, 1950.

ERIKSON, E. H. Identity and the life cycle: selected papers. *Psychol. Issues*, 1959, Monograph 1.

FREUD, ANNA. *The ego and the mechanisms of defence.* (Trans. by C. Baines.) London: Hogarth, 1937.

FREUD, ANNA. Adolescence. *Psychoanal. Stud. Child,* 1958, *13*, 255–278.

FREUD, S. *Three contributions to the theory of sex.*
(1905). (Trans. by A. A. Brill.) New York and Washington: Nerv. and Ment. Dis. Pub. Co., 1930.

FREUD, S. Character and anal erotism (1908). *Collected papers.* (Trans. under supervision of J. Riviere.) New York: Basic Books, 1959. Vol. II, 45–50.

FREUD, S. The predisposition to obsessional neurosis (1913). *Collected papers.* (Trans. under supervision of J. Riviere.) New York: Basic Books, 1959. Vol. II, 122–131.

FREUD, S. The infantile genital organization of the libido (1923). *Collected papers.* (Trans. under supervision of J. Riviere.) New York: Basic Books, 1959. Vol. II, 244–249.

FROMM, E. *Man for himself.* New York: Rinehart, 1947.

FROMM, E. *The sane society.* New York: Rinehart, 1955.

HARLOW, H. F. Mice, monkeys, men, and motives. *Psychol. Rev.,* 1953, *60*, 23–32.

HORNEY, KAREN. *New ways in psychoanalysis.* New York: Norton, 1939.

KRIS, E. *Psychoanalytic explorations in art.* New York: International Univer. Press, 1952.

MARCUSE, H. *Eros and civilization.* Boston: Beacon Press, 1955.

MONTGOMERY, K. C. The role of the exploratory drive in learning. *J. comp. physiol. Psychol.,* 1954, *47*, 60–64.

MYERS, A. K., AND MILLER, N. E. Failure to find a learned drive based on hunger; evidence for learning motivated by "exploration." *J. comp. physiol. Psychol.,* 1954, *47*, 428–436.

OLDS, J., AND MILNER, P. Positive reinforcement produced by electrical stimulation of septal area and other regions of rat brain. *J. comp. physiol. Psychol.,* 1954, *47*, 419–427.

PIAGET, J. *The origins of intelligence in children.* (Trans. by M. Cook.) New York: International Univer. Press, 1952.

SCHILDER, P. *Goals and desires of men.* New York: Columbia Univer. Press, 1942.

SHEFFIELD, F. D., AND ROBY, T. B. Reward value of a non-nutritive sweet taste. *J. comp. physiol. Psychol.,* 1950, *43*, 471–481.

SHEFFIELD, F. D., ROBY, T. B., AND CAMPBELL, B. A. Drive reduction vs. consummatory behavior as determinants of reinforcement. *J. comp. physiol. Psychol.,* 1954, *47*, 349–354.

SHEFFIELD, F. D., WULFF, J. J., AND BACKER, R. Reward value of copulation without sex drive reduction. *J. comp. physiol. Psychol.,* 1951, *44*, 3–8.

SILVERBERG, W. V. *Childhood experience and personal destiny.* New York: Springer, 1952.

SULLIVAN, H. S. *The interpersonal theory of psychiatry.* New York: Norton, 1953.

THOMPSON, C. *Psychoanalysis: evolution and development.* New York: Hermitage, 1950.

WHITE, R. W. Motivation reconsidered: The concept of competence. *Psychol. Rev.,* 1959, *66*, 297–333.

---

* For a more extensive list of references, see original paper. —EDITOR

40

Learning Capacities
of the Human Infant [1]

LEWIS P. LIPSITT [2]

This article describes a program of research in infant behavior. Infancy, an age period that received very little attention for many years, is now a topic of great interest and concern. Lewis Lipsitt, professor of psychology at Brown University, has an extensive laboratory in a large maternity hospital in Providence, Rhode Island. The recent advances in technology have been fully utilized to insure the reliability of his experimental methods.

INTRODUCTION

HISTORICAL ORIENTATION

The field of child development has traditionally relied on psychometric or "maturity-measuring" techniques. Though these are founded on the use of morphological models borrowed from structural biology (Gesell, 1954; Harris, 1957), they have been used even for assessing the behavioural properties of the young organism and for seeking

principles explaining the origins of later behaviour in the history of the organism (Lipsitt, 1963). It has been implicitly assumed that intellectual endowment is genetically determined and essentially constant; proper attention has not been paid to the behavioural consequences of experiential precursors. These attitudes and assumptions have almost pre-empted the search for, and discovery of, the special capacities of infants to receive sensory stimulation in all modalities and to learn. The studies of Pratt (1954), Irwin (1943), and Marquis (1931, 1941) were notable exceptions.

No thoughtful observer or researcher of infant behaviour would deny the obvious fact that some behavioural differences are related to age. Nevertheless the human newborn can no longer be regarded as a spinal creature who can have no capacity for learning or cognitive activity because of absence or reduction of myelination or cerebral convolutions (Elkonin, 1957).

The normal human infant shows an exceptional talent for differential responding, conditioning, and discrimination learning. These are often achieved in a matter of minutes, particularly when the responses are relevant to the maintenance of life, or to evolutionary selection, or when they provide opportunity to explore the environment. I hold no brief for any particular mode of learning or for any special theoretical model for the understanding of specific learning effects that may be induced in the immature organism. A constricted view of the possible mechanisms whereby experimental circumstances may work their wonders would limit the accumulation of knowledge in this area, as did the premature conclusion that the structural properties of the immature organism could not possibly permit learning to occur. It would be equally senseless to allow a monolithic learning-theory orientation to shut off possible lines of inquiry as it was to permit the tyranny of an exclusive developmental-structural dogma. Indeed, it may well be that we are only beginning to understand some of the very special learning skills of the young human (Hinde, 1966).

It should no longer surprise us that organisms do not inevitably get better and better at whatever they do with increasing age. Of course there has always been acceptance of a statute of limitations for the aged in this connection; but apologists have generally considered the frailties of age to be the result of a superimposition of disease and deformity rather than a "true" developmental effect. The effectiveness of some types of stimulation, and the organism's capacity for response, become dimin-

[1] The research reported here and the writing of the present paper were supported largely by a grant to the author from the U.S. Public Health Service, National Institutes of Health (Grant No. HD 03911).

[2] The author expresses his gratitude to the staff of Providence Lying-In Hospital, where so much of the newborn research reported here has been carried out.

Lewis P. Lipsitt, "Learning capacities of the human infant," in *Brain and Early Behavior: Development in the Fetus and Infant*, R. J. Robinson, ed. New York: Academic Press, 1969, 227–249. Reprinted with abridgement by permission.

ished in many different ways with increasing age; with respect to some human attributes the developmental decline or social destruction of a response may begin at birth. The human newborn is as good at the palmar grasp, at the Babkin response, at rooting, and even at sucking soon after birth as he will ever be again. [The Babkin response is an inborn rooting reflex in which the mouth opens in response to pressure on the palm.—EDITOR] Some of the body's glands decrease proportionally in size from birth on, while others increase and then decrease in both size and function. So, too, may certain behavioural capacities of the "growing" organism either "atrophy" or wax then wane with increasing age. It is perhaps time for someone to present the thesis that the newborn human creature is about as competent a learning organism as he can become.

RESEARCH PROGRAMME

For the past decade, I have been fortunate to have a laboratory for sensory assessment and conditioning in one of the larger U.S. maternity hospitals. Many of the infants first studied during the newborn period, along with small populations of infants from private paediatric practices, have been available subsequently for behaviour studies at various intervals throughout the first year. The eventual aim of this research programme is to document longitudinal changes (or constancies) in the learning and sensory properties of the child at least through the first year of life. The success of such studies depends heavily upon the prior development of appropriately reliable experimental stimulation techniques and upon the initial documentation of behaviour-phenomena worth pursuing across an extensive age-span. For these reasons, and because longitudinal data-cells require more time to fill, the results available thus far are concerned predominantly with the behaviours that occur at specific young ages and with the stimulating conditions necessary to elicit them. Although our concern is with processes or changes in behaviour occurring over periods of time or with repetitive stimulation, the time courses to which I shall refer here will, with two exceptions, be of relatively short duration.

. . .

BRIEF REVIEW OF PREVIOUS FINDINGS

As a background for the present paper, some of the previous studies carried out in these laboratories and reported in detail elsewhere will first be reviewed. Several studies (Lipsitt, 1967; Engen and Lipsitt, 1965; Engen, Lipsitt, and Kaye, 1963)

have clearly demonstrated that habituation occurs in the human newborn; repetitive presentation of stimulation of moderate intensity, in this case odorants, produces response decrement over successive trials, and subsequent recovery of response whether to totally new odorants or to olfactory stimuli which were components of previously habituated compounds. Such behaviour suggests that the human newborn processes information in a rather sophisticated way, suppressing response to non-threatening stimulus signals but alerting once again if a novel stimulus, even in the same sensory modality, should be introduced suddenly. Moreover, the phenomenon of response recovery to components of previously habituated compounds indicates that some central nervous system mechanism is probably involved in the discrimination, since peripheral factors and fatigue are ruled out by the technique.

With respect to sucking behaviour, it has been established that the human newborn is keenly sensitive to momentary differences in intraoral stimulation and that reinforcing circumstances associated with the sucking act may increase (or diminish) sucking-response frequency. In a study (Lipsitt and Kaye, 1965) which compared the sucking behaviour of infants who were administered either nipple, tube, or nipple-tube-alternation sequences of trials, it was shown that the sucking rate is greater with an ordinary nipple than with a less flexible and less rounded tube, that nipple-sucking is adversely affected by the previous administration of the tube, and that tube-sucking is made easier by previous nipple-sucking. The evidence of these lasting effects of previous experience brings us closer to an understanding of the role of prior experience in the determination of infants' behaviour.

. . .

The work of our laboratory has recently been increasingly concerned with the exploration of conditioning techniques using responses of the infant that may be presumed to have functional significance for the survival of the organism and for the maximization of exploratory arousal. The human infant seems capable of making many responses which have the consequence of increasing stimulus input. The assimilation of such stimulus input often results in arousing still further "searching" activity. When this relationship between the organism and the environment has progressed to a maximum (to be determined for each subject, for each type of stimulus, and for various reinforcing conditions) the stimulation loop is often "turned off" by the subject who now manifests satiation, fatigue, or habituation. This cycle of events can perhaps be best understood in operant behavioural terms, but it must be acknowledged, if not insisted, that respondent behaviour has an important role in the cycle.

RECENT STUDIES

THE NEWBORN INFANT

Conditioned head-turning. Elaborating upon techniques earlier reported by Papoušek (1959, 1960, 1961), Siqueland and Lipsitt (1966) used both tactile stimulation and nutritive reinforcement to condition head-turning in neonates. The general procedure requires tactile stimulation of the infant at the corner of the mouth, a procedure that characteristically elicits ipsilateral head-turning in 25–35 per cent of the trials prior to conditioning. Such "rooting" is usually considered to be respondent behaviour, since it requires a specific eliciting stimulus. The procedure used in these studies involved the systematic reinforcement of the respondent as if it were an operant or instrumental behaviour. Thus, on conditioning trials in which the infant turned his head appropriately in response to the tactile stimulus, a nipple was quickly placed in the baby's mouth, allowing it to suck and to be nutritively reinforced. In all these studies, auditory stimuli preceded and occurred simultaneously with the tactile stimulus, in order (1) to determine whether classically-conditioned anticipatory head-turning might increase in frequency over conditioning trials, and (2) to afford an opportunity to study discriminative behaviour as well as non-differential conditioning behaviour.

In our first study the procedure was to sound a buzzer for 5 seconds, during the latter half of which the left cheek of the subject was stroked. If the infant responded ipsilaterally, dextrose was administered for 2 seconds. Eighteen subjects in the second and third days of life received thirty trials of conditioning, with 30-second inter-trial intervals, while another 18 matched control subjects received the same programme of stimulation, subject for subject, but were given the dextrose, on appropriate trials, 8–10 seconds after termination of the tactile stimulus. Response to the tactile stimulus increased strikingly in the experimental group— from approximately 30 per cent to 80 per cent— while the matched control group merely declined in the frequency of ipsilateral head-turning.

In an elaboration of the technique, two groups of infants 2–4 days old were studied to see whether differential reinforcement for two responses, left versus right head-turning, would lead to discriminative responding. Now two auditory stimuli were used, a tone and the buzzer, and trials were alternated between the left and the right cheeks, the buzzer being associated with touch to one side and tone with touch to the other. The tone and buzzer were each the positive stimulus for a random half of the subjects, and a basal assessment period enabled application of the positive stimulus to the less favoured head-turning side. For the 20 experimental subjects, reinforcement was presented after ipsilateral turns to the positive stimulus (R^{S+}), but not after turns to the negative stimulus (R^{S-}). Twenty control subjects received the same total number of reinforcements, subject for subject, but dextrose reinforcement was presented 8–10 seconds after tactile stimulation and was not contingent upon head-turning. Learning was reflected in relative shifts in percentages of R^{S+} and R^{S-} over trials. The shift occurred in the experimental group, which rose in R^{S+} responding from approximately 20 per cent to 75 per cent, while the control group declined from 20 per cent. Learned differentiation of head-turning behaviour in the newborn was thus substantiated.

Next, in an attempt to induce a still more difficult differentiation, the two auditory stimuli served as positive and negative cues for reinforcement at one side only. Sixteen infants, aged 48 to 116 hours, were divided into two groups: for one the tone was positive and the buzzer negative, while for the other the designations were reversed. Turns to right-sided stimulation in the presence of one auditory stimulus were reinforced, while right turns in the presence of the other auditory stimulus were not. After original training $S+$ became $S-$, and $S-$ became $S+$ in each group. As previously, stimulus presentations occurred on a 30-second inter-trial interval basis, and tactile stimulation overlapped the last half of the tone or buzzer. Under such conditions, responding to the positive stimulus increased sharply, from approximately 25 per cent to 70 per cent, while response to the negative stimulus changed negligibly. Upon reversal of the stimulating conditions, the expected shift in behaviour was such that the previously negative and now positive stimulus eventually generated reliably more ipsilateral responses than the previously positive and now negative stimulus.

In none of these three studies did conditioned subjects demonstrate a reliable increase in classical anticipatory responding during the sound-stimulus presentations, but it is apparent from the differential behaviour established in the third study that the auditory stimuli had discriminative signal functions.

Free-operant head-turning. In a further study of reinforcement patterns and extinction in human newborns Siqueland (1968) demonstrated large differences in free-operant head-turning behaviour, during extinction, as a function of differences in reinforcement schedules during acquisition. An apparatus for the continuous polygraphic monitoring of head-turning activity was used, and a 10° head-turn arc in either direction was adopted as the required operant. Three groups of eight newborns each in the third and fourth days of life were given 5-second presentations of a non-nutritive nipple as reinforcement. Conditioning procedures involved a 3-minute baseline period, 25 reinforcements, a 5-minute extinction period, 15 additional reinforcements, and a second extinction period of 3 minutes. Training in one group was on a continuous (100 per cent) schedule, and a Ratio group received one reinforcement for every two responses early in learning and one for every three responses later. A third group received reinforcement for each 20-second period in which a head movement was *not* made (that is, a 10° movement delayed reinforcement for 20 seconds). The groups were thus equated on total number of reinforcements, prior to each extinction period, while their patterns of reinforcement varied.

The analysis of data was concerned with extinction behaviour. It is very clear that the three groups varied greatly in frequency of head-turns during both of the extinction conditions. The Ratio group gave reliably more responses than the Continuous Reinforcement group, and the third group produced the fewest responses. In fact, reliable increases in responding over the course of extinction were evidenced by the third group, as would be expected by the fact that for this group conditioning involved the suppression of head-turns.

While the Siqueland-Lipsitt studies demonstrated strong learning effects in a situation involving nutritive reinforcement, the Siqueland study shows very clearly that opportunity to suck non-nutritively may also serve as a powerful reinforcing event. This study is also the first clear demonstration of free operant conditioning in a situation that does not rely on eliciting stimulation as in the Papoušek and the Siqueland-Lipsitt studies.

Temporal conditioning. Marquis (1941) has shown that human infants within the first 10 days of life are capable of adjusting their activity patterns and sleep-waking cycles (Irwin, 1930) to temporally controlled feeding schedules. To explore the capacity of the neonate for short-term temporal conditioning Ambrose and Lipsitt (unpublished) studied temporal responsivity under three different modes of stimulation: auditory, vestibular, and olfactory. Two methods were used to assess whether temporal conditioning occurred: (1) presentation of mock or test trials after a series of stimulations to determine whether responses would occur at the accustomed time of stimulus presentation, and (2) examination of increased responding, over training trials, to determine whether there is an increased tendency for anticipatory responses to be made in the interval immediately preceding the customary stimulus presentation time. To provide vestibular stimulation Ambrose designed a motor-driven baby rocker which automatically moves the baby up and down through an excursion of 3 inches at controlled rates of speed. Besides the vestibular stimulation of rocking, the infants in the present study received olfactory stimulation from anise oil on a cotton-swab, and sound stimulation produced by dropping a pegged wooden ball through a constant distance to a wooden surface. The auditory stimulus was an 87-dB clack of noise, of essentially momentary duration, while the odorant presentation and rocking stimulation lasted 5 seconds on each trial. Three groups, each of five infants, received the stimulus types in different orders: (1) sound, odorant, rocking, (2) odorant, sound, rocking, and (3) rocking, sound, odorant. Each of the three stimuli was presented to each infant on eight successive occasions, then was followed by three "mock" trials during which the polygraph record was marked at the regular 30-second interval (the interval between all stimulations). No stimulation whatever was administered on mock trials.

The analysis of responding was concerned with respiration, heart rate, and motility, the latter represented in either the electromyographic or stabilimetric records (these being almost perfectly correlated). The response of greatest concern was that occurring during the nine mock trials. The period for response-assessment was a 5-second unit of time. The first such period began 30 seconds after the previous stimulus presentation and the subsequent ones were at 30-second intervals. A response was defined simply as any change in pattern form or frequency relative to a baseline period. Baseline was the 5-second interval immediately preceding this time unit, unless an anticipatory response occurred, in which case the 5-second unit immediately preceding that interval was used. When two judges were unable to make identical judgements concerning the occurrence of response on mock trials, the trial was scored "uncertain." In the case of heart-rate change a stringent criterion was adopted: a change of two beats or more per 5-second interval (24 beats per minute) was required. Responding during the mock trials was compared with control intervals which were of comparable duration but which followed each mock trial by 15 seconds. Each subject then had nine opportunities to respond during mock trials and nine opportunities during control intervals. The mean number of responses made during mock trials was 4·53, as compared with mean control-interval responding of 2·46, a difference resulting in a t of 4·55, significant at the ·01 level (df = 14).

Although the magnitude of the temporal-conditioning effect as found here is not great, further corroboration of infant capacity for such learning has been found by Fitzgerald and associates (1967) for pupillary responding (although not for eyelid blinking), and further study of such phenomena seems warranted.

The "Bronshtein effect." Ever since the reports of Bronshtein and his colleagues (1958) American researchers in neonatal behaviour have been fascinated by the possibility of suppressing ongoing behaviour by external stimulation. The phenomenon is now commonly referred to as the Bronshtein effect; for example, if an infant has a nipple in his mouth and is sucking ordinarily (that is, is engaging in sucking behaviour dictated by his idiosyncratic congenital patterns under no special conditions of external stimulation), the sudden introduction of an extraneous stimulus such as a sound, visual stimulus, or odour will tend to disrupt the sucking pattern. The phenomenon has been interpreted as one of external inhibition or the arousal of orienting behaviour which competes with other ongoing behaviour (Sokolov, 1963; Lynn, 1966).

In connection with the disruption of ongoing behaviour through the introduction of external competing stimulation, Bronshtein reported that habituation of such disruption occurs over successive stimulus presentations. Thus although the introduction of a tone at first had a marked effect upon the sucking pattern this effect diminished progressively with increasing experience. In our laboratory two studies have failed to replicate the Bronshtein suppression effect (Kaye and Levin, 1963), but other investigators (Keen, 1965; Haith, 1966) have been able to document it clearly.

Semb and Lipsitt (1968) completed an investigation in which the Bronshtein suppression effect without habituation has been clearly demonstrated in newborns. The study was designed to provide optimal conditions for its occurrence in that the tonal stimulation was introduced on specific occasions when the child was sucking, not on a random-presentation or a temporally locked basis. At the same time, and in the same subjects, the obverse response to that of sucking-suppression was studied. On occasions when the infant was not sucking, the same tone was systematically introduced. Under these conditions activation of sucking is readily induced; in fact activation of sucking in the presence of a non-sucking state of the infant

occurs about twice as frequently as the sucking-suppression phenomenon.

· · ·

OLDER INFANTS IN THE FIRST YEAR

Conjugate reinforcement. At this point I should like to leave consideration of the newborn to discuss recent advances in techniques for studying behaviour in the older infant. It is our eventual aim to have techniques for longitudinal study of learning proficiency and for the study of specific stimulating circumstances and their short-term effects on behaviour. In studies of learning in infants, various environmental events must be sought which promote and sustain some measured behaviour. Although it is apparent to most investigators of child behaviour that infants and children engage in much behaviour that seems "self-reinforcing" only recently have there been systematic attempts to incorporate such behaviour into basic psychological theory or to study its origins parametrically. White (1959) introduced the term "competency striving," Butler (1953) the term "curiosity motivation," and Harlow, Harlow and Meyer (1950) spoke of the "manipulation drive" to refer to behaviour occurring in the absence of apparent or traditional primary drives. Hunt (1965) has spoken of infants as having a need for sensory input and opportunity to experience "recognitive familiarity," and in a physiological context Pfaffmann (1960) spoke of "the pleasures of sensation." However, in studies involving sensory input as reinforcement rather than more vital consequences of response, reinforcers often lose their effectiveness, due to adaptation or boredom, before the associative process has been demonstrated or explored extensively (Lipsitt, 1963). Recently Lindsley and co-workers (1961) and Lindsley (1962, 1963) implemented and investigated a type of reinforcement that shows promise in infant conditioning.

Conjugate reinforcement involves the presentation of a continuously available event contingent upon response, such that the event's intensity varies directly and immediately with response strength (for example, rate or intensity). The prototype is the hand-generator flashlight in which illumination intensity is controlled directly by the response rate and pressure on a trigger or dynamometer handle. Compared with episodic schedules in which reinforcement is provided either by delivery of pellets or candies, or by punitive circumstances with discrete onsets and offsets, the conjugate type of response-consequent permits (1) closer analysis of periodic changes in the value of reinforcing stimuli, and (2) maintenance of the subject in the observation situation for fairly long periods of time.

In our first use of the conjugate reinforcement technique (Lipsitt *et al.,* 1966) 12-month-old subjects were seated in an infant chair attached to a box containing a manipulandum, a clear plastic panel. Response to the manipulandum activated a power supply which was designed to vary the light intensity inside the box according to changes in the response rate. Opportunity to see inside the box, which was otherwise dark, was proportionate to the response rate, and transition from low to high brightness and *vice versa* was gradual rather than sudden. In the box a colourful clown picture was rotated continuously. An electrical counter enabled cumulative recording of response every 15 seconds. The procedure involved the use of a basal period of no reinforcement for responding, followed by a conditioning session in which visual reinforcement was available, followed by extinction, then reconditioning, then re-extinction. The behaviour of infants in this situation even for as short a period as 15 minutes supported the efficacy of conjugate reinforcement in the study of infant learning; response rates increased from basal levels through conditioning and decreased when reinforcement was withheld.

Mobiles for conjugate reinforcement. Recently a former student of our laboratory conducted a study using her own 2-month-old infant and five other children of the same age. Following suggestions of Uzgiris and Hunt (1965), Rovee and Rovee (1969) hung a mobile over the infants' cribs. The infants were familiarized with the mobile for several weeks before the experimental procedure began. For four of the infants, the experimental session lasted 27 minutes, and for two others the session lasted 46 minutes. For the experimental session, the infants were loosely clothed with legs exposed and feet bare. Observations were made from the foot of the crib, with the observer out of view of the child. The 27-minute procedure involved a 3-minute baseline period during which the operant level of right-foot kicks was established, a 15-minute acquisition period involving conjugate reinforcement wherein the mobile was linked to the child's leg via a light string, and a 5-minute extinction period in which the string connecting the child's limb with the mobile was detached. The two subjects serving in the 46-minute session received a 10-minute re-acquisition period followed by 5 minutes of re-extinction. The operant response conditioned was that of leg flexions, and the reinforcement was that of visual feedback from the moving mobile. It should be emphasized that the mobile always remained in position during the basal and extinction phases, but limb movements during these phases were not instrumental in activating movement of the object.

Reliability tests indicated that limb movement increased, relative to the basal level, when the mobile could be moved by the leg and that detachment of the string connection resulted in diminution of leg activity.

The Rovees observed that the behaviour of the infants changed qualitatively as well as quantitatively over the course of the sessions. Gross, diffuse body activity occurred early in the sessions, but after experience in operating the mobile the infant used smooth direct thrusts of the limb to which the cord was attached. During the reinforcement phases intense kicking was often followed by rather long pauses, during which the infant remained still but kept his gaze fixed on the swaying figures.

Following the Rovees' work, another study was conducted by Leslie Smith on her own child between the ages of 2 and 5 months. She tested the infant with a multitude of mobile objects varying in colour and form; some were offered with associated sound stimulation. In this study, movements were registered by an automatic counter. As in Rovee's study, it was shown that a 2-month-old infant quickly learns to move his limb appropriately to activate the visual reinforcer, and that limb movement increases during reinforcement periods and diminishes during extinction periods. Interesting findings from this pilot investigation include the strong suggestion that with increased experience in the situation the infant begins to "test" the effect of the response, so that after some training the infant comes to recognize quickly when his responses are effective and when not and adjusts his behaviour accordingly and rapidly. The mobile-reinforcement situation provides a potentially sensitive procedure by which to assess infants' preferences for various types of stimulation. For example, when the child in the Smith study was presented with a red mobile its response rate was consistently higher than when it was presented with an otherwise identical but white mobile.

The Smith data show clearly that infants will behave in a mobile-movement situation for very long periods of time without apparent fatigue or satiation except as indicated by occasional pauses. To be sure, the technique is hampered by the occasional occurrence of fussy or crying behaviour— such activity increases limb-movement responses considerably—and for purposes of assessing cognitive processes it would appear that the procedure ought to be "shut off" during fussy periods of this sort. On the other hand these studies suggest that crying itself might become an important subject for study. It seems that crying occurs rather frequently some minutes after the onset of an extinction condition, as if the crying may be generated by the frustration of expectation. It was noted that the crying could sometimes be abated by re-institution of a conditioning period.

Sucking and visual stimulation. Over the past 2 years Siqueland has developed a line of research in which infants as young as 3 months of age can control the visual input which they receive by sucking on an automatic nipple linked to a slide projector. The presentation of visual stimuli or the experimental withdrawal of these stimuli is contingent upon the infants' making high-amplitude sucking responses. When high-amplitude sucking is required to activate the projector light, infants rapidly adjust the intensity of sucks to produce higher illumination, much as previously described in the conjugate reinforcement situation.

In one experiment Siqueland sought to determine whether non-nutritive sucking could be studied in 4-month-old children by the use of visual reinforcers. Subjects were 30 infants assigned to one of three groups: *Gp C* (control baseline), *Gp R* (reinforcement group), and *Gp W* (stimulus withdrawal group). The first group provided a baseline reference for 10 minutes of non-reinforced sucking, and the other groups received a 13-minute session consisting of conditioning, extinction, reconditioning, and re-extinction. For *Gp R* reinforcement was contingent on sucking during the conditioning periods, and for *Gp W* sucking resulted in withdrawal of the visual stimulus, each criterion suck resulting in a 5-seconds delayed onset of the visual stimulus. For both groups, eight chromatic 35 mm slides showing geometric forms, cartoon figures, and human faces were presented for 30 seconds each in 4-minute conditioning blocks.

The reinforcement group showed rapid acquisition of criterion sucks, while the baseline group showed negligible change in such behaviour. *Gp W* showed a slight decrease in the ratio of high-amplitude sucking. The evidence clearly shows that heterogeneous visual stimulation may function in a reinforcing capacity to maintain sucking behaviour in infants of 4 months.

Another of Siqueland's studies compared the sucking behaviour of three age groups (4-, 8- and 12-months) in the visual reinforcement situation again using the sucking response as the operant. Highly reliable differences in sucking rates were obtained among the three age groups during a baseline-assessment session lasting 5 minutes.

Siqueland next attempted re-establishment of sucking behaviour in 12-month-old infants when such behaviour is operative in enhancing visual

stimulation. Two groups of ten infants received different sets of visual stimuli. One group was shown four coloured slides four times each over two 4-minute sessions, and the other group was shown a set of eight slides twice each. The results showed dramatic increases in sucking rate for both groups as compared with baseline controls of the same age. Reliable response decrements were also obtained after reinforcement ended. Moreover, although predicted differences between the two groups were not obtained during initial conditioning and extinction phases, apparent stimulus familiarization (satiation) effects were reflected in a decreasing response rate for the 4-stimulus group during reconditioning as compared with high stable rates for the 8-stimulus group. Siqueland's work continues to explore which stimulus parameters, including comparisons across modalities, are influential in controlling an infant's sucking behaviour. The apparent ease with which infants learn to control their visual environment by appropriate sucking behaviour is interesting because many observers of infants have noted that visual exploratory behaviour is often most intense in a child that is engaged in sucking. Many a mother has reported that she can most easily attract the child's gaze to hers when the infant is feeding. In the earliest days of life, sucking and visual exploratory behaviour seem to have an intimate relationship.

PROSPECTS FOR THE FUTURE

It only remains to be said that as we progress in our studies of human behaviour in the first year of life some of the seeming complexities become better understood through experimental analyses and careful measurement of the relationships between the response and the environmental feedback. Experimental techniques based on some traditional notions about the reinforcing functions of environmental stimulation have been immensely useful in leading to knowledge about the control of behaviour by stimuli. However, it must also be admitted that experimentalists must pay more attention to the ordinary non-laboratory circumstances under which the human organism generally lives and to which he seems, all things considered, remarkably well adapted. The ecologists in America (for example, Wright, 1960; Barker, 1951) and the ethologists in Europe (for example, Hinde, 1966; Eibl-Eibesfeldt, 1967) have done the field of experimental child psychology a great service in calling for increased attention to the naturalistic habitat and the built-in response repertoire of the human child. A healthy consequence is that conjugate reinforcement phenomena, for instance, are now being seriously explored by child experimentalists.

It does appear at present that modifications and embellishments of traditional classical and operant conditioning techniques seem quite in order for the further advance of understanding of infant learning behaviour. The enormous amount of effective learning which takes place during the first year of life in infants reared "naturally" is seldom accomplished under conditions exactly like those used in the laboratory to study basic acquisition and extinction processes. In real life learning trials are almost never deliberately spaced, the stimulating conditions are seldom well-controlled, and much of the infant's learning gives the appearance of occurring fortuitously.

The proper scientific study of a natural phenomenon is not usually the exploration of the fortuitous. Nevertheless it is quite possible that by taking advantage of the changing state of the baby from moment to moment, including the momentary changes in its condition of curiosity, and by using variant rather than constant stimulation conditions experimenters might understand better some of the learning processes that have often proved refractory in the well-controlled laboratory situation. It is apparent to me, for instance, that most early learning is neither of a purely classical conditioning nor of a purely operant variety, but is some sort of amalgamation of these. The Siqueland-Lipsitt finding with respect to conditioned head-turning is a case in point, inasmuch as the procedure fulfilled both respondent and operant requirements, providing both eliciting and emitting stimulus conditions. It is sometimes necessary or desirable to use an eliciting stimulus to potentiate a response which can then be reinforced operantly, thus increasing the probability of the occurrence of that response in the absence of the eliciting stimulation on future occasions. For example, the process of conditioning the sucking behaviour of a newborn with an initially low-probability level of sucking might be facilitated by pressing the infant's palms when the nipple is in the mouth, thus eliciting a higher sucking rate. This higher sucking rate may then be reinforced through feeding, eventually allowing the eliciting stimulation of the palm-press to be faded out. In a sense, we might most readily engender learned behaviour in the immature organism by violating the basic requirements of the classical and operant conditioning paradigms. The head-retraction response in the presence of a smothering stimulus may well be of this type, whereby it first occurs as an elicited or respondent behaviour but becomes a learned operant in the course of development; thus the older child positions his head so as to preclude smothering even before an actual threat of respiratory occlusion occurs. Similarly, it is not unlikely that smiling behaviour in children first occurs primarily as respondent behaviour which is supplanted or overshadowed later in ontogeny by a predominantly operant mode of occurrence (Bijou and Baer, 1965).

REFERENCES

BARKER, R. G. 1951. *One boy's day*. Harper, New York.

BIJOU, S. W. and BAER, D. M. 1965. *Child development II: Universal stage of infancy*. Appleton-Century-Crofts, New York. Pp. 3–7.

BRONSHTEIN, A. I., ANTONOVA, T. G., KAMENSTKAYA, A. G., LUPPOVA, N. N. and SYTOVA, V. A. 1958. On the development of the functions of analysers in infants and some animals at the early stage of ontogenesis. In *Problemy evolyutaii fisiolgicheskikh funkisii*. Academiya Nauk, Moscow and Leningrad. Transl. (Off. of Tech. Servs. Report No. 60–61066, 1960. Pp. 106–116) obtainable from U.S. Dept. of Commerce, Office of Technical Services, Washington, D.C.

BUTLER, R. A. 1953. Discrimination learning by rhesus monkeys to visual exploration motivation. *J. comp. physiol. Psychol. 46*, 95–98.

EIBL-EIBESFELDT, I. 1967. Concepts of ethology and their significance in the study of human behaviour. In H. W. Stevenson, E. Hess, and H. L. Rheingold (Eds.), *Early behavior: comparative and developmental approaches*. Wiley, New York. Pp. 127–146.

ELKONIN, D. B. 1957. The physiology of higher nervous activity and child psychology. In B. Simon (Ed.), *Psychology in the Soviet Union*. Routledge & Kegan Paul, London. Pp. 47–68.

ENGEN, T. and LIPSITT, L. P. 1965. Decrement and recovery of responses to olfactory stimuli in the human neonate. *J. comp. physiol. Psychol. 59*, 312–316.

ENGEN, T., LIPSITT, L. P. and KAYE, H. 1963. Olfactory responses and adaptation in the human neonate. *J. comp. physiol. Psychol. 56*, 73–77.

FITZGERALD, H. E., LINTZ, L. M., BRACKBILL, Y. and ADAMS, G. 1967. Time perception and conditioning of an autonomic response in human infants. *Percept. Mot. Skills. 24*, 479–486.

GESELL, A. 1954. The ontogenesis of infant behavior. In L. Carmichael (Ed.), *Manual of child psychology*. Wiley, New York. Pp. 335–373.

HARLOW, H. F., HARLOW, M. K. and MEYER, D. R. 1950. Learning motivated by a manipulation drive. *J. exp. Psychol. 40*, 228–234.

HARRIS, D. B. 1957. (Ed.), *The concept of development*. Univ. of Minnesota Press, Minneapolis.

HINDE, R. A. 1966. *Animal behaviour: a synthesis of ethology and comparative psychology*. McGraw-Hill, New York.

HUNT, J. McV. 1965. Traditional personality theory in the light of recent evidence. *Am. Scient. 53*, 80–96.

IRWIN, O. C. 1930. Amount and nature of activities of

newborn infants under constant external stimulating conditions during the first ten days of life. *Genet. Psychol. Monogr. 8*, 1–92.

IRWIN, O. C. 1943. The activities of newborn infants. In R. G. Barker, J. S. Kounin, and H. F. Wright (Eds.), *Child behavior and development.* McGraw-Hill, New York. Pp. 29–47.

KAYE, H. and LEVIN, G. R. 1963. Two attempts to demonstrate tonal suppression of non-nutritive sucking in neonates. *Percept. Mot. Skills. 17*, 521–522.

KEEN, R. 1965. Effects of auditory stimuli on sucking behavior in the human neonate, *J. exp. child Psychol. 1*, 348–354.

LINDSLEY, O. R. 1962. A behavioral measure of television viewing. *J. advert. Res. 2*, 2–12.

LINDSLEY, O. R. 1963. Experimental analysis of social reinforcement: terms and methods. *Am. J. Orthopsychiat. 33*, 624–633.

LINDSLEY, O. R., HOBIKA, J. H. and ETSTEN, B. E. 1961. Operant behavior during anesthesia recovery: a continuous and objective method. *Anesthesiology. 22*, 937–946.

LIPSITT, L. P. 1963. Learning in the first year of life. In L. P. Lipsitt and C. C. Spiker (Eds.), *Advances in child development and behavior.* Vol. 1. Academic Press, New York. Pp. 147–195.

LIPSITT, L. P. 1967. Learning in the human infant. In H. W. Stevenson, E. H. Hess, and H. L. Rheingold (Eds.), *Early behavior: comparative and developmental approaches.* Wiley, New York. Pp. 225–247.

LIPSITT, L. P. and KAYE, H. 1965. Changes in neonatal response to optimizing and non-optimizing sucking stimulation. *Psychon. Sci. 2*, 221–222.

LIPSITT, L. P., PEDERSON, L. J. and DeLUCIA, C. A. 1966. Conjugate reinforcement of operant responding in infants. *Psychon. Sci. 4*, 67–68.

LYNN, R. 1966. *Attention, arousal and the orienting reaction.* Pergamon, Oxford.

MARQUIS, D. P. 1931. Can conditioned responses be established in the newborn infant? *J. genet. Psychol. 39*, 479–492.

MARQUIS, D. P. 1941. Learning in the neonate: the modification of behavior under three feeding schedules, *J. exp. Psychol. 29*, 263–282.

PAPOUŠEK, H. 1959. A method of studying conditioned food reflexes in young children up to the age of six months. *Pavlov J. Higher Nerv. Activ. 9*, 136–140.

PAPOUŠEK, H. 1960. Conditioned motor alimentary reflexes in infants. *Cesk. Pediat. 15*, 861–872, 981–988.

PAPOUŠEK, H. 1961. Conditioned head rotation reflexes in the first months of life. *Acta paediat., Stockh. 50*, 565–576.

PFAFFMANN, C. 1960. The pleasures of sensation. *Psychol. Rev. 67*, 253–268.

PRATT, K. C. 1954. The neonate. In L. Carmichael (Ed.), *Manual of child psychology.* Wiley, New York. Pp. 215–291.

ROVEE, C. K. and ROVEE, D. 1969. Conjugate reinforcement of infant exploratory behaviour. *J. exp. Child Psychol. 8*, 33–39.

SEMB, G. and LIPSITT, L. P. 1968. The effects of acoustic stimulation on cessation and initiation of non-nutritive sucking in neonates. *J. exp. Child Psychol. 6*, 585–597.

SIQUELAND, E. R. 1968. Reinforcement patterns and extinction in human newborns. *J. exp. Child Psychol. 6*, 431–442.

SIQUELAND, E. R. and LIPSITT, L. P. 1966. Conditioned head-turning in human newborns. *J. exp. Child Psychol. 3*, 356–376.

SOKOLOV, E. N. 1963. Higher nervous functions: the orienting reflex. *A. Rev. Physiol.* 545–580.

UZGIRIS, I. and HUNT, J. McV. 1965. A longitudinal study of recognition learning. Paper read at the biennial meeting of the Society for Research in Child Development, Minneapolis, Minnesota.

WHITE, R. W. 1959. Motivation reconsidered: the concept of competence. *Psychol. Rev. 66*, 297–333.

WRIGHT, H. F. 1960. Observational Child Study. In P. H. Mussen (Ed.), *Handbook of research methods in child development.* Wiley, New York. Pp. 71–139.

41

Adolescence[1]

ANNA FREUD

An article by Anna Freud of London, England, follows. Her contributions to psychoanalytic theory are probably exceeded only by those of her father, Sigmund Freud. In her discussion of the problems of the adolescent, she emphasizes personality differences among adolescents in coping with the stresses of their age period. Among her books are The Ego and the Mechanisms of Defense *(1948, rev. 1966) and* Normality and Pathology in Childhood: Assessments of Development *(1965), both published by the International Universities Press, New York City.*

This paper is a provocative version of her long-famed descriptions of adolescent defenses against anxiety and guilt. Freud closes her article with an important discussion of the normality of adolescent difficulties.

I. ADOLESCENCE IN THE PSYCHOANALYTIC THEORY

INTRODUCTION

I return to the subject of adolescence after an interval of twenty years. During this time much has happened in analytic work to throw added light on the problems concerned and to influence the conditions of life for young people, whether normal or abnormal. Nevertheless, in spite of partial advances, the position with regard to the analytic study of adolescence is not a happy one, and especially unsatisfactory when compared with that of early childhood. With the latter period, we feel sure of our ground, and in possession of a wealth of material and information which enables us to assume authority and apply analytic findings to the practical problems of upbringing. When it comes to adolescence, we feel hesitant and, accordingly, cannot satisfy the parents or educational workers who apply for help to us and to our knowledge. One can hear it said frequently that adolescence is a neglected period, a stepchild where analytic thinking is concerned.

These complaints, which come from two sides, from the parents as well as from the analytic workers themselves, seem to me to warrant closer study and investigation than they have received so far. . . .

II. CLINICAL APPLICATIONS

What follows is an attempt to apply at least some of our hard-won insights to three of the most pressing problems concerning adolescence.

IS THE ADOLESCENT UPSET INEVITABLE?

There is, first, the ever recurrent question whether the adolescent upheaval is welcome and beneficial as such, whether it is necessary and, more than that, inevitable. On this point, psychoanalytic opinion is decisive and unanimous. The people in the child's family and school, who assess his state on the basis of behavior, may deplore the adolescent upset which, to them, spells the loss of valuable qualities, of character stability, and of social adaptation. As analysts, who assess personalities from the structural point of view, we think otherwise. We know that the character structure of a child at the end of the latency period represents the outcome of long drawn-out conflicts between id and ego forces. The inner balance achieved, although characteristic for each individual and precious to him, is preliminary only and precarious. It does not allow for the quantitative increase in drive activity, nor for the changes of drive quality which are both inseparable from puberty. Consequently, it has to be abandoned to allow adult sexuality to be integrated into the individual's per-

[1] The content of this paper is based on material collected in the Hampstead Child-Therapy Clinic with the aid of grants by The Field Foundation, Inc., New York, The Foundations' Fund for Research in Psychiatry, New Haven, Connecticut, The Ford Foundation, New York, The Psychoanalytic Foundation, Inc., and The Grant Foundation, Inc., New York.

Anna Freud, Adolescence, *Psychoanalytic Study of the Child,* 1958. Reprinted by permission of International Universities Press and the author.

sonality. The so-called adolescent upheavals are no more than the external indications that such internal adjustments are in progress.

On the other hand, we all know individual children who as late as the ages of fourteen, fifteen or sixteen show no such outer evidence of inner unrest. They remain, as they have been during the latency period, "good" children, wrapped up in their family relationships, considerate sons of their mothers, submissive to their fathers, in accord with the atmosphere, ideas and ideals of their childhood background. Convenient as this may be, it signifies a delay of normal development and is, as such, a sign to be taken seriously. The first impression conveyed by these cases may be that of a quantitative deficiency of drive endowment, a suspicion which will usually prove unfounded. Analytic exploration reveals that this reluctance to "grow up" is derived not from the id but from the ego and superego aspects of the personality. These are children who have built up excessive defenses against their drive activities and are now crippled by the results, which act as barriers against the normal maturational processes of phase development. They are, perhaps more than any others, in need of therapeutic help to remove the inner restrictions and clear the path for normal development, however "upsetting" the latter may prove to be.

IS THE ADOLESCENT UPSET PREDICTABLE?

A second question which we are asked to answer frequently concerns the problem whether the manner in which a given child will react in adolescence can be predicted from the characteristics of his early infantile or latency behavior. Apart from the more general affirmative answer given by Ernest Jones (1922), only one among the authors named above has made clear and positive assertions in this respect. Siegfried Bernfeld (1923), when discussing his protracted type of male adolescence and its characteristics, established the links between this form of puberty and a specific type of infantile development based on the following three conditions: (a) that the frustration of infantile sex wishes has been shattering for the child's narcissism; (b) that the incestuous fixations to the parents have been of exceptional strength and have been maintained throughout the latency period; (c) that the superego has been established early, has been delineated sharply from the ego, and that the ideals contained in it are invested with narcissistic as well as with object libido.

Other and less precise answers to the same question are scattered through the literature. We find the opinion that, in the majority of cases, the manifestations of the adolescent process are not predictable since they depend almost wholly on quantitative relations, i.e., on the strength and suddenness of drive increase, the corresponding increase in anxiety causing all the rest of the upheaval.

I suggested in another place (1936) that adolescence brings about occasionally something in the nature of a spontaneous cure. This happens in children whose pregenital activities and characteristics remained dominant throughout latency until the increase in genital libido produces a welcome decrease in pregenitality. This latter occurrence, on the other hand, can be matched by a corresponding one which produces the opposite effect: where phallic characteristics have remained dominant during latency, the increase in genital libido produces the effect of an exaggerated and threatening aggressive masculinity.

It seems to be generally accepted that a strong fixation to the mother, dating not only from the oedipal but from the preoedipal attachment to her, renders adolescence especially difficult. This latter assertion, on the other hand, has to be correlated with two recent findings of a different nature which we owe to work done in our Hampstead Child-Therapy Clinic. One of these findings is derived from the study of orphaned children who were deprived of the relationship to a stable mother figure in their first years. This lack of a mother fixation, far from making adolescence easier, constitutes a real danger to the whole inner coherence of the personality during that period. In these cases adolescence is preceded frequently by a frantic search for a mother image; the internal possession and cathexis of such an image seems to be essential for the ensuing normal process of detaching libido from it for transfer to new objects, i.e., to sexual partners.

The second finding mentioned above is derived from the analyses of adolescent twins, in one case children whose twin relationship in infancy had been observed and recorded in minute detail (Burlingham, 1952). In their treatments it transpired that the "adolescent revolt" against the love objects of infancy demands the breaking of the tie to the twin in no lesser degree than the breaking of the tie to the mother. Since this libidinal (narcissistic as well as object-directed) cathexis of the twin is rooted in the same deep layer of the personality as the early attachment to the mother, its withdrawal is accompanied by an equal amount of structural upheaval, emotional upset, and resulting symptom formation. Where, on the other hand, the twin relationship survives the adolescent phase, we may expect to see a delay in the onset of maturity or a restrictive hardening of the character of the latency period similar to the instances mentioned above in which the childhood love for the parents withstands the onslaught of the adolescent phase.

To return to the initial question: it seems that we are able to foretell the adolescent reactions in certain specific and typical constellations but certainly not for all the individual variations of infantile personality structure. Our insight into typical developments will increase with the number of adolescents who undergo analysis.

PATHOLOGY IN ADOLESCENCE

This leaves us with a third problem which, to my mind, outweighs the preceding ones so far as clinical and theoretical significance are concerned. I refer to the difficulty in adolescent cases to draw the line between normality and pathology. As described above, adolescence constitutes by definition an interruption of peaceful growth which resembles in appearance a variety of other emotional upsets and structural upheavals.[3] The adolescent manifestations come close to symptom formation of the neurotic, psychotic or dissocial order and merge almost imperceptibly into borderline states, initial, frustrated or fully fledged forms of almost all the mental illnesses. Consequently, the differential diagnosis between the adolescent upsets and true pathology becomes a difficult task.

For the discussion of this diagnostic problem I leave most other authors in the field to speak for themselves and summarize my own impressions based on past and present clinical experience.

In 1936, when I approached the same subject from the aspect of the defenses, I was concerned with the similarity between the adolescent and other emotional disturbances rather than with the differences between them. I described that adolescent upsets take on the appearance of a neurosis if the initial, pathogenic danger situation is located in the superego with the resulting anxiety being felt as guilt; that they resemble psychotic disturbances if the danger lies in the increased power of the id itself, which threatens the ego in its existence or integrity. Whether such an adolescent individual impresses us, then, as obsessional, phobic, hysterical, ascetic, schizoid, paranoid, suicidal, etc., will depend on the one hand on the quality and quantity of the id contents which beset the ego, on the other hand on the selection of defense mechanisms which the latter employs. Since, in adolescence, impulses from all pregenital phases rise to the surface and

defense mechanisms from all levels of crudity or complexity come into use, the pathological results —although identical in structure—are more varied and less stabilized than at other times of life.

Today it seems to me that this structural description needs to be amplified, not in the direction of the similarity of the adolescent to other disorders but in that of their specific nature. There is in their etiology at least one additional element which may be regarded as exclusive to this period and characteristic for it: namely that the danger is felt to be located not only in the id impulses and fantasies but in the very existence of the love objects of the individual's oedipal and preoedipal past. The libidinal cathexis to them has been carried forward from the infantile phases, merely toned down or inhibited in aim during latency. Therefore the reawakened pregenital urges, or— worse still—the newly acquired genital ones, are in danger of making contact with them, lending a new and threatening reality to fantasies which had seemed extinct but are, in fact, merely under repression.[4] The anxieties which arise on these grounds are directed toward eliminating the infantile objects, i.e., toward breaking the tie with them. Anny Katan (1937) has discussed this type of defense, which aims above all at changing the persons and the scene of conflict, under the term of "removal." Such an attempt may succeed or fail, partially or totally. In any case, I agree with Anny Katan that its outcome will be decisive for the success or failure of the other, more familiar line of defensive measures which are directed against the impulses themselves.

A number of illustrations will serve to clarify the meaning of this assumption.

(I) Defense Against the Infantile Object Ties. Defense by Displacement of Libido. There are many adolescents who deal with the anxiety aroused by the attachment to their infantile objects by the simple means of flight. Instead of permitting a process of gradual detachment from the parents to take place, they withdraw their libido from them suddenly and altogether. This leaves them with a passionate longing for partnership which they succeed in transferring to the environment outside the family. Here they adopt varying solutions. Libido may be transferred, more or less unchanged in

---

[3] Adolescence, of course, is not the only time in life when alterations of a physiological nature cause disturbances of mental equilibrium. The same happens in later years in the climacterium; and recently, Grete L. Bibring has given a convincing description of similar damage to the equilibrium of mental forces during pregnancy.

[4] An important clinical instance of this can be found in adolescent girls with anorexia nervosa. Here the infantile fantasies of oral impregnation receive added impetus from the new real possibilities of motherhood opened up by genital development. Consequently, the phobic measures adopted against the intake of food on the one hand and identification with the mother on the other hand are overemphasized to a degree which may lead to starvation.

form, to parent substitutes, provided that these new figures are diametrically opposed in every aspect (personal, social, cultural) to the original ones. Or the attachment may be made to so-called "leaders," usually persons in age between the adolescent's and the parents' generation, who represent ideals. Equally frequent are the passionate new ties to contemporaries, either of the same or of the opposite sex (i.e., homosexual friendships) and the attachments to adolescent groups (or "gangs"). Whichever of these typical solutions is chosen, the result makes the adolescent feel "free," and revel in a new precious sense of independence from the parents who are treated, then, with indifference bordering on callousness.

Although the direction taken by the libido in these instances is, in itself, on lines of normality, the suddenness of the change, the carefully observed contrast in object selection, and the overemphasis on the new allegiances mark it as defensive. It represents an all too hasty anticipation of normal growth rather than a normal developmental process.

It makes little further difference to the emotional situation whether the libidinal flight is followed by actual flight, i.e., whether the adolescent also "removes" himself bodily from his family. If not, he remains in the home in the attitude of a boarder, usually a very inconsiderate one so far as the older and younger family members are concerned.

On the other hand, the withdrawal of cathexis from the parents has most decisive consequences for the rest of the defensive processes. Once the infantile objects are stripped of their importance, the pregenital and genital impulses cease to be threatening to the same degree. Consequently, guilt and anxiety decrease and the ego becomes more tolerant. Formerly repressed sexual and aggressive wishes rise to the surface and are acted on, the actions being taken outside the family in the wider environment. Whether this acting out will be on harmless, or idealistic, or dissocial, or even criminal lines will depend essentially on the new objects to which the adolescent has attached himself. Usually the ideals of the leader, of the adolescent group, or of the gang, are taken over wholeheartedly and without criticism.

Adolescents of this type may be sent for treatment after their actions have brought them into conflict with their schools, their employers, or the law. As far as psychoanalytic therapy is concerned, they seem to offer little chance for the therapeutic alliance between analyst and patient without which the analytic technique cannot proceed. Any relationship to the analyst and, above all, the transference to him would revive the infantile attachments which have been discarded; therefore the adolescent remains unresponsive. Also, the escape from these attachments has suspended the feeling of internal conflict, at least temporarily; consequently, the adolescent does not feel in need of psychological help. A. Aichhorn had these points in mind when he maintained that adolescents of the dissocial and criminal type needed a long period of preparation and inner rearrangement before they could become amenable to analytic treatment. He maintained that the latter would be successful only if, during this preparation in a residential setting, the adolescent made a new transference of object love, reawakened his infantile attachments, internalized his conflicts once more, in short, became neurotic.

To try and analyze an adolescent in his phase of successful detachment from the past seems to be a venture doomed to failure.

Defense by Reversal of Affect. A second typical reaction to the same danger situation, is, although less conspicuous outwardly, more ominous in nature inwardly.

Instead of displacing libido from the parents—or, more likely, after failing to do so—the adolescent ego may defend itself by turning the emotions felt toward them into their opposites. This changes love into hate, dependence into revolt, respect and admiration into contempt and derision. On the basis of such reversal of affect the adolescent imagines himself to be "free" but, unluckily for his peace of mind and sense of conflict, this conviction does not reach further than the conscious surface layer of his mind. For all deeper intents and purposes he remains as securely tied to the parental figures as he has been before; acting out remains within the family; and any alterations achieved by the defense turn out to his disadvantage. There are no positive pleasures to be derived from the reversed relationships, only suffering, felt as well as inflicted. There is no room for independence of action, or of growth; compulsive opposition to the parents proves as crippling in this respect as compulsive obedience to them can prove to be.[5] Since anxiety and guilt remain undiminished, constant reinforcement of defense is necessary. This is provided in the first place by two methods: denial (of positive feeling) and reaction formations (churlish, unsympathetic, contemptuous attitudes). The behavioral picture that emerges at this stage is that of an uncooperative and hostile adolescent.

Further pathological developments of this state of affairs are worth watching. The hostility and

[5] S. Ferenczi has pointed to this effect of "compulsive disobedience" many years ago.

aggressiveness, which serve as a defense against object love in the beginning, soon become intolerable to the ego, are felt as threats, and are warded off in their own right. This may happen by means of projection; in that case the aggression is ascribed to the parents who, consequently, become the adolescent's main oppressors and persecutors. In the clinical picture this appears first as the adolescent's suspiciousness and, when the projections increase, as paranoid behavior.

Conversely, the full hostility and aggression may be turned away from the objects and employed inwardly against the self. In these cases, the adolescents display intense depression, tendencies of self-abasement and self-injury, and develop, or even carry out, suicidal wishes.

During all stages of this process, personal suffering is great and the desire to be helped intense. This, in itself, is no guarantee that the adolescent in question will submit to analytic therapy. He will certainly not do so if treatment is urged and initiated by the parents. Whenever this happens, he will consider analysis as their tool, extend his hostility or his suspicions to include the person of the analyst, and refuse cooperation. The chances are better if the adolescent himself decides to seek help and turns to analysis, as it were, in opposition to the parents' wishes. Even so, the alliance with the analyst may not be of long duration. As soon as a true transference develops and the positive infantile fantasies come into consciousness, the same reversal of affect tends to be repeated in the analytic setting. Rather than relive the whole turmoil of feelings with the analyst, many adolescent patients run away. They escape from their positive feelings, although it appears to the analyst that they break off treatment in an overwhelmingly strong negative transference.

Defense by Withdrawal of Libido to the Self. To proceed in the direction of increasing pathology:

Withdrawal of libido from the parents, as it has been described above, does not, in itself, decide about its further use, or fate. If anxieties and inhibitions block the way toward new objects outside the family, the libido remains within the self. There, it may be employed to cathect the ego and superego, thereby inflating them. Clinically this means that ideas of grandeur will appear, fantasies of unlimited power over other human beings, or of major achievement and championship in one or more fields. Or, the suffering and persecuted ego of the adolescent may assume Christ-like proportions with corresponding fantasies of saving the world.

On the other hand, the cathexis may become attached to the adolescent's body only and give rise there to the hypochondriacal sensations and feelings of body changes that are well known clinically from initial stages of psychotic illness.

In either case analytic therapy is indicated as well as urgent. Treatment will dispel the appearance of severe abnormality if it reopens a path for the libido, either to flow backwards and recathect the original infantile objects, or to flow forward, in the direction described above, to cathect less frightening substitutes in the environment.

What taxes the analyst's technical skill in these cases is the withdrawn state of the patient, i.e., the problem of establishing an initial relationship and transference. Once this is accomplished, the return from narcissistic withdrawal to object cathexis will relieve the patient, at least temporarily.

I believe there are many cases where the analyst would be wise to be content with this partial success without urging further treatment. A further, and deeper, involvement in the transference may well arouse all the anxieties described above and, again, lead to abrupt termination of the analysis due to the adolescent's flight reaction.

Defense by Regression. The greater the anxiety aroused by the object ties, the more elementary and primitive is the defense activity employed by the adolescent ego to escape them. Thus, at the extreme height of anxiety, the relations with the object world may be reduced to the emotional state known as "primary identification" with the objects. This solution with which we are familiar from psychotic illnesses implies regressive changes in all parts of the personality, i.e., in the ego organization as well as in the libido. The ego boundaries [6] are widened to embrace parts of the object together with the self. This creates in the adolescent surprising changes of qualities, attitudes and even outward appearance. His allegiance to persons outside himself betrays itself in these alterations of his own personality (i.e., his identifications) rather than in an outflow of libido. Projections, together with these identifications, dominate the scene and create a give-and-take between the self and object which has repercussions on important ego functions. For example, the distinction between the external and internal world (i.e., reality testing) becomes temporarily negligible, a lapse in ego functioning which manifests itself in the clinical picture as a state of confusion.

Regression of this kind may bring transitory relief to the ego by emptying the oedipal (and many of the preoedipal) fantasies of their libidinal cathexis.[7] But this lessening anxiety will not be long-

---

[6] See P. Federn (1952) and, following him, T. Freeman et al. (1958).

[7] See in this connection M. Katan (1950).

lived. Another and deeper anxiety will soon take its place which I have characterized on a former occasion (1951) as the fear of emotional surrender, with the accompanying fear of loss of identity.

(II) Defense Against Impulses. Where the defenses against the oedipal and preoedipal object ties fail to achieve their aim, clinical pictures emerge which come nearest to the borderline toward psychotic illness.

The "Ascetic" Adolescent. One of these, the "ascetic" adolescent, I have described before as fighting all his impulses, preoedipal and oedipal, sexual and aggressive, extending the defense even to the fulfillment of the physiological needs for food, sleep, and body comfort. This, to me, seems the characteristic reaction of an ego, driven by the blind fear of overwhelming id quantities, an anxiety which leaves no room for the finer distinctions between vital or merely pleasant satisfactions, the healthy or the morbid, the morally permitted or forbidden pleasures. Total war is waged against the pursuit of pleasure as such. Accordingly, most of the normal processes of instinct and need satisfaction are interfered with and become paralyzed. According to clinical observation, adolescent asceticism is, with luck, a transitory phenomenon. For the analytic observer it provides precious proof of the power of defense, i.e., of the extent to which the normal, healthy drive derivatives are open to crippling interference by the ego.

On the whole, analytic treatment of the ascetic type does not present as many technical difficulties as one would expect. Perhaps, in these individuals, defense against the impulses is so massive, that they can permit themselves some object relationship to the analyst and, thus, enter into transference.

The "Uncompromising" Adolescent. Another, equally abnormal adolescent, is described best as the "uncompromising" type. The term, in this instance, does refer to more than the well-known conscious, unrelenting position adopted by many young people who stand up for their ideas, refuse to make concessions to the more practical and reality-adapted attitudes of their elders, and take pride in their moral or aesthetic principles. "Compromise," with these adolescents, includes processes which are as essential for life as, for example, the cooperation between impulses, the blending of opposite strivings, the mitigation of id strivings by interference from the side of the ego. One adolescent whom I observed in analysis did his utmost, in pursuit of this impossible aim, to prevent any interference of his mind with his body, of his activity with his passivity, his loves with his hates, his realities with his fantasies, the external de-

mands with his internal ones, in short, of his ego with his id.

In treatment this defense was represented as a strong resistance against any "cure," the idea of which he despised in spite of intense suffering. He understood correctly that mental health is based in the last resort on harmony, i.e., on the very compromise formations which he was trying to avoid.

III. The Concept of Normality in Adolescence

Where adolescence is concerned, it seems easier to describe its pathological manifestations than the normal processes. Nevertheless, there are in the above exposition at least two pronouncements which may prove useful for the concept: (1) that adolescence is by its nature an interruption of peaceful growth, and (2) that the upholding of a steady equilibrium during the adolescent process is in itself abnormal. Once we accept for adolescence disharmony within the psychic structure as our basic fact, understanding becomes easier. We begin to see the upsetting battles which are raging between id and ego as beneficent attempts to restore peace and harmony. The defensive methods which are employed either against the impulses, or against the object cathexis, begin to appear legitimate and normal. If they produce pathological results, this happens not because of any malignancy in their nature, but because they are overused, overstressed, or used in isolation. Actually, each of the abnormal types of adolescent development, as it is described above, represents also a potentially useful way of regaining mental stability, normal if combined with other defenses, and if used in moderation.

To explain this last statement in greater detail: I take it that it is normal for an adolescent to behave for a considerable length of time in an inconsistent and unpredictable manner; to fight his impulses and to accept them; to ward them off successfully and to be overrun by them; to love his parents and to hate them; to revolt against them and to be dependent on them; to be deeply ashamed to acknowledge his mother before others and, unexpectedly, to desire heart-to-heart talks with her; to thrive on imitation of and identification with others while searching unceasingly for his own identity; to be more idealistic, artistic, generous, and unselfish than he will ever be again, but also the opposite: self-centered, egoistic, calculating. Such fluctuations between extreme opposites would be deemed highly abnormal at any other time of life. At this time they may signify no more than that an adult structure of personality takes a long time to emerge, that the ego of the individual in question does not cease to experiment and is in no hurry to close down on possibilities. If the temporary solutions seem abnormal to the onlooker, they are less so, nevertheless, than the hasty decisions made in other cases for one-sided suppression, or revolt, or flight, or withdrawal, or regression, or asceticism, which are responsible for the truly pathological developments described above.

While an adolescent remains inconsistent and unpredictable in his behavior, he may suffer, but he does not seem to me to be in need of treatment. I think that he should be given time and scope to work out his own solution. Rather, it may be his parents who need help and guidance so as to be able to bear with him. There are few situations in life which are more difficult to cope with than an adolescent son or daughter during the attempt to liberate themselves.

IV. Summary

In the foregoing papers the author has reviewed and summarized some of the basic literature on adolescence, as well as her own views on the subject. Her former description of the defensive processes in adolescence has been amplified to include specific defense activities directed against the oedipal and preoedipal object ties.

BIBLIOGRAPHY

AICHHORN, A. (1925), *Wayward Youth*. New York: Viking Press, 1948.

BERNFELD, S. (1923), Uber eine typische Form der männlichen Pubertät. *Imago*, IX.

BURLINGHAM, D. (1952), *Twins*. New York: International Universities Press.

FEDERN, P. (1952), *Ego Psychology and the Psychoses*. New York: Basic Books.

FREEMAN, T., CAMERON, L. J. and McGHIE, A. (1958), *Chronic Schizophrenia*. New York: International Universities Press.

FREUD, A. (1936), *The Ego and the Mechanisms of Defense*. New York: International Universities Press, 1946. See Chapters X and XI.

FREUD, A. (1951), A Connection between the States of Negativism and of Emotional Surrender (Horigkeit). Paper read at the International Psycho-Analytical Congress, Amsterdam, August 1951. Summary in *Int. J. Psa.*, XXXIII, 1952, p. 265.

JONES, E. (1922), Some Problems of Adolescence. *Papers on Psycho-Analysis*. London: Bailliere, Tindall & Cox, fifth edition, 1948.

KATAN-ANGEL, A. (1937), The Role of Displacement in Agoraphobia. *Int. J. Psa.*, XXXII, 1951.

KATAN, M. (1950), Structural Aspects of a Case of Schizophrenia. *This Annual*, V.

42

Crises in Normal Personality Development

GORDON W. ALLPORT

This article, by the late Gordon W. Allport, deals with crises in the personality development of "normal" college students. Allport deals with his topic in relation to autobiographical materials supplied by his students. His discussion is not from a Freudian point of view. Vicissitudes of adjustment to college, motherhood, etc., have a lesson for preventive work in mental health. A study of the transition points in life may permit forecasting (or at least early recognition of) periods of emotional difficulty, which then may be palliated, often in fairly simple ways. Examples of such role changes are getting a new brother or sister, entering school, developing sexually in early adolescence, leaving home in late adolescence, and experiencing major changes in adulthood (entering military service, marrying, being pregnant, giving birth, moving, changing jobs, and being bereaved). Indeed, the relatively fixed age, within our society, of some of these role changes may contribute to the apparent relation of developmental periods to chronological age.

There is one trick every teacher knows: When trapped in a state of ignorance throw the question back to the class. Without suspecting the teacher's predicament, bright students will often rescue him.

This is the strategy I employed to learn something about crises in normal personality development. I passed along the assignment to my class of 100 captive undergraduates, and they obligingly provided me, through their own autobiographical writing, with the insights that I articulate now. Parenthetically, let me say that in my opinion no teacher or counselor has the right to require intimate autobiographical documents from students. Yet when given a completely free choice, the large majority will choose to write in the autobiographical vein. For the few who would find the experience too threatening, it should not be prescribed.

. . .

It is in middle and late adolescence, . . . according to Erikson (3), that the identity crisis is in the ascendance.* The young person seems to be moving from past childhood into present adulthood in a jerky manner. Development is not continuous like a hill; rather, it is episodic like a flight of stairs. It is this episodic or crisis character of development that brings both challenge and opportunity to the guidance officer.

NATURE OF CRISIS

What precisely is a "crisis"? It is a situation of emotional and mental stress requiring significant alterations of outlook within a short period of time. These alterations of outlook frequently involve changes in the structure of personality. The resulting changes may be progressive in the life or they may be regressive. By definition, a person in crisis cannot stand still; that is to say, he cannot redact his present traumatic experience into familiar and routine categories or employ simple habitual modes of adjustment. He must either separate himself further from childhood and move toward adulthood, or else move backward to earlier levels of adjustment which may mean becoming disorganized, dropping out of school, escaping from the field, developing hostilities and defenses, and in general becoming a thorn in the flesh of the teacher, the parent, the counselor, the dean, and occasionally of the police. Sometimes, following a crisis, the adolescent will become stabilized anew after four or five weeks of severe disorganization; but in many cases the trauma retards development for a year or more, and may even leave a life-long scar.

---

* Erikson's views are stated at the beginning of this section in "A Healthy Personality for Every Child."—EDITOR

Gordon W. Allport, "Crises in normal personality development," *Teachers College Record*, 1964, 66 (3), 235–241. Reprinted, with slight abridgement, by permission.

Turning now to my data, drawn from college undergraduates, we ask first about the phenomenology of crisis. What does it "feel" like to the student? Common is a sense of numbness and apathy. Upon entering college, the youth finds fewer strict role-prescriptions than at home. He is no longer tied to his domestic filial role, to the highly structured routine of high school, to his siblings, to his church connections, to his teen-age sub-cultures. He has left his possessions behind—his stamp collection, his television, his girl friends, his boy friends. All his familiar roles are in suspension. As one students writes,

The complete freedom of college is itself a crisis. For the first time I live in close contact with people who are not members of my family. They don't even resemble people I have known before. They have different opinions, different origins, and different emotions. I feel numbed by it all.

Interestingly enough, this sense of hollowness does not necessarily have its maximum effect during the freshman year. The excitement of new scenes and especially frequent correspondence with and visits back to the home town keep the silver cord intact. The student feels that he should prove to his parents, teachers, friends, that he can master the college environment and thus please them and win their approval as he has done in the past. The impending crisis has not yet overwhelmed him (or her—for what I am saying is as true for college girls as for boys).

It is the sophomore year that seems (from my data) to be the year of crisis *par excellence*. Suddenly it becomes no longer tolerable to live one's life for the edification of people "back home." The time has come for the child of the past to be separated once and for all from the adult of the present. Here are typical phenomenological statements of this stage of the crisis:

I feel I have been dragged into something against my will.

I feel like a rat in a maze.

I want to be a law unto myself, but cannot.

It seems suddenly that the decisions I make must be valid for the rest of my life.

To shake off parental norms and values seems to me the most important thing I must do.

The life of the past and the life of the future seem suddenly to be at cross purposes. There is often an intolerable feeling of suspended animation. Recrystallization is not yet possible. The youth is waiting still to make a choice of careers, a suitable marriage, and to find an integrative philosophy of life which his diverse college courses are too discordant to supply.

APATHY AND ANXIETY

It is small wonder that apathy and a paralysis of will often occur. But apathy is only a mask for anxiety. The whole framework of life is disturbed. Whereas the majority of students contrive gradually to build a new framework in spite of, or perhaps because of, the goads of anxiety, yet a large minority cannot cope with the situation unaided.

From my data, I would estimate that three-quarters are able to take the progressive road in creating their new frame of existence. About one-quarter cannot immediately do so. Proof of this point is that the dropout rate during undergraduate years is surprisingly high—over 20 per cent at Harvard, about three-quarters of the cases representing voluntary withdrawals (2). The dropouts present a special problem of guidance. Blaine and McArthur (2) write,

The drop-outs as a group ultimately do quite well if properly handled. We attempt to establish a relationship, however brief or tenuous, with these students, not so much to prevent their leaving school, but rather in the hope of giving them some insight into the determinants of their difficulties so that their dropping out can be ultimately converted into a meaningful constructive experience instead of mere failure.

After a year or two of constructive work elsewhere, the majority of voluntary dropouts return to college and graduate. But they could not have met their crisis by remaining in the environment that was the context of their conflict.

The regressive road is surprisingly common. Among eventual dropouts, but also among other students, we find such self-destroying behavior as quitting classes, a compulsion to do trivial things, playing bridge until four A.M., drinking bouts, feelings of unreality, fugues, and general debauchery. The candid documents received startle me a bit by the extent of plain juvenile delinquency among my innocent-appearing students:

One student finding himself unable to handle his conflicts over choice of career and over friction with his roommate, indulged in plagiarism on a term paper in such a way that he would be caught and forcibly separated from college. In this case a wise instructor, catching him in the transgression, turned the occasion into constructive counseling, forgave the deed, and put the lad onto the progressive rather than regressive road.

Here I venture a theoretical digression. The problem, as I see it, is one of interiorizing motivation. To put it in a student's words: "I am fed up with having everybody else cheer me on. I want to work to please myself rather than others, but I don't know how to do it." This plaintive statement points to a serious dilemma in our educational process. In school, the child is rewarded and punished by good grades and bad grades. Even in college, As and Bs are pats on the back, Ds and Fs are punishment. To gain love, the student must read books and toe the academic line. Finally, he obtains his degree (which is a symbol of academic love) and is freed from this external form of motivation. What then happens?

We know that a shockingly high percentage of college graduates rarely or never read another book after receiving their bachelor's degree. Why should they? Their love now comes from their employer, their wife, their children, not from the approval of parents and teachers. For them, intellectual curiosity never became a motive in its own right. External rewards are appropriate props in early childhood. But we educators, being limited by current inadequate theories of learning, do not know how to help the student free himself from the props of reward and develop a functionally autonomous zeal for learning. With our slavish dependence on reinforcement theory, I think it surprising that we arouse as much internal motivation as we do. In any event, we cannot be proud of the many educational cripples who after graduation, lacking the routine incentive of college, sink into intellectual apathy.

CRISIS AREAS

The counselor or teacher, of course, cannot wait for better theories of learning. He is confronted here and now with crises in the concrete. Four areas of conflict, judging from my data, are especially common.

INTELLECTUAL CRISES

First, there are students whose problem is one of intellectual malplacement. Among my cases, a large number report that in primary and secondary school they were too bright for their class. The penalty is one of boredom lasting down into college work, which they still do not find challenging enough for their abilities. At the same time, double promotions in elementary and high school are not a solution. To be placed with older children often creates social difficulties far more serious than boredom. In fact, the evil consequences reported from double promotion are so numerous that we

should challenge this particular solution of the bright child's dilemma.

The opposite type of intellectual crisis is also common. It is the deep disturbance that often results in college from intensified competition. It is statistically impossible for most students to maintain the same relative superiority in college that they enjoyed in high school. While this fact does not trouble the majority, it is a critical experience for those who depend on scholarship aid or who frame their self-image almost entirely in terms of scholarly preeminence. They are suffering a severe narcissistic wound.

SPECIFIC INFERIORITIES

A second area of crisis is the old, familiar "inferiority complex." Besides the sense of intellectual inferiority just described, we encounter deep disturbance due to physical handicaps or to plain physical appearance, with resulting shyness, loneliness, and misery. To be poor at athletics creates a crisis for males, probably more acute in high school than in college. To be a member of a minority group likewise creates an inevitable crisis somewhere along the line. Here again I suspect the major adjustments and defenses are prepared before the college age. Occasionally, the inferiority concerns guilt due to moral lapses. One student is still haunted by her dishonesty which enabled her to pass a certain course three years ago. She has felt miserable ever since about this critical experience and badly needs a means of expiation.

In this connection we may speak of religious crises. While they are uncommon in my sample, Havens (5) estimates that at any given time 12 per cent of college students have a critical concern, and sometimes acute crises, due to their religious conflicts. I suspect the concern is even more widespread, but since it pertains to one's whole ground of being, it is seldom configured as a specific crisis at a given moment of time.

Another area, seldom mentioned but surely important, is the ideological crisis of modern society as a whole. Youth is inevitably worried, as are adults, by our uncertain future. Elsewhere I have discussed the withdrawal of American youth from their social and political context (4). Both the earlier and present data show an almost exclusive concern among American youth with their own lives. Compared with autobiographies of youth in other cultures, the American documents are far more self-centered, more privatistic. They are too baffled to articulate their distress, and so take refuge in their private concerns.

Sex and Family *

SEX CONFLICTS

Needless to say, our candid discussions of crises frequently, in fact usually, report acute sex conflicts. Extremely common are breakups in boy-girl relationships which are usually taken as a disaster only slightly less fatal than the end of the world. Such breakups are so recently experienced that college students do not realize that they will, in spite of their present feelings, eventually make a good recovery.

We should face the fact that at least in the early years of college life crises in the sexual sphere are for the most part frankly genital in their reference. The biological drive is so powerful that the youth is concerned with it almost by itself. Its integration into mature love, into marriage, into career plans, into an embracing philosophy of life, exceeds his present capacity. He is likely to think that genitality by itself is maturity. Sexual gratification is frankly the aim, often with devastating consequences. At this stage of development, the students have much to say about sex and little to say about mature love.

FAMILY CONFLICTS

I have left until last the most pervasive area of conflict and crisis. I am referring, of course, to the situation that exists between every adolescent and his parents. It is not enough to say that adolescent rebellion against the parents is the rule. Of course it is; but my documents show that the whole history of the relationships from the time of earliest memories is important. Almost any irregularity in normal family life is felt bitterly and may trouble a student even into adulthood. A mother who is neglectful or self-centered, or perhaps overpossessive and neurotic, leaves traumatic traces in the child's life. A father who is ineffectual and weak, or cruel, or absent (if only for wartime service) leaves the child with a lasting feeling of protest.

One document of unusual maturity notes that many college students seem to need their parents as scapegoats. They find it comfortable to blame parents for their own shortcomings. Perceiving that their parents are not all-powerful, all-wise, and all-perfect, they can say, "Well, no wonder I am having a hard time growing up; they didn't raise me right." Thus, an adolescent, having no genuine ground for complaint, may yet soak himself in self-pity, not being mature enough to relate his re-

stricted image of his parents to the totality of human nature—not yet ready to appreciate the fact that his parents, considering human limitations, may have done a good job. Even if the job was not especially good, the adolescent seems not yet able to appreciate his parents' good intentions as an important value in their own right. From talking with many parents, I hazard the hypothesis that normally it is not until the age of 23 that a child encounters his parents on a mature, adult-to-adult basis.

This brief account of crises emanating from the parent-child relationship leads me to a final point. My students were required to discuss their crises from the point of view of personality theory. They were free to employ any of the theories they were studying in my course. Most of them took Freud. (I may add that the reason was not because Freud was their instructor's favorite author.)

THE CONDITIONS OF THEORY

Now my observation is this: Their Freudian interpretations seemed to fit well if and when the family situation in early life was disturbed. When the father was absent or ineffectual, when the mother was notably aggressive, when there was deliberate sex stimulation within the family—in such cases, it seems that the Oedipal formula provides a good fit, together with all its theoretical accoutrements of identification, superego conflict, defense mechanisms, castration threats, and all the rest.

When, on the other hand, the family life is reasonably normal and secure, a Freudian conceptualization seems forced and artificial. If we say, by way of rough estimate, that 60 per cent of the students try a Freudian conceptualization of their own cases, about 10 per cent turn out to be wholly convincing and theoretically appropriate. The remaining 50 per cent appear to be somehow contrived and badly strained.

I am wondering whether the same ratio might be applicable to cases that come to counselors. If a counselor or a therapist approaches every client or patient with the preconceived belief that his life must fit a Freudian frame of conceptualization, he may win in a minority of the cases, but lose in the majority.

Even where a Freudian approach is clearly justified, exclusive adherence to it may distract the counselor from many significant developments within the life—for example, from the present functional significance of religious and aesthetic values, from the competence and interests that extend beyond the neurotic core, from the client's conscious plans for the future, and from his "will to meaning" and existential concern with life as a whole.

---

* In order to interpet the material which follows, the reader should know that the majority of students in this study were males.—EDITOR

Every person concerned with guidance, or for that matter with teaching, needs as background some general theory of the nature of human personality (1).* Our tendency, I fear, is to draw our theories from the realm of illness and deviance. It is somehow tempting to apply psychiatric rubrics to all personalities, for psychiatric rubrics are vivid, incisive, dramatic, and easy. Our conceptual banners bear such sloganized concepts as Oedipal complex, character disorder, identity diffusion, schizoid, acting out, and maybe an array of dimensions drawn from the Minnesota Multiphasic Personality Inventory. All such concepts, of course, have their proper place. But personality theory for guidance and teaching needs also to be woven of less lurid fabrics.

Youth, whatever neurotic threads may lie in his nature, is busy with his realistic perceptions, with his gradual learning and quiet coping, with the slow extension of selfhood, with noncritical failures and successes, with developing a generic conscience and a personal style of life. Even in the throes of crisis, he seeks in undramatic ways to consolidate his gains and continue on the path of becoming. A theory of personality adequate to undergird the art of guidance will keep such nondramatic facts in mind. Crises in normal personality development are important, but so too is the slow growth of each youth's unique style of life.

---

* The article cited here is to be found in Section I of this book.—EDITOR

REFERENCES

1. ALLPORT, G. W. Psychological models for guidance. *Harvard educ. Rev.,* 1962, *32,* 373–381.

2. BLAINE, G. B., & McARTHUR, C. C. *Emotional problems of the student.* New York: Appleton-Century-Crofts, 1961.

3. ERIKSON, E. *Childhood and society.* New York: Norton, 1950.

4. GILLESPIE, J. M., & ALLPORT, G. W. *Youth's outlook on the future.* New York: Doubleday, 1955.

5. HAVENS, J. A study of religious conflict in college students. *J. sci. Stud. Relig.,* 1963, *3,* 52–69.

43

Student Unrest: Sources and Consequences

LEON EISENBERG

We have recently seen a tremendous increase in restlessness and sometimes violence among students. Leon Eisenberg, professor of psychiatry at Harvard Medical School and chief of psychiatry at Massachusetts General Hospital, suggests that the experience of being young has changed radically. The period of adolescence is prolonged, for one thing. Not only the university but the whole of society has changed. It appears that both are continuing to evolve at an unprecedented pace. Eisenberg discusses implications of these changes for the behavior of adolescents.

. . . They will rediscover rules of behavior which their predecessors have let fall into disuse, including matters supposed to be of little importance: how the young should be silent in the presence of their elders, give up their seats to them, and take dutiful care of their parents; not to mention details of personal appearance, such as the way their hair is cut and the clothes and shoes they wear. It would be silly, I think, to make laws on these matters; such habits cannot be established or kept up by written legislation. It is probable, at any rate, that the bent given by education will determine the quality of later life, by that sort of attraction which like things always have for one another, till they finally mount up to one imposing result, whether for good or ill. For that reason I should not myself be inclined to push legislation to that length.— SOCRATES, as quoted in Plato's *"Republic"*

This article is based on a paper presented at the annual meeting of the American Academy of Pediatrics, held in Chicago, Illinois, 21 October 1969.

Does psychiatry have anything useful to say about student unrest? I am uncertain. My reluctance to give a positive answer stems from the role ascribed to the psychiatrist. When he speaks, he is heard as though his comments are based solely on his knowledge of the mentally ill; his remarks on this topic will be taken to imply that student unrest is a manifestation of illness—and that, as I shall try to point out, is just what I do *not* think it is. I do not deny that some students, indeed some student leaders, are ill; any social movement that involves large numbers of people must, on the basis of statistical probability, include some who are ill. But that fact is tangential to any attempt to understand the fundamental sources of contemporary student behavior. If psychiatrists have anything useful to add, it will be from our knowledge of the interrelation between social forces and psychological development—that is, of normal adolescent and young adult psychology as these arise from, and in turn affect, the social and cultural history of this epoch (*1*).

Student unrest in countries on every continent stirs passions and polarizes opinions. Urgent decisions are forced upon administrators by the vehemence of student activists. Traditional academic reliance on committees of investigation and prolonged faculty debates is precisely what students will not tolerate; they insist that delay sanctions immorality. Their tactic of confrontation is designed to provoke a response; clearly, it succeeds in doing so. Without the grace of leisurely contemplation, official reaction rapidly becomes reflex, as unreasoned and as impulsive as that of which we accuse the students. The rapidity of events puts a premium on hastily contrived and simpleminded "explanations" of extraordinarily complex phenomena.

That there is little time does not relieve us of the need to take time to try to understand lest we destroy the virtues of the University in the name of "defending" it. The greatness of the academic tradition lies precisely in its responsiveness to human needs. Needs change, styles change, societies change; many of our students perceive the very university life which we found so meaningful for our own development as irrelevant to theirs; they regard it as counterproductive in solving the major social problems of this era. It is often the brightest, the most committed, the most creative, who so regard it (*2*). It falls upon us to try to understand what it is about them, and what it is about the world they live in, that can account for this turning away from the Academy. Without such understanding, this nation may set forth upon a course of action that will destroy the University and its students—and us as well.

ACADEMIC TURBULENCE NOT NEW

First, a historical note.

The American student revolution that began in the 1960's is regarded by the general public as unprecedented; this is partly because of the unhealthy quietude that prevailed in the previous decade of witch-hunting congressional committees. In fact, Harvard, recently the scene of a building take-over and a police bust after years of relative tranquility, was wracked by student revolutions in the 18th and 19th centuries. These revolts were not over high moral issues but over the more mundane matter of the quality of the food served in the commons. From this each took its name: the Bread and Butter Rebellion of 1805; the Cabbage Rebellion of 1807. The new commons built in 1814, called University Hall (the name of the building seized in 1969), was the scene of general turmoil which led to the dismissal of the entire sophomore class, one of whose members (John Washington Adams) was the son of the then President of the United States, John Quincy Adams.

Indeed, the European universities, on which the American were modeled, had been marked by serious and bloody fights between the academics and townspeople in France and in England (3). Cambridge University itself was founded by migrating scholars from Oxford after that university was closed. Perhaps half the universities in Europe owe their origin to such migrations—and the constitutions of others were formalized only after riots had forced change.

If I mention the past, it is to remind us that the phenomena that beset us have not appeared *de novo*, but *not* to suggest that the causes are identical or to imply that we can simply await the passing of the tide. The university occupies a far more central position in contemporary society; students form so much larger a proportion of the young population as to have altered the social role and significance of student life qualitatively; although food or dormitory life can be a trigger for unrest, the public slogans behind which the students rally demand changes in society, not the privilege of the monastic pursuit of isolated scholarship.

My remarks are confined to the North American scene. The phenomenon itself, as each day's newspapers reveal, is worldwide. Some of the motivating factors are similar here and abroad (and thus this article may have at least limited relevance elsewhere). Others are ecologically specific; the antiquated and authoritarian structure of Italian and French universities, the role of military oligarchies in Latin America; the lack of professional opportunities in undercapitalized countries; the suppression of cultural freedom in eastern Europe—each shapes student response. But it is my contention that the United States, by virtue of its enormous productive capacity, its technological finesse, and its relative, but uneven, affluence, offers in its present a view of a future inevitable for the youth of other nations—unless they (and we) recognize the sociological revolution in the status of young people that is part of the "post-industrial" state.

PROLONGATION OF ADOLESCENCE

Let me now sketch in broadly some of the identifiable forces which shape the characteristics of contemporary youth. Of these, the most often mentioned, but by no means the most important, is biological.

There has been a marked secular trend toward a lowering of the mean age at which puberty occurs. Tanner (4) has estimated that "the age at menarche has been getting earlier by some four months per decade in Western Europe over the period of 1830–1960." By this projection, *biological* adolescence begins 4 years earlier than it did a century and a half ago, presumably because of improvements in nutrition and health. Obviously, this is not an infinite regression. There is a biological lower bound; nations, and classes within nations, undergoing the most rapid economic gains experience the most marked changes. The relevance to our topic is simply this: the attainment of the biological capacity for assuming adult roles now antecedes by a significantly longer period than in the past the time at which the young person is admitted to adult status, and would do so even if the age of adulthood had remained constant.

More significant, however, is a second set of factors. With the increasing technological development of modern society, the age at which the necessary training for adult roles can be mastered extends the interval between childhood and acknowledged adulthood still further, thus prolonging adolescence *socially*, just as it has been prolonged *biologically*. I need not spell out the psychological significance of possessing physical, intellectual, and social capacities the responsible exercise of which is denied by the rules and conventions of societies which have not accommodated to change.

Yet, on the other hand, by virtue of this very prolongation of the time available, not to a small elite, but to an ever larger number of our youth, it is also true that adolescent and young-adult psychological development is permitted a time for flowering unknown to earlier generations.

CHILDHOOD, ADOLESCENCE, AND YOUTH AS CONCEPTS

Philip Aries (5) has provided evidence that the *idea* of childhood is a relatively recent cultural invention. In the Middle Ages, only infancy was recognized as a separate stage. It lasted until the age of 7, when the child was assimilated into the adult world by apprenticeship, with little or no formal education for the vast majority of children. The concept of childhood as a separate stage of human development was first advanced in the educational writings of the French philosophers of the Enlightenment.

As infant mortality began to decrease, and as the amount of leisure time began to increase, the experience of childhood began to change. With the growth of industrialization and the need for a better-trained working class, education of the child and his segregation from adult society in the special institutions appropriate to the new concept of childhood began to be the norm for an ever larger percentage of the world's children.

Kenneth Keniston (6) has carried this argument one step further: he suggests that the *concept* of adolescence is a 20th-century idea, resulting from the further evolution of society. Freud, writing at the turn of the century, spoke of puberty as a biological event and had relatively little to say about it in contrast to the profusion of publications on adolescence that appeared in the post-World War II period. In this country, mandatory schooling up to the age of 18 has become the rule; the period of being sheltered from work roles and of being assigned formal educational tasks has been extended to an increasingly large percentage of the 12- to 18-year-old population, for whom the job market has in any event no openings.

With some 7 million young Americans in colleges and universities, Keniston argues that the ground has been set for a new stage of psychological development: the postadolescent stage of *youth*.

These are young people who have completed the psychological tasks of adolescence in Erikson's terms—emancipation from the family of origin, comfort with sexuality, attainment of a sense of identity and a capacity for intimacy (7). But, in their extended role as students, given a moratorium from the need to assume adult responsibilities, they continue to experiment with adult roles and to reassess their relation to society. Unlike so many of us a generation ago, they are not willing simply to be enrolled in the society made for them by their elders but, instead, question the very foundations of that society. They fluctuate between moods of euphoria, convinced that they can make real a world of beauty and idealism, and moods of alienation, wanting nothing to do with an ugly reality

they despair of changing. It is true that they have not learned the necessity of translating idealistic ambition into effective tactics for progress. But have we?

I do not wish to be misunderstood. There have been children, adolescents, and youth in all recorded history. But the self-conscious awareness of these epochs as stages of development and the creation of social institutions to provide the time and the means for their flowering are new phenomena, new at least in the sense that more than a handful of young people participate in this further personal development.

The very newness of the concept of adolescence and the explosive growth in the numbers of those sharing in it contribute to a social hiatus: the absence of traditional mores for behavior appropriate to this prolonged and massed stage of youth. Ruth Benedict, 30 years ago (8), pointed out that primitive societies provide rites of passage in puberty—feats of strength and courage and tribal ceremonies that formally acknowledge the beginning of manhood. Contemporary society has blurred as well as prolonged this transition. For many—the poor, the black, the Mexican, the Puerto Rican, the Indian—there is no assurance of an adult role with meaning and dignity. I have argued elsewhere (9) that the striking absence of adolescent unrest in Israeli collective farms is in part explicable in terms of the need for the labor of the young, upon whom the collective depends for its existence (9). Perhaps I exaggerate the absence of norms for youth. In our time, riots and rowdyism were hardly uncommon; they occurred after football games and in panty raids. But these were the prerogatives of the college-bound elite; their elders smiled indulgently at these momentary excesses of young gentlemen en route to executive roles. Can it be that our ire is aroused by a difference in *causes,* by the *seriousness* of the challenge, by the *social character* of the crowd, no longer a privileged elite but an unwashed generation?

SOCIAL CHARACTERISTICS OF STUDENT LIFE

Let me shift now from the psychology of individual development to follow Coleman's sociological analysis (10). To repeat, we confront a large segment of the population who experience an enforced delay of the time at which they enter socially productive work. Moreover, their families are becoming far less important units of social cohesion, as more and more of the roles once borne by the family are taken on by other institutions in society. Third, these young people are segregated into mass educational institutions, which have a special value system: the student is given the task of improving himself on an individualistic basis—indeed, a competitive one—in which the success of one student is at the expense of another; grading is likely to be on a distribution curve. The funnel narrows as the student moves from one level to the next.

Moreover, the university itself has grown larger and consequently more bureaucratic and impersonal. Small group and tutorial sessions, once the hallmark of higher education, have been replaced by computer assignments, large lecture halls, and televised instruction. Funding mechanisms, which make each scientist an entrepreneur in securing money to support his own research establishment, have weakened faculty loyalties to the university and to its students. Faculty advancement has been based on numbers of papers published and grants obtained, rather than on capacity to inspire the young. Regimented in large cohorts, pressed toward egoistic goals, isolated from the governance of the campus, the students' experience is one of disconnectedness from society. Moreover, the growing legions of college students (estimated at 10 million by 1975!) include many who are "social draftees" rather than "volunteers." Most immediately, this results from the search for an alternative to military conscription. But even were the Vietnam war to end, social pressures from parents and peers, together with occupational demands for credentials in the form of diplomas certifying, not competence, but completion, conspire to assign the university the role of producer of a managerial class rather than that of a haven for personal development.

Contrast this with the traditional social function of the young worker who must collaborate with others in producing for society. Though each worker may be motivated by his paycheck, he can earn it only in a common effort by virtue of the very nature of mass production; he can increase it only by joining with others in a trade union. If even the adults in contemporary society feel atomized and alienated, how much more must this be true of the student who has no immediate usefulness to society and who has had little to say in controlling the destiny of the society of which he is, willy-nilly, a member? It may be this very characteristic that makes joining in common causes so exhilarating an experience for students. As one reads the accounts of those who have participated in the seizure of buildings, one is struck by the repetitive assertion of the sense of euphoria and communal love that characterizes the immediate experience, whatever depression and dismay may follow its failure, and however ineffective the tactic may have been in attaining its professed aims. Some of these revolutionaries of ours are existential revolutionaries; for many it is the experience that matters rather than the accomplishments. In this emphasis on *feeling* lies the threat to the political mechanisms that must be preserved if social change is to be attained.

Just as these young people differ from the youth of an earlier day by virtue of these psychological and social characteristics, the world in which they live differs from the world of our adolescence in equally important ways. Industrialization has been succeeded by automation. To the machines that permitted man to augment his muscles have been added machines that permit him to augment his brain. This awesome power has resulted in a society that changes at an exponential pace. In a sense, the machines do outthink us, for they promise immediate gains so glittering in their appeal that we introduce them before we have been able to calculate their consequences. We are only just becoming aware of the pollution of our environment by the very technology that brings us creature comforts but whose price is the corruption of the quality of life. Some economists predict a future in which there will be work for no more than a fraction of the population. If this comes to pass, the religious ethic of work, common to the Judeo-Christian tradition, may be as out of date as the horse and the gas light. If the young regard the traditions we wish to pass on to them as irrelevant, they may not be wrong. Those traditions, even those only a generation old, may no longer be functional in a world that is radically different from the one in which they may have made sense. The hippie movement is dying, but its insistence on a degree of hedonism that infuriates those conditioned to a lifetime of hard work may in fact be a harbinger of future trends.

REVOLUTION AS THEATER OF THE ABSURD

Of the technical innovations that have special impact upon the young, none is more insistent and relentless than television. Television serves not only to transmit selectively, and by selection to determine, what is "news" but often to affect the course of the news by virtue of the presence of cameras on the scene. Its ubiquity and intrusiveness lend every contemporary happening the quality of living theater. Events are made "events" by the camera, whose presence inspires dramatic performances by providing an audience. Styles of behavior, once slowly spread by personal travel, now command instant imitation—and produce instant boredom, thus forcing a search for ever greater flamboyance if an audience is to be captured. The pace is accelerated, and overstatement is demanded, for the watcher has quickly had enough and turns the knob in search of new and more prurient excitement. It has become standard operating procedure to alert the mobile television truck as to the time and place of the next demonstration; without coverage, its value as witness is diminished. I do not suggest that the similarity of student tactics the world over is solely determined by the visual transmission of style—social urgencies the world over have their own resemblances—but each new stratagem becomes at once available to the rebel discouraged by the bankruptcy of his former repertoire. In *La Dolce Vita*, Fellini employed hordes of news photographers to symbolize the avidity with which the public devours scandal and destroys privacy. How pale the photograph in contrast to the moving image which converts political assassination into a commodity for home viewing!

Pervasive social problems press upon the young from every side. They inhabit a world that hangs upon the edge of instant nuclear destruction. The ideology of some is bitterly evident in the current one-line joke, "When you sail on the S.S. *Titanic*, why not go first class!" American students face enforced service in a savage and unpopular war in Vietnam or the equally unpalatable alternatives of jail or emigration. Their brief flurry into conventional political activity in support of Eugene McCarthy ended in the debacle at Chicago. In their view, the universities they attend have become corrupted in the process of serving the needs of the military-industrial complex, against which President Eisenhower had warned the nation. The major iniquities of society—poverty and racism—continue unchecked in the midst of affluence and plenty.

Unlike the last generation, this one rejects ideologies, capitalist and communist alike. The young insist on unconditional morality, a goal no society has yet attained, and they demand it now. Their insistence on immediate change together with their disdain for tactics and practicality, their emphasis on resurrection through personal witness, and their substitution of rhetoric for the hard work of politics, understandable though these manifestations may be, jeopardize the realization of the very social aims behind which they rally.

Irresponsible calls for social revolution when the social conditions for change do not yet exist can endanger the very possibility of change.

But perhaps we have been addressing ourselves to the wrong question all along. Perhaps we should be asking, not why there is student unrest, but why there is no *adult* unrest, except in response to students. Why are we content to tolerate an immoral and futile war? Why do we as physicians permit health services to be cut back while $100 million each day is committed to the war in Vietnam? Is it perhaps because we have been complacent that the young are frantic?

If I have referred to students as "they" and have written as though so multifarious a group shared a single ideology—even that of "rejecting ideologies"—this has been no more than a device of rhetoric. To have qualified each statement with appropriate reservations would have made each sentence a labored paragraph and this brief article an unreadable monograph. One need only cite the bitter schisms that have ripped apart the once pluralistic and decentralized Students for a Democratic Society as testimony to the diversity and contradictions within the student movement. There simply are no reliable data for identifying that fraction of the student population that is "activist" in the broad sense of the term; sections of the country differ, and this month's answers almost certainly will not obtain next month. Indeed, there *are* students who accept traditional academic paths—some in pursuit of scholarship, others en route to professional roles, still others as a means of achieving occupational mobility—and some who maintain a precarious equilibrium by *not* raising questions.

Whatever the fraction of the disaffected who are explicitly committed to the goal of radical social change, what is striking is the large reservoir of support from their peers, who rally in substantial numbers when sanctions are brought to bear against the initially small bands. It is conventional wisdom to dismiss this secondary response as irrelevant to the initial issues and to attribute it to the cleverness of radical tacticians (and the ineptness of university authorities) in "politicizing" the student body. This is no more than another expression of disbelief in the salience of the issues that arouse students. The post-bust slogans may broaden to include demands for amnesty, but the initial banners are still very much in evidence. They continue to provide, because they are viewed as legitimate, the moral justification in the minds of the many for the defense of the beleaguered few. This remains true whatever may have been the intent of self-proclaimed revolutionaries.

One further distinction must, however, be emphasized. The concerns, the tactics, and the special circumstances of black students, while having attributes in common with those of white students, require a special analysis that is beyond the scope of this article. White student radicals are still in search of a constituency beyond the bounds of the campus; as of this writing, at least, they have had no evident success in their call for an alliance with labor. Black students command greater, if still limited, sympathy in their own off-campus communities and have begun to voice demands more immediately relevant to the needs of those communities; witness the current emphasis on jobs for construction workers rather than on purely academic reforms. The experience of growing up black in white America so burns itself into the consciousness of black adolescents and youths as to become the central issue in their development (*11*).

The attitudes manifested by the student vanguard, white and black, are more significant than can be ascertained merely through counting numbers. For they bring to awareness, by sharpening to the point of caricature, the very issues, so easily blinked at by those of us who have it made, that threaten the fabric of society. To the extent that they reflect views shared in some part by a substantial percentage of their fellow students, they speak for some millions of young people. And that is a sociological phenomenon without parallel in our—or any nation's—history.

WHO SHALL GUARD THE GUARDIANS?

To diagnose student unrest as though it were symptomatic of individual psychopathology is to fall into the error of confusing history with biography. The label of sickness provides a rationalization for avoiding an examination of the criticism the "patient" makes of his "family" and "doctor." To label unrest as "sick" is no more than a sophisticated version of the rage of adults at the effrontery of the child who pointed out that the Emperor had no clothes on. In part, adult fury stems from the very accuracy of the charge the young lodge against us. This is not to say that the correctness of the accusation warrants abject surrender by our generation; the young have no greater wisdom than we possess, and a good deal less practicality. But it is to say that resort to harsh punishment will perpetuate angry rebellion and block meaningful change.

The danger is dramatically clear. The anarchy of the young; the recklessness of some in threatening the university, the last remaining platform for rational dissent; their isolation from the mainstream of the community—all combine to offer the right wing a prime and long-sought opportunity to smash the university in the name of protecting it. Our difficult task is to defend the legitimacy of student criticism at the same time that we find a way to make students aware that more is needed than sloganeering.

What must be combatted among students is the romantic movement to substitute feeling for knowing. If cold logic without ethics is what enables the engineer or the scientist to hire himself out to be a hangman and produce weapons of mass destruction, it is also true that the romantic revolutionary gets himself and his disciples slaughtered in the mountains by the guns of mercenaries.

Yet students have been perhaps the most potent single force in mobilizing public opinion against the

war. Consider only the remarkable support for the Vietnam moratorium generated primarily by student groups. Indeed, 79 university presidents, notably silent until now, have petitioned the government for troop withdrawal. If it is argued that the university has been politicized, let it likewise be recognized that compliant silence is also a political act, particularly when it is accompanied by war-related research at the expense of comparable efforts to solve the staggering domestic problems that confront our nation. The irrational and often self-destructive actions of the minority of self-proclaimed revolutionaries represent only a small part of the youth scene. Indeed, what must be combated is the stereotyping of all students in the image of the few whose unacceptable behavior provides a convenient excuse for ignoring the real issues at the core of present-day unrest.

The energy, idealism, and intelligence of youth are the prime resources of each nation; if those resources are to be wisely spent, our youth must be involved in the mainstream of national life. Youth is impatient—as it should be—with excuses for perpetuating evil. In the excess of its zeal, it sometimes abandons reason. But he who does not lose his mind over certain things has no mind to lose.

REFERENCES

1. L. EISENBERG, *Children,* 1965, *12,* 131; _____, in *Crosscurrents in Psychiatry and Psychoanalysis,* R. Gibson (Ed.), Philadelphia: Lippincott, 1967, p. 65; _____, *Bull. At. Sci.,* 1966, *22,* 27.

2. K. KENISTON, *Young Radicals,* New York: Harcourt, Brace & World, 1968; R. Coles, *Psychiatry,* 1964, *27,* 305.

3. H. RASHDALL, *The Universities of Europe in the Middle Ages,* Oxford: Clarendon, 1895.

4. J. M. TANNER, *Growth at Adolescence,* Oxford: Blackwell, ed. 2, 1962.

5. P. ARIES, *Centuries of Childhood,* New York: Knopf, 1962.

6. K. KENISTON, in *Psychopathology of Adolescence,* J. Zubin and A. Freedman (Eds.), New York: Grune & Stratton, 1970.

7. E. H. ERIKSON, *Psychol. Issues,* 1959, *1,* No. 1.

8. R. BENEDICT, *Psychiatry,* 1938, *1,* 161.

9. L. EISENBERG & P. NEUBAUER, *J. Amer. Acad. Child Psychiat.,* 1965, *4,* 426.

10. J. S. COLEMAN, in *Psychopathology of Adolescence,* J. Zubin and A. Freedman (Eds.), New York: Grune & Stratton, 1970.

11. W. E. B. DuBois, *Souls of Black Folk,* New York: New American Library, 1969; K. B. CLARK, *Dark Ghetto,* New York: Harper & Row, 1965; C. BROWN, *Manchild in the Promised Land,* New York: Macmillan, 1965; MALCOLM X, *The Auto-*

biography of Malcolm X, New York: Grove, 1965; R. COLES, *Children of Crisis,* Boston: Little, Brown, 1967; L. EISENBERG, *Ment. Hyg.,* 1968, *52,* 512; C. M. PIERCE, *Amer. J. Ortho-psychiat.,* 1969, *39,* 553; C. A. PINDERHUGHES, *Amer. J. Psychiat.,* 1969, *125,* 1552; A. F. POUSSAINT and J. LADNER, *Arch. Gen. Psychiat.,* 1968, *18,* 385.

VIII

Sex as a Determinant of Behavior

Under many conditions, knowing a person's gender is important if one wishes to predict how he or she will behave. As an explanatory concept, sex or gender is (and has been) the center of considerable controversy. Are behavioral sex differences rooted in the contrasting biological make-up of males and females? Are they determined by differences in the ways boys and girls are taught to act in conformity with the role ascribed to each sex, as culturally prescribed or as viewed by the particular parents?

Anthropologists have contributed some answers. The contrasts between males and females observed in certain societies are different from the contrasts in others. By providing us with knowledge of the range of behaviors adopted by each of the sexes in various cultures, anthropologists have shown us that certain behaviors are clearly not determined by biological sex. The work of Margaret Mead on this topic is particularly well known (e.g. *Male and Female,* Morrow, 1949).

The differences between the sexes are not to be found solely in the biological aspects of anatomy and reproductive functions. M. F. Ashley Montagu has said that "females are more durable and males more unendurable." The female appears to be biologically sounder than the male at every stage, and can expect to outlive the male. Although more males are conceived than females, more males are lost in spontaneous abortion or miscarriage, and in neonatal and infant deaths. In the living of life, males appear to have more problems. Reading disabilities are more frequent among males, as are at least certain types of emotional disturbances (according to some data in our society). The second part of Montagu's statement refers to the fact that differences in activity level and metabolic rates may contribute to making the male more assertive, more difficult to live with—more "unendurable."

Once we leave the area of biological viability, all differences in behavior between the sexes are due to the action of experience on the genetic substrate. One should note that even genetically there are not just two separate populations (male and female) in the world. The genetic anomalies of the sex chromosomes provide numerous combinations, or "sexes." [1] However, the behavioral effects of the genetic anomalies are poorly understood, though behavioral gender roles seem to be determined primarily by child rearing.

The anthropological evidence that many or perhaps most sex differences other than anatomical are learned has led some psychologists to act as though sex differences did not really exist—that is, as if they were not "real," *only* learned. Researchers even formed their samples by including males and females together as though sex would not affect the results. At present, interest in sex differences has come in for a revival. One reason for this is the fact that research data analyzed separately for the two sexes have frequently revealed that girls and boys responded to the experimental conditions disparately or even in opposite directions.

At the 1961 meeting of the American Psychological Association, Dorothy

---

[1] See Section II, article 5, for further discussion relevant to this topic.

Eichorn, on the basis of some of her work, commented: "If you want to predict the behavior of a male, you must know the male. If you want to predict the behavior of a female, you must know the situation." This statement implies not only that there are differences between males and females, but that male behavior and female behavior must be explained or predicted by different theories. Such a statement does not prejudge whether the differences exist because of biology or because of the interaction of our culture with biological factors. Indeed, any time we use classifications such as sex and race, which appear to be biologically based, or such as "first-born," which appears to reflect experiential differences, we lose a great deal of information that might help us understand or predict behavior. We would always improve our prediction if we knew an individual's personal characteristics, not just which group he belonged to. However, when we have access to no other information, knowledge of membership in such groups may be helpful in predicting behavior.

One must carefully distinguish between using classifications like race, sex, or birth order as an aid in scientific understanding and using them to assign individuals to one treatment or another. This is especially true when the treatment affects opportunities for schooling or jobs. The values of democracy call for equal opportunity for each sex. Even if it should turn out that one kind of educational milieu would be better, on the average, for males and another for females, children should be assigned to educational programs on the basis of their individual characteristics, not just because they happen to be members of a particular biological or social group. This point is not only relevant for sex or race, which are biologically defined groups, but for groups defined by age, birth position in the family, or social class. Age is an imperfect way of defining readiness for school (or readiness for retirement). While position in the family, or birth order, is not an important basis for discrimination in the United States today, some Western cultural groups of the past have accorded great favoritism (in terms of education and inheritance) to the first-born son, regardless of his individual merits or characteristics. Such practices still exist in some parts of the world and to some degree in Western cultures.

Sex differences, conceived of as a product of both biological attributes and learning, may be created or molded in a variety of ways:

1. Certain behaviors are often reinforced more in one sex than in the other.
2. Interpersonal experiences are frequently different according to one's sex.
3. Individuals may belong to groups that have members of only one sex and that mold their behavior accordingly.

To recapitulate, *sex* as an explanatory concept can be *biological* (Section II), or it can be an intermediate variable in such explanatory systems as those stressing *learning* (Section III), *interpersonal experiences* (Section IV), *settings and instigations* (Section V), or *group memberships* (Section VI). From whichever of these standpoints one conceives of sex as a variable in determining behavior, it may also play a role in relation to the other determinants considered in this book (e.g., cognitive and motivational). In most sections, some papers have analyzed or discussed their research data in terms of each sex separately. Some have limited their studies to subjects of only one sex. Such a decision may have been dictated by theoretical or practical concerns. Some theoretical issues are best investigated in one sex only. Discrepant findings for the two sexes may be difficult to deal with in theoretical terms, or the money may be lacking to permit study of a sample large enough to be analyzed for each sex separately.

For those students interested in pursuing this topic in greater depth, we recommend the following sources (listed alphabetically):

1. Daniel G. Brown, "Sex Role Development in a Changing Culture," *Psychological Bulletin,* 1958, *55,* 232–242 (or in either previous edition of this book).
2. Josef E. Garai and Amram Scheinfeld, "Sex Differences in Mental and Behavioral Traits," *Genetic Psychology Monographs,* 1968, *77,* 169–299.
3. David B. Lynn, *Parental and Sex Role Identification* (McCutcheon, 1969). This small book incorporates materials from a number of his articles.
4. John Money, "Developmental Differentiation of Femininity and Masculinity Compared," in *Potential of Women,* edited by S. M. Farber and R. H. L. Wilson (McGraw-Hill, 1963).
5. Paul Mussen and Eldred Rutherford, "Parent-Child Relations and Parental Personality in Relation to Young Children's Sex Role Preferences," *Child Development,* 1963, *34,* 589–607 (and in the second edition of *The Causes of Behavior,* 1966).
6. Robert R. Sears, "Development of Gender Role" in *Sex and Behavior,* edited by Frank A. Beach (Wiley, 1965).

In addition, numerous references will be found in the bibliographies of the various articles in this section.

44

A Cross-cultural Survey
of Some Sex Differences
in Socialization [1]

HERBERT BARRY III,
MARGARET K. BACON,
AND IRVIN L. CHILD

This article gives some cross-cultural perspective on the socialization practices for the two sexes. It thus exemplifies the type of anthropological contribution referred to in the introduction to this section. The paper is based on materials from the Human Relations Area Files developed at Yale University, where the authors were located. The files, copies of which now exist at various universities, contain information about the living practices of human beings in societies around the globe. They are an important source of data for testing hypotheses in psychology and child development, as well as in anthropology.

The survey shows that there are common elements across societies in how the sexes are differentiated. These findings could be used to bolster the idea that biology dictates the communalities. However, the data also show that there are exceptions, thus highlighting the role of cultural determinism. The authors' analysis indicates that the needs of a society or culture influence the variations. This is congruent with the relatively small sex differentiation in our own society. The fact that

the differentiation made between maleness and femaleness is less in the United States (and in modern or technological cultures generally) than in many other cultures does not mean that there is an absence in the U.S. of discrimination based on sex.

Barry, a psychologist interested in psychopharmacology as well as cross-cultural research, has a research appointment in the School of Pharmacy at the University of Pittsburgh. Bacon is in the Department of Anthropology at Livingston College of Rutgers University. Child is professor of psychology at Yale University.

In our society, certain differences may be observed between the typical personality characteristics of the two sexes. These sex differences in personality are generally believed to result in part from differences in the way boys and girls are reared. To the extent that personality differences between the sexes are thus of cultural rather than biological origin, they seem potentially susceptible to change. But how readily susceptible to change? In the differential rearing of the sexes does our society make an arbitrary imposition on an infinitely plastic biological base, or is this cultural imposition found uniformly in all societies as an adjustment to the real biological differences between the sexes? This paper reports one attempt to deal with this problem.

DATA AND PROCEDURES

The data used were ethnographic reports, available in the anthropological literature, about socialization practices of various cultures. One hundred and ten cultures, mostly nonliterate, were studied.[2] They were selected primarily in terms of the existence of adequate ethnographic reports of socialization practices and secondarily so as to obtain a wide and reasonably balanced geographical distribution. Various aspects of socialization of infants and children were rated on a 7-point scale by two judges (Mrs. Bacon and Mr. Barry). Where the ethnographic reports permitted, separate ratings were made for the socialization of boys and girls. Each rating was indicated as either confident or doubtful; with still greater uncertainty, or with

[1] This research is part of a project for which financial support was provided by the Social Science Research Council and the Ford Foundation. We are greatly indebted to G. P. Murdock for supplying us with certain data, as indicated below, and to him and Thomas W. Maretzki for suggestions that have been used in this paper.

[2] Most of the societies we used are listed by name in H. Barry III, I. L. Child, and M. K. Bacon, Relation of child training to subsistence economy, *American Anthropologist*, 1959, *61*, 51–63.

Herbert Barry III, Margaret K. Bacon, and Irvin L. Child, "A cross-cultural survey of some sex differences in socialization," *Journal of Abnormal and Social Psychology*, 1957, *55*, 327–332. Reprinted by permission.

complete lack of evidence, the particular rating was of course not made at all. We shall restrict the report of sex difference ratings to cases in which both judges made a confident rating. Also omitted is the one instance where the two judges reported a sex difference in opposite directions, as it demonstrates only unreliability of judgment. The number of cultures that meet these criteria is much smaller than the total of 110; for the several variables to be considered, the number varies from 31 to 84.

The aspects of socialization on which ratings were made included:

1. Several criteria of attention and indulgence toward infants.
2. Strength of socialization from age 4 to 5 years until shortly before puberty, with respect to five systems of behavior; strength of socialization was defined as the combination of positive pressure (rewards for the behavior) plus negative pressure (punishments for lack of the behavior). The variables were:

   (a) Responsibility or dutifulness training. (The data were such that training in the performance of chores in the productive or domestic economy was necessarily the principal source of information here; however, training in the performance of other duties was also taken into account when information was available.)
   (b) Nurturance training, i.e., training the child to be nurturant or helpful toward younger siblings and other dependent people.
   (c) Obedience training.
   (d) Self-reliance training.
   (e) Achievement training, i.e., training the child to orient his behavior toward standards of excellence in performance, and to seek to achieve as excellent a performance as possible.

Where the term "no sex difference" is used here, it may mean any of three things: (a) the judge found separate evidence about the training of boys and girls on this particular variable, and judged it to be identical; (b) the judge found a difference between the training of boys and girls, but not great enough for the sexes to be rated a whole point apart on a 7-point scale; (c) the judge found evidence only about the training of "children" on this variable, the ethnographer not reporting separately about boys and girls.

SEX DIFFERENCES IN SOCIALIZATION

On the various aspects of attention and indulgence toward infants, the judges almost always agreed in finding no sex difference. Out of 96 cultures for which the ratings included the infancy period, 88 (92%) were rated with no sex difference by either judge for any of those variables. This result is consistent with the point sometimes made by anthropologists that "baby" generally is a single status undifferentiated by sex, even though "boy" and "girl" are distinct statuses.

On the variables of childhood socialization, on the other hand, a rating of no sex difference by both judges was much less common. This finding of no sex difference varied in frequency from 10% of the cultures for the achievement variable up to 62% of the cultures for the obedience variable, as shown in the last column of Table 1. Where a sex difference is reported, by either one or both judges, the difference tends strongly to be in a particular direction, as shown in the earlier columns of the same table. Pressure toward nurturance, obedience, and responsibility is most often stronger for girls, whereas pressure toward achievement and self-reliance is most often stronger for boys.

For nurturance and for self-reliance, all the sex differences are in the same direction. For achievement there is only one exception to the usual direction of difference, and for obedience only two; but for responsibility there are nine. What do these exceptions mean? We have reexamined all these cases. In most of them, only one judge had rated the sexes as differently treated (sometimes one judge, sometimes the other), and in the majority of these cases both judges were now inclined to agree that there was no convincing evidence of a real difference. There were exceptions, however, especially in cases where a more formal or systematic training of boys seemed to imply greater pressure

TABLE 1
RATINGS OF CULTURES FOR SEX DIFFERENCES OF FIVE VARIABLES OF CHILDHOOD SOCIALIZATION PRESSURE

Variable	Number of Cultures	Both Judges Agree in Rating the Variable Higher in		One Judge Rates No Difference, One Rates the Variable Higher in		Percentage of Cultures with Evidence of Sex Difference in Direction of		
		Girls	Boys	Girls	Boys	Girls	Boys	Neither
Nurturance	33	17	0	10	0	82%	0%	18%
Obedience	69	6	0	18	2	35%	3%	62%
Responsibility	84	25	2	26	7	61%	11%	28%
Achievement	31	0	17	1	10	3%	87%	10%
Self-reliance	82	0	64	0	6	0%	85%	15%

on them toward responsibility. The most convincing cases were the Masai and Swazi, where both judges had originally agreed in rating responsibility pressures greater in boys than in girls. In comparing the five aspects of socialization we may conclude that responsibility shows by far the strongest evidence of real variation in the direction of sex difference, and obedience much the most frequently shows evidence of no sex difference at all.

In subsequent discussion we shall be assuming that the obtained sex differences in the socialization ratings reflect true sex differences in the cultural practices. We should consider here two other possible sources of these rated differences.

1. The ethnographers could have been biased in favor of seeing the same pattern of sex differences as in our culture. However, most anthropologists readily perceive and eagerly report novel and startling cultural features, so we may expect them to have reported unusual sex differences where they existed. The distinction between matrilineal and patrilineal, and between matrilocal and patrilocal cultures, given prominence in many ethnographic reports, shows an awareness of possible variations in the significance of sex differences from culture to culture.

2. The two judges could have expected to find in other cultures the sex roles which are familiar in our culture and inferred them from the material on the cultures. However, we have reported only confident ratings, and such a bias seems less likely here than for doubtful ratings. It might be argued, moreover, that bias has more opportunity in the case ambiguous enough so that only one judge reported a sex difference, and less opportunity in the cases where the evidence is so clear that both judges agree. Yet in general, as may be seen in Table 1, the deviant cases are somewhat more frequent among the cultures where only one judge reported a sex difference.

The observed differences in the socialization of boys and girls are consistent with certain universal tendencies in the differentiation of adult sex role. In the economic sphere, men are more frequently allotted tasks that involve leaving home and engaging in activities where a high level of skill yields important returns; hunting is a prime example. Emphasis on training in self-reliance and achievement for boys would function as preparation for such an economic role. Women, on the other hand, are more frequently allotted tasks at or near home that minister most immediately to the needs of others (such as cooking and water carrying); these activities have a nurturant character, and in their pursuit a responsible carrying out of established routines is likely to be more important than the development of an especially high order of skill.

Thus training in nurturance, responsibility, and, less clearly, obedience, may contribute to preparation for this economic role. These consistencies with adult role go beyond the economic sphere, of course. Participation in warfare, as a male prerogative, calls for self-reliance and a high order of skill where survival or death is the immediate issue. The childbearing which is biologically assigned to women, and the child care which is socially assigned primarily to them, lead to nurturant behavior and often call for a more continuous responsibility than do the tasks carried out by men. Most of these distinctions in adult role are not inevitable, but the biological differences between the sexes strongly predispose the distinction of role, if made, to be in a uniform direction.[3]

The relevant biological sex differences are conspicuous in adulthood but generally not in childhood. If each generation were left entirely to its own devices, therefore, without even an older generation to copy, sex differences in role would presumably be almost absent in childhood and would have to be developed after puberty at the expense of considerable relearning on the part of one or both sexes. Hence, a pattern of child training which foreshadows adult differences can serve the useful function of minimizing what Benedict termed "discontinuities in cultural conditioning" (1).

The differences in socialization between the sexes in our society, then, are no arbitrary custom of our society, but a very widespread adaptation of culture to the biological substratum of human life.

VARIATIONS IN DEGREE OF SEX DIFFERENTIATION

While demonstrating near-universal tendencies in direction of difference between the socialization of boys and girls, our data do not show perfect uniformity. A study of the variations in our data may allow us to see some of the conditions which are associated with, and perhaps give rise to, a greater or smaller degree of this difference. For this purpose, we classified cultures as having relatively large or small sex difference by two different methods, one more inclusive and the other more selective. In both methods the ratings were at first considered separately for each of the five variables. A sex difference rating was made only if both judges made a rating on this variable and at least one judge's rating was confident.

In the more inclusive method the ratings were

---

[3] For data and interpretations supporting various arguments of this paragraph, see Mead (2), Murdock (3), and Scheinfeld (6).

dichotomized, separately for each variable, as close as possible to the median into those showing a large and those showing a small sex difference. Thus, for each society a large or a small sex difference was recorded for each of the five variables on which a sex difference rating was available. A society was given an over-all classification of large or small sex difference if it had a sex difference rating on at least three variables and if a majority of these ratings agreed in being large, or agreed in being small. This method permitted classification of a large number of cultures, but the grounds for classification were capricious in many cases, as a difference of only one point in the rating of a single variable might change the over-all classification of sex difference for a culture from large to small.

In the more selective method, we again began by dichotomizing each variable as close as possible to the median; but a society was now classified as having a large or small sex difference on the variable only if it was at least one step away from the scores immediately adjacent to the median. Thus only the more decisive ratings of sex difference were used. A culture was classified as having an over-all large or small sex difference only if it was given a sex difference rating which met this criterion on at least two variables, and only if all such ratings agreed in being large, or agreed in being small.

We then tested the relation of each of these dichotomies to 24 aspects of culture on which Murdock has categorized the customs of most of these societies [4] and which seemed of possible significance for sex differentiation. The aspects of culture covered include type of economy, residence pattern, marriage and incest rules, political integration, and social organization. For each aspect of culture, we grouped Murdock's categories to make a dichotomous contrast (sometimes omitting certain categories as irrelevant to the contrast). In the case of some aspects of culture, two or more separate contrasts were made (e.g., under form of marriage we contrasted monogamy with polygyny, and also contrasted sororal with nonsororal polygyny). For each of 40 comparisons thus formed, we prepared a 2×2 frequency table to determine relation to each of our sex-difference dichotomies. A significant relation was found for six of these 40 aspects of culture with the more selective dichotomization of overall sex difference. In four of these comparisons, the relation to the more inclusive dichotomization was also significant. These relationships are all given in Table 2, in the form of phi

---

[4] These data were supplied to us directly by Professor Murdock.

TABLE 2
CULTURE VARIABLES CORRELATED WITH LARGE SEX DIFFERENCES IN SOCIALIZATION, SEPARATELY FOR TWO TYPES OF SAMPLE

Variable	More Selective Sample		More Inclusive Sample	
	ϕ	N	ϕ	N
Large animals are hunted	.48*	(34)	.28*	(72)
Grain rather than root crops are grown	.82**	(20)	.62*	(43)
Large or milking animals rather than small animals are kept	.65*	(19)	.43*	(35)
Fishing unimportant or absent	.42*	(31)	.19	(69)
Nomadic rather than sedentary residence	.61**	(34)	.15	(71)
Polygyny rather than monogamy	.51*	(28)	.38**	(64)

* $p < .05$.
** $p < .01$.
Note.—The variables have been so phrased that all correlations are positive. The phi coefficient is shown, and in parentheses, the number of cases on which the comparison was based. Significance level was determined by x^2, or Fisher's exact test where applicable, using in all cases a two-tailed test.

coefficients, along with the outcome of testing significance by the use of x^2 or Fisher's exact test. In trying to interpret these findings, we have also considered the nonsignificant correlations with other variables, looking for consistency and inconsistency with the general implications of the significant findings. We have arrived at the following formulation of results:

1. Large sex difference in socialization is associated with an economy that places a high premium on the superior strength, and superior development of motor skills requiring strength, which characterize the male. Four of the correlations reported in Table 2 clearly point to this generalization: the correlations of large sex difference with the hunting of large animals, with grain rather than root crops, with the keeping of large rather than small domestic animals, and with nomadic rather than sedentary residence. The correlation with the unimportance of fishing may also be consistent with this generalization, but the argument is not clear.[5] Other cor-

---

[5] Looking (with the more inclusive sample) into the possibility that this correlation might result from the correlation between fishing and sedentary residence, a complicated interaction between these variables was found. The correlation of sex differentiation with absence of fishing is found only in nomadic societies, where fishing is likely to involve cooperative activity of the two sexes, and its absence is likely to mean dependence upon the male for large game hunting or herding large animals (whereas in sedentary societies the alternatives to fishing do not so uniformly require special emphasis on male strength). The correlation of sex differentiation with nomadism is found only in nonfishing societies; here nomadism is likely to imply large game hunting or herding large animals, whereas in fishing

relations consistent with the generalization, though not statistically significant, are with large game hunting rather than gathering, with the hunting of large game rather than small game, and with the general importance of all hunting and gathering.

2. Large sex difference in socialization appears to be correlated with customs that make for a large family group with high cooperative interaction. The only statistically significant correlation relevant here is that with polygyny rather than monogamy. This generalization is, however, supported by several substantial correlations that fall only a little short of being statistically significant. One of these is a correlation with sororal rather than nonsororal polygyny; Murdock and Whiting (4) have presented indirect evidence that co-wives generally show smoother cooperative interaction if they are sisters. Correlations are also found with the presence of either an extended or a polygynous family rather than the nuclear family only; with the presence of an extended family; and with the extreme contrast between maximal extension and no extension of the family. The generalization is also to some extent supported by small correlations with wide extension of incest taboos, if we may presume that an incest taboo makes for effective unthreatening cooperation within the extended family. The only possible exception to this generalization, among substantial correlations, is a near-significant correlation with an extended or polygynous family's occupying a cluster of dwellings rather than a single dwelling.[6]

In seeking to understand this second generalization, we feel that the degree of social isolation of the nuclear family may perhaps be the crucial underlying variable. To the extent that the nuclear family must stand alone, the man must be prepared to take the woman's role when she is absent or incapaci-

tated, and vice versa. Thus the sex differentiation cannot afford to be too great. But to the extent that the nuclear family is steadily interdependent with other nuclear families, the female role in the household economy can be temporarily taken over by another woman, or the male role by another man, so that sharp differentiation of sex role is no handicap.

The first generalization, which concerns the economy, cannot be viewed as dealing with material completely independent of the ratings of socialization. The training of children in their economic role was often an important part of the data used in rating socialization variables, and would naturally vary according to the general economy of the society. We would stress, however, that we were by no means using the identical data on the two sides of our comparison; we were on the one hand judging data on the socialization of children and on the other hand using Murdock's judgments on the economy of the adult culture. In the case of the second generalization, it seems to us that there was little opportunity for information on family and social structure to have influenced the judges in making the socialization ratings.

Both of these generalizations contribute to understanding the social background of the relatively small difference in socialization of boys and girls which we believe characterizes our society at the present time. Our mechanized economy is perhaps less dependent than any previous economy upon the superior average strength of the male. The nuclear family in our society is often so isolated that husband and wife must each be prepared at times to take over or help in the household tasks normally assigned to the other. It is also significant that the conditions favoring low sex differentiation appear to be more characteristic of the upper segments of our society, in socioeconomic and educational status, than of lower segments. This observation may be relevant to the tendency toward smaller sex differences in personality in higher status groups (cf. Terman and Miles, 8).

The increase in our society of conditions favoring small sex difference has led some people to advocate a virtual elimination of sex differences in socialization. This course seems likely to be dysfunctional even in our society. Parsons, Bales, *et al.* (5) argue that a differentiation of role similar to the universal pattern of sex difference is an important and perhaps inevitable development in any social group, such as the nuclear family. If we add to their argument the point that biological differences between the sexes make most appropriate the usual division of those roles between the sexes, we have compelling reasons to expect that the decrease in differentiation of adult sex role will not

societies nomadism evidently implies no such special dependence upon male strength. Maximum sex differentiation is found in nomadic nonfishing societies (15 with large difference and only 2 with small) and minimum sex differentiation in nomadic fishing societies (2 with large difference and 7 with small difference). These findings further strengthen the argument for a conspicuous influence of the economy upon sex differentiation.

[6] We think the reverse of this correlation would be more consistent with our generalization here. But perhaps it may reasonably be argued that the various nuclear families composing an extended or polygynous family are less likely to develop antagonisms which hinder cooperation if they are able to maintain some physical separation. On the other hand, this variable may be more relevant to the first generalization than to the second. Occupation of a cluster of dwellings is highly correlated with presence of herding and with herding of large rather than small animals, and these economic variables in turn are correlated with large sex difference in socialization. Occupation of a cluster of dwellings is also correlated with polygyny rather than monogamy and shows no correlation with sororal vs. nonsororal polygyny.

continue to the vanishing point. In our training of children, there may now be less differentiation in sex role than characterizes adult life—so little, indeed, as to provide inadequate preparation for adulthood. This state of affairs is likely to be especially true of formal education, which is more subject to conscious influence by an ideology than is informal socialization at home. With child training being more oriented toward the male than the female role in adulthood, many of the adjustment problems of women in our society today may be partly traced to conflicts growing out of inadequate childhood preparation for their adult role. This argument is nicely supported in extreme form by Spiro's analysis of sex roles in an Israeli kibbutz (7). The ideology of the founders of the kibbutz included the objective of greatly reducing differences in sex role. But the economy of the kibbutz is a largely nonmechanized one in which the superior average strength of men is badly needed in many jobs. The result is that, despite the ideology and many attempts to implement it, women continue to be assigned primarily to traditional "women's work," and the incompatibility between upbringing or ideology and adult role is an important source of conflict for women.

NOTE ON REGIONAL DISTRIBUTION

There is marked variation among regions of the world in typical size of sex difference in socialization. In our sample, societies in North America and Africa tend to have large sex difference and societies in Oceania to have small sex difference. Less confidently, because of the smaller number of cases, we can report a tendency toward small sex differences in Asia and South America as well. Since most of the variables with which we find the sex difference to be significantly correlated have a similar regional distribution, the question arises whether the correlations might better be ascribed to some quite different source having to do with large regional similarities, rather than to the functional dependence we have suggested. As a partial check, we have tried to determine whether the correlations we report in Table 2 tend also to be found strictly within regions. For each of the three regions for which we have sizable samples (North America, Africa, and Oceania) we have separately plotted 2 x 2 tables corresponding to each of the 6 relationships reported in Table 2. (We did this only for the more inclusive sample, since for the more selective sample the number of cases within a region would have been extremely

small.) Out of the 18 correlations thus determined, 11 are positive and only 3 are negative (the other 4 being exactly zero). This result clearly suggests a general tendency for these correlations to hold true within regions as well as between regions, and may lend further support to our functional interpretation.

SUMMARY

A survey of certain aspects of socialization in 110 cultures shows that differentiation of the sexes is unimportant in infancy, but that in childhood there is, as in our society, a widespread pattern of greater pressure toward nurturance, obedience, and responsibility in girls, and toward self-reliance and achievement striving in boys. There are a few reversals of sex difference, and many instances of no detectable sex difference; these facts tend to confirm the cultural rather than directly biological nature of the differences. Cultures vary in the degree to which these differentiations are made; correlational analysis suggests some of the social conditions influencing these variations, and helps in understanding why our society has relatively small sex differentiation.

REFERENCES

1. BENEDICT, RUTH. Continuities and discontinuities in cultural conditioning. *Psychiatry*, 1938, *1*, 161–167.
2. MEAD, MARGARET. *Male and female.* New York: Morrow, 1949.
3. MURDOCK, G. P. Comparative data on the division of labor by sex. *Social Forces*, 1937, *15*, 551–553.
4. MURDOCK G. P., and WHITING, J. W. M. Cultural determination of parental attitudes. The relationship between the social structure, particular family structure and parental behavior. In M. J. E. Senn (Ed.), *Problems of infancy and childhood: Transactions of the Fourth Conference*, March 6–7, 1950. New York: Josiah Macy, Jr. Foundation, 1951. Pp. 13–34.
5. PARSONS, T., BALES, R. F., *et al. Family, socialization and interaction process.* Glencoe, Ill.: Free Press, 1955.
6. SCHEINFELD, A. *Women and men.* New York: Harcourt, Brace, 1944.
7. SPIRO, M. E. *Kibbutz: Venture in Utopia.* Cambridge: Harvard Univer. Press, 1956.
8. TERMAN, L. M., and MILES, CATHERINE C. *Sex and personality.* New York: McGraw-Hill, 1936.

45

On the Meaning of Behavior: Illustrations from the Infant

JEROME KAGAN

This paper raises methodological, or even philosophical, issues that are crucial to an understanding of most of the articles in this book.

One often forgets that a given behavior may have many different meanings. The author deals with this and other important general points in the context of specific data. He considers changes in the meaning of certain behaviors (visual fixation and vocalization) that depend on the age or sex of the infant. We have chosen to put the paper in this section rather than in Section VII because we feel that the points raised apply to sex as a determinant of behavior more than age. Meanings of behaviors are also considered in relation to the social class of the infants, so that a portion of the paper is relevant to Section VI.

Professor Kagan is a leading figure in child psychology. He has been at Harvard University since 1964, after some years at the Fels Research Institute.

Psychology's assigned responsibility in the scientific academy is to understand the relations

Presidential address to Division 7 of the American Psychological Association, San Francisco, California, September 2, 1968. Preparation of this manuscript was facilitated by research grant MH 08792 from the National Institute of Mental Health and a grant from the Carnegie Corporation of New York.

Jerome Kagan, "On the meaning of behavior: illustrations from the infant," *Child Development*, 40, 1969, 1121–1134. Reprinted by permission. © 1969 by The Society for Research in Child Development, Inc.

among events, behaviors, and internal psychological structures. The laws that link psychological structures to stimulus events, on the one hand, and to behaviors, on the other, seem to be of preferential importance, and modern biology may provide useful analogies as we search for the form of these laws. Specifically, the problems inherent in the relation of genetic structure to manifest characteristics (the genotype-phenotype relation) are remarkably similar to the problems inherent in the relation between psychological structures and overt behaviors. Consider two central principles from modern genetics as illustrations.

The first principle states that phenotypes resist change and remain constant despite changes in genotype (Mayr 1966). The experimental proof of this principle is contained in the observation that the distribution of phenotypes for a particular trait in the F_1 generation does not always reveal the true genetic structure of each offspring. Analogously, the pattern of overt responses remains similar despite changes in internal structure. A newly acquired idea does not typically change the overt action of the individual, and powerful probes are required to reveal the presence of new acquisitions.

A second genetic principle states that there is a greater potential for variability in the genotype than in the phenotype (Mayr 1966). There are, for example, a limited number of visible hues that a given flower can exhibit, but a much larger number of different biochemical structures, each of which results in the same hue. It is estimated that man's approximately 150,000 genes permit a potential variety of 6.4×10^{13} different genotypes but actually produce a far smaller number of phenotypically different individuals. Analogously, it is proposed that there is far less potential variety in the classes of overt responses a human being can display than there is in the combinations of psychological structures that can mediate responses. That is, there are more constraints on variety in behavior than there are on variety in psychological structures. Anatomical as well as social constraints (which take the form of rules) limit seriously the total variety of responses an organism can issue. There are a limited number of ways one can press a bar, sip martinis, or cry. But each of these delineated responses can serve many different combinations of motives, expectancies, standards, and beliefs. This image of a relatively limited set of behaviors to be mapped on a larger set of internal psychological structures provides the central theme of this paper.

One of psychology's problems is to discern the meaning of its behavioral phenotypes, which is a way of saying that it must find the psychological structures each response class serves. Since responses do not exist independent of organisms and situations, it is necessary, at a minimum, to acknowledge the species, age, and sex of the organism and the stimulus context in which he is behaving. We should not inquire about the cause of smiling, but must constrain the question by denoting, at a minimum, the age, sex, and context in which the behavior occurred. Consider some popular dependent variables in contemporary psychology: anxiety, rapid eye movements, ease of conditioning, EEG desynchronization, achievement themes, risk taking, or affiliative behavior. These are vital and extensively researched phenomena, but the flavor of the work occasionally implies that a particular score or magnitude on one of these variables has a univocal meaning, regardless of the age or sex of the organism or the context in which he is behaving.

This general issue could be discussed in relation to many different response dimensions. This paper shall consider the issue with relation to two easily quantified responses displayed by the infant: duration of orientation toward a visual stimulus (typically called fixation time) and nonmorphemic vocalization. The intention is to persuade the reader that the meaning of these responses is a serious function of the age and sex of the agent making the response, in children under 2 years of age. Investigation of fixation time has the longer history; Fantz (1961) chose this variable in his pioneering studies of perceptual dynamics in the young infant. Nonmorphemic vocalization, oddly enough, has not been popular with investigators. Less than 1 percent of studies of infants during the last 50 years chose nonmorphemic vocalization in the first year as a dependent variable worthy of quantification. Investigation of reflexes, sitting, crawling, creeping, and morphemic speech have been, by contrast, extremely popular. It is possible that the pragmatic and evaluative biases of these early investigators led to this selectivity. One can see positive progression or growth in motor skill and vocabulary, whereas babbling of infants appears to idle. Let us turn now to the differential meaning of fixation time as a function of age.

AGE AND FIXATION TIME

Duration of fixation of a visual stimulus seems to change its primary loyalty at least three times during the first 3 years of life. During the first 6–8 weeks the infant has an unlearned disposition to fixate events that have a high rate of change in their physical parameters. Movement and contour contrast possess high rates of change, and newborns are dramatically more attentive to moving lights than to static ones, to stimuli with a high degree of black-white contour than to stimuli with minimal contour contrast (Haith 1966; Salapatek & Kessen 1966). But this apparently unlearned disposition eventually competes with an acquired determinant by the time the infant is 12 weeks old.

The degree of discrepancy between the stimulus and an acquired schema becomes an important determinant of fixation time at this age. A schema is an internal representation of a stimulus, where the term *representation* refers to a particular arrangement of the distinctive elements of the stimulus. The principles by which elements acquire distinctiveness are not known, and this is one of psychology's most challenging problems. However, the hypothesis states that once a schema has been formed, events that are discrepant from that schema—alterations in the arrangement or form of the distinctive elements of the schema—will elicit longer fixations from the infant than events perfectly representative of the schema or events having no relation to schema. That is, there is a curvilinear relation between fixation time and degree of discrepancy between schema and external event. Support for this hypothesis is found in the pattern of fixation times of 4-month-old infants to schematic representations of human faces and meaningless designs. Achromatic illustrations of male faces elicit fixation times twice as long as those elicited by random shapes of varying number of turns which are extremely novel and contain greater contour contrast than the faces (McCall & Kagan 1967a). Moreover, the 4-month-old studies a regular schematic face longer than one which has the same facial components disarranged (Haaf & Bell 1967). Final support for the discrepancy hypothesis comes from a study in which 3-month-old infants were exposed to a novel three-dimensional stimulus at home for 1 month and then shown that stimulus and three transformations of the standard at 4 months of age. Control children viewed all four stimuli for the first time at 4 months. The experimental infants who viewed the standard at home showed shorter fixation times to all four stimuli than the controls. The discrepancy effect emerged for girls who showed longer fixation times to the transformations than to the standard they viewed at home (McCall & Kagan 1967b).

Although the definitive study is yet to be performed, there is tentative support for the notion that very familiar and very novel stimuli elicit shorter fixation times than events that are only moderately discrepant from established schema. But this generalization is probably not true until the infant is at least 3–4 months old and has had time to establish some schema. [The advanced psychology student may want to compare with Helson's concept of adaptation level.—EDITOR]

A third determinant of fixation time—in addition to high rate of change and discrepancy—first appears during the last third of the first year and becomes prominent by 2 years. It concerns the meaningfulness of the event and is defined by the density of hypotheses associated with a class of events. With age, a child acquires both a more articulated schema for a particular class of events, as well as a set of associations and hypotheses which he activates when he is exposed to an event that is discrepant from his schema. The activation of these hypotheses leads to prolonged fixations. The child's attention is maintained because he is trying to construct the familiar from the discrepant; he is actively trying out cognitive hypotheses that will permit him to assimilate the event. The more knowledge he has about a class of stimuli, the longer he can work at this construction. The child's attention remains riveted on the stimulus in approximate proportion to the density of these hypotheses.

In sum, three factors appear to control duration of fixation in the infant: high rate of change in the physical parameters of the stimulus operating during the opening weeks of life, to which is added moderate discrepancy at about 3 months and activation of hypotheses at 9–10 months. It is suggested that these factors supplement each other; an event that has contrast, is discrepant, and engages meaningful hypotheses should elicit longer fixations from an 18-month-old than a stimulus with only one or two of these characteristics.

Data on age changes in fixation time to representations of human faces provide a test of the usefulness of these assumptions. A set of four different three-dimensional representations of a male face was presented to the same sample of 150 children at 4, 8, 13, and 27 months of age. All infants were Caucasian and first born. Figure 1 illustrates the four faces.

Fixation times were highest at 4 months, lowest at 8–13 months, and intermediate at 27 months. The long fixations at 4 months reflect the fact that the stimuli were discrepant from the infant's acquired schema for his parent's face. Fixation times dropped at 8–13 months because the faces were much less discrepant but did not elicit any hypotheses. The fixation times began to rise between 13 and 27 months as a consequence of the meaningfulness vector. The largest increase in fixation time between 13 and 27 months occurred for the face that had eyes, nose, and mouth rearranged (scrambled face), suggesting the comple-

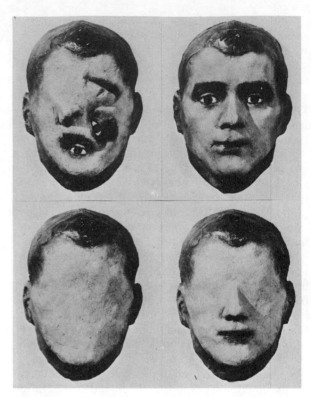

FIGURE 1. *Flesh-colored clay faces presented to the infants.*

mentary action of discrepancy and meaningfulness.

Independent data gathered by Finley (1967) corroborate these ideas and extend the age function to 3 years of age. Finley saw three cross-sectional samples of 1-, 2-, and 3-year-old children. One group was composed of peasant Mayan Indians living on the Yucatan peninsula; the second was a middle-class group from Cambridge. The Indian children saw the faces of a Mayan male; the Cambridge children saw a Caucasian male face. The fixation times increased linearly with age and also showed a stimulus by age interaction, with the rearranged face showing the largest increase in fixation time between 2 and 3 years of age. Figure 2 combines the longitudinal data with those gathered by Finley for the regular, rearranged, and blank faces—three faces that were used in both investigations. There was an almost perfect U-shaped function relating fixation time and age; and the greatest increase in fixation time from 1 to 3 years occurred for the rearranged, or scrambled, face. This stimulus by age interaction reflects the joint action of discrepancy and density of hypotheses. The scrambled face was more difficult to assimilate than the other two and elicited a richer set of hypotheses in the service of this assimilation. Some of the children's spontaneous comments are consonant with this suggestion. One 2-year-old

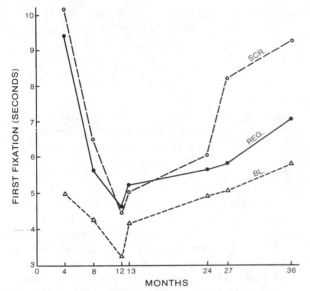

FIGURE 2. *Relation between fixation time to faces and age (several samples combined).*

child said, "What happened to his nose, who hit him in the nose?" Another said, "Who that, mommy? A monster, that a monster, mommy?"

SOCIAL CLASS AND FIXATION TIME

Additional support for the assumption that meaningfulness begins to control fixation time toward the end of the first year is found in the degree of covariation between educational level of the child's family and fixation time from 4 through 27 months. There was no relation between educational level of the infant's family and duration of fixation at 4 months for either sex. At 13 and 27 months, however, there were significant positive correlations—in the high 30s—between these variables, although slightly higher for girls than for boys. Since upper-middle-class children are likely to be taught a richer set of symbolic structures surrounding faces than lower-middle-class infants, the former should possess richer nests of hypotheses to the faces and display longer fixations. The increasing correlation between educational level of the parents and fixation time as the child grows is congruent with the presumed role of meaningfulness on fixation time.

STABILITY OF FIXATION TIME

The data on intraindividual stability of fixation time support the assumptions regarding the changing determinants of this response. If fixation time at 4 months is primarily controlled by degree of discrepancy, whereas at 8 and 13 months it begins

to be controlled by activation of hypotheses, there should be minimal continuity for fixation time from 4 to 8 or from 4 to 13 months. But if a child's rate of acquisition of hypotheses to the faces remains relatively constant, there might be moderate stability from 8 to 13 months. These expectations were generally confirmed. There was minimal intraindividual stability of fixation time from 4 to 8 or from 4 to 13 months for this group of 150 infants. However, there was moderate stability of fixation time to the faces from 8 to 13 months for girls ($r = 0.51$, $p < .01$). The correlation for boys was lower and nonsignificant. The sex difference in degree of continuity of fixation time to the faces is concordant with the sex differences in magnitude of association between educational level of the family and fixation time at 1 year. Rate of acquisition of hypotheses to the faces seems to be more constant and more closely tied to the educational level of the family among girls than boys.

The entire corpus of data is, at the least, congruent with the proposition that duration of fixation of a visual event comes under the influence of different processes during the opening 3 years. The meaning of a 10-second fixation time to a face depends on the age of the child, which is shorthand for implying a particular stage of cognitive development.

SEX AND VOCALIZATION

The vocalization data illustrate the importance of the child's sex in understanding the meaning of a response. Students of comparative psychology often find sexual dimorphisms in behavior (i.e., a given situation leads to different responses in the two sexes; see Hamburg & Lunde 1966). For example, a fear-inducing stimulus more often leads to motor freezing in the female monkey than in the male but leads to motor excitability in the male. The babbling of the young infant may display a sexual dimorphism. Nonfretful, nonmorphemic vocalization to auditory and visual stimulation during the first half year seems to be more clearly in the service of an excitability that accompanies information processing in girls than in boys. The boys' vocalizations seem to reflect an excitability that more often accompanies boredom or motor restlessness than the processing of information. Before considering evidence for this suggestion, it should be noted that the average vocalization time during a 30-second stimulus presentation averaged only 2 seconds at 4, 8, and 13 months. Vocalization, like fixation time, was longer at 4 months than at 8 or 13 months. With only one major exception, vocalization time was independent of fixation time, cardiac deceleration, or frequency of smiling during the first year. Moreover, there were no sex differences in mean vocalization time or variability at any age. Boys and girls vocalized equally often, but the pattern of correlates of this response was unequivocally different for the two sexes. [Remember Eichorn's point (see Intro., Sec. 8)—ED.]

THE LINK TO ATTENTIVENESS

Vocalization was more closely associated with independent indexes of active information processing among girls than boys. For example, among girls, duration of vocalization to representations of faces at 4 months predicted duration of orientation, at 8 months of age, to a speaker baffle which was the source of human speech. At 8 months, each child listened to a set of four taped stimuli, read by a male voice, in which meaning and inflection were varied. There were four sets of sentences, each lasting 20 seconds. The four stimuli were (1) high meaning read with high inflection, (2) high meaning read with low inflection, (3) low meaning (nonsense) read with high inflection, and finally (4) low meaning read with low inflection. The girls who vocalized to a photograph of a male face at 4 months looked longer at the speaker baffle than the girls who did not vocalize ($r = 0.35$, $p < .01$). No such relation emerged for boys ($r = -0.01$). This relation was even more dramatic when general attentiveness at 4 months was controlled. All infants who showed short fixation times to the faces at 4 months (based on a median split) were eliminated from the analysis. The group of highly attentive 4-month infants was then divided into those who vocalized versus those who did not vocalize at 4 months. The vocalizing girls looked significantly longer at the speaker than the nonvocalizing girls; the relation for boys was in the reverse direction.

A second instance of covariation between vocalization and an index of attentiveness involved a contemporaneous relation between vocalization and magnitude of cardiac deceleration to the presentation of the male voice at 8 months. Investigation of cardiac deceleration has a short history, partly for technical reasons concerning amplifiers, but partly because of the theoretical prejudices spawned by arousal theory. The Laceys (Lacey 1959; Lacey, Kagan, Lacey, & Moss 1963) demonstrated that cardiac deceleration, not acceleration, was a common reaction when an adult was attending to an auditory or visual event. Subsequent work verified this phenomenon in infants and indicated its usefulness in studies of attention distribution in preverbal children (Lewis, Kagan, Campbell, & Kalafat 1966). A working hypothesis is that, other things being equal, an obvious deceleration is most likely to occur in an infant when the stimulus is a moderate discrepancy from an existing schema, that is, when the event surprises the infant. A long fixation is least likely to be accompanied by a cardiac deceleration when the event is very novel or too familiar. The phrase "double take" is an apt description of the infant's appearance when he shows a deceleration to a visual or auditory stimulus. This look of surprise is typically accompanied by a sudden quieting and a large cardiac deceleration. It is assumed that the infants who showed large decelerations to the auditory sentences at 8 months were more attentive than those who did not decelerate. Many infants showed large cardiac decelerations to the sentences at 8 months, but there were no sex differences in average deceleration. Similarly, many infants vocalized after the auditory stimulus terminated, during the 10-second interstimulus period when the room was silent. Again, there were no sex differences in average vocalization during this quiet period. But if vocalization is an index of excitability occasioned by information processing, then the girls who were most attentive to the sentences as they were being presented—as indexed by cardiac deceleration—should have vocalized the most when the voice terminated. This relation held for girls but not for boys. There was a significant positive association between magnitude of deceleration during the stimulus and vocalization following its termination for the girls ($r = 0.3$, $p < .01$) but not for the boys ($r = 0.1$, $p = $ N.S.).

A third instance of covariation between attentiveness and vocalization among girls is seen in the degree of correlation between fixation time and vocalization time to the regular face at 4 months. There was a significant positive association between looking and babbling for the girls, but none for the boys.

A fourth instance of a preferential link between early babbling and later attentiveness in girls was contained in the significant correlation between vocalization to the faces at 8 months and the tendency to engage in long periods of uninterrupted play with toys when these children were 27 months old. Once again, this relation was absent for the boys.

Finally, vocalization among the girls differentiated among stimuli that elicited equal fixation times, while vocalization among the boys failed to differentiate among these stimuli. The 4-month-old girls vocalized significantly more to the regular face than to the scrambled clay face on the first presentation of these two stimuli. The boys showed equivalent vocalization to these two faces.

Independent data gathered by Michael Lewis and the author on 6-month-old infants seen at the Fels Institute also revealed differentiated use of vocalization by girls, but not by boys. The infants were shown a series of faces and geometric forms in random order. Girls vocalized significantly more to the faces than to the forms; the boys showed equivalent vocalization to both classes of stimuli. An auditory episode that followed the visual series contained a strange male voice and a strange female voice reading prose. Girls vocalized more to the female than to the male voice; the boys babbled equally to both voices.

In addition to the preferential association between vocalization and varied indexes of information processing, vocalization was also more stable across ages for girls than for boys. Vocalization to all four clay faces at 4 or 8 months predicted vocalization to these faces at 13 months ($r = 0.34$, $p < .05$; $r = 0.47$, $p < .01$ for girls); there was no stability for the boys ($r = 0.00$; $r = -.14$).

The sex differences in stability of vocalization and degree of association with indexes of attentiveness imply that nonmorphemic babbling reflects the excitement generated by information processing more faithfully in girls than in boys. This speculation is supported by the work of others. Cameron, Livson, and Bayley (1967) have reported that high scores on a vocalization factor derived from the Bayley Intelligence Scale during the second half of the first year predicted Stanford-Binet IQ scores during childhood and adulthood for girls (r ranged from 0.4 to 0.6), but not for boys. Moore's (1967) longitudinal study of middle- and working-class London infants also provides relevant evidence. At 6 and 18 months of age, each of 41 boys and 35 girls was assigned a speech quotient from the Griffith's Infant Scale. High scores index frequency and variety of babbling to people's voices and music. The speech quotient was more stable for girls than for boys across the period 6–18 months ($r = 0.52$ for girls but only -0.01 for boys).

There are two complementary interpretations of this sexual dimorphism for infant babbling. One explanation assumes, first, that samples of Cambridge, Berkeley, or London mothers differ in their tendency to accelerate the cognitive development of their infants. Second, the disposition to accelerate the infant leads mothers to initiate different actions with daughters than with sons. It is suggested that an accelerating mother is more likely to engage in frequent, reciprocal vocalization with her daughter than with her son. As a result, the infant girl establishes a strong disposition to babble when excited by interesting events. In essence, it is suggested that there is greater variability among mothers of daughters than among mothers of sons in practices that involve reciprocal vocalization and stimulation of vocalization when the child is processing information. There is some support for this point of view.

Part of our longitudinal sample was observed in the home when the infants were 4 months old. As reported elsewhere, well-educated mothers of daughters were more likely than poorly educated ones to engage in distinct face-to-face vocalization with their daughters and to respond to the girls' babbling within 10 seconds of its occurrence. Among boys, there was no relation between the mother's education and the occurrence of these practices (Kagan 1968). Additional support for this argument comes from a study in which mothers were interviewed during their pregnancy and rated on a variable called "quality and affective excitability of mother's speech." When the infants of these mothers were 3 months old, the mother-child interaction was observed in the home. The personality dimension rated during pregnancy covaried with auditory and visual stimulation of daughters (but not sons), and with physical affection toward sons (but not daughters). These data support the idea that a particular type of mother may display different patterns of handling toward sons and daughters as early as 12 weeks of age (Moss and Robson 1968).

A second interpretation, not exclusive of the first, argues for a basic sex difference in organization of the central nervous system. It is possible that vocalization is a more prepotent reaction for girls than boys when the infant is in the state of arousal created by processing information. This suggestion gains credence from comparative studies showing dramatic sex differences within primate strains in typical reactions to arousal states (Hamburg & Lunde 1966; Harlow 1965), and from observations of primates in natural contexts, suggesting that specific vocal sounds (such as squeals) are more often noted in females than males (Jay 1965). This explanation assumes that the sexes differ in their preferred reaction to that state designated as "stimulus excitement." The infant girl is likely to vocalize; the infant boy is more likely to react with motor quieting or skeletal motor discharge. If this is true, then babbling in the 4–8-month-old infant will be a more faithful index of attentional dynamics for girls than for boys.

SUMMARY

In general, there was minimal intraindividual continuity for the fixation and vocalization variables from 4 to 8 months, but moderate, and in some cases surprisingly good, continuity from 8 to 13 months, especially for girls. The emergence of this stability during the latter half of the first year is concordant with anthropometric data suggesting that stable physical growth dimensions begin to emerge about 6 months of age (Acheson 1966).

The more impressive stability of fixation and vocalization time for girls over boys matches the human biological data. Acheson (1966) has written that it is difficult to find a physiological or physical growth dimension that is not more stable for girls than for boys, and we are tempted to call upon biological factors as agents lobbying for continuity of these psychological dimensions in the girl. The stronger correlation for girls between social class and fixation time at 13 months has an interesting analogue in the fact that similar results emerge for older children. For example, grades in school, IQ scores, and decision times each show greater covariation with social class among girls than among boys. This pattern is not restricted to white populations; the correlation between maternal and child IQ at 4 years is markedly higher for girls ($r = 0.39$, $p < .001$) than for boys ($r = 0.15$) from black, urban families (Hess, Shipman, Brophy, & Bear 1968). It is suggested that this phenomenon is due to the fact that mothers of different social classes in the United States differ more dramatically in their acceleratory practices toward their daughters than toward their sons.

Finally, these data are relevant to the problem of mapping behavior on psychological structure. The U-shaped function relating age and fixation time to faces over the period 4–36 months is persuasive of the need to invent different determinants for fixation time. The importance of sex is a bit more controversial. It is not common for a psychologist to give the same task to subjects varying widely in age and assume that the behavior of all the age cadres derives from the same structures. However, there are many psychologists who deny the relevance of sex differences. They either pool sexes regularly or fail to specify whether the subjects were boys or girls. Most of the responses psychologists quantify are not sexually dimorphic. But some are, and since we do not know which ones, it seems appropriate to examine all corpuses of data for such differences before accepting the null hypothesis. This examination means not only checking means and variances but also looking at patterns of relations among variables.

A specific magnitude for a specific response often serves many different forces. The mapping of these magnitudes on the set of varied determinants will require rigorous theory and a keen sensitivity to nature's subtle messages. Von Békésy (1964, p. 728) gave a hint about the source of his own inductive creations when he noted that he chose da Vinci as his model because "da Vinci did not try to outdo nature with his fantasy, but, quite the opposite, he tried to learn from nature. It was this simple finding that gave me, in my student years, the hope that perhaps I would be able to produce something of enduring interest."

REFERENCES

ACHESON, R. M. Maturation of the skeleton. In F. Falkner (Ed.), *Human development*. Philadelphia: Saunders, 1966. Pp. 465–502.

CAMERON, J.; LIVSON, N.; & BAYLEY, N. Infant vocalizations and their relationship to mature intelligence. *Science*, 1967, *157*, 331–333.

FANTZ, R. L. The origin of form perception. *Scientific American*, 1961, *204*, 66–72.

FINLEY, G. E. Visual attention, play and satiation in young children: a cross-cultural study. Unpublished doctoral dissertation, Harvard University, 1967.

HAAF, R. A., & BELL, R. Q. The facial dimension in visual discrimination by human infants. *Child Development*, 1967, *38*, 893–899.

HAITH, M. M. The response of the human newborn to visual movement. *Journal of Experimental Child Psychology*, 1966, *3*, 235–243.

HAMBURG, D. A., & LUNDE, D. T. Sex hormones in the development of sex differences in human behavior. In E. E. Maccoby (Ed.), *The development of sex differences*. Stanford, Calif.: Stanford University Press, 1966. Pp. 1–24.

HARLOW, H. F. Sexual behavior in the rhesus monkey. In F. A. Beach (Ed.), *Sex and behavior*. New York: Wiley, 1965. Pp. 234–265.

HESS, R. D.; SHIPMAN, V. C.; BROPHY, J. E.; & BEAR, R. M. The cognitive environments of urban preschool children. Project report, Graduate School of Education, University of Chicago, November 1968.

JAY, P. The common langur of North India. In I. DeVore (Ed.), *Primate behavior*. New York: Holt, Rinehart & Winston, 1965. Pp. 197–249.

KAGAN, J. On cultural deprivation. In D. C. Glass (Ed.), *Biology and behavior: environmental influences*. New York: Rockefeller University Press, 1968. Pp. 211–250.

LACEY, J. I. Psychophysiological approaches to the evaluation of psychotherapeutic process and outcome. In E. A. Rubenstein & M. B. Parloff (Eds.), *Research in psychotherapy*. Washington, D.C.: National Publishing Co., 1959. Pp. 160–208.

LACEY, J. I.; KAGAN, J.; LACEY, B.; & MOSS, H. A. The visceral level: situational determinants and behavioral correlates of autonomic response patterns. In P. H. Knapp (Ed.), *Expressions of the emotions in man*. New York: International Universities Press, 1963. Pp. 161–196.

LEWIS, M.; KAGAN, J.; CAMPBELL, H.; & KALAFAT, J. The cardiac response as a correlate of attention in infants. *Child Development*, 1966, *37*, 63–72.

MCCALL, R. B., & KAGAN, J. Attention in the infant: effects of complexity, contour, perimeter, and familiarity. *Child Development*, 1967, *38*, 939–952. (a)

McCall, R. B., & Kagan, J. Stimulus-schema discrepancy and attention in the infant. *Journal of Experimental Child Psychology*, 1967, *5*, 381–390. (b)

Mayr, E. *Animal species and evolution*. Cambridge, Mass.: Belknap Press, 1966.

Moore, T. Language and intelligence: a longitudinal study of the first eight years. *Human Development*, 1967, *10*, 88–106.

Moss, H. A., & Robson, K. The role of protest behavior in the development of the mother-infant attachment. Paper presented at the meeting of the American Psychological Association, San Francisco, 1968.

Salapatek, P., & Kessen, W. Visual scanning of triangles by the human newborn. *Journal of Experimental Child Psychology,* 1966, *3*, 113–122.

Von Békésy, G. Concerning the pleasure of observing and the mechanics of the inner ear. Nobel Lecture in Physiology or Medicine for 1961. In *Nobel lectures in physiology or medicine*. Vol. 3. *1942–1962*. Amsterdam: Elsevier, 1964. Pp. 722–746.

46

Behavioral Differences Related to Experience of Mother and Sex of Infant in the Rhesus Monkey[1]

G. MITCHELL AND E. M. BRANDT

This brief note by Mitchell and Brandt shows differences in the ways monkey mothers treat their offspring according to the sex of the baby. While the sexes receive different treatment, the data suggest that individual differences in offspring (as well as in mothers) may play a considerable role in child rearing among the Rhesus. Differences in the behavior of male and female infant monkeys are also shown. On the one hand, the findings of these differences in the rhesus (a species less influenced than humans are by culture) could be taken to underline the importance of biological factors. On the other hand, the mother's experience as a mother has the most influence on her behavior in the first three months of her infant's life, even though the sex of the infant becomes more important after three months. These facts complicate the interpretation.

Dr. Mitchell and Dr. Brandt are both at the National Center for Primate Biology of the University of California at Davis.

[1] This research was supported by National Institutes of Health Grant FR–00169 to the National Center for Primate Biology, and Grants MH 17425–01 to the first author and HD 04335–01 to the second author.

An extended report of this study may be obtained without charge from G. Mitchell, National Center for Primate Biology, University of California, Davis, California 95616, or for a fee from the National Auxiliary Publications Service. Order Document No. 00956 from National Auxiliary Publications Service of the American Society for Information Science, c/o CCM Information Sciences, Inc., 909 Third Avenue, New York, New York 10022. Remit in advance $2.00 for microfiche or $5.00 for photocopies and make checks payable to: Research and Microfilm Publications, Inc.

The Mitchell and Stevens (1968) *Macaca mulatta* mothers and infants, studied from 1 to 3 months, were used in the present study. The effects of maternal experience and the sex of the infant on maternal and infant behavior were evaluated again in the second 3 months.

Eight multiparous monkey mothers were matched with eight primiparous mothers for date of delivery and sex of infant. An observation cage was divided into two $3 \times 3 \times 3$ foot cubicles by a $3/8$-inch sheet of transparent Acrylite. In six of twelve 16-minute sessions for any given matched pair, each mother-infant pair was observed in one side of the cage with a neutral mother-infant stimulus pair in the other side. A different stimulus pair was used for the next six sessions. Frequencies and durations were recorded on a clock counter device. All reported results are significant beyond the .05 level.

Primiparous mothers stroked their own infants and, particularly mothers of females, threatened the stimulus infants more often than multiparous mothers (stroke, $\bar{X} = 20$ versus 5 times; threat, $\bar{X} = 19$ versus 5 times); multiparous mothers bit their own infants (particularly male infants) while the primiparous did not ($\bar{X} = 2$ versus 0 times).

While mothers of females, particularly multiparous, looked at the environment longer than mothers of males ($\bar{X} = 17$ versus 14 minutes), mothers of males, particularly primiparous, looked at and lipsmacked at the stimulus infant longer than mothers of females (look, $\bar{X} = 5$ versus 3 minutes; lipsmack, $\bar{X} = .5$ versus .2 minute). Mothers of males threatened and (especially the multiparous mothers) bit their own infants more often than mothers of females (threat, $\bar{X} = 3$ versus 0 times; bite, $\bar{X} = 2$ versus 0 times), but they also submitted passively to their infants more often ($\bar{X} = 14$ versus 4 times). Mothers of females, more often than mothers of males, restrained ($\bar{X} = 2$ versus 0 times) and retrieved their infants ($\bar{X} = 5$ versus 1 time) and threatened the stimulus mothers ($\bar{X} = 5$ versus 1 time).

Male infants looked at their mothers' bodies longer than female infants ($\bar{X} = 1.4$ versus .7 minutes), who looked at their mothers' faces more often ($\bar{X} = 29$ versus 18 times). Female infants (particularly of multiparous mothers) looked at the observers and at the stimulus mothers more often than male infants (looked at observer, $\overline{X} = 24$ versus 13 times; looked at stimulus mother, $\overline{X} = 106$ versus 71 times); while male infants, as compared to female infants, play-imitated with the stimulus infants longer ($\overline{X} = 1$ versus 0 minute), oral-explored the environment more often (especially primiparous infants) ($\overline{X} = 37$ versus 15 times), climbed longer ($\overline{X} = 4$ versus 2 minutes), ran-jumped more often ($\overline{X} = 56$ versus 12 times), and threatened the stimulus infant longer ($\overline{X} = .1$ versus .0 minute).

The factors of maternal experience and sex of infant do affect the behaviors of mother and infant rhesus monkeys. In the second 3 months, maternal experience wanes in importance as a factor influencing maternal or infant behavior, as the sex of the infant becomes the more important factor. One can best characterize mothers of males as "punishers," mothers of females as "protectors," male infants as "doers," and female infants as "watchers." The mother plays a role in prompting the greater independence and activity that is typical of males.

[Primiparous mothers are those with first offspring. Multiparous mothers have had previous offspring.—EDITOR]

REFERENCE

MITCHELL, G., & STEVENS, C. W. Primiparous and multiparous monkey mothers in a mildly stressful social situation: First three months. *Development Psychobiology*, 1968, *1*, 280–286.

47

Race, Social Class, and the Motive to Avoid Success in Women [1]

Peter J. Weston [2]
and Martha Shuch Mednick

The final article in this section presents a study of college women and deals with a kind of variable that is of particular concern to the women's liberation movement. The motive to avoid success has often been alleged to be one of the chief handicaps to woman's achievement in our society. Here we have an empirical study of the problem in the context of both race and class differences. It could thus have been put in Section VI.

Such a motive, which seems in the majority culture in the United States to be more characteristic of women than men, is greatly influenced by experiential factors. This, at least, is the implication of the differences found between races. Because the samples do not permit all of the possible race and class comparisons, one is glad to see that the authors anticipate further work in this area. Indeed some of that work is alluded to in the additional results that Dr. Mednick has provided for us. Dr. Martha Shuch Mednick is on the faculty of University of Michigan. See article 58 for a related paper on women's need for power.

Horner (1968) successfully reconciled some of the confusion in research on achievement motiva-

tion in women by postulating and demonstrating an avoidance motive called the motive to avoid success (M-s).[3] This psychological barrier to intellectual achievement is defined as "the expectancy or anticipation of negative consequences as a result of success in competitive achievement situations." In the case of women, the specific negative consequences may be social rejection by men, loss of affection, friendship or one's datable or marriageable quality (Horner, 1968, p. 22). According to Horner, when a girl achieves intellectually, she anticipates that she will be regarded as unfeminine. Horner's data support the existence of such a motive in fantasy productions; she also successfully predicted women's problem solving behavior in intellectually competitive situations by using M-s scores. Tangri (1969) also demonstrated that senior level college women express M-s with greater frequency than do junior level girls.

It has been observed by a number of investigators that the motivations and aspirations expressed by black women follow a pattern different from those expressed by white women (Moynihan, 1965; Frazier, 1939, 1962; Pettigrew, 1965). Forces inherent in the social system have had a deleterious effect on black family life as evidenced, for example, by the high percentage of black families headed by women (Clark, 1965; U.S. Department of Labor, 1965). It is commonly asserted that this has resulted in a sex-role identity pattern in which women are more dominant and aggressive and permitted, and indeed, encouraged to be aspiring and intellectually striving. This overt image is partially confirmed by studies of aspirations of black high school students in which girls express higher aspirations than boys (Thompson, 1965); black parents' aspirations for their daughters are higher than for their sons. This finding was not obtained by Gurin and Katz (1966) in their massive study of motivation and level of aspiration in students in Southern black colleges in which college women expressed lower aspirations than the men, seemingly following the pattern of the larger society. The aspirations of these women seemed to be a reflection of the women's realistic perceptions of the opportunities available to them. We maintain, however, that while a girl may lower and be realistic about her aspirations, she may nevertheless maintain fantasies of success and achievement and not avoid dominance and aggressive intellectual

[1] Based on a thesis by the senior author submitted to Howard University in partial fulfillment of the requirements for the M.A. in Psychology.

[2] Now at the University of Michigan.

[3] This study addresses itself to a comparison of women from several cultural subgroups within the American (U.S.) society. Cross-society or national comparisons are projected for future research by the second author.

Peter J. Weston and Martha T. Mednick, "Race, social class, and the motive to avoid success in women," *Journal of Cross-Cultural Psychology, 1,* 1970, 284–291. Reprinted by permission.

mastery. Furthermore, the dynamics involved in her achievement orientation may still be quite different from those of the white women. With this in mind, a series of studies have been undertaken with the goal of exploring the personality and motivational dynamics influencing expressed aspirations and actual career planning in black college women.

A few words must be added about the variable of social class. The possibility of social class differences among black women must be anticipated. The black middle class has been described as "out-middle classing" white middle class in terms of their values. Furthermore, since middle class life is generally more male dominated and family life more stable (Frazier, 1962), it is reasonable to expect that the black middle class college woman will be less dominant and striving than her lower class counterpart.

The present study simply sought to compare black women with white women, not on aspirations, but in fantasy productions to a situation with an intrinsic theme of intellectual competition.

The following hypotheses were tested:

1. Black college women will exhibit fewer M-s responses than white college women.
2. Lower class black women will have fewer M-s responses than middle class black women.

METHOD

SUBJECTS

The *S*s were 63 undergraduate women enrolled at Bluefield State College and 22 enrolled at American University.[4] The breakdown of these *S*s by race and social class is given in Table 1. Social class was determined by occupation and educational level of the parents.

TABLE 1
NUMBER OF SUBJECTS FROM EACH SCHOOL BY RACE AND SOCIAL CLASS

	American University		Bluefield State	
Race	Middle class	Lower class	Middle class	Lower class
Black	10	1	22	28
White	11	0	13	0

----

[4] Bluefield State is a four year liberal arts college in West Virginia whose undergraduate population is approximately 50.8% black. (U.S. Department of Health, Education and Welfare, 1967; Bluefield Registrar's Office, 1969). The undergraduate population of American University (Washington, D.C.) is 4–4.8% black (Statistical Office, American University, 1969).

MATERIALS

Verbal TAT cues[5] such as those used by Horner and a brief questionnaire requesting socio-economic information were administered to each subject. The four cues in order of presentation were as follows:

1. After first term finals, Anne finds herself at the top of her medical school class.
2. A young woman is talking about something important with an older person.
3. Jennifer has just been informed that her three-act play will be produced in New York this coming season.
4. Susan is sitting in a chair with a smile on her face.

Cues 1 and 3 were designed to elicit success imagery while cues 2 and 4 were non-arousal or neutral cues and, as such, were not scored for M-s but served as buffers in the experimental situation.

PROCEDURE

The *S*s were seated in a classroom and given a questionnaire containing the four verbal cues. The cues were presented in the order stated above. All *S*s received the following instructions:

> You are going to see a series of verbal leads or cues and I would like you to tell a story that is suggested to you by each one. Try to imagine what is going on in each. Then tell what the situation is, what led up to the situation, what the people are thinking and feeling and what they will do. In other words, write as complete a story as you can, a story with plot and characters. You will have twenty seconds to look at each verbal cue and then five minutes to write your story about it. Write your first impressions and work rapidly. I will keep time and tell you when it is time to finish your story and to get ready for the next cue. Remember there are no right or wrong answers or kinds of stories, so please feel free to write whatever story is suggested to you when you look at a cue. Spelling, punctuation, and grammar are not important. What is important is to write out as fully and as quickly as possible the story that comes into your mind as you imagine what is going on in each cue.

Thus, the *S*s were required to write brief five-minute stories in response to each of the four cues which were observed for twenty seconds. The stories were written around the following four questions spaced on an answer sheet:

----

[5] The use of verbal cues appear as effective in eliciting imagery as the TAT pictures and have been used by numerous investigators (Atkinson, Horner, Tangri, McClelland, 1959; Bachman et al., 1967). Of course, these are ideally suited to studies in which race comparisons are to be made, since the problem of changing the pictures of identity figures does not arise.

1. What is happening? Who are the persons?
2. What has led up to this situation? What has happened in the past?
3. What is being thought? What is wanted? By whom?
4. What will happen? What will be done?

The instructions given are standard for the TAT; their general tone is to urge the *S*s to produce stories and not to think in terms of right or wrong answers.

The M-s scores were obtained from a content analysis of the fantasies. The first and third cues were scored for M-s independently by two trained raters using the coding directions described by Horner (1968). A general decision was made concerning the presence or absence of M-s imagery and only results agreed upon by both raters were considered.[6] Any imagery (i.e., statement in the story) which suggested or anticipated negative consequences as a result of success was considered fear of success imagery. More specifically, this meant that someone in the story was being placed in an undesirable or negative situation (e.g., losing the friendship of close associates, being socially rejected especially by men, feeling guilt, despair, or doubting one's normality or femininity) because of success in an intellectually competitive situation.

Thus, in scoring the stories for M-s when there was negative imagery reflecting concern about the success, the following criteria were used:

a. negative consequences because of the success
b. anticipation of negative consequences because of the success
c. negative affect because of the success
d. instrumental activity away from present or future success
e. any direct expression of conflict about success.

Also scored was any evidence of:

f. denial of the situation described by the cue
g. bizarre, inappropriate, unrealistic or non-adaptive responses to the situation described by the cue.

No score was given when the stories contained no indication of negative consequences, negative affect

or concern about negative consequences of success. This comprised the "low M-s" category in analysis. A score of 1 indicated that the *S*'s responses reflected mild concern about possible negative consequences of success while a score of 2 was given when there was mention of severe negative consequences of success.[7] Scores of 1 and 2 comprised the "high M-s" category. A score of 3 was assigned to those stories of a bizarre, inappropriate or unrealistic nature. These stories were not used in the analysis of M-s.

After writing the stories, each *S* was asked to answer the questionnaire described above. The designation of social class level was determined on the basis of the answers to those questions.

RESULTS

The M-s data were evaluated separately for each success cue and for the two schools. These means and standard deviations are presented in Table 2.

The significance level of all group differences was evaluated by means of the Fisher Exact Probability Test (1956). Table 3 shows the findings from the Bluefield and American University samples.

The hypothesis with regard to race differences was supported for both cues and at both schools. Class differences within the Black group were not significant, in contradiction to our second hypothesis. This, of course, was only observed at Bluefield State, but was consistent for both cues.

[The absence of a social class difference has since been confirmed in additional samples, according to Dr. Mednick. In a Master's Thesis by Bright conducted at Howard University in 1970, 28% of 125 women tested (all Black) manifested M-s on the "Anne" cue. Other studies at Black schools in the Southeast by Puryear (M.S. Thesis, 1971) found a similar rate (N = 165). In all samples, incidence of M-s and social class level were unrelated. The stability of this finding is suggested further by the fact that sex of experimenter does not affect the results: in all these additional samples the experimenter was a woman, in contrast with the first,

---

[6] For the sample of 85 *S*s the raters agreed upon 91.8% of the responses to cue 1; there was 81.2% agreement on responses to cue 3.

[7] There were seven such stories in the Bluefield sample: five were in response to cue 1 and two to cue 3. No such stories appeared in the American University sample.

TABLE 2
M–S MEANS AND STANDARD DEVIATIONS FOR THE TWO SCHOOLS AND THE TWO CUES

| | Bluefield State | | | | | | American University | | | | | |
| | Cue 1 | | | Cue 3 | | | Cue 1 | | | Cue 3 | | |
Race and class	N	M	SD	N	M	SD	N	M	SD	N	M	SD
White Middle	13	1.25	.59	13	.73	.75	11	1.13	.73	11	.44	.50
Black Middle	22	.16	.49	22	.11	.31	10	.30	.64	10	0	0
Black Lower	28	.24	.42	28	0	0	1	0	0	1	0	0

TABLE 3
MOTIVE TO AVOID SUCCESS AS RELATED TO RACE AND SOCIAL CLASS

Race and class	Bluefield State sample				American University sample			
	Cue 1		Cue 3		Cue 1		Cue 3	
	High M–s	Low M–s	High M–s	Low M–s	High M–s	Low M–s	High M–s	Low M–s
White Middle	11	1	6	5	6	2	4	5
Black Middle	2	17	2	16	2	8	0	9
	$p = .00001$		$p = .018$		$p = .28$		$p = .041 \ (\alpha = .05)$[1]	
Black Lower	6	19	0	19	NR[2]	NR	NR	NR
Black Middle	2	17	2	16	NR	NR	NR	NR
	$p = .170$		$p = .23$					

Note—Fisher probability test used for all analyses.
[1] $\alpha = .05$ for all tests
[2] NR—no respondents

wherein the instruments were administered by a man.—EDITOR]

DISCUSSION

The race difference hypothesis was supported; social class, on the other hand, does not seem to affect M-s imagery.

The stories of black Ss displayed very little M-s. The following are examples of stories written by these Ss. A response to cue 1:

Anne is very pleased because upon completion of finals she finds herself at the top of her medical school class. Anne has studied diligently for long and hard hours. She has always wanted to be a part of the medical profession. Although she studied constantly, she never dreamed of being number one in her class. She wants to pursue a medical career and she is convinced that she can master the work. Her parents and boyfriend will be proud of her. She will continue in medical school graduate and go on to become a leader in her profession.

An example of a response to cue 3:

Jennifer has majored in drama school. Although she is only a junior, she has been writing little three-act plays, one of which has brought her much success. She is, of course, delighted because she never anticipated that any of her work would ever be produced. Jennifer had fancied herself more as an actress than a playwright. She will continue to write more plays. Eventually, Jennifer will write and star in her own productions, moving on to Hollywood, making motion pictures and receiving an Oscar.

In contrast, the display of fear of success imagery is quite clear in the stories of white Ss. Examples

of such stories are the following: Typical responses to cue 1:

Anne and her fellow classmates are sitting around 'shooting the bull.' Final exams, naturally, is the topic of discussion. Two or three people seem to dominate the conversation, and Anne is sitting quietly off to one side, her facial expression is one of mixed emotions. Anne has always been a good student and medicine is her 'thing.' She has worked many long and hard hours to achieve the goal she has reached, with very little time for fun. Anne wonders whether it is really worth it, as she seems to be left out of the 'fun crowd' and ignored by the guys because she is a 'brain.' The only time she is noticed is when someone needs help with homework. Anne will let her studies go and become a party girl.

and

Anne is in George Washington Medical School. The persons involved are the ten girls and fifty guys in Anne's first year in medical class. Anne graduated at the top of her class at Jackson College for Women. She was an anthropology major. Anne's friends and parents are proud. Some of the guys in her class are jealous and there's some tension in the class. Anne will marry Jack, a second year medical student and she won't finish medical school.

A response to cue 3:

Jennifer has worked very hard to achieve this success despite lack of encouragement from Bill, her boyfriend. Bill feels that success will change her. She will go to New York and her play will be a flop. She will come back to Bill. However, Bill is engaged. Jennifer realizes her mistake and lost dream and becomes a nun.

Horner (1968) has suggested that the high M-s found in white Ss is probably due to the aggressive overtones of intellectual competition needed for success in these areas, since aggression has been socially linked to a lack of femininity and its display is seen as leading to negative consequences (i.e., social rejection). The present findings suggest that success in intellectually competitive situations does not elicit similar fear in the black college woman. This may be related to the different sex role patterns since, as noted above, the nature of American society has placed black women in more dominant roles than those assumed by black men or by white women. Accordingly, intellectual mastery is not threatening and professional achievement may in fact not lead to rejection by the male. A successful woman is an economic asset and attractive rather than threatening to a black man. Hence, success as here projected is not to be feared. It may also be argued that the aspirations depicted in these situations are so unrealistic for any black person that the girls do not actually project themselves into their stories, do not identify with the characters and therefore have nothing to fear. For the present this must stand as an alternative explanation though there is some evidence that this is not the case. It would be difficult to argue that the American University sample sees such career goals as completely unattainable. While the Bluefield women may view themselves, as well as their potential husbands, as being unlikely to achieve high status professional careers, the girls attending a white urban university may have realistic aspirations of this sort. It is interesting to note here that in a study of black upper-middle class sorority women attending the University of Michigan, M-s scores matched those of white women on that campus, indicating that at some point up the social-educational status ladder fears of such success may appear.[8] We are now proceeding with several studies designed to illuminate the dynamics of M-s in these women as well as their actual career aspirations and the degree of their commitment to these aspirations. Problem solving performance of high and low M-s scorers in competition with men will be examined. Of course, if low M-s is simply a result of the unreality of the goals implied in the cue, and fear of being intellectually dominant over men does exist, this should be demonstrated in a face to face competitive task.

A final comment about the absence of social

class differences needs to be made. It has been suggested (Horner, personal communication) that a black woman needs to be of upper-middle or upper class status before a fear of success is generated. The Michigan findings tend to support this notion but we could not examine this in our data. Social class differences will be examined in more detail in data about to be collected at Howard University.

REFERENCES

CLARK, KENNETH B. *Dark ghetto.* New York: Harper and Row, 1965.

DAVIS, A., & HAVIGHURST, R. J. Social class and color differences in child-rearing. In C. Kluckhohn, H. A. Murray, & D. M. Schneider. (Eds.), *Personality in nature, society and culture.* (third ed.) New York: Alfred A. Knopf, 1959, chap. 18.

FRAZIER, E. F. *Black bourgeoisie.* New York: Collier Books, 1962.

GURIN, P., & KATZ, D. *Motivation and aspiration in the Negro college.* Final report, U.S. Department of Health, Education and Welfare, 1966.

HORNER, M. S. Sex differences in achievement motivation and performance in competitive and non-competitive situations. Unpublished doctoral dissertation, University of Michigan, 1968.

MOYNIHAN, D. P. *The Negro family.* Washington, D.C.: Office of Policy Planning and Research, United States Department of Labor, 1965.

PETTIGREW, L. *A profile of the Negro American.* Princeton: D. Van Nostrand Company, 1964.

SIEGEL, S. *Non-parametric statistics for the behavioral sciences.* New York: McGraw-Hill, 1956.

TANGRI, SANDRA S. Role-innovation in occupational choice among college women. Unpublished doctoral dissertation, University of Michigan, 1969.

THOMPSON, D. In Moynihan, D. (Ed.). *The Negro family.* U.S. Department of Labor, 1965.

UNITED STATES DEPARTMENT OF LABOR. *The Negroes in the United States: their economic and social situations.* Bulletin No. 1511, U.S. Department of Labor, 1965.

UNITED STATES DEPARTMENT OF LABOR. *Extent of unemployment among non-white men, 1955–63.* Bureau of Labor Statistics, 1965.

WESTON, P. J. *Race, social class and the motive to avoid success in women.* Unpublished Master's Thesis, Howard University, 1969.

[8] Personal communications from Matina S. Horner and Sandra G. Tangri.

IX

Cognitive Determinants and Resultants

Among American psychologists, a fundamental challenge to the tradition of behaviorism has emerged within the last few years—cognitive psychology. Behaviorists, especially learning theorists of the S–R (stimulus–response) reinforcement persuasion featured in Section III, focus on overt acts. In order to learn how behavior is determined, they study the ways responses can be changed by environmental events (stimuli) under the control of the experimenter. Cognitive theorists, on the other hand, emphasize the *knowledge* that an individual has, how he organizes his world, and how he integrates new information with that which he already possesses. The impetus giving rise to the cognitive point of view arose from the enormous difficulty—some say impossibility—of dealing with complex human behavior in S–R terms. The complexity of language, especially, argues for this approach. Man is qualitatively different from lower animals in terms of his symbolic capacities—his ability to use language. The production of novel utterances is a creative accomplishment that cannot be accounted for in simple S–R terms.[1] Noam Chomsky's major contributions to linguistic theory (transformational-generative grammar) have done much to further the acceptance of the cognitive point of view. Bruner (see Section XI) represents a cognitive orientation, an attitude that is rapidly becoming the theoretical preference of many workers in child development and educational psychology.

Jean Piaget has probably been the single most important influence on today's conceptions of cognitive development. According to Piaget, the child passes through a series of stages, the order of which is invariant; that is, the same for all children. In this section there are two articles about Piagetian notions.

The measurement of intelligence has been a primary concern of many psychologists, especially those in the field of education. Intelligence is one of the key variables in influencing the outcome of education and in determining the nature of the training that should be given. The problems of intelligence and its measurement are related to biological issues. Indeed, historically the question of hereditary *vs.* experiential determinants has dominated discussions of intelligence. Not content to think of intelligence as merely that which is measured by intelligence tests, many psychologists (as well as lay people) have tended to reify intelligence and then to engage in lengthy discussions about the degree to which "it" is innately or biologically determined. Recently, psychologists have found it more fruitful to think in terms of *intelligent behaviors* rather than "intelligence" and to turn attention to the interactions of heredity and environment in determining intelligent behaviors. The introduction to Section II and Tulkin's article in Section VI deal with the influence of race and social class on intelligence. So, less directly, does the introduction to Section VIII.

---

[1] The behaviorists, of course, argue that this phenomenon can indeed be accounted for in S–R terms. See B. F. Skinner's *Verbal Behavior* (New York: Appleton-Century-Crofts, 1957).

48

Cognitive Capacity
and Cognitive Competence[1]

Morton Bortner
and Herbert G. Birch

*One of the central theses of the cognitivist's po-
sition is that actual performance is quite different
from underlying capacity (often called "competence"). While in the behaviorist tradition performance is usually accepted as a fairly good in-
dicator of "what has been learned" (even though
the theoretical distinction between learning and
performance is often acknowledged), the cognitive viewpoint emphasizes that one must know a
considerable amount about the particular concepts, abilities, and strategies of the subject, as
well as the particular conditions of training and
task demand, in order to determine the degree to
which performance accurately reflects capacity.
Morton Bortner is professor and Kennedy Foundation Scholar at Yeshiva University. Herbert Birch,
who holds both the Ph.D. and the M.D. degree, is
professor of pediatrics at the Albert Einstein College of Medicine.*

[1] This is a revision of a paper read at the annual conference
of the American Association on Mental Deficiency, San Francisco, May 12–17, 1969. The report is based on projects supported, in part, by the Joseph P. Kennedy, Jr., Foundation, the
U.S. Office of Education Grant OEG–0–8–071272–3317
(032), the National Institute of Child Health and Human Development Grant HD 00719, the Association for the Aid of
Crippled Children, and the National Association for Retarded
Children.

In this paper we wish to argue that it is essential
to make a distinction between cognitive capacity
and cognitive performance if we are to be most
effective in developing approaches to the habilitation and education of mentally subnormal children. Such a distinction, though rarely stated
explicitly, is not new and has its roots in the very
first efforts directed at developing special training
procedures for the improvement of function in the
mentally subnormal. It was a distinction which
underlay Itard's disagreement with Pinel as to the
worthwhileness of trying to teach Victor, the "wild
boy" of Aveyron (Itard, 1801). Pinel was dominated by the 18th Century attitude which tended
to view mental subnormality as a unitary phenomenon in which cognitive functions were fixed,
and to lump mentally defective children into a
homogeneous mass with individuals differing from
one another primarily in the severity of their deficits and in the nature of associated physical and
behavioral signs.

Itard, stimulated by the French revolution and
its doctrine of the improvability of man, argued
that Victor's defects derived at least as much from
his faulty opportunities for development as from
his biologic limitations. In Itard's view, Victor's
behavior did not reflect his capacity but only his
currently available competence. Itard saw his task
as that of raising performance to the limits imposed
by capacity. The difference between Itard and Pinel
was therefore not merely a disagreement between
persons, but between epochs. When Itard decided
to work with Victor, it was therefore in courageous
opposition to established opinion expressed by
Pinel that the child was "an incurable idiot, inferior to domestic animals" (Kanner, 1964). Itard's
experience over a 5-year period—though depressing for him since Victor failed to reach a normal
level of intellectual and social functioning—constituted one of the most successful failures in the
history of special education. It demonstrated that
even a severely mentally subnormal child could
learn, and produced a variety of training strategies,
methods, and approaches through which such improvement could be effected. Itard's work made
it clear that Victor's performance did not necessarily reflect his capacity directly, and that special
methods were essential in dealing with handicapped
children if competence were to approach the limits
of capacity.

Despite Itard's demonstration that mentally subnormal children could improve in their adjustment to their environment, Seguin had to transcend
authoritative gloom and doom, as exemplified by

Morton Bortner and Herbert G. Birch, "Cognitive capacity and cognitive competence," *American Journal of Mental Deficiency, 74,* 1970, 735–744. Reprinted by permission.

Esquirol's opinion that educational efforts were useless and that "no means are known by which a larger amount of reason or intelligence can be bestowed upon the unhappy idiot, even for the briefest period" (Kanner, 1964). Seguin's insistence that something could be done to bridge the gap between capacity and performance, however, foreshadowed the common assumption underlying the work of such modern researchers as Luria, Tizard, Lewis, House and Zeaman, O'Connor and Hermelin, Zigler, and the Clarkes. All these workers view cognitive performance as not necessarily providing an accurate reflection of cognitive capacity. They have been able to demonstrate that changes in training procedures, task organization, social circumstances, and motivation, as well as characteristics of the examiner, all significantly influence the level of performance.

The scope of the present paper did not permit us to review in detail the history of attitudes toward capacity and performance. Rather, it was our feeling that studies relevant to the question have been so scattered that at no point have they been sufficiently integrated and related to general principles of psychological development. We have attempted, therefore, to relate them to work in the general psychology of development in the hope that a more fully expressed conceptualization of the distinction between cognitive capacity and cognitive performance would be helpful in the guidance and development of practices for the care and habilitation of mentally subnormal children.

We began this effort by considering some of the studies from our own laboratories. In these studies, we raised the question of the degree to which children possessed concepts which were not available for use when they performed under ordinary free-field conditions (Birch & Bortner, 1966). It was found that when young children were presented with a model object and asked to select from among three alternatives that object which "belonged" with the model, the children matched on the basis of stimulus properties. Thus, if the model object were a red button, and the alternatives for matching were a red lipstick case, a blue poker chip, and a spool of thread, the young children selected either the lipstick case, which agreed with the model in color, or the poker chip, which had the same shape. Older children, in contrast, ignored the stimulus properties and selected the thread, which had a functional relation to the button, as the object which "belonged" with it. Did the younger children fail to select the thread because they did not understand its functional relationship to the button, or did they possess the concept but not have it available for use? This question could be examined by testing the hypothesis that

the younger children did indeed possess the concept, i.e., had it as one of their capacities but did not utilize it under conditions in which their behavior could be guided by information at a sensory level. If this hypothesis were true, it would be expected that a comparable group of young children, confronted with the task under conditions in which competition from sensory properties was reduced, would manifest their possessed functional concept in performance. We presented this and other problems under conditions in which the alternative choices contained no striking sensory attributes which matched the model. Behavior was not dominated by sensory properties under these altered conditions, and almost all of the young children made functional selections. Many of them, when requested to rationalize their choice of thread to go with a red button, stated, "You sew a button with it."

Clearly, these normal young children possessed functional concepts, but they were not available for use when the task was presented in such a way as to place their hierarchically organized and age-specific determining tendencies in competition with their much weaker tendency to be responsive to functional attributes. Such a tendency is not restricted to children and is, in a more general sense, a feature of human problem solving (Birch & Rabinowitz, 1951; Duncker, 1945; Maier, 1930; Woodworth & Sells, 1935).

When this technique for differentiating between capacity and competence was applied to brain-damaged children, essentially the same findings obtained (Birch & Bortner, 1967). The tendency to use such abstractions as class membership and functional characteristics as bases for matching was facilitated in brain-damaged children when the competition of immediately present stimulus properties was systematically reduced. Moreover, the brain-damaged children were able to match in terms of function as frequently and correctly under conditions where the competition between conceptual category or function and stimulus properties was reduced as did normal children who had to choose in the context of stimulus competition. These results demonstrated that brain-damaged children did in fact possess, and under certain conditions could use, higher-order abstractions. However, their expression of such abstract capacity was inhibited in the presence of stimulus competition and only became evident when such competition was reduced.

The findings in these studies suggested the possibility that changes in problem solving and cognitive style as a function of age are based upon alterations in hierarchical selection set rather than simply on the acquisition of new concepts or new capacities. This suggestion received support in the study by Mehler and Bever (1967) in which conservation of number was studied in very young children. In general, Piaget's approach was utilized. Clay pellets were arranged in two rows, with the shorter row containing the larger number of pellets. When the children were asked to point to the row with "more," Piaget's reported finding of nonconservation was confirmed, with the children choosing the longer row (the one containing fewer pellets). However, when M & M candies were substituted for the pellets and the response called for was nonverbal, i.e., when the children were permitted to take and eat the row of their choice, the children more frequently took the shorter row with more candies—apparently demonstrating conservation in action. Some children responded incorrectly in their verbal judgments of which clay row had "more" whereas in the M & M row they chose the correct row to eat. Apparently, in one case (clay pellets) "more" meant visual extent, whereas in the other (M & M candies) it meant "more" things to eat. Hence, the particular task set appeared to have influenced both the children's definitions of "more" and their performance. The content of the task apparently defined a set which drew selectively upon the children's possessed capacities—leading to selections based on visual-perceptual responses to extent in one instance and on responses linked to an amount concept in the other.

Dryman, Birch, and Korn (1970) found a similar dissociation between capacity and performance in the problem solving of older children. In their study, 6-year-old children were presented with a task in which a floating bead had to be extracted from a test tube that was one-third full of water. The children were asked how they would get the bead out. First responses were manipulative. Approximately a third of the children offered or verbalized a float-up solution. They were then confronted with the tube and bead on a table with tweezers and other tools as well as two bottles of water. Not one of the children who had verbalized the correct solution poured water into the tube as his *first* response. All the children tended to be dominated by the manipulative opportunities present despite the fact that the tweezers and other objects were not effective tools. After failing with these objects, some of the children used the water, but half of the children who had verbalized a float-up solution *never* used this strategy in their efforts. Instead, they perseveratively and repetitively were dominated by their manipulative sets.

Thus, there are age-specific sets, motive-specific sets (M & M), and task-specific sets, all of which define different fragments of capacity which are expressed in performance. The gap is broader or narrower in accordance with the goodness of fit between the structure of the task demand and the nature of the relation between the subject's motivation and his capacities.

These studies supported the assumption that a meaningful distinction could be made between capacity (representing the potential of the individual) and performance (representing the level at which the individual responds). Moreover, the performance of the individual did not appear directly to reflect his capacity, but rather seemed to represent that fragment of his capacities which was in accord with the particular conditions of demand. This general proposition has led workers in Britain, Russia, and America to be concerned with delineating the appropriate conditions for making demands which, in turn, would lead to performance that more truly reflected the capacities of the subnormal individual than he ordinarily exhibited.

These different workers have had different emphases. The British group emphasized work habilitation and the productivity of subjects, with special concern for the development of training methods that would permit the individual to engage in productive work through an appropriate tapping of potentials that are dormant under most task conditions. The American work, which has overlapped somewhat with this view, has had a primarily motivational emphasis, and has, in general, shown how level of performance varies both qualitatively and quantitatively as a result of the selective manipulation of conditions of demand and of reward. The Russian emphasis has been on the "second signal system" (language) and ways in which deficiencies in this area could be overcome with appropriate training, resulting in a fuller expression of capability. All three groups have been concerned with the gap between capacity and performance in the cognitive functioning of subnormal children.

Lewis (1960) summarized the British approach to the distinction between capacity and performance by pointing to such studies as those of O'Connor and Tizard (1956), who demonstrated that acquisition of a skill improved strikingly for retarded individuals when social conditions in the workshop were manipulated. The focus of British concern was on work habilitation, productivity, defining of work conditions and motives, and the development of training methods. Manipulation of work (learning) conditions (Clarke, 1957; Tizard & Loos, 1954) resulted in the employment of retarded patients who for years had been viewed as unemployable.

Another approach to the problem of the influence of motivational factors on cognitive functioning has been pursued by the Clarkes, who have advanced the notion that the complexity of the task may be a factor in the transfer of learning and that this can be used to advantage by the retarded child. They have reported that transfer is facilitated when practice in categorizing is offered to the subject, and when superordinate categories are formed. Manipulation of conditions is thus possible which then enhances and improves cognitive performance (Clarke & Cookson, 1962; Clarke & Cooper, 1964; Clarke, Cooper, & Clarke, 1967; Clarke & Clarke, 1967; Clarke & Cooper, 1967; Clarke, Clarke, & Cooper, in press; Clarke, 1968).

More generally, Tizard and Grad (1961) found considerable differences in the abilities of retarded individuals which could not be attributed to differences in level of intelligence, i.e., defects of temperament were among the noncognitive handicaps exhibited by these individuals. Such a view has much in common with the American tendency to shift the emphasis from intelligence alone to other features of personality. The work of Thomas, Chess, Birch, Hertzig, and Korn (1963), with normal children, has constituted one such search for those relatively stable noncognitive characteristics which are identifiable from early infancy and which help to define the child's later functioning.

Another search for the motivational or noncognitive components of learning is illustrated in the work of Zigler and his associates. In response to suggestions by Lewin (1936) and Kounin (1941) that retarded children are more cognitively rigid (e.g., more perseverative) than normal children, and thus less capable in satiation, motoric, and concept-switching tasks, Zigler and others have proposed a motivational hypothesis. They suggested that the observed differences on these tasks were related to the child's responsiveness to verbal support, approval, and in general, social reinforcement (Shallenberger & Zigler, 1961; Zigler, 1966; Zigler & Butterfield, 1966). The effectiveness of such reinforcement was seen as interacting with a number of factors in the child's personal and social context, including anxiety level of the subject (Walters & Ray, 1960), sex of the examiner in relation to sex of the subject (Gewirtz & Baer, 1958; Stevenson, 1961), chronological age or mental age of subject (Stevenson, 1961), social class of the subject (Douvan, 1956; Zigler, 1962; Zigler & DeLabry, 1962) relationship of the examiner to the subject (McCoy & Zigler, 1965), imitativeness of the subject (Turnure & Zigler, 1964) and nature of the incentive (Cantor & Hottell, 1955; Ellis, 1962; Gordon, O'Connor & Tizard, 1955; Heber, 1959; Wolfensberger, 1960; Zigler & Unell, 1962). Most importantly, social reinforcement was thought to be related to the nature and extent of the social deprivation in the child's background (Butterfield

& Zigler, 1965; Clarke & Clarke, 1959; Clarke, Clarke & Reiman, 1958; Green & Zigler, 1962; Shepps & Zigler, 1962; Zigler, 1961, 1962; Zigler, Hodgden & Stevenson, 1958), with greater deprivation leading to greater responsiveness to social reinforcement.

House and Zeaman have sought to define those conditions of a noncognitive nature which lead to improved cognitive performance, and have identified such contributing factors as novelty (Zeaman, House & Orlando, 1958), sequence of easy to hard (House & Zeaman, 1960), and various conditions of reward (House, Orlando & Zeaman, 1957; House & Zeaman, 1958a, 1958b; Zeaman & House, 1962).

Luria and his colleagues have emphasized the significance of language development for the more general process of mental development (Liublinskaya, 1957; Luria, 1961; Luria & Vinogradova, 1959). Luria also stressed the interaction of the child and the teacher (offering verbal help) as an educational event wherein "what the child can do today with the help of the teacher he will be able to do by himself tomorrow." This rise in performance level, then, was related to what Vygotsky had called the "zone of potential development"—an apparent reference to capacity. Luria appeared to be concerned with the distinction between capacity and performance, in his implicit focus upon the fact that the child was capable of doing more, and with the consequent need to bridge this gap through verbal help from the teacher.

Luria suggested that there are two signal systems, one governing motor behavior and the other verbal behavior. In the normal child, the second system (language) guides and regulates action, and this regulation forms the basis for voluntary behavior. In the severely subnormal child, language does not develop sufficiently to assume this orienting function, and the result is a loose connection between verbal and motor behavior. This theory has led a number of investigators to study language functions in subnormal children in order to explore the conditions which facilitate learning of words (Hermelin & O'Connor, 1964; O'Connor & Hermelin, 1963), learning sets (O'Connor & Hermelin, 1959a) and the relation of words to sensory-motor behavior (O'Connor & Hermelin, 1959b).

In comparative psychology, too, the problem of possession and availability was exemplified in the work of Lashley and Yerkes. They sought to determine whether or not rats were capable of distinguishing geometric forms one from another. Yerkes and Watson's (1911) work with the discrimination box had clearly indicated that, under the conditions of performance defined by the use of the box at that time, rats were totally incapable of making form discriminations but, instead, made discriminations based merely upon relative brightness. Lashley, on the basis of his naturalistic observations of rats, believed that this was an underestimation of the rat's capacity and repeated Yerkes' experiments. However, after thousands of trials of experience, the performance of the rats in Lashley's experiments was no better than was the case with completely naive rats. It was not until 19 years later (Lashley, 1930) that he conceptualized the problem in a new way. He argued that the rat was an organism that was primarily responsive to the kinesthetic, tactile, and olfactory aspects of a situation, and that when the conditions of a task were ones in which these nonvisual cues dominated the animal's responsiveness, the response made to a visual stimulus would be at a level considerably below his capacity. Thus, it could be argued that the rat possessed the ability to discriminate forms but did not exhibit this capacity under the particular conditions of testing. With the goal of reducing nonvisual stimuli and of focusing "attention" on the visual task, Lashley developed the jumping apparatus in which the movements of the animal were restricted by placing him upon a small platform. Under these conditions, the animal's attention was more readily directed to, and forced to focus upon, the properties of the visual stimuli. Once this technique was introduced, Lashley was able to demonstrate that those rats which previously could not make form discriminations in thousands of trials were now able to exhibit this capacity in 20 to 30 trials. An organism, therefore, which for years had been declared as lacking in the capacity to develop form discriminations now evidenced such a capacity.

An analogous controversy existed in physiological psychology between Malmo and Jacobsen with respect to the functions of the frontal lobes. Jacobsen (1934) found that monkeys which had their frontal lobes removed bilaterally lost their ability to engage in a delayed response. Malmo and Kleinsasser (1942) questioned whether the animals really had lost this ability, and suggested the alternative view that bilateral frontal lobe extirpation led to increased vulnerability to retroactive inhibition. Such inhibition, they asserted, interfered with the learning upon which the delayed response was based. If this were true, then the performance of the animals was not truly reflecting their capacity with respect to either single-trial learning or the ability to engage in delay. They changed the nature of the delay period from one in which the lights were on (giving the animals the opportunity to respond to other visual stimuli and so, retroactively, to inhibit the initial visual learn-

ing) to a delay period sustained in total darkness. When this was done, delayed response was exhibited by animals with bilateral frontal lobectomy. These results, again, indicated that a distinction had to be made between an animal's capacity to engage in a given level of behavior and its manifestation of this capacity in performance.

Related findings are those of Geschwind, who described a patient with neurological impairment who could not name colors but who could nevertheless recognize their correct names when this information was presented in either oral or written form (Geschwind & Fusillo, 1966). Another patient (Geschwind & Kaplan, 1962), even while giving an incorrect verbal description of an object, effectively demonstrated the correct use of the object. In both of these cases, the performance of the patients did not reflect their understanding until the task requirements were adapted from ones requiring a verbal response to ones requiring some other kind of response.

Similar concerns have been expressed by Pribram and others in their judgments of the consequences of brain extirpations on behavior. They have argued that deterioration in performance need not always be interpreted as a loss of the capacity to perform, that the primary mechanism that has been interfered with in many instances is the motivation of the animal to perform, and that if this motivation is restored, performance will again reflect intact capacity (Pribram, 1966; West, 1960).

Additional conclusions deriving from experimental and comparative psychology dealing with the difference between capacity and performance can be found in the studies of Tryon (1940) on the genetics of intelligence in rats. Tryon selectively bred a group of rats which performed well and a group which performed poorly on an enclosed alley maze. By breeding bright with bright and dull with dull animals, he raised two colonies of rats which were consistent in their maze brightness and maze dullness. Tryon's data were interpreted as demonstrating that intelligence was heritable, and that breeding bright with bright and dull with dull resulted in increased differentiation between the two groups of rats with respect to general intellectual capacity. Overlooked in Tryon's discussion was the possibility that the specific learning task he was using was one that was dependent rather explicitly upon information deriving from nonvisual cues. Therefore, what Tryon might have been breeding for was not intelligence in general but, rather, responsiveness to certain features of environmental information in one of his groups of rats, as contrasted with responsiveness to alternative features of environmental information in his other rats. The failure to consider this problem became apparent when one of Tryon's students, Searle, repeated the experiment with these strains.

Searle (1949) found that, on elevated mazes which permitted greater opportunities for visual cues to operate, Tryon's dull rats performed as well as the so-called bright rats. Moreover, he noted that temperamental differences of a complex nature existed between the two strains and concluded:

> [When] all types of apparatus situations are considered there is no evidence that Dulls are generally inferior . . . [and] differences in the maze learning ability represent differences in patterns of behavior traits rather than in *degrees* of any single psychological capacity [pp. 319–320].

This suggested that what had been bred for was not a difference in general intellectual capacity but, rather, differences in sensory sensitivity and temperamental stability.

The latter conclusion was supported more recently by the findings of Fuller and Thompson (1960) in the area of behavior genetics. They compared five dog breeds on seven behavioral measures. Although there were differences among the breeds, different breeds appeared to be superior learners on different types of learning tasks. On tasks eliciting motivational and emotional responses, even greater differences were found among breeds. These findings led Birch (1968) to conclude that:

> learning ability is by no means a unitary trait, and that in different organisms different patterns of responsiveness, of motivation, of emotionality, and of antecedent history contribute substantially to determining which sub-grouping will learn most effectively under conditions of different instruction and task demand . . . [and] that differences in learning achievement whether measured by intelligence tests or by school achievement in human beings, represent the products of different degrees of goodness of fit between the learner, the task, and, in particular, the instructional mode [p. 56].

All of the findings discussed thus far involve the following concepts. The first is the concept that stimuli in the environment compete to dominate the behavior of the individual. The second is the concept that preponderant set or directional style in individuals determines (either on an habitual basis, or on the basis of prior focused training, or on the basis of intrinsic physiologic differences) those aspects of environmental stimulation to which the individual will respond. The third concept involves the motivation of the organism and

the degree to which this motivation acts both to elevate level of activity and to make explicit the direction of activity. (In this sense, one differentiates between drive, which represents an elevation of action level, and motive, which is a directed and selective organization of such increased energetics toward defined goals and specified features of the environment.) The fourth point is the problem of interference with competences, as illustrated by the Malmo–Jacobsen controversy. The fifth point embraces the totality of ideas considered above and involves the idea that differences in learning achievement represent products of different degrees of goodness of fit between the organism and the environment. Certain kinds of fit between organism and environment result in directionalities of behavior and in the successful expression of selected features of the individual's capacities, whereas environmental modifications may encourage other types of performance which reflect quite different capacities.

The concept of the hierarchical organization of response systems is relevant here. This general concept was recently advanced by Birch (1962) and suggests that one of the ways in which organisms differ from one another is in the hierarchical organization of their sense systems. In the development of the normal individual, the telereceptor system gradually comes to dominate over visceral and proximal reception. Complex patterning of behavior, e.g., reading readiness, comes to be organized around the dominant use of auditory and visual information. Thus, certain kinds of reading disability may stem from the inadequate development of an appropriate hierarchical organization of sensory systems, and thus may be the result of the failure of visual system dominance.

Little empirical work is available in this area. Bakker (1966, 1967) has been doing systematic studies within the context of this hypothesis on individuals with reading disabilities, and has demonstrated certain differences in the hierarchy of visual and kinesthetic responsiveness of normal and backward readers. Using a psychophysical method to determine differences in responsiveness to visual and kinesthetic stimuli, and using a difference-threshold procedure, he reported that visual and kinesthetic discrimination capacities were more similar in backward readers than in normal readers in whom visual discrimination was far superior to kinesthetic discrimination. He inferred that there was less dominance of the visual over the kinesthetic system in backward readers.

Clearly, the point of view being developed is related to the issue of behavioral individuality. We have been focusing upon those features of cognitive individuality which may contribute to the gap between capacity and performance. The areas of social psychology and personality development yield related findings. For example, examiner effects on intelligence test scores represent manifestations of the ways in which incorrect estimates of capacity may be obtained on the basis of differences in attitude or in style of approach of the examiner to the child. Thus, the studies of Haggard (1954) and of Anastasi and DeJesus (1953) on social background, atmosphere, and examiner effects indicate that the ethnicity of the examiner, the style with which the examiner approaches the child, and the degree to which the child is familiar with the test circumstances and test atmosphere all contribute to both the level of performance itself and the degree to which the child's performance is a more or less accurate reflection of his capacity.

Our consideration of the relation between cognitive capacity and cognitive performance in mentally subnormal children, as well as in normal children and experimental animals, permits a general conclusion. It is clear from all these data that performance levels under particular conditions are but fragmentary indicators of capacity. Possessed concepts and skills, and particular conceptual abilities, as well as levels of learning when manifested in performance, all reflect the interaction between possessed potentialities and the particular conditions of training and task demand. Glaring differences occur in the estimates of potential when meaningful alterations are made in the conditions for performance. It is clear that we have but begun to explore the universe of conditions for learning and performance which will facilitate most effectively the expression of the potentialities for adaptation which exist in mentally subnormal children. Clearly, the most effective facilitation of development will be dependent on the ingenuity with which such conditions are elaborated. It is to be hoped that placing this question in the broader context of psychology will contribute to the invention of more effective strategies for training and for the maximation of competence.

REFERENCES

ANASTASI, A., & DeJESUS, C. Language development and non-verbal IQ of Puerto Rican preschool children in New York City. *Journal of Abnormal and Social Psychology,* 1953, *48,* 357–366.

BAKKER, D. Sensory dominance in normal and backward readers. *Perceptual and Motor Skills,* 1966, *23,* 1055–1058.

BAKKER, D. Sensory dominance and reading ability. *Journal of Communication Disorders,* 1967, *1,* 316–318.

BIRCH, H. G. Dyslexia and the maturation of visual function. In J. Money (Ed.), *Reading disability: Progress and research needs in dyslexia.* Baltimore: Johns Hopkins Press, 1962. Pp. 161–169.

BIRCH, H. G. Boldness and judgment in behavior genetics. In M. Mead, T. Dobzhansky, E. Tobach, & R. Light (Eds.), *Science and the concept of race.* New York: Columbia University Press, 1968. Pp. 49–58.

BIRCH, H. G., & BORTNER, M. Stimulus competition and category usage in normal children. *Journal of Genetic Psychology,* 1966, *109,* 195–204.

BIRCH, H. G., & BORTNER, M. Stimulus competition and category utilization in brain damaged children. *Developmental Medicine and Child Neurology,* 1967, *9,* 402–410. (Also in S. Chess & A. Thomas, (Eds.), *Annual progress in child psychiatry and child development.* New York: Bruner/Mazel, 1968.)

BIRCH, H. G., & RABINOWITZ, H. S. The negative effect of previous experience on productive thinking. *Journal of Experimental Psychology,* 1951, *41,* 121–125.

BUTTERFIELD, E. C., & ZIGLER, E. The influence of differing institutional social climates on the effectiveness of social reinforcement in the mentally retarded. *American Journal of Mental Deficiency,* 1965, *70,* 48–56.

CANTOR, G. N., & HOTTELL, J. V. Discrimination learning in mental defectives as a function of magnitude of food reward and intelligence level. *American Journal of Mental Deficiency,* 1955, *60,* 380–384.

CLARKE, A. D. B. A symposium: The social adjustment of the mentally deficient: I. Recent English research. *American Journal of Mental Deficiency,* 1957, *62,* 295–299.

CLARKE, A. D. B. The need of the mentally retarded for complex learning experiences. Paper read at Symposium on Education of the Moderately and Severely Retarded, Ostend, Belgium, April 1968.

CLARKE, A. D. B., CLARKE, A. M., & REIMAN, S. Cognitive and social changes in the feebleminded: Three further studies. *British Journal of Psychology,* 1958, *49,* 144–157.

CLARKE, A. D. B., & CLARKE, A. M. Recovery from the effects of deprivation. *Acta Psychologica, Amsterdam,* 1959, *16,* 137–144.

CLARKE, A. M., & CLARKE, A. D. B. Learning transfer and cognitive development. In G. Jervis, & J. Zubin (Eds.), *Psychopathology of mental development.* New York: Grune & Stratton, 1967.

CLARKE, A. M., CLARKE, A. D. B., & COOPER, G. M. The development of a set to perceive categorical relations. In H. C. Haywood (Ed.), *Social-Cultural Aspects of Mental Retardation.* New York: Appleton-Century-Crofts, 1970, in press.

CLARKE, A. D. B., & COOKSON, M. Perceptual-motor transfer in imbeciles: A second series of experiments. *British Journal of Psychology,* 1962, *53,* 321–330.

CLARKE, A. D. B., & COOPER, G. M. Age and perceptual-motor transfer of training. *Perceptual and Motor Skills,* 1964, *19,* 849–850.

CLARKE, A. M., & COOPER, G. M. Conceptual transfer in preschool children as a function of prior training. *Psychonomic Science*, 1967, *9*, 307–308.

CLARKE, A. M., COOPER, G. M., & CLARKE, A. D. B. Task complexity and transfer in the development of cognitive structures. *Journal of Experimental Child Psychology*, 1967, *5*, 562–576.

DOUVAN, E. Social status and success striving. *Journal of Abnormal and Social Psychology*, 1956, *52*, 219–223.

DRYMAN, I., BIRCH, H. G., & KORN, S. J. Verbalization and action in the problem-solving of six-year-old children. Unpublished manuscript, Yeshiva University, 1970.

DUNCKER, K. On problem-solving. *Psychological Monographs*, 1945, *58*, (5, Whole No. 270). (Translated by L. S. Lees.)

ELLIS, N. R. Amount of reward and operant behavior in mental defectives. *American Journal of Mental Deficiency*, 1962, *66*, 613–617.

FULLER, J. L., & THOMPSON, W. R. *Behavior genetics*. New York: Wiley, 1960.

GESCHWIND, N., & FUSILLO, M. Color naming defects in association with alexia. *Archives of Neurology*, 1966, *15*, 137–146.

GESCHWIND, N., & KAPLAN, E. A human cerebral deconnection syndrome. *Neurology*, 1962, *12*, 675–685.

GEWIRTZ, J., & BAER, D. The effect of brief social deprivation on behaviors for a social reinforcer. *Journal of Abnormal and Social Psychology*, 1958, *56*, 49–56.

GORDON, S., O'CONNOR, N., & TIZARD, J. Some effects of incentives on the performance of imbeciles on a repetitive task. *American Journal of Mental Deficiency*, 1955, *60*, 371–377.

GREEN, C., & ZIGLER, E. Social deprivation and the performance of retarded and normal children on a satiation type task. *Child Development*, 1962, *33*, 499–508.

HAGGARD, E. A. Social status and intelligence: An experimental study of certain cultural determinants of measured intelligence. *Genetic Psychology Monographs*, 1954, *49*, 141–186.

HEBER, R. Motor task performance of high grade mentally retarded males as a function of the magnitude of incentive. *American Journal of Mental Deficiency*, 1959, *63*, 667–671.

HERMELIN, B., & O'CONNOR, N. Short term memory in normal and subnormal children. *American Journal of Mental Deficiency*, 1964, *69*, 121–125.

HOUSE, B. J., ORLANDO, R., & ZEAMAN, D. Role of positive and negative cues in the discrimination learning of mental defectives. *Perceptual and Motor Skills*, 1957, *7*, 73–79.

HOUSE, B. J., & ZEAMAN, D. Visual discrimination learning in imbeciles. *American Journal of Mental Deficiency*, 1958, *63*, 447–452. (a)

HOUSE, B. J., & ZEAMAN, D. Reward and non-reward in the discrimination learning of imbeciles. *Journal of Comparative and Physiological Psychology*, 1958, *51*, 614–618. (b)

HOUSE, B. J., & ZEAMAN, D. Transfer of a discrimination from objects to patterns. *Journal of Experimental Psychology*, 1960, *59*, 298–302.

ITARD, J. M. G. *De l'éducation d'un homme sauvage*. Paris: Goujon, 1801.

JACOBSEN, C. F. The effects of extirpation of the frontal association in monkeys upon complex adaptive behavior. *Psychological Bulletin*, 1934, *31*, 636–637.

KANNER, L. *A history of the care and study of the mentally retarded*. Springfield, Ill.: Charles C Thomas, 1964.

KOUNIN, J. Experimental studies of rigidity: I. The measurement of rigidity in normal and feebleminded persons. *Character and Personality*, 1941, *9*, 251–273.

LASHLEY, K. The mechanism of vision: I. A method for rapid analysis of pattern vision in the rat. *Journal of Genetic Psychology*, 1930, *37*, 353–460.

LEWIN, K. *A dynamic theory of personality*. New York: McGraw-Hill, 1936.

LEWIS, A. The study of defect. *American Journal of Psychiatry*, 1960, *117*, 289–305.

LIUBLINSKAYA, A. A. The development of children's speech and thought. In B. Simon (Ed.), *Psychology in the Soviet Union*. Translated by J. Ellis, M. Ellis, and others. Stanford, Calif.: Stanford University Press, 1957.

LURIA, A. R. An objective approach to the study of the abnormal child. *American Journal of Orthopsychiatry*, 1961, *31*, 1–16.

LURIA, A. R., & VINOGRADOVA, O. S. An objective investigation of the dynamics of semantic systems. *British Journal of Psychology*, 1959, *50*, 89–105.

MAIER, N. R. F. Reasoning in humans: I. On directions. *Journal of Comparative Psychology*, 1930, *10*, 115–143.

MALMO, R. B., & KLEINSASSER, A. J. Interference factors in delayed response in monkeys after removal of the frontal lobes. *Psychological Bulletin*, 1942, *39*, 492–493.

McCOY, N., & ZIGLER, E. Social reinforcer effectiveness as a function of the relationship between child and adult. *Journal of Personality and Social Psychology*, 1965, *1*, 604–612.

MEHLER, J., & BEVER, T. G. Cognitive capacity of very young children. *Science*, 1967, *158*, 141–142.

O'CONNOR, N., & HERMELIN, B. Some effects of word learning in imbeciles. *Language and Speech*, 1959, *2*, 63–71. (a)

O'CONNOR, N., & HERMELIN, B. Discrimination and reversal learning in imbeciles. *Journal of Abnormal and Social Psychology*, 1959, *59*, 409–413. (b)

O'CONNOR, N., & HERMELIN, B. Recall in normals and subnormals of like mental age. *Journal of Abnormal and Social Psychology*, 1963, *66*, 81–84.

O'CONNOR, N., & TIZARD, J. *The social problem of mental deficiency*. London: Pergamon Press, 1956.

PRIBRAM, K. H. (ED.), *Brain and behavior*. Baltimore: Penguin, 1966. 2 vols.

SEARLE, L. V. The organization of hereditary maze-brightness and maze-dullness. *Genetic Psychology Monographs*, 1949, *39*, 279–325.

SHALLENBERGER, P., & ZIGLER, E. Rigidity, negative reaction tendencies, and cosatiation effects in normal and feebleminded children. *Journal of Abnormal and Social Psychology*, 1961, *63*, 20–26.

SHEPPS, R., & ZIGLER, E. Social deprivation and rigidity in the performance of organic and familial retardates. *American Journal of Mental Deficiency*, 1962, *67*, 262–268.

STEVENSON, H. Social reinforcement with children as a function of CA, sex of E and sex of S. *Journal of Abnormal and Social Psychology*, 1961, *63*, 147–154.

THOMAS, A., CHESS, S., BIRCH, H. G., HERTZIG, M., & KORN, S. *Behavioral individuality in early childhood*. New York: New York University Press, 1963.

TIZARD, J., & GRAD, J. C. *The mentally handicapped and their families; a social survey*. London: Oxford University Press, 1961.

TIZARD, J., & LOOS, F. The learning of a spatial relations test by adult imbeciles. *American Journal of Mental Deficiency*, 1954, *59*, 85–90.

TRYON, R. C. Genetic differences in maze learning ability in rats. *Yearbook of the National Society for the Study of Education*, 1940, *39*(1), 111–119.

TURNURE, J., & ZIGLER, E. Outer-directedness in the problem solving of normal and retarded children. *Journal of Abnormal and Social Psychology*, 1964, *69*, 427–436.

WALTERS, R., & RAY, E. Anxiety, isolation and reinforcer effectiveness. *Journal of Personality*, 1960, *28*, 358–367.

WEST, R. W. *Childhood aphasia: Proceedings of Institute on Childhood Aphasia. Stanford University School of Medicine*. Chicago: National Society for Crippled Children and Adults, 1960.

WOLFENSBERGER, W. Differential reward as motivating factors in mental deficiency research. *American Journal of Mental Deficiency*, 1960, *64*, 902–906.

WOODWORTH, R. S., & SELLS, S. B. An atmospheric effect in formal syllogistic reasoning. *Journal of Experimental Psychology*, 1935, *18*, 451–460.

YERKES, R. B., & WATSON, J. B. Methods of studying vision in animals. *Behavior Monographs*, 1911, *1*, 1–90.

ZEAMAN, D., & HOUSE, B. J. Approach and avoidance in the discrimination learning of retardates. *Child Development*, 1962, *33*, 355–372.

ZEAMAN, D., HOUSE, B. J., & ORLANDO, R. Use of special training conditions in visual discrimination learning with imbeciles. *American Journal of Mental Deficiency*, 1958, *63*, 453–459.

ZIGLER, E. Social deprivation and rigidity in the performance of feebleminded children. *Journal of Abnormal and Social Psychology*, 1961, *62*, 413–421.

ZIGLER, E. Social deprivation in familial and organic retardates. *Psychological Reports*, 1962, *10*, 370.

ZIGLER, E. Motivational determinants in the performance of retarded children. *American Journal of Orthopsychiatry*, 1966, *36*, 848–856.

ZIGLER, E., & BUTTERFIELD, E. C. Rigidity in the retarded: A further test of the Lewin-Kounin formulation. *Journal of Abnormal Psychology*, 1966, *71*(3), 224–231.

ZIGLER, E., & DELABRY, J. Concept switching in middle class, lower class and retarded children. *Journal of Abnormal and Social Psychology*, 1962, *65*, 267–273.

ZIGLER, E., HODGDEN, L., & STEVENSON, H. W. The effect of support and nonsupport on the performance of normal and feebleminded children. *Journal of Personality*, 1958, *26*, 106–122.

ZIGLER, E., & UNELL, E. Concept-switching in normal and feebleminded children as a function of reinforcement. *American Journal of Mental Deficiency*, 1962, *66*, 651–657.

49

The Effect of Task Complexity on Reflection-Impulsivity [1]

Regina M. Yando
and Jerome Kagan

Children differ substantially in the way in which they approach problem-solving and other cognitive tasks, and they manifest their own particular style in many different circumstances. Jerome Kagan, professor of developmental psychology at Harvard, has done extensive investigation of one such cognitive style, the tendency of a child to be reflective or impulsive. Regina Yando is a member of the Research Department of the Fernald School, Waltham, Massachusetts.

Though substantial progress has been made in recent years in studying and modelling human problem solving, relatively little account has been taken of the effects of individual differences upon the problem-solving process. This paper describes research investigating the effects of one such individual difference variable. The disposition to evaluate one's cognitive product is likely to be an important determinant of the quality of the final solution, especially in problem situations where multiple solution hypotheses are available. Decision time is often a good index of the degree to which a problem solver pauses to evaluate his answer.

Classical studies of the decision time variable (e.g., Morin & Forrin, 1963; Hyman, 1953) have largely been concerned with establishing the relation between decision time and the amount of information (either stimulus or response) available to the subject. Other investigations (Kagan, 1966b), however, have studied decision time in problem situations that hold the amount of information constant. These studies have revealed that some individuals consistently display fast or slow decision times when faced with problems containing a fixed number of alternative responses. This individual difference variable has been described as the reflection-impulsivity dimension.

Previous investigations of reflection-impulsivity have demonstrated its long-term stability, generality across varied task situations, and predictive validity to a variety of problem-solving situations (Kagan, 1965a,b). However, the stability of this disposition across problems with varying numbers of alternative responses has not been investigated. Specifically, this study asks whether children previously classified as reflective or impulsive retain their preferred style of response under conditions which vary the number of alternative responses.

Method

Subjects

The *S*s were second-grade children from four public elementary schools in Fargo, North Dakota. The schools were chosen from a total of 13 elementary schools as being most representative of the general socioeconomic level of this city of 50,000 people. The parents of all second-grade children in the four selected schools were sent a letter requesting permission to test their children. An affirmative reply was received from approximately 200 of the 360 families, and 60 boys and 60 girls were randomly selected from the 200 for the initial phase of testing.

The age range was 6–11 to 8–6, and the IQ range (Kuhlmann-Anderson) was 91 to 135 (mean of 106 for boys, 109 for girls). These scores were obtained at the beginning of the school year; the technical manual for the seventh edition of the Kuhlmann-Anderson reports for grade 2 a test-retest reliability of .85 and an odd-even score reliability of .95. The correlation of the Kuhlmann with the Stanford-Binet (forms L and L–M) is reported to be .65 for grades 2 and 3. No child had been retained in any grade, and no gross physical anomalies (specifically visual) were detected in any of the children.

[1] Supported by NSF University Grant GU–1877 (North Dakota State University) and MH–8792 from NIMH. The assistance of the North Dakota State University psychology students, particularly Sheila Emblin, is gratefully acknowledged. The cooperation of the administrative officials, principals, and teachers of the Fargo City school system made this study possible.

Regina M. Yando and Jerome Kagan, "The effect of task complexity on reflection-impulsivity," *Cognitive Psychology, I,* 1970, 192–200. Reprinted with abridgement by permission.

TEST MATERIALS

Performance on the Matching Familiar Figures (MFF) Test has been regarded as the primary index of the reflection-impulsivity dimension. In the standard form of this task, the child is presented a picture of a familiar object (standard) and six similar variants, only one of which is identical to the standard. The test consists of two initial practice items and 10 test items, each comprised of a standard and six variants. The standard appears alone on the top page of a book and the variants on the bottom page. The instructions request the child to find the picture on the bottom page that is exactly like the picture on the top page. If the child makes the correct response, he is praised; if incorrect, he is told that his response is not correct, and he is asked to try again until he finds the correct variant. The two major variables scored are: *(a)* response time to the child's first solution hypothesis and *(b)* total number of errors on each test item. The child's final scores are the mean response time to the first solution hypothesis across all 10 test items and the total number of errors. Figure 1 shows a typical test item.

In order to test the stability of a child's preferred style of response in problems having varying numbers of alternative responses, 10 different forms of the MFF were constructed. Like the original MFF, the new forms consisted of 10 items (standard and variants), each item on a given form having the same number of variants. Where the original MFF had six variants per item, however, the 10 new forms had 2, 3, 4, 5, 7, 8, 9, 10, 11, and 12 variants per item. Each item was entirely different from any other item appearing on any of the forms. The same directions and the same two practice items (containing six variants) were used with each of the 10 new forms.

PROCEDURE

Ten trained male and female advanced psychology students were randomly assigned to test individually 8 to

9 *S*s each week. *E*s tested a different group of children each week and were never aware of the previous test results on the children. Neither the examiners nor the children were aware of the purpose of the study.

Initially, each child was administered the original six variant MFF as a classification test. On the basis of his performance on this test, a child was classified as reflective (response time above the median, error score below the median), impulsive (response time below the median, error score above the median), or nonextreme (all children not identified as reflective or impulsive). Median splits were performed within each sex separately. Random selection from this remaining group narrowed the sample to 14 boys and 14 girls in each of the three classifications (84 children total).

Following the initial classification, each of the 84 *S*s was seen weekly on the same day for 10 consecutive weeks. A different form of the MFF was administered to each *S* each week in order of increasing difficulty (i.e., during the first week, all *S*s were administered the 2 variant form; during the second week, the 3 variant form, etc.).

RESULTS

RESPONSE TIME

Mean response times across the 10 weeks are presented in Fig. 2. Response time data were subjected to a $3 \times 2 \times 10$ (Classification Tempo $\times$ Sex $\times$ Number of Alternatives) repeated measures analysis of variance. The between aspects of the analysis revealed significant main effects for Classification Tempo [$F(2/78) = 21.11$, $p < .001$] and Sex [$F(1/78) = 5.63$, $p < .05$]. The Classification Tempo $\times$ Sex interaction was not significant. Newman-Keuls (Winer, 1962) analysis of the nature of the tempo effect revealed that reflective children obtained significantly higher response times than both nonextreme ($p < .01$) and impulsive children ($p < .01$). The difference between the nonextreme and impulsive children was also significant at the .05 level. The sex differ-

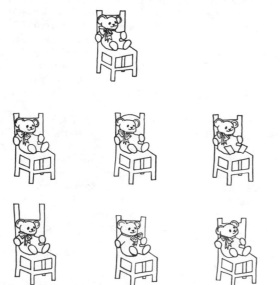

FIGURE 1. *Sample item from Matching Familiar Figures Test.*

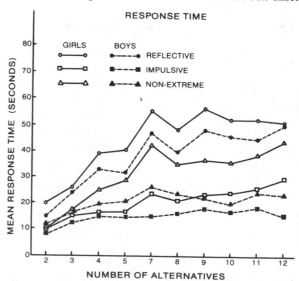

FIGURE 2. *Response time as a function of number of alternatives for the initial classification group.*

ence was produced by the nonextreme girls who showed significantly longer response times than nonextreme boys ($p < .05$). The within portion of the analysis revealed a significant main effect for Number of Alternatives [$F(9/702) = 42.81$, $p < .001$] and significant interactions between Sex × Number of Alternatives [$F(9/702) = 2.71$, $p < .001$] and Classification Tempo × Number of Alternatives [$F(2/702) = 4.11$, $p < .001$]. The triple interaction was not significant. The nature of these effects can be clearly seen in Fig. 2. Although all groups showed a gradual increase in time as the number of alternatives increased, this effect was more dramatic for reflective children and nonextreme girls than for impulsive children and nonextreme boys.

ERROR SCORES

Mean total error scores across the 10 weeks are presented in Fig. 3. Error data were subjected to a 3 × 2 × 10 (Classification Tempo × Sex × Number of Alternatives) repeated measures analysis of variance. The between aspects of the analysis revealed significant main effects for Classification Tempo [$F(2/78) = 17.93$, p $< .001$] and Sex [$F(1/78) = 8.54$, $p < .01$], but the interaction was not significant. Newman-Keuls analysis revealed all tempo groups (reflective $\overline{X} = 3.10$, nonextreme $\overline{X} = 6.84$, impulsive $\overline{X} = 11.64$) to be significantly different from each other at the .01 level. Moreover, the girls in each classification group made significantly fewer errors than the boys in the corresponding group. The within portion of the analysis revealed a significant main effect for Number of Alternatives [$F(9/702) = 38.67$, $p < .001$] and significant interactions between Sex × Number of Alternatives [$F(1/702) = 5.03$, $p < .001$] and Classification Tempo × Number of Alternatives [$F(2/702) = 6.09$, $p < .001$]. The triple interaction was not significant. The nature of these effects can be clearly seen in Fig. 3.

Impulsive children and boys in general showed the most significant increase in errors as the number of alternatives on each task increased. However, task complexity had little, if any, effect on reflective girls.

STABILITY

The children tended to retain their rank order for response time and errors, for the interweek Pearson Product Moment correlations were high. The median correlation was .73 ($p < .01$) for response time and .68 ($p < .01$) for errors. The range was .46 to .92 ($p < .01$) for response time and .22 to .87 ($p < .01$) for errors. The relation between errors and response time was in accord with earlier findings; there was a negative relation between errors and response time for each of the 10 tests (median $r = -.57$).

CLASSIFICATION

Although the data reveal that as a group children maintained their respective classifications over time and across problems with varying alternative responses, it is of interest to inspect the individual cases within each classification. In order to do this, each child was reclassified (reflective, impulsive, or nonextreme) on the basis of the median response time and error scores obtained for each of the 10 sets of data; thus yielding 10 classifications for each child. This analysis revealed that 7 boys and 9 girls of the 28 children initially classified as impulsive retained an impulsive classification for *each* of the 10 forms of the MFF; of the 28 initially classified as reflective, 7 boys and 8 girls retained a reflective classification; and 10 boys and 8 girls retained a nonextreme classification.

The trends evidenced for the total group (Figs. 2 and 3) were more dramatic for this select sample. The consistently reflective Ss showed no increase in errors despite increasing task difficulty across the 10 weeks. Impulsive Ss, on the other hand, showed no increase in response time over the 10 weeks despite increasing task difficulty. The mean response time for impulsive Ss for the 12 variant test was about 12 sec, only slightly larger than the mean response time of 9 sec for the 2 variant test. These values are to be contrasted with mean response times for the reflective Ss; 58 sec for the 12 variant test and 17 sec for the easy 2 variant test.

RELATION TO IQ

Among boys, the group administered IQ score was independent of response time (range: $r = .06$ to $.22$, none significant) and errors (range: $r = .00$ to $-.36$, with only one coefficient significant at the .05 level). Among girls, however, there was a weak positive relation between IQ and response time (5 of 11 coefficients significant at the .05 level; range: $r = .14$ to $.36$), and a consistent negative relation between IQ and errors (8 of 11 coefficients significant at the .05 level; range: $r = -.26$ to $-.40$).

DISCUSSION

The reflection-impulsivity dimension was remarkably stable across problems with differing numbers

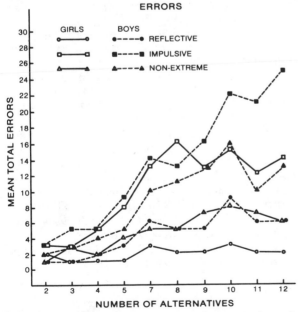

FIGURE 3. *Errors as a function of the number of alternatives for the initial classification group.*

of alternative responses. The child's preferred approach to the task was a better predictor of both errors (for reflective children) and response time (for impulsive children) than task difficulty. That is, regardless of task difficulty, reflective children committed few errors; impulsive children responded quickly and committed many errors. These findings, together with the apparent stability of this dimension over a 10-week period, support the notion that reflection-impulsivity is an important characteristic of the child's psychological organization. It should be noted, however, that since the number of alternatives increased linearly each week there is a confounding of difficulty with previous experience with the task.

The reflective children are actively considering alternative hypotheses during their longer decision times, for earlier work has demonstrated that they make many more visual scans of the standard and variants than the impulsives (Kagan, Pearson, & Welch, 1966a). Moreover, the reflective children tend to examine all the variants before offering a solution; the impulsives often respond after examining only a few (Vurpillot, 1968; Nelson, 1968; Sigelman, 1966).

The tendency to be reflective or impulsive is likely to have multiple determinants. Our preferred interpretation is that reflective children experience greater anxiety over error than impulsives. Reflectives seem to be overly concerned with making a mistake and thus subject their answers to scrutiny. A recent experimental study indicated that response times increase following a failure experience designed to arouse anxiety over error (Messer, 1968). Moreover, 11-year-old boys who display symptoms associated with low anxiety (aggression, cheating) were more impulsive than boys of the same social class who displayed symptoms associated with high anxiety (fears, obsessions, nightmares).[2] Although anxiety over error is admittedly only one potential determinant of reflection-impulsivity, we view it as the most salient.

Lower class and "culturally deprived" children tend to be impulsive (Kagan, 1966a). The inferior intellectual performance displayed by these children may be due, in part, to an impulsive attitude, in addition to deficits in cognitive resources. Although impulsivity is not the sole cause of error, a child who consistently attacks a problem with this preferred strategy may experience repeated failure.

Agents of educational change have typically con-

centrated upon curriculum and the incentive value of classroom materials and paid less attention to individual differences in children of similar competence. The concern has been with *what* rather than *how* the child is to be taught. Previous data (Yando & Kagan, 1968; Kagan, Pearson, & Welch, 1966b) suggest that modification of the decision strategy of the children may have subsequent effects on his problem-solving ability. It is urged that research in instructional and testing procedures acknowledge the significance of the preferred strategy of the learner.

REFERENCES

HYMAN, R. Stimulus information as a determinant of reaction time. *Journal of Experimental Psychology,* 1953, *45,* 188–196.

KAGAN, J. Individual differences in the resolution of response uncertainty. *Journal of Personality and Social Psychology,* 1965, *2,* 154–160. (a)

KAGAN, J. Reflection-impulsivity and reading ability in primary grade children. *Child Development,* 1965, *36,* 609–628. (b)

KAGAN, J. Reflection-impulsivity: the generality and dynamics of conceptual tempo. *Journal of Abnormal Psychology,* 1966, *71,* 17–24. (a)

KAGAN, J. Developmental studies in reflection and analysis. In A. H. Kidd & J. L. Rivoire (Eds.), *Perceptual development in children.* New York: International Press, 1966. Pp. 497–522. (b)

KAGAN, J., PEARSON, L., & WELCH, L. Conceptual impulsivity and inductive reasoning. *Child Development,* 1966, *37,* 583–594. (a)

KAGAN, J., PEARSON, L., & WELCH, L. The modifiability of an impulsive tempo. *Journal of Educational Psychology,* 1966, *57,* 359–365. (b)

MORIN, R. E., & FORRIN, B. Response equivocation and reaction time. *Journal of Experimental Psychology,* 1963, *66,* 30–36.

NELSON, T. F. The effects of training in attention deployment on observing behavior in reflective and impulsive children. Unpublished doctoral dissertation, University of Minnesota, 1968.

SIGELMAN, E. Y. Observing behavior in impulsive and reflective children. Unpublished doctoral dissertation, University of Minnesota, 1966.

VURPILLOT, E. The development of scanning strategies and their relation to visual discrimination. *Journal of Experimental Child Psychology,* 1968, *6,* 637–650.

WINER, B. J. *Statistical principles in experimental design.* New York: McGraw-Hill, 1962.

YANDO, R., & KAGAN, J. The effect of teacher tempo on the child. *Child Development,* 1968, *39,* 27–34.

---

[2] S. Weintraub, personal communication.

50

Children's Conceptions of Psychological Causality

Martin Whiteman

This article is another example of the extensive literature that has been based on the seminal works of Jean Piaget. In this article, Martin Whiteman, a member of the faculty of the Columbia University School of Social Work, looks at the development of children's notions about psychological causality. The article is also valuable for its discussion of how the interview technique was used with young children.

Piaget's pioneering explorations have brought forth a number of investigations of the child's conception of physical causality. However, there has been relatively little investigation of the child's conceptions of psychological causality. It would

seem as appropriate to ask a child, "What makes people angry?" as it is to ask him "What makes clouds move?" Yet, systematic explorations of the child's developing awareness of the causes of another person's behavior are lacking. This lack is particularly poignant since, as adults, we are continually making inferences about the causes of other people's behavior. An important problem, then, is how and when such causal inferences are learned.

A major set of concepts used by people in explaining behavior comprises the so-called mechanisms of adjustment. People, in their everyday behavior, do seem to use as explanatory devices those behaviors that psychologists have conceptualized as rationalizations or displacements or projections, for example, rationalization ("He's using that as an excuse"), displacement ("He's just taking out all his troubles on me"), projection ("Well, that's the way he is himself and he thinks everybody is that way"). From a theoretical point of view, it is important to understand how and when such explanatory ideas become part of the conceptual repertoire of the child. Psychologists of such widely differing theoretical persuasion as Anna Freud (1946) and Hilgard (1949) have pointed to the importance of such mechanisms for maintenance of self-esteem. However, there has been no attempt to study directly the cognitive development of such notions, which are as important in their own right as the development by the child of conceptions of space, time, and physical causality.

Piaget has drawn a basic distinction between the preoperational intuitive stage (around 4–7 years) and the concrete operational stage (around 7–11 years). According to Piaget (1950) and Flavell (1963), there is a major revision in the child's thought at around 7 years, enabling him to conceptualize certain types of relations and classes. A major achievement of the operational child is his ability to decenter from a focus on the perceptually dominant to an emphasis on the more invariant but less salient properties of stimulus displays, as illustrated by the operational child's ability to conserve conceptually an object's substance or length despite changes in the object's appearance or location. Similarly, one would expect that the operational as compared to the younger preoperational child should have greater ease in decentering from the more obvious overt behaviors to the less obvious underlying motivations as described by the adjustment mechanisms. Furthermore, Laurendeau and Pinard (1962), replicating early Piaget investigations (1929; 1930),

This research was supported by a grant from the National Institute of Mental Health (No. MH–10578–01). A preliminary report was made at the 1965 meeting of the Eastern Psychological Association at Atlantic City. Grateful acknowledgment is made to Anita G. Bardin, Judith F. Levine, Sherrie F. Miller, and Judith L. Ryan for their contribution to the interviewing and to the coding of the data gathered in phase 2. Dr. Lassar K. Gotkin of the Institute for Developmental Studies, Department of Psychiatry, New York Medical College, was most helpful in securing the cooperation of the teachers and of the administration of the public schools in which the work was done. Miss Jean Lloyd and Mrs. Goldie Haile, kindergarten teachers, are thanked for their cooperation in expediting the interviewing of the children.

have shown striking differences between these two age levels in their ability to apprehend physical causality. It becomes pertinent, therefore, to explore the differences between such contrasting age groups in their explanations of psychological causality as well as to relate such differences to conceptions of physical causality.

The general aim of this study is to explore the feasibility of using interviews with children at two age levels, the 5–6-year range and the 8–9-year-old span, in order to study developing conceptions of psychological causality.

The study comprised two separate phases. The specific aims of phase 1 were to (a) devise usable categorizations and scoring systems for the assessment of psychological causality, (b) study the homogeneity among items in order to determine whether reliable and meaningful indexes might be formed, and (c) study developmental and intellectual differences with respect to such indexes of psychological causality. The second phase had as its purposes: (a) the objectification and standardization of the interviewing procedure devised in phase 1, (b) the replication of phase 1 with comparable but somewhat larger samples to assess the reliability of phase 1 findings with respect to developmental and intellectual differences in the understanding of psychological causality, and (c) the extension of phase 1 results through the study of the relation between grasp of psychological causality and understanding of physical causality.

PHASE 1

METHOD

Subjects. The subjects comprised 42 children. The 21 younger children comprised an experimental kindergarten class in Harlem, New York City. Stanford-Binet IQ's were available for these children. For each kindergarten child, a separate roster of third-grade children from the same school was prepared. The third graders on each roster had been matched with the kindergarten child with respect to sex and IQ as assessed by group test. For each kindergarten child, a third grader was then selected from the appropriate roster by random sampling. For each grade, the average IQ was 101 with a standard deviation of 10. All children were Negro or Puerto Rican. The kindergarten children were in the 5–6-year range, while the third graders fell in the 8–9-year span.

The interview. The interviews were conducted by the writer and dealt with the child's tape-recorded responses to questions about each of seven stories. Each story read to the child exemplified

in rudimentary form a different mechanism of adjustment, that is, displacement, wishful dreaming, projection, regression, repression, rationalization, and denial. The instructions to the child and the stories themselves were as follows:

"I'm going to tell you some stories about a little girl called Jane. In each of these stories Jane does something different from what she usually does. I want you to tell me why she did it. Here's the first story." (For boys, "Johnnie" was substituted for "Jane" in all the stories, and "toy soldiers" for "dolls" in the first story.)

1. Displacement: "There was once a little girl named Jane. One day her mother promised that Jane's favorite dessert, ice cream, would be served at supper. But Jane's mother forgot to buy the ice cream, and so there wasn't any ice cream for dessert. Jane didn't say anything to her mother about the ice cream. After supper Jane went to play with her dolls and did something she never did before. She spanked her dolls. Why did she spank her dolls?"

2. Wishful dreaming: "One day Jane looked at T.V. and saw a girl who had a wonderful bicycle. Jane herself didn't have a bicycle and couldn't even ride one. That night Jane dreamed that her father bought her a bicycle and that she was riding all over the block on it. How come she had such a dream?"

3. Projection: "Jane was a good girl, but there was one thing she never liked to do. She didn't like to share her toys with the other kids. She always wanted to keep her toys to herself and not let the other kids use them. One day Jane's mother told her that they were going to visit another family where there was another little girl who was Jane's age. Jane and this other little girl could play together. But Jane looked unhappy and said, 'I bet she won't want to share any of her games and toys.' Why did Jane say this when she didn't even know the other little girl?"

4. Regression: "One day Jane didn't feel well. She had a headache and didn't want to eat. She began to act just like her baby brother. She talked baby talk; she wanted to suck her baby brother's milk bottle; and she even wanted to be held in her mother's arms just like a baby. Why did she act this way?"

5. Repression: "One day Jane's mother bought her a new pair of gloves. She warned Jane not to lose the gloves, because Jane had lost the last pair. One afternoon Jane lost her gloves coming back from school. She knew she had to tell her mother. But when she got home, she forgot to tell her. When Jane went out to play in the afternoon, she told her friends about the lost gloves. But that night she forgot to tell her mother. The next morning at breakfast Jane again forgot to tell her mother. Why did she keep forgetting to tell her mother about the lost gloves?"

6. Rationalization: "One day Jane's mother gave her a big bowl of spinach. Jane said, 'I'm not going to eat the spinach because it makes you very fat!' Why did Jane say that about the spinach when she liked to eat fattening things like ice cream and candy?"

7. Denial: "Jane wanted very much to go to her friend's birthday party. On the day of the party she fell

sick and couldn't go. But Jane said, 'I didn't want to go to that party anyway!' Why did Jane say that?"

There was an attempt in each story to focus questions or probes on certain key elements, for example, whether the child grasped the role of the ice cream disappointment in arousing anger in the displacement story, or whether the child saw Jane as really wanting to go to the party in the denial story.

In order to gain some control on memory and language differences, an attempt was made to pose alternatives, to recapitulate part of the stories in the questions, and in some cases to suggest causal possibilities as a kind of testing-of-the-limits procedure.

Each story was coded according to the degree in which the motivation of the child in the story situation was grasped. Thus, in the displacement story, the highest score was given to the children who attributed the spanking of the doll to the ice cream deprivation, who spontaneously or in response to probes cited an appropriate emotional reaction to the ice cream deprivation, that is, being mad or sad, and had some psychological explanation for spanking the doll rather than the mother. A lower score was assigned to sequences which related the ice cream deprivation to the spanking, but offered no psychological reason for spanking the doll rather than the mother. At a lower level, the spanking was conceived as the doll's fault, with no apprehension of the possible causal role of the ice cream incident. Thus, the doll was conceived as bad or dirty or ugly or jumping too much.

Statistical treatment. The feasibility of combining the responses to the various stories into an index was explored. A Motivation Index was constructed by cumulating weights for each of the seven stories. For the entire group, this total index score was then correlated with each of the subscores derived from particular stories.

RESULTS

The individual stories. Table 1 indicates that the stories proved difficult even for the older children. The percentage of older children showing the highest level of understanding (level 4 in Table 1) ranges from 5 per cent for the rationalization story to 38 per cent for the displacement story, with a median of 19 per cent. The repression and displacement stories proved the easiest for the older children, while the rationalization and regression stories proved the most difficult. For the younger children, the highest level could be reached only in the case of the repression story, and this with only one child. With more lenient criteria (success

TABLE 1
DISTRIBUTION OF 21 YOUNGER CHILDREN (AGES 5 AND 6) AND MATCHED OLDER CHILDREN (AGES 8 AND 9) IN RESPONSE CATEGORIES OF PHASE 1 STORIES

Story and Age Group	Level of Understanding					x^{2a}
	0	1	2	3	4	
Displacement:						
Younger	...	3	15	3	0	
Older	...	0	5	8	8	11.08***
Wishful dreaming:						
Younger	3	10	3	5	0	
Older	0	4	5	8	4	2.77
Projection:						
Younger	4	4	12	1	0	
Older	0	0	9	9	3	9.09**
Regression:						
Younger	6	6	4	5	0	
Older	0	5	12	2	2	4.08*
Repression:						
Younger	...	...	10	10	1	
Older	...	...	6	8	7	.75
Rationalization:						
Younger	2	18	1	0	0	
Older	0	11	8	1	1	4.90*
Denial:						
Younger	...	14	3	4	0	
Older	...	8	3	6	4	2.08

^{a} Corrected for discontinuity. Adjacent scoring categories for each story combined to form median dichotomies for the x^2 analysis.
* Significant at .05 level.
** Significant at .01 level.
*** Significant at .001 level.

at levels 3 or 4), the percentage of success for the younger children ranged from 48 per cent in the case of the repression story to 0 per cent for the rationalization story, with a median of 10 per cent. Rationalization and projection were the most difficult stories for the younger children while repression, regression, and wishful dreaming proved relatively easier. Most of the older children (71 per cent as compared to 10 per cent of the younger children) were able to show comprehension of Jane's underlying motivation in at least three stories (using the more lenient level 3 or 4 criterion). The application of more rigorous criteria for comprehension, with greater concentration on the spontaneous answers of the child (level 4), disclosed that 76 per cent of the older children were able to reach the highest level on at least one story as compared to 5 per cent of the younger group.

Table 1 also indicates that, when the scores for each story were dichotomized at the median, significant age differences appeared in the case of the displacement, projection, regression, and rationalization stories.

With respect to the displacement story, the older children tended to attribute the spanking to the ice cream deprivation. The younger children tended to attribute the spanking to the intrinsic naughtiness of the doll. In the projection story, some of the older children tended to attribute Jane's statement about the other girl's not sharing to Jane's own behavior. Thus, Jane's remark is seen as a projection of her own disinclination to share. As one child put it: "Just because she don't share her things, she might believe that girl would be as evil as she." More usually, however, Jane's remark was seen as occasioned by the other girl's reaction to Jane's own habit of not sharing. The younger children had difficulty seeing Jane's own nonsharing as the direct or indirect cause of her thinking the other child would not share. The younger children tended to refer more to the other girl as directly causing Jane's remark, for example: "Jane says the other girl won't share because the girl was strange." In the regression story, the older children more readily perceived the advantages of acting like a baby. The younger children may have mentioned the illness as cause, but had difficulty in seeing the child wanting to be treated as a baby when ill. Finally, in the rationalization story, the younger child was more prone to believe that Jane said she would not eat the spinach because it makes you very fat because Jane actually thought that the spinach made you very fat, that she did not just say it but really believed it. The older child tended to attribute Jane's saying that spinach makes you very fat because she didn't want to eat it.

. . .

The Motivation Index. The analysis of variance of the Motivation Index revealed the expected and highly significant age differences. Ninety per cent of the younger children scored below the median score of the older children. The more intelligent children tended to score significantly higher when the dichotomies of those above 100 IQ and those at 100 or below were used. Rhos of .40 and .15 between IQ and Motivation Index were found for the older and younger children, respectively. Neither of these coefficients is significant. However, the analysis of variance revealed a significant interaction between grade and IQ. Thus, IQ differences on the Motivation Index were stronger among the older children than among the younger children. Sex differences on the Motivation Index were not significant, but there was a significant interaction between sex and intelligence. Differences between intelligence levels were more clearly related to the Motivation Index in the case of the boys, with the less intelligent boys scoring lower. However, among the girls, the difference between intelligence levels on the Motivation Index was minimal and in a reversed direction, with the less

intelligent girls scoring slightly but not significantly higher.

PHASE 2

METHOD

Subjects. The phase 2 subjects comprised seventy children—36 kindergarten children and 34 third graders. As in phase 1, the younger children were in the 5–6-year range, the older in the 8–9-year span, and all children were Negro or Puerto Rican. Two kindergarten classes were used, both taught by the same teacher. Of the 47 kindergarten children interviewed, the records of 11 children were not used either because of difficulty in comprehending their answers or, more frequently, because they simply replied "don't know" to most of the questions on the psychological causality interview. The 34 third-grade children were randomly selected from the entire third-grade roster of this particular school. The IQ data based on group tests were available for 27 of the 34 third graders. The mean IQ was 97, with a range from 75 to 133. For the kindergarten group, Stanford-Binet IQ data were available, but only for 24 out of the 36 children. However, these IQ's were based on a random sample of children from the two kindergarten classes. For the kindergarten group, the mean IQ was 94, with a range from 71 to 116. Forty-two per cent and 53 per cent of the kindergarten and third graders, respectively, were male. In order to replicate an analysis performed on 21 matched pairs in phase 1, twenty pairs of kindergarten and third-grade children matched in IQ were selected. The mean IQ of the twenty phase 2 kindergarteners and twenty matched third graders was 93.

Procedure. Six of the seven stories used in phase 1 were administered to the two groups. The repression story was omitted in order to shorten the administration time. In addition, the projection story was revised so as to impress upon the respondent that Jane did not know the other child. However, the paramount change in phase 2 was the use of a standardized interview with standardized probes and a standard sequence of probes. The standardized probes were explicit wordings of questions to be asked the child. The sequence of such probes was also specified for the interviewers. Directions were given to the interviewers about when to probe for a new element of the concept in question and when to stay with the same point, altering the question in order to see whether the child could succeed with more information. The stories were administered in a randomized order.

In contrast to phase 1, the interviews were not conducted by the writer but by four graduate students of the Columbia University School of Social Work. A number of sessions were devoted to a discussion of the specific rationales of the study, of underlying theoretical issues, and of methodological problems in interviewing young children. Pilot interviewing was conducted by three of the students at a neighboring day-care center, after which further discussion was held regarding ambiguities or difficulties arising in the interviewing situation.

Scoring categories were devised, both for the initial responses to the story and the responses to questions by the interviewer. As in phase 1, there was an attempt to arrange the categories in each story hierarchically, with the higher-numbered categories including more of the elements of the concept studied. The scoring system involved categorizing the children for each story at three levels. Level 3 was assigned to children whose responses at any point in the interview included all of the elements of the concept for any particular story, whether or not the grasp of the concept was maintained or lost following further questioning. Level 2 included children whose responses at any point showed comprehension of some but not all elements of the concept, while level 1 was assigned to children whose responses at no point showed an understanding of any of the key elements of the explanatory concept.

In addition to the questionnaire on psychological causality, a series of questions dealing with physical causality was also posed. These questions dealt with the attribution of life to various objects and were designed to reveal animistic tendencies in the child. The questionnaire was originally constructed by Laurendeau and Pinard (1962) in their replication of Piaget's work on physical causality. The child was asked whether each of 21 objects was alive. In the present study, the score of this Animism Scale was the number of correct responses given by child. The reliability of this measure for the combined group was .84, as assessed by the Kuder-Richardson Formula 20 (Gulliksen, 1950, pp. 220–227).

RESULTS AND DISCUSSION

The individual stories. The stories were scored independently by two sets of raters. For the coding of the elements of each story based on the initial response of 36 children, the percentage of agreement was 96 per cent. The percentage of agreement ranged from 89 per cent for the Denial story to 100 per cent for the dream wishing story. For the coding of the elements of each story based on both initial and probed-for responses of 28 children, the overall percentage of agreement was 85 per cent, with a range from 75 per cent for rationalization to 93 per cent for the wishful dreaming story. Table 2 reveals that the older children consistently scored higher than the younger group, with five of the six items significant at least on the .01 level. The failure of the rationalization story to yield significant differences between the two graders may be due to the relatively low interrater reliability of coding for this item. From the point of view of age differentiation, the new interview procedure seems at least as effective as the one reported on in phase 1. However, the increment in significant age differentiation on the part of the stories may be at least partly due to the increased sample size in phase 2. The displacement, projection, and regression stories which were significant differentiators between age levels in phase 1 also show significant differentiation in phase 2. Additionally, the denial and wishful dreaming stories which did not yield significant differences in phase 1 do so in phase 2.

· · ·

Motivation Index 2. [The analysis of variance] reveals that the age differences on Motivation In-

TABLE 2

PERCENTAGES OF 36 YOUNGER CHILDREN (AGES 5 AND 6) AND 34 OLDER CHILDREN (AGES 8 AND 9) IN RESPONSE CATEGORIES OF PHASE 2 STORIES

	Level of Understanding [a]			
Story and Age Group	1	2	3	x^2
Displacement:				
Younger	31	69	0	7.52*
Older	3	79	18	$df = 1$
Wishful dreaming:				
Younger	30	61	9	17.83**
Older	3	50	47	$df = 2$
Projection:				
Younger	78	8	14	25.41**
Older	15	15	70	$df = 1$
Regression:				
Younger	25	67	8	10.59*
Older	12	47	41	$df = 2$
Rationalization:				
Younger	36	64	0	.75
Older	26	65	9	$df = 1$
Denial:				
Younger	50	42	8	13.70**
Older	24	29	47	$df = 2$

[a] For displacement, projection, and rationalization, scoring categories 2 and 3 were combined in the x^2 analysis, with correction for discontinuity.

* Significant at .01 level.
** Significant at .001 level.

dex 2 were highly significant. As anticipated, the older children scored considerably higher than the younger. Ninety-four per cent of the kindergarten group fell below the median score of the third graders, which parallels the comparable figure of 90 per cent found with Motivation Index 1. However, this and a separate analysis of variance (not shown) failed to reveal significant IQ differences, nor IQ interactions with age and sex—contrary to the results of phase 1. The younger children were significantly more animistic than the older ones. Twice as many kindergarten children as third graders fell into a high animism group ($P <$ .01). The above analyses suggest that conceptions of psychological causality (as assessed by Motivation Index 2) and of physical causality (as assessed by the Animism Scale) both develop with age. However, the limited relation between the two measures points to the independence in the rate and timing of their respective development within the individual child.

The relation between age and conceptions of psychological causality appears stronger than the relation between age and conceptions of physical causality (see Table 3). Thus when one selects children who are relatively homogeneous with respect to the Motivation Index, the relation between age and the Animism Scale is not statistically significant. However, when the selection is of children who are relatively homogeneous on animism score, the relation between age and Motivation Index is still highly significant. Similarly, a comparison of the five kindergarten children and eight third graders with comparable MA's (about 7 years)

revealed that the younger children averaged about four points *below* the older on the Motivation Index but about four points *above* the older on the Animism Scale. This suggests the importance of chronological rather than mental age in the development of conceptions of psychological causality.

SOME CONCLUDING POINTS

The relative difficulty of the younger child in (a) differentiating between observed locus of effect and inferred locus of cause and (b) decentering from a focus on overt behavior to a more covert intent would not be inconsistent with Piaget's distinction between the "intuitive" child (ages 4–7) and the "concrete operational" child (ages 7–11). It would, therefore, be worthwhile to explore the Motivation Index scores of children who have and have not attained conservation of substance, for example, since the latter is a criterion for the concrete operation stage. However, the operation of more specific experiential factors is suggested by the differential ease of the items within age groups, the lack of strong or consistent correlations of the Motivation Indexes with IQ, the importance of chronological age over and above mental age differences, the relative independence of the Motivation Indexes from the Animism Scale, and the sex differences on Motivation Index 1. It is also possible that age differences in psychological causality may take a different form within groups of higher socioeconomic standing where the child's linguistic experiences and explanatory encounters with adults are differently patterned.

Behavioral correlates need exploration. Certain patternings of responses to the stories may be related to particular behavioral patterns. Thus, ease in grasping projection stories, where blame is externalized, may be related to acting-out behavior. The Motivation Index might be correlated with measures of ability to shift role, to understand the other's viewpoint, and with avoidance of what Piaget (1932) has conceptualized as objective morality. One would expect the growth of understanding of psychological causality to parallel the growth of moral judgments based on the other's underlying intentions, rather than on his overt behaviors.

TABLE 3
RELATIONS BETWEEN AGE AND (a) ANIMISM SCALE, WITH MOTIVATION INDEX 2 CONTROLLED; (b) MOTIVATION INDEX 2, WITH ANIMISM SCALE CONTROLLED

| | Age Group | | | | | |
| | 5 and 6 years | | 8 and 9 years | | | |
	N	$\%$	N	$\%$	x^2	P
Animism Scale [a]:						
Higher	9	64	8	35		
					1.98	$> .05$
Lower..............	5	36	15	65		
Motivation Index 2 [b]:						
Higher	0	0	14	82		
					14.97	$< .001$
Lower..............	11	100	3	18		

[a] Higher and lower levels defined by score ranges on the Animism Scale of 5–12, and 13–21, respectively. The 37 subjects are all within the 11–14 range on the Motivation Index 2.

[b] Higher and lower levels defined by score ranges on the Motivation Index of 13–16 and 7–12, respectively. The 28 subjects are all within the 16–19 range on the Animism Scale.

REFERENCES

FLAVELL, J. *The developmental psychology of Jean Piaget.* Princeton, N.J.: Van Nostrand, 1963.

FREUD, ANNA. *The ego and the mechanisms of defence.* New York: International Universities Press, 1946.

GULLIKSEN, N. *Theory of mental tests.* New York: Wiley, 1950.

HILGARD, E. Human motives and the concept of the self, *American Psychologist,* 1949, *4,* 374–382.

LAURENDEAU, MONIQUE, & PINARD, A. *Causal thinking in the child.* New York: International Universities Press, 1962.

PIAGET, J. *The child's conception of the world.* New York: Harcourt, Brace, 1929.

PIAGET, J. *The child's conception of physical causality.* London: Kegan Paul, 1930.

PIAGET, J. *The moral judgment of the child.* London: Kegan Paul, 1932.

PIAGET, J. *The psychology of intelligence.* New York: Harcourt, Brace, 1950.

51

Egocentrism in Adolescence

David Elkind

David Elkind, professor of psychology at the University of Rochester, is one of the leading interpreters of Piaget in the United States. One of his latest books is Children and Adolescents: Interpretive Essays on Jean Piaget *(New York: Oxford University Press, 1970). In this article, Elkind describes the forms in which egocentrism appears at each stage of cognitive development, up to adolescence.*

Within the Piagetian theory of intellectual growth, the concept of egocentrism generally refers to a lack of differentiation in some area of subject-object interaction (Piaget, 1962). At each stage of mental development, this lack of differentiation takes a unique form and is manifested in a unique set of behaviors. The transition from one form of egocentrism to another takes place in a dialectic fashion such that the mental structures which free the child from a lower form of egocentrism are the same structures which ensnare him in a higher form of egocentrism. From the developmental point of view, therefore, egocentrism can be regarded as a negative by-product of any emergent mental system in the sense that it corresponds to the fresh cognitive problems engendered by that system.

Preparation of this paper was supported in part by grant No. 6881 from the Office of Education.

David Elkind, "Egocentrism in adolescence," *Child Development, 38,* 1967, 1025–1034. Reprinted by permission. Copyright 1967 by The Society for Research in Child Development, Inc.

Although in recent years Piaget has focused his attention more on the positive than on the negative products of mental structures, egocentrism continues to be of interest because of its relation to the affective aspects of child thought and behavior. Indeed, it is possible that the study of egocentrism may provide a bridge between the study of cognitive structure, on the one hand, and the exploration of personality dynamics, on the other (Cowan, 1966; Gourevitch & Feffer, 1962). The purpose of the present paper is to describe, in greater detail than Inhelder and Piaget (1958), what seems to me to be the nature of egocentrism in adolescence and some of its behavioral and experiential correlates. Before doing that, however, it might be well to set the stage for the discussion with a brief review of the forms of egocentrism which precede this mode of thought in adolescence.

FORMS OF EGOCENTRISM IN INFANCY AND CHILDHOOD

In presenting the childhood forms of egocentrism, it is useful to treat each of Piaget's major stages as if it were primarily concerned with resolving one major cognitive task. The egocentrism of a particular stage can then be described with reference to this special problem of cognition. It must be stressed, however, that while the cognitive task characteristic of a particular stage seems to attract the major share of the child's mental energies, it is not the only cognitive problem with which the child is attempting to cope. In mental development there are major battles and minor skirmishes, and if I here ignore the lesser engagements it is for purposes of economy of presentation rather than because I assume that such engagements are insignificant.

SENSORI-MOTOR EGOCENTRISM (0–2 YEARS)

The major cognitive task of infancy might be regarded as *the conquest of the object.* In the early months of life, the infant deals with objects as if their existence were dependent upon their being present in immediate perception (Charlesworth, 1966; Piaget, 1954). The egocentrism of this stage corresponds, therefore, to a lack of differentiation between the object and the sense impressions occasioned by it. Toward the end of the first year, however, the infant begins to seek the object even when it is hidden, and thus shows that he can now differentiate between the object and the "experience of the object." This breakdown of egocentrism with respect to objects is brought about by mental representation of the absent object.[1] An internal representation of the absent object is the earliest manifestation of the symbolic function which develops gradually during the second year of life and whose activities dominate the next stage of mental growth.

PRE-OPERATIONAL EGOCENTRISM (2–6 YEARS)

During the preschool period, the child's major cognitive task can be regarded as *the conquest of the symbol*. It is during the preschool period that the symbolic function becomes fully active, as evidenced by the rapid growth in the acquisition and utilization of language, by the appearance of symbolic play, and by the first reports of dreams. Yet this new capacity for representation, which loosed the infant from his egocentrism with respect to objects, now ensnares the preschool children in a new egocentrism with regard to symbols. At the beginning of this period, the child fails to differentiate between words and their referents (Piaget, 1952b) and between his self-created play and dream symbols and reality (Kohlberg, 1966; Piaget, 1951). Children at this stage believe that the name inheres in the thing and that an object cannot have more than one name (Elkind, 1961a, 1962, 1963).

The egocentrism of this period is particularly evident in children's linguistic behavior. When explaining a piece of apparatus to another child, for example, the youngster at this stage uses many indefinite terms and leaves out important information (Piaget, 1952b). Although this observation is sometimes explained by saying that the child fails to take the other person's point of view, it can also be explained by saying that the child assumes words carry much more information than they actually do. This results from his belief that even the indefinite "thing" somehow conveys the properties of the object which it is used to represent. In short, the egocentrism of this period consists in a lack of clear differentiation between symbols and their referents.

Toward the end of the pre-operational period, the differentiation between symbols and their referents is gradually brought about by the emergence of concrete operations (internalized actions which are roughly comparable in their activity to the elementary operations of arithmetic). One consequence of concrete operational thought is that it enables the child to deal with two elements, properties, or relations at the same time. A child with concrete operations can, for example, take account of both the height and width of a glass of colored liquid and recognize that, when the liquid is poured into a differently shaped container, the changes in height and width of the liquid compensate one another so that the total quantity of liquid is conserved (Elkind, 1961b; Piaget, 1952a). This ability, to hold two dimensions in mind at the same time, also enables the child to hold both symbol and referent in mind simultaneously, and thus distinguish between them. Concrete operations are, therefore, instrumental in overcoming the egocentrism of the preoperational stage.

CONCRETE OPERATIONAL EGOCENTRISM (7–11 YEARS)

With the emergence of concrete operations, the major cognitive task of the school-age child becomes that of *mastering classes, relations, and quantities*. While the preschool child forms global notions of classes, relations, and quantities, such notions are imprecise and cannot be combined one with the other. The child with concrete operations, on the other hand, can nest classes, seriate relations, and conserve quantities. In addition, concrete operations enable the school-age child to perform elementary syllogistic reasoning and to formulate hypotheses and explanations about concrete matters. This system of concrete operations, however, which lifts the school-age child to new heights of thought, nonetheless lowers him to new depths of egocentrism.

Operations are essentially mental tools whose products, series, class hierarchies, conservations, etc., are not directly derived from experience. At this stage, however, the child nonetheless regards these mental products as being on a par with perceptual phenomena. It is the inability to differentiate clearly between mental constructions and perceptual givens which constitutes the egocentrism of the school-age child. An example may help to clarify the form which egocentrism takes during the concrete operational stage.

In a study reported by Peel (1960), children and adolescents were read a passage about Stonehenge and then asked questions about it. One of the questions had to do with whether Stonehenge was a place for religious worship or a fort. The children (ages 7–10) answered the question with flat statements, as if they were stating a fact. When they were given evidence that contradicted their statements, they rationalized the evidence to make it conform with their initial position. Adolescents, on the other hand, phrased their replies in proba-

---

[1] It is characteristic of the dialectic of mental growth that the capacity to represent internally the absent object also enables the infant to cognize the object as externally existent.

bilistic terms and supported their judgments with material gleaned from the passage. Similar differences between children and adolescents have been found by Elkind (1966) and Weir (1964).

What these studies show is that, when a child constructs a hypothesis or formulates a strategy, he assumes that this product is imposed by the data rather than derived from his own mental activity. When his position is challenged, he does not change his stance but, on the contrary, reinterprets the data to fit with his assumption. This observation, however, raises a puzzling question. Why, if the child regards both his thought products and the givens of perception as coming from the environment, does he nonetheless give preference to his own mental constructions? The answer probably lies in the fact that the child's mental constructions are the product of reasoning, and hence are experienced as imbued with a (logical) necessity. This "felt" necessity is absent when the child experiences the products of perception. It is not surprising, then, that the child should give priority to what seems permanent and necessary in perception (the products of his own thought, such as conservation) rather than to what seems transitory and arbitrary in perception (products of environmental stimulation). Only in adolescence do young people differentiate between their own mental constructions and the givens of perception. For the child, there are no problems of epistemology.

Toward the end of childhood, the emergence of formal operational thought (which is analogous to propositional logic) gradually frees the child from his egocentrism with respect to his own mental constructions. As Inhelder and Piaget (1958) have shown, formal operational thought enables the young person to deal with all of the possible combinations and permutations of elements within a given set. Provided with four differently colored pieces of plastic, for example, the adolescent can work out all the possible combinations of colors by taking the pieces one, two, three and four, and none, at a time. Children, on the other hand, cannot formulate these combinations in any systematic way. The ability to conceptualize all of the possible combinations in a system allows the adolescent to construct contrary-to-fact hypotheses and to reason about such propositions "as if" they were true. The adolescent, for example, can accept the statement, "Let's suppose coal is white," whereas the child would reply, "But coal is black," This ability to formulate contrary-to-fact hypotheses is crucial to the overcoming of the egocentrism of the concrete operational period. Through the formulation of such contrary-to-fact hypotheses, the young person discovers the arbitrariness of his own

mental constructions and learns to differentiate them from perceptual reality.

ADOLESCENT EGOCENTRISM

From the strictly cognitive point of view (as opposed to the psychoanalytic point of view as represented by Blos [1962] and A. Freud [1946] or the ego psychological point of view as represented by Erikson [1959]), the major task of early adolescence can be regarded as having to do with *the conquest of thought*. Formal operations not only permit the young person to construct all the possibilities in a system and construct contrary-to-fact propositions (Inhelder & Piaget, 1958); they also enable him to conceptualize his own thought, to take his mental constructions as objects and reason about them. Only at about the ages of 11–12, for example, do children spontaneously introduce concepts of belief, intelligence, and faith into their definitions of their religious denomination (Elkind, 1961a; 1962; 1963). Once more, however, this new mental system which frees the young person from the egocentrism of childhood entangles him in a new form of egocentrism characteristic of adolescence.

Formal operational thought not only enables the adolescent to conceptualize his thought, it also permits him to conceptualize the thought of other people. It is this capacity to take account of other people's thought, however, which is the crux of adolescent egocentrism. This egocentrism emerges because, while the adolescent can now cognize the thoughts of others, he fails to differentiate between the objects toward which the thoughts of others are directed and those which are the focus of his own concern. Now, it is well known that the young adolescent, because of the physiological metamorphosis he is undergoing, is primarily concerned with himself. Accordingly, since he fails to differentiate between what others are thinking about and his own mental preoccupations, he assumes that other people are as obsessed with his behavior and appearance as he is himself. *It is this belief that others are preoccupied with his appearance and behavior that constitutes the egocentrism of the adolescent.*

One consequence of adolescent egocentrism is that, in actual or impending social situations, the young person anticipates the reactions of other people to himself. These anticipations, however, are based on the premise that others are as admiring or as critical of him as he is of himself. In a sense, then, the adolescent is continually constructing, or reacting to, *an imaginary audience.* It is an audience because the adolescent believes that he will be the focus of attention; and it is imaginary because, in actual social situations, this is not usually the case (unless he contrives to make it so). The construction of imaginary audiences would seem to account, in part at least, for a wide variety of typical adolescent behaviors and experiences.

The imaginary audience, for example, probably plays a role in the self-consciousness which is so characteristic of early adolescence. When the young person is feeling critical of himself, he anticipates that the audience—of which he is necessarily a part—will be critical too. And, since the audience is his own construction and privy to his own knowledge of himself, it knows just what to look for in the way of cosmetic and behavioral sensitivities. The adolescent's wish for privacy and his reluctance to reveal himself may, to some extent, be a reaction to the feeling of being under the constant critical scrutiny of other people. The notion of an imaginary audience also helps to explain the observation that the affect which most concerns adolescents is not guilt but, rather, shame, that is, the reaction to an audience (Lynd, 1961).

While the adolescent is often self-critical, he is frequently self-admiring too. At such times, the audience takes on the same affective coloration. A good deal of adolescent boorishness, loudness, and faddish dress is probably provoked, partially in any case, by a failure to differentiate between what the young person believes to be attractive and what others admire. It is for this reason that the young person frequently fails to understand why adults disapprove of the way he dresses and behaves. The same sort of egocentrism is often seen in behavior directed toward the opposite sex. The boy who stands in front of the mirror for 2 hours combing his hair is probably imagining the swooning reactions he will produce in the girls. Likewise, the girl applying her makeup is more likely than not imagining the admiring glances that will come her way. When these young people actually meet, each is more concerned with being the observed than with being the observer. Gatherings of young adolescents are unique in the sense that each young person is simultaneously an actor to himself and an audience to others.

One of the most common admiring audience constructions, in the adolescent, is the anticipation of how others will react to his own demise. A certain bittersweet pleasure is derived from anticipating the belated recognition by others of his positive qualities. As often happens with such universal fantasies, the imaginary anticipation of one's own demise has been realized in fiction. Below, for example, is the passage in *Tom Sawyer* where Tom sneaks back to his home, after having run away with Joe and Huck, to discover that he and his friends are thought to have been drowned:

> But this memory was too much for the old lady, and she broke entirely down. Tom was snuffling, now, himself—and more in pity of himself than anybody else. He could hear Mary crying and putting in a kindly word for him from time to time. He began to have a nobler opinion of himself than ever before. Still, he was sufficiently touched by his aunt's grief to long to rush out from under the bed and overwhelm her with joy—and the theatrical gorgeousness of the thing appealed strongly to his nature too—but he resisted and lay still.

Corresponding to the imaginary audience is another mental construction which is its complement. While the adolescent fails to differentiate the concerns of his own thought from those of others, he at the same time over-differentiates his feelings. Perhaps because he believes he is of importance to so many people, the imaginary audience, he comes to regard himself, and particularly his feelings, as something special and unique. Only he can suffer with such agonized intensity, or experience such exquisite rapture. How many parents have been confronted with the typically adolescent phrase, "But you don't know how it feels. . . ." The emotional torments undergone by Goethe's young Werther and by Salinger's Holden Caulfield exemplify the adolescent's belief in the uniqueness of his own emotional experience. At a somewhat different level, this belief in personal uniqueness becomes a conviction that he will not die, that death will happen to others but not to him. This complex of beliefs in the uniqueness of his feelings and of his immortality might be called *a personal fable*, a story which he tells himself and which is not true.

Evidences of the personal fable are particularly prominent in adolescent diaries. Such diaries are often written for posterity in the conviction that the young person's experiences, crushes, and frustrations are of universal significance and importance. Another kind of evidence for the personal fable during this period is the tendency to confide in a personal God. The search for privacy and the belief in personal uniqueness leads to the establishment of an I-Thou relationship with God as a personal confidant to whom one no longer looks for gifts but rather for guidance and support (Long, Elkind, & Spilka, 1967).

The concepts of an imaginary audience and a personal fable have proved useful, at least to the writer, in the understanding and treatment of troubled adolescents. The imaginary audience, for example, seems often to play a role in middle-class delinquency (Elkind, 1967). As a case in point, one young man took $1,000 from a golf tournament purse, hid the money, and then promptly revealed himself. It turned out that much of the motivation for this act was derived from the anticipated response of "the audience" to the guttiness of his action. In a similar vein, many young girls become pregnant because, in part at least, their personal fable convinces them that pregnancy will happen to others but never to them and so they need not take precautions. Such examples could be multiplied but will perhaps suffice to illustrate how adolescent egocentrism, as manifested in the imaginary audience and in the personal fable, can help provide a rationale for some adolescent behavior. These concepts can, moreover, be utilized in the treatment of adolescent offenders. It is often helpful to these young people if they can learn to differentiate between the real and the imaginary audience, which often boils down to a discrimination between the real and the imaginary parents.

The Passing of Adolescent Egocentrism

After the appearance of formal operational thought, no new mental systems develop and the mental structures of adolescence must serve for the rest of the life span. The egocentrism of early adolescence nonetheless tends to diminish by the age of 15 or 16, the age at which formal operations become firmly established. What appears to happen is that the imaginary audience, which is primarily an anticipatory audience, is progressively modified in the direction of the reactions of the real audience. In a way, the imaginary audience can be regarded as hypothesis—or better, as a series of hypotheses—which the young person tests against reality. As a consequence of this testing, he gradually comes to recognize the difference between his own preoccupations and the interests and concerns of others.

The personal fable, on the other hand, is probably overcome (although probably never in its entirety) by the gradual establishment of what Erikson (1959) has called "intimacy." Once the young person sees himself in a more realistic light as a function of having adjusted his imaginary audience to the real one, he can establish true rather than self-interested interpersonal relations. Once relations of mutuality are established and confidences are shared, the young person discovers that others have feelings similar to his own and have suffered and been enraptured in the same way.

Adolescent egocentrism is thus overcome by a twofold transformation. On the cognitive plane, it is overcome by the gradual differentiation between his own preoccupations and the thoughts of others;

while on the plane of affectivity, it is overcome by a gradual integration of the feelings of others with his own emotions.

Summary and Conclusions

In this paper I have tried to describe the forms which egocentrism takes and the mechanisms by which it is overcome, in the course of mental development. In infancy, egocentrism corresponds to the impression that objects are identical with the perception of them, and this form of egocentrism is overcome with the appearance of representation. During the preschool period, egocentrism appears in the guise of a belief that symbols contain the same information as is provided by the objects which they represent. With the emergence of concrete operations, the child is able to discriminate between symbol and referent, and so overcome this type of egocentrism. The egocentrism of the school-age period can be characterized as the belief that one's own mental constructions correspond to a superior form of perceptual reality. With the advent of formal operations and the ability to construct contrary-to-fact hypotheses, this kind of egocentrism is dissolved because the young person can now recognize the arbitrariness of his own mental constructions. Finally, during early adolescence, egocentrism appears as the belief that the thoughts of others are directed toward the self. This variety of egocentrism is overcome as a consequence of the conflict between the reactions which the young person anticipates and those which actually occur.

Although egocentrism corresponds to a negative product of mental growth, its usefulness would seem to lie in the light which it throws upon the affective reactions characteristic of any particular stage of mental development. In this paper I have dealt primarily with the affective reactions associated with the egocentrism of adolescence. Much of the material, particularly the discussion of the *imaginary audience* and the *personal fable* is speculative in the sense that it is based as much upon my clinical experience with young people as it is upon research data. These constructs are offered, not as the final word on adolescent egocentrism, but rather to illustrate how the cognitive structures peculiar to a particular level of development can be related to the affective experience and behavior characteristic of that stage. Although I have here only considered the correspondence between mental structure and affect in adolescence, it is possible that similar correspondences can be found at the earlier levels of development as well. A consideration of egocentrism, then, would seem to be a useful starting point for any attempt to reconcile cognitive structure and the dynamics of personality.

REFERENCES

BLOS, P. *On adolescence.* New York: Free Press, 1962.

CHARLESWORTH, W. R. Development of the object concept in infancy: methodological study. *American Psychologist,* 1966, *21,* 623. (Abstract)

COWAN, P. A. Cognitive egocentrism and social interaction in children. *American Psychologist,* 1966, *21,* 623. (Abstract)

ELKIND, D. The child's conception of his religious denomination, I: The Jewish child. *Journal of genetic Psychology,* 1961, *99,* 209–225. (a)

ELKIND, D. The development of quantitative thinking. *Journal of genetic Psychology,* 1961, *98,* 37–46. (b)

ELKIND, D. The child's conception of his religious denomination, II: The Catholic child. *Journal of genetic Psychology,* 1962, *101,* 185–193.

ELKIND, D. The child's conception of his religious denomination, III: The Protestant child. *Journal of genetic Psychology,* 1963, *103,* 291–304.

ELKIND, D. Conceptual orientation shifts in children and adolescents. *Child Development,* 1966, *37,* 493–498.

ELKIND, D. Middle-class delinquency. *Mental Hygiene,* 1967, *51,* 80–84.

ERIKSON, E. H. Identity and the life cycle. *Psychological issues.* Vol. 1, No. 1, New York: International Universities Press, 1959.

FREUD, ANNA. *The ego and the mechanisms of defense.* New York International Universities Press, 1946.

GOUREVITCH, VIVIAN, & FEFFER, M. H. A study of motivational development. *Journal of genetic Psychology,* 1962, *100,* 361–375.

INHELDER, BÄRBEL, & PIAGET, J. *The growth of logical thinking from childhood to adolescence.* New York: Basic Books, 1958.

KOHLBERG, L. Cognitive stages and preschool education. *Human Development,* 1966, *9,* 5–17.

LONG, DIANE, ELKIND, D., & SPILKA, B. The child's conception of prayer. *Journal for the scientific Study of Religion,* 1967, *6,* 101–109.

LYND, HELEN M. *On shame and the search for identity.* New York: Science Editions, 1961.

PEEL, E. A. *The pupil's thinking.* London: Oldhourne, 1960.

PIAGET, J. *The child's conception of the world.* London: Routledge & Kegan Paul, 1951.

PIAGET, J. *The child's conception of number.* New York: Humanities Press, 1952. (a)

PIAGET, J. *The language and thought of the child.* London: Routledge & Kegan Paul, 1952. (b)

PIAGET, J. *The construction of reality in the child.* New York: Basic Books, 1954.

PIAGET, J. *Comments on Vygotsky's critical remarks concerning "The language and thought of the child" and "Judgment and reasoning in the child."* Cambridge, Mass.: M.I.T. Press, 1962.

WEIR, M. W. Development changes in problem solving strategies. *Psychological Review,* 1964, *71,* 473–490.

52

Language and Cognition: Current Perspectives from Linguistics and Psychology

JOHN B. CARROLL

The view that non-standard dialects in general, and lower-class black English in particular, are not adequate for the development of organized, higher-order thought has been widespread. The counter-view is maintained with at least equal fervor. John B. Carroll, as chairman of the Linguistic Society of America's Committee on Language and Cognitive Development, presents very cogently the alternative point of view. It becomes apparent quickly that the controversy is far from being solely a theoretical one; it has important educational, social, and political implications. The paper by Labov and Robins in Section VI is also relevant.

Dr. Carroll, a leading educational psychologist, psychometrician, and psycholinguist, was formerly at Harvard University and is now Senior Research Psychologist at Educational Testing Service, Princeton, New Jersey.

In a series of papers published in the late 1950's and early 1960's, the British sociologist Basil Bernstein (*3, 4*) proposed a distinction between two forms of language that has caught the attention of educators and educational psychologists on both sides of the Atlantic. One form is what he called "public" language, the other is what he called "formal" language. Later, he renamed these forms as the "restricted code" and the "elaborated code," respectively. It was not Bernstein's drawing of the distinction between these two forms of language that was of particular moment; it was what Bernstein said about them, namely that the "public" or "restricted" code tended to be limited to short, highly stereotyped utterances whose symbolism is descriptive and concrete, whereas the "formal" or "elaborated" language is rich in qualification and complexity. The implication was that the user of the "restricted" code is unable to convey any careful, logical analysis of a situation, or even to conceive of a situation in any analytic terms, whereas the user of the "formal" or "elaborated" code was not so handicapped. In a number of empirical studies, Bernstein claimed to have been able to demonstrate the existence of these two types of language and to show their correlation with social-class differentiation.

Actually, Bernstein's views on the difference between these two codes and the effect of the difference on thinking have never been entirely clear, and as has been pointed out by Lawton (*7*), these views have undergone certain changes in emphasis over the course of the years. Lawton believes that Bernstein did not really mean to say that the linguistic code actually influences the form of thought; rather he argued that thought, and the kind of language used to express that thought, is a function of the social situation and the individual's perception of his role in society. Lawton also points out that the alleged correlation between language code and social class is not as great as some of those who quote Bernstein might have us think: on occasion, lower-class persons can use the "elaborated" code, and even in Bernstein's early presentations of his theory, it was emphasized that middle-class persons use *both* the restricted code and the elaborated code, depending upon the social situation.

Be that as it may, Bernstein's ideas have been much discussed. As frequently happens when new ideas are discussed by people who hear about them only second-hand, Bernstein's ideas have been watered down, modified, and oversimplified. It has been assumed that Bernstein's "restricted code" is one in which it is impossible to formulate thought of any high degree of logical complexity, and it has also been assumed that lower-class persons, being limited to the use of a "restricted" code, are unable to formulate logical thought. Bernstein did not make any such simplistic claims. I refer you to Lawton's analysis of Bernstein's writings for a more accurate statement of what Bernstein actually said.

John B. Carroll, "Language and cognition: Current perspectives from linguistics and psychology." Presented April 19, 1971, at the IRA Pre-Convention Institute on Reading, Language and Non-Standard Dialects. Reprinted by permission.

In their book *Teaching Disadvantaged Children in the Pre-School*, the educational psychologists Bereiter and Engelmann (*1*) cited Bernstein's theories as claiming that "the speech of lower-class people follows a linguistic code . . . that is inadequate for expressing personal or original opinions, for analysis and careful reasoning, for dealing with anything hypothetical or beyond the present, and for explaining anything very complex." According to these writers, Bernstein "sees the [lower-class] child . . . as being trapped by the restrictions of [his] linguistic code and unable to operate at the high conceptual and logical level that is required in formal education." They go on to describe the "language problems of culturally deprived children" (i.e., lower-class black children), making such points as these:

1. "The speech of the severely deprived children seems to consist not of distinct words, but rather of whole phrases or sentences that function like giant words. . . . These 'giant word' units cannot be taken apart by the child and recombined. . . . Instead of saying 'He's a big dog,' the deprived child says 'He bih daw.' Instead of saying 'I ain't got no juice,' he says 'Uai-ga-na-ju'" (p. 34).

2. It is not merely a problem of "faulty pronunciation," but of an "inability to deal with sentences *as sequences of meaningful parts*" (italics in the original). The lower-class black child cannot repeat sentences with any degree of complexity; he tends to "give merely an approximate rendition of the over-all sound profile of the sentence" (p. 35).

3. The "culturally deprived" child cannot distinguish sentences that differ with respect to structure words or inflections (p. 35).

4. "Many disadvantaged children of preschool age come very close to the total lack of ability to use language as a device for acquiring and processing information" (p. 39).

It is true that Bereiter and Engelmann acknowledge that "studies by Loban and others have been cited as evidence that culturally deprived children do possess all the necessary elements of English grammar and syntax, even though they make scanty use of some of them." But, they continue, "what is crucial . . . is not the extent to which their language is technically capable of conveying thoughts and information but the extent to which the children themselves are able to use language in this way" (p. 39).

It is worthy of note that Bereiter and Engelmann apply Bernstein's notion of a "restricted code" to the language of lower-class black children, who speak a form of English that is a distinct, nonstandard dialect. While there are dialect differences in England between middle-class and lower-class speech, Bernstein was thinking not so much of dialect differences as of differences in speech styles and modes of formulating thought. Thus, it is easy to gain the false impression, from Bereiter and Engelmann's statements, that lower-class black English *is* what Bernstein would call a restricted code, whereas standard English is an "elaborated code." The fact of the matter is that if there is any validity in Bernstein's distinction between "restricted" and "elaborated" codes, it could operate just as well in standard English as in some nonstandard form of English such as what is loosely called "lower-class black English." We all use a "restricted" code when we are in casual social situations in which there is quick interchange of simple information, feelings, and opinions that we do not have to formulate carefully.

I have quoted extensively from Bereiter and Engelmann only because they give the most explicit statement available of a view that seems to be widespread: that lower-class black English is "a basically nonlogical mode of expressive behavior which lacks the formal properties necessary for the organization of thought" (*2*, pp. 112–113). It may be that Bereiter and Engelmann no longer hold to this view, but the impression that it has made is sufficiently common among educators that it deserves comment and rebuttal. Also, this view reflects social attitudes toward nonstandard languages that linguists feel are misguided and wrong. There are, in fact, many myths about language that are commonly believed and repeated: that simple folk have exceedingly small vocabularies, that the languages of "primitive" tribes are extremely simple and incapable of expressing thought, and that when a person does not speak "grammatically," he is not thinking correctly. The widespread acceptance of such ideas is alarming to linguists, not only because they are scientifically untenable, but also because they reflect social attitudes that are rightly to be regarded as snobbish, undemocratic, and antithetical to social progress.

It was for this reason that the Linguistic Society of America last year appointed a Committee on Language and Cognitive Development, of which I am chairman, to prepare materials that would seek to inform educators and the public at large concerning linguists' knowledge about the nature of language, the adequacy of different languages or forms of language for formulating thought, and the nature of language development in the individual. The present address is a brief summary of some of the facts, principles, and views that linguists hope to have made more widely known. These include not only things that linguists as linguists know, but also some facts and conclusions that have been reached in the psychology of language.

Let me lay down some general principles that

will guide our later consideration of the particular problems of nonstandard dialects:

1. Language is a complex human phenomenon that takes the same general form wherever it is found. It permits the expression of a certain very wide range of information, experiences, feelings, and thoughts, and it does so in somewhat the same way regardless of the particular form of the language or the culture of the user, as long as the language is a so-called "natural language" that is used from childhood on as a native language by its users. This is true whether the language is one such as English, Russian, Chinese, or Indonesian used by a highly developed culture, or one such as Bantu, Navaho, or Fijian, used by a less technically advanced culture. (There are, of course, certain modes of expression, such as music or higher mathematics, that are outside the province of language, but they are equally excluded from all natural languages.)

2. In saying that all languages have the same general form, we mean that all languages possess units for expressing particular concepts and rules whereby utterances are constructed to indicate the social purpose of the utterance and the particular relationships among concepts that are to be communicated. Languages do, of course, differ somewhat in the concepts they select for use in expression, and they vary widely in the particular rules they employ for constructing utterances. Nevertheless, all languages have ways of referring to all the kinds of beings, objects, substances, events, and relationships encountered in common human experience. They all have ways of communicating ideas of space, time, number, negation, condition, opposition, specificity, class membership, quality, and the like, many of these ideas being of a highly abstract nature. In general, it is true that anything that can be said in one language can be said in any other language, if one ignores the special cultural connotations and conceptual references that may attach to the utterances of a given language, and if one excludes the problem of translating advanced technical ideas from one language to another.

3. Language systems are neutral with respect to truth or logic; a language system does not force its speakers to make true or logical statements as opposed to untrue or illogical statements.

4. Except for languages with very small numbers of speakers living in close association, it is common to find minor or even major variations in the pronunciation, vocabulary, or grammar of a language across the various groups using it. Different forms of a language are technically known as *dialects*, and to say that a person speaks a dialect has no derogatory or pejorative force. (I am speaking a particular dialect of English right now!) Dialect variation occurs both in the languages of advanced civilization (witness all the dialects of English) and in those of aboriginal groups. It is often the case, too, that one or more dialects of a language acquire higher status than others; high-status dialects are generally called standard dialects, while dialects of lesser status are often regarded as "nonstandard." This is not at all because a high-status form of a language is necessarily any better equipped to communicate ideas or formulate thought, but simply because the speakers of that dialect have attained generally higher social status and power (and often, more education) than the speakers of other dialects, through the operation of political, economic, and other social forces. The phenomenon of "standard" vs. "nonstandard" dialects is found throughout the world, even in the case of aboriginal languages like Bantu or Fijian, and speakers of nonstandard dialects are generally well aware of the low status accorded their dialects, regardless of their actual social status.

5. Speakers of any language, or any dialect, use that language in many different styles, depending upon the particular social situation in which they find themselves on a given occasion. These styles or registers vary in many ways, generally along a dimension of formality vs. informality. For example, Martin Joos in his essay *The Five Clocks* (5) distinguishes five styles that speakers and writers of standard English may affect: frozen, formal, consultative, casual, and intimate. But he also notes that styles vary in the dimensions of age, "breadth," and "responsibility" (with some overtones of relations with the "standard-nonstandard" dimension mentioned above). Speakers of nonstandard dialects are capable of similar variation in styles of speech.

6. It is usually the case that the various dialects of a language, whether standard or nonstandard, are mutually intelligible at least to some extent. The more similar the dialects are in their pronunciation, vocabulary, and grammar, the more they are mutually intelligible. Depending upon the amount of exposure to them, and other factors, speakers can learn to understand a number of different dialects better than would otherwise be normal for them. Some speakers can speak and be understood in two or more dialects, often in different levels or registers of these dialects.

7. Within the speakers of a given dialect, there will be certain variations in *competence*, that is, knowledge of the system of the language and the rules by which the system is put together, so to speak. In the main, this variation occurs in the individual's knowledge of vocabulary. That is, some speakers know more words, and more about the different uses of words, than others. There may

be some variation also in competence with respect to grammatical rules, and even some variation with respect to basic pronunciation rules. These variations in competence depend to an unknown extent on differences in basic mental capacities, in amount of education, or in amount of exposure to other speakers of the language. Through appropriate education or training, individuals can be helped to reach higher levels of competence, but we do not necessarily know what the best training methods are to achieve this goal, nor do we know how to predict the maximum level of competence that an individual can achieve after such training.

8. In addition, even among speakers who have the same degree of "competence" (technically defined as above), there will be variation in what we may call *performance characteristics*, that is, in verbal fluency and creativeness, in reasoning power, in social perception, and other individual traits that affect the individual's use of language, whether in speaking, understanding, reading, or writing. Of course, the more the individual knows about the language, the more likely it is that he will be able to use it fluently, creatively, and intelligently, but it remains true that skill in language use is not only a matter of language competence but of many other factors in the individual's make-up.

9. The course of a child's acquisition of his native language, whatever that language may be, is normally regular and predictable. While there are individual differences in rate of development that may be associated with some combination of hereditary and environmental factors, every child passes through certain distinct stages of development in his learning of the phonological, lexical, and grammatical characteristics of his language. Furthermore, he learns whatever language or variety of language he is exposed to. (Sometimes he learns several languages, or varieties of language, at the same time.) By the time he is about five, the normal child has learned *most* of the characteristics of his language that enable him to use it in ordinary communication with peers and with adults, although he will learn much more about his language as he grows older and is exposed to more advanced uses of it.

10. The developmental stages through which a child passes in learning his language are quite possibly correlated with the child's mental development. Frankly, we do not know much, as yet, about this correlation or how it operates. There are those who believe that language development leads and guides mental development, and there are those who believe that, on the contrary, mental development leads language development. There is no *a priori* way of resolving this question, and it is difficult even to interpret the few empirical studies that bear on it. On the basis of several lines of reasoning and the available evidence, I incline to the belief that mental development tends to lead and proceed in advance of language development— that a given stage of language development cannot be attained until the appropriate mental capacity for that development has matured. I believe also that the adequate development of mental maturity is only a *necessary* condition, not a sufficient condition, for language development. Obviously, the child must be exposed to language in situations that are meaningful to him before he can learn it. If this view is correct, the absence of a given phase of language development cannot be taken necessarily as evidence for a deficit in mental maturity; it could equally well be evidence for a deficiency in the environmental conditions in which the child is placed.

Armed with these general propositions and principles, we may now re-examine some of the views that have been put forth by such writers as Bernstein, Bereiter and Engelmann, and others.

To say that there exists a "restricted code" in no sense implies that the basic form of a speaker's language is incapable of allowing him to formulate thought of any degree of logical complexity. If one takes the total range of linguistic devices available to the speaker of any natural language, and in fact usually within the competence of that speaker, one finds that these devices would permit the expression of any thought or relationship that one might desire to express (except, of course, for highly technical discourse for which vocabulary might be lacking). Neither British lower-class English, nor lower-class black English is incapable of expressing complex thought. The linguist William Labov (6) has given a number of examples of lower-class black English in which quite complex thoughts are expressed, for example, one in which a youngster tells a slightly older black interviewer that there can't be a heaven because it could only have been made by a God, but since nobody really knows what God is like, he doesn't exist and therefore couldn't have made a heaven.

Note, however, that this youngster was speaking in a social situation in which he felt perfectly free to talk. If Bereiter's slum children appeared to speak in "grunts" or "giant words," it may have been because they found themselves in a situation which inhibited their speech in certain ways.

Bernstein's "restricted code" is properly to be interpreted as a style or mode of speaking in which the speaker finds no need to formulate thoughts carefully and with adequate qualification. It has little or nothing to do with the basic language system in which the speech is couched, and it is merely an accident if the particular speech patterns used under such conditions appear to be less complex on the average.

Bereiter and Engelmann's notion that their slum children speak in "giant words" and are unable to perceive speech as a sequence of meaningful sounds is patently wrong, as it violates the second proposition I have enunciated above, that all languages have a certain form, with rules for constructing utterances out of basic elements. No language has any provision for constructing "giant words" that are unanalyzable in terms of simpler elements and that would convey what might otherwise be conveyed by a sentence. Neither the famous compound words of German nor the polysynthetic words of a language like Eskimo can be conceived of as "giant words" constructed out of whole cloth, independent of other elements in the language. Bereiter and Engelmann's very examples belie their allegations: The child who said "Uai-ga-na-ju" (for "I ain't got no juice") *constructed* his utterance from basic elements according to a fairly complex set of rules; he could have said "I ain't got no milk" or "I got some juice" or "If you don't give me no juice, I ain't got none" or literally hundreds of other utterances on this general pattern.

Since all languages are neutral with respect to truth or logic, it cannot be the case that nonstandard forms of English are illogical. Under certain conditions, black English omits the copula *to be*, as in the utterance "He sick," a fact from which it is sometimes concluded that black English is "illogical." As it happens, standard Russian also omits the copula in sentences of this type, but I hope nobody would argue that Russian is "illogical." The same goes for the argument that languages that use the double negative are illogical. Black English is similar to French, Spanish, and Old English in using the double negative.

Lower-class black English is admittedly a nonstandard dialect of English but I believe the status in which it is regarded, like the status of many other nonstandard dialects, would be improved if the public realizes that it is just as highly structured and just as capable of communicating thought as a standard dialect. Even if Bernstein's distinction between "restricted" and "elaborated" codes is accepted, there can be both "restricted" and "elaborated" codes, or modes of speaking, in nonstandard dialects as well as in standard ones.

Also, just as standard dialects can be used in various styles, so also can nonstandard dialects be used in various styles. It is possible to reinterpret Bereiter and Engelmann's reports of the speech of their slum children by saying that these children were speaking in a special style—a style

adopted whenever the children found themselves in a minority position.

Children speaking a nonstandard dialect cannot be expected necessarily to comprehend standard English, although the evidence says that they understand standard English better than speakers of standard English understand *their* dialect. This fact is not adequately taken into account in a variety of psychological tests. For example, children who speak nonstandard dialects get unfairly low scores on certain subtests of the widely-used Illinois Test of Psycholinguistic Abilities (8) that require the child to follow the grammatical distinctions observed by standard English. It is a grave mistake, often made, to interpret these low scores as indicating a retarded state of language development or, worse still, a retarded state of mental development. The Manual of the ITPA fails to recognize this problem or to warn against such misinterpretations. A fairer test would be one that is designed in terms of the nonstandard dialect in question.

There may be some justice in the claims of Bereiter and Engelmann, and others who have prepared programs of language improvement for speakers of nonstandard English, that some of these children have not learned the words for certain concepts, even in their own dialects, because one can expect differences in the extent to which children have learned such words. The mistake that is often made, however, is to assume that the nonstandard dialect in question lacks these words or has no way of expressing these concepts. Programs of language "improvement," i.e., programs in which children are taught the standard dialect, should be based on careful analyses of what stock of words and concepts is possessed by the nonstandard dialect. It will frequently turn out that a child who seems not to possess a particular feature of a standard dialect already knows a corresponding feature in his nonstandard dialect.

From the proposition that language acquisition is a natural and regular course of development we can draw the inference that the child who learns a nonstandard dialect learns it in much the same way as do children who acquire standard dialects. If the child's acquisition of a nonstandard dialect is viewed in its own terms rather than in terms of the extent to which he acquires the standard dialect, it will not appear as distorted and unusual as it is often thought to be.

To sum up the argument of this paper, I would emphasize the incorrectness and fallaciousness of the apparently widespread belief that speaking a nonstandard dialect is somehow a sign of a deficiency in thought or of mental development.

There may be some connection between language and thought, but it is not exhibited in nonstandard speech. Our children who are speakers of nonstandard dialects—whether they be blacks, Puerto Ricans, or Chicanos, are not the victims of undeveloped language codes. Their languages have principles and rules similar to those that govern any language.

REFERENCES

1. BEREITER, CARL, and SIEGFRIED ENGELMANN. *Teaching Disadvantaged Children in the Pre-School.* Englewood Cliffs, N.J.: Prentice-Hall, 1966.

2. BEREITER, CARL; S. ENGELMANN; JEAN OSBORN; and P. A. REIDFORD. "An Academically Oriented Pre-School." In Fred M. Hechinger (Ed.), *Pre-School Education Today.* New York: Doubleday, 1966. Pp. 105–135.

3. BERNSTEIN, BASIL. "Some Sociological Determinants of Perception: An Inquiry into Sub-Cultural Differences." *British Journal of Sociology, 9* (June, 1958), 159–174.

4. BERNSTEIN, BASIL. "Linguistic Codes, Hesitation Phenomena, and Intelligence." *Language and Speech, 5* (January, 1962), 31–46.

5. JOOS, MARTIN. *The Five Clocks.* New York: Harcourt Brace Jovanovich, 1967.

6. LABOV, WILLIAM. "The Logic of Non-Standard English." In Frederick Williams (Ed.), *Language and Poverty: Perspectives on a Theme.* Chicago: Markham Publishing Co., 1970. Pp. 153–189.

7. LAWTON, DENIS. *Social Class, Language, and Education.* New York: Schocken Books, 1968.

8. PARASKEVOPOULOS, JOHN N., and SAMUEL A. KIRK. *The Development and Psychometric Characteristics of the Revised Illinois Test of Psycholinguistic Abilities.* Urbana: University of Illinois Press, 1969.

53

Personality and IQ Change [1]

Jerome Kagan, Lester W. Sontag,
Charles T. Baker,
and Virginia L. Nelson

This article addresses itself to the interactions between personality and intelligence in terms of IQ change. The paper is from The Fels Research Institute for the Study of Human Development, the locus of one of the earliest-begun and broadest longitudinal studies. (Honzik's article in Section II is another example of the longitudinal approach.) The techniques used by Kagan et al. to assess personality are two well-known projective techniques—the Rorschach Ink Blots and the TAT or Thematic Apperception Test. As mentioned earlier, Professor Kagan is now at Harvard University. Lester W. Sontag is Director Emeritus of Fels Research Institute, Antioch College; Charles T. Baker is assistant resident psychiatrist at Vancouver General Hospital, University of British Columbia, Canada; and Virginia L. Nelson was formerly a research assistant at the Fels Research Institute.

Research on mental development during the last twenty years has indicated that a child's IQ score does not necessarily remain constant with age (2, 3, 4, 10). Several reports (9, 10, 12) suggest that changes in environmental conditions can depress or raise IQ level and it is sometimes implied that these changes may be explained by recourse to personality variables. The purpose of this paper is to demonstrate that changes in IQ during childhood are correlated with certain personality predispositions as inferred from projective test data. The personality variables under study include (a) need for achievement, (b) competitive strivings, (c) curiosity about nature, and (d) passivity.

Performance on an IQ test is assumed to be a function of at least two major variables: the variety of skills and abilities the person brings to the test situation and his motivation to perform well on the test (2, 6). Since the IQ scores of some children change markedly during the school years, it seems plausible to assume that those children who show marked increases in IQ have a very strong motivation to acquire or develop the various intellectual skills tapped by an IQ test and to perform well in a testing situation. It is suggested that need for achievement, competitive strivings, and curiosity about nature motivate the acquisition and improvement of cognitive abilities and by so doing facilitate increases in tested IQ.

The social environment often awards praise and recognition for intellectual accomplishment, and school age children with a high need for achievement might seek to gratify this need through intellectual activity. Thus it was predicted that children showing marked increases in IQ would produce more achievement imagery on the TAT than those with minimal gains in IQ.

Secondly, the school environment emphasizes competitive intellectual activity, and children with strong competitive needs would be highly motivated to acquire the intellectual skills which result in successful competition with one's classmates. Thus it was predicted that children showing IQ gains would show more competitive strivings than children displaying minimal gains in IQ. In choosing an index of competitive strivings, besides the related measure of TAT achievement fantasy, it was decided to use aggressive content on the Rorschach. The bases for this choice rested on the assumptions that (a) incidence of aggressive imagery reflected degree of aggressive motivation and (b) competition was a socially accepted form of aggressive behavior. For in competition, as in aggression, the child desires to defeat another individual and assert his superiority over him. The population of children in this study is predominantly middle class and apt to place strong inhibitions on

[1] This investigation was supported in part by a research grant (PHS M 1260) from the National Institute of Mental Health of the National Institutes of Health, United States Public Health Service. The writers wish to thank Dr. Seymour B. Sarason for his critical reading of the manuscript.

Jerome Kagan, Lester W. Sontag, Charles T. Baker, and Virginia L. Nelson, "Personality and IQ change," *Journal of Abnormal and Social Psychology*, 1958, 56, 261–266. Reprinted by permission.

direct overt expression of aggression. Therefore, there would be a tendency for the individual with high aggressive motivation to seek socially accepted channels for aggressive expression such as competitive activity with peers. Thus it was predicted that children showing IQ gain would report more Rorschach aggressive content than those with minimal gain because of their greater competitive predisposition.

A third motive that might facilitate a child's acquisition of knowledge and skills in dealing with the environment could be curiosity about nature. Interest in birth, death, sexual anatomy, and other processes of nature is a frequent phenomenon in young children. It is suggested that the more intense this curiosity the greater the motivation to acquire the habits which would gratify this motive. Since reading, questioning, and manipulating the environment are effective behavioral methods of gratifying one's curiosity, it might be expected that the highly curious child would be more likely to develop these skills and therefore apt to gain in IQ score. The TAT measure used to evaluate curiosity was presence of themes of interest in nature and its phenomena. For the Rorschach, it was hypothesized that concern with the body might reflect, in part, heightened interest in natural processes, and it was suggested that anatomy content might be more frequent for children who showed marked IQ gains than for those with minimal increases in IQ. It is recognized that many clinical psychologists regard anatomy content in adults as indicative of psychopathology. This study is concerned with the correlates of IQ gain rather than psychopathology, and it is not implied that children who show increases in IQ are completely free of conflict. Secondly, it was felt that the determinants of anatomy content for children might be different from those which produce this content in adults.

A final prediction dealt with the predisposition to behavioral passivity. The children who show IQ gains have been characterized as having high need achievement, competitive strivings, and curiosity about the environment. This constellation of motives implies that when these children are confronted with a problem, they would have a tendency to attack and attempt to solve the problem rather than withdraw from the situation or seek help. On this basis, it was predicted that children who showed IQ gains would be less likely than those with minimal IQ increases to characterize their TAT heroes as passive in attitude or behavior.

The Fels Research Institute is uniquely equipped to test these ideas about IQ change since it has continuous longitudinal information on the development of a sample of normal children. These data include intelligence and projective tests, observations of the children, and reports on the parent-child interaction. In a recent study, Sontag, Baker, and Nelson (11) related personality information on a sample of children with changes in IQ and found that those children who showed marked increases in IQ were rated as more competitive, more likely to display self-initiated behavior and less passive than those who showed decreases in IQ. The TAT and Rorschach protocols were not utilized in making these personality ratings, and the results from this study served as a major stimulus for the present investigation.

METHOD

A sample of 140 Fels subjects (Ss), 70 of each sex, were chosen for study because a fairly complete record of test information was available on them. From ages $2\frac{1}{2}$ to 6, the Stanford-Binet intelligence test (1916 or 1937 revision) was administered to most Ss twice yearly, on their birthdays and six months after their birthdays. From ages 6 to 12, most Ss received alternately Form L or Form M of the 1937 revision annually on or near each S's birthday. All of the tests were administered by one of the authors (VLN). The mean IQ of the Fels population is near 120, with standard deviation varying from 14 to 20 IQ points.

In order to obtain groups of Ss who showed the most change in IQ score from ages 6 to 10, a smoothed longitudinal plot of each S's IQ was prepared by averaging the mean of three consecutive test scores around each age. This procedure is explained in detail in other reports (1, 10, 11). This technique tends to eliminate erratic variations in IQ and hopefully furnishes a more valid measure of IQ changes. Then each S's smoothed IQ at age 6 was subtracted from his smoothed IQ at age 10, and this distribution of differences, positive if S gained in IQ and negative if S lost in IQ, was divided into quartiles. This report deals with the projective test information on those S's in the two extreme groups: those who increased and those who decreased the most in IQ score. These will be called Group A, the IQ ascenders, and Group D, the IQ descenders, respectively. There was no significant difference between the mean IQ of the two extreme quartiles at age six, the means being 119 and 116 for Groups A and D respectively. The average amount of increase in IQ for Group A was larger (plus 17 points) than the corresponding decrease for the members of Group D (minus 5 points) and while 46 per cent of Group D lost five or more points, every child in Group A gained 10 or more points during the years 6 through 10. The mean IQ of the entire sample of 140 tends to increase slightly from ages 6 to 10, probably as a result of practice effects with the same test. Since every S in Group D showed a decrease in IQ, it might be inferred that the members of Group D did not benefit from practice and familiarity with the test, and it is probably more accurate to view Group D Ss in this light rather than as Ss who showed marked decreases in IQ score.

The projective tests used in the analysis were the Rorschach and selected TAT pictures. Two factors governed the choice of the TAT cards which were analyzed. Because the protocols were gathered over a period of years, there was not complete comparability for all Ss for the number of cards administered. Secondly, the specific hypotheses of the study dictated the cards chosen for analysis and Cards 1, 3 BM, 3 GF, 5, 6 BM, 12 F, 14, and 17 BM were selected for analysis. The age at which the TAT protocols were administered ranged from 8-9 to 14-6 with median at 11-6 and 80 per cent of the protocols obtained between the ages of 11 and 12. The age at which the Rorschachs were administered ranged from 6-5 to 13-6 with median at 10-5 and 63 per cent of the sample having had the test between ages 10 and 11. Since the Rorschach and TAT were administered by different examiners there was no comparability with respect to inquiry or probing. Thus, the analysis of both the Rorschach and TAT were restricted to the S's spontaneous verbalization to the stimulus before any questions or inquiry were conducted by the examiner. The protocols were scored for the following fantasy categories.

1. *Need achievement on the TAT.* Achievement imagery on the TAT was scored according to the definition of McClelland et al. (8); and themes involving a reference to competition with a standard of excellence were scored achievement imagery.

2. *Rorschach aggression.* The definition of aggressive content on the Rorschach included (*a*) people, animals, or creatures engaged in physical or verbal aggression, e.g., fighting or quarreling, (*b*) explosive objects or explosions, e.g., volcanoes, bombs exploding, fireworks, and (*c*) objects or animal parts normally regarded as instruments of aggression, e.g., spears, rifles, clubs, guns, knives, horns, and claws.

3. *Intellectual curiosity about nature.* For the TAT, curiosity was defined in terms of themes in which someone is interested in the processes or phenomena of nature. Curiosity on the Rorschach was restricted to anatomy or X-ray responses of internal organs or boney parts, e.g., stomach, backbone, ribs.

4. *Passivity.* Because of the limited amount of thematic material in the spontaneous performance, themes of passivity were limited to stories in which the central figure was described as sleepy, tired, or resting.

The fantasy categories were independently scored by the senior author and an assistant without knowledge of the S's IQ scores.[2] Reliability was very high because of the limited amount of content scored for each response and the objectivity of the definitions. Percentage of agreement for the three TAT categories was 95 per cent and for the two Rorschach categories 99 per cent.

RESULTS

Although there was a total of 70 Ss in the two extreme quartiles, not all of the Ss had Rorschach or TAT data for the age range under study. Table 1 shows the distri-

---

[2] The writers wish to thank Mary Schnurer for her assistance in assessing the reliability of the scoring.

TABLE 1

DISTRIBUTION OF Ss BY SEX AND DIRECTION OF IQ CHANGE USED IN THE ANALYSIS OF THE TAT AND RORSCHACH

Group	TAT		Rorschach	
	Boys	*Girls*	*Boys*	*Girls*
Group A	22	11	22	10
Group D	10	20	9	18
Both groups	32	31	31	28

bution of Ss, by sex and direction of IQ change, for the TAT and Rorschach analyses. Because there are approximately twice as many boys as there are girls in Group A, all comparisons were first made separately by sex and results were only combined if the direction of the result for both boys and girls in the same IQ group was in the predicted direction.

1. *Need Achievement.* All achievement themes, save one, occurred to Cards 1 and 17 BM. The typical achievement story to Card 1 concerned a boy who wanted to master the violin and/or become a famous violinist, while the typical achievement theme to 17 BM involved competitive activity with regard to rope climbing. Table 2 shows the percentage of Ss in each group reporting achievement imagery plots to Cards 1, 17 BM, and to both pictures.

For both Cards 1 and 17 BM, more male and female Ss in Group A report achievement imagery than the boys or girls of Group D. For Card 1, the difference between Group A and Group D girls is reliable at the .03 level; the difference for boys is in the predicted direction but not significant. For Card 17 BM, the difference between Group A and Group D boys is significant ($P = .03$) and in the predicted direction for girls. All P values are for one tail and were evaluated using the exact method suggested by Fisher (5). When the sexes were pooled, comparisons between Groups A and D were significant not only for Cards 1 and 17 BM separately but also for the number of Ss telling achievement imagery to both Cards 1 and 17 BM ($P < .10$, .03, and .01 respectively). Thus, the Ss who showed increases in IQ were more prone to structure Cards 1 and 17 BM in terms of achievement oriented behavior than the Ss in Group D.

2. *Aggressive Content on Rorschach.* There was no significant difference between Groups A and D or be-

TABLE 2

PERCENTAGE OF Ss REPORTING ACHIEVEMENT IMAGERY TO CARDS 1 AND 17 BM

TAT Card	Group A			Group D		
	Boys	*Girls*	*Boys and Girls*	*Boys*	*Girls*	*Boys and Girls*
Card 1	36.4	50.0	40.6	27.3	15.0	19.4
Card 17 BM	36.4	30.0	34.4	0.0	15.0	9.7
Cards 1 and 17 BM	22.7	10.0	18.8	0.0	0.0	0.0

tween boys and girls with respect to the mean number of responses per protocol, and the mean for the entire sample was 27 responses. There was no difference between Group A and Group D girls with respect to percentage of each group reporting one or more aggressive responses per protocol (30.0 per cent for Group A versus 33.0 per cent for Group D). However, the difference between Group A and D boys approached significance with 59.1 per cent of the former and 22.2 per cent of the latter reporting one or more aggressive images ($P = .07$). Thus, the prediction of a correlation between IQ increase and aggressive imagery held only for the boys. Because of the tentativeness of this result and the more speculative nature of the hypothesis relating competitive striving and aggressive content, an attempt was made to validate this finding by analyzing a later Rorschach protocol for the boys in Groups A and D. Not all of the boys had Rorschachs administered to them at a later age, and only 15 *S*s in Group A and five in Group D were available for analysis. The median ages at the time of administration were 13-8 and 15-0 for Groups A and D respectively, and there was no significant difference in the lengths of the protocols of the two groups. The results were in the same direction for 86.7 per cent of Group A, and 20.0 per cent of Group D reported one or more aggressive images, and this difference is highly significant ($P = .01$).

3. *Intellectual Curiosity.* The only TAT card eliciting curiosity plots was Card 14, and the typical theme described a person gazing at or interested in the stars or the heavens. Table 3 shows the percentage of each group telling such themes to Card 14.

Both the boys and girls in Group A told more themes of interest in the stars or heavens than the males and females in Group D ($P = .14$, $P = .10$, respectively) and combining of the sexes yielded a highly significant difference between Groups A and D ($P < .01$).

4. *Anatomy and X-Ray Responses on the Rorschach.* There was no difference between Group A and Group D girls reporting one or more anatomy responses (30.0 per cent versus 38.9 per cent for Groups A and D respectively). For the boys, 31.8 per cent of Group A and 0.0 per cent of Group D reported anatomy or X-ray imagery, a difference that approached significance ($P = .06$). This finding was also validated on the same sample of 20 boys that was used to check the differences in aggressive content. The results were in the same direction with 60.0 per cent of Group A and 20.0 per cent of Group D reporting anatomy content ($P = .15$).

5. *Passivity.* Card 3 BM accounted for most of the passivity themes and the groups were compared with respect to the incidence of stories to Card 3 BM in which the central figure was sleepy, tired, or resting. Table 4

TABLE 3
PERCENTAGE OF *S*s REPORTING THEMES OF CURIOSITY TO CARD 14

Sex	Group A	Group D
Boys	40.9	18.2
Girls	30.0	5.0
Boys and girls	37.5	9.7

TABLE 4
PERCENTAGE OF *S*s REPORTING THEMES OF PASSIVITY TO CARD 3 BM

Sex	Group A	Group D
Boys	9.1	27.3
Girls	10.0	45.0
Boys and girls	9.4	38.7

shows the percentage of each group telling such themes. Both the boys and girls in Group D showed more passivity themes than the boys and girls in Group A. Although only the difference for the girls was significant ($P = .06$), when the sexes were pooled the difference was highly reliable ($P < .03$).

Cards 3 GF, 5, 6 BM, and 12 F did not furnish data relevant to the hypotheses under test and these results are not summarized.

DISCUSSION

In the main, the hypotheses about the differences between Groups A and D have been verified. Boy and girl ascenders produced more TAT achievement imagery and curiosity about nature than Group D children and male ascenders displayed more aggressive content on the Rorschach than the boys in Group D. The higher incidence of aggressive imagery for the boys who gained in IQ was interpreted as reflecting stronger competitive motivation. Finally, the *S*s in Group D were presumed to have a more passive orientation since they were more likely to perceive the ambiguous figure on Card 3 BM as sleeping or tired. The relation between Rorschach anatomy content and IQ gain was the most tentative finding.

The results are interpreted as indicating that high motivation to achieve, competitive strivings, and curiosity about nature may motivate the acquisition of intellectual skills and knowledge which, in turn, facilitates increases in tested IQ. If one accepts the generally assumed notion that boys are more competitive and achievement oriented than girls, the fact that there were twice as many boys in Group A as there were girls supports the present interpretation. A recent study using the Edwards Personal Preference Schedule found that high school boys obtained higher need achievement scores than high school girls (7).

These results are not interpreted as indicating that strong achievement, competitive, and curiosity motives are the only variables involved in producing gains in IQ. The *S*s in this study are all average or above in IQ and there is not adequate sampling of children with lower IQ levels. One would not expect *S*s with low IQs or language handicaps to suddenly show an interest in reading despite achievement needs or intellectual curiosity.

The child who spends increased time reading be- . cause of a heightened interest in natural processes must have already learned the basic reading skills so that his behavior is not a difficult or unlikely choice for him.

Similarly, needs for achievement and successful competition should only motivate attempts at improvement of intellectual abilities in a social milieu where praise, recognition, and superior status are awarded for such accomplishment. That is, achievement-oriented children from homes in which intellectual activity was praised would probably be more likely to master intellectual skills than achievement-oriented children from homes in which such accomplishment was not rewarded. In a cultural environment where athletic ability, fighting prowess, or success with the opposite sex was highly valued, one might expect the child to choose these behavioral channels to gratify his achievement and competitive needs. The parents in the Fels population are predominantly middle class and tend to place importance on intellectual accomplishment. A large majority of the parents have attended college, and since enrollment in the Fels program is voluntary it might be inferred that only parents who valued knowledge and scientific pursuits would be predisposed to become part of the research population. Thus, the children under study tend to come from homes which value intellectual ability.

Study of the educational attainment of the parents of the Ss in Groups A and D revealed no significant difference between the groups with respect to the percentage of families in which both parents attended college (57.1 per cent for Group A versus 42.9 per cent for Group D; $P > .30$). Although there is a slight difference favoring the educational level of Group A families, the difference was not dramatic. There may be important differences between Groups A and D with respect to the differential encouragement of intellectual achievement, but measurement of these differences would probably require variables more refined than educational level of the parents. However, even though parental emphasis on intellectual activity may increase the child's desire to improve his cognitive skills, the child's predisposition to adopt or rebel against parental values should selectively influence his motivation to strive for intellectual accomplishment. Thus, the type of relation between parent and child may be an important factor in this process.

Finally, there is the possibility that genetic and/ or constitutional variables may play a role in facilitating marked IQ changes. There is considerable data indicating that genetic factors influence IQ level but less evidence relevant to the role of these variables in producing childhood increases in IQ score. For most of the children in our population, IQs tend to level off during the ages 6–10 and most of the marked changes in level occur during the preschool years. However, the exact relationship between genetic variables and IQ change has yet to be determined. The phenomenon of IQ increase during the school years is admittedly complex and it is not implied that the child's motives are the major factor. However, it is suggested that personality needs may influence this process. Perhaps the most accurate generalization is that for middle-class children with average or above IQ levels, strong achievement, competitive, and curiosity needs may facilitate IQ gains by motivating the child to master intellectual skills.

A final implication of these findings is that they add indirect evidence for the usefulness of the Rorschach and TAT as research instruments. Validation of a predicted relationship between TAT achievement imagery and IQ gain increases one's confidence in the hypothesis that TAT plots can serve as an index of achievement-oriented tendencies. The results of the Rorschach analysis suggest that aggressive content may be an index of an individual's aggressive predispositions but not necessarily a measure of his tendency to express direct, physical aggression. Although Sontag, Baker, and Nelson (11), using behavioral observations, rated the boys in Group A as more competitive than those in Group D, there was no difference between these groups with respect to intensity or incidence of direct verbal or physical aggression or destruction of property. We have assumed that competition is a socially approved form of aggressive behavior and the higher incidence of aggressive content for Group A boys was presumed to be a result of their more intense competitive strivings. Some clinicians who use projective tests are too prone to focus on predictive statements about direct, physical aggression when confronted with a protocol containing aggressive content. One is apt to overlook the fact that the individual may have alternative behavioral channels for expression of aggressive motives.

SUMMARY

For a group of 140 boys and girls in the Fels Research population on whom continuous Binet IQ data were available, a distribution of IQ change was obtained by subtracting each S's smoothed IQ at age 6 from his smoothed IQ at age 10. This distribution of differences was divided into quartiles, and the Rorschach and TAT protocols of the upper (maximum increase in IQ) and lower (maximum decrease in IQ) quartiles were analyzed and compared. The results showed that in comparing the *S*s who showed IQ increases with those showing IQ decreases, the former had, on the TAT, significantly more (*a*) achievement imagery on Cards 1 and 17 BM and (*b*) themes of curiosity about nature on Card 14, and significantly fewer themes of passivity on Card 3 BM. For the boys only, more of the *S*s who increased in IQ had anatomy responses and aggressive imagery on the Rorschach. The results were interpreted as indicating that high need achievement, competitive striving, and curiosity about nature are correlated with gains in IQ score because they may facilitate the acquisition of skills that are measured by the intelligence test.

REFERENCES

1. BAKER, C. T., SONTAG, L. W., and NELSON, VIRGINIA L. Specific ability in IQ change. *J. consult, Psychol.,* 1955, *19*, 307–310.
2. BAYLEY, NANCY. Mental growth in young children. *Yearb. Nat. Soc. Stud. Educ.,* 1940, *39*, (II), 11–47.
3. BAYLEY, NANCY. Consistency and variability in the growth in IQ from birth to eighteen years. *J. genet. Psychol.,* 1949, *75*, 165–196.
4. BRADWAY, KATHERINE. IQ constancy on the Revised Stanford-Binet from the preschool to the junior high school level. *J. genet. Psychol.,* 1944, *65*, 197–217.
5. FISHER, R. A. *Statistical methods for research workers.* (5th ed.) Edinburgh: Oliver & Boyd, 1934.
6. HAGGARD, E. A., DAVIS, A., and HAVIGHURST, R. J. Some factors which influence performance of children on intelligence tests. *Amer. Psychol.,* 1948, *3*, 265–266.
7. KLETT, C. J. Performance of high school students on the Edwards Personal Preference Schedule. *J. consult. Psychol.,* 1957, *21*, 68–72.
8. MCCLELLAND, D. C., ATKINSON, J. W., CLARK, R. A., and LOWELL, E. L. *The achievement motive.* New York: Appleton-Century-Crofts, 1953.
9. RICHARDS, T. W. Mental test performance as a reflection of the child's current life situation: A methodological study. *Child Develpm.,* 1951, *22*, 221–233.
10. SONTAG, L. W., BAKER, C. T., and NELSON, VIRGINIA L. Personality as a determinant of performance. *Amer. J. Orthopsychiat.,* 1955, *25*, 555–562.
11. SONTAG, L. W., BAKER, C. T., and NELSON, VIRGINIA L. Mental growth and personality development. *Monogr. Soc. Res. Child Develpm.,* in press.
12. WELLMANN, BETH L., and MCCANDLESS, B. R. Factors associated with Binet IQ changes of preschool children. *Psychol. Monogr.,* 1946, *60*, No. 2 (Whole No. 278).

"I think that children are more intelligent and less experienced than most parents realize. I have tried to treat my son as if he were a beloved companion with whom I was traveling in a country where I had been before and he had not."

Frederick Lewis Allen
(quoted in *Reader's Digest,*
February 1959, page 28)

54

Stimulation, Enjoyment, and Originality in Dyadic Creativity

E. Paul Torrance

*The final paper in this section is addressed to a topic that has aroused great interest in recent years—creativity. Many tests of creativity have been devised; typically, such tests require that a student (1) produce answers instead of choosing from among a set of suggested answers, and (2) give multiple answers, not just one. For example, a student is asked to list all the ways he can think of to use a brick; this type of item comes from one of the most widely used tests, developed by J. P. Guilford (see his "Three Faces of Intellect," * American Psychologist, 14, 469–479). *Unfortunately, the correlation among the several tests of creativity is not very high, so that the identification of "creative" children depends strongly on which test you use!*

One of the psychologists whose names are most associated with the investigation of creativity is E. Paul Torrance of the University of Georgia, the author of this article.

The history of creative achievement as it has been written is largely the story of individual creativity. There have been of course the rare but well-known instances of dyadic creativity such as that of Wilbur and Orville Wright, Marie and Pierre Curie, Charles and William Mayo, William and Karl Menninger, and Frederick Banting and Charles Best. Less well known was Alexander

Graham Bell's Thomas A. Watson; Robert H. Goddard's wife, Esther; Thomas Edison's John Krueski and other collaborators. In behavioral science there have been the well-known husband and wife teams such as Sheldon and Eleanor Glueck, and Lois and Gardner Murphy, Thelma and Edward L. Thurstone, Margaret and Harry Harlow, Anne Roe and George Gaylord Simpson, and others. Also familiar is the expression, "Behind every great man is a great woman." Perhaps the underlying dynamic of this truth springs from the dyadic creativity of the husband-wife interaction. Thus, dyadic creativity may be more common and more important than is apparent from the history of creative achievement.

Neither the literature of social psychology and group dynamics nor creativity has anything specific to say about dyadic creativity. One of the few psychologists who have attempted to describe the nature of dyadic creativity is Henry A. Murray (1964). He conceptualizes dyadic creativity as dealing with two interdependent regions of imagination operating as a single system. In the dyadic interaction, both members of the dyad try to translate their imaginations into actual, overt reciprocations and collaborations. Murray (1964) uses the analogy of "two people singing a duet and making up the music as they go along [p. 639]." He attempts to formulate the concept of dyadic creativity in terms of different kinds of zestful and capable transmissions resulting in appreciative receptions. In this formulation, the member of the dyad who acts as the transmittor in one instance may function as the receptor in another.

The present investigation arose from the author's research in the broader area of group dynamics and creative functioning and his interest in classroom procedures that facilitate creative functioning. In a study with 5-year-old children he (Torrance, 1969) had found a greater willingness to undertake difficult tasks in dyads than in individual and large group conditions. In a pilot study with both 5-year-old children and college students he (Torrance, 1970) had found that a higher level of originality is attained on creative thinking tests by both members of a dyad than by individuals working alone. The investigation reported herein represents an attempt to explore further the dynamics of dyadic creativity with particular emphasis on the feelings of members of dyads about their own stimulation, enjoyment, and originality. It was hypothesized that individuals taking a test of creative thinking in dyads would attain a higher level of creativity and experience stronger feelings of stimulation, enjoyment, and originality of expression than individuals working alone under standard conditions.

METHOD

SUBJECTS

The subjects were 100 juniors and seniors enrolled in three classes of introductory educational psychology at the University of Georgia. They were about equally divided between majors in elementary education and secondary education; 74 were female and 26 were male. The subjects were assigned randomly to the experimental and control conditions.

MEASURES

The Ask-and-Guess Test of the Torrance Tests of Creative Thinking, Form A (Torrance, 1966) was used as the warm-up task and the Product Improvement Test of this same battery was used as the test task. This task calls for the subject to produce ideas for improving a stuffed toy elephant so that it will be more fun for children to play with and requires 10 minutes. Responses are scored according to a standardized scoring guide for fluency, flexibility, and originality. Extensive reliability and validity data are reported in the norms-technical manual.

A set of 10-point rating scales was used in obtaining self-ratings of feelings of stimulation, enjoyment, and originality of expression. To permit chi-square analyses the 10-point scales for stimulation and enjoyment were collapsed to 3-point scales (High, points 1 and 2; Moderate, 3 and 4; Low, 5 and above). The 10-point scale for self-ratings of originality was collapsed to a 4-point scale (Highly Original, points 1 and 2; Fairly Original, points 3 and 4; Not Very Original, points 5 and 6; Unoriginal and Commonplace, 7 and above).

EXPERIMENTAL TREATMENT

The subjects within each of the three classes were assigned to dyads and to standard, individual, or control conditions. The test booklets had been marked in advance to designate specific dyads and were shuffled thoroughly before being drawn by subjects. Members of dyads were instructed to sit side by side and to call out their responses to one another as they wrote them. They were encouraged to hitchhike on one another's responses and permit themselves to be sparked by one another. They were forbidden, however, to copy or repeat one another's responses.

To provide warm-up and practice in working in dyads, the Ask-and-Guess Test was administered. This test consists of three 5-minute tasks: asking questions about a picture, making guesses about the causes of the action depicted in the picture, and making guesses about the consequences of the action depicted. Instructions for the test task were as follows:

In the middle of this page is a sketch of a stuffed toy elephant of the kind you can buy in most dime stores for about one to two dollars. It is about six inches tall and weighs about a half pound. In the spaces on this page and the next one, list the cleverest, most interesting and unusual ways you can think of for changing this toy elephant so that children will have more fun playing with it. Do not worry about how much the change would cost. Think only about what would make it more fun to play with as a toy.

The rating scales were administered immediately after the subjects completed the test task.

Data were obtained for 100 subjects on the test task but the rating scales of two of the experimental and two of the control subjects could not be used.

RESULTS

The means, standard deviations, and F ratios for the scores on fluency, flexibility, and originality on the Product Improvement Test under dyadic and standard, individual, or control conditions are reported in Table 1. These data indicate that the experimental treatment had a very strong effect on the creative functioning of the subjects in this study as measured by the fluency, flexibility, and originality scores of the Product Improvement Test. The results for flexibility and originality are especially strong.

Table 2 presents the data to permit a comparison of the self-ratings of the experimental and control subjects on feelings of stimulation and enjoyment

TABLE 1

MEANS, STANDARD DEVIATIONS, AND F RATIOS
FOR SCORES OF FLUENCY, FLEXIBILITY, AND
ORIGINALITY ON PRODUCT IMPROVEMENT
TEST UNDER DYADIC AND INDIVIDUAL
CONDITIONS

| | Dyads | | Individual | | |
Measure	M	SD	M	SD	F
Fluency	23.7	8.75	19.0	6.32	9.38*
Flexibility	10.0	2.63	7.6	2.35	22.27*
Originality	27.1	13.86	18.2	9.13	14.36*

Note.—$n = 50$ for each condition.
* $p < .01$.

TABLE 2

SELF-RATINGS OF FEELINGS OF STIMULATION AND
ENJOYMENT ON CREATIVITY TEST TASK IN
DYADS AND INDIVIDUAL CONDITION

| | Dyads | | | Individual | | | |
Variable	High	Moderate	Low	High	Moderate	Low	x^2
Stimulation	34	12	2	25	17	6	4.20*
Enjoyment	39	7	2	27	13	8	7.56*

Note.—$n = 50$ for each condition.
* $p < .05$.

on the test task. It will be noted from these data that the subjects in the experimental or dyadic condition expressed greater feelings of stimulation and enjoyment than the subjects in the control or standard administration of the test.

The data on the self-ratings of originality on the test task are reported in Table 3 for the experimental and control subjects. From these data, it is clear that the subjects in dyads sensed in their performance on the test task a stronger feeling of having produced highly original responses than did subjects working alone as under standard testing conditions.

DISCUSSION

The data yielded by the experiment described herein give strong support to the author's hypothesis that individuals taking a test of creative thinking in dyads would attain a higher level of functioning and experience stronger feelings of stimulation, enjoyment, and originality of expression than individuals working alone under standard test conditions. It should be recognized that these results were obtained from college students who have reasonably good skills in communicating with one another. If similar results could be obtained from disadvantaged children and young people and potential school dropouts, the implications for compensatory education for these groups would be quite promising. It is known from a variety of studies that students in these groups are deficient in verbal skills and perform rather poorly on verbal tests of the kind used in this study. Many observers (Riessman, 1962; Taba & Elkins, 1966), however, have noted that disadvantaged children and youth are quite articulate in their peer groups.

TABLE 3
SELF-RATINGS OF ORIGINALITY ON CREATIVITY TEST TASK
IN DYADS AND INDIVIDUAL CONDITION

Rating	Dyads	Individual
Highly original	17	3
Fairly original	18	20
Not very original	10	15
Unoriginal, commonplace	3	10

Note.—$n = 50$ for each condition. $x^2 = 14.64$, $p < .001$.

The rationale supported by the findings of this study offers promise as a guide in devising classroom procedures to facilitate a higher level of creative functioning in the classroom. The production of original responses places the thinker in a minority of one and being a minority of one makes a person uncomfortable psychologically and requires courage and considerable ego strength. This makes children and young people in formal classroom situations reluctant to express their original ideas even on paper. Since disadvantaged children and youth, potential school dropouts, and the like are especially lacking in self-esteem and weak in ego strength, they are especially vulnerable to classroom pressures against originality of expression. If dyadic interaction can provide the support and stimulation necessary to reduce the pressures against originality of expression, the use of dyadic arrangements in classrooms might possibly result in a higher level of mental functioning among students, especially among disadvantaged children and young people, potential school dropouts, and others who require such psychological support and stimulation. The data also suggest that greater attention might profitably be given the entire problem of dyadic creativity.

REFERENCES

MURRAY, H. A. Dyadic creations. In W. G. Bennis, E. E. Schein, D. E. Berlew, & F. I. Steele (Eds.) *Interpersonal dynamics.* Homewood, Ill.: Dorsey Press, 1964.

RIESSMAN, F. *The culturally deprived child.* New York: Harper & Row, 1962.

TABA, H., & ELKINS, D. *Teaching strategies for the culturally disadvantaged.* Chicago: Rand McNally, 1966.

TORRANCE, E. P. *Torrance Tests of Creative Thinking: Norms-technical manual.* Princeton, N.J.: Personnel Press, 1966.

TORRANCE, E. P. Peer influences on preschool children's willingness to try difficult tasks. *Journal of Psychology,* 1969, *72,* 189–194.

TORRANCE, E. P. Influence of dyadic interaction on creative functioning. *Psychological Reports,* 1970, *26,* 391–394.

X

MOTIVATIONAL DETERMINANTS AND RESULTANTS

Here we deal with psychological conditions, states, or processes that influence human behavior. In the main, these affect a person's use of his abilities more than the existence of the abilities, a topic that was covered in Section IX; hence, our somewhat oversimplified use of the term "motivational." An example of the kinds of inner disposition with which the present section deals is level of aspiration as it bears on school achievement.

Also discussed in this motivational section are the role of fantasy, the positive trait of generosity, and the need for power. While the attributes presented in this section are themselves determinants of behavior, they are also the resultants of other determinants—those described in the foregoing parts of this book.

55

Success and Failure in the Classroom

ROGER G. BARKER

School is an acceptable arena for many pupils who have a high need for scholastic achievement. However, other students lack academic motivation. Roger G. Barker of the University of Kansas discusses the ways those pupils fare. Barker, one of the psychologists influenced by the Gestalt concept, is active in the field of child psychology. Other child psychologists with a Gestalt orientation include the late Heinz Werner and Herman Witkin, who has pioneered the work on perceptual development studied longitudinally. That work is discussed in Personality Through Perception *(Harper, 1954), by Witkin, Lewis, Hertzman, Machover, Meissner, and Wapner, and in* Psychological Differentiation, *by Witkin, Dyk, Faterson, Goodenough, and Karp (Wiley, 1962).*

The influence of Barker and his colleagues led us to see the need to devote a section of this book to "settings" (Section V). Their work on psychological ecology is unique. See, for example, Barker's book with Herbert Wright, Midwest and its Children: The Psychological Ecology of an American Town *(Row, Peterson, 1955).*

Of the numerous roles which the classroom teacher plays, that of dispenser of success and failure is undoubtedly the most impressive and worrisome to the pupils, and one of the most crucial for their present and future adjustment. It is also the role in which many teachers meet their severest conflicts; to fail John or not to fail him, whichever is done, frequently leaves feelings of guilt and anxiety. Clearly an understanding of the conditions and effects of success and failure would be of greatest value to teachers.

When does a child experience success? When does he experience failure? In what ways do these experiences affect behavior? Do the schools make it possible for children to achieve a sufficient number of important success experiences? If not, what can be done about it? A small but very important body of verified knowledge is now available bearing upon these crucial questions. In this article only a very small segment of these data can be presented.

Professor Kurt Lewin, then at the University of Berlin, and his student Ferdinand Hoppe initiated an experimental approach to these questions in the late 1920's.[1] Hoppe first considered the fundamental problem of when a person experiences success and when failure. He presented his adult subjects with simple motor and intellectual tasks such as hanging sixteen rings upon as many hooks as they passed upon a rapidly moving belt, and solving puzzles. During each trial with the tasks, Hoppe observed the subjects secretly and after the completion of each trial he interviewed them thoroughly in an effort to find out the circumstances under which they experienced success and failure. One result was clearly apparent: the experiences of success and failure were unrelated to the actual achievements of the individual. One subject might experience success when he placed four rings on the hooks; another experienced failure when he placed fifteen correctly. In addition, for a particular person, the achievement experienced as success (or failure) continually changed; at one time a single ring correctly placed might give rise to an experience of success, while on a later occasion the placing of six rings would result in an experience of failure. These findings led Hoppe to a conclusion which seems very obvious once it is stated, but one that is so fundamental that it has very wide implications: *the occurrence of success and failure experiences is independent of actual achievement; it is determined, rather, by the goals, expectations and aspirations of the person at the time of the action.* These expected achievements Hoppe called *the level of aspiration.*

---

[1] Hoppe, F., "Erfolg und Misserfolg," *Psychol. Forsch.*, 1930, *14*, 1–62.

Roger G. Barker, "Success and failure in the classroom," *Progressive Education*, 1942, *19*, 221–224. Reprinted by permission.

It is obvious that the level of aspiration is important for on it depends the occurrence of success and failure. Hoppe therefore directed his study to the effects of success and failure experiences on the level of aspiration. He found that after success the level of aspiration is usually raised (i.e. a new and higher goal is set after a lower one is achieved), and that after failure the level of aspiration is usually lowered (i.e. a new and lower goal is set after a high one has not been achieved). He found, in other words, that the level of aspiration shifts in such a way that, whatever the actual achievement of the person, the frequency of his success and failure experiences remains fairly constant. This means that the level of aspiration operates as a mental hygiene factor of great significance. It constitutes a sort of governor; it protects the person against continual failure on the one hand, and against easy achievements which do not give the feeling of success, on the other hand. This fact is behind the frequent observation that feelings of success accompany the process of achieving but disappear after attainment.

Sometimes, however, this mechanism is thrown out of balance and it fails to perform this protective function. In some cases, aspirations are maintained consistently above achievement. The individual is then subjected to continual failure with its disastrous consequences for adjustment and happiness. In other cases, aspirations are placed consistently below achievement with resulting lack of ambition, exaggerated caution, broken morale, cynicism, etc. In both instances very serious personal and social difficulties may develop. It is of the greatest importance, therefore, to determine why the level of aspiration does not function protectively for these persons.

Hoppe suggested that the level of aspiration is set as a compromise between two conflicting tendencies: (1) the desire to avoid the hurt accompanying failure, operating to force aspirations safely below the level of achievement; and (2) the desire to succeed at the highest possible level, operating to push goals above achievement levels. Subsequent investigations suggested that the latter tendency derives from social pressures to do what is most highly approved by society, irrespective of a realistic assessment of one's own capabilities. This conflict between fear of failure and desire to maintain goals that are socially approved results, usually, in a level of aspiration at or near the upper limit of one's ability range.

If this interpretation is correct, it would be expected that an increase in social pressure should alter the level of aspiration. This is, in fact, the case. Subsequent investigations have shown that pupils at the low end of the class achievement distribution aspire, on the average, above the level of their achievement possibilities (and therefore experience failure), while those at the upper end of the achievement distribution set their aspirations below their level of achievement (and therefore experience success).[2]

Although the differences between aspiration and achievement are not great in a quantitative sense, they are psychologically very important. So far as success and failure are concerned, "a miss is as good as a mile." This difference in relation of aspiration to achievement appears to mean that the social pressures of the school situation may operate to throw off-balance the protective mechanism of the level of aspiration, thus subjecting children to exaggerated failure and success experiences.

It is not difficult to understand why these pressures arise in many schools. Social acceptability in an intimate group such as a school class requires a high degree of conformity to group standards in all sorts of public behavior. The first step in achieving such acceptability is to set goals in accordance with the group standards. In schools where evaluation is largely on the basis of academic achievements this means that poor students are forced, by the social pressure of the classroom, to set goals they cannot achieve or else to admit that they are mavericks; both are undesirable alternatives from a mental hygiene viewpoint. There is pressure upon bright students, also, to set their goals in conformity with the achievements of their roommates, rather than with their own.

Adults on the other hand are infrequently subjected to such pressures for long periods of time, for adults are able with considerable success to hide from others certain crucial symbols of their divergence from what is considered good or desirable (such as age, income, family background), and they are able to withdraw when the pressures become too great. Furthermore, achievement in most adult activities is not estimated with the precision that is attempted in many schools. Doctors, lawyers, plumbers and bakers can vary within a considerable range of effectiveness and no one is wiser; they are still adequate. This gives a fundamental security which is denied to pupils who are frequently and publicly evaluated, i.e., acclaimed or humiliated by an authority from whose decisions there is no recourse and in a group from which there is no escape.

---

[2] Hilgard, E. R., E. M. Sait, and G. A. Magaret, "Level of aspiration as affected by relative standing in an experimental social group," *J. Exper. Psychol.,* 1940, *27,* 411–421.

Anderson, H. H. and H. F. Brandt, "Study of motivation involving self-announced goals of fifth grade children and the concept of level of aspiration," *J. Soc. Psychol.,* 1939, *10,* 209–232.

Middle-class pupils are unusually sensitive to these pressures. They are, in effect, subjected to the demands of a single dominating institution, for the family supports the demands of the school. This means that the pressures, the demands, the rewards, the punishments, the successes and the failures of the school are frequently of overwhelming importance to these children. No one with influence will question the righteousness of the school's verdicts or the correctness of its values. If the school is one in which the rewards are all centered about a very limited variety of achievements, for example academic achievements, the child who is relatively dull or uninterested in academic activities must experience continual failure. He will fail even though he is kind, or good looking, or has a sense of humor or has physical prowess, even though he is full of energy, graceful, courageous, friendly or with mechanical abilities. He will fail in school even though these behavior characteristics are very highly valued by many other institutions, until in adolescence he becomes sufficiently independent to establish affiliations with other groups which do reward nonacademic achievement.

Compared with life outside school, many schools distribute success and failure in an extremely unrealistic way. Adults, for example, are inevitably influenced by various pressures, and rewarded according to conflicting values of a variety of institutions and social groups (family, vocation, clique, church, lodge, union, etc.), and these influences are likely to be of somewhat equal potency in their lives. This means that the adult can to some extent balance the failures in one region of his life by successes in other regions. The effects of vocational failures may be mitigated by successes in family and recreational relationships where quite different achievements are valued. In schools that emphasize academic achievement, this kind of balancing is impossible for middle-class children.

What is the consequence of the chronic failure and success that many schools enforce upon great numbers of pupils? We do not know a great amount from scientific experiment but what we do know is very suggestive.

Sears studied the level of aspiration of a group of fifth grade children who had long histories of chronic school failure in reading and arithmetic, and another group with equally consistent histories of school success in reading and arithmetic.[3]

She found that the children who had experienced continual success set their aspirations at a realistic level, i.e., at a level where success was frequently achieved. The children with a history of chronic failure, on the other hand, set their aspirations with little regard for their achievements. Of those in this latter group, some children apparently lived almost exclusively in terms of their aspirations, ignoring completely the fact that their achievements were entirely out of line with their expectations. In these cases the desire for respectability may have forced the children to an imaginary world where the mere gesture of achieving by setting high goals was accepted in lieu of real achievement. The seriousness of this behavior is sufficiently obvious to need no special emphasis. The institutionalized person for whom a gesture is sufficient to convince him he is Napoleon has traveled further along the same path.

The cases where the children failed to set goals even at the level of their poor achievement may involve withdrawal from the activity in any except a very peripheral sense; they may be cases of extreme caution or they may represent attempts to depreciate the importance of the activity by refusing to take it seriously. None of these outcomes of educational effort are desirable.

What can schools do to avoid throwing out of gear the protective mechanism of the level of aspiration with the resulting unfortunate consequences for the success and failure experiences of pupils? The answers are implied in the discussion, but they may be summarized as follows:

(1) broaden the basis for evaluating pupils;

(2) reduce to a minimum the prominence of the relative standing of the pupils;

(3) allow maximum freedom to pupils to set their own goals and to alter them as their success and failure experiences require; i.e., make success possible at all levels of achievement;

(4) reduce the dominance of the teacher.

These conditions can be achieved in different ways. It is interesting to note, however, that they can hardly be avoided if democratic teaching procedures are used, if the interests of the child are followed and if group undertakings are an important part of school activities.

---

[3] Sears, P. S., "Levels of aspiration in academically successful and unsuccessful children," *J. Abnor. and Soc. Psychol.*, 1940, *35*, 498–536.

At times, motives that might disrupt concentration find expression in behaviors that are harmless and sometimes even beneficial. In the first paper of this double selection, Lili Peller conveys the idea that enjoyment of literature, one of the more grace- ful self-indulgences available to man or woman, stems in large part from the need to deal with inner conflicts that are not fully resolved—even in adults. She describes the latent meanings she discerns in the plots of children's books—meanings that ac- count for the satisfaction readers gain from specific types of literature. Prior to her death, Peller was a lay analyst in New York and a member of the faculty of the Philadelphia Association for Psy- choanalysis.

Adding a footnote to the discussion of the mean- ings of children's literature, we quote the conclu- sion of a classic paper written by one of the pioneers of psychoanalytic theory, the late Sandor Ferenczi.

. . . In recent decades the esteem for writers of children's books has greatly risen, in line with the general tendency to relish a much wider range of productions in all fields of art (for instance, primi- tive, exotic, psychotic, and frankly amateurish art). In keeping with this trend, a publisher sometimes even brings out a story written and illustrated by a child. Such a book may be very appealing because its author is so genuine, so earnest, so involved in his own writing—but as a story it usually falls flat.

But a child can spin a daydream with such emo- tional intensity that he will remember it in later years; indeed, he may live his life under its spell. This is especially true when at a time of inner turmoil, he encounters his own, his private day- dream woven into a story. Sometimes we discover only in analysis the strong grip that an early story has had on a person's life. Usually it is one scene of the story or one story character which is vested with emotional significance.

"The poet arouses in us emotions of which we hardly believed ourselves capable" (Freud, 1908). If the adult reader cherishes this ability of the poet, the child with his unlimited eagerness to savor life is wide open to the magic of the storyteller.

A fear or anxiety which remains covered up in everyday life may become broadly visible through the child's reaction to a story. But while a tale may frighten a child, it may give relief too. He discovers that he is not the only one in the world who harbors fears or hatred or spite, emotions that are socially unacceptable. Thus the recent well-meant en- deavors to purge stories of all cruelties, of all mean feelings and of vengeance may actually increase a child's guilt feelings and the burden he carries unaided. . . .

I am going to discuss a number of typical child- hood fantasies and some of the stories built on them. [Not all the story types discussed in the original are included in these excerpts.—EDITOR] Let us start with a plot intended for the very young.

THE FANTASY OF LOSS AND RETURN

A child loses his mother and, after dangerous ad- ventures, is reunited with her. Any number of

[1] Paper presented at the Annual Meeting of the American Psychoanalytic Association in Chicago, May, 1957. A first version had been presented at the Hampstead Child Therapy Clinic, London, 1956.

* Lili Peller, "Daydreams and children's favorite books," *The Psychoanalytic Study of the Child*, 1959, *14*, taken from 414–433. Reprinted by permission of the International Universities Press, Inc., New York

† Excerpt from "Stages in the development of the sense of reality," in Sandor Ferenczi, *Sex in Psychoanalysis* (New York: Basic Books, Inc., 1950), pp. 238–239. Reprinted by permission.

stories use this plot. Because it appeals to the youngest listener, the child in the story is often an animal child. This has the advantage that more gruesome adventures can be included. With an animal as the central figure, the storyteller can introduce the cannibalistic fears and fantasies of young children and thus increase the drama (see, e.g., *The Story about Ping, the Duckling; Peter Rabbit; Curious George, the Monkey*). It is the child who acts out, who runs away, but his leaving is often preceded by some fault or negligence of his mother (or protector) mentioned very casually, and hardly noticed by the reader—the story really gains momentum with the child's escapade.

Let us look at the best known story for very young children, *The Tale of Peter Rabbit*. His mother warns him not to go *near* Mr. McGregor's garden. She has hardly left on her shopping trip when Peter runs right into that forbidden territory. He finds it absolutely full of delicacies, young radishes and tender salad leaves, but Peter's happiness in stuffing himself is very short-lived. He is chased and almost caught and killed. Is it all Peter's fault? It looks this way, yet it never would have happened if his mother had not considered a shopping trip more important than looking after her children.

And so it goes also in the other stories. Curious George would not have ended up in jail had his protector not left him alone on their very first day in the big city where George was surrounded by gadgets tempting him to manipulate them. It is the mother who, by turning her attention temporarily to other matters, loosens the bond between herself and the child (A. Freud, 1953). Even in this simplest type of story there is a conscious plot and another one which reaches consciousness for a brief moment, then sinks back to the preconscious or unconscious. Yet this part contributes to the story's emotional appeal as well as to the motivation and the plausibility of the story hero's conduct. In all art, essential parts remain on the unconscious or preconscious level, and the nursery tale is no exception.

In these stories for very young readers, animals feel, behave, and talk like human beings. But these fantastic elements are not essential; the very same daydream may also be expressed in a cogently realistic story; see e.g., *Oley, the Sea Monster*. Oley is a baby seal that gets picked up and carried away by a sailor while his mother dives for some food. An exciting adventure story follows, with funny and deeply moving events—but nothing that could not have happened in reality. The book even carries a map showing the route through the Great Lakes, the St. Lawrence and around Nova Scotia by which Oley swam back to his mother.

Tales of *fantasy* and realistic "true" stories are considered to be basically different, yet we find that every childhood fantasy can become the backbone for either type of story.

THE FANTASY OF THE REVERSAL OF ROLES

The young son (the small one, the simpleton), the shy one who always is left out of things, proves to be stronger than all his older brothers when a great danger arises. Thus he not only slays the dragon and wins the princess, he also rescues his friends or his father's kingdom—in short, he becomes the beloved and admired benefactor. This is the core of many fairy tales, in which it is often the third, the youngest son whom nobody has taken seriously, and who wins after his older brothers have failed.[3] This is the plot of *Hop o' My Thumb*, of John Ruskin's famous *The King of the Golden River*, and also of the Biblical legend of Joseph and his brothers. The contrast of who seems to be strong and powerful and who is small and helpless, and the sudden unexpected reversal of roles provide the spice of these stories. Again there are completely realistic stories with the same plot, for instance the French story *Moustachio*. Moustachio is the smallest dog in his village, indeed, ridiculously small. Yet on the day of the great hunt, he is the one who finds and holds the vicious wild boar at bay until his master comes and fires the deadly shot. The storyteller's skill, his use of relevant details, makes the improbable victory plausible. . . .

HEROIC TALE—OEDIPAL-LEVEL STORIES

In these tales the hero obtains the goals of oedipal wishes in a form which is acceptable to the ego of the latency child. What we know of other latency fantasies also applies here: their ingredients are akin to those which in stories, dramas, operas, and ballads appeal to an adult audience. The essentials of these fantasies have been presented by Freud (1908, 1909b), and its juvenile version was studied

---

[3] Why is it usually the *third* son who wins? We may think of the symbolic significance of the number three (Abraham, 1923). However, reasons of plot construction offer another explanation. Were the story to speak of one older and one younger brother, the contest between them would resemble too closely the father-son contest, and thus conjure up the oedipal struggle; on the other hand, the account of deeds of a larger number of brothers might be too lengthy, too repetitious—three is the smallest crowd. Finally, the story of the youngest son who succeeds where his older brothers lost out may be a faint memory of archaic conditions where elder sons were murdered or exiled while the youngest, born when the father's strength was declining, stood a better chance of becoming his heir.

by Friedlaender (1942), whose work remains to be of basic importance.

The hero or the heroine lives with one parent or some relatives. Thus at the outset of the story the parents, or at least the parent of the same sex, have been eliminated without the hero's guilt. The grownups in the story accept the child hero as one of them, not as a child. The story depicts the hero's struggle against adverse circumstances and against the villain or villains. But being fearless, resourceful, and a paradigm of many virtues, his eventual triumph is assured.

Friedlaender mentions the following favorite books which use this fantasy: *David Copperfield, Jane Eyre, Treasure Island, Emil and the Detectives;* Anna Freud (1936) has already pointed to *Little Lord Fauntleroy,* and to various fairy tales. Friedlaender attributes the overwhelming popularity of *Jane Eyre* to the fact that in this story the oedipal wish attains a "relatively undisguised" fulfillment. Here I do not follow her. It is the very art of storytelling that the fulfillment of the primal wish is achieved and at the same time skillfully veiled. Occasionally, it even remains barred from consciousness. There is only one other alternative left to the artist: a hero (or heroine) who attains undisguised gratification goes to his own destruction—like Oedipus. But Jane, after long and tragic trials and tribulations, eventually marries her man, and they live fairly happily ever after. Throughout the story, Jane is a very proper girl. I do not agree that in her story the oedipal fantasies "break through in almost bare-faced fashion." Yet Friedlaender is right in one point: the gratification in *Jane Eyre* seems more direct than, for instance, in *Treasure Island* or *David Copperfield.*

A remark of Freud helps us to understand Jane Eyre's seemingly more overt wish fulfillment. In his story the poet may incorporate the boy's version of the oedipal wish—centering on gratification of aggression and ambition—or the poet may build the story on the feminine counterpart and focus on direct libidinal gratification: a prince charming who leads the heroine home. But it is a difference of focus only—both versions contain or allude to both gratifications, the erotic and the ambitious one. . . .

THE STORIES FOR "HAVE NOTS"

This group may not seem to be a counterpart to the others mentioned so far, but rather a catch-all term for a number of types, namely, for all stories which owe their special appeal less to the tale they spin or to the story characters they bring to life than to the *milieu* they describe. This discrepancy disappears when we extend the meaning of the term "daydream" to indicate not only a narrative, a sequence of events, but also a static *tableau,* the vision of a blissful scene, which includes the daydreamer in his enjoyment of a coveted environment. The readers of these tales are recruited from the ranks of those who pine for an ambient not attainable to them in reality. Here we think of the story describing ways and joys of *teenagers* for those who are still too timid or too young for them; there are the stories of *school life,* i.e., life in a British public school for those who are too young, or, more often, who do not quite belong to the socioeconomic strata who can afford such a school (Orwell, 1939). There are *nature, mystery, adventure, big game* and *Wildwest* stories for those who are barred from these experiences in reality. One generation ago, youthful readers loved historical novels which took them into a romanticized past. Today, stories of space travel have partly replaced them.

Of course, all these stories have also a hero; he has satellites and adversaries; there is a plot, and the story may represent hack-writing or may be well done—in either event a great deal of the attraction is due to the coveted milieu into which the readers are transposed. This is their bait; and this formula is by no means restricted to juveniles but accounts for the popularity of many books, movies, and plays for all ages.

Books may give pleasure through more than one fantasy. Biographies enable the reader to identify with a father image. You have to be famous to rate a biography, and achieving fame can be translated into psychoanalytic concepts as achieving a flamboyant oedipal victory. But a well-written biography does more than this: by reporting personal anecdotes, by letting the reader in on trivial day-by-day incidents, it fosters in him the illusion of hobnobbing with the great and the mighty. This is our reason for mentioning biographies here among the "Have Not" stories. (Receiving factual information may of course be also highly pleasurable, but is outside our topic.)

I suspect that the countless "How-To-Do-It" books, pamphlets and magazines describing hobbies and skills of amateurs are cherished not only by the "doers," to whom they deliver technical information, but also (or mainly?) by the "idlers," for whom they substitute for the doing. Not only an imaginative tale, also a sober step-by-step account can incite and feed daydreams.

I have presented typical daydreams paraphrasing the important emotional constellations of childhood. There is the relationship of the little child to the protective and despotic preoedipal mother. The young child cannot fight her, nor oppose her—the drama is restricted to the possibility of escape and return or rescue. The Loss-and-Return fantasy is really an elaboration of the infant's earliest play activity, the peek-a-boo game. There the plot also consists of separation and reunion.

Several types of daydream mirror the oedipal tension. The Reversal-of-Roles fantasy deals with the relationship to older siblings and to the early father, experienced as fearfully big and strong. The Hero and Heroine fantasies refer more directly to the oedipal constellation. The Bad-Boy stories glorify open defiance of all father images. Actually both the Hero and the Bad-Boy stories tell of oedipal victory, but the bad boy's triumph is quickly attained and short-lived, while the hero attains his goal the slow and arduous way. There are the fantasies of having a twin, an alter ego, or a most faithful companion; and finally the last-mentioned omnibus group which "sells" admission to the coveted but unattainable milieu. Thus daydreams born and fomented by all basic childhood constellations seem covered—but the best group of stories for the young child is still to be discussed.

THE EARLY TALE

I am speaking of such universal favorites as the *Christopher Robin* stories, *The Story of Dr. Dolittle,* the *Mary Poppins* books, and Grahame's *The Wind in the Willows.* In some respect, the books of *Babar, the Elephant* also belong here.

In all groups discussed so far we find books which are little masterpieces and others where the writer has learned the formula and uses it glibly. But in this last group I know of no such hackwriting. These are tales which cannot easily be imitated. If not handled by a literary master, the plot would fall apart, and there would not be left a story worth the telling.

In *Winnie-the-Pooh,* for instance, there is a group of toy animals who for all intents and purposes are alive, although they are at the same time plain stuffed animals. Each one lives in his own house—but all are within easy walking distance from each other. They share adventures and expeditions and all kinds of pleasures and hardships. Winnie-the-Pooh is not their leader, but ranks first in seniority, he is *primus inter pares.* And he is a conceited, greedy, but lovable toy bear. The real leader, the figure who turns up in emergencies, is Christopher Robin, the five-year-old to whom they all belong. Only a few lines of each chapter deal with C.R. in person, but when he is badly needed he is right at hand. The personality of each toy animal emerges clearly and so do the positive, the likeable as well as the weaker qualities of its character.

Now let us take a quick glance at *Dr. Dolittle.* He is an elderly, smallish, shy doctor. The drawings show him pot-bellied, bald, a rather ridiculous figure. His outstanding qualities are his simplicity and kindness. No part of the globe is too distant to travel to when he learns about sick animals in need of his magical cure. His home

is in the English country side; originally his sister kept house for him, but she became disgusted and left when the doctor refused to give up the crocodile who ate up the linoleum. As the tale begins, the good doctor lives all alone with his faithful animals, a parrot, a dog, a baby pig, an owl, a duck, and a monkey. These, his household companions, are introduced by name and drawn as individual characters. Besides them are nameless throngs of animals who move in and out of the story.

The central figure of another classic series is *Mary Poppins,* the governess whom the eastwind blows into the home of four children at number Seventeen Cherry Tree Lane. The pictures show her rather unkindly as an old-fashioned, bony spinster with quite shabby yet frilly clothing and accessories. She is at times harsh, moody, often snappy in her commands and answers—but she works magic and enjoys a terrific reputation with various mysterious personages. Her children have wonderful adventures and thus are willing to put up with her occasional bad days.

And, finally, *The Wind in the Willows (The Wind in the Reeds,* as it was originally called) tells the story of four devoted friends, Toad, Rat, Mole and Badger. Each one has his own house and each house is quite different from the others. Rat lives at the bank of the busy river. Toad is rich and keeps residence in a splendid mansion, Badger's ancient and many-chambered home is in the Wild Woods, and Mole has very modest ("compact," his friends call it) quarters underground. Among the friends there is continuous visiting, passing by and dropping in, and staying for hours and days and sumptuous meals. These casual visits alternate with adventures undertaken jointly by two or three of them. The Almighty Protector of this chummy group appears only once. He is the Piper-at-the-Gates-of-Dawn, whose presence is felt long before he is seen, whose sweet chant is heard before he appears as a faun-shaped figure. Yet his animals know that in distress he will be at their side.

The togetherness of these friends, their deep loyalty, fills the books and shows in their cozy visits as well as in their wild and glorious adventures. Their enemies are nameless and faceless flocks of animals. A few incidentally introduced humans stay at the fringe of the narrative and their feelings remain hazy and are not really woven into the story. They appear and disappear as their function in the story requires not growing into story characters.

Here are four obviously very diverse tales. They differ not only in plot, in characters, in style, they also appeal to different age groups and are far apart in their literary levels. What, then, do they have in common? In each story we find a Group of loyal friends and we find a Protector who can work magic (at least in the eyes of his entourage; whatever five-year-old Christopher plans or figures out appears as magic to his toy animals). Every member of this group has unique gifts and skills and foibles. In the animal stories there is usually one of a kind, one of a species, and animals who in reality could never live together, like a badger and a toad, or a pig and a parrot, are intimates. No member of the circle is defined as either young or old, as male or female.[5] The magician-protector's sex is given, but he (or she) is of an age or appearance where genital maleness or femaleness is of little consequence. . . .

The magician-protector stays offstage or near the wings and the friends' actions and their feelings really carry the story. The character of each one of them is etched distinctly, although age and sex are left vague. In these tales *the two great dichotomies, male-female, old-young,* which pervade and shape our life and bring so much pressure upon the ego of the young child, are mostly nonexistent. These stories seem to say: "See what good times and how much adventure you can have if you just forget and ignore those things."

The friends in these stories are devoted to one another, yet their love is conflict-free. There is no jealousy. Let us see what else is absent. Family relations of all kinds are nonexistent or they are at the very fringe of the story, and the feelings of these incidental relatives for one another are lukewarm in comparison with the ardent loyalty and the intimacy welding the friends together. The exception here is a parent's love for its small, helpless baby. Kanga loves Roo, Otter loves Little Portly.

In all the chapters of contented home life or risky adventures nothing happens that would suggest a comparison between what Tom does and what Dick does, or between their appearance. And perhaps as a further assurance against the pressure of comparison, of jealousy and competition, most of them belong to different species. Who will compare a monkey with an owl or a mole with a toad? The members of the closely knit circle are not measured against one another. And more than this: their earlier self is not compared with their later self. They are the same people at the end of the story as they were when we first met them. This, too, is in sharp contrast to the hero of the oedipal tale, who at the close of the story is not only in different circumstances, but is changed, an "improved" person. The good and the sly and bad people he met, the events he went through, joy and sorrow, love and loneliness—have molded him. The endearing characters of Lofting's, of Milne's and of Grahame's tales remain throughout the story what they were at the very beginning. Each one is as boastful or greedy, or as kind or gullible as we found him when he first entered. This is not because these stories, by and large, appeal to younger children who are but little aware of the passage of time. After all, heroes intended for a very young age group (e.g., Pinocchio or Bambi) grow up and change, and this recasting of their inner self becomes an essential part of the story. But the heroes of the Early Tale are static characters.[6]

The reader of the oedipal story identifies with the hero and with his success, and by doing so he vicariously shares the hero's pressures, The charm of the Early Tale may be due to their complete absence.

Frequently the characters of these stories wear animal masks.[7] These are the masks of animals rather than real animals. Not only do they talk and wear clothes, but besides giving them a few convincing and specific animal features, there is no attempt to present a biologically correct picture of their animal life. Why, then, are these animal masks employed by the writer? A human character who in a story is not defined according to his approximate age remains so vague, so insipid, that he does not win our interest, and a human being whose sex remains undefined arouses anxiety. In the Early Tale the animals are depicted with just enough authentic detail to screen the absence of those features which are usually indispensable for creating a plausible character, i.e., the missing age and sex. *The animal mask supports the mechanism of denial.* The paucity of concrete features gives them a heraldic quality.

In the preoedipal phase the child is almost unaware that there are men and women. The difference he perceives is between him and the adults, the persons who can fulfill his wishes or deny them all. The world is divided into children and grown-ups. In the oedipal phase he is aware of sexual differences but likely to forget that other division which formerly loomed so large, he is cocky enough to consider himself the equal of his parents. I know that I am over-simplifying—yet basically this is correct: from being innocent of one of the great dichotomies (male-female) the child turns to ignore the other one (child-adult). Time and again, however, this dichotomy is sharply brought to his attention. He is only a child and thus can neither

---

[5] Exception: the children in the *Mary Poppins* stories. And the general principle may as well be stated here: I am presenting a story structure which exists in the abstract, yet is violated in one or the other point in each story. In relation to the perfect fantasy each story is like a web torn in a different spot in every instance and thus the pattern, i.e., the basic daydream, can be reconstructed by bringing them side by side and comparing them.

[6] In the discussion in London, 1956, Dr. B. Lantos pointed to their similarity with the inhabitants of the Garden Eden whose serene life flowed along without strife, murder, or sexuality.

[7] The Pogo characters of Walt Kelly, which use the childish form of the comic strip to amuse adults and to bootleg some biting social and political criticism, also are animal masks, also one of a kind and nondescript in their sex and age.

be his mother's partner nor his father's successful competitor. In his happy moments he succeeds in denying that he is small and unequipped for being a lover, but painful experiences bring him brusquely back to reality. That a child envies the grownups has always been known, but Freud pointed to the direct and gross male (or female) aspirations which go with the wish to be big. These fantastic aspirations make the child's happy illusions and his downfalls so intense and potentially traumatic.

At this point I thought I had discovered a new way of looking at the oedipal constellation. But then I happened to scan the last pages of Little Hans's case history and came across the daydreams he produced at the end of his analysis (Freud, 1909b). Hans has two "happiness fantasies" (*"Glücksfantasien"*), which testify to his newly-won ability to cope with the pressures in his life. The plumber comes in one fantasy to screw off his buttocks and his penis and to give him larger ones instead; in the other, Hans has many children and takes them to the toilet, wipes their behind, their "podl," in short, does everything a mother does with her little children.

With these fantasies Hans has regained his former cheerfulness. They provide the gratifications from which reality excludes him because he is only a little boy. With the first fantasy he denies the gulf separating the boy from the grown man, while the second cancels the difference between male and female. The Early Tale employs the opposite technique: the confining and often painful dichotomies are blissfully absent or irrelevant for the story characters.

The Early Tale builds on the defense mechanisms of denial. A quick glance at another story character may clarify what is being done here. *Peter Pan* is a little boy who refuses to grow up—that is, he is well aware of the difference between old and young, but says NO to something he does not like, he *negates* the need to grow up. The Early Tale goes one step further: there nobody heard of such a thing as growing up. The animal friends are a delightful mixture of childishness and grownupness.[8]

At the core of every successful story there is a universal daydream. The tale begins, the curtain rises, the reader identifies with the hero, and enjoys experiences inaccessible to him in reality. The intensity and the grip of emotions he finds in the story would at times be painful in real life.

The pleasure yielded by a daydream is intense, yet definitely restricted. The storyteller makes the daydream articulate, hence communicable, and he

makes it ego-syntonic, thereby changing and multiplying the enjoyment. The hack-writer takes the daydream and uses it pretty much "as is." The poet paraphrases and veils it, and he even destroys some of its easy and glib gratification.

Earlier studies had assumed that the story in which we meet our own daydream makes it fully conscious by lending words to it. I believe that essential parts of a story, of its plot, of the story characters' motivations and conflicts remain unconscious or preconscious and *for this very reason* arouse our emotions, our sympathy most effectfully. Here a good children's story shares the dynamics of all art.

Many nursery tales employ magical features, i.e., denial in fantasy. Miracles happen with complete ease and make the story possible. The well-known traditional fairy tales are very old and come to us from a time when adults, too, believed in magic. In a preliterate world the laws of reality have less validity, they are less stringent for the reasoning of anyone, child or adult.

The storyteller, like the poet, must believe in the tale he spins. If he makes a conscious effort to write "for little children," his story is likely to sound concocted or it becomes pedantic. This may explain why the majority of fairy tales written today are so trite and syrupy. But recent decades have given us one type of story where fantastic happenings are closely interwoven with highly realistic and prosaic details which in a way deny the first denial. The reader is shuttled between the two, and this double denial may account for the story's ability to hold his interest.

The sincere modern fairy tale is at home in both the world of magic and denial in fantasy *and* in the well-observed world of sober, everyday reality.

We have discussed daydreams, paraphrasing important human relationships and aspirations, and we also took a close look at one type of contemporary fairy tales. Because these stories usually appeal to young children and because they remind us of a simple, carefree age, we called them "Early Tales." In these stories, problems of genital sexuality and the slow encroachments of death are eliminated. Yet thanks to the poet's art, the sutures where these powerful realities were cut out from the fabric of human life are invisible.

---

[8] Suppression is the conscious attempt to forget something, while repression refers to the unconscious mechanism. I am using negation and denial in a parallel fashion.

BIBLIOGRAPHY

JUVENILES AND NOVELS

BARRIE, J. M. (1906), *Peter Pan*.
BRONTË, C. (1847), *Jane Eyre*.
BURNETT, F. H. (1886), *Little Lord Fauntleroy*.
COLLODI, C. (1880), *The Adventures of Pinocchio*.

DE BRUNHOFF, J. (1933), *Babar, the Elephant.**

DICKENS, C. (1850), *David Copperfield.*

ETS, M. (1947), *Oley, the Sea Monster.*

FLACK, M. (1933), *The Story about Ping.*

GRAHAME, K. (1908), *The Wind in the Willows.*

KÄSTNER, E. (1929), *Emil and the Detectives.*

LOFTING, H. (1920), *The Story of Dr. Dolittle.**

MILNE, A. A. (1926), *Winnie-the-Pooh.**

POTTER, B. (1902), *The Tale of Peter Rabbit.**

REY, A. H. (1941), *Curious George.**

RIGBY, D. (1947), *Moustachio.*

RUSKIN, J. (1851), *The King of the Golden River.*

SALTEN, F. (1926), *Bambi.*

STEVENSON, R. L. (1883), *Treasure Island.*

TRAVERS, P. (1934), *Mary Poppins.**

PSYCHOANALYTIC AND GENERAL

ABRAHAM, K. (1923), Two Contributions to the Study of Symbols. *Clinical Papers and Essays on Psychoanalysis.* New York: Basic Books, 1955.

BUXBAUM, E. (1941), The Role of Detective Stories in a Child's Analysis, *Psa. Quart.,* X.

FRAIBERG, S. (1954), Tales of the Discovery of the Secret Treasure. *This Annual,* IX.

FREUD, A. (1936), Chapter VI: Denial in Phantasy. *The Ego and the Mechanisms of Defense.* New York: International Universities Press, 1946.

FREUD, A. (1953), On Losing and Getting Lost. Presented at the International Psychoanalytical Congress, London.

FREUD, S. (1906), The Relation of the Poet to Day-Dreaming. *Collected Papers,* IV. London: Hogarth Press, 1925.

FREUD, S. (1909b), Family Romances. *Collected Papers,* V. London: Hogarth Press, 1950.

FRIEDLAENDER, K. (1942), Children's Books and Their Function in Latency and Prepuberty. *Am. Imago,* III.

ORWELL, G. (1939), Boys' Weeklies. In *A Collection of Essays by George Orwell.* New York: Doubleday, 1954.

* *First volume of a series.*—EDITOR

(Stages in the Development of the Sense of Reality)

In fairy-tales . . . phantasies of omnipotence are and remain the dominating ones. Just where we have most humbly to bow before the forces of Nature, the fairy-tale comes to our aid with its typical motives. In reality we are weak, hence the heroes of fairy-tales are strong and unconquerable; in our activities and our knowledge we are cramped and hindered by time and space, hence in fairy-tales one is immortal, is in a hundred places at the same time, sees into the future and knows the past. The ponderousness, the solidity, and the impenetrability of matter obstruct our way every moment: in the fairy-tale, however, man has wings, his eyes pierce the walls, his magic wand opens all doors. Reality is a hard fight for existence; in the fairy-tale the words "little table, be spread" are sufficient. A man may live in perpetual fear of attacks from dangerous beasts and fierce foes; in the fairy-tale a magic cap enables every transformation and makes us inaccessible. How hard it is in reality to attain love that can fulfill all our wishes! In the fairy-tale the hero is irresistible, or he bewitches with a magic gesture.

Thus the fairy-tale, through which grown-ups are so fond of relating to their children their own unfulfilled and repressed wishes, really brings the forfeited situation of omnipotence to a last, artistic presentation.

57

Generosity in Nursery School Boys

ELDRED RUTHERFORD
AND PAUL MUSSEN

*Psychologists have focused a great deal of their energy and attention on the study of human difficulties—on the troubled or the anti-social and troublesome. Since the classic study by Lois Barclay Murphy (*Social Behavior and Child Personality: An Exploratory Study of Some Roots of Sympathy* [*Columbia University Press, 1937*]), relatively little research has been done on prosocial behaviors. Recently, there has been a cheering trend toward more work on desirable attributes. One instance is the work of Staub (see Section V). This study of generosity by Eldred Rutherford and Paul Mussen is another instance of such investigations.*

Rutherford and Mussen have long collaborated, as evidenced by selections authored by them in previous editions of this book. Mussen is professor of psychology at the University of California at Berkeley. In 1970 he edited a new edition of the famous Carmichael's Manual of Child Psychology *(Wiley). Rutherford has taught psychology for some years at California's San Jose State College.*

This study was supported by the National Institute of Child Health and Human Development, U.S. Public Health Service, under research grant HD 01650. The authors wish to express their appreciation to Mrs. Natasha Wist, of San Jose State College, for her invaluable assistance in collecting and analyzing the data for this study.

Eldred Rutherford and Paul Mussen, "Generosity in nursery school boys," *Child Development*, 1968, *39*, 755–765. Reprinted by permission. © 1968 by the Society for Research in Child Development, Inc.

The now classic studies of Hartshorne and May (1928–1930) started a long series of investigations of children's conscience, strength of character, moral characteristics, and judgments. While there are some exceptions (Grinder, 1962; Sears, Maccoby, & Levin, 1957; Sears, Rau, & Alpert, 1965), these have generally been less concerned with the personality correlates and familial antecedents of moral behavior and standards than with establishing patterns of behavior reflecting underlying moral dispositions or traits (e.g., Aronfreed, 1961; Burton, 1963; Johnson, 1962; Kohlberg, 1963). This is somewhat surprising in view of the fact that parental teaching, guidance, and treatment have ordinarily been considered crucial for the acquisition of high standards of moral behavior.

Students of socialization view the development of superego or conscience, like sex typing, as a major product of the child's identification with his parents. There is evidence that the acquisition of sex-appropriate patterns of interests and activities (sex typing) is a consequence of what Mowrer has termed "developmental identification" (Mowrer, 1952)—identification motivated by warmth and affection toward the model, in this case, the like-sexed parent.

But the relation between moral behavior and developmental identification, if it exists, has yet to be established empirically. Data from several investigations indicate that high levels of conscience development are associated with positive, affectionate attachment to nurturant parents, but the correlations are small and the evidence does not seem compelling. For example, Sears et al. (1957) showed that a child's tendency toward confessing transgression, as reported by the mother, was related to parental warmth, as rated by an interviewer. Resistance to temptation has also been found to be related to some criteria of dependency (and, presumably, parental nurturance) among nursery school children (Sears et al., 1965).

Most research on moral development, like that mentioned above, has been focused on prohibitions, the proscriptive "thou shalt not" aspects of morality, such as resistance to temptation, cheating, and stealing. Although Hoffman (1963) dealt with "consideration for others" as a dependent variable, relatively little research attention has been given to other behaviors that reflect more altruistic, interpersonally oriented kinds of morality—compassion, generosity, cooperation, sympathy. Operational definitions of high conscience typically involve either compliance with rules about prohibited behavior or guilt about transgressions. Perhaps this research emphasis on prohibitions is due to the fact that, in the moral training of young children in our culture, proscriptive rules are more readily conveyed and more strongly emphasized than more positive, altruistic values. Certainly parents and other agents of socialization have many opportunities to "teach" children those proscriptive rules by rewarding approved responses and by punishing behaviors that violate such rules. Direct tuition may be the primary source of the child's acquisition of these proscriptions; parental identification—modeling one's behavior after the parents'—may play a comparatively minor role here.

Moreover, the products of identification are presumably *patterns* of behavior rather than isolated, restricted, discrete responses. If the tendency to resist temptation is a result of the process of identification, this characteristic would be positively related to other moral behaviors. But Hartshorne and May (1928–1930) found only low, though positive, correlations among various types of moral behavior. Children were not highly consistent in their behavior. For example, cheating in one situation was not generally predictive of cheating in another situation. This suggests that acquiring proscriptive rules of morality depends upon specific learning experiences rather than on identification with parents.

It is, of course, possible that proscriptive rules of behavior are "taught" by means of reward and punishment, while more positive—perhaps more complex—characteristics are acquired by means of developmental identification with a model. If this is true, the development of such characteristics as altruism, cooperation, generosity, and sympathy would be associated with warm, nurturant parent-child relationships.

This is in fact the first hypothesis of the present study, which is focused on one aspect of moral behavior—generosity. More specifically, this hypothesis states that high levels of generosity in young children will be related to perceptions of their like-sexed parent (the primary identificand) as warm, affectionate, and nurturant.

In addition, if a high level of generosity is a consequent of the identification process, it should be one aspect of a *pattern* of moral behaviors correlated with other positive characteristics. The second major hypothesis of the study, therefore, is that generosity is positively related to such characteristics as cooperation, altruism, sympathy, and kindness.

METHODS

The subjects of the study were middle-class Caucasian boys between the ages of 4-6 and 4-11, enrolled in nursery schools in a large California city. This age group was considered most appropriate to test the hypothesis about the relation between parent-child interactions and the acquisition of moral behavior, since it may be assumed that during these years parental and familial influences predominate over the kinds of peer influences that may be prepotent later on.

THE ASSESSMENT OF GENEROSITY

The initial sample consisted of 63 boys in seven nursery school classes who were observed individually in a structured situation designed to assess level of generosity. Subjects considered high and low in generosity on the basis of their performance in this situation were selected for further study.

Each subject was taken to a small room by a "teacher" (investigator's assistant). The teacher presented him with 18 identical pieces of candy, all of them of a kind he had previously chosen from a wide assortment as the most desirable. He was also given three plastic bags and was told that one was for him and the other two were for "the two children in the nursery school you like best." He was then asked to divide the candies into the three bags, putting as many as he wanted in his own bag, which he could take home with him at the end of the day. Pretesting of this technique indicated that children of this age readily understood the instructions and knew that keeping more candies for themselves meant that there would be fewer candies for their two friends. The *generosity score* was simply the number of candies the subject gave away.

The range of possible scores was, of course, 0–18. The mean for all 63 boys tested initially was 10.7. Fourteen of the 63 subjects, the nongenerous group, got scores of zero, that is, they kept all 18 candies. The generous (high) group, 17 boys, donated 15 or more candies to their friends. These two groups of boys were selected for further study.

Ratings of generosity by the boys' teachers were used to assess the validity of this situational measure of generosity. These teachers were asked to sort name cards, each giving the name of a boy in her class, into five piles, pile one for those "who are among the most generous, least selfish nursery school boys I have ever known" and pile five for those "who are among the most selfish, least generous nursery school boys I have known." Pile three contained the names of boys "who seem about average in generosity, neither highly generous nor highly selfish in their behavior." Ratings of 1–5 were assigned to the boys on the basis of this sort. The mean ratings for the groups of boys who scored generous and nongenerous in their disposition of the candy were 2.12 and 3.36, respectively

($t = 3.13$, $p < .01$, $df = 20$). It may be assumed that teachers' ratings were based on extensive observations of their pupils' behavior. The generosity measure used in this study therefore appears to be generally valid, that is, scores in the structured situational test reflect generalized tendencies to behave generously.

DOLL PLAY

The hypotheses were tested by relating generosity scores to data derived from children's responses in doll play, a situational test of competitiveness, and a series of 21 teachers' ratings (the Fels scales [Baldwin, 1948]).

Twenty-two of the subjects (12 generous and 10 nongenerous boys) responded to a projective, semi-structured doll-play situation, administered by *E*, using a standardized set of instructions. The boys' responses were used in testing both major hypotheses of the study. Using a simple set of family dolls (mother, father, and child), each subject played out, and thus completed, seven incomplete stories. These were specifically designed to elicit the child's attitudes toward his parents and his perceptions of them, as well as some self-concepts —particularly those aspects related to feelings of generosity, hostility, and sympathy. The following two stories are illustrative:

PARENT-CHILD RELATIONS STORY

SCENE.—In the house, parent dolls are in their bed, and the child doll is in his.
INSTRUCTIONS.—"It's late at night. Everyone is asleep. Suddenly the boy has a bad dream and wakes up very frightened. What do you think he will do? Show me."

SELF-CONCEPT STORY

SCENE.—Mother in kitchen by window looking into yard, child doll and two other children are in yard.
INSTRUCTIONS.—"Mother calls to her son to come in and get cookies. The boy brings the last three cookies in the house—there are no more—for him and friends. But just then, another friend comes to play. Now there are four children and only three cookies. What will the boy do? Show me."

The assumption underlying the interpretation and scoring of these stories is that the child's descriptions of the hero reflect his self-concepts, and what he says about the parent dolls reveals his attitudes toward his own parents. Thus it is assumed that the child who portrays the child hero as behaving generously sees himself as a generous person and the one who describes the doll father as nurturant considers his own father to be nurturant.

Each story was recorded verbatim and scored for presence or absence of the following variables: (*a*) Father Nurturance or Mother Nurturance (FN or MN) (the hero or other children receive help, attention, or reassurance from the father or mother); (*b*) Father Sympathy or Mother Sympathy (FS or MS) (the father or the mother comforts a child in distress); (*c*) Child Dependency (CD) (a child seeks help from another person—usually a parent or parents); (*d*) Child Sympathy (CS) (the hero attends to another child's distress); (*e*) Child Generosity (CG) (the hero shares a limited supply of valuable goods, e.g., toys, cookies, with other children); and (*f*) Interpersonal Hostility (IH) (verbal or physical expression of aggression between participants in the story).

In order to eliminate bias, all scoring was done "blind," that is, the scorer had no knowledge of the subject's generosity status. The reliability of the scoring system was checked by having two psychologists score the stories independently. The two scorers agreed perfectly in 91 per cent of the scores of the 22 protocols (154 stories).

The subject's score for each doll-play variable was the total number of stories in which it appeared.

COMPETITION GAME

After the doll-play stories had been completed, each subject participated with the investigator in a "racing game," which was based on one of Murphy's situational tests (Murphy, 1956). In nine races, the child raced a doll against the investigator's doll along the length of a yardstick on the floor. The investigator moved his doll at a constant, moderately slow speed, and the child could win or lose the race with a large or small margin of victory. In no instance did the subject permit the investigator to win. The competitiveness score was the subject's average margin of victory for all nine races.

TEACHER'S RATINGS

Nursery teachers rated each of the 31 generous and nongenerous subjects they knew on 21 nine-point rating scales, the Fels scales (Baldwin, 1948). These scales describe a number of characteristics directly relevant to a test of the second major hypothesis of the study. These were: affectionateness, aggressiveness, competitiveness, conscience, friendliness, gregariousness, kindness, leadership, obedience, patience, quarrelsomeness, sensitiveness, shyness, suggestibility, tenacity.

Unfortunately, it was impossible to evaluate the interrater reliability of these ratings because no child was rated by more than one teacher.

RESULTS AND DISCUSSION

The first hypothesis of the study maintains that the acquisition of moral behavior is a product of developmental identification. If this hypothesis is valid, high levels of generosity in young boys, an index of moral development, should be related to perceptions of their fathers as warm, nurturant, and affectionate. The boy's relation with his father was assumed to be most crucial, since that parent is ordinarily the boy's principal identificand.

The hypothesis was tested by comparing the doll-play FN scores of the generous and nongenerous groups. The results of this comparison are presented in Table 1, which gives the mean scores of the two groups in FN and MN and in the child variables assessed by means of the doll-play techniques.

The data clearly support the first hypothesis: the mean FN score of the highly generous boys was significantly higher than that of the boys low in generosity. Generosity in young boys is in fact related to variables underlying developmental identification, specifically to their perceptions of their fathers as warm and nurturant. These data may therefore be interpreted as being entirely consistent with, and thus supportive of, the developmental identification hypothesis which holds that a child's identification with a parent is motivated by his feelings of warmth and affection for that parent.

Since the child's perceptions of his parents were assessed on the basis of his verbalized responses in a doll-play situation, it might be argued that the child's generosity is an antecedent rather than a consequent of his perceptions of his father. The child's descriptions of the doll-play figures may be projections of his own generous characteristics. If this were the case, these findings would have no bearing on the problem of the relation between strength of identification and the acquisition of behaviors related to superego development.

While there are no data in this study that permit direct refutation of this argument, there are a number of reasons for believing that it is not valid. For one thing, while the generous and nongenerous boys differed significantly in FN scores, the two groups did not differ significantly in MN scores, in the degree to which they attributed nurturant, affectionate characteristics to the mother in their stories. If characteristics attributed to doll-play figures were simply projections of the subjects' feelings about themselves, the generous boys would portray *both* parents as highly nurturant and giving. The fact that generous boys view the father as more nurturant does not seem consistent with the argument that descriptions of him are projections of the child's self-concepts. The finding is more consistent with the developmental identification hypothesis.

Furthermore, although there were no direct assessments of parent-child relationships in the present study, the findings of other investigations indicate that the child's perceptions of parental warmth and nurturance are highly correlated with actual parental behavior, at least as the latter is evaluated in parental interviews (Mussen & Distler, 1960; Mussen & Rutherford, 1963). For these reasons, it seems most plausible to regard these positive, nurturant perceptions of the fathers as determinants, rather than consequents, of the child's level of generosity. This is of course what would be predicted on the basis of the developmental identification hypothesis.

Another finding from the doll-play data seems particularly pertinent to the first hypothesis. This involves parental sympathy, a characteristic that was seldom depicted in these subjects' stories. In fact, only six subjects told stories in which the father comforted a child in distress (e.g., holding a hurt child; telling a child "don't worry, you'll feel all right in a minute"; taking a child into the house "for a cookie so he will feel better"). All six of

TABLE 1

MEAN SCORES OF BOYS HIGH AND LOW IN GENEROSITY ON PARENTAL AND SELF-PERCEPTION (DOLL PLAY) VARIABLES

Variable	High (N = 12)	Low (N = 10)	d	t	p[a]
Parental:					
Mother Nurturance (MN)	2.25	1.90	0.35	0.83	N.S.
Father Nurturance (FN)	1.40	0.17	1.23	2.24	< .05
Child:					
Generosity	2.00	1.10	0.90	2.65	< .02
Sympathy	1.08	1.10	0.02	0.06	N.S.
Hostility	0.42	1.20	0.78	2.17	< .05
Dependency	1.67	3.70	2.03	3.43	< .01

[a] *p* is for two-tail tests (*df* = 20).

these boys were in the highly generous group; none of the boys in the nongenerous groups told a story involving parental sympathy. Application of a χ^2 test to the data, with Yates's correction, yielded a a value of 4.59 ($p < .05$).

This finding, although based on only relatively few subjects, suggests that fathers of generous boys, in addition to being warm and nurturant in their relationships with their sons, are more likely to respond to a child's distress with sympathy and attempts to comfort him. If, as we assumed, the child's descriptions of the fathers in his stories accurately reflect his perceptions of his own father's behavior, the fathers of generous boys are apparently more likely than the others to provide models of sympathy, generosity, altruism, and compassion. It may be suggested that paternal nurturance serves a double function: it motivates the child to emulate the father's behavior and, at the same time, it provides a model of behavior that is essentially kind and considerate. The father's sympathy and compassion may be conceptualized by the child as generosity. In identifying with the father, he incorporates this characteristic and behaves in generous ways.

The second general hypothesis of the study holds that, if a high level of generosity is a consequent of identification with the parents, it should be part of a *pattern* of moral behaviors, not a discrete, isolated characteristic. If this hypothesis is valid, level of generosity would be positively correlated to such characteristics as cooperation, altruism, lack of interpersonal aggression, and sympathy.

Several of the techniques used in the study provided data for testing this hypothesis. Certain aspects of the child's self-concept—some of them related to morality—were assessed by means of doll play. Comparisons of the means of the generous and nongenerous groups on the relevant doll-play child scores are summarized in Table 1. These data provide some general support for the hypothesis that moral characteristics are positively intercorrelated. On the basis of the characteristics attributed to the children in their doll-play stories, it may be inferred that highly generous boys, in contrast to those low in generosity, are motivated to behave generously and have less feeling of hostility and aggression toward others.

As Table 1 indicates, generous boys show significantly less dependency in their stories than the nongenerous group. While dependency (or its reverse, independence) is not generally considered a moral quality, this finding seems highly consistent with the second hypothesis. Being generous to others undoubtedly requires some impulse control, some capacity for suppressing desires for immediate gratification (such as taking all the available candy). The development of such capacity—and the maturity it implies—would certainly seem to depend upon identification with an adult model. This would be particularly true of boys identifying with their fathers because independent behavior, in our culture, is commonly regarded as a masculine sex-typed characteristic. The relation between high levels of generosity and a strong sense of independence may therefore be interpreted as indicating that generosity is part of a pattern of characteristics acquired through identification with the father.

Children who manifest high levels of generosity would be expected to be less fiercely competitive than those who are not generous. The subjects' reactions in the structured competitive situation (racing) in which they all participated indicated that this is true. The average lead of the nongenerous boys over the investigator-competitor, based on nine races, was 3.69 inches, while the corresponding margin for boys who were highly generous was only 2.65 inches ($t = 2.13$, $p < .05$). Behaviorally, then, high generosity seems to be part of a pattern which involves less intense interpersonal competition, less need to win out over a competitor by a great margin.

Each subject was rated by his teacher on 21 characteristics (the Fels scales), and these ratings were also used to test the second hypothesis. Table 2 summarizes the data for the two groups.

The groups differed significantly, or nearly significantly, in 5 of the 21 rated characteristics. Four of the five differences were in directions consistent with findings from doll play or the competition situation and were supportive of the second hypothesis. Thus, in comparison with boys low in generosity, those who were highly generous were rated as more kindly, less competitive (or more cooperative)—consistent with the behavioral measure—less aggressive and less quarrelsome—consistent with less interpersonal hostility in doll play.

In addition, the generous boys were regarded by their nursery school teachers as less gregarious than their nongenerous peers. Apparently their activities are less directed toward others and toward the group. They appear to be more independent and self-sufficient. This is very likely another reflection of their relatively low dependency needs, already noted in their doll-play stories. From this point of view, relatively low ratings in gregariousness may be regarded as an indication of a sense of independence that is a product of identification with the father.

In sum, the relevant data from the doll-play techniques, from a behavioral test of competitiveness, and from teachers' ratings (which are pre-

TABLE 2
PERSONAL CHARACTERISTICS OF BOYS HIGH AND LOW IN GENEROSITY

Rating Variable	High (N = 17)	Low (N = 14)	d	t	p[a]
Gregariousness	3.00	5.23	2.23	2.75	< .02
Competitiveness	3.18	5.07	1.89	2.44	.02
Quarrelsomeness	3.53	4.78	1.25	1.91	< .10
Kindness	3.35	2.28	1.07	1.92	< .10
Aggressiveness	3.12	4.50	1.38	1.66	.10
Patience	4.65	3.64	1.01	1.20	N.S.
Tenacity	3.88	3.31	0.57	0.79	N.S.
Affectionateness	3.53	4.54	1.01	1.19	N.S.
Leadership	3.29	4.64	1.35	1.48	N.S.
Masculinity	2.53	3.15	0.62	0.95	N.S.
Obedience	3.65	2.78	0.87	1.21	N.S.
Apprehensiveness	3.76	4.57	0.81	1.02	N.S.
Sensitiveness	3.29	3.50	0.21	0.26	N.S.
Shyness	4.88	4.21	0.67	0.74	N.S.
Suggestibleness	3.18	3.77	0.59	0.84	N.S.
Cheerfulness	2.53	2.36	0.17	0.24	N.S.
Conscience	4.38	4.57	0.19	0.24	N.S.
Curiosity	2.53	3.56	1.03	1.47	N.S.
Emotional control	3.71	3.77	0.06	0.07	N.S.
Gross activity	2.53	3.26	1.09	1.57	N.S.
Friendliness	2.59	2.00	0.59	1.07	N.S.

[a] p is for two-tail tests ($df = 20$).

sumably based on extensive sampling of the overt behavior of the children) are highly supportive of the second hypothesis. Generosity as tested in the situational tests used in this study does appear, as the second hypothesis predicts, to be part of a pattern of interrelated, altruistic characteristics. Apparently, then, generosity is not an isolated, discrete bit of moral behavior that develops independently of other types of behavior that are manifestations of high moral standards governing interpersonal relations. This is precisely what one would expect if this characteristic were a result of an identification process in which the identificand is actually a model of behavior indicative of generosity, rather than the outcome of specific experiences involving positive and negative reinforcements for generous and nongenerous behavior.

REFERENCES

ARONFREED, J. The nature, variety, and social patterning of moral responses to transgression. *Journal of Abnormal and Social Psychology*, 1961, *63*, 223–241.

BALDWIN, A. Socialization and the parent-child relationship. *Child Development*, 1948, *19*, 127–136.

BURTON, R. V. The generality of honesty reconsidered. *Psychological Review*, 1963, *70*, 481–500.

GRINDER, R. Parental child-rearing practices, conscience, and resistance to temptation of sixth grade children. *Child Development*, 1962, *33*, 802–820.

HARTSHORNE, H., & MAY, M. A. *Studies in the nature of character*, Vol. 1: *Studies in deceit;* Vol. 2, *Studies in self-control;* Vol. 3, *Studies in the organization of character*. New York: Macmillan, 1928–1930.

HOFFMAN, M. L. Parent discipline and the child's consideration for others. *Child Development*, 1963, *34*, 573–588.

JOHNSON, R. A study of children's moral judgments. *Child Development*, 1962, *33*, 327–354.

KOHLBERG, L. The development of children's orientations toward a moral order, I: Sequence in the development of moral thought. *Vita Humana*, 1963, *6*, 11–33.

MOWRER, O. H. Identification: a link between learning theory and psychotherapy. In *Learning theory and personality dynamics*. New York: Ronald, 1952. Pp. 573–616.

MURPHY, L. B. *Personality in young children*. New York: Basic Books, 1956.

MUSSEN, P., & DISTLER, L. Child-rearing antecedents of masculine identification in kindergarten boys. *Child Development*, 1960, *31*, 89–100.

MUSSEN, P., & RUTHERFORD, E. Parent-child relations and parental personality in relation to young children's sex-role preferences. *Child Development*, 1963, *34*, 589–607.

SEARS, R. R., MACCOBY, E. E., & LEVIN, H. *Patterns of child-rearing*. Evanston, Ill.: Row, Peterson, 1957.

SEARS, R. R., RAU, L., & ALPERT, R. *Identification and child-rearing*. Stanford, Calif.: Stanford University Press, 1965.

58

Women and the Need for Power—Two Alternative Manifestations[1]

DAVID G. WINTER

The following study of the need for power among college women reflects the recent interest in the fact that certain motivations traditionally recognized as "male" are also important in determining the behavior of females. In this pioneering article, the similarities and the differences in the power motive for the two sexes are discussed. The author, David G. Winter, is a member of the faculty at Wesleyan College in Connecticut.

Many psychologists now recognize that their concentration on men as research subjects (Schultz, 1969) is perceived as political oppression. Moreover, it is surely harmful to the validity and generalizability of their findings and, hence, of their science. This fault is particularly evident in the research on variables which are intimately involved with present-day social stereotypes of sex roles—topics such as power, aggression, achievement, and dependency. This paper is a preliminary report on behaviors associated with the need for power (*n* Power) among college women. Previous *n* Power research, conducted exclusively with men, has shown that *n* Power predicts office-holding, owning prestige possessions, and drinking (Winter, 1968a; 1971a). Among women the action correlates may be quite different, and so it is important that they be studied separately.

PRELIMINARY ANALOGIES FROM ACHIEVEMENT MOTIVATION RESEARCH

The research strategy, measurement techniques, and general psychometric properties associated with *n* Power are similar to those of *n* Achievement; both variables are also deeply bound up with sex roles and sex stereotypes. Therefore, it is useful to note the issues that were raised, and the findings that were obtained when researchers began to study the achievement motive in women (French and Lesser, 1964; Horner, 1969). These are noted below under three headings:

I. Arousal experiments. McClelland et al. (1953, pp. 178–181) reported that "women do not show an increase in *n* Achievement scores as a result of achievement-involving instructions . . . [referring to] leadership capacity and intelligence;" but that reference to social acceptability appears to arouse *n* Achievement. Subsequent research presented a confusing picture. French and Lesser (1964) clarified the findings with the following interpretation: Arousal of *n* Achievement among women will "work" if the arousal situation is congruent with the woman's conception of her own sex role (or "value orientation" with respect to sex roles); references to intelligence will arouse *n* Achievement among intellectually-oriented women; references to "Women's Role" success worked with women who valued that role.[2]

II. Performance Correlates of the Motive. French and Lesser found that *n* Achievement related to performance when that performance was perceived as related to, or congruent with, the woman's conception of her own sex role. Moreover, the sex of the stimulus figures used in measuring the motive was important. In general, motive scores derived from stories written to sentence stems (or pictures) involving women predicted performance better than those derived from stories written to male stimulus figures, for women with both kinds of sex role conception. There were complex interactions.

[1] The findings reported in this paper are based on research carried out for an Honors Thesis at Connecticut College by Carol Feinstein, and at Wheaton College by David Hamilton. Barbarajean McNeill, Cynthia Hamilton, Connie Sutherland, and Frances Viggiani helped in the administration and analysis. Loretta Konstan scored the stories. Abigail Stewart made suggestions and criticized the interpretations. I am grateful for the help of these people. The work was supported by NIH Grant MH 16,687.

[2] With respect to this heading, it is interesting to note that a re-analysis of TATS collected by S. Winter (Characteristics of fantasy while nursing. *J. Pers.*, 1969, *37*, 58–72), showed no differences in *n* Power between mothers nursing babies and those not nursing.

Based on a paper presented at the Eastern Psychological Association, April, 1971. Used by permission.

III. *Structure of the Scoring System.* So far, no one had found reason to question the usefulness of the basic scoring definitions and subcategories of *n* Achievement when applied to women. However, Horner (1969) identified a distinct motive, "Fear of Success," among college women. Here there was a reversal of the linkages between outcome (success vs. failure) and affect (happiness vs. sadness) that made up the achievement motive scoring system. Horner argued that this reversal of fantasy linkage, such that positive outcome was associated with negative affect, was derived from a woman's socialization into a traditional sex-role.

This paper is focused mainly on the second heading: What are the performance correlates of the power motive in women? Under what conditions do the correlates observed for men also apply to women? What are the female correlates of *n* Power, and how are they related to different conceptions of the female role?

SUBJECTS AND PROCEDURES

Three different groups of college undergraduate women were asked to write stories to TAT-type pictures, and were then given a variety of other questionnaires and procedures. Table 1 gives data about the characteristics of the sample, pictures used, and other details. The questionnaires contained a variety of different items, which were designed to explore the widest possible variety of things that might relate to the power motive. Only in a few cases was there direct overlap between questions asked of one group and those asked of another, because the studies were originally carried out independently. Thus the present survey of findings should really be considered as a gathering of fruitful early data that should be further investigated and cross-validated on other groups of women.

All stories were scored for *n* Power according to a revised system (Winter, 1968b) by a trained, expert scorer. In addition, each scored story was further classified as "Hope of Power" or "Fear of Power," a distinction which Winter (1971b) devised as a parallel to Atkinson and Feather's "Hope of Success" and "Fear of Failure" aspects of the achievement motive. Thus there are scores for three power-related motives: An overall *n* Power score; a "Hope of Power" score which is conceived

TABLE 1
CHARACTERISTICS OF SAMPLES

	1. Wheaton College (Norton, Mass.); tested in Spring, 1970.	2. Wheaton College tested in Autumn, 1970.	3. Connecticut Coll. tested in Autumn, 1970.
Abbreviations used in this paper:	W-1	W-2	CT
Number of Subjects	49	59	67
Undergraduate class	upperclassmen	31 freshmen 23 sophomores 2 juniors 3 seniors	40 sophomores 19 juniors 8 seniors
"TAT" pictures used		1. A middle-aged woman with a young boy. 2. A tired-looking couple sitting on a marble bench. 3. An older man and a younger man in an office. 4. A man and a woman in a restaurant with a guitarist.	1. A young woman alone in contemplation. 2. A man and a woman in a restaurant with a guitarist. 3. Two women in lab coats, with scientific apparatus. 4. A couple on a roof, at night. 5. A middle-aged woman with a young boy. 6. A man and a woman on a trapeze.
Additional data collected	Questionnaire	"Who Am I?" Test Draw-a-Person test Questionnaire	Questionnaire

TABLE 2
INTERCORRELATIONS OF SCORES ON
POWER-RELATED MOTIVES

W-1 Sample (N = 59)

	Hope of Power	Fear of Power
N Power	.80**	.48**
Hope of Power		−.13

CT Sample (N = 67)

	Hope of Power	Fear of Power
N Power	.77**	.55**
Hope of Power		−.16

** p < .01

as the approach motive, and a "Fear of Power" score which is conceived as the avoidance motive. The latter two sum to the total *n* Power score. Table 2 shows the intercorrelations for these three scores. The approach and avoidance aspects of the power motive are essentially uncorrelated with each other, but both are significantly related to the total score. This pattern is consistent both with results obtained with men and with the theoretical framework of approach and avoidance motives constructed by Atkinson and Feather (1966, pp. 89–90).

RESULTS I: VALIDATION OF SOME MALE *n* POWER CORRELATES

First, we shall present findings which suggest that, at least under some circumstances, the *n* Power measures predict behaviors for women that are sim- ilar to those predicted for men. The Connecticut College sample were asked "What offices have you held while at college?" Those who had been officers were higher in Hope of Power, lower in Fear of Power, but not different in overall *n* Power than those who had not held office. (See Table 3.) These findings, which only approach the usual level of significance for Fear of Power, increase dramatically when we consider only the motive scores based on stories written to pictures of women (Numbers 1, 3, and 5 in the Connecticut sample; see Table 1). In other words, under just those conditions predicted by French and Lesser, we find the power motive scores related to this basic power-related behavior.

Some additional findings are also consistent with previous studies of men; undergraduate women who own prestige possessions (in this case both an automobile and a television set, at college) are higher in *n* Power than those who do not (1st **W** sample.)* Those women who have had two or more traffic accidents are higher in the Fear of Power than those who have had none or only one. (Winter, 1971b, interprets this finding as indicating that the motive to avoid power leads to a generalized problem of dealing with structure, particularly under stress.) *N* Power is also related to hostile verbal behavior, in this case to the intensity of the person's favorite expressions of profanity as determined by answers to the question: "Imagine a situation where you feel like swearing. What expression would you use?" Expressions were scaled from 0 to 5, where

* It is, of course, possible that this relation is a reflection of SES variables.—EDITOR

TABLE 3
VALIDATION OF SOME MALE *n* POWER CORRELATES

I. Office-Holding (CT Sample)

		Mean scores on:	
	n Power	Hope of Power	Fear of Power
Officers in organizations (N = 20)	8.40	6.90	1.50
Not officers (N = 47)	7.30	4.34	2.96
Differences	1.10	2.56	−1.46
	t = .92	t = 2.53	t = 1.93
		p < .02 (2 tailed)	p < .07 (2 tailed)

II. Consumption of alcohol (CT Sample)

		Correlations with:	
	n Power	Hope of Power	Fear of Power
Amount of wine consumed (average)	.53**	.39*	.31
Amount of liquor consumed (average)	.06	−.07	.32
Wine index[a]	.50**	.31	.36
Liquor index[a]	.03	−.10	.30

* p < .05
** p < .01

[a] Index of quantity consumed on average occasion times frequency of these occasions; both measured on a 5-point scale.

1 was for a polite expression (rats, etc.) and 5 was for a sex/perversion expression (r = .24, p .10).

McClelland et al. (1971) report relationships between the power motive and drinking liquor. In the Connecticut study, n Power was related to drinking wine (both the average amount drunk, and an index of average quantity times frequency). (See Table 3.) This difference may suggest a sex difference in the choice of beverage as related to the power motive, or it may suggest changes in the drinking correlates of n Power among the present generation of college students, for whom wine is often an adjunct to marijuana usage.

These findings are important because they help to give some very basic construct validity to the measure of n Power. Indeed, we would be reluctant to call the measure n Power if it did not predict such actions. Of more importance in the present context, however, are the relationships of the power motive scores to various behaviors that involve a woman's conception of her role, vis-a-vis existing cultural stereotypes and patterns.

RESULTS II: ACTION CORRELATES RELATED TO SEX ROLE CONCEPTIONS

We shall consider Hope of Power and Fear of Power separately. Table 4 presents some correlates of the approach motive. When asked, "What religious figures, male or female, do you admire?" women high in n Power (Wheaton) tend to mention women more often (p < .07 two tailed). When the request is broadened to "Name a few people you admire," women high in Hope of Power tend more often to mention "famous" women (those of national or historical prominence, generally because of their careers), (p < .15, one tailed because it was a cross validation) and less often to mention their own mother (including the more general term "parents") (p < .15 two tailed). On the "Who Am I?" questionnaire, women high in Hope of Power (Wheaton, 2nd sample) tend more often to use categories of sex (e.g., "a woman"), religion, occupation (e.g., "studying to be a teacher") (all of this at p < .05 or .01), and territory, e.g., "living in Massachusetts" (p < .10). They are less likely to use attributes of self-determination of goals (e.g., "trying to get ahead") (p < .01). There is no relationship between Hope of Power and the number of phrases or categories used in the test as a whole. All of the categories used more frequently by women high in Hope of Power are basic *ascribed categories of social identity* (Gordon, 1968). In contrast, Hope of Power seems unrelated to *personal attributes* or subjective feelings about the self. We might conclude that for women, the Hope of Power is related to having a relatively greater sense of one's exter-

nal, social identity—or at least a greater salience of this aspect of identity.

While Hope of Power is not related to reported sexual behavior (Connecticut College sample), among those women who say that they have had sexual intercourse, Hope of Power is higher among those who describe themselves as "aggressive" rather than "passive" in a sexual relationship (p < .02, two tailed).

Taking all of the results together, we could conclude that women high in Hope of Power find it important that they are women; they tend to define themselves in terms of occupations; they tend to hold offices in organizations. This suggests that for women, the Hope of Power is related to behavior in much the same way as for men. Alternatively, for women high in the Hope of Power, traditional cultural stereotypes about sex-roles seem to have less importance in channeling their power-related behavior (through complexes of expectancies and incentives). Nevertheless, the identification of self as a woman is *more* salient. Over all, we could call the Hope of Power, in women, a "Joan of Arc" or "Liberated" style of seeking power goals. In some respects the pattern is similar to that for men; yet sex—and sex-role—is very salient even if only as something not to be followed (see George Bernard Shaw's play "St. Joan").

The results concerning Fear of Power are presented in Table 4. The pattern seems to fit, rather closely, the traditional stereotype of how women are supposed to behave in order to get power, and how they are supposed to use the power they have. First, Fear of Power is negatively related to describing the self in terms of "Intellectual" attributes (p < .10, two tailed). In other words, college women high on Fear of Power are inclined to avoid getting too close to intellectual activity. If they plan a career at all, it is far less likely to be a "male" career (i.e., a career which is "appropriate" for men according to the cultural stereotype); and more likely to be something such as a teacher, to have a "part-time" career, or else simply marry and raise a family (p < .05 two tailed). Women at Wheaton whose fathers attended the Spring "Fathers' Weekend" are significantly higher in Fear of Power than those whose fathers did not attend (p < .02 two tailed). Those who regularly read two or more "women's magazines" tended to be high in Fear of Power (p < .12). Finally, among the Connecticut College women, Fear of Power is related to taking courses at Wesleyan University (a nearby college which was largely male) and to the frequency of using marijuana (rs = .27 and .24 respectively, both are significant at .05 level). These all suggest a concern with meeting men and doing things that will attract them. One final response is of interest: When

TABLE 4
CORRELATES OF THE FEAR OF POWER SCORE

	Mean Fear of Power score
I. The "Who Am I?" Questionnaire (W-2 Sample)	
Those mentioning two or more Intellectual ($N = 10$)	.70
Those mentioning none or one ($N = 49$)	2.41
Difference	−1.71; $t = 1.85$
	$p < .10$ 2-tailed
II. Career Plans (CT Sample)	
Those mentioning a "male" career (i.e. one which is "appropriate" for men in terms of cultural sex-role stereotypes) ($N = 11$)	.82
Those mentioning a "female" career, a part-time career, "working until marriage," or only marriage ($N = 45$)	2.44
Difference	−1.62; $t = 2.08$
	$p < .05$ 2-tailed
III. Suitcase Question (W-1 and W-2 Samples)	
Those mentioning an evaluative adjective ("Cute," "nice," "sexy," etc.) in describing clothing to be taken in a suitcase "if you were to pack a suitcase for a date at another college. . . ." ($N = 17$)	3.88
Those not mentioning such adjectives ($N = 31$)	2.06; $t = 2.60$
	$p = .01$, 2-tailed
Those mentioning an evaluative adjective, W-2 Sample ($N = 11$)	4.18
Those not mentioning, W-2 sample ($N = 48$)	1.65; $t = 2.98$
	$p < .005$ 1-tailed
IV. Women's Magazines (W-2 Sample)	
Those who report reading regularly two or more "Women's magazines" ($N = 13$)	3.15
Those who report reading none or one ($N = 46$)	1.82; $t = 1.59$
	$p < .12$ 2-tailed

	Correlations with Fear of Power Score: ($N = 67$)
V. Aspects of College Living (CT Sample)	
Reported frequency of smoking marijuana (6-point scale)	.24*
Reported frequency of using dexedrine (ibid.)	.11
Reported frequency of using LSD (ibid.)	−.04
Number of courses taken at Wesleyan University	.27*

* $p < .05$

asked ". . . if you were to pack a suitcase for a date at another college, . . . what would you put in the suitcase?" Women high on Fear of Power tended more often to use evaluative adjectives such as "cute," "nice," or "sexy" to describe some article of clothing that they would pack ($p < .01$ for each W sample).

All of these findings seem to relate to a concern with playing the "cute" girl who shuns the life of the mind, is interested in "women's things," is conscious of the impact of her appearance when out in public, and finally, who is literally "Daddy's girl." Our cultural folklore has it that this is the way (or at least the major way) for women to get power: in the words of Gloria Steinem (1969), they "marry power." It probably originates as the young girl learns to shape her power behaviors and concerns in such a way as to preserve the tie of affection to

her father, as Stewart (1971) suggests. What is the Fear of Power pattern in adult fantasy? That is, how is it scored? It means that power needs are either fused with explicit altruistic concerns, or else that the power impulse is checked by anxiety, doubt, disapproval, or irony (See Winter, 1971b). In later life, it means having continually to channel power needs into behaviors which will please men and capture their power for one's own vicarious enjoyment as a "power behind the throne." It is a story even older than Cleopatra.

DISCUSSION

These two patterns of the power motive in women (i.e., "Joan of Arc" and "Cleopatra"), with their historical labels, seem to overlap rather closely with the approach and avoidance aspects of the motive. This is not to say that further specification, and use of sex-role conceptions as a moderator variable, would not improve the prediction of behavior from motive scores. However, our cultural stereotypes do seem to be that women should fear power and seek it in an indirect way, while men—and liberated women—can approach it directly.

REFERENCES

ATKINSON, J. W., & FEATHER, M. T. A theory of achievement motivation. New York: John Wiley & Sons, Inc., 1964.

FRENCH, ELIZABETH G., & LESSER, G. S. Some characteristics of the achievement motive in women. J. Ahearn, Soc. Psychol., 1964, *68,* 119–128.

GORDON, C. Self-conceptions: configurations of content. In C. Gordon and K. J. Gorgon (Eds.) *The self in social interaction.* New York: John Wiley & Sons, Inc., 1968, pp. 115–136.

HORNER, MATIMA. Fear of success in women. *Psychology Today,* October, 1969, pp. 36–38, 62.

MCCLELLAND, D. C., ATKINSON, J. W., CLARK, R. A., & LOWELL, E. L. *The achievement motive.* New York: Appleton-Century-Crofts, 1953.

MCCLELLAND, D. C., DAVIS, W. M., WANNER, E., & KALIN, R. *Alcohol and human motivation.* New York: The Free Press, 1971.

SCHULTZ, D. P. The human subject in psychological research. *Psychol. Bull.,* 1969, *72,* 214–228.

STEINEM, GLORIA. Women and power. In C. Falker (Ed.) *The power game.* New York: Simon & Schuster, Inc., 1969, pp. 161–171.

STEWART, ABIGAIL J. The nature of women: a study of female responses to male definition. Unpublished honors thesis, Wesleyan University, 1971.

WINTER, D. G. Need for power in thought and action. *Proceedings of the 76th annual convention of the American Psychological Association.* Washington: American Psychological Association, 1968, 429–430 (a).

WINTER, D. G. A revised scoring system for the need for power (*n* Power). Unpublished manuscript, Wesleyan University, 1968 (b).

WINTER, D. G. The need for power in college men: action correlates and relationship to drinking. In McClelland et al., *Alcohol and human motivation,* ch. 5. New York: The Free Press, 1971 (a).

WINTER, D. G. The power motive. Unpublished manuscript, Wesleyan University, 1971 (b).

XI

SPECIFIC EDUCATIONAL IMPLICATIONS

The papers in this section focus on instructional issues. To varying degrees all of the determinants of behavior discussed in previous parts of the book affect the behaviors subsumed under the label "educational implications." It will be obvious to the reader that many of the articles in other sections might well have been placed here. We have chosen to place those items elsewhere, instead of concentrating them all in this section, to underscore the fundamental continuity of the fields of child development and educational psychology.

The important distinction to be made is not between child development and educational psychology, but, rather, between (1) both of these topics, as aspects of the science of psychology, and (2) educational practice. The aim of psychology is to develop systematic knowledge about behavior, to seek answers to questions that might be highly abstract; the goal of education is to determine policy, to design and implement educational programs. The psychologist's role, in the search for knowledge, allows him the luxury of waiting until all the data are in—until he is satisfied with his answer to a question. The educator, on the other hand, must make decisions: he must select and train teachers, and adopt a curriculum for the year. The classroom teacher must make myriad decisions every day—there is often no opportunity to test out alternative strategies. When faced by a first-grader who has a temper tantrum during the arithmetic lesson, the teacher *must* adopt a course of action.

How can the practitioner use the general knowledge that is offered by the psychologist? He must take from the research and theory whatever he can use to make informed decisions and to make his actions as effective as possible. It is hoped that he will look closely at what he has done, in order to evaluate his decisions. One can indeed conceptualize the role of the teacher as one of "hypothesis-making" and "hypothesis-testing." That is done by Frederick J. McDonald in his book *Educational Psychology*, second edition (Belmont, California: Wadsworth Publishing Co., 1965).*

Is the task fundamentally one of applying findings from basic research? N. L. Gage, professor of educational psychology at Stanford University and editor of the extremely useful *Handbook of Research on Teaching* (Chicago: Rand McNally and Co., 1963), says:

> What *must* [the teacher] do, if his behavior is to have the desired effect on the comprehension of his youngsters? How can the behavior of one person, a teacher, have an effect on another person's comprehension of a concept or principle? . . .
> My answer, in very general terms, is that the teacher will manipulate the learner's environment, in accordance with the laws of logic and cognition, in the same way that he can influence another person's perceptions by manipulating the environment in accordance with the laws of perception. . . .
> The teacher, by the same token, can compel us to comprehend concepts and principles, depending on whether the stimuli or ideas themselves exist in certain patterns, whether they have certain relationships to one another,

---

* On this theme, see the quotation by William James that follows the preface of this volume.

and, of course, on whether the pupil has certain cognitive capacities, sets, and the like.[1]

Compare this with Bruner's statement:

> ... Part of the failure of educational psychology was its failure to grasp the full scope of its mission. It has too readily assumed that its central task was the application of learning theory to education—or, in turn, the application of personality or of group dynamics or whatnot. In fact, none of these efforts produced a major contribution to educational practice largely because the task was not really one of application in any obvious sense, but of formulation. Learning theory, for example, is distilled from descriptions of behavior in situations where the environment has been arranged either for the convenience of observing learning behavior or out of a theoretical interest in some special aspect of learning—reinforcement, cue distinctiveness, or whatnot. But a theory of instruction, which must be at the heart of educational psychology, is principally concerned with *how* to arrange environments to *optimize* learning according to various criteria—e.g., to optimize transfer or retrievability of information or whatnot.[2]

When you have finished your reading (and the course) you may lean toward one or the other of these views. And if you get practical experience, you may modify these views over time.

Recent work on the psychology of reading provides a good example of a "new style" in educational research. The plethora of studies of educational methods, comparing their effectiveness in typical classrooms, has, unfortunately, produced very little useful information. This has resulted in more stress on basic research. At first, much of the basic research focused on a rather narrow definition of "reading," that is, the ability to "decode" from an unfamiliar orthographic code to the already-mastered speech code. Most recently, other aspects of reading— especially comprehension—have attracted attention, reflecting the strong influence of cognitive psychology. The articles on reading in this section will show the student how a curriculum area is attacked. The reader is also urged to examine other articles which involve reading, including those by Litcher and Johnson in Section V and by Labov and Robins in Section VI.

In today's rapidly changing world, the promise of technology is great. Programmed instruction is now coming of age in the form of computer-assisted instruction. Teaching machines have provoked both a great deal of work and a good deal of debate. The current models (both theoretical and actual) are based on the earlier work of B. F. Skinner. Sidney L. Pressey, long at Ohio State University and now at the University of Arizona, is generally credited with being the first to devise a "teaching machine." As is frequently the case, the climate was not favorable at the time, and not much development occurred. (This is in marked contrast to what happened to Skinner's invention of a teaching machine.) Pressey has written an article critical of the ways the new devices are being used.[3]

Educational technology provides one way to cope with an important reality, the enormous amount of individual variation among students. There has been a long history of research on individual differences—witness the development

---

[1] From N. L. Gage, Toward a cognitive theory of teaching, *Teachers College Record*, 1964, *65*, 408–412 (p. 410).

[2] From J. S. Bruner, Education as social invention, *The Journal of Social Issues*, 1964, *20*, 21–33 (p. 32).

[3] "A puncture of the huge 'programming' boom?" *Teachers College Record*, 1964, *65*, 413–418.

and importance of testing. However, as Gerald S. Lesser, professor of developmental psychology at Harvard University, points out, knowledge of individual differences is not enough. We must add to that knowledge a "... range of instructional alternatives to fit particular children. We must discover how to adjust and adapt our instructional strategies—the choice of curriculum, its content, level, sequence, pace, and style of presentation—to the differences we have identified among students. Given an enlarged understanding of individual differences, it becomes obvious that, instead of seeking a single 'best' instructional arrangement, the teacher's task is that of building options in the instructional arrangements needed to fit particular learners." These words are taken from Professor Lesser's new book *Psychology and Educational Practice* (Glenview, Ill.: Scott, Foresman and Co., 1971). The student may wish to look at that book after reading the relevant articles in this volume, such as the one by Yando and Kagan in Section IX.

59

The Growth of Mind[1]

Jerome S. Bruner

This selection, by Jerome S. Bruner (long a professor of psychology and director of the Center for Cognitive Studies at Harvard University, and now the Watts Professor of Psychology at Oxford University), was Bruner's presidential address to the American Psychological Association. In the paper he probes the relation between cognitive development and pedagogy.

These past several years, I have had the painful pleasure—and it has been both—of exploring two aspects of the cognitive processes that were new to me. One was cognitive development, the other pedagogy. I knew, as we all know, that the two were closely related, and it was my naive hope that, betimes, the relation would come clear to me. Indeed, 2 years ago when I first knew that in early September 1965 I would be standing here, delivering this lecture, I said to myself that I would use the occasion to set forth to my colleagues what I had been able to find out about this vexed subject, the relation of pedagogy and development. It seemed obvious then that in 2 years one could get to the heart of the matter.

The 2 years have gone by. I have had the privilege of addressing this distinguished audience

(Bruner, 1964) on some of our findings concerning the development of cognitive processes in children, and I have similarly set forth what I hope are not entirely unreasonable ideas about pedagogy (Bruner, in press). I am still in a very deep quandary concerning the relation of these two enterprises. The heart of the matter still eludes me, but I shall stand by my resolve. I begin on this autobiographical note so that you may know in advance why this evening is more an exercise in conjecture than a cataloguing of solid conclusions.

What is most unique about man is that his growth as an individual depends upon the history of his species—not upon a history reflected in genes and chromosomes but, rather, reflected in a culture external to man's tissue and wider in scope than is embodied in any one man's competency. Perforce, then, the growth of mind is always growth assisted from the outside. And since a culture, particularly an advanced one, transcends the bounds of individual competence, the limits for individual growth are by definition greater than what any single person has previously attained. For the limits of growth depend on how a culture assists the individual to use such intellectual potential as he may possess. It seems highly unlikely—either empirically or canonically—that we have any realistic sense of the furthest reach of such assistance to growth.

The evidence today is that the full evolution of intelligence came as a result of bipedalism and tool using. The large human brain gradually evolved as a sequel to the first use of pebble tools by early near-man. To condense the story, a near-man, or hominid, with a slightly superior brain, using a pebble tool, could make out better in the niche provided by nature than a near-man who depended not on tools but on sheer strength and formidable jaws. Natural selection favored the primitive tool user. In time, thanks to his better chance of surviving and breeding, he became more so: The ones who survived had larger brains, smaller jaws, less ferocious teeth. In place of belligerent anatomy, they developed tools and a brain that made it possible to use them. Human evolution thereafter became less a matter of having appropriate fangs or claws and more one of using and later fashioning tools to express the powers of the larger brain that was also emerging. Without tools the brain was of little use, no matter how many hundred cubic centimeters of it there might be. Let it also be said that without the original programmatic capacity for fitting tools into a sequence of acts, early hominids would never have started the epigenetic progress

[1] Address of the President to the Seventy-third Annual Convention of the American Psychological Association, Chicago, September 4, 1965.

that brought them to their present state. And as human groups stabilized tools became more complex and "shaped to pattern," so that it was no longer a matter of reinventing tools in order to survive, but rather of mastering the skills necessary for using them. In short, after a certain point in human evolution, the only means whereby man could fill his evolutionary niche was through the cultural transmission of the skills necessary for the use of priorly invented techniques, implements, and devices.

Two crucial parallel developments seem also to have occurred. As hominids became increasingly bipedal, with the freed hands necessary for using spontaneous pebble tools, selection also favored those with a heavier pelvic bony structure that could sustain the impacting strain of bipedal locomotion. The added strength came, of course, from a gradual closing down of the birth canal. There is an obstetrical paradox here: a creature with an increasingly larger brain but with a smaller and smaller birth canal to get through. The resolution seems to have been achieved through the immaturity of the human neonate, particularly cerebral immaturity that assures not only a smaller head, but also a longer period of transmitting the necessary skills required by human culture. During this same period, human language must have emerged, giving man not only a new and powerful way of representing reality but also increasing his power to assist the mental growth of the young to a degree beyond anything before seen in nature.

It is impossible, of course, to reconstruct the evolution in techniques of instruction in the shadow zone between hominids and man. I have tried to compensate by observing contemporary analogues of earlier forms, knowing full well that the pursuit of analogy can be dangerously misleading. I have spent many hours observing uncut films of the behavior of free-ranging baboons, films shot in East Africa by my colleague Irven DeVore with a very generous footage devoted to infants and juveniles. I have also had access to the unedited film archives of a hunting-gathering people living under roughly analogous ecological conditions, the !Kung Bushmen of the Kalahari, recorded by Laurence and Lorna Marshall, brilliantly aided by their son John and daughter Elizabeth.[2] I have also worked directly but informally with the Wolof of Senegal, observing children in the bush and in French-style schools. Even more valuable than my own in-

formal observations in Senegal were the systematic experiments carried out later by my colleague, Patricia Marks Greenfield (in press).

Let me describe very briefly some salient differences in the free learning patterns of immature baboons and among !Kung children. Baboons have a highly developed social life in their troops, with well-organized and stable dominance patterns. They live within a territory, protecting themselves from predators by joint action of the strongly built, adult males. It is striking that the behavior of baboon juveniles is shaped principally by play with their peer group, play that provides opportunity for the spontaneous expression and practice of the component acts that, in maturity, will be orchestrated into either the behavior of the dominant male or of the infant-protective female. All this seems to be accomplished with little participation by any mature animals in the play of the juveniles. We know from the important experiments of Harlow and his colleagues (Harlow & Harlow, 1962) how devastating a disruption in development can be produced in subhuman primates by interfering with their opportunity for peer-group play and social interaction,

Among hunting-gathering humans, on the other hand, there is *constant* interaction between adult and child, or adult and adolescent, or adolescent and child. !Kung adults and children play and dance together, sit together, participate in minor hunting together, join in song and story telling together. At very frequent intervals, moreover, children are party to rituals presided over by adults—minor, as in the first haircutting, or major, as when a boy kills his first Kudu buck and goes through the proud but painful process of scarification. Children, besides, are constantly playing imitatively with the rituals, implements, tools, and weapons of the adult world. Young juvenile baboons, on the other hand, virtually never play with things or imitate directly large and significant sequences of adult behavior.

Note, though, that in tens of thousands of feet of !Kung film, one virtually never sees an instance of "teaching" taking place outside the situation where the behavior to be learned is relevant. Nobody "teaches" in our prepared sense of the word. There is nothing like school, nothing like lessons. Indeed, among the !Kung children there is very little "telling." Most of what we would call instruction is through showing. And there is no "practice" or "drill" as such save in the form of play modeled directly on adult models—play hunting, play bossing, play exchanging, play baby tending, play house making. In the end, every man in the culture knows nearly all there is to know about how to get on with life as a man, and every woman as a woman—

---

[2] I am greatly indebted to Irven DeVore and Educational Services Incorporated for the opportunity to view his films of free-ranging baboons, and to Laurence and Lorna Marshall for the opportunity to examine their incomparable archives. DeVore and the Marshalls have been generous in their counsel as well.

the skills, the rituals and myths, the obligations and rights.

The change in the instruction of children in more complex societies is twofold. First of all, there is knowledge and skill in the culture far in excess of what any one individual knows. And so, increasingly, there develops an economical technique of instructing the young based heavily on *telling* out of context rather than *showing* in context. In literate societies, the practice becomes institutionalized in the school or the "teacher." Both promote this necessarily abstract way of instructing the young. The result of "teaching the culture" can, at its worst, lead to the ritual, rote nonsense that has led a generation of critics from Max Wertheimer (1945) to Mary Alice White (undated) of Teachers' College to despair. For in the detached school, what is imparted often has little to do with life as lived in the society except insofar as the demands of school are of a kind that reflect *indirectly* the demands of life in a technical society. But these indirectly imposed demands may be the most important feature of the detached school. For school is a sharp departure from indigenous practice. It takes learning, as we have noted, out of the context of immediate action just by dint of putting it into a school. This very extirpation makes learning become an act in itself, freed from the immediate ends of action, preparing the learner for the chain of reckoning remote from payoff that is needed for the formulation of complex ideas. At the same time, the school (if successful) frees the child from the pace setting of the round of daily activity. If the school succeeds in avoiding a pace-setting round of its own, it may be one of the great agents for promoting reflectiveness. Moreover, in school, one must "follow the lesson" which means one must learn to follow either the abstraction of written speech—abstract in the sense that it is divorced from the concrete situation to which the speech might originally have been related—or the abstraction of language delivered orally but out of the context of an ongoing action. Both of these are highly abstract uses of language.

It is no wonder, then, that many recent studies report large differences between "primitive" children who are in schools and their brothers who are not: differences in perception, abstraction, time perspective, and so on. I need only cite the work of Biesheuvel (1949) in South Africa, Gay and Cole (undated) in Liberia, Greenfield (in press) in Senegal, Maccoby and Modiano (in press) in rural Mexico, Reich (in press) among Alaskan Eskimos.

What a culture does to assist the development of the powers of mind of its members is, in effect, to provide amplification systems to which human beings, equipped with appropriate skills, can link themselves. There are, first, the amplifiers of action —hammers, levers, digging sticks, wheels—but more important, the programs of action into which such implements can be substituted. Second, there are amplifiers of the senses, ways of looking and noticing that can take advantage of devices ranging from smoke signals and hailers to diagrams and pictures that stop the action or microscopes that enlarge it. Finally and most powerfully, there are amplifiers of the thought processes, ways of thinking that employ language and formation of explanation, and later use such languages as mathematics and logic and even find automatic servants to crank out the consequences. A culture is, then, a deviser, a repository, and a transmitter of amplification systems and of the devices that fit into such systems. We know very little in a deep sense about the transmission function, how people are trained to get the most from their potential by use of a culture's resources.

But it is reasonably clear that there is a major difference between the mode of transmission in a technical society, with its schools, and an indigenous one, where cultural transmission is in the context of action. It is not just that an indigenous society, when its action pattern becomes disrupted falls apart—at a most terrifying rate—as in uncontrolled urbanization in some parts of Africa. Rather, it is that the institution of a school serves to convert knowledge and skill into more symbolical, more abstract, more verbal form. It is this process of transmission—admittedly very new in human history—that is so poorly understood and to which, finally, we shall return.

There are certain obvious specifications that can be stated about how a society must proceed in order to equip its young. It must convert what is to be known—whether a skill or a belief system or a connected body of knowledge—into a form capable of being mastered by a beginner. The more we know of the process of growth, the better we shall be at such conversion. The failure of modern man to understand mathematics and science may be less a matter of stunted abilities than our failure to understand how to teach such subjects. Second, given the limited amount of time available for learning, there must be a due regard for saving the learner from needless learning. There must be some emphasis placed on economy and transfer and the learning of general rules. All societies must (and virtually all do) distinguish those who are clever from those who are stupid—though few of them generalize this trait across all activities. Cleverness in a particular activity almost universally connotes strategy, economy, heuristics, highly generalized skills. A society must also place emphasis upon how one derives a course of action from what one has learned. Indeed, in an indigenous society, it is almost impossible to separate what one does from what one knows. More advanced societies often have not found a way of dealing with the separation of knowledge and action—probably a result of the emphasis they place upon "telling" in their instruction. All societies must maintain interest among the young in the learning process, a minor problem when learning is in the context of life and action, but harder when it becomes more abstracted. And finally, and perhaps most obviously, a society must assure that its necessary skills and procedures remain intact from one generation to the next—which does not always happen, as witnessed by Easter Islanders, Incas, Aztecs, and Mayas.[3]

Unfortunately, psychology has not concerned itself much with any of these five requisites of cultural transmission—or at least not much with four of them. We have too easily assumed that learning is learning is learning—that the early version of what was taught did not matter much, one thing being much like another and reducible to a pattern of association, to stimulus-response connections, or to our favorite molecular componentry. We denied there was a problem of development beyond the quantitative one of providing more experience, and with the denial, closed our eyes to the pedagogical problem of how to represent knowledge, how to sequence it, how to embody it in a form appropriate to young learners. We expended more passion on the part-whole controversy than on what whole or what part of it was to be presented first. I should except Piaget (1954), Kohler (1940), and Vygotsky (1962) from these complaints—all until recently unheeded voices.

Our neglect of the economy of learning stems, ironically, from the heritage of Ebbinghaus (1913), who was vastly interested in savings. Our nonsense syllables, our random mazes failed to take into account how we reduce complexity and strangeness to simplicity and the familiar, how we convert what we have learned into rules and procedures, how, to use Bartlett's (1932) term of over 30 years ago, we turn around on our own schemata to reorganize what we have mastered into more manageable form.

Nor have we taken naturally to the issue of knowledge and action. Its apparent mentalism has repelled us. Tolman (1951), who bravely made the distinction, was accused of leaving his organisms wrapt in thought. But he recognized the problem and if he insisted on the idea that knowledge might be organized in cognitive maps, it was in recognition (as a great functionalist) that organisms go somewhere on the basis of what they have learned. I believe we are getting closer to the problem of how knowledge affects action and vice versa, and offer in testimony of my conviction the provocative book by Miller, Galanter, and Pribram (1960), *Plans and the Structure of Behavior.*

Where the maintenance of the learner's interest is concerned, I remind you of what my colleague Gordon Allport (1946) has long warned. We have been so concerned with the model of driven behavior, with drive reduction and the *vis a tergo* that, again, until recently, we have tended to overlook the question of what keeps learners interested in the activity of learning, in the achievement of competence beyond bare necessity and first payoff. The work of R. W. White (1959) on effectance motivation, of Harlow and his colleagues (Butler, 1954; Harlow, 1953) on curiosity, and of Heider (1958) and Festinger (1962) on consistency begins to redress the balance. But it is only a beginning.

The invention of antigradation devices, guarantors that skill and knowledge will be maintained intact, is an exception to our oversight. We psychologists have been up to our ears in it. Our special contribution is the achievement test. But the achievement test has, in the main, reflected the timidity of the educational enterprise as a whole. I believe we know how to determine, though we have not yet devised tests to determine, how pupils use what they learn to think with later in life—for there is the real issue.

I have tried to examine briefly what a culture must do in passing on its amplifying skills and knowledge to a new generation and, even more briefly, how we as psychologists have dealt or failed to deal with the problems. I think the situation is fast changing—with a sharp increase in interest in the conversion problem, the problems of economy of learning, the nature of interest, the relation of knowledge and action. We are, I believe, at a major turning point where psychology will once again concern itself with the design of methods of assisting cognitive growth, be it through the invention of a rational technology of toys, of ways of enriching the environment of the crib and nursery, of organizing the activity of a school, or of devising a curriculum whereby we transmit an

---

[3] I have purposely left out of the discussion the problems of impulse regulation and socialization of motives, topics that have received extended treatment in the voluminous literature on culture and personality. The omission is dictated by emphasis rather than evaluation. Obviously, the shaping of character by culture is of great importance for an understanding of our topic as it bears, for example, upon culture-instilled attitudes toward the uses of mind. Since our emphasis is upon human potential and its amplification by culturally patterned instrumental skills, we mention the problem of character formation in passing and in recognition of its importance in a complete treatment of the issues under discussion.

organized body of knowledge and skill to a new generation to amplify their powers of mind.

I commented earlier that there was strikingly little knowledge available about the "third way" of training the skills of the young: the first being the play practice of component skills in prehuman primates, the second the teaching-in-context of indigenous societies, and the third being the abstracted, detached method of the school.

Let me now become highly specific. Let me consider a particular course of study, one given in a school, one we are ourselves constructing, trying out, and in a highly qualitative way, evaluating. It is for schools of the kind that exist in Western culture. The experience we have had with this effort, now in its third year, may serve to highlight the kinds of problems and conjectures one encounters in studying how to assist the growth of intellect in this "third way."

There is a dilemma in describing a course of study. One begins by setting forth the intellectual substance of what is to be taught. Yet if such a recounting tempts one to "get across" the subject, the ingredient of pedagogy is in jeopardy. For only in a trivial sense is a course designed to "get something across," merely to impart information. There are better means to that end than teaching. Unless the learner develops his skills, disciplines his taste, deepens his view of the world, the "something" that is got across is hardly worth the effort of transmission.

The more "elementary" a course and the younger its students, the more serious must be its pedagogical aim of forming the intellectual powers of those whom it serves. It is as important to justify a good mathematics course by the intellectual discipline it provides or the honesty it promotes as by the mathematics it transmits. Indeed, neither can be accomplished without the other. The content of this particular course is man: his nature as a species, the forces that shaped and continue to shape his humanity. Three questions recur throughout:

> What is human about human beings?
> How did they get that way?
> How can they be made more so?

In pursuit of our questions we explore five matters, each closely associated with the evolution of man as a species, each defining at once the distinctiveness of man and his potentiality for further evolution. The five great humanizing forces are, of course, tool making, language, social organization, the management of man's prolonged childhood, and man's urge to explain. It has been our first lesson in teaching that no pupil, however eager, can appreciate the relevance of, say, tool making or language in human evolution without first grasping the fundamental concept of a tool or what a language is. These are not self-evident matters, even to the expert. So we are involved in teaching not only the role of tools or language in the emergence of man, but, as a necessary precondition for doing so, setting forth the fundamentals of linguistics or the theory of tools. And it is as often the case as not that (as in the case of the "theory of tools") we must solve a formidable intellectual problem ourselves in order to be able to help our pupils do the same. I should have said at the outset that the "we" I employ in this context is no editorial fiction, but rather a group of anthropologists, zoologists, linguists, theoretical engineers, artists, designers, camera crews, teachers, children, and psychologists. The project is being carried out under my direction at Educational Services Incorporated, with grants from the National Science Foundation and the Ford Foundation.

While one readily singles out five sources of man's humanization, under no circumstances can they be put into airtight compartments. Human kinship is distinctively different from primate mating patterns precisely because it is classificatory and rests on man's ability to use language. Or, if you will, tool use enhances the division of labor in a society which in turn affects kinship. So while each domain can be treated as a separate set of ideas, their teaching must make it possible for the children to have a sense of their interaction. We have leaned heavily on the use of contrast, highly controlled contrast, to help children achieve detachment from the all too familiar matrix of social life: the contrasts of man versus higher primates, man versus prehistoric man, contemporary technological man versus "primitive" man, and man versus child. The primates are principally baboons, the prehistoric materials mostly from the Olduvai Gorge and Les Eyzies, the "primitive" peoples mostly the Netsilik Eskimos of Pelly Bay and the !Kung Bushmen. The materials, collected for our purposes, are on film, in story, in ethnography, in pictures and drawings, and principally in ideas embodied in exercises.

We have high aspirations. We hope to achieve five goals:

1. To give our pupils respect for and confidence in the powers of their own minds
2. To give them respect, moreover, for the powers of thought concerning the human condition, man's plight, and his social life
3. To provide them with a set of workable models that make it simpler to analyze the nature of the social

world in which they live and the condition in which man finds himself

4. To impart a sense of respect for the capacities and plight of man as a species, for his origins, for his potential, for his humanity

5. To leave the student with a sense of the unfinished business of man's evolution

One last word about the course of study that has to do with the quality of the ideas, materials, and artistry—a matter that is at once technological and intellectual. We have felt that the making of such a curriculum deserved the best talent and technique available in the world. Whether artist, ethnographer, film maker, poet, teacher—nobody we have asked has refused us. We are obviously going to suffer in testing a Hawthorne effect * of some magnitude. But then, perhaps it is as well to live in a permanent state of revolution.

Let me now try to describe some of the major problems one encounters in trying to construct a course of study. I shall not try to translate the problems into refined theoretical form, for they do not as yet merit such translation. They are more difficulties than problems. I choose them, because they are vividly typical of what one encounters in such enterprises. The course is designed for 10-year-olds in the fifth grade of elementary school, but we have been trying it out as well on the fourth and sixth grades better to bracket our difficulties.

One special point about these difficulties. They are born of trying to achieve an objective and are as much policy bound as theory bound. It is like the difference between building an economic theory about monopolistic practices and constructing policies for controlling monopoly. Let me remind you that modern economic theory has been reformulated, refined, and revived by having a season in policy. I am convinced that the psychology of assisted growth, i.e., pedagogy, will have to be forged in the policy crucible of curriculum making before it can reach its full descriptive power as theory. Economics was first through the cycle from theory to policy to theory to policy; it is happening now to psychology, anthropology, and sociology.

---

* A Hawthorne effect is an effect often observed when new procedures are introduced. It consists of an increase in productivity, irrespective of changing conditions of work, because of improvement in mental attitude of the workers as a result of their being subjects in an experiment. For example, not only may production increase if lighting conditions are bettered, it may also increase if they are worsened. Because of discovery of this effect, we know that heightened performances of workers or students who are participants in a new plan or program may not be indicative of the long-term value of the innovation but may, in some cases, be solely the consequence of raised morale.—EDITOR

Now on to the difficulties. The first is what might be called *the psychology of a subject matter*. A learned discipline can be conceived as a way of thinking about certain phenomena. Mathematics is one way of thinking about order without reference to what is being ordered. The behavioral sciences provide one or perhaps several ways of thinking about man and his society—about regularities, origins, causes, effects. They are probably special (and suspect) because they permit man to look at himself from a perspective that is outside his own skin and beyond his own preferences—at least for awhile.

Underlying a discipline's "way of thought," there is a set of connected, varyingly implicit, generative propositions. In physics and mathematics, most of the underlying generative propositions like the conservation theorems, or the axioms of geometry, or the associative, distributive, and commutative rules of analysis are by now very explicit indeed. In the behavioral sciences we must be content with more implicitness. We traffic in inductive propositions: e.g., the different activities of a society are interconnected such that if you know something about the technological response of a society to an environment, you will be able to make some shrewd guesses about its myths or about the things it values, etc. We use the device of a significant contrast as in linguistics as when we describe the territoriality of a baboon troop in order to help us recognize the system of reciprocal exchange of a human group, the former somehow provoking awareness of the latter.

There is nothing more central to a discipline than its way of thinking. There is nothing more important in its teaching than to provide the child the earliest opportunity to learn that way of thinking—the forms of connection, the attitudes, hopes, jokes, and frustrations that go with it. In a word, the best introduction to a subject is the subject itself. At the very first breath, the young learner should, we think, be given the chance to solve problems, to conjecture, to quarrel as these are done at the heart of the discipline. But, you will ask, how can this be arranged?

Here again the problem of conversion. There exist ways of thinking characteristic of different stages of development. We are acquainted with Inhelder and Piaget's (1958) account of the transition from preoperational, through concrete operational, to propositional thought in the years from preschool through, say, high school. If you have an eventual pedagogical objective in mind, you can translate the way of thought of a discipline into its Piagetian (or other) equivalent appropriate to a given level of development and take the child onward from there. The Cambridge Mathematics

Project of Educational Services, Incorporated, argues that if the child is to master the calculus early in his high school years, he should start work early with the idea of limits, the earliest work being manipulative, later going on to images and diagrams, and finally moving on to the more abstract notation needed for delineating the more precise idea of limits.

In "Man: A Course of Study," (Bruner, 1965) there are also versions of the subject appropriate to a particular age that can at a later age be given a more powerful rendering. We have tried to choose topics with this in mind: The analysis of kinship that begins with children using sticks and blocks and colors and whatnot to represent their own families, goes on to the conventional kinship diagrams by a meandering but, as you can imagine, interesting path, and then can move on to more formal and powerful componential analysis. So, too, with myth. We begin with the excitement of a powerful myth (like the Netsilik Nuliajik myth), then have the children construct some myths of their own, then examine what a set of Netsilik myths have in common, which takes us finally to Lévi-Strauss's (1963) analysis of contrastive features in myth construction. A variorum text of a myth or corpus of myths put together by sixth graders can be quite an extraordinary document.

This approach to the psychology of a learned discipline turns out to illuminate another problem raised earlier: the maintenance of interest. There is, in this approach, a reward in understanding that grows from the subject matter itself. It is easier to engineer this satisfaction in mathematics, for understanding is so utter in a formal discipline—a balance beam balances or it does not: therefore there is an equality or there is not. In the behavioral sciences the payoff in understanding cannot be so obviously and startlingly self-revealing. Yet, one can design exercises in the understanding of man, too—as when children figure out the ways in which, given limits of ecology, skills, and materials, Bushmen hunt different animals, and then compare their predictions with the real thing on film.

Consider now a second problem: *how to stimulate thought in the setting of a school.* We know from experimental studies like those of Bloom and Broder (1950), and of Goodnow and Pettigrew (1955), that there is a striking difference in the acts of a person who thinks that the task before him represents a problem to be solved rather than being controlled by random forces. School is a particular subculture where these matters are concerned. By school age, children have come to expect quite arbitrary and, from their point of view, meaningless demands to be made upon them by

adults—the result, most likely, of the fact that adults often fail to recognize the task of conversion necessary to make their questions have some intrinsic significance for the child. Children, of course, will try to solve problems if they recognize them as such. But they are not often either predisposed to or skillful in problem finding, in recognizing the hidden conjectural feature in tasks set them. But we know now that children in school can quite quickly be led to such problem finding by encouragement and instruction.

The need for this instruction and encouragement and its relatively swift success relates, I suspect, to what psychoanalysts refer to as the guilt-ridden oversuppression of primary process and its public replacement by secondary process. Children, like adults, need reassurance that it is all right to entertain and express highly subjective ideas, to treat a task as a problem where you *invent* an answer rather than *finding* one out there in the book or on the blackboard. With children in elementary school, there is often a need to devise emotionally vivid special games, story-making episodes, or construction projects to reestablish in the child's mind his right not only to have his own private ideas but to express them in the public setting of a classroom.

But there is another, perhaps more serious difficulty: the interference of intrinsic problem solving by extrinsic. Young children in school expend extraordinary time and effort figuring out what it is that the teacher wants—and usually coming to the conclusion that she or he wants tidiness or remembering or to do things at a certain time in a certain way. This I refer to as extrinsic problem solving. There is a great deal of it in school.

There are several quite straightforward ways of stimulating problem solving. One is to train teachers to want it and that will come in time. But teachers can be encouraged to like it, interestingly enough, by providing them and their children with materials and lessons that *permit* legitimate problem solving and permit the teacher to recognize it. For exercises with such materials create an atmosphere by treating things as instances of what *might* have occurred rather than simply as what did occur. Let me illustrate by a concrete instance. A fifth-grade class was working on the organization of a baboon troop—on this particular day, specifically on how they might protect against predators. They saw a brief sequence of film in which six or seven adult males go forward to intimidate and hold off three cheetahs. The teacher asked what the baboons had done to keep the cheetahs off, and there ensued a lively discussion of how the dominant adult males, by showing their formidable mouthful of teeth and making threatening gestures had turned the trick.

A boy raised a tentative hand and asked whether cheetahs always attacked together. Yes, though a single cheetah sometimes followed behind a moving troop and picked off an older, weakened straggler or an unwary, straying juvenile. "Well, what if there were four cheetahs and two of them attacked from behind and two from in front. What would the baboons do then?" The question could have been answered empirically—and the inquiry ended. Cheetahs *do not* attack that way, and so we do not know what baboons *might* do. Fortunately, it was not. For the question opens up the deep issues of what might be and why it is not. Is there a necessary relation between predators and prey that share a common ecological niche? Must their encounters have a "sporting chance" outcome? It is such conjecture, in this case quite unanswerable, that produces rational, self-consciously problem-finding behavior so crucial to the growth of intellectual power. Given the materials, given some background and encouragement, teachers like it as much as the students.

I should like to turn now to the *personalization of knowledge.* A generation ago, the progressive movement urged that knowledge be related to the child's own experience and brought out of the realm of empty abstractions. A good idea was translated into banalities about the home, then the friendly postman and trashman, then the community, and so on. It is a poor way to compete with the child's own dramas and mysteries. A decade ago, my colleague Clyde Kluckhohn (1949) wrote a prize-winning popular book on anthropology with the entrancing title *Mirror for Man.* In some deep way, there is extraordinary power in "that mirror which other civilizations still hold up to us to recognize and study . . . [the] image of ourselves [Lévi-Strauss, 1965]." The psychological bases of the power are not obvious. Is it as in discrimination learning, where increasing the degree of contrast helps in the learning of a discrimination, or as in studies of concept attainment where a negative instance demonstrably defines the domain of a conceptual rule? Or is it some primitive identification? All these miss one thing that seems to come up frequently in our interviews with the children. It is the experience of discovering kinship and likeness in what at first seemed bizarre, exotic, and even a little repellant.

Consider two examples, both involving film of the Netsilik. In the films, a single nuclear family, Zachary, Marta, and their 4-year-old Alexi, is followed through the year—spring sealing, summer fishing at the stone weir, fall caribou hunting, early winter fishing through the ice, winter at the big ceremonial igloo. Children report that at first the three members of the family look weird and un-couth. In time, they look normal, and eventually, as when Marta finds sticks around which to wrap her braids, the girls speak of how pretty she is. That much is superficial—or so it seems. But consider a second episode.

It has to do with Alexi who, with his father's help, devises a snare and catches a gull. There is a scene in which he stones the gull to death. Our children watched, horror struck. One girl, Kathy, blurted out, "He's not even human, doing that to the seagull." The class was silent. Then another girl, Jennine, said quietly: "He's got to grow up to be a hunter. His mother was smiling when he was doing that." And then an extended discussion about how people have to do things to learn and even do things to learn how to feel appropriately. "What would you do if you had to live there? Would you be as smart about getting along as they are with what they've got?" said one boy, going back to the accusation that Alexi was inhuman to stone the bird.

I am sorry it is so difficult to say it clearly. What I am trying to say is that to personalize knowledge one does not simply link it to the familiar. Rather one makes the familiar an instance of a more general case and thereby produces awareness of it. What the children were learning about was not seagulls and Eskimos, but about their own feelings and preconceptions that, up to then, were too implicit to be recognizable to them.

Consider finally the problem of *self-conscious reflectiveness.* It is an epistemological mystery why traditional education has so often emphasized extensiveness and coverage over intensiveness and depth. We have already commented on the fact that memorizing was usually perceived by children as one of the high-priority tasks but rarely did children sense an emphasis upon ratiocination with a view toward redefining what had been encountered, reshaping it, reordering it. The cultivation of reflectiveness, or whatever you choose to call it, is one of the great problems one faces in devising curriculum. How lead children to discover the powers and pleasures that await the exercise of retrospection?

Let me suggest one answer that has grown from what we have done. It is the use of the "organizing conjecture." We have used three such conjectures —what is human about human beings, how they got that way, how they could become more so. They serve two functions, one of them the very obvious though important one of putting perspective back into the particulars. The second is less obvious and considerably more surprising. The questions often seemed to serve as criteria for determining where they were getting, how well they were understanding, whether anything new was emerging. Recall Kathy's cry: "He's not human doing that to the seagull." She was hard at work in her rage on the conjecture what makes human beings human.

There, in brief, are four problems that provide some sense of what a psychologist encounters when he takes a hand in assisting the growth of mind in children in the special setting of a school. The problems look quite different from those we encounter in formulating classical developmental theory with the aid of typical laboratory research. They also look very different from those that one would find in an indigenous society, describing how children picked up skills and knowledge and values in the context of action and daily life. We clearly do not have a theory of the school that is sufficient to the task of running schools—just as we have no adequate theory of toys or of readiness building or whatever the jargon is for preparing children to do a better job the next round. It only obscures the issue to urge that some day our classical theories of learning will fill the gap. They show no sign of doing so.

I hope that we shall not allow ourselves to be embarrassed by our present ignorance. It has been a long time since we have looked at what is involved in imparting knowledge through the vehicle of the school—if ever we did look at it squarely. I urge that we delay no longer.

But I am deeply convinced that the psychologist cannot alone construct a theory of how to assist cognitive development and cannot alone learn how to enrich and amplify the powers of a growing human mind. The task belongs to the whole intellectual community: the behavioral scientists and the artists, scientists, and scholars who are the custodians of skill, taste, and knowledge in our culture. Our special task as psychologists is to convert skills and knowledge to forms and exercises that fit growing minds—and it is a task ranging from how to keep children free from anxiety to how to translate physics for the very young child into a set of playground maneuvers that, later, the child can turn around upon and convert into a sense of inertial regularities.

And this in turn leads me to a final conjecture, one that has to do with the organization of our profession, a matter that has concerned me greatly during this past year during which I have had the privilege of serving as your President. Psychology is peculiarly prey to parochialism. Left to our own devices, we tend to construct models of a man who is neither a victim of history, a target of economic forces, or even a working member of a society. I am still struck by Roger Barker's (1963) ironic truism that the best way to predict the behavior of a human being is to know where he is: In a post office he behaves post office, at church he behaves church.

Psychology, and you will forgive me if the image seems a trifle frivolous, thrives on polygamy with her neighbors. Our marriage with the biological sciences has produced a cumulation of ever more powerful knowledge. So, too, our joint undertakings with anthropology and sociology. Joined together with a variety of disciplines, we have made lasting contributions now that the emphasis is shifting to the problems of alleviating stress and arranging for a community's mental health. What I find lacking is an alignment that might properly be called the growth sciences. The field of pedagogy is one participant in the growth sciences. Any field of inquiry devoted to assisting the growth of effective human beings, fully empowered with zest, with skill, with knowledge, with taste is surely a candidate for this sodality. My friend Philip Morrison once suggested to his colleagues at Cornell that his department of physics grant a doctorate not only for work in theoretical, experimental, or applied physics, but also for work in pedagogical physics. The limits of the growth sciences remain to be drawn. They surely transcend the behavioral sciences cum pediatrics. It is plain that, if we are to achieve the effectiveness of which we as human beings are capable, there will one day have to be such a field. I hope that we psychologists can earn our way as charter members.

REFERENCES

ALLPORT, G. Effect: A secondary principle of learning. *Psychological Review*, 1946, *53*, 335–347.

BARKER, R. On the nature of the environment. *Journal of Social Issues*, 1963, *19*, 17–38.

BARTLETT, F. *Remembering*. Cambridge, England: Cambridge Univer. Press, 1932.

BIESHEUVEL, S. Psychological tests and their application to non-European peoples. *Yearbook of Education*. London: Evans, 1949. Pp. 87–126.

BLOOM, B., & BRODER, L. Problem solving processes of college students. *Supplementary Educational Monograph, No. 73*. Chicago: Univer. Chicago Press, 1950.

BRUNER, J. The course of cognitive growth. *American Psychologist*, 1964, *19*, 1–15.

BRUNER, J. Man: A course of study. *Educational Services Inc. Quarterly Report*, 1965, Spring-Summer, 3–13.

BRUNER, J. *Toward a theory of instruction*. Cambridge: Harvard Univer. Press, in press.

BUTLER, R. A. Incentive conditions which influence visual exploration. *Journal of Experimental Psychology*, 1954, *48*, 19–23.

EBBINGHAUS, H. *Memory: A contribution to experimental psychology.* New York: Teachers College, Columbia University, 1913.

FESTINGER, L. *A theory of cognitive dissonance.* Stanford: Stanford Univer. Press, 1962.

GAY, J., & COLE, M. Outline of general report on Kpelle mathematics project. Stanford: Stanford University, Institute for Mathematical Social Studies, undated. (Mimeo)

GOODNOW, JACQUELINE, & PETTIGREW, T. Effect of prior patterns of experience on strategies and learning sets. *Journal of Experimental Psychology,* 1955, *49,* 381–389.

GREENFIELD, PATRICIA M. Culture and conservation. In J. Bruner, Rose Olver, & Patricia M. Greenfield (Eds.), *Studies in cognitive growth.* New York: Wiley, in press. Ch. 10.

HARLOW, H., & HARLOW, MARGARET. Social deprivation in monkeys. *Scientific American,* 1962, November.

HARLOW, H. F. Mice, monkeys, men, and motives. *Psychological Review,* 1953, *60,* 23–32.

HEIDER, F. *The psychology of interpersonal relations.* New York: Wiley, 1958.

INHELDER, BARBEL, & PIAGET, J. *The growth of logical thinking.* New York: Basic Books, 1958.

KLUCKHOHN, C. *Mirror for man.* New York: Whittlesey House, 1949.

KOHLER, W. *Dynamics in psychology.* New York: Liveright, 1940.

LÉVI-STRAUSS, C. The structural study of myth. *Structural anthropology.* (Trans. by Claire Jacobson & B. Grundfest Scharpf) New York: Basic Books, 1963. Pp. 206–231.

LÉVI-STRAUSS, C. Anthropology: Its achievements and future. Lecture presented at Bicentennial Celebration, Smithsonian Institution, Washington, D. C., September 1965.

MACCOBY, M., & MODIANO, NANCY. On culture and equivalence. In J. Bruner, Rose Olver, & Patricia M. Greenfield (Eds.), *Studies in cognitive growth.* New York: Wiley, in press. Ch. 12.

MILLER, G., GALANTER, E., & PRIBRAM, K. *Plans and the structure of behavior.* New York: Holt, 1960.

PIAGET, J. *The construction of reality in the child.* New York: Basic Books, 1954.

REICH, LEE. On culture and grouping. In J. Bruner, Rose Olver, & Patricia M. Greenfield (Eds.), *Studies in cognitive growth.* New York: Wiley, in press. Ch. 13.

TOLMAN, E. Cognitive maps in rats and men. *Collected papers in psychology.* Berkeley & Los Angeles: Univer. California Press, 1951. Pp. 241–264.

VYGOTSKY, L. *Thought and language.* (Ed. & trans. by Eugenia Hanfmann & Gertrude Vakar) New York: Wiley, 1962.

WERTHEIMER, M. *Productive thinking.* New York & London: Harper, 1945.

WHITE, MARY A. The child's world of learning. Teachers College, Columbia University, undated. (Mimeo)

WHITE, R. W. Motivation reconsidered: The concept of competence. *Psychological Review,* 1959, *66,* 297–333.

60

Cues Used in Visual Word Recognition[1]

JOANNA P. WILLIAMS, ELLEN L.
BLUMBERG, AND DAVID V. WILLIAMS

How do children recognize words? Do they respond to the overall shape of the word or to individual letters? The following selection attacks this question, which has important implications for the development of instructional methods. The results of the study also point up some of the difficulties we run into when we use data collected on adults to predict what a child's response is likely to be. Joanna P. Williams, an editor of this volume, is visiting professor of psychology and education at Teachers College, Columbia University, and editor of the Journal of Educational Psychology; *Ellen L. Blumberg is at the Graduate School of Education of the University of Pennsylvania; David V. Williams is assistant professor of psychology at Ithaca College.*

Many different theories have been proposed to explain the manner in which words are "recognized." One frequently encountered hypothesis is that children recognize words as wholes, that is, by configuration—overall shape (Tinker & Paterson, 1940). Others have thought that individual letters (perhaps the initial and terminal ones) provide the important cues (Levin, Watson, & Feldman, 1964). The most recent suggestion, proposed on the basis of work done by Gibson (1965) and her colleagues, is that familiarity with grapheme-phoneme correspondences is fundamental to word recognition. The effective cue might also prove to be some combination of these factors.

In spite of the quantity of research on this topic, the bases of word recognition are not yet well understood. Since many of these studies have held contradictory implications for reading instruction, determining the bases of word recognition remains an important problem (Williams, 1970).

Early research is still being cited widely. For example, a study by Cattell in 1885 (see Cattell, 1947) is often quoted to justify the use of curriculum materials and methods that are based on the whole word as the fundamental unit of recognition. These are the so-called "look-say" methods, such as the Scott-Foresman series featuring Dick and Jane. Cattell, using tachistoscopic presentation and adult subjects, found that given a specific exposure time, two unconnected letters *or* two unconnected words could be recognized. There are a number of serious weaknesses in this early study. For example, it is not clear that the subjects did not simply recognize a few of the letters in the word and identify the words on this basis, rather than by its configuration. Therefore it is not possible to interpret these findings as support for "whole word" methods of instruction.

This experiment is representative of much of the data in the area. Many studies have used adult subjects, whose familiarity with written language makes them different from 5-year-old beginning readers. Yet very few such studies have explicitly compared adults and children on any given task. Moreover, many studies to date have employed tachistoscopic or other types of presentation that may involve methods of word recognition that are different from those used in reading.

A 1965 study by Marchbanks and Levin suggested a useful experimental task for investigating this matter. Their data, collected on a sample of middle-class kindergarten and first-grade children, indicated that specific letters and not configuration of the words form the basis for recognition. The present experiment was conducted in order to extend these initial findings.

First, the authors were interested in replicating Marchbanks and Levin's study on a sample of socioeconomically disadvantaged urban children. All of Marchbanks and Levin's subjects probably

[1] This study was supported in part by a Faculty Research Grant from the University of Pennsylvania. The authors thank Harris N. Miller for designing the circuitry for the apparatus and Gerald Satlow for his help in the statistical analysis.

had some knowledge of the alphabet, even though the kindergarten children had not had formal reading instruction. The present authors were interested in how subjects much less familiar with the alphabet would perform on this task.

Second, Marchbanks and Levin did not provide any data on an adult population. Since their task was designed to simulate conditions of the actual reading situation more closely than the tasks used in many of the earlier studies, we felt that it would be useful to determine whether the literate adult would show the same choice strategies as the young child.

Finally, the present study included certain methodological improvements in the presentation of stimuli and recording of responses.

METHOD

TASK

The task, as developed by Marchbanks and Levin (1965), consisted of a delayed matching-to-sample procedure. The stimuli were three-letter and five-letter artificially constructed words (trigrams and quingrams). A single "word" was presented. Then this word was removed from sight and an array of several randomly arranged words appeared, from which the subject was to choose one that most resembled the stimulus word. These words were so structured that each choice represented one of a systematic series of errors that might be made. As in Table 1, Example a, it was possible to match the stimulus CUG on the basis of the first letter (*che*), the second letter (*tuk*), the third letter (*ilg*), or on the basis of configuration (*arp*). For the quingrams, it was possible to evaluate six cues: each letter and configuration, as in the case of Example b in Table 1. Configuration was determined by the height of the letters and whether or not they extended below the line.

TABLE 1
WORDS USED IN MATCHING-TO-SAMPLE PROCEDURE

Stimulus	Word
a. cug	che
	tuk
	ilg
	arp
b. moged	mythi
	borsu
	pagle
	fimet
	jukad
	raqub
c. sajuk	sapef
	sojit
	segub
	siqok

There was one trial in both the trigram and quingram series in which all cues were varied. On the remaining trials, certain cues were held constant in the responses in order to determine which of several cues were used when the use of others was restricted. This is the case in Example c, in which both shape and first letter were held constant and second, third, fourth, and fifth letter varied. The subject had an equal opportunity to respond on the basis of any one of the individual letter cues. In the case of the trigrams, there were half as many chances to choose shape as any of the other three cues. For the quingrams, there were 26 chances to choose shape as a cue, and 30 chances for the other cues. Scores were corrected for this differential opportunity to respond. There were 8 trigram items and 52 quingram items which were combined and presented in random order.[2]

The words were typed on Kodak Ektagraphic slides using a primer type-face. At the beginning of each trial, a single word was presented on a rear projection screen by a Carousel projector. After 3 seconds the response choices appeared, and the timer started. The subject indicated his choice by pressing a large button next to the vertical array of responses. This registered his choice, stopped the timer, and in 3 seconds presented the next stimulus word. These events were automatically sequenced by time-delay relay circuitry.

In order to be sure that all subjects understood the task, practice trials were given. First, pictures of objects were presented. On the first slide, the subject saw a picture of a house as stimulus and then, on the next slide, had to pick out the house from an array of other pictured objects. Five such items were used. In each practice item, the number of response choices was increased, starting at two and working up to six. Next, the subject saw a series of five similar items containing geometric forms, and had to find the one that was "most like" the stimulus.

Following this pretraining, the experiment was run as described above. Upon completion of the experimental task, all subjects in the first grade and kindergarten groups were given an alphabet recognition test. Each letter, printed on a 2 × 3 card, was presented individually, in a random order, and the subject was asked to name each letter.

After each adult had completed the task, he filled out a brief questionnaire which provided opportunity for him to indicate any strategy used in the recognition of the words. The questions made no mention of specific strategies.

---

[2] Marchbanks and Levin had used twice as many items, such that each trial was "doubled." That is, each item was matched with a second item, which involved an analogous cue choice, but with different letters. They did this so that reliability of choice could be estimated. Reliability was measured by the consistency of choice when analogous cues were varied on different trials, and the reliability was approximately .65. Tables giving the design of the trigram and quingram tasks have been deposited with the National Auxiliary Publications Service. Order NAPS Document No. 8250 from ASIS National Auxiliary Publications Service, *c/o* CCM Information Sciences, Inc., 909 3rd Avenue, New York, New York 10022, remitting $1.00 for microfiche or $3.00 for photocopies.

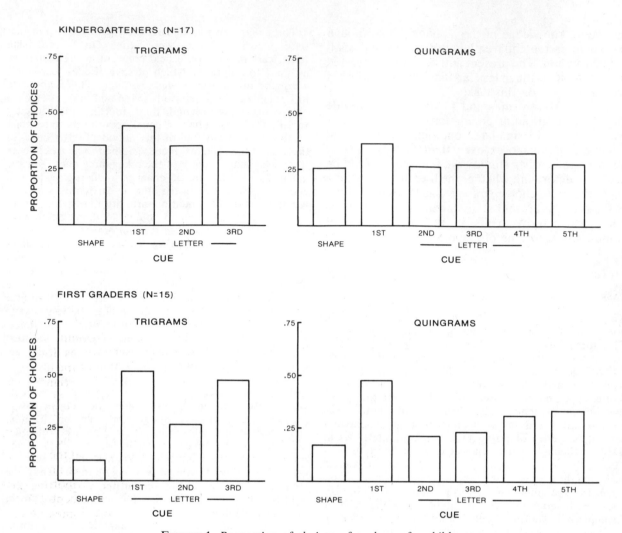

FIGURE 1. *Proportion of choices of each cue for children.*

SUBJECTS

The subjects were 17 kindergarten children, 15 first graders and 32 undergraduate and graduate students. They represented, respectively, nonreaders, beginning readers, and proficient readers. All were attending Philadelphia schools. The children attended a public school in a socioeconomically disadvantaged area. At the time of testing, the kindergarten subjects had had no instruction in reading or letter recognition. The first graders' reading instruction stressed word-attack skills (as opposed to "look-say" techniques).

RESULTS

The number of times subjects matched words on the basis of each cue was determined, and the proportion of choices of each cue relative to the total numbers of opportunities to choose that cue was calculated.

Figure 1 presents these data for kindergarten subjects and first graders, for both trigrams and quingrams. A Friedman analysis of variance was computed, to determine whether there was significant variation among the proportion of choices of the various cues available. Differences were not significant for kindergarten subjects, either for the trigrams ($\chi^2 = 1.05$, $df = 3$) or the quingrams ($\chi^2 = 7.53$, $df = 5$). However, for first-graders, analysis of the trigram data showed variation significant at the .001 level ($\chi^2 = 21.62$, $df = 3$) and for the quingram data at the .005 level ($\chi^2 = 19.68$, $df = 5$).

Specific comparisons were made on the first grade data using Nemenyi's test (Kirk, 1968), which indicated that, for the trigrams, shape was chosen significantly less often ($p < .01$) than the first and last letters, which did not differ. For the quingrams, shape was again chosen significantly less often than the first letter ($p < .05$) and the other differences were not reliable.

On the basis of the alphabet-recognition task scores, the children were divided into high and

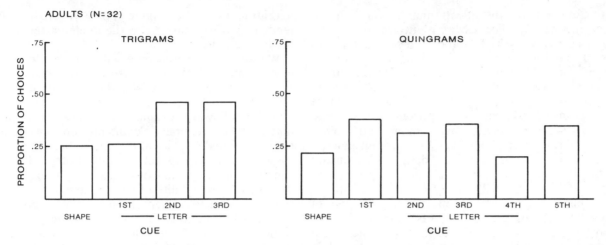

FIGURE 2. *Proportion of choices of each cue for adults.*

low groups: those who correctly named 20 or more letters, and those whose scores were less than 16. There were five zero scores in this low group. The high group was composed entirely of first graders ($N = 11$). The low group contained the kindergarten children and four first graders.

The same analyses described previously were performed on these two groups. The results were similar to those found when the subjects were divided by grade level. That is, for those subjects who had little knowledge of the alphabet, there were no differences in the proportion of times that the several cues were chosen. For the subjects who scored high on the alphabet test, however, the variation both for the trigrams and the quingrams was significant at the .001 level. It is interesting to

note that none of the five subjects who scored zero on the alphabet test showed any tendency to make choices on the basis of configuration.

In Figure 2 the data for the 32 adult subjects are presented. The pattern of choices for these subjects is quite different from that of the children. The overall Friedman analysis of variance was significant at the .01 level ($\chi^2 = 12.84$, $df = 3$) for trigrams and the .001 level ($\chi^2 = 41.27$, $df = 5$) for quingrams. On trigrams, there was a greater tendency to match on the basis of second or third letter (these two cues did not differ), and the proportion of choices of the initial letter was no greater than of shape. On quingrams, proportions of choices on the basis of all cues except for the fourth letter and configuration were comparable.

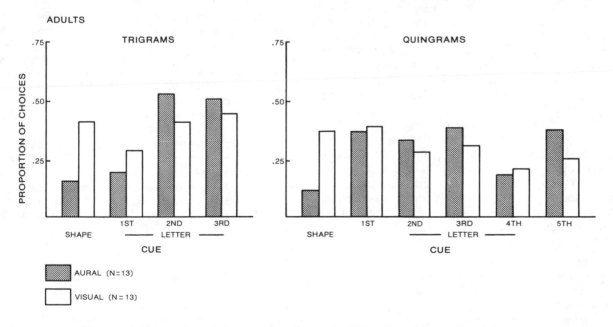

FIGURE 3. *Proportion of choices of each cue for "visual" and "aural" subgroups.*

On the basis of the questionnaire data, two distinct groups of subjects were identified: those who reported that they had used one of several types of visual matching strategy, and those who described the use of aural matching strategies. Thirteen of the 32 subjects were classified as "visual," and another 13 as "aural." Figure 3 presents the data for these two subgroups. Those who reported using a visual strategy showed no differences among their choices ($\chi^2 = 2.03$, $df = 3$; $\chi^2 = 8.10$, $df = 5$), but an analysis done on the "aural" subjects' data was significant at the .01 level ($\chi^2 = 11.37$, $df = 3$) for trigrams, and the .001 level ($\chi^2 = 29.50$, $df = 5$) for quingrams. The main aural strategy reported was the use of rhyme (by 10 of the 13 subjects). Further inspection of the questionnaire responses of the visual group indicated that 6 of the 13 subjects described their strategy as one in which they tried to match on the basis of overall shape, which had been the *least* salient cue for the first-grade group.

DISCUSSION

The principal conclusion to be drawn from these data is that children do not match words on the basis of configuration as much previous data and a good bit of lore would have it. Rather, children who have some ability to identify letters of the alphabet, and who thus can be considered "beginning readers,"—that is, the first graders in this experiment—showed a strong tendency to match on the basis of individual letters, the initial letter being particularly salient. Even those children with less acquaintance with the alphabet show no "natural" tendency to regard shape as a salient cue. These results replicate Marchbanks and Levin's (1965) data on middle-class children. As they suggest, the preponderance of choices on initial and then final letter may be explainable in terms of the theory of primacy and/or recency of cues.

What implications are there for instruction? In view of these and other findings, there seems to be no justification for developing instructional methods or primer materials based on the use of configuration as the primary cue. Shape seems a poor choice after reading training is begun, for when children know the alphabet, individual letters become quite salient. Also, if one's instructional strategy were to attempt to capitalize on tendencies seen before any instruction is given, con-figuration would be a poor choice. There was no tendency to use this cue in the kindergarten (nonreading) children.

We have considered here only the development of recognition of those words actually presented in training. Even more crucial is the problem of transfer, which must form the basis for the development of the wide reading vocabulary of the proficient reader. Relying on configuration as a cue for effective transfer is not at all reasonable—even if a subject were in fact skilled in this strategy. Even a simple transfer from lower case to upper case removes the possibility of using shape as a cue.

There were yet different patterns of responding in the adult sample, indicating a variety and in some cases a quite complex strategy. The results suggest that it should not be assumed that adults and children behave in the same manner on this type of verbal matching task. Indeed, it is worth noting that the most widely used reading method over the past 30 years (the "look-say" or "whole word" method) has stressed identification of words on the basis of configuration. But it is adults, not children, who sometimes show this strategy in word recognition, and it is clear that implications for instruction that are based on data collected on adult readers can be seriously misleading.

REFERENCES

CATTELL, J. M. *Man of science*, Vol. 2. York, Pa.: Science Press, 1947.

GIBSON, E. J. Learning to read. *Science*, 1965, *148*, 1066–1072.

KIRK, R. E. *Experimental design: Procedures for the behavioral sciences.* Belmont, Calif.: Brooks/Cole, 1968.

LEVIN, H., WATSON, J., & FELDMAN, M. Writing as pretraining for association learning. *Journal of Educational Psychology*, 1964, *55*, 181–184.

MARCHBANKS, G., & LEVIN, H. Cues by which children recognize words. *Journal of Educational Psychology*, 1965, *56*, 57–61.

TINKER, M., & PATERSON, D. Eye movements in reading a modern face and Old English. *American Journal of Psychology*, 1940, *54*, 113–115.

WILLIAMS, J. P. From basic research on reading to educational practice. In H. Levin & J. P. Williams, *Basic studies on reading*. New York: Basic Books, 1970.

61

Letter-name Versus Letter-sound Knowledge in Learning to Read

S. JAY SAMUELS

How much emphasis should be placed on teaching beginning readers to name the letters of the alphabet? The controversy on this issue has had a long history. In this article, S. Jay Samuels, professor of educational psychology at the University of Minnesota, reviews the evidence and suggests that skills other than letter-naming facilitate reading acquisition.

There is a considerable interest at the present time in teaching children to name letters of the alphabet in the belief that letter-name knowledge facilitates learning to read. This interest is manifest at kindergarten and first grade levels where instruction in naming letters is commonly given as part of the reading readiness program. Sesame Street, the television program for preschoolers, also includes instruction in letter naming. Durrell and Murphy (1964, P. 143) claim that: "Most letter-names contain their sounds, and this assists the child in relating the phoneme in the spoken word to its form in print. Children who know letter-names learn words more readily. . . ."

HISTORICAL PERSPECTIVES

Belief that letter-name knowledge facilitates learn-ing to read has a longer history than most would suspect. The purpose of this article is to explore the origin of this belief and to test the validity of the assumption.

Huey (1908, P. 265) wrote: "The alphabetic method, used almost universally in Greece and Rome, and in European countries generally until well into the nineteenth century, and which was nearly universal in America until about 1870, is now chiefly of historical interest.

"In the alphabet method of reading instruction, as practiced in Europe and this continent, the child learned to name letters before learning to read words. After mastering the names of the letters, nonsense syllables such as *ab*, *ob*, and *ib* were introduced. The student first spelled each letter and then pronounced the syllable. He progressed to three letter nonsense syllables, short words, and finally, sentences. Naming the letters generally preceded pronouncing the syllables or words."

In 1840, Bumstead commented that the practice of drilling the child month after month on letter names was irksome to student and teacher. Thayer (1857) found that a large majority of teachers were still using the alphabet method, although the whole word method was known. Horace Mann (Huey, 1908, P. 259), an advocate of the whole-word method, ridiculed the en-o—*no*, pee-you-tee—*put*, tee-aitch-ee—*the* method of beginning reading. The chief criticism of the alphabet method was that spelling the word before pronoucing it interfered with comprehension. As an alternative, the whole-word method was suggested. During the 1840's the controversy in reading was not over phonic versus whole-word methods, but over the alphabet versus the whole-word method. By 1870 the conflict appeared to be settled in favor of the whole-word method. Like a pendulum swinging, the alphabet letter-naming method is reappearing on the American scene in another form.

The current belief that letter-name knowledge facilitates learning to read probably originates with the numerous studies which find a high positive correlation between letter-name knowledge upon entry to first grade and reading achievement at the end of first grade. For example, Barrett (1965), de Hirsch, Jansky and Langford (1966), Bond and Dykstra (1967), and Dykstra (1967) found letter-name knowledge to be the best single predictor of first grade reading. The addition of factors such as mental age, auditory and visual discrimination, and socio-economic status to a letter identification score contributed little to prediction of first grade reading achievement (Silvaroli, 1965).

S. Jay Samuels, "Letter-name versus letter-sound knowledge in learning to read," *The Reading Teacher, 24,* 1971, 604–608, 662. Reprinted with permission of S. Jay Samuels and the International Reading Association.

CORRELATIONAL AND EXPERIMENTAL EVIDENCE

The mistake which some educators have made regarding letter-name knowledge and success in reading is to impute causation to correlational findings. Wilson and Flemming (1937, 1940), who found high correlations between letter knowledge and reading achievement, concluded that alphabet knowledge contributed to reading progress.

In the well known Durrell (1958) monograph, Nicholson reported that the correlation between ability to identify lowercase letters and rate of learning to read words was higher than the correlation between I.Q. and rate of learning to read these words. In the same report, Linehan stated that letter name and sound training seemed to facilitate first grade reading achievement. Since the group which received name and sound training received auditory discrimination training as well, it is impossible to determine if the facilitative effect was produced by name, sound or discrimination training. Durrell concluded, however, that reading difficulties could be prevented if, in addition to other kinds of training, instruction in letter names and sounds was given.

Whereas correlational studies have found letter name knowledge to be related to reading achievement, experimental classroom studies generally have not. Ohnmacht (1969) used intact classrooms to study the effects of letter name and sound training. One group was given early training in just letter names. A second group was given training in names and sounds. A third group served as a control. She found the group getting training on names and sounds was superior to the other groups. The group getting training only on letter names was no better than the control. Johnson (1969) also found that early classroom training in letter names failed to produce superior end-of-the-year reading achievement in comparison to the control.

The studies to be reported here represent an attempt to determine under experimental laboratory conditions what component of letter-name training, if any, facilitates reading acquisition. It may be argued that it is only the ability to visually discriminate the letters, one from another, which is important. Or, it is the ability to visually discriminate each letter and produce its name which is important. A third possibility exists. The correlation between letter-name knowledge and reading achievement is an artifact; that in an experimental setting, subjects getting letter-name training or letter discrimination training will be no better in learning to read than control subjects getting no training. To answer these questions, two experiments were done.

In experiment one, 100 first grade students midway through the first year of public elementary school were used. The students were randomly assigned to one of four treatment groups.

The letter-discrimination group was trained to visually discriminate one letter from another. No names were attached.

The letter-name group was given the same letters as the letter discrimination group but they were trained to name the letters.

Two control groups were used. Both control groups were trained on an irrelevant task. This task consisted of learning the names of dogs.

Following training, all four groups were given the same transfer task. This consisted of learning to recognize four words by the look-say method. The words were spelled using the letters used in training the letter-discrimination and naming groups.

Comparing the four groups on speed of learning the transfer task revealed by analysis of variance no significant difference among the groups. The finding that there was no difference between the letter-name group and the control group in learning a transfer list was a surprising finding, especially in view of the consistent results from the correlational studies indicating that letter-name knowledge is the best single predictor of reading achievement.

To check on the first study, a replication was done the next year, using a new sample of students and a new research assistant who was not told the results of the previous study. The results of the second study were exactly the same as the first study, that is, no significant difference on speed of learning the transfer task was found for any of the groups.

The results of the two studies indicate that letter-name knowledge does not facilitate learning to read words made up of the same letters. The fact that subjects in both studies were first graders and well into the process of reading acquisition amplifies these findings. Had the subjects been kindergarteners and naive to the fact that graphemes and phonemes were combined to form words and that some letter-names were similar to the phonemes they represented, one could argue that the transfer test was inappropriate for their level of sophistication. The fact that two studies failed to find facilitation for the letter-name groups on the transfer tasks strongly suggests that letter-name knowledge does not help the student learn to read. These results support the experimental classroom findings of Johnson (1969) and Ohnmacht (1969), who also failed to find that letter-name knowledge produced greater reading achievement. A recent communication from Jenkins (1970), who did an experimental study comparing a letter-name trained group with a control, indicated that letter-name training did not facilitate learning to read.

OTHER VARIABLES

The failure in the experimental studies to find that letter-name knowledge facilitates word recognition leads one to suspect that the correlational findings between letter-name knowledge and reading may be a product of some other factor, such as intelligence or socio-economic status. None of the correlational studies controlled for these variables.

Stevenson, *et al.*, (1968) and Anderson and Samuels (1970) found that paired associate learning ability is significantly correlated with intelligence. Speed of learning to name letters of the alphabet is a paired-associate task and may be taken as an index of intelligence. Since in the elementary school I.Q. is highly correlated with reading achievement, it is not surprising that letter-name knowledge is also correlated with reading achievement.

Another explanation for the correlation between letter-name knowledge and reading achievement is that the kind of home background which enables a child to enter first grade knowing many of the letters of the alphabet would be the kind of home in which academic achievement is stressed. Again, it is well known that socio-economic status and home environment are highly correlated with school achievement.

TASK ANALYSIS FOR TRAINING

Although letter-name knowledge does not seem to have any beneficial effect on reading, there is evidence that letter-sound training does have a positive effect. The Linehan and Ohnmacht studies both suggest this. Jeffrey and Samuels (1967) found that when letter-sound training was combined with other types of training suggested by a Gagne-type (1962) task analysis, improved reading acquisition resulted.

In the Jeffrey and Samuels (1967) study, a task analysis was done to determine what sub-skills were required for the student to independently decode a set of four words. The four words used in the 1967 study were identical to the ones used in the two studies reported here. A task analysis of the desired terminal performance indicated that left to right scanning, letter-sound training, and phonic blend training were required. When this combination of sub-skills was provided, the letter-sound trained group was superior to the other groups in independently decoding words, and they learned the set of four words to criterion significantly faster than the other groups. It is important to note that all the groups in the study got identical training on left-to-right scanning and blending. The only difference was that in addition to scanning and blending, one group got training in letter-sound

correspondence. This 1967 study indicates that when letter-sound training is combined with the other prerequisite skills, facilitation in decoding [is] produced.

The success of the 1967 study points to the importance of identifying in behavioral terms the specific terminal reading behaviors required. Then a task analysis must be done to determine the sub-skills required for successful completion of the terminal objective. Task analysis would suggest that it is not letter-name, but letter-sound training in combination with the other prerequisite sub-skills which is useful in facilitating the reading acquisition process. While there is no argument with the importance of letter-name knowledge, it seems ill-advised to suggest to teachers that this type of training will help the child learn to read.

REFERENCES

ANDERSON, R. H., and SAMUELS, S. J. Visual recognition memory, paired-associate learning, and reading achievement. Paper presented at American Educational Research Association, Minneapolis, 1970.

BARRETT, T. Predicting reading achievement through readiness tests. In J. Allen Figurel (Ed.) Reading and inquiry. *Proceedings of International Reading Association*, 1965, *10*, 26–28.

BUMSTEAD, J. F. *My little primer*. Boston: Perkins and Marwin, 1840.

BOND, G. L., and DYKSTRA, R. Coordinating center for first grade reading instruction programs. Minneapolis: University of Minnesota, 1967.

DE HIRSCH, K., JANSKY, J. J., and LANGFORD, W. D. *Predicting reading failure: a preliminary study*. New York: Harper and Row, 1966.

DURRELL, D. Success in first grade reading. *Boston University Journal of Education*, 1958, *3*, 2–47.

DURRELL, D., and MURPHY, H. *Speech to print phonics*, Teacher's manual. New York: Harcourt, Brace and World, 1964.

DYKSTRA, R. Coordinating center for first grade reading instruction programs. Minneapolis: University of Minnesota, 1967.

GAGNE, R. M. The acquisition of knowledge. *Psychological Review*, 1962, *69*, 355–365.

HUEY, E. *The psychology and pedogogy of reading*. New York: The Macmillan Company, 1908. Reissued by M.I.T. Press, 1968.

JEFFREY, W. E., and SAMUELS, S. J. The effect of method of reading training on initial learning and transfer. *Journal of Verbal Learning and Verbal Behavior*, 1967, *6*, 354–358.

JENKINS, J. Personal communication. University of Delaware, 1970.

JOHNSON, R. J. The effect of training in letter names on success in beginning reading for children of differing abilities. Doctoral dissertation, University of Minnesota, 1969.

Ohnmacht, D. D. The effects of letter-knowledge on achievement in reading in the first grade. Paper presented at American Educational Research Association, Los Angeles, 1969.

Silvaroli, N. J. Factors in predicting children's success in first grade reading. Reading and inquiry. *Proceedings of International Reading Association*, 1965, *10*, 296–298.

Stevenson, H. W., Hale, G. A., Klein, R. E., and Miller, L. K. Interrelations and correlates in children's learning and problem solving. *Monographs of the Society for Research in Child Development*, 1968, *33*, 1–68.

Thayer, G. Letters to a young teacher. *Barnard's Journal of Education*, 1857, *4*.

Wilson, F. T., and Flemming, C. Correlations of perception with other abilities and traits in grade seven. *Child Development*, 1937, *8*, 223–240.

62

The Politics of Reading *

Neil Postman

One of the most reasonable assumptions, one might think, is that reading is essentially a skill that is extremely valuable for everyone. Neil Postman, professor of English Education at New York University, argues the other side: That the literacy process is far from politically neutral and that a curriculum including "multi-media literacy" would be much more generally useful.

Teachers of reading comprise a most sinister political group, whose continued presence and strength are more a cause for alarm than celebration. I offer this thought as a defensible proposition, all the more worthy of consideration because so few people will take it seriously.

My argument rests on a fundamental and, I think, unassailable assumption about education: namely, that all educational practices are profoundly political in the sense that they are designed to produce one sort of human being rather than another—which is to say, an educational system always proceeds from some model of what a human being *ought* to be like. In the broadest sense, a political ideology is a conglomerate of systems for pro-

moting certain modes of thinking and behavior. And there is no system I can think of that more directly tries to do this than the schools. There is not one thing that is done to, for, with, or against a student in school that is not rooted in a political bias, ideology, or notion. This includes everything from the arrangement of seats in a classroom, to the rituals practiced in the auditorium, to the textbooks used in lessons, to the dress required of both teachers and students, to the tests given, to the subjects that are taught, and most emphatically, to the intellectual skills that are promoted. And what is called reading, it seems to me, just about heads the list. For to teach reading, or even to promote vigorously the teaching of reading, is to take a definite political position on how people should behave and on what they ought to value. Now, teachers, I have found, respond in one of three ways to such an assertion. Some of them deny it. Some of them concede it but without guilt or defensiveness of any kind. And some of them don't know what it means. I want to address myself to the latter, because in responding to them I can include all the arguments I would use in dealing with the others.

In asserting that the teaching of reading is essentially a political enterprise, the most obvious question I am asking is, "What is reading good for?" When I ask this question of reading teachers, I am supplied with a wide range of answers. Those who take the low ground will usually say that skill in reading is necessary in order for a youngster to do well in school. The elementary teacher is preparing the youngster for the junior high teacher, who prepares him for the senior high teacher, who, in turn, prepares him for the college teacher, and so on. Now, this answer is true but hardly satisfactory. In fact, it amounts to a description of the *rules* of the school game but says nothing about the purpose of these rules. So, when teachers are pushed a little further, they sometimes answer that the school system, at all levels, makes reading skill a precondition to success because unless one can read well, he is denied access to gainful and interesting employment as an adult. This answer raises at least a half-dozen political questions, the most interesting of which is whether or not one's childhood education ought to be concerned with one's future employment. I am aware that most people take it as axiomatic that the schooling process should prepare youth for a tranquil entry into our economy, but this is a political view that I think deserves some challenge. For instance, when one considers that the second most common cause of death among adolescents in the U.S. is suicide, or that more

---

* An earlier version of this article was presented as the keynote address at the Lehigh University Reading Conference, January 24, 1970.

Neil Postman, "The politics of reading," *Harvard Educational Review*, *40*, 1970, 244–259. Copyright 1970 by Harvard Educational Review. Reprinted by permission.

people are hospitalized for mental illness than all other illnesses combined, or that one out of every 22 murders in the United States is committed by a parent against his own child, or that more than half of all high school students have already taken habit-forming, hallucinogenic, or potentially addictive narcotics, or that by the end of this year, there will be more than one-million school drop-outs around, one can easily prepare a case which insists that the schooling process be designed for purposes other than vocational training. If it is legitimate at all for schools to claim a concern for the adult life of students, then why not pervasive and compulsory programs in mental health, sex, or marriage and the family? Besides, the number of jobs that require reading skill much beyond what teachers call a "fifth-grade level" is probably quite small and scarcely justifies the massive, compulsory, un-relenting reading programs that characterize most schools.

But most reading teachers would probably deny that their major purpose is to prepare students to satisfy far-off vocational requirements. Instead, they would take the high ground and insist that the basic purpose of reading instruction is to open the student's mind to the wonders and riches of the written word, to give him access to great fiction and poetry, to permit him to function as an informed citizen, to have him experience the sheer pleasure of reading. Now, this is a satisfactory answer in-deed but, in my opinion, it is almost totally untrue.

And to the extent that it is true, it is true in a way quite different from anything one might expect. For instance, it is probably true that in a highly complex society, one cannot be governed unless he can read forms, regulations, notices, catalogues, road signs, and the like. Thus, some minimal read-ing skill is necessary if you are to be a "good citizen," but "good citizen" here means one who can follow the instructions of those who govern him. If you cannot read, you cannot be an obedient citizen. You are also a good citizen if you are an enthusiastic consumer. And so, some minimal reading competence is required if you are going to develop a keen interest in all the products that it is necessary for you to buy. If you do not read, you will be a relatively poor market. In order to be a good and loyal citizen, it is also necessary for you to believe in the myths and superstitions of your society. Therefore, a certain minimal reading skill is needed so that you can learn what these are, or have them reinforced. Imagine what would happen in a school if a Social Studies text were introduced that described the growth of American civilization as being characterized by four major developments: 1) insurrection against a legally constituted govern-ment, in order to achieve a political identity; 2)

genocide against the indigenous population, in order to get land; 3) keeping human beings as slaves, in order to achieve an economic base; and 4) the im-portation of "coolie" labor, in order to build the railroads. Whether this view of American history is true or not is beside the point. It is at least as true or false as the conventional view *and* it would scarcely be allowed to appear unchallenged in a school-book intended for youth. What I am saying here is that an important function of the teaching of reading is to make students accessible to political and historical myth. It is entirely possible that the main reason middle-class whites are so concerned to get lower-class blacks to read is that blacks will remain relatively inaccessible to standard-brand beliefs unless and until they are minimally literate. It just may be too dangerous, politically, for any substantial minority of our population *not* to believe that our flags are sacred, our history is noble, our government is representative, our laws are just, and our institutions are viable. A reading public is a responsible public, by which is meant that it be-lieves most or all of these superstitions, and which is probably why we still have literacy tests for voting.

One of the standard beliefs about the reading process is that it is more or less neutral. Reading, the argument goes, is just a skill. What people read is their own business, and the reading teacher merely helps to increase a student's options. If one wants to read about America, one may read De-Toqueville or *The Daily News;* if one wants to read literature, one may go to Melville or Jacqueline Susann. In theory, this argument is compelling. In practice, it is pure romantic nonsense. *The New York Daily News* is the most widely read news-paper in America. Most of our students will go to the grave not having read, of their own choosing, a paragraph of DeToqueville or Thoreau or John Stuart Mill or, if you exclude the Gettysburg Ad-dress, even Abraham Lincoln. As between Jacque-line Susann and Herman Melville—well, the less said, the better. To put it bluntly, among every 100 students who learn to read, my guess is that no more than one will employ the process toward any of the lofty goals which are customarily held before us. The rest will use the process to increase their knowledge of trivia, to maintain themselves at a relatively low level of emotional maturity, and to keep themselves simplistically uninformed about the social and political turmoil around them.

Now, there are teachers who feel that, even if what I say is true, the point is nonetheless irrele-vant. After all, they say, the world is not perfect. If people do not have enough time to read deeply, if people do not have sensibilities refined enough to read great literature, if people do not have interests broad enough to be stimulated by the unfamiliar, the fault is not in our symbols, but in ourselves. But there is a point of view that proposes that the "fault," in fact, *does* lie in our symbols. Marshall McLuhan is saying that each medium of communication contains a unique metaphysic—that each medium makes special kinds of claims on our senses, and therefore, on our behavior. McLuhan himself tells us that he is by no means the first person to have noticed this. Socrates took a very dim view of the written word, on the grounds that it diminishes man's capacity to memorize, and that it forces one to follow an argument rather than to participate in it. He also objected to the fact that once something has been written down, it may easily come to the attention of persons for whom it was not intended. One can well imagine what Socrates would think about wire-tapping and other electronic bugging devices. St. Ambrose, a prolific book writer and reader, once complained to St. Jerome, another prolific writer and reader, that whatever else its virtues, reading was the most anti-social behavior yet devised by man. Other people have made observations about the effects of communications media on the psychology of a culture, but it is quite remarkable how little has been said about this subject. Most criticism of print, or any other medium, has dealt with the content of the medium; and it is only in recent years that we have begun to understand that each medium, *by its very structure*, makes us do things with our bodies, our senses, and our minds that in the long run are probably more important than any other messages communicated by the medium.

Now that it is coming to an end, we are just beginning to wonder about the powerful biases forced upon us by the Age of the Printed Word. McLuhan is telling us that print is a "hot" medium, by which he means that it induces passivity and anesthetizes almost all our senses except the visual. He is also telling us that electronic media, like the LP record and television, are reordering our entire sensorium, restoring some of our sleeping senses, and, in the process, making all of us seek more active participation in life. I think McLuhan is wrong in connecting the *causes* of passivity and activity so directly to the structure of media. I find it sufficient to say that whenever a new medium—a new communications technology—enters a culture, *no matter what its structure*, it gives us a new way of experiencing the world, and consequently, releases tremendous energies and causes people to seek new ways of organizing their institutions. When Gutenberg announced that he could manufacture books, as he put it, "without the help of reed, stylus, or pen but by wondrous agreement, proportion, and harmony of punches and types," he

could scarcely imagine that he was about to become the most important political and social revolutionary of the Second Millenium. And yet, that is what happened. Four hundred and fifty years ago, the printed word, far from being a medium that induced passivity, generated cataclysmic change. From the time Martin Luther posted his theses in 1517, the printing press disseminated the most controversial, inflammatory, and wrenching ideas imaginable. The Protestant Reformation would probably not have occurred if not for the printing press. The development of both capitalism and nationalism were obviously linked to the printing press. So were new literary forms, such as the novel and the essay. So were new conceptions of education, such as written examinations. And, of course, so was the concept of scientific methodology, whose ground rules were established by Descartes in his *Discourse on Reason*. Even today in recently illiterate cultures, such as Cuba, print is a medium capable of generating intense involvement, radicalism, artistic innovation, and institutional upheaval. But in those countries where the printed word has been pre-eminent for ever 400 years, print retains very few of these capabilities. Print is not dead, it's just old—and old technologies do not generate new patterns of behavior. For us, print is the technology of convention. We have accommodated our senses to it. We have routinized and even ritualized our responses to it. We have devoted our institutions, which are now venerable, to its service. By maintaining the printed word as the keystone of education, we are therefore opting for political and social stasis.

It is 126 years since Professor Morse transmitted a message electronically for the first time in the history of the planet. Surely it is not too soon for educators to give serious thought to the message he sent: "What hath God wrought?" We are very far from knowing the answers to that question, but we do know that electronic media have released unprecedented energies. It's worth saying that the gurus of the peace movement—Bob Dylan, Pete Seeger, Joan Baez, Phil Ochs, for instance—were known to their constituency mostly as voices on LP records. It's worth saying that Viet Nam, being our first television war, is also the most unpopular war in our history. It's worth saying that Lyndon Johnson was the first president ever to have resigned because of a "credibility gap." It's worth saying that it is now commonplace for post-TV college sophomores to usurp the authority of college presidents and for young parish priests to instruct their bishops in the ways of *both* man and God. And it's also worth saying that black people, after 350 years of bondage, want their freedom—now. Post-television blacks are, indeed, our true *now* generation.

Electronic media are predictably working to un-loose disruptive social and political ideas, along with new forms of sensibility and expression. Whether this is being achieved by the structure of the media, or by their content, or by some com-bination of both, we cannot be sure. But like Guten-berg's infernal machine of 450 years ago, the electric plug is causing all hell to break loose. Mean-while, the schools are still pushing the old tech-nology; and, in fact, pushing it with almost hysterical vigor. Everyone's going to learn to read, even if we have to kill them to do it. It is as if the schools were the last bastion of the old culture, and if it has to go, why let's take as many down with us as we can.

For instance, the schools are still the principal source of the idea that literacy is equated with in-telligence. Why, the schools even promote the idea that *spelling* is related to intelligence! Of course, if any of this were true, reading teachers would be the smartest people around. One doesn't mean to be unkind, but if that indeed is the case, no one has noticed it. In any event, it is an outrage that chil-dren who do not read well, or at all, are treated as if they are stupid. It is also masochistic, since the number of non-readers will obviously continue to increase and, thereby, the schools will condemn themselves, by their own definition of intelligence, to an increasing number of stupid children. In this way, we will soon have remedial reading-readiness classes, along with remedial classes for those not yet ready for their remedial reading-readiness class.

The schools are also still promoting the idea that literacy is the richest source of aesthetic experience. This, in the face of the fact that kids are spending a billion dollars a year to buy LP records and see films. The schools are still promoting the idea that the main source of wisdom is to be found in li-braries, from which most schools, incidentally, carefully exclude the most interesting books. The schools are still promoting the idea that the non-literate person is somehow not fully human, an idea that will surely endear us to the non-literate peoples of the world. (It is similar to the idea that salvation is obtainable only through Christianity—which is to say, it is untrue, bigoted, reactionary, and based on untenable premises, to boot.)

Worst of all, the schools are using these ideas to keep non-conforming youth—blacks, the politi-cally disaffected, and the economically disadvan-taged, among others—in their place. By taking this tack, the schools have become a major force for political conservatism at a time when everything else in the culture screams for rapid reorientation and change.

What would happen if our schools took the drastic political step of trying to make the new technology the keystone of education? The thought will seem less romantic if you remember that the start of the Third Millenium is only 31 years away. No one knows, of course, what would happen, but I'd like to make a few guesses. In the first place, the physical environment would be entirely differ-ent from what it is now. The school would look something like an electric circus—arranged to accommodate TV cameras and monitors, film projectors, computers, audio and video tape ma-chines, radio, and photographic and stereophonic equipment. As he is now provided with textbooks, each student would be provided with his own still-camera, 8 mm. camera, and tape casette. The school library would contain books, of course, but at least as many films, records, video-tapes, audio-tapes, and computer programs. The major effort of the school would be to assist students in achieving what has been called "multi-media literacy." Therefore, speaking, film-making, picture-taking, televising, computer-programming, listening, per-haps even music playing, drawing, and dancing would be completely acceptable means of express-ing intellectual interest and competence. They would certainly be given weight at least equal to reading and writing.

Since intelligence would be defined in a new way, a student's ability to create an idea would be at least as important as his ability to classify and remember the ideas of others. New evaluation procedures would come into being, and standard-ized tests—the final, desperate refuge of the print-bound bureaucrat—would disappear. Entirely new methods of instruction would evolve. In fact, schools might abandon the notion of teacher in-struction altogether. Whatever disciplines lent themselves to packaged, lineal, and segmented presentation would be offered through a computer-ized and individualized program. And students could choose from a wide variety of such programs whatever they wished to learn about. This means, among other things, that teachers would have to stop acting like teachers and find something useful to do, like, for instance, helping young people to resolve some of their more wrenching emotional problems.

In fact, a school that put electric circuitry at its center would have to be prepared for some serious damage to all of its bureaucratic and hierarchical arrangements. Keep in mind that hierarchies derive their authority from the notion of unequal access to information. Those at the top have access to more information than those at the bottom. That is in fact why they are at the top and the others, at the bottom. But today those who are at the bottom of the school hierarchy, namely, the students, have access to at least as much information about most subjects as those at the top. At present, the only way those at the top can maintain control over them is by carefully discriminating against what the students know—that is, by labelling what the students know as unimportant. But suppose cinematography was made a "major" subject instead of English literature? Suppose chemotherapy was made a "major" subject? or space technology? or ecology? or mass communication? or popular music? or photography? or race relations? or urban life? Even an elementary school might then find itself in a situation where the faculty were at the bottom and its students at the top. Certainly, it would be hard to know who are the teachers and who the learners.

And then perhaps a school would become a place where *everybody*, including the adults, is trying to learn something. Such a school would obviously be problem-centered, *and* future-centered, *and* change-centered; and, as such, would be an instrument of cultural and political radicalism. In the process we might find that our youth would also learn to read without pain and with a degree of success and economy not presently known.

I want to close on this thought: teachers of reading represent an important political pressure group. They may not agree with me that they are a sinister political group. But I should think that they would want to ask at least a few questions *before* turning to consider the *techniques* of teaching reading. These questions would be: What is reading good for? What is it better or worse than? What are my motives in promoting it? And the ultimate political question of all, "Whose side am I on?"

63

The Changing World of Mental Measurement and Its Social Significance [1]

WAYNE H. HOLTZMAN

Recent criticism of normative testing for college admission and grading in courses is discussed in Wayne Holtzman's article, along with current attempts at educational reform. Holtzman is director of the Hogg Foundation for Mental Health, University of Texas, and was editor of the Journal of Educational Psychology *from 1967 to 1972.*

One of the great success stories of modern psychology is the development of objective tests for measuring human abilities that are of importance to society. During the past half century, the standardized mental test with nationally based norms has proven to be a highly effective instrument for selection and classification of men in the armed forces; for evaluation of educational progress within our school systems; for selective admission of college students; for selection of employees within government, business, and industry; and for clinical assessment of individuals in need of psychological services. It is estimated that within American schools alone, over 250 million standardized tests of ability are administered each year (Brim, Glass, Neulinger, Firestone, & Lerner, 1969). It is a rare individual indeed, especially

[1] Presidential Address of Division 5, presented at the annual meeting of the American Psychological Association, Miami Beach, Florida, September 1970.

among children and young adults, who has not been evaluated by a standardized mental test, a test that has played a significant role in determining his place in society.

From World War I until the late 1950s, the testing movement enjoyed a degree of public acceptance it is unlikely to see again. Judging each person on the basis of his measured performance rather than on his family background, social status, or political connections has been a powerful agent of social change. Assuming unbiased, reliable measurement, what could be more just within the American concept of an egalitarian society than recognizing merit by objective tests of ability? Even today, college entrance examinations have made it possible for able but financially poor students to obtain scholarships in the best private colleges.

CRITICISMS OF TESTING

By the late 1950s, it became generally apparent that the large-scale normative use of objective tests for rewarding selected individuals among many in competition has serious social consequences of debatable value. The testing movement has always had its critics, but they failed to gain a foothold until the impact of adverse decisions based on tests had been felt by millions of individuals. In the post-Sputnik period, a growing number of critics have claimed that mental tests are unfair to the bright but unorthodox person, to the culturally disadvantaged, and to the naïve individual who lacks experience in taking standardized tests (Anastasi, 1967; Commission on Tests, 1970).

The growing controversies surrounding mental tests have become especially acute within educational institutions. It is generally recognized that the educated person enjoys the riches of society as well as enhanced self-esteem and personal development, while the person who prematurely drops out of school is cast into an inferior role. It is not surprising that the angry cries of black students are directed at normative tests that deprive them of entrance to the better colleges, jobs, and social positions.

A major dilemma arises in attempting to meet these criticisms. The traditional academic curricula of our schools and colleges are becoming increasingly dependent on verbal communication, verbal memory, and the same kind of abstract reasoning as measured by scholastic aptitude tests. Therefore, sufficiently high correlations arise between standardized multiple-choice aptitude tests and course examinations to justify the use of tests for prediction of academic achievement and selective admissions. The rapid growth of higher education and the greatly increased number of students per course have forced more and more instructors to employ multiple-choice objective examinations for grading students. As a result, the relevance of scholastic aptitude tests for prediction of academic grades has increased, rather than decreased, in recent years. The compelling economics of mass education and objective normative testing are exceedingly difficult to resist in a rapidly expanding system of higher education. Tests that are designed for normative use, whether for college admissions or course examinations, discriminate against those who are culturally different from the majority.

Such incidental discrimination might be more justifiable if there were a close correspondence between success in school and subsequent occupational success. But for a number of reasons, the correlation between grades and later success is too low to argue generally that measured performance in the traditional academic curriculum is that critical. The issue is made more complex by the fact that entry to many occupations is denied an individual who fails to complete the prescribed academic program, regardless of the program's relevance. The growing meritocracy built around traditional curricula that are uniformly prescribed, normative tests that are competitively graded, and restrictive credentials for job entry may be efficient means of building a technological society, but it does so by exacting a heavy toll on those members of society who fail to conform to the majority. The more tightly the meritocracy is drawn, the more self-fulfilling the prophecies.

Educational Reform and the New Technologies

A way out of this dilemma may be closer at hand than many realize. The number of pressures within American society and new developments in measurement and instruction are moving in the same general direction. Led by students, spokesmen for minority rights, and concerned academicians, the general public is becoming increasingly aware of serious inequities within our educational system. As higher education becomes more essential to vocational advancement and personal fulfillment, the fruits of education cannot be denied to anyone who is motivated and capable of profiting from it.

The growing attacks on normative testing for college admission and course grading are having an impact as more and more individuals call for less emphasis on scholastic aptitude measures and more

on other abilities and new forms of instruction. The kinds and variety of curricula recognized as appropriate for various forms of education are increasing markedly. Courses aimed at social problems and individual self-development are eroding the traditional, discipline-oriented curricula in many colleges. This new thrust may involve individual competencies in such things as social leadership, self-awareness, regard for human rights and social responsibilities, or other aspects of behavior that typically have not been important in traditional academic pursuits. As the curriculum moves through reform, there will be opportunities for new kinds of measurement as well.

Emphasis is being given in many circles to the idea of individualized instruction in which the learner moves at his own pace and at a time and place that is appropriate for him as an individual. The units of instruction emphasize self-paced learning with regular social reinforcement to maintain a high degree of motivation and relevance, coupled with the concept of continuous progress from one unit to the next. These "microcurriculum units" or modules have fairly well-defined behavioral objectives or performance criteria by which mastery can be recognized. The curriculum itself is viewed in a more global manner as consisting of strings of modules arranged according to an explicit hierarchy of values that are in harmony with the future goals of individual development. In many fields of learning, these specific modules involve training objectives where criterion testing for standardized mastery is employed rather than normative testing for measuring individual differences. Much of what goes on in education is susceptible to treatment in this form. The broader educational objectives differ considerably from one individual to the next in order to maximize potentiality for individual development.

A major force for social change in educational reform is the emergence of new educational technology and related techniques of measurement. Keeping track of a person moving at his own pace in a continuous progress environment, where the particular branching of the curriculum is tailor-made for the student's own learning aptitudes and level, requires a computer to manage the curriculum and assist with the instruction (Holtzman, 1970). In a traditional setting, the instructor keeps a record of how well each student does on each achievement test for the course, while the periodically collected scores from standardized normative tests are stored centrally. When instruction is individualized, testing must be done more frequently and at different times for each student. In many cases, performance testing and instruction are so closely interwoven that they appear as one integrated learning activity. Except for periodic testing at a later date to determine how much a person has retained, even the conceptual nature of measurement shifts from a normative basis, where each person is compared with a general population, to a criterion-referenced basis, where the only decision made is whether or not the student has achieved the desired objective for a specific instructional module. Not only are more short tests given, but many more have to be constructed, again requiring a computer for generating tests from item pools as well as scoring and storing them for each student.

Several large-scale programs of individualized instruction are sufficiently advanced to demonstrate the feasibility and power of this approach to educational reform. Now in its fourth year of operation under the leadership of John Flanagan, and jointly developed by the American Institutes for Research and Westinghouse Learning Corporation, Project PLAN consists of over 1,000 modules divided across nine operating grades and four subject-matter areas (Dunn, 1969). Each teaching unit is coded as to reading difficulty, required teacher supervision, media richness, required social involvement, and a number of other characteristics. A profile is prepared for each student containing measures of abilities, interests, aspirations, and background data for use by the computer in matching the curriculum to the student. The combination of normative measurement on nationality standardized tests for initial guidance and placement of the student and criterion-referenced tests for assessing progress in mastering the curriculum modules is especially noteworthy. Experience to date with over 10,000 students indicates that most individuals like the new freedom provided by PLAN, and that learning proceeds at a faster pace.

A still more detailed form of individualized instruction can be found in the program of individually prescribed instruction developed by Glaser and associates at the University of Pittsburgh's Learning Research and Development Center (Cooley & Glaser, 1969). A specific lesson plan is prescribed individually for each child every day, depending on his performance and desires of the previous day. Thousands of curriculum modules are stored and retrieved manually by clerks at the end of each day until the experimental system can be perfected and stored electronically in computers. Interwoven with each module is a criterion-referenced achievement test that provides a basis for decision making in selecting the next module.

A recent study by Ferguson (1969) serves to illustrate computer-assisted branched testing with elementary arithmetic materials in the Pittsburgh individually prescribed instruction program. A

model was developed and tested in which items are selected on the basis of previous responses and are thus tailored to the competencies of the student. A learning hierarchy of prerequisite relationships among 18 objectives in addition and subtraction was formulated on the basis of previous studies. Two major sequences emerged as dominant in the hierarchy, one involving only addition skills and the other exclusively concerned with subtraction. A third sequence integrated both addition and subtraction. Initially, an examinee was presented with a randomly generated item for the specific objective being tested. The computer scored his response as correct or incorrect and generated another item. The process continued until a sufficient number of items had been answered for the computer to make a decision regarding the individual's proficiency on the objective. The decision model involved assigning a priori probability values to the two types of error constituting incorrect decisions and applying Wald's sequential probability ratio test to terminate the testing on the objective in question. Selection of the next objective to be tested depended on the examinee's proficiency on the first objective as well as the proposed learning hierarchy. When given to 74 students in Grades 1–6 at the Oakleaf Elementary School, Pittsburgh, Pennsylvania, the sequential branched testing method proved to be three times as efficient as a fixed-length conventional test, requiring, on the average, only 52 items instead of 150.

A sequential branched testing procedure proves far superior to conventional testing when one.has a computer for generating and scoring items, a suitable communication terminal for interaction of computer and examinee, and a good basis for arranging the skills to be tested in a learning hierarchy. The procedure is ideally suited to criterion-referenced testing but is of questionable value where normative testing is employed. As Lord (1970) has demonstrated, little is to be gained by the use of tailored testing with conventional items for normative measurement except in the case of best and worst students.

Integrating the elements of programmed learning and sequential branched testing into a single curriculum requires a computer for electronic storage and retrieval of the material to be learned, the test items for measuring mastery, and the instructional branching strategy for both the curriculum and the tests. Suitable multimedia teaching terminals with visual display devices, light pens, audio units, and typewriters under either student or computer control, depending on the nature of the curriculum and purpose of the student, must be provided in large numbers at reasonable cost before computer-assisted instruction, testing, and guidance can become operational. Several major companies are now designing hardware configurations that will soon have the required functional capabilities for fully implementing computer-assisted instruction. It is now fairly certain that the cost of such a system can be sharply reduced by mass production to the point where it is economically feasible to think of large-scale implementation (Alpert & Bitzer, 1970). Psychological laboratories for computer-assisted instruction at Stanford University, the University of Texas, the University of Illinois, Florida State University, System Development Corporation, the Mitre Corporation, and a dozen other universities and research institutes have already demonstrated the feasibility of this new technology as well as its dramatic impact on individual learning in many areas.

Such new technologies as Project PLAN, individually prescribed instruction, and computer-assisted instruction are highly promising in their eventual impact on educational practices and the concomitant measurement of standardized mastery using criterion-referenced tests instead of normative testing for competitive selection. Successful prototypes have been developed, but these represent only a small beginning compared to what must be done in the way of research and development before individualized instruction in the true sense of the term can be properly implemented on a large scale.

NATIONAL ASSESSMENT OF EDUCATIONAL CHANGE

Still another important departure from standardized normative measurement of individual differences in mental abilities grows out of the increased concern for developing a national system of social indicators, measures that reflect the quality of life, the rate of educational progress, and the value of human resources for the nation as a whole as well as for different regional, ethnic, and socio-economic groups. A recent report of the Behavioral and Social Sciences Survey Committee (1969) has recommended the establishment of a system of social indicators by the federal government that would lead to an annual social report for measuring changes in many aspects of society. A step in this direction has already been taken by the National Assessment of Educational Progress, a project of the Education Commission of the States (Womer, 1970).

Under the leadership of Ralph Tyler and support from the Carnegie Corporation, the Exploratory Committee on Assessing the Progress of Education

began in 1964 to collect information about the knowledge and skills held by 9-year-olds, 13-year-olds, and 17-year-olds and of young adults in 10 subject areas taught in schools. After five years of planning and public debate as to the merits of the project, National Assessment launched its first annual survey for all four age levels in three subject areas—citizenship, science, and writing. The national sample contained a total of approximately 100,000 persons carefully chosen on a stratified random basis involving 52 sampling units from each of four geographic regions.

The first step in preparing materials for National Assessment was to determine a list of educational objectives for each subject. Using these objectives as guides, various measurement research organizations took responsibility for preparing exercises designed to assess what young people actually know. A variety of approaches—questionnaires, interviews, observations, and performance tasks—were employed in addition to traditional multiple-choice and short-answer questions similar to those used in standardized mental tests.

Five important distinctions can be made between the National Assessment exercises and multiple-choice items employed in normative tests. First, the assessment exercises are designed to discover what defined segments of the nation's population can do or what they know, rather than to distribute people normatively according to measured individual differences. For example, what percentage of the 9-year-olds in the country know that most plants get most of their water directly from the soil? Or know how to report a fire? Or report that they had ever taken part in some organized civic project to help other people? Does this percentage shift significantly across different segments of the population or over time?

Second, while items in a test are summed to give a score for each individual, exercises in National Assessment are each analyzed in their own right by pooling data across individuals. For this reason, it is particularly important that the exercises be meaningful to specialist and layman alike, that they be directly related to the stated objectives, and that they have high content validity. Extensive review sessions involving a variety of judges were held for every exercise retained for National Assessment.

Third, the exercises are designed for a broad range of difficulty in order to report to the American public examples of knowledges, skills, and understandings that are common to almost all American youth of a given age, examples that are common to a typical or average American youth, and examples that are common to only the most knowledgeable youth. Ideally, one-third of the exercises should be passed by most of the population, one-third by about half, and one-third by only a small percentage. By contrast, item difficulty level in the typical normative test is likely to hover near the 50% level or to be evenly distributed throughout the range.

Fourth, all exercises, except those in reading, are presented aurally as well as visually, so that no one is severely penalized in responding, say, to citizenship or science questions.

And fifth, the exercises are assembled in heterogeneous packages with different sets of exercises given to different individuals on a sampling basis. A package for 17-year-olds last year, for example, contained seven multiple-choice science exercises, three free-response citizenship exercises, and one essay exercise for writing. Exercises are packaged in any convenient fashion that adds up to no more than 50 minutes of assessment time for each person. Items in a normative test, on the other hand, are assembled in relatively homogeneous scales so that they can be added together to give a reliable score.

Unlike most measurement applications in psychology and education, in National Assessment a person is never asked to record his name. Responses are clustered and analyzed by sex, age, race, region, community, and family characteristics in order to obtain censuslike information about the educational progress of various segments of the population. Repeated applications in the years ahead will provide a wealth of data dealing with change over time—data that should be useful in national planning, particularly when examined together with other social indicators.

Individuals and schools approached by National Assessment were given the option of declining to participate in order to respect their rights to privacy. Exceedingly few refused to participate under these permissive conditions, testifying to the wisdom of this policy. My own experience in soliciting the cooperation of 13,000 high school students in a probability statewide sample (Moore & Holtzman, 1965) and in asking for the continued participation of 420 families in a longitudinal study of personality development (Holtzman, Diaz-Guerrero, Swartz, & Lara Tapia, 1968) has been similarly favorable. Unbiased samples can be obtained in most measurement studies without coercion of even a mild sort. National Assessment provides an exemplary model of how one should proceed in order to protect the privacy of individual participants and their freedom to decline.

Preserving the confidentiality of data is a related problem that continues to worry many thoughtful individuals. As we move into large-scale programs with extensive, centralized data banks stored in computers, the possibility of harm to an individual cannot yet be completely eliminated. The files that may do greatest damage to the individual are those that are kept secret from him but not from those who can take action affecting him. While much of the national concern expressed in recent congressional hearings deals with personal information that psychologists are unlikely to find interesting, specific attention has been directed at potential abuses of individual privacy involving psychological test data, biographical information, and social attitudinal data typically employed in psychological research. The proper balance between protecting the individual against the misuse of information about himself and collating data to help solve major social, economic, and educational problems has not yet been achieved. On the other hand, continuation of the present highly decentralized systems will not cure present abuses of individual privacy, although it will prevent the integration of information required for future social development. As Ruggles (1969) has pointed out, the key to the problem of protecting privacy is not to depend blindly on the inefficiency that accompanies the present situation. Properly developed centralized data banks can eventually assure greater protection for the individual while also providing essential information for basic research as well as future national planning.

One interesting solution to the problem of protecting the confidentiality of data from individual respondents is the Link system that has been devised for the national study of college student characteristics by the American Council on Education's Cooperation Institutional Research Program (Astin & Boruch, 1970). Measurement data and biographical information on several hundred thousand college freshmen are collected each year as part of an ongoing educational data bank. Initially, a more or less traditional system was instituted. Two physically separate tape files were created, one containing the student's answers to research questions together with an arbitrary identification number, and a second containing only the student's name and address and the same arbitrary number. The first tape with the research data file was openly accessible for analysis. The second tape with the name and address file was locked in a vault and used only to print labels for follow-up mailings. The original questionnaires and punched cards were then destroyed.

Good as it may seem, this system still did not offer complete protection against government subpoena or unauthorized disclosure by staff members with access to both files. A third file, the Link file, was created which contained two sets of numbers—

the original arbitrary identification numbers from the research data file, and a completely new set of random numbers which were substituted for the original identification numbers in the second file. The final step in establishing the new system was to deposit the new Link file at a computer facility in a foreign country with a firm agreement that the foreign facility would never release it to anyone, including the American Council on Education. Follow-up mailing tapes now have to be prepared by the foreign facility. There is no way that anyone can identify individual responses in the research file.

Such elaborate steps to guarantee the complete confidentiality of personal information in research files may seem far too expensive. Why go to this extreme when the chances are exceedingly remote that any harm could be done to an individual by using a more traditional system? The reason for foolproof data files is that the public demands it. However unlikely, there does exist the possibility of court subpoena or improper invasion of privacy when the data files and decoding files are under the control of the same organization.

RECOGNITION OF SOCIAL, CULTURAL, AND LINGUISTIC VARIABILITY

One of the most important changes of the past decade in the field of mental measurement as well as in society as a whole is the greatly increased respect for social, cultural, and linguistic variability among different kinds of people. Until recently, the "American way of life" was defined almost entirely by middle-class values of white, English-speaking people of largely western-European origin. In general, school curricula, symbols of social status and privilege, occupations, the more highly valued life styles, and to some extent even suggested definitions of intelligence, all conformed to the dominant values of which most Americans were proud. The forgotten minorities were expected to adjust to these values if they were to enjoy the fruits of the nation. As recently as 10 years ago, school principals in the Southwest often pointed proudly to the fact that the speaking of Spanish by Mexican-American children was prohibited on their school grounds, English being the only permissible language in which to receive an education.

The emergence of black culture, the Chicano movement, and the stirring of the American Indian as well as other forgotten groups in the wake of desegregation and civil rights legislation have forced white America to reexamine its soul. The result in the field of mental measurement has been a recognition and acceptance of cultural variability,

a search for new kinds of cognitive, perceptual, and affective measures by which to gauge mental development, and a renewed determination to contribute significantly to the task of overcoming educational and intellectual deprivation.

A generation ago, the typical study involving mental measurement and social variability consisted of giving tests, standardized largely on middle-class whites, to people of other ethnic, linguistic, and socioeconomic backgrounds. Countless individual and group differences were observed and classified in a descriptive manner. Today, more attention is given to devising procedures for measurement and evaluation which are indigenous to the culture under study. Illustrative of this new approach is the work of Freeberg (1970), who developed a test battery specifically tailored in content, format, and administration to disadvantaged adolescents drawn largely from the black and Puerto Rican ghettos of New York. The extensive six-year longitudinal study of 2,000 Headstart children undertaken last year by the Educational Testing Service also contains a large variety of new measures that are specifically designed for culturally disadvantaged children (Anderson, 1969). The problem with most such tailored procedures is that they may be just as ill-suited for use with other markedly different individuals as are tests standardized on middle-class whites when employed for assessing educationally disadvantaged children.

The most difficult methodological problems arise in cross-cultural research where two or more distinctly different cultures are compared systematically (Holtzman, 1968). The translation, calibration, and administration of psychological measures across cultures require close and continual collaboration of specialists from each culture who have learned to trust each other fully. In a similar manner, measurement across subcultures within a given nation requires the full participation of representatives from each subculture, a condition that is met by all too few investigators thus far. In spite of such problems, studies dealing systematically with cultural, social, and linguistic variability are growing rapidly in number while also increasing greatly in the power of their research designs. Is it too much to hope that by the end of the coming decade the lingering ethnocentrism of the testing movement will disappear?

· · ·

In the short span of this article, it has been possible to highlight only selected topics within the broad field of mental measurement. It should be obvious to even the casual observer of trends in the field that other areas also deserve attention. It is worth noting that every one of the new advances reviewed is heavily dependent on the modern electronic computer for its implementation. Fundamental to the changing world of mental measurement is the rapid growth in power, versatility, and accessibility of high-speed computers. Large-scale testing; new educational technology such as individually prescribed instruction, sequential branched testing within the curriculum, Project PLAN, and computer-assisted instruction; national assessment of educational change and the development of a system of social indicators; new techniques for preserving the confidentiality of personal data; and even new programs for assessing the mental development of culturally different people—all require a computer for implementation.

In focusing primarily on the social implications of new advances, it is easy to overlook the numerous theoretical and methodological contributions to the field of measurement and evaluation that have been made in the past few years. New techniques of scaling, test theory, factor analysis, and multivariate experimental designs are being produced and extended in a lively manner. The immediate social significance of these developments may not be readily apparent because of their indirect, long-range nature as basic research contributions. And yet, without the continued, vigorous support of such theoretical and methodological advances, the truly great potentiality of the changing world of measurement would fail to materialize. Each of the promising new developments surveyed above is heavily dependent on the solution of difficult basic research problems before it can be fully realized to the benefit of society. There is every reason to be optimistic about the next 10 years in the field of mental measurement, given the recognized social significance of new developments and the rapid rate at which basic work is advancing.

REFERENCES

ALPERT, D., & BITZER, D. L. Advances in computer-based education. *Science,* 1970, *167,* 1582–1590.

ANASTASI, A. Psychology, psychologists, and psychological testing. *American Psychologist,* 1967, *22,* 297–306.

ANDERSON, S. B. The ETS–OEO longitudinal study of disadvantaged children. In, *Untangling the tangled web of education.* Princeton, N. J.: Educational Testing Service, 1969.

ASTIN, A. W., & BORUCH, R. E. A "Link" system for assuring confidentiality of research data in longitudinal studies. *ACE Research Reports,* 1969, *5*(3).

BEHAVIORAL AND SOCIAL SCIENCES SURVEY COMMITTEE. *The behavioral and social sciences: Outlook and needs.* Washington, D. C.; National Academy of Sciences, 1969.

BRIM, O. G., JR., GLASS, D. C., NEULINGER, J., FIRESTONE, I. J., & LERNER, S. C. *American beliefs and attitudes about intelligence.* New York: Russell Sage Foundation, 1969.

COMMISSION ON TESTS. *Report of Commission on Tests: 1. Righting the balance.* New York: College Entrance Examination Board, 1970.

COOLEY, W. W., & GLASER, R. The computer and individualized instruction. *Science,* 1969, *166,* 574–582.

DUNN, J. A. The accommodation of individual differences in the development of personal programs of study. In J. C. Flanagan (Chm.), Project PLAN: A computer-supported individualized education program. Symposium presented at the meeting of the American Psychological Association, Washington, D. C., September 1969.

FERGUSON, R. L. Computer-assisted criterion-referenced testing. Working Paper No. 49, Learning Research and Development Center, University of Pittsburgh, 1969.

FREEBERG, N. E. Assessment of disadvantaged adolescents: A different approach to research and evaluation measures. *Journal of Educational Psychology,* 1970, *61,* 229–240.

HOLTZMAN, W. H. Cross-cultural studies in psychology. *International Journal of Psychology,* 1968, *3,* 83–91.

HOLTZMAN, W. H. Computers in education. In W. H. Holtzman (Ed.), *Computer-assisted instruction, testing, and guidance.* New York: Harper & Row, 1970.

HOLTZMAN, W. H., DIAZ-GUERRERO, R., SWARTZ, J. D., & LARA TAPIA, L. Cross-cultural longitudinal research on child development: Studies of American and Mexican school children. In J. P. Hill (Ed.), *Minnesota Symposia on Child Psychology.* Vol. 2. Minneapolis: University of Minnesota Press, 1968.

LORD, F. Some test theory for tailored testing. In W. H. Holtzman (Ed.), *Computer-assisted instruction, testing, and guidance.* New York: Harper & Row, 1970.

MOORE, B. M., & HOLTZMAN, W. H. *Tomorrow's parents.* Austin: University of Texas Press, 1965.

RUGGLES, R. How a data bank might operate. *Think,* 1969, *35*(3), 22–23.

WOMER, F. G. *What is National Assessment?* Denver, Colo.: Education Commission of the States, 1970.

XII

TEACHERS AND TEACHING

We have devoted a section of this book specifically to the teacher in order to emphasize the enormous importance of the role. The teacher is undoubtedly the most crucial factor in the classroom. Whatever the method, whatever the materials, the teacher's own knowledge and sensitivity count most heavily. Does he know his field? Is he able to structure lessons and explanations in an effective way? How closely is he attuned to the student's responses, and how well can he provide appropriate rewards contingent on the desired output? Does he know his students? In what ways should he attempt to arouse and sustain motivation?

Despite the acknowledged importance of the teacher—and despite widespread criticism of teachers today—there has been a dearth of research into the psychology of teaching. We do not really know what teaching is all about; what the teacher actually says and does in the classroom; how effective his teaching is, etc.

There have recently been some attempts to develop objective methods for studying the behavior of teachers. Interaction analysis, for example, developed by Ned A. Flanders, is a technique of systematic classroom observation, in which verbal statements during spontaneous classroom communication are coded and analyzed and the frequencies of different types of coded statements are related to students' achievement and attitudes. Flanders' most recent book, for those interested in learning more about his interaction analysis, is *Analyzing Teaching Behavior* (Reading, Mass.: Addison-Wesley, 1970).

The Center for Research and Development in Teaching at Stanford University has worked for several years in this problem area. N. L. Gage, in his book *Teacher Education and Teacher Effectiveness: The Search for a Scientific Basis* (Palo Alto, Calif.: Pacific Books, 1970), has presented the Stanford group's point of view. They reject the idea that we must find *the* criterion of "teacher effectiveness" before we can select and train good teachers. Such an overall criterion is much too gross for scientific investigation, as well as for use in teacher-education. Rather, they use criteria of effectiveness in limited, specifically defined aspects of the role (micro-criteria). They analyze the teaching process into small, discrete components—technical skills—which can be taught, practiced, and evaluated (micro-teaching) in a teacher education program. Gage's approach is most promising, but concrete work in these areas has a long way to go.

64

Teachers' Attitudes Toward Children's Behavior Revisited

ALEXANDER TOLOR,
WILLIAM L. SCARPETTI,
AND PAUL A. LANE

How sensitive are teachers to the behavior problems of their pupils? Wickman's classic study in 1928 indicated an enormous difference between the views of teachers and clinicians. In 1959, Harry Beilin updated that study and found that there had been some rapprochement between the two groups. Beilin's article, "Teachers' and Clinicians' Attitudes Toward Behavior Problems of Children: A Reappraisal," was published in Child Development, *volume 30, pages 9–25, and was reprinted in the second edition of* The Causes of Behavior. *The following article is a very recent study on the topic. It points out that while the gap has closed to some extent, there are still large differences between teachers and clinicians. It examines the reasons for the discrepancy. Alexander Tolor is associate professor of psychology and director of the Institute of Human Development at Fairfield University; William L. Scarpetti is in the Division of Psychology, Northwestern University Medical School; and Paul A. Lane is associate professor of psychology at the University of Bridgeport.*

A classic study by E. K. Wickman (1928) found a great discrepancy between the views of teachers and mental health workers toward the behavior problems of children. Although this study has been criticized on methodological grounds, its influence on American education has been profound. Several more recent investigations (Griffiths, 1952; Schrupp & Gjerde, 1953; Stouffer, 1952) suggest that while there has been considerable change in the attitudes of teachers to make them more congruent with those of clinicians, marked differences between the two groups continue to exist. These differences are still in the direction of teachers being more concerned with management, sexual adjustment, and adherence to authority problems whereas the mental health professionals are more sensitive to withdrawal behavior and behavior not directly related to the school routine but suggesting a deterioration of social or emotional patterns.

The purpose of this study was to explore further the relationship between the evaluations by teachers and psychologists of a wide range of child behavior patterns. More specifically, it was anticipated that by employing a comprehensive scale of unambiguous behavioral items, which can be grouped on an empirical or theoretical basis to focus on patterns of functioning, it would be possible to identify the types of behavioral patterns that teachers and psychologists perceive most differently. The effect that the teachers' experience level has on the ratings was also to be determined.

METHOD

The teacher respondents consisted of 90 female and 28 male elementary public school teachers randomly selected from a large urban school system. They were drawn from all grades ranging from the kindergarten to the seventh grade level, inclusively. There were 9 teachers at the kindergarten level, 13 at Grade 1, 16 at Grade 2, 15 at Grade 3, 17 at Grade 4, 16 at Grade 5, 15 at Grade 6, and 17 at Grade 7. The professional experience of the teachers encompassed the range of less than 1 year to 44 years (mean 11.9 years).

The psychologist respondents consisted of 17 males and 6 females, all of whom were functioning in clinical settings in the same state as the teachers. The highest degree held by the psychologists was the Ph.D. for 15 and the M.A. or M.S. by eight. In experience the psychologists ranged from under one year to over 30 years (mean 10.7 years).

The measuring device was the Staten Island Behavior Scale (Mandell & Silberstein, 1965) which consists of 295 items descriptive of children's behavior. The items were originally selected from published and unpublished scales used to evaluate children's adjustment and from an analysis of a large number of case records in the files of a child guidance clinic.

The items were classified for the purposes of the present study by six raters (5 advanced students and 1

Alexander Tolor, William L. Scarpetti, and Paul A. Lane, "Teachers' attitudes toward children's behavior revisited," *Journal of Educational Psychology, 58,* 1967, 175–180. Copyright 1967 by the American Psychological Association, and reproduced by permission.

414

Diplomate in Clinical Psychology), making independent judgments, into the following classifications: psychosomatic and physical disturbance (71 items); phobias (18 items); aggressiveness (56 items); affect expression (58 items); communication disturbance (21 items); regressive behavior (15 items); inefficiency indicators (25 items); and fantasy involvement or withdrawal (31 items).

Each item was placed into the category that represented the rating of the majority of the judges. An indication of the high degree of interrater agreement is provided by the fact that on 203 of the 295 items (69%) at least five of the raters were in complete agreement in regard to the classification of an item.

Illustrations of the different types of items are the following: For the psychosomatic and physical disturbance classification—"Is slow in his movements"; for the phobic classification—"Is afraid of being alone in a wide open space"; for aggressiveness—"Hits or attacks other child"; for affect expression—"Shows inappropriate feeling"; for communication disturbance—"Talks and talks"; for regressive behavior—"Carries blanket"; for inefficiency indicators—"Does not complete his chores"; and for fantasy involvement or withdrawal—"Doesn't join in competitive games."

The written instructions accompanying the administration of the scale are presented below:

For each of the following items please indicate whether the behavior in question, in your opinion, indicates normal or abnormal behavior in a child falling in the age range from 1 to 16 inclusive.

Please answer all items without omitting any, and try to check either the "Normal" or "Abnormal" category. In the event that you really cannot decide whether the behavior is normal or abnormal, you may check the "Unknown" line. However, you will probably be able to arrive at a definite decision in all or nearly all instances.

The respondents were not given any time limit, but were cautioned against collaborating with anyone else in completing the scale.

The very broad age range was quite deliberately employed in the instructions since our intent was not so much to obtain reactions to a child's behavior at a specific point in time—even though we recognized that the appropriateness of behavior is age related—but more to distill from a less structured frame of reference behavior patterns that most frequently tend to be regarded as being normal or abnormal, even in the absence of a specific anchoring point.

RESULTS AND DISCUSSION

The main findings indicated that teachers and psychologists, when their responses for each item on the questionnaire are compared by chi-square, differ significantly ($p < .05$) on 66 of the 295 items, that is, on 22.4% of the items, in regard to whether they rated the behavior to be normal or abnormal. This number of differentiating items is significantly greater than would be expected on a chance basis

alone. Of the 66 critical descriptions of behavior, 7, or 11%, are in the psychosomatic and physical disturbance category, 1, or 2%, in the phobias category, 21, or 32%, in the aggressiveness category, 19, or 29%, in the affect expression category, 3, or 5%, in the communication disturbance category, 6, or 9%, in the regressive behavior category, 3, or 5%, in the inefficiency indicators category, and 6, or 9%, in the fantasy involvement or withdrawal category.

Since the categories consisted originally of unequal numbers of scale items, the percentages reported above may be somewhat misleading. Another way of analyzing the same data is to determine the proportion of items within each category that differentiates the teachers' judgments from the psychologists' ratings. Employing this approach, we note from Table 1 that the greatest disagreement occurs in the areas of regressive behavior, aggressiveness, and affect expression. Next in order are fantasy involvement or withdrawal, communication disturbance, and inefficiency indicators in which areas the two groups are in relatively close agreement. In regard to phobias and psychosomatic and physical disturbance, the judgments of psychologists and teachers are very much in accord, as can be seen by the negligible item disagreement.

These results indicate, therefore, that elementary school teachers in general tend to evaluate behavior that may be described as regressive, aggressive, and emotional quite differently than do psychologists. In view of the fact that nearly all of the differentiating items, that is, 61 of 66, or 92.4%, were rated predominantly normal by psychologists and abnormal by teachers, it is obvious that elementary school teachers perceive regressive, aggressive, and emotional behavior to be considerably more pathological than do mental health professionals.

Two subgroups of teachers were selected based on amounts of teaching experience. The Highs consisted of the top third in experience of the over-

TABLE 1

DEGREE OF DISAGREEMENT BETWEEN TEACHERS AND
PSYCHOLOGISTS IN SPECIFIC SCALE CATEGORIES

Category	Items in scale	Percentage of items disagreed upon
Physical-psychosomatic	71	10
Phobic	18	6
Aggressive	56	38
Affect	58	33
Communication	21	14
Regressive	15	40
Inefficiency	25	12
Fantasy-withdrawal	31	19

all group of teachers. The Lows consisted of the lowest third in teaching experience. The 39 teachers in the High subgroup ranged in professional experience from 14 to 44 years with a median of 24.5 years; the 39 teachers in the Low subgroup ranged in experience from less than 1 year to 6 years with a median of 3 years.

When the attitudes toward child behavior of the Lows are compared with those of the psychologists, 83 items were rated significantly differently by the two groups. Eighty of the 83 items, or 96%, were rated normal more often by psychologists than by teachers with relatively little experience. There was disagreement primarily in regard to the significance of aggressive behavior (57% of the items in that category were rated differently), regressive behavior (33% of the items here were differently rated), and affect expressions (31% of the items were judged differently). There was no difference in the ratings of the 18 phobic items, and relatively little disparity in judgments for inefficient behavior (16%) and fantasy-withdrawal behavior (16%). Communication problems and physical-psychosomatic disturbances produced only moderate disagreements (19% and 21%).

A similar chi-square analysis was done comparing the attitudes of teachers high in experience with psychologists on each of the scale items. In this comparison only 45 behavioral descriptions significantly differentiated the groups. Moreover, the patterns of disagreements between highly experienced teachers and psychologists, on the one hand, and less experienced teachers and psychologists, on the other hand, is very different. For one thing, the more experienced teachers did not nearly as often differ from psychologists in the direction of ascribing abnormality to a description of child behavior as did the less experienced teachers. As a matter of fact, the differences between the more experienced teachers and psychologists were likely to be as often in the direction of teachers considering the behavior to be benign when psychologists regarded it as being pathological as it was to be considered pathological when the psychologists rated it as being normal. (Only 52% of the differentiating items were rated normal by psychologists more often than by highly experienced teachers.) Second, the area in which the differences become manifest for the highly experienced teachers is very different from the Lows. More specifically, the Highs do not differ from the psychologists particularly in regard to aggressive, regressive, and affect behavior as do the Lows. The least disparity (0%), as a matter of fact, occurs in relation to regressive behavior; the greatest discrepancy (28% of the items in the category), occurs with the ratings of phobic behavior.

Finally, chi-square analyses of the item ratings

for teachers high and teachers low in experience yielded the largest degree of discrepancy of all comparisons. Ninety-six, or 32.5% of the total number of behavioral descriptions, were rated significantly differently by these two subgroups. Interestingly, all 96 critical items were perceived to be normal more often by the highly experienced teachers as compared with the less experienced teachers.

Table 2 presents the percentage of items within each of the scale categories rated differently by highly experienced and relatively inexperienced teaching personnel. It will be noted that phobic behavior tends most often to be viewed differently by teachers of varying degrees of experience, and that there is considerable disagreement about behavior involving communication facility and efficiency.

Illustrative of the specific differences in ratings between the more experienced and the relatively less experienced teachers are the following items, all of which were regarded to be normal by the more experienced teachers and abnormal by the less experienced teachers:

> Cries or whimpers
> Plays with or fingers his mouth
> Headache
> At the slightest upset, coordination becomes poor
> Is frightened in crowds
> Is afraid of being alone in a wide open space
> Child's thoughts are hard to understand
> Lying

Lewis (1965), in reviewing the literature bearing on the "Continuity hypothesis," which states that ". . . emotional disturbance in a child is symptomatic of a continuing psychological process that may lead to adult mental illness [p. 465]," concluded that the acting-out child is more likely to become seriously disturbed as an adult than the

TABLE 2

DEGREE OF DISAGREEMENT BETWEEN HIGHLY EXPERIENCED AND RELATIVELY INEXPERIENCED TEACHERS IN SPECIFIC SCALE CATEGORIES

Category	Items in scale	Percentage of items disagreed upon
Physical-psychosomatic	71	28
Phobic	18	67
Aggressive	56	32
Affect	58	28
Communication	21	48
Regressive	15	13
Inefficiency	25	40
Fantasy-withdrawal	31	26

timid, withdrawn child. He suggested that perhaps the judgments of teachers, as derived from the Wickman (1928) study, represented a more accurate appraisal of the pathology of children than the evaluations of clinicians, at least when adult psychiatric status is taken as the criterion. Irregardless of the validity of the perceptions of each of these groups, the study of the nature of the attitudes remains an important research problem since attitudes will influence markedly the interactions between the child and his teachers.

Beilin (1959) pointed out cogently that the attitudinal patterns of teachers and clinicians toward adjustment difficulties reflect in part their different roles, and that their roles, in turn, "influence the organization of their respective experiences [p. 22]." Since Beilin regards teachers to be essentially task-oriented, that is, concerned with the imparting of information and skills, and since mental health professionals are more concerned with preventing poor adjustment and promoting good adjustment, it is not surprising that these two groups will continue to perceive child behavior differently.

The present findings suggest that psychologists tend to be more accepting, or at least more tolerant, of a greater variety of child behavior than teachers, and tend to regard a wider range of behavior as being normal. Teachers, especially those who are relatively inexperienced, label much more behavior as being abnormal. Teachers are especially critical of categories of behavior that may be referred to as aggressive, regressive, and emotionally expressive. The fact that the greatest degree of disagreement is found between experienced and inexperienced teachers reinforces the impression that actual exposure to child behavior is an important determinant of attitudes toward pathology.

The present study also bears on the frequently voiced criticism of clinicians as being overly sensitive to the pathological aspects of others and not sufficiently sensitive to their assets. The findings indicate that this criticism is probably unjustified since the clinicians were in fact much less prone to interpret behavior as being abnormal than the teachers.

Brief reference should be made to several methodological limitations. First, a number of teachers and psychologists who were given the Staten Island Scale either did not complete the form or failed to follow instructions and had to be eliminated for that reason. Thus, of the original sample of 145 teachers, only 118 could be employed for the analysis. Whether the respondents who cooperated differ in any essential respect from those who did not is not known. Second, although some precautions were taken against the respondents being influenced by others in making

their ratings, the possibility still remains that some judgments were not made entirely independently.

Perhaps a more important problem is related to the ambiguous instructions provided the subjects. Many respondents found the task to be extremely difficult. A number took great pains to comment that since what is considered normal and abnormal is so closely related to the age level of the child, they could not arrive at a decision. Moreover, some stated that since the degree, severity, frequency, nature of onset, duration, and circumstances surrounding the appearance of the symptom remained unspecified, their confidence level in arriving at a decision was extremely low. Nevertheless, it should be noted that since both the professionals and the teachers were faced with the same need to impose structure on the scale items, there is little likelihood that the ratings reflect systematic response biases that differ for the two groups.

It is suggested that the question of whether anchoring the concept of normality versus abnormality to specific age levels affects the ratings of groups of experts and teachers merits further research attention. Also, it might be possible to investigate the effect of increased structure in the description of each item, in terms of such characteristics as frequency of the symptom, on the judgments. Other extensions of this project would concern themselves with the variance contributed to teacher ratings of such variables as their age, teaching competence, and socioeconomic status.

REFERENCES

BEILIN, H. Teachers' and clinicians' attitudes toward the behavior problems of children: A reappraisal. *Child Development*, 1959, *30*, 9–25.

GRIFFITHS, W. *Behavioral difficulties of children as perceived and judged by parents, teachers and children themselves.* Minneapolis: University of Minnesota Press, 1952.

LEWIS, W. W. Continuity and intervention in emotional disturbance: A review. *Exceptional Children*, 1965, *31*, 465–475.

MANDELL, W., & SILBERSTEIN, R. M. Children's psychopathology behavior rating scale. Paper presented at the meeting of the Eastern Psychological Association, Atlantic City, April 1965.

SCHRUPP, M. H., & GJERDE, C. M. Teacher growth in attitudes toward behavior problems of children. *Journal of Educational Psychology*, 1953, *44*, 203–214.

STOUFFER, G. A. W., JR. Behavior problems of children as viewed by teachers and mental hygienists. *Mental Hygiene*, 1952, *36*, 271–285.

WICKMAN, E. K. *Children's behavior and teachers' attitudes.* New York: Commonwealth Fund, 1928.

65

Influence of Pupils' Attitudes on Perception of Teachers' Behaviors and on Consequent School Work[1]

JANICE B. GOLDBERG

How do pupils perceive their teachers? Are their perceptions related in any way to their classroom performance? Janice B. Goldberg's study of these questions is based on a doctoral dissertation submitted to the Harvard Graduate School of Education. Goldberg is now professor of psychology at the University of Maryland, Baltimore.

Pupils who achieve well in one teacher's classroom may achieve poorly in another teacher's class. Similarly, in any classroom some pupils achieve well, while others, equally intelligent, achieve poorly. Little is known about *differential* pupil reaction to teachers and its consequent effect upon pupils' school performance.

Some investigations of pupil-teacher relationships have used pupils' ratings of teachers' classroom behaviors which are conceptualized along personality dimensions related to the authoritarian versus the nonauthoritarian personality pattern (Amidon & Flanders, 1961; Cogan, 1954; Flanders, 1951). The intent of these studies has been to show that authoritarian-related teacher behaviors elicit pupil anxiety which results in lowered pupil achievement. The findings of these studies are inconclusive. The validity of using pupils' ratings as a method for determining differential pupil reaction to teachers stems from the fact that pupils observe more of the teacher's typical behavior than is usually available to the outside observer. Moreover, pupils are directly involved in the teaching-learning process.

There are two major shortcomings in most pupil rating studies. One is the pooling of all pupils' ratings without consideration of individual differences in pupils' perceptions despite the fact that extensive research has shown that individual personality factors influence perception (Bruner, 1958). The other is the use of broad variables, for example, "liking the teacher." Such global variables do little to clarify the complexity of teacher-pupil relationships and require considerable inference on the part of pupils. To avoid these shortcomings this study investigated the relationships between pupils differentiated in their attitudes toward authority and their perceptions of specific, denotable teacher behaviors. These specific behaviors require less inference by pupils.

The study rests on the premise that differential pupil reaction to teachers may be due to underlying attitudinal factors which influence pupils' perceptions of teachers' behaviors and their consequent performance of school work. It is also assumed that teachers' attitudinal factors predispose them to behave in a particular fashion and that these behaviors can be identified.

While many personality factors influence perception and behavior, this study relies upon the measurement of attitudinal variables comprising the authoritarian versus the nonauthoritarian personality dimension (Adorno, Frenkel-Brunswik, Levinson, & Sanford, 1950) as a significant determinant of teacher behavior and as an influence on pupil perception. In view of findings that high and low authoritarians differ in their perceptions of others (Scodel & Mussen, 1953), in their study habits (Gladstein, 1957), and in their ability to learn different kinds of subject matter (Neel, 1959), it is suggested that pupils who are differentiated in their attitudes toward authority will differ in their perceptions of teachers' behaviors related to the authoritarian versus the nonauthoritarian personality dimension (Adorno et al., 1950).

[1] This study is based on a dissertation submitted to the Graduate School of Education of Harvard University in partial fulfillment of the requirements for the Doctor of Education degree. The research was supported by a grant from the Milton Fund. The author wishes to thank her advisors, D. W. Oliver and G. W. Goethals, for their assistance in the execution of the study.

These hypotheses were tested: (*a*) Pupils differentiated as high or low on the California F Scale,* on the Flexibility Scale, and on the Compulsivity Scale will differ in their perceptions of teachers' classroom behaviors. (*b*) The ratings of teachers' classroom behaviors by pupils differentiated as high or low on the three attitude scales are related to the amount of required and self-initiated work pupils report they perform.

METHOD

There are three important features in the research design. One is the use of specific, denotable classroom teacher behaviors which are operationally defined in terms of the variables underlying the California F Scale (Adorno et al., 1950) rather than the more common use of global variables to describe teachers' behaviors. The characterization of teachers' behaviors is based on a well-defined personality theory, that is, the authoritarian personality dimension, since the variables comprising this dimension are expressed by teachers in many ways in the classroom. The second is the assessment of pupils' attitudes on a personality dimension which taps attitudes toward authority. This seems appropriate since the authority vested in the teacher is an important construct in the pupil's daily school life. The third important feature is the use of two unique criterion variables devised by Cogan (1954)—the amount of required work and self-initiated work performed by pupils. While these criteria do not directly measure pupil change, for example, as measured by standardized achievement tests, they avoid the pitfalls of these tests. Cogan argued that performance of pupil *work* is closely related to pupil *change* (or gain) and "intervenes just prior to pupil change."

SUBJECTS

Subjects were 254 eighth- and ninth-grade boys and their 12 male social studies teachers in three junior high schools in a Boston suburb.

INSTRUMENTS

All measures (pupils' attitudes, pupils' ratings of teacher behaviors, and pupils' reports of required and self-initiated work) were secured from one questionnaire. Administration procedures were standardized, and pupils were given assurances of anonymity.

INDEPENDENT VARIABLES

To differentiate pupils according to their attitudes toward authority, three instruments were used: (*a*) McGee's (1955) revised version of the California F Scale was modified for this study. High scorers (authoritarians) tend to be intolerant of ambiguity, to be rigid in their thinking, and to show perceptual distortion when rating others.

---

* A questionnaire developed for research on authoritarian personalities—EDITOR

Split-half reliability is .86. (*b*) Gough's (1956) Flexibility Scale was also modified for this study. This scale measures desire for order and certainty, especially in intellectual matters. High scorers resist learning ambiguous material found in social studies content, a resistance associated with the authoritarian's intolerance of ambiguity. The scale correlates ($r = .59$, $p < .01$) with the F Scale described above. Inter-item reliability is .75. (*c*) Berlak's (1959) Compulsivity Scale was shortened for this study. This scale measures attention to detail and order, particularly in school work. High scorers (high compulsives) may be said to have a strong desire to do well in school while the converse is true for low compulsives. These assumptions regarding the differences in the attitudes of high and low compulsive pupils seem tenable in view of Oliver and Shaver's (1962) finding of a strong relationship ($r = .57$, $p < .005$) between Compulsivity and "need cognition," defined as "a desire to do well in school." The overall rigidity of behavior measured by the scale reflects attitudes consistent with authoritarianism. The scale correlates ($r = .20$, $p < .05$) with the F Scale. Inter-item reliability is .76. A Likert-type scale is provided for each of the three attitude measures with six possible responses to each item. The responses range from "strong agreement" to "strong disagreement."

DEPENDENT VARIABLES

Descriptive teacher behaviors were related, by hypothesis, to variables representing the underlying personality trends measured by the California F Scale. In turn, these descriptive behaviors, hypothesized to be manifestations of the authoritarian versus the nonauthoritarian personality pattern, were matched with *specific, denotable teacher behavior items* drawn from Cogan's (1954) Pupil Survey. The criterion guiding the process of determining which *denotable behavior item* corresponded to the *descriptive* behavior was the functional relevance of the item to the behavior. The process of matching descriptive behaviors and thereby relating F-Scale variables to denotable teacher behaviors is demonstrated as follows. One F-Scale variable comprising the authoritarian personality structure is termed "Anti-intraception." This personality trend is characterized by impatience with the subjective and the tender-minded. It was hypothesized that such a teacher would tend to be unconcerned with what pupils think and feel, and might be contemptuous of the academically poor pupil. The descriptive behavioral manifestation of this variable is the statement, "Teacher is unsympathetic with a pupil's failure at a task." The operational definition of this behavior and, therefore, of the F-Scale variable is the questionnaire item: "When we give a wrong answer in class, our teacher says we are 'slow,' 'not smart,' etc."

The 25 specific authoritarian teacher behavior items characterize the authoritarian teacher, in part, as strongly directive, impatient with academically inferior pupils, and generally rejecting of pupils. High scores on these items represent the extent to which pupils perceive teachers as authoritarian.

A similar procedure was used to relate descriptive nonauthoritarian teacher behaviors to specific Pupil Survey items. The 23 specific nonauthoritarian teacher behaviors represent personality trends hypothesized to be *opposite* to the meaning of the F-Scale variables.[2] These items characterize the nonauthoritarian teacher, in part, as permissive, more concerned with individual pupils' needs, and generally accepting of pupils. High scores on these items represent the extent to which pupils perceive teachers as nonauthoritarian.

A 5-point frequency scale was provided for each of the items. Responses to the items range from "Almost never" to "Very often." Cogan (1954) reports a reliability coefficient of .96 for these teacher behavior items. Pupils' ratings of these items are the dependent variables of the study.

CRITERION VARIABLES

To determine the amount of school work performed by pupils, two measures were used: (*a*) 24 items concerned with homework represent the amount of *required work* a pupil does, and (*b*) 21 items represent the extent to which a pupil does extra, unassigned (*self-initiated*) school work. Some examples are:

Required work: "Give a report"

Self-initiated work: "I make extra graphs, charts, etc."

The items were rated on a 6-point frequency scale. Responses to the items range from "Almost never" to "Almost always." The reliability coefficient for the required work items is .94 and .89 for the self-initiated work items (Cogan, 1954).

RESULTS AND DISCUSSION

Hypothesis 1 is partially confirmed. Table 1 shows that compulsivity in the total sample is strongly related to pupils' perceptions of teachers' behaviors. Pupils' F-Scale and Flexibility Scale scores are not related to their perceptions of teachers' behaviors.

While compulsivity is a component of the F Scale ($r = .20, p < .05$) and of the Flexibility Scale ($r = .27, p < .005$), its influence on pupil perception of teacher behavior may be due to the fact that it measures school-related attitudes rather than the generalized attitudes measured by the F Scale and the Flexibility Scale.

The *t* tests in Table 2 show that when pupils are differentiated as high or low on the Compulsivity Scale their ratings of teachers' behaviors are significantly different. High compulsives, those who work carefully in order to do well in school, perceive teachers as more nonauthoritarian. Low compulsives, those who may be less concerned with

---

[2] Complete tables of descriptive teacher behaviors and specific items may be found in the author's unpublished doctoral dissertation (Goldberg, 1965).

TABLE 1
CORRELATIONS BETWEEN PUPILS' SCORES ON THE ATTITUDE SCALES AND THEIR PERCEPTIONS OF TEACHERS' BEHAVIORS AND THE AMOUNT OF REQUIRED AND SELF-INITIATED WORK PERFORMED

	Pupils' scores		
	F Scale	Flexibility Scale	Compulsivity Scale
Teachers' behaviors			
Authoritarian	−0.07	−0.08	−0.23*
Nonauthoritarian	0.04	0.08	0.23*
Work performed			
Required	0.02	0.08	0.35**
Self-initiated	0.01	0.02	0.43**

Note.—$N = 254$.
* $p < .01$.
** $p < .005$.

doing well in school, perceive teachers as more authoritarian.

The differences in perception by the two groups of pupils may lie in differential treatment of these pupils. The authoritarian teacher is characterized, in part, as strongly directive, impatient with academically poor pupils, and may be unconcerned with pupils' personal needs and goals. The authoritarian teacher tends to demand good school performance, to insist on strict order, and to conform to a rigid routine.

Since the Compulsivity Scale measures attention to detail and order in school work, it has been assumed that the high compulsive wants to do well in school. He is probably the academically strong pupil who conforms to teacher expectations of good work. It may be that less demand is made of him by his teacher since he does good work in accordance with his own inner needs. He may be favorably treated in that he gets less criticism from his teacher. Thus, he perceives the teacher as more nonauthoritarian. The low compulsive may care less about good school performance. He is

TABLE 2
MEANS OF HIGH AND LOW COMPULSIVE PUPILS' RATINGS OF TEACHERS' BEHAVIORS

	Mean pupil ratings			
Teachers' behaviors	Low-compulsive	High compulsive	df	t
Authoritarian	57.21	51.99	252	2.29*
Nonauthoritarian	80.16	84.97	252	−2.51**

* $p < .05$.
** $p < .01$.

probably the academically weak pupil who does not meet teacher expectations of good work. The teacher may excessively criticize him and may persistently require him to do more careful work. Thus, the low-compulsive pupil perceives the teacher as more authoritarian. It is also possible that pupils' attitudes toward the teacher as an authority figure may result in perceptual distortion of the teacher's behavior. The high compulsive, with his need to do well in school, may perceive teacher demands for good work as aiding him to do well in school and, therefore, as reasonable behavior. Thus, he rates the teacher as less authoritarian. The low compulsive, having less need to do well in school, may perceive this kind of teacher behavior as unreasonable and he rates the teacher as more authoritarian.

Hypothesis 2 is partially confirmed. Table 1 also shows that compulsivity in the total sample is positively related to the amount of work pupils perform. However, no significant relationship exists between either F-Scale or Flexibility Scale scores and amount of school work performed.

Two-way analyses of variance show differences in pupils' compulsivity and differences in pupils' perceptions of teachers' nonauthoritarian behaviors do influence their performance of required and self-initiated work. There is a highly significant interaction effect between pupils' compulsivity and pupils' perceptions of nonauthoritarian teacher behaviors with self-initiated work as their criterion measure ($F = 19.17$, df 1/218, $p < .01$). The required F ratio at this level is 6.76. Interaction between pupils' compulsivity and their perceptions of nonauthoritarian teacher behaviors with required work as the criterion measure is significant at the .05 level.

The cell means for these analyses show that high-compulsive pupils do *less* work when the teacher is perceived as nonauthoritarian. Low-compulsive pupils do *more* work when the teacher is perceived as nonauthoritarian. Although the data derived for Hypothesis 1 indicate that high-compulsive pupils *perceive* teachers as more nonauthoritarian, these same cell means show that this perception of the teacher influences their performance of school work. These findings suggest that perception of teacher behavior as nonauthoritarian may conflict with high-compulsive pupils' need for a directive, demanding teacher. Thus, perception of nonauthoritarian behavior appears to serve as cues for anxiety in high-compulsive pupils, resulting in less performance of school work. Conversely, perception of nonauthoritarian behavior seems to encourage low-compulsive pupils to do more work, probably because this kind of teacher tends to have warmer relationships with pupils—even those who have less desire to do well in school.

Two-way analyses of variance of pupils' compulsivity and their perceptions of teachers' authoritarian behaviors show no significant interaction effects. However, trends in the cell means reveal that high-compulsive pupils do more work when they perceive the teacher as authoritarian than do low-compulsive pupils. This lends weight to suggestions made earlier that high-compulsive pupils perceive this kind of teacher behavior as enabling them to fulfill their need to do well in school. Low-compulsive pupils do less work when the teacher is perceived as authoritarian. Thus, it is possible that such teacher behaviors may serve as cues for anxiety resulting in lowered school performance for those pupils who are less concerned about good school work.

The findings tend to support the conclusion that pupils differentiated in their attitudes—in this case on a measure of compulsivity—do perceive different kinds of teachers' behaviors differently and that this differential in perception influences the consequent amount of school work performed.

In view of contemporary concern for teaching "disadvantaged" children who tend to have little interest in good school performance, these results may be helpful in selecting teachers for these children as well as for studying their learning patterns.

REFERENCES

ADORNO, T. W., FRENKEL-BRUNSWIK, E., LEVINSON, D. J., & SANFORD, R. N., *The authoritarian personality.* New York: Harper, 1950.

AMIDON, E., & FLANDERS, N. A. The effects of direct and indirect teacher influence on dependent-prone students learning geometry. *Journal of Educational Psychology*, 1961, *52*, 286–291.

BERLAK, H. Rigidity scale. Unpublished manuscript. Cambridge: Harvard Graduate School of Education, 1959.

BRUNER, J. S. Social psychology and perception. In E. E. Maccoby, T. R. Newcomb, & E. L. Hartley (Eds.), *Readings in social psychology.* (3rd ed.) New York: Holt, 1958. Pp. 85–94.

COGAN, M. L. The relation of the behavior of teachers to the productive behavior of their pupils. Unpublished doctoral dissertation, Harvard University, 1954.

FLANDERS, N. A. Personal-social anxiety as a factor in experimental learning situations. *Journal of Educational Research*, 1951, *45*, 100–110.

GLADSTEIN, G. A. The relationship between study behavior and personality for academically successful students. Unpublished doctoral dissertation, University of Chicago, 1957.

GOLDBERG, J. B. The influence of pupils' attitudes on their perceptions of teachers' behaviors and on their consequent performance of school work. Unpublished doctoral dissertation, Harvard University, 1965.

GOUGH, H. G. *Manual for the California Psychological Inventory*. Palo Alto: Consulting Psychologists Press, 1956.

McGEE, H. M. Measurement of authoritarianism and its relation to teachers' classroom behavior. *Genetic Psychology Monographs*, 1955, *52*, 89–146.

NEEL, A. F. The relationship of authoritarian personality to learning: F Scale scores compared to classroom performance. *Journal of Educational Psychology*, 1959, *50*, 195–199.

OLIVER, D. W., & SHAVER, J. P. *The analysis of public controversy: A study in citizenship education.* (Report from the Laboratory for Research in Instruction.) Cambridge: Harvard Graduate School of Education, 1962.

SCODEL, A., & MUSSEN, P. Social perceptions of authoritarians and non-authoritarians. *Journal of Abnormal and Social Psychology*, 1953, *48*, 181–184.

66

Reach, Touch, and Teach

Terry Borton

Curriculum projects in the post-Sputnik years stressed cognitive development. The new math, for example, introduced elementary school pupils to mathematical concepts previously taught to high school and college students. While these curriculum projects in subject-matter fields are continuing, a different type of curriculum reform has sprung up. Schools are beginning to educate students about their feelings, their values, and their own psychological growth. Terry Borton, director of the Dual-Audio Television Project in the Philadelphia public schools, has written an excellent report of this new trend.

There are two sections to almost every school's statement of educational objectives—one for real, and one for show. The first, the real one, talks about academic excellence, subject mastery, and getting into college or a job. The other discusses the human purpose of school—values, feelings, personal growth, the full and happy life. It is included because everyone knows that it is important, and that it ought to be central to the life of every school. But it is only for show. Everyone knows how little schools have done about it.

In spite of this, the human objectives describe the things all of us cite when we try to remember what "made a difference" in our school careers:

the teacher who touched us as persons, or the one who ground out our lives to polish our intellects; the class that moved with the strength and grace of an Olympic team, or the dozens of lessons when each of us slogged separately toward the freedom of 3 o'clock. What we learned, and what we became, depended to a significant degree on how we felt about ourselves, our classmates, and our teachers. The schools were right—the human purposes *were* important. But with the exception of those teachers who were so rare we never forgot them, the schools did little to put their philosophy into practice.

Recently, however, a variety of programs have begun to build curricula and teaching methodology that speak directly to the human objectives. These programs, stemming both from within the schools and from various branches of psychology, point the way to a school practice which not only recognizes the power of feelings, but also combines academic training with an education directly aimed at the student's most important concerns. Schools may soon be explicitly teaching students such things as how to sort out and guide their own psychological growth, or increase their desire to achieve, or handle their aggressive instincts in non-violent forms.

The new impetus has a variety of names: "psychological education," "affective," "humanistic," "personological," "eupsychian," "synoetic." Some of these names are a bit bizarre, and none has yet gained wide acceptance. But taken together their presence indicates a growing recognition that in the world's present state of social and moral turmoil, the schools' traditional second objective can no longer be for show. Riots, poverty, war, student rebellion, swollen mental hospitals, and soaring crime rates have involved an enormous number of people. They have generated a broadening conviction that society is as responsible for the psychological well-being of each of its members as is each individual. And that conviction has created a receptive audience for new kinds of educational critics.

The new critics do not simply attack the schools for their academic incompetence, as did the Rickovers of a decade ago. They are equally concerned with the schools' basic lack of understanding that students are human beings with feelings as well as intellects. Jonathan Kozol has given a gripping sense of the "destruction of the hearts and minds of Negro children" in his *Death at an Early Age*. In *How Children Fail* John Holt has shown that even in the best "progressive" schools, children live in constant fear which inhibits their learning, and Paul

Goodman's *Compulsory Mis-Education* has made a powerful case for his contention that "the present school system is leading straight to 1984." The intuitive warnings of these "romantic critics" have been backed up by statistical evidence from the largest survey of education ever conducted, James Coleman's *Equality of Educational Opportunity*. This survey correlates academic achievement with attitudes such as a student's self concept, sense of control over his fate, and interest in school. The study concludes that these attitudes and feelings are more highly correlated with how well a student achieves academically than a combination of many of the factors which educators have usually thought were crucial, such as class size, salary of teachers, facilities, curriculum.

The pressure to deal more directly with student feelings (increasingly a pressure from students as well as critics) has given rise to dozens of different projects. None of the three examples which I will discuss here has yet reached the size or influence of the giant curriculum centers (such as the Educational Development Corporation) which grew up as a result of the post-Sputnik criticism. But in the long run they may be much more important. For the post-Sputnik curriculum reforms were essentially attempts to find better ways to teach the traditional disciplines of math, science, or social studies—often with the effect of moving the college curriculum into elementary and secondary schools. The programs I am describing not only operate with different techniques, but also begin to define and develop new curriculum subjects and a new school orientation toward practical and applied psychology. If expanded, they will make a profound change in American education—hopefully a change toward a more humane educational process, and a more human student.

The project which I co-directed with Norman Newberg, the Philadelphia School Board's specialist in "affective education," is an example of such a curriculum. It is being developed from within the schools—in this case by a group of urban teachers trying to find a philosophy and method which would work with the students they were asked to teach. The program is based on the assumption that every person handles massive amounts of information, and needs to be taught both logical and psychological processes for handling it. Two semester-long courses, one in communications, and one in urban affairs, isolate such processes as symbolization, simulation, dreaming, and de-escalating pressure, and teach them in an explicit fashion. At the same time the classes are designed to tie these processes to the amorphous undercurrent of student concerns for self-identity, power, and relationship.

I dropped into a high school communications class one hot day during last summer's field testing, when the teacher was working on "taxonomy of process," or a way of looking at what, why, and how behavior occurs and changes. The purpose of the class was to show the students a simple technique for analyzing their own habitual forms of processing the world around them, and then to show them how they could develop new responses if they wanted to. The class was working in groups of twos, filling in "What Wheels" for each other. One boy in the back was without a partner, so I joined him, and we agreed that I would make a What Wheel for him, and he would make one for me. I drew a circle, filled in the spokes, and wrote down my first impressions of him: "strong, quick, Afro, shy, bright."

The teacher asked us to read each other our What Wheels, select one adjective which interested us most, and ask our partner to draw a "Why Wheel" to explain *why* that adjective was meaningful to him.

Charlie read me his What Wheel—he was perceptive, as students usually are about teachers. Then I read him mine.

"Why'd you write 'shy'? I ain't shy."

"Well, I just met you, so I can't fill out a whole Why Wheel about it. But when I first sat there, I noticed you looked down at your desk instead of up at me. So I just guessed you were shy with strangers—maybe just with strange teachers."

Charlie took his What Wheel from me and looked at it. "You know, that's the truth. I thought nobody, except maybe my mother, knew that about me, but well, it's the truth anyhow."

The murmur of the class's conversation quieted while the teacher told us how to make up "How Wheels" with our partners. We were supposed to write down the range of actions which would either increase or decrease the trait we had been discussing.

"Aw, man, it would be easy to increase being shy," laughed Charlie. "I just wouldn't look at nobody."

"And decreasing it?"

"I'd look at you like I'm looking at you right now," he said, looking me straight in the eye. "And more than that, I'd look at you like that when you first came in here. Teacher, or white man, I wasn't afraid of you; no reason why I should act like I was."

We talked for a while—about my wheels, about the effectiveness of the what, why, how process questions for looking at behavior, and about school. When the bell rang, we shook hands. "See ya around," he said.

"See ya around," I said.

While many teachers have been experimenting

with techniques similar to ours, research psychologists usually have been rather disdainful of the messy problems in the schools. Increasingly, however, psychologists such as David McClelland of Harvard are beginning to work on problems of motivation and attitude in schools. The progression of McClelland's study is a good example of how basic research may be applied to problems in education. McClelland began working on problems of measuring the motivation of rats deprived of food, performed a series of experiments to measure hunger motivation in humans, and then devised a system for measuring "achievement motivation" in men by counting the frequency of its appearance in fantasy images. He defined the need for achievement (n-Ach) as a pattern of thought and fantasy about doing things well, and discovered that those people who had such a pattern were characterized by a preference for moderate risk goals, a desire for immediate feedback on their performance, and a liking for personal responsibility. McClelland reasoned that if a society had a great number of such individuals, the society itself should show outstanding achievement. Twenty years were spent in a mammoth research effort to substantiate his claim that achievement research provided a "factual basis for evaluating theories that explain the rise and fall of civilizations." The next step was to devise educational methods for increasing the achievement motive in people who did not have much of it, and to test out these methods in this country and abroad.

Dr. Alfred Alschuler, director of the Harvard Achievement Motivation Development Project, which is one result of McClelland's research, is in charge of a federally funded five-year research project to assess what factors lead to effective achievement training. The project has devised many classroom techniques for increasing achievement motivation in students, most of them involving experiential learning that takes place in a game situation. I visited one training program for teachers in a nearby city, and sat in on a session that used a contest in making paper airplanes to demonstrate to the teachers how achievement motivation affects their students.

There was a lot of joking around the table, as everyone was a little nervous.

"Now they're going to use the old carrot on us," cracked a little physics teacher sitting on my right.

The head of the math department, an enormous man, smiled broadly, first at the physics teacher, and then at me. "Feeling cut-throat?" he asked.

I didn't say so, but I was, and he knew it. My "n-Ach" was way up. We eyed each other while we set our own quotas for the number of planes we would make.

Dr. Alschuler gave us the start sign. I was making

planes feverishly; out of the corner of my eye, I could see the math department head moving more slowly, but doing a better job—the quality control check at the end of the game might go in his favor. The physics teacher was using mass production techniques, making one fold at a time.

At the end of five minutes the game was up, and we were all laughing at the tension it had produced. The physics teacher had more planes than any of us, but his mass production assembly had failed— all the planes were missing one wing. I had the second largest number of planes, but several had sloppy folds and were disqualified.

"Nuts to this," said the physics teacher. "I'm not going to get another heart attack over a bunch of paper airplanes. Next time I'm dropping my quota in half. I'm only going to make six."

I was swearing at myself—I should have been more careful. Next time through the game I would set a slightly lower quota and do a better job.

The math teacher was smiling broadly. He had won.

Later we all talked about our experience in the game and how our own behavior did or did not reflect the characteristics of a high achiever. Did we set moderate risk goals? Did we utilize information on our success or failure? Then we began to dig into the more fundamental value issues that were involved. Suppose that we could use games like the paper plane construction to teach students the characteristics of a high achiever, and through a variety of such exercises could actually train him to think and act as one. Was that a good thing? Did we want to subject our students to the pressure that we had felt? Could we decide that achievement training was good for some students who were not achieving up to our standards, and bad for those who were too competitive? On what basis?

Just as researchers are becoming involved in the practical questions of education, so clinical psychotherapy is getting up off its couch and finding ways to add its skill to solving school problems. Dr. Carl Rogers, founder of client-centered therapy, is presently working with Western Behavioral Sciences Institute and a group of Catholic schools to devise ways to use "sensitivity groups" in the schools. (A "sensitivity group" or "T-group" is composed of about a dozen people who meet for the purpose of giving feedback on how each person's behavior affects the other people in the group.) The National Training Laboratory, an associate of the National Education Association, is now running a year-round series of T-groups and related experiences for teachers and administrators. And in San Diego, child psychiatrist Dr. Harold Bissell and educator Dr. Uvaldo Palomares have set up the Human Development

Training Institute which has written a two-year sequence of lesson plans to improve a primary school child's self-confidence and awareness, and has trained 1,000 teachers to use it.

One of the most eclectic approaches in the clinical tradition is the project run by Dr. George Brown of the University of California at Santa Barbara. Brown's project, sponsored by the Ford Foundation through the ebullient Esalen Institute, utilizes many different approaches, but particularly the theories of Gestalt therapy which attempt to get youth in touch with how they are feeling in the "here and now." With such theoretical orientations in their background, the teachers in Brown's project are encouraged to devise their own techniques to integrate academic with affective or emotional learning in order to achieve a more "humanistic education."

I joined the teachers at one of the monthly meetings where they learn about new ideas, and share with each other the techniques they have developed. Gloria Siemons, a pretty first-grade teacher, was describing an exercise that she had first conducted with the entire class, and then used when one child became angry at another. She lined the class up in two rows on the playground, had them find a partner, put their hands up facing each other, and push.

Push they did, laughing all over the field, especially at their teacher, who was being pushed around in a circle by several of the bigger kids.

Later, when two kids got into an argument at recess, Mrs. Siemons simply asked them: "Are you angry now? Would you like to push?"

"Yes, I'm angry. I'm angry at him."

Both agreed to the contest, pushed for a minute as hard as they could, and then collapsed into each other's arms giggling. Their anger was worked out, but without hurting each other.

"What would happen," I asked Mrs. Siemons, "if one kid pushed another hard enough to hurt him?"

"We have a rule about that. 'It's OK to be angry with someone, and it's OK to push, but it's *not* OK to push him into the rosebush.'"

Good teachers, particularly good first-grade teachers such as Mrs. Siemons, have always responded to the emotional side of their students' lives, and it is precisely this intuitive gift which Dr. Brown is capitalizing on. By systematizing such techniques and relating them to a general theoretical framework, he and the teachers of his staff have begun to generate hundreds of ways to integrate the feelings of students with the regular curriculum taught from kindergarten to high school.

The techniques being developed, the dozens of programs, and the various theories differ in many respects, but they have several features in common. First, and most important, all of them deal in a very explicit and direct way with the student's feelings, interpersonal relations, or values. It is the fact that they are so explicit and direct which sets them apart from the vague protestations that schools have usually made about this area. While schools were concentrating on math, science, or English, they often ignored or actively suppressed feelings. The new programs make what was covert behavior the subject of overt discussion; they make the implicit explicit. They legitimize feelings, clarify them for the student, and suggest a variety of behaviors which he can use to express them. They do so on the assumption that these feelings exert a powerful effect on a student's behavior, both in the present and in the future. If schools want to influence behavior, then it makes sense to deal directly with its major sources, not just with the binomial theorem, the gerund, or the Seventeenth Amendment.

A factor in the new field which often causes misunderstanding is that most of the programs use non-verbal experiences, either through physical expression and involvement, or through art, sculpture, or music. For the most part, this involvement with the *non*-verbal is not *anti*-verbal or *anti*-intellectual. Non-verbal educational techniques are based on the obvious but little-utilized fact that a child learns most of his emotional response patterns at a very young age—before he can talk. His knowledge of love, rejection, anger, and need does not come through words, but through his physical senses— touch, a flushed face, a gnawing in his stomach. Even later, when he begins to talk, the words he learns are "Mama," "doggie," "see"—words for things and actions, not feelings. Indeed, many children seem entirely unable to give a name to their current feelings—they have been taught how to say "I am bad," but not "I feel bad." Education that deals with feelings is often facilitated by skipping over the verbal labels which have been learned relatively late in life, regaining the other senses, and then reintegrating them with verbal thought and new behaviors.

Another common technique which causes confusion is the reliance of many of the programs on games, dramatic improvisations, and role-playing. Again, though those utilizing the techniques believe in fun and use games, few of them are simply advocating "fun and games." Their interest stems from an insight into the learning process of small children. By playing games—house, fireman, office, war —little children learn what it will be like to be an adult, and begin to develop their own style in that role. But our culture provides few such opportunities for older children or adolescents, even though the society is changing so fast that many of the response patterns they learned as a three-year-old may be no longer relevant, or even dangerous. Games and improvisation allow a simulation of the self. While they are real and produce real emotions, their tightly defined limits provide a way to try out new behavior without taking the full consequences which might occur if the same action were performed in ordinary relationships.

There are answers for questions about non-verbal and gaming emphasis, but there are many other questions which the programs raise for which there are no answers. At best, solutions will come slowly, and that is bound to produce tremendous strain in a time when events wait for no one. Many of these problems are already developing. Though Dr. Alschuler at Harvard and Dr. Willis Harmon at the Stanford Research Institute are both engaged in large surveys to find out what techniques and philosophies are presently being employed in the field, there is still no common theoretical base for the programs, and very little research on their effectiveness. The Achievement Motivation Development Project has by far the most extensive research program, and Dr. Alschuler's experience with it has made him feel strongly about the need for additional evidence before program expansion:

We have very little hard evidence that programs in this new field accomplish much more than natural maturation. We have claims, promises, and fascinating anecdotes. But we should not institute these programs without first using the most sophisticated research techniques we have to improve them and explore their consequences.

In addition to unanswered questions about effectiveness, there are practical limitations to all of the programs. Few have done an adequate job of integrating their material with the usual skills and knowledge that everyone recognizes the schools must continue to teach. No attempt has yet been made to work together with the free-flowing academic programs (such as the Leicestershire movement) which seem natural complements. Though all of the projects I have discussed here stress their responsiveness to student concerns, it is not yet clear how they can do that and yet not be heavily dependent on the skills and personalities of a few teachers like Mrs. Siemons who can both legitimize anger and make the rosebush out of bounds.

Politically, programs with both the potential and the liabilities of these are obvious hot potatoes. It is unclear as yet how projects designed by psychologists will fit in with current efforts toward more community control and what seems to be the re-

sulting concentration on "teaching the basics." Even a mode of politics that is in consonance with the ideals and methods of the new programs is unknown, for the vision they present is often as utopian as that in George Leonard's exciting new book, *Education and Ecstasy*. How to get from here to there without waiting until 2001 is a complex political problem. Suppose, for instance, that a school district decided to adopt an entirely new curriculum and school organization based on the concepts I have been discussing. Would the teachers be able to change? Great care would have to be taken with their feelings and concerns, for not only are they as human as the children, but—as recent events in New York have indicated—they will strike if they feel they are being treated unfairly.

The most fundamental problem, and the one which is likely to get people the most upset, is the ethical question caused by changing the expectations of what schools are for. At present, students go to school to "learn stuff," and though they may expect schools to provide information, they do not expect schools to change them in any fundamental way, or even to offer that opportunity. As long as schools continue to have relatively little explicitly acknowledged impact on the students' values, attitudes, and behaviors, no one is likely to worry much about ethical issues. If schools consciously begin to make important changes in students' lives, people will suddenly become very concerned about what is happening to immature minds that are forced to accept this kind of education for twelve years. They will begin to ask whether there should be compulsory education, or whether students should be free to accept or reject schooling. And they will begin to ask hard questions about what should be taught, and how it should be presented.

If, for instance, all children should be motivated, should they also be "achievement motivated"? At what age? Who decides? And who teaches? What is to stop teachers from working out of their own needs rather than for those of their pupils? Should teachers who share an important confidence have the same legal privilege which a lawyer or a minister has? How can parents and children be assured of the privacy which is their right?

The ethical problems are likely to be compounded by the reporting of the mass media. The new field is peculiarly open to parody ("HARVARD PROF TEACHES PAPER AIRPLANE CONSTRUCTION") and to easy association with the exotic and erotic. (*Life* recently stuck a single misleading paragraph on Brown's project into a long article on Esalen Institute. By far the most arresting thing in the article was a two-page picture spread on a nude sensitivity group that had nothing to do with either Brown's project or Esalen.) Sensational publicity is not what the new field needs. It does need the time, the careful research and planning, and the critical reporting which will allow it to grow or decline on its merits. The alternative is a series of fads, created by ignorance and publicity, and death—after a short and enthusiastic life—in disillusionment.

The new programs are too important to allow that to happen. They are delicate, and they are moving into an area which is fundamentally new, so they can be expected to suffer from the attention they attract, to make mistakes, and to run into blind alleys. If it takes the big curriculum development corporations a million dollars and three years to build a single course in science or social studies, it will be even more difficult to build a fully developed curriculum in a new field. But the effort should be encouraged. For while it may not be novel to assert that a man's feelings are a crucial determinant of his public behavior and private well-being, there is no question about the novelty and significance of school programs that explicitly educate both the feelings and the intellect. Such programs raise many of society's basic questions about purpose and meaning—tough questions which will not be easy to answer. But they also offer a possibility for building a saner world—a world where people are more open about their feelings, careful in their thinking, and responsible in their actions.

INDEX

A

Abraham, K., 360n
Abramowicz, M., 227
Accomplishment, sense of, 246–247
Acheson, R. M., 304
Achievement:
  as acquired drive, 63
  and experience of success or failure,
      356–358
  motive for among women, 372–373
  need for, 212, 216, 425
  of pupils, related to teacher behavior,
      418, 420–421
  and race, SES and family, 223–228
Achievement motivation:
  of first-borns, 167
  and IQ, 346
  social factors in, 212, 213
  training for, 293
Achievement scores:
  of blacks and whites, 224
  by socioeconomic status, 225–226
Adams, J. Q., 282
Adams, J. W., 282
Adler, A., 175
Adler, M., 15
Adolescence, 240
  competence model of, 257, 259
  concept of, 274–275, 283
  egocentrism in, 336–338
  identity crisis in, 276–279
  inevitable stress during, 269–270
  in the kibbutz, 211
  pathology of, 271–274
  persistence of personality traits
      from, 48
  predictability of stress in, 270–271
  prolongation of, 282
  in psychoanalysis, 256
  and sense of identity, 247–249
  unrest during, 281–287
  use of power during, 113–114
Adorno, T. W., 418, 419
Adults, social reinforcement by, 68–75
Affect:
  defense by reversal of, 272–273
  expression of, 416
Affiliation, and birth order, 166, 169
Age:
  and concept of causality, 329–332
  and conformity, 186, 189–190

as determinant of behavior, 239–240
developmental periods by, 45–46
and fixation time, 299–301
and frequency of Down's syndrome,
    39
and maternal deprivation, 85–88, 90
and teaching of complex subjects,
    387–388
Aged, care of, 32
Aggression, 63, 79, 117–124
  and anxiety, 119
  definitions of, 117–118
  exposure to models of, 178
  home sources of, 121–124
  and IQ, 346, 348
  mother's permissiveness for,
      119–121
  punishment for, 121
  sex differences in, 48
  teachers vs. clinicians on, 415–416
  and television-watching, 28–29, 178
Aichhorn, A., 272
Allen, F. L., 351
Allen, K. E., 70, 71
Allen, L., 45
Allen, V. L., 201
Allen, 169
Allinsmith, W., 355
Allport, G. W., 24, 179, 385
  on personality, 276–280
  on psychological models, 13–18
Alpert, R., 158, 366, 409
Alphabet:
  knowledge of, 397, 399
  naming of, 396
Alschuler, A., 425, 427
Altruism (see also Generosity)
  imitation as determinant of, 159,
      163–164
Altus, W. D., 166n, 175
Ambiguity, and conformity, 186, 189–
    191
Ambivalence, 63
Ambrose, A., 263
Amidon, E., 418
Amniocentesis, 37
Anaclitic identification, 158, 164
Anastasi, A., 41–42, 320, 406
Anaximander, 8, 12
Anderson, H. H., 357
Anderson, J. E., 44
Anderson, R. H., 399